★ **San Clemente** ⑫
See pages 186–7

★ **Trajan's Markets** ⑩
see pages 88–9

Piazza di Spagna

Via Veneto

Piazza della Rotonda

⑦

Quirinal

★ **Santa Maria del Popolo** ⑥
See pages 138–9

⑬

⑧

★ **Santa Maria Maggiore** ⑬
See pages 172–3

⑩

Esquiline

⑨

Capitol

Forum

⑪

Palatine

⑫

Lateran

⑭

Caracalla

★ **San Giovanni in Laterano** ⑭
See pages 182–3

Aventine

★ **Santa Maria in Trastevere** ⑤
See pages 212–13

★ **Colosseum** ⑪
See pages 92–5

EYEWITNESS TRAVEL GUIDES

ROME

EYEWITNESS TRAVEL GUIDES

ROME

DK PUBLISHING

LONDON • NEW YORK • MUNICH
MELBOURNE • DELHI

PROJECT EDITOR Fiona Wild
ART EDITOR Annette Jacobs
EDITORS Ferdie McDonald, Mark Ronan, Anna Streiffert
US EDITORS Mary Ann Lynch, Mary Sutherland
DESIGNER Lisa Kosky
DESIGN ASSISTANT Marisa Renzullo

PRODUCTION CONTROLLER Hilary Stephens
PICTURE RESEARCH Catherine O'Rourke
RESEARCH IN ROME Sam Cole
DTP EDITOR Siri Lowe

MAIN CONTRIBUTORS
Olivia Ercoli, Ros Belford, Roberta Mitchell

MAPS
Andrew Heritage, James Mills-Hicks, John Plumer,
Chez Picthall (Dorling Kindersley Cartography)

PHOTOGRAPHERS
John Heseltine, Mike Dunning, Kim Sayer

ILLUSTRATORS
Studio Illibill, Kevin Jones Associates,
Martin Woodward, Robbie Polley

This book was produced with the assistance of
Websters International Publishers.

Reproduced by Colourscan (Singapore)
Printed and bound by South China Printing Co. Ltd., China
First American Edition, 1993
03 04 05 10 9 8 7
Published in the United States by DK Publishing, Inc.,
375 Hudson Street, New York, New York 10014

Reprinted with revisions 1996, 1997, 1999 (twice), 2001,
2002, 2003

Copyright © 1993, 2003 Dorling Kindersley Limited, London

Library of Congress Cataloging-in-Publication Data
Rome.
    p.   cm. – – (DK eyewitness travel guides)
Includes index.
ISBN 0-7894-9421-3 (alk.paper)
1. Rome (Italy) – – Guidebooks. I. Eyewitness travel guides
DG804.R68256 2003
914.5'6320493– –dc21   2002031329

FLOORS ARE REFERRED TO THROUGHOUT IN ACCORDANCE WITH EUROPEAN USAGE,
IE THE "FIRST FLOOR" IS THE FLOOR ABOVE GROUND LEVEL.

See our complete product line at
www.dk.com

**The information in this Dorling Kindersley
Travel Guide is checked annually.**
Every effort has been made to ensure that this book is as up-to-date as
possible at the time of going to press. Some details, however, such as
telephone numbers, opening hours, prices, gallery hanging arrangements
and travel information are liable to change. The publishers cannot accept
responsibility for any consequences arising from the use of this book, nor
for any material on third party websites, and cannot guarantee that any
website address in this book will be a suitable source of travel information.
We value the views and suggestions of our readers very highly. Please write
to: Publisher, DK Eyewitness Travel Guides, Dorling Kindersley,
80 Strand, London WC2R 0RL, Great Britain.

CONTENTS

Colosseum

INTRODUCING
ROME

Moses by Michelangelo in
San Pietro in Vincoli

Fresco in Villa Farnesina

ROME AREA BY AREA

The Tempietto

Arch of Titus

TRAVELERS' NEEDS

Mosaic in Santa Prassede

SURVIVAL GUIDE

Roman antipasto

The basilica of St. Peter's in the Vatican City

How to Use this Guide

THIS EYEWITNESS TRAVEL GUIDE helps
you get the most from your stay
in Rome with the minimum of
practical difficulty. The opening
section, *Introducing Rome*, locates the
city geographically, sets modern Rome
in its historical context and explains
how Roman life changes through the
year. *Rome at a Glance* is an overview
of the city's attractions. The main
sightseeing section is section two,
Rome Area by Area, starting on page

62. It describes all the important sights
with maps, photographs and detailed
illustrations. In addition, six planned
walks take you step by step through
special areas of Rome.

Carefully researched tips for hotels,
shops and markets, restaurants and
cafés, sports and entertainment are
found in section three, *Travelers'
Needs*, and section four, *Survival
Guide* has advice on everything from
mailing a letter to catching the Metro.

ROME AREA BY AREA

The city has been divided
into the 16 central sightseeing areas, each separately
color-coded. Each chapter
opens with a portrait of the
area and a list of the sights
to be covered. These are
located by numbers on an
Area Map. This is followed
by a large-scale *Street-by-
Street Map* focusing on the
most interesting part of the
area. The main body of the
chapter consists of detailed
descriptions of all the listed
sights. Finding your way
around the chapter is made
simple by the numbering
system used throughout.
This refers to the order in
which the sights are
described in the chapter.

Sights at a Glance lists
the sights in the area
by category: Churches
and Temples, Museums
and Galleries, Historic
Streets and Piazzas,
Historic Buildings,
Arches and Gates,
Columns, Obelisks
and Statues, Fountains,
Ancient Sites and
Parks and Gardens.

The area covered in
greater detail on the
Street-by-Street Map
is shaded red.

Numbered circles pinpoint all
the listed sights on the *Area
Map*. Palazzo Doria Pamphilj,
for example, is ❻.

1 Area Map

*For easy reference, the
sights in each area are
numbered and located on
a map of the area. To help
the visitor, the map also
shows Metro stations and
parking areas.*

Photographs of distinctive
details of buildings help
you identify the sights.

Color-coding on
each page makes
the area easy to find
in the book.

2 Street-by-Street Map

*This gives a bird's-eye view of
the heart of each sightseeing
area. To help you locate and
identify important sights as
you walk around, these are
highlighted in stronger color.*

A locator map shows you
exactly where you are in
relation to surrounding areas.
The area shown in the *Street-
by-Street Map* is marked in red.

**Palazzo Doria
Pamphilj** ❻ is shown
on this map as well.

A suggested route for a walk
takes in the most interesting
and attractive streets in the area.

Stars indicate the sights that
no visitor should miss.

Travel tips help you to
reach the area quickly.

ROME AT A GLANCE
Each map in this section covers a specific theme: *Churches and Temples, Museums and Galleries, Fountains and Obelisks, Celebrated Visitors and Residents*. The top sights are shown on the map; other sights are described on the two pages following.

Each sightseeing area is color-coded.

The theme is explored in greater detail on the two pages following the map.

3 Detailed information on each sight
All the important sights in each area are described individually. They are listed in order, following the numbering on the Area Map. Practical information is also provided.

PRACTICAL INFORMATION
Each entry provides all the information needed to visit the sight. A key to the symbols used is inside the back cover.

Map reference to *Street Finder* at back of book   **Sight number**

Address   **Telephone number**

Palazzo Doria Pamphilj 6

Piazza del Collegio Romano 2.
Map 5 A4 & 12 E3. **[** 06-679 Z3 23. **]** 64, 70, 81, 85, 95, 117, 119, 492. **Open** 10am–1pm Fri–Wed. **Closed** Jan 1, May 1, Dec 25. **Adm charge**. **&** limited. **[]** compulsory for private apartments; notify attendant. **[]**

Opening hours

Useful bus routes   **Services and facilities available**

4 Rome's major sights
These are given two or more full pages in the sightseeing area in which they are found. Historic buildings are dissected to reveal their interiors, and museums and galleries have color-coded floor plans to help you find important exhibits.

The Visitors' Checklist provides the practical information you will need to plan your visit.

The façade of each major sight is shown to help you spot it quickly.

Stars indicate the most interesting architectural details of the building, and the most important works of art or exhibits on display inside.

A timeline charts the key events in the history of the building.

INTRODUCING ROME

Putting Rome on the Map

Sᴵɴᴄᴇ ɪᴛꜱ ꜰᴏᴜɴᴅᴀᴛɪᴏɴ ᴏᴠᴇʀ 2,700 years ago on seven hills near the banks of the River Tiber, Rome has grown into a city of three million people covering 580 sq miles (1,500 sq km) of central Italy. Within this area is the independent Vatican City State. Rome was made capital of the newly united Italy in 1870. It is about 17 miles (28 km) from the sea and has good rail and road links to many other historic Italian towns and cities.

KEY

☐ Rome and Environs

— Main railroad

✈ Airport

═ Highway

═ A road

0 kilometers   50

0 miles   25

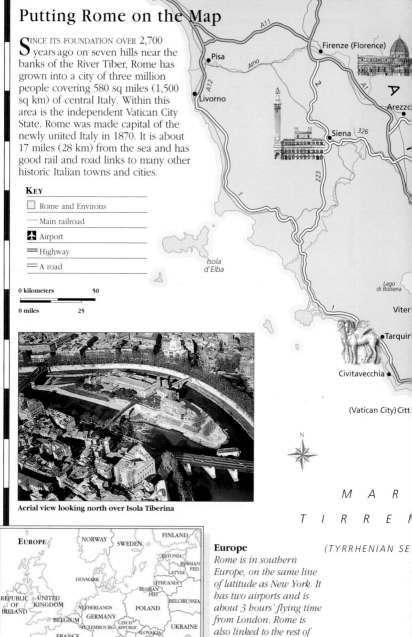

Aerial view looking north over Isola Tiberina

Europe
Rome is in southern Europe, on the same line of latitude as New York. It has two airports and is about 3 hours' flying time from London. Rome is also linked to the rest of Europe by road and rail. It is about 15 hours from Paris by train. It is also at the center of Italy's main road network, parts of which follow the routes of ancient Roman roads.

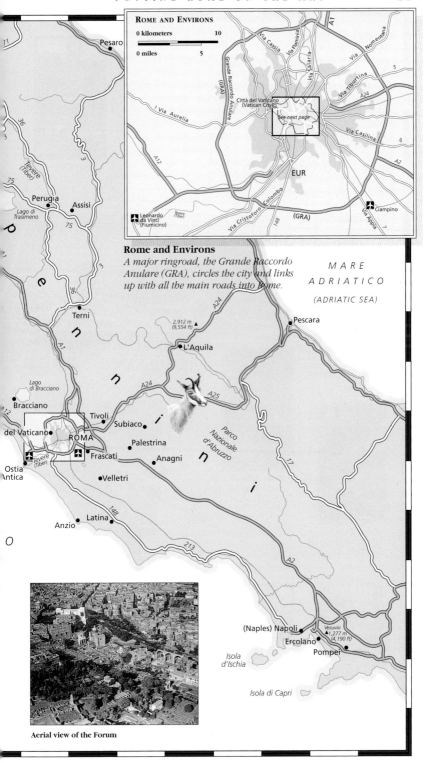

ROME AND ENVIRONS

0 kilometers 10

0 miles 5

Città del Vaticano
(Vatican City)

see next page

1 Via Aurelia

Via Cassia

Via Flaminia

A1

Via Nomentana

Via Salaria

Via Tiburtina

A24

Via Casilina

6

EUR

A12

Grande Raccordo Anulare (GRA)

Via Cristoforo Colombo

148

(GRA)

Leonardo
da Vinci
(Fiumicino)

Tevere
(Tiber)

Via Appia

7

Ciampino

5

Rome and Environs

*A major ringroad, the Grande Raccordo
Anulare (GRA), circles the city and links
up with all the main roads into Rome.*

MARE
ADRIATICO
(ADRIATIC SEA)

Pesaro

71

36

3

Tevere
(Tiber)

75

Perugia

Assisi

Lago di
Trasimeno

75

36

Terni

A1

Lago
di Bracciano

Bracciano

12

del Vaticano

ROMA

Ostia
Antica

Tevere
(Tiber)

Tivoli

Subiaco

Palestrina

Frascati

Anagni

Velletri

A24

2,912 m
(9,554 ft)

L'Aquila

A25

Parco
Nazionale
d'Abruzzo

Pescara

17

Anzio

Latina

148

213

A2

O

(Naples) Napoli

Ercolano

Pompei

Vesuvio
1,277 m
(4,190 ft)

Isola
d'Ischia

Isola di Capri

Aerial view of the Forum

Central Rome

M OST OF THE SIGHTS described in this book lie
within the old city wall in 16 areas shown on
the map below. Each of the areas has its own
chapter. If you are on a short visit, you may have to
restrict yourself to just a few of the central areas: the
Forum to see ancient Rome; the Capitol, Piazza
della Rotonda and Piazza Navona for the historic
center of the city; Campo de' Fiori for its grand
Renaissance palazzi; Piazza di Spagna for its
reminders of the 18th-century Grand Tour and its
smart modern shops; and the Vatican to see St.
Peter's and the center of Roman Catholicism.

PAGES 128–41
Street Finder maps
4, 5

0 meters 500

0 yards 500

N

*Piazza d.
Spagna*

PAGES 222–49
Street Finder maps
3, 4

Vatican

*Piazza
della
Rotonda*

*Piazza
Navona*

*Campo de'
Fiori*

Janiculum

T I B E R

PAGES 116–27
Street Finder maps
4, 11, 12

PAGES 142–53
Street Finder maps
4, 8, 11, 12

Trastevere

PAGES 214–21
Street Finder maps
3, 4, 7, 11

PAGES 206–13
Street Finder maps
4, 7, 8, 11

PAGES 102–15
Street Finder maps
4, 5, 12

PAGES 198–205
Street Finder maps
7, 8, 12

PAGES 154–65
Street Finder maps
5, 6, 12

PAGES 250–55
Street Finder maps
5, 6

PAGES 64–75
Street Finder maps
5, 12

PAGES 166–75
Street Finder maps
5, 6

PAGES 76–95
Street Finder maps
5, 8, 9, 12

PAGES 96–101
Street Finder map 8

PAGES 188–97
Street Finder maps
8, 9

PAGES 176–87
Street Finder maps
6, 9, 10

Via Veneto

Quirinal

Esquiline

Capitol

Forum

Palatine

Lateran

Aventine

Caracalla

THE HISTORY OF ROME

ONE OF THE most ancient cities in Europe, Rome was founded over 2,700 years ago. Since then, it has been continuously inhabited, and, as the headquarters first of the Roman Empire and then of the Catholic Church, it has had an immense impact on the world. Many European languages are based on Latin; many political and legal systems follow the ancient Roman model; and buildings all around the world utilize styles and techniques perfected in ancient Rome. The city itself retains layers of buildings spanning over two millennia. Not surprisingly, all this history can seem a little overwhelming.

Roman eagle (2nd century AD)

Rome began as an Iron Age hut village, founded in the mid-8th century BC. In 616, the Romans' sophisticated Etruscan neighbors seized power but were ousted in 509, when Rome became a Republic. It conquered most of the rest of Italy, then turned its attentions overseas, and by the 1st century BC it ruled Spain, North Africa and Greece. The expansion of the Empire provided opportunities for power-hungry individuals, and the clashing of egos led to the collapse of democracy. Julius Caesar ruled for a time as dictator, and his nephew, Octavian, became Rome's first emperor, assuming the title Augustus. During the reign of Augustus, Christ was born, and though Christians were persecuted until the 4th century AD, the new religion took hold, and Rome became its main center.

Even though it was the seat of the papacy, during the Middle Ages Rome went into decline. The city recovered spectacularly in the mid-15th century and for over 200 years was embellished by the greatest artists of the Renaissance and the Baroque. Finally, in 1870, Rome became the capital of the newly unified Italy.

15th-century map of Rome from the north

Detail from 2nd-century AD Roman mosaic from the Temple of Fortune in Palestrina

Rome's Early Development

ACCORDING TO THE HISTORIAN Livy, Romulus founded
Rome in 753 BC. Sometime later, realizing his tribe
was short of females, he invited the neighboring
Sabines to a festival and orchestrated the mass
abduction of their women. Although Livy's account is
pure legend, there is evidence that Rome was founded
around the middle of the 8th century BC, and that the
Romans and Sabines united shortly afterward. Historical
evidence also gives some support to Livy's claim that
after Romulus's death Rome was ruled by a series of
kings, and that in the 7th century BC it was conquered
by the Etruscans and ruled by the Tarquin family. Last
of the dynasty was Tarquinius Superbus (Tarquin
the Proud). His despotic rule led to the Etruscans
being expelled and the founding of a Republic
run by two annually elected consuls. The uprising
was led by Lucius Junius Brutus, the model of the
stern, patriotic Roman Republican.

EXTENT OF THE CITY

▨ *750 BC*   ☐ *Today*

Ceremonial trumpets

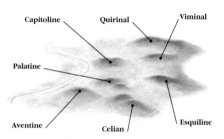

Capitoline   Quirinal   **Viminal**

Palatine

Aventine   Celian   **Esquiline**

The Seven Hills of Rome
*By the 8th century BC, shepherds and
farmers lived on four of Rome's seven hills.
As the population grew, huts were built in the
marshy valley later occupied by the Forum.*

Iron Age Hut
*Early settlers lived
in crude thatch
huts. Traces of
their original
foundations
have been
found on the
Palatine.*

**Augur, digging
foundation**

TEMPLE OF JUPITER
*This Renaissance painting by Perin del
Vaga shows Tarquinius Superbus
founding the Temple of Jupiter on the
Capitol, the sacred citadel of Rome.*

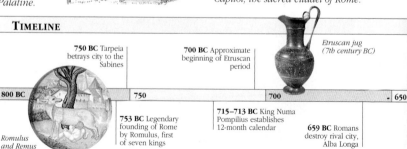

TIMELINE

750 BC Tarpeia
betrays city to the
Sabines

700 BC Approximate
beginning of Etruscan
period

*Etruscan jug
(7th century BC)*

800 BC   **750**   **700**   **650**

*Romulus
and Remus*

753 BC Legendary
founding of Rome
by Romulus, first
of seven kings

715–713 BC King Numa
Pompilius establishes
12-month calendar

659 BC Romans
destroy rival city,
Alba Longa

The Legend of the She-Wolf
The evil King of Alba threw his baby nephews, Romulus and Remus, into the Tiber but they were washed ashore and suckled by a she-wolf.

Raven, guardian of the citadel

Apollo of Veio
Etruscan culture and religion were influenced by the Greeks. This 5th- or 6th-century statue of the Greek god Apollo comes from Veio, a powerful, wealthy Etruscan city.

King Tarquin, holding the stone worshiped as a thunderbolt

The Legend of Aeneas
Some Roman legends make the Trojan hero Aeneas the grandfather of Romulus and Remus.

WHERE TO SEE ETRUSCAN ROME

The Cloaca Maxima sewer still functions, but there are few other traces of Etruscan Rome. Most finds come from Etruscan sites outside Rome like Tarquinia, with its tomb paintings of sumptuous banquets *(see p271)*, but there are major collections in the Villa Giulia *(pp262–3)* and Vatican Museums *(p238)*. The most famous object, however, is a bronze statue of the legendary she-wolf in the Capitoline Museums *(p73)*. The Antiquarium Forense *(p87)* displays objects from the necropolis that once occupied the site of the Roman Forum.

Funeral urns shaped like huts were used for cremation starting in the mid-8th century BC.

Etruscan jewelry, like this 7th-century BC gold filigree brooch, was lavish. Treasures of this kind have given the Etruscans a reputation for luxurious living.

600 BC Possible date of construction of Cloaca Maxima sewer

578 BC Servius Tullius Etruscan King

565 BC Traditional date of the Servian Wall around Rome's seven hills

Statue of Jupiter

510 BC Temple of Jupiter consecrated on Capitoline

600	550	500

616 BC Tarquinius Priscus, first Etruscan king. Forum and Circus Maximus established

534 BC King Servius murdered

509 BC L J Brutus expels Etruscans from Rome and founds the Republic

L J Brutus

507 BC War against Etruscans. Horatius defends wooden bridge across Tiber

Kings, Consuls and Emperors

R OME HAD OVER 250 RULERS in the 1,200 years between its
foundation by Romulus and AD 476, when the last emperor
was deposed by the German warrior Odoacer. Romulus was the
first of seven kings, overthrown in 509 BC when Rome became a
Republic. Authority was held by two annually elected consuls, but
provision was made for the appointment of a dictator in times of
crisis. In 494 BC, the office of Tribune was set up to protect the
plebeians from injustice at the hands of their patrician rulers.
Roman democracy, however, was always cosmetic. It was
discarded completely
in 27 BC, when
absolute power
was placed in
the hands of
the emperor.

70–63 BC Pompey

107–87 BC
Marius is
consul
seven times

205 BC Scipio
Africanus

218 BC Quintus Fabius
Maximus

*Romulus, his twin Remus and
the she-wolf who suckled them*

456 BC Lucius
Quintus
Cincinnatus

c.753–715 BC
Romulus

800 BC	700	600	500	400	300	200	100
SEVEN KINGS			**REPUBLIC**				
800 BC	700	600	500	400	300	200	100

c.715–673 BC
Numa
Pompilius

c.673–641 BC
Tullus Hostilius

c.641–616 BC
Ancus Marcius

c.534–509 BC
Tarquinius Superbus

c.579–534 BC
Servius Tullius

616–579 BC
Tarquinius Priscus

c.509 BC Lucius
Junius Brutus and
Horatius Pulvillus

396 BC Marcus
Furius Camillus

133 BC Tiberius Gracchus

122–121 BC
Gaius Gracchus

82–80 BC
Sulla

63 BC
Cicero

60–50 BC Triumvirate
of Julius Caesar,
Pompey and Crassus

45–44 BC Julius
Caesar is sole ruler

Tarquinius Priscus consulting an augur

*Julius Caesar,
whose rise to
power marked the
end of the
Roman Republic*

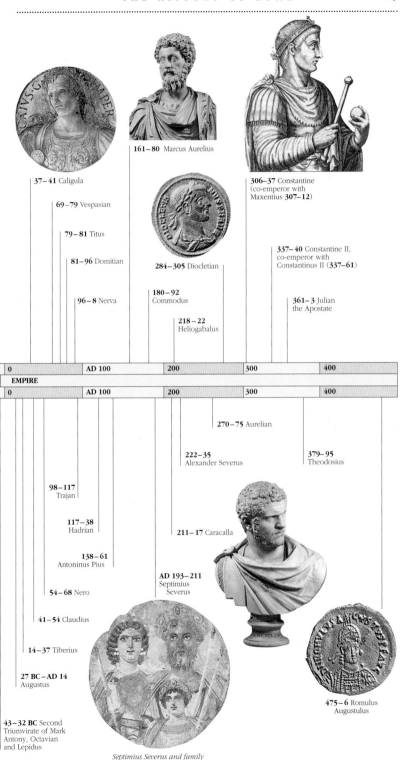

161–80 Marcus Aurelius

37–41 Caligula

69–79 Vespasian

79–81 Titus

81–96 Domitian

96–8 Nerva

284–305 Diocletian

180–92 Commodus

218–22 Heliogabalus

306–37 Constantine (co-emperor with Maxentius 307–12)

337–40 Constantine II, co-emperor with Constantinus II (337–61)

361–3 Julian the Apostate

0	AD 100	200	300	400

EMPIRE

0	AD 100	200	300	400

270–75 Aurelian

222–35 Alexander Severus

379–95 Theodosius

98–117 Trajan

117–38 Hadrian

211–17 Caracalla

138–61 Antoninus Pius

AD 193–211 Septimius Severus

54–68 Nero

41–54 Claudius

14–37 Tiberius

27 BC–AD 14 Augustus

475–6 Romulus Augustulus

43–32 BC Second Triumvirate of Mark Antony, Octavian and Lepidus

Septimius Severus and family

The Roman Republic

Bronze coin, showing Temple of Vesta (c.57 BC)

BY THE MID-2ND CENTURY BC, Rome controlled the west Mediterranean, policing and defending it with massive armies. The troops had more loyalty to the generals than to distant politicians, giving men like Marius, Sulla, Pompey and Caesar the muscle to seize political power. Meanwhile, peasants whose land had been destroyed during the invasion of Hannibal in 219 BC had flooded into Rome. They were followed by slaves and freedmen from conquered lands such as Greece, swelling the population to half a million. There was plenty of work for immigrants: constructing roads, aqueducts, markets and temples, all financed by taxes on Rome's expanding trade.

EXTENT OF THE CITY

▢ 400 BC	▢ Today

Cut stone blocks

Covered water channels

Arch spanning road

The gradient of an aqueduct was about 1 in 1,000.

How an Aqueduct Worked
Water from a spring in the hills was collected in a reservoir to build up pressure and ensure a steady supply to the city.

High ground

Cleaning vent

Reservoir

Underground water channel

Arches carrying water across low ground

Cicero Denounces Catiline
In 62 BC, Catiline planned a coup. Cicero discovered the plot and persuaded the Senate to condemn the conspirators to death.

TIMELINE

499 BC Battle against Latin tribes; Temple of Castor and Pollux built to commemorate the victory

Via Appia

380 BC Servian Wall rebuilt

396 BC Definitive victory over rival Etruscan city, Veio

312 BC Construction of Via Appia and Rome's first aqueduct, the Aqua Appia

500 BC	450 BC	400 BC	350 BC	300 BC

390 BC Rome invaded by Celtic Gauls: quacking geese on Capitoline hill warn of impending attack

264–241 BC First Punic War (against Carthage)

Relief of Capitoline geese

Roman Street
In the 1st century BC, most buildings in Rome were made from brick and concrete. Only a few public buildings were of marble.

AQUEDUCT (2ND CENTURY BC)
Rome owed much of its prosperity to its skilled civil engineers. When the city's wells were no longer sufficient, aqueducts were built to bring water from surrounding hills. Some were over 50 miles (80 km) long.

Arches for maintaining a constant gradient over low-lying land

Scipio Africanus
In 202 BC, the Roman general Scipio defeated Hannibal. Rome replaced Carthage as master of the Mediterranean.

Temple of Juno
The ruins of this 197 BC temple are embedded in the church of San Nicola in Carcere (see p151). Romans consulted their gods before all important ventures.

WHERE TO SEE REPUBLICAN ROME

This fresco depicting a group of slaves building a wall can be seen at the Museo Nazionale Romano *(see p163)*.

The Temple of Saturn, first built in 497 BC, now consists of eight majestic columns overlooking the Forum at the end of the Via Sacra *(see p83)*.

Rome's loveliest Republican buildings are the two Temples of the Forum Boarium *(see p203)*. Four more temples can be seen in the Area Sacra of Largo Argentina *(p150)*. Most monuments from this period, however, lie underground. Only a few, like the Tomb of the Scipios *(p195)*, have been excavated. One of the bridges leading to Tiber Island *(p153)*, the Ponte Fabricio, dates from the 1st century BC and is still used by pedestrians.

Ponte Fabricio, built in 62 BC

220 BC Via Flaminia built, linking Rome to the Adriatic coast	**168 BC** Victory in Macedonian War completes Roman conquest of Greece	**133–120 BC** Gracchi brothers killed for trying to introduce land reforms	**51 BC** Caesar conquers Gaul
250 BC	**200 BC**	**150 BC**	**100 BC**
218–202 BC Second Punic War; Scipio Africanus defeats Carthaginians	**149–146 BC** Third Punic War; Carthage destroyed	**71 BC** Spartacus's slave revolt crushed by Crassus and Pompey	**60 BC** Rome has three joint rulers: Pompey, Crassus and Caesar

Hannibal

Imperial Rome

Statue of Bacchus, god of wine

I N 44 BC, Caesar became dictator for life, only to be assassinated a month later. The result was 17 years of civil war, which ended in 27 BC, when Augustus became Rome's first emperor. The Empire expanded in fits and starts, but by the late 3rd century it was so huge that Diocletian decided to place it under the rule of four emperors. Thanks to trade and taxes from its vast domains, Rome was the most magnificent city in the world, studded with the lavish buildings of emperors advertising their civic munificence and military triumphs.

EXTENT OF THE CITY

☐ *AD 250*   ☐ *Today*

Cross-vaulted ceiling with mosaic decoration

Natatio (swimming pool)

Apotheosis of Augustus
The first and perhaps the greatest Roman emperor, Augustus ruled for 27 years and was deified by the Senate after his death.

ROMA CAPVT MVNDI

The baths could hold up to 3,000 people. They met to gossip in the central *frigidarium* (cold room).

Area for exercise and gymnastics

The Roman Empire under Trajan
By the 2nd century AD, the Roman Empire stretched from Britain to Syria, and Rome was known as the Caput Mundi, *the head of the world.*

TIMELINE

Emperor Nero

49 BC Caesar crosses the Rubicon and takes Rome

27 Augustus becomes first emperor

64 Fire during Nero's rule destroys much of city

65 First persecution of Christians under Nero

72 Colosseum begun

50 BC	0	AD 50	100

44 Caesar becomes dictator for life, and is murdered by Brutus and Cassius

AD 42 St Peter the Apostle comes to Rome

13 Ara Pacis is erected to celebrate the peace Augustus has secured in the Empire

67 St Peter is crucified and St Paul executed in Rome

Statue of St Peter in San Paolo fuori le Mura

Roman Revelry
Banquets could last for up to 10 hours, with numerous courses, between which guests would retire to a small room to relax.

WHERE TO SEE IMPERIAL ROME

There are relics of Imperial Rome throughout the city center, some hidden below churches and palazzi, others – like the Forum *(see pp76–87)*, the Palatine *(pp97–101)* and the Imperial Fora *(pp88–91)* – fully excavated. The magnificence of the era, however, is best conveyed by the Pantheon *(pp110–11)* and the Colosseum *(pp92–5)*.

BATHS OF DIOCLETIAN (AD 298)

Rome's public baths were not just places to keep clean. They also had bars, libraries, barbershops, brothels and sports facilities.

The Arch of Titus *(p87)*, erected in the Forum in AD 81, commemorates Emperor Titus's sack of Jerusalem in AD 70.

Tepidarium (warm room)

Virgil (70–19 BC)

Virgil was Rome's greatest epic poet. His most famous work is the Aeneid, *the story of the Trojan hero Aeneas, and his journey to the future site of Rome.*

A relief of Mithras, a popular Persian god (3rd century AD), can be seen beneath the church of San Clemente *(pp186–7)*.

164–180 Plague rages in Roman Empire

212 Citizenship granted to virtually all inhabitants of the Empire

270 Aurelian Wall begun

Section of Aurelian Wall

| 150 | 200 | 250 |

125 Hadrian redesigns the Pantheon

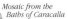
Mosaic from the Baths of Caracalla

216 Baths of Caracalla completed

247 Rome's Millennium is celebrated

284 Empire divided into West and East

Early Christian Rome

Crucifixion in Santa Maria Antiqua

IN THE 1ST CENTURY AD, during the reign of Tiberius, a rebellious pacifist was crucified in a distant corner of the Empire. This was nothing unusual, but within a few years, the followers of that man – Jesus Christ – became notorious in Rome, and they and Christ's teachings were perceived as a threat to public order, and many Christians were executed. Even so, the new religion spread through all levels of Roman society. When the Apostles Peter and Paul arrived in Rome, there was a small Christian community, and in spite of persecution by the state, Christianity flourished. In AD 313, the Emperor Constantine issued an edict granting Christians freedom of worship and soon after founded a shrine on the site of St. Peter's tomb. This secured Rome's position as a center of Christianity, but in the 5th century Rome's political importance declined, and the city fell to Goths and other invaders.

EXTENT OF THE CITY

☐ *AD 395*   ☐ *Today*

Youthful, beardless representation of Christ

St. Paul

Classical-style border decorated with fruit

4TH-CENTURY MOSAIC, SANTA COSTANZA
Beautiful mosaics, often with palm trees and other Oriental motifs suggesting Jerusalem, helped spread the message of early Christianity.

Santo Stefano Rotondo
This 17th-century engraving shows how a Roman temple (top) might have been transformed (above) into the 5th-century round church of Santo Stefano.

The Good Shepherd
The pagan image of a shepherd sacrificing a lamb became a Christian symbol.

TIMELINE

c.320 Building of first St. Peter's

356 Legendary founding of Santa Maria Maggiore

Gold solidus of Theodosius

410 Rome sacked by Alaric's Goths

455 Rome sacked again by Vandals

| 300 | 350 | 400 | 450 |

312 Control of Empire won by Constantine after battle at Milvian Bridge

Battle of the Milvian Bridge

380 Emperor Theodosius makes Christianity the official religion of the Roman Empire

395 Division of the Empire between Ravenna and Constantinople

422 Founding of Santa Sabina

Epigraph of Peter and Paul
This is one of hundreds of early Christian graffiti housed in the Lapidary Gallery of the Vatican (see p237).

Crucifixion, Santa Sabina
This 5th-century panel on the door of Santa Sabina (see p204) is one of the earliest known representations of the Crucifixion. Interestingly, Christ's cross is not actually shown.

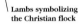

St. Peter receiving peace from the Savior

Lambs symbolizing the Christian flock

Constantine's Cross
Constantine's vision of the True Cross during the Battle of the Milvian Bridge made him convert to Christianity.

WHERE TO SEE EARLY CHRISTIAN ROME

There are traces of early Christianity all over Rome. Many ancient churches were built over early Christian meeting places and sites of martyrdoms: among them are San Clemente *(see pp186–7),* Santa Pudenziana *(p171)* and Santa Cecilia *(p211).* Outside the walls of the old city are miles of underground catacombs *(pp265–6),* many decorated with Christian frescoes, while the Vatican's Pio-Christian Museum *(p240)* has the best collection of early Christian art.

This statuette, carved out of bone, is embedded in the rock of the Catacombs of San Panfilo, just off the Via Salaria **(map 2 F4).**

The Cross of Justin, in the Treasury of St. Peter's *(p232),* was given to Rome by the Emperor Justin in AD 578.

475 Fall of Western Roman Empire; Byzantium becomes seat of Empire

A Byzantine image of St. Paul

609 Pantheon is consecrated as a Christian church

500　　　550　　　600

496 Anastasius II is first pope to assume title *Pontifex Maximus*

590–604 Pope Gregory the Great strengthens the papacy

630 Sant'Agnese fuori le Mura is built in Roman Byzantine style

The Papacy

THE POPE is considered Christ's representative on earth, claiming his authority from St. Peter, the first Bishop of Rome. Though some popes have been great thinkers and reformers, the role has rarely been purely spiritual. In the Middle Ages, many popes were involved in power struggles with the Holy Roman Emperor. Renaissance popes like Julius II and Leo X, the patrons of Raphael and Michelangelo, lived as luxuriously as any secular prince. The popes listed here include all those who exercised significant political or religious influence, up as far as the end of the Counter-Reformation, when the power of the papacy began to wane.

St. Ludovic Kneels before Boniface VIII *by Simone Martini*

314–35 St. Sylvester I

222–30 St. Urban I

217–22 St. Callixtus I

590–604 St. Gregory the Great

496–8 Anastasius II

Gregory the Great leading a procession to end the plague

931–5 John XI

891–6 Formosus

955–64 John XII

1227–41 Gregory IX

1216–27 Honorius III Savelli

0	200	400	600	800	1000	1200

PAPACY BASED IN ROME

0	200	400	600	800	1000	1200

336 St. Mark

352–66 Liberius

88–97 St. Clement

42–67 St. Peter

579–90 Pelagius II

608–15 St. Boniface IV

731–41 St. Gregory III

772–95 Adrian I

847–55 St. Leo IV

817–24 St. Paschal I

795–816 St. Leo III

1032–44, 1047–8 Benedict IX

1073–85 St. Gregory VII

1099–1118 Paschal II

1130–43 Innocent II

1154–9 Adrian IV

1198–1216 Innocent III

St. Peter, *from a mosaic in Santa Prassede* (see p171)

Innocent III's Vision of the Church, *from a fresco by Giotto*

Portrait of Gregory XIII by Lavinia Fontana

1560–65 Pius IV Medici

1555–9 Paul IV

1523–34 Clement VII Medici

1513–21 Leo X Medici

1492–1503 Alexander VI Borgia

1294–1303 Boniface VIII

1484–92 Innocent VIII Cybo

1471–84 Sixtus IV della Rovere

1464–71 Paul II Barbo

1458–64 Pius II Piccolomini

1572–84 Gregory XIII Boncompagni

1670–76 Clement X Altieri

1667–9 Clement IX

1655–67 Alexander VII Chigi

1605 Leo XI Medici

1700–21 Clement XI

1300	1400	1500	1600	1700
AVIGNON	**PAPACY AGAIN BASED IN ROME**			
1300	1400	1500	1600	1700

1417–31 Martin V Colonna

1447–55 Nicholas V

1584–7 Sixtus V

1644–55 Innocent X Pamphilj

1623–44 Urban VIII Barberini

Nicholas V Receiving a Book, *illustration from a contemporary manuscript*

1503–13 Julius II della Rovere

1592–1605 Clement VIII Aldobrandini

1605–21 Paul V Borghese

Urban VIII Approving a Building Project *in the Vatican's Gallery of Tapestries* (see p241)

Raphael's portrait of Julius II

1534–49 Paul III Farnese

Paul III Gives His Approval to the Capuchin Order *by Sebastiano Ricci*

Medieval Rome

Mosaic, San Clemente

Supplanted by Constantinople as capital of the Empire in the 4th century, Rome was reduced to a few thousand inhabitants by the early Middle Ages, its power just a memory. In the 8th and 9th centuries, the growing importance of the papacy revived the city and made it once more a center of power. But continual conflicts between the Pope and the Holy Roman Emperor soon weakened the papacy. The 10th, 11th and 12th centuries were among the bleakest in Roman history: violent invaders left Rome poverty-stricken, and the constantly warring local barons tore apart what remained of the city. Despite this, the first Holy Year was declared in 1300 and thousands of pilgrims arrived in Rome. But by 1309, the papacy was forced to move to Avignon, leaving Rome to slide into further squalor and strife.

EXTENT OF THE CITY

▨ 1300   ☐ Today

Charlemagne Crowned in St. Peter's
On Christmas Day in 800, Charlemagne was made emperor of the Holy Roman Empire, a new Christian dominion to replace that of ancient Rome.

Trajan's Column

Column of Marcus Aurelius

Madonna and Child Mosaic
The Chapel of St. Zeno (817–24) in the church of Santa Prassede (see p171) has some of the best examples of Byzantine mosaics in Rome.

San Giovanni in Laterano

Aurelian Wall

MEDIEVAL PLAN OF ROME
Maps like this one, illustrating the principal features of the city, were produced for pilgrims, the tourists of the Middle Ages.

TIMELINE

Emperor Otto I

700	800	900	1000
725 King Ine of Wessex founds the first hostel for pilgrims in the Borgo	**852** The Vatican is fortified with walls following a raid by Saracens		**961** King Otto the Great becomes first German Holy Roman Emperor
778 Charlemagne, King of the Franks, conquers Italy	**800** Charlemagne crowned emperor in St. Peter's	**880–932** Rome is ruled by two women, Theodora and then her daughter, Marozia	

Stefaneschi Triptych *(1315)*
Giotto and his pupils painted this triptych for Cardinal Stefaneschi as an altarpiece for St. Peter's. It is now in the Vatican Museums (see p240).

Colosseum

Capitol

Pyramid of Caius Cestius

Old St. Peter's

Castel Sant'Angelo

Pantheon

Cosmati Tabernacle
Marblework by the Cosmati family, like this tabernacle in Santa Sabina (see p204), decorates many of Rome's medieval churches.

WHERE TO SEE MEDIEVAL ROME

Among the most interesting churches of the period are San Clemente, with a fine apse mosaic and Cosmati floor *(see pp186 – 7)*, Santa Maria in Trastevere *(pp212–13)* and Santa Maria sopra Minerva, Rome's only Gothic church *(p108)*. Santa Cecilia in Trastevere *(p211)* has a Cavallini fresco, and there is fine Cosmati work in Santa Maria in Cosmedin *(p202)*.

Charlemagne's Dalmatic in the Treasury of St. Peter's *(p232)* was supposedly worn by the Holy Roman Emperor at his coronation. In fact, the richly embroidered vestment probably dates from the 14th century.

Santa Sabina *(p204)* on the Aventine Hill has a medieval bell tower.

Mosaic façade, Santa Maria in Trastevere (pp212–13)

1084 Rome is attacked by Normans

1100

1108 San Clemente is rebuilt

1140 Santa Maria in Trastevere is restored

1200 Rome is an independent commune under Arnaldo di Brescia

1200

1232 Cloister of San Giovanni in Laterano completed

1309 Pope Clement V moves the papacy to Avignon

1300 First Holy Year proclaimed by Pope Boniface VIII

1300

Cola di Rienzo

1347 Cola di Rienzo – an Italian patriot – tries to restore the Roman Republic

1348 Black Death strikes Rome

Renaissance Rome

POPE NICHOLAS V came to the throne in 1447 determined to make Rome a city fit for the papacy. Among his successors, men like Julius II and Leo X eagerly followed his lead, and the city's appearance was transformed. The Classical ideals of the Renaissance inspired artists, architects and craftsmen, such as Michelangelo, Bramante, Raphael and Cellini, to build and decorate the churches and palaces of a newly confident Rome.

Detail of Botticelli's *Youth of Moses* **(1480s)**

EXTENT OF THE CITY

▨ *1500*	☐ *Today*

Hemispherical dome

Balustrade of small columns

Classical colonnade of 16 Doric columns

School of Athens by Raphael
In this fresco (see p243), Raphael complimented many of his peers by representing them as ancient Greek philosophers. The building shown is based on a design by Bramante.

THE TEMPIETTO
The Tempietto (1502) at San Pietro in Montorio (see p219) was one of Bramante's first works in Rome. A simple, perfectly proportioned miniature Classical temple, it is a model of High Renaissance architecture.

Cosmati-style mosaic floor

Palazzo Caprini
Bramante's design had a strong influence on later Renaissance palazzi. Parts of the building survive in Palazzo dei Convertendi (see p227).

TIMELINE

1377 Papacy returns to Rome from Avignon under Pope Gregory XI

1409–15 Papacy moves to Pisa

1452 Demolition of old St. Peter's basilica begins

1444 Birth of Bramante

1350		1400		1450

1378–1417 The Great Schism, a division in the papacy in Avignon

1417 Pope Martin V ends the Great Schism in the papacy

Pope Martin V, reigned 1417–31

Sack of Rome
In 1527, the unruly troops of Charles V of Spain pillaged the city, destroying countless works of art. Pope Clement VII took refuge in Castel Sant'Angelo.

WHERE TO SEE RENAISSANCE ROME

The Campo de' Fiori area (see pp142–53) is full of grand Renaissance palazzi, especially along Via Giulia (pp276–7). Across the river stands the delightful Villa Farnesina (pp220–21). The most typical church of the period is Santa Maria del Popolo (pp138–9), and the best collection of Renaissance art is in the Vatican Museums (pp234–47). These include the Sistine Chapel (pp244–7) and the Raphael Rooms (pp242–3).

The Madonna di Foligno by Raphael (1511–12) is one of the fine Renaissance paintings in the Vatican Pinacoteca (p241).

Pope Nicholas V
Nicholas ordered the demolition of the old St. Peter's.

The Pietà, commissioned for St. Peter's in 1501, was one of Michelangelo's first sculptures executed in Rome (p233).

Statue of St. Peter, believed to have been crucified on this site

Underground chapel

1475 Birth of Michelangelo

1483 Birth of Raphael

1486 Building of Palazzo della Cancelleria

1506 Pope Julius II orders start of work on new St. Peter's

1500

1508 Michelangelo begins painting the Sistine Chapel ceiling

Cumaean Sibyl, Sistine Chapel

1519 Frescoes completed in Villa Farnesina

1527 Troops of Emperor Charles V sack Rome

1550

1547 Pope Paul III appoints Michelangelo architect of St. Peter's

Emperor Charles V

Baroque Rome

BY THE 16TH CENTURY, the Catholic Church had become immensely rich – one of the chief criticisms of the Protestant reformers. The display of grandeur and extravagance by the papal court contrasted sharply with the poverty of the people, and **Baroque putto** wealthy Roman society was characterized by sumptuous luxury and a ceaseless round of entertainment. To make the Catholic faith more appealing than Protestantism, scores of churches were built and monuments and fountains were erected to glorify the Holy See. The finest architects in the ornate, dramatic style of the Baroque were Bernini and Borromini.

EXTENT OF THE CITY

▨ 1645	☐ Today

Ceiling portraying heavenly scenes

Monument to Pope Alexander VII
This Bernini tomb in St. Peter's (pp230–33) includes a skeleton brandishing an hourglass.

Gian Lorenzo Bernini *(1598–1680)*
The favorite artist of the papacy, Bernini transformed Rome with his churches, palaces, statues and fountains.

Holy Family fresco

Tapestry of Pope Urban VIII
Bernini's most devoted patron, Pope Urban VIII Barberini (1623– 44), is shown here receiving the homage of the nations.

A marble rose marks the best place to stand to appreciate the illusion of space created by the artist.

TIMELINE

1568 The Jesuits build the Gesù, prototypical church of the early Baroque

Altar carving from the Gesù

1595 Annibale Carracci begins to fresco Palazzo Farnese

1624 Bernini's sculpture of *Apollo and Daphne*

1626 Work on St. Peter's is completed

1550	1575	1600	1625

1571 Birth of Caravaggio

1585 Pope Sixtus V plans new streets

1600 Philosopher Giordano Bruno is burned at the stake for heresy

Galileo

1633 Galileo condemned to house arrest for heresy

Illusionistic beams in ceiling

Chapel painted on flat slanting wall

Figures painted to be viewed from an angle

Queen Christina of Sweden
In a coup for Catholicism, Christina renounced Protestantism and abdicated her throne. In 1655, she moved to Rome, where she became the center of a lively literary and scientific circle.

St. Ignatius, founder of the Jesuits

Francesco Borromini
(1599 – 1667)
In the many churches he built in Rome, Borromini made use of revolutionary geometric forms.

POZZO CORRIDOR
The use of perspective to create an illusion of depth and space was a favorite Baroque device. Andrea Pozzo painted this illusionistic corridor in the 1680s in the Rooms of St. Ignatius near the Gesù (see pp114–15).

San Carlo alle Quattro Fontane
One of Borromini's most influential designs was this tiny oval church (see p161) on the Quirinal hill.

1651 Bernini redesigns much of Piazza Navona

Bernini's Fontana dei Fiumi in Piazza Navona

1694 Palazzo di Montecitorio is completed

1735 Spanish Steps are designed

1732 Work starts on the Trevi Fountain

1650	1675	1700	1725

1657 Borromini completes Sant'Agnese in Agone

1656 Work starts on Bernini's colonnade for St. Peter's Square

Bonnie Prince Charlie, pretender to the throne of England

1721 Bonnie Prince Charlie is born in Rome

1734 Clement XII makes Palazzo Nuovo world's first public museum

Understanding Rome's Architecture

Arch of Titus

THE ARCHITECTURE of Imperial Rome kept alive the Classical styles of ancient Greece, at the same time developing new, uniquely Roman forms based on the arch, the vault and the dome. The next important period was the 12th century, when many Romanesque churches were built. The Renaissance saw a return to Classical ideals, inspired by the example of Florence, but in the 17th century Rome found a style of its own again in the flamboyance of the Baroque.

The entablature above these columns has both straight and arched sections (Hadrian's Villa).

CLASSICAL ROME

Most Roman buildings were of concrete faced with brick, but from the 1st century BC, the Romans started to imitate earlier Greek models, using marble to decorate temples and other public buildings.

Plain frieze

Corinthian capital

Triangular pediment

Cornice (projecting section along facade)

Architrave (horizontal section resting on columns)

Fluted column shaft

Podium

Cella (inner sanctuary)

Colonnade enclosing portico

Roman temples were usually built on a raised dais or podium, to make them prominent. Many were fronted by a portico, a roofed porch with columns.

Caryatids were sculpted columns, usually in the form of a female figure. Roman caryatids, like this one in the Forum of Augustus, were often copied in detail from earlier Greek examples.

The orders of Classical architecture were building styles, each based on a different column design. The three major orders were borrowed by the Romans from the Greeks.

Aedicules were small shrines, framed by two pillars, usually containing a statue of a god.

Coffers were decorative sunken panels that reduced the weight of domed and vaulted ceilings.

Doric order   **Ionic order**   **Corinthian order**

EARLY CHRISTIAN AND MEDIEVAL ROME

The first Christian churches in Rome were based on the basilica: oblong, with three naves, each usually ending in an apse. From the 10th to the 13th centuries, most churches were built in the Romanesque style, which used the rounded arches of ancient Rome.

Basilicas in Rome have, in most cases, kept their original rectangular shape. The nave of San Giovanni in Laterano retains its 4th-century floorplan.

The triumphal arch divides the nave of a church from the apse. Here, in San Paolo fuori le Mura, it is decorated with mosaics.

RENAISSANCE AND BAROQUE ROME

Renaissance architecture (15th–16th centuries) drew its inspiration directly from Classical models. It revived the use of strict geometric proportions. The Baroque age (late 16th–17th centuries) broke many established rules, favoring grandiose decoration over pure Classical forms.

Putti were a popular decorative feature in the Baroque. A *putto* is a painting or sculpture of a child like a Cupid or cherub.

A loggia is an open-sided gallery or arcade. It may be a separate structure or part of a building, as here at San Saba.

A tabernacle is used to house the Sacrament for the mass. This 13th-century Gothic wall tabernacle is in San Clemente.

A baldacchino is a canopy, supported on columns, rising over the main altar. This Baroque example is in St Peter's.

Rusticated masonry decorates the exterior of many Renaissance palazzi. It consists of massive blocks divided by deep joints.

COSMATESQUE SCULPTURE AND MOSAICS

The Cosmati family, active in Rome during the 12th and 13th centuries, have given their name to a particularly Roman style of decoration. They worked in marble, producing various elements for churches, including cloisters, episcopal thrones, tombs, pulpits, fonts and candlesticks. These were often decorated with bands of colorful mosaic. They also left many fine floor mosaics, usually of white marble with an inlay of red and green porphyry. Ancient Roman columns were cut up to provide the materials. Several other families of stonemasons used a similar style, and their work is also described as Cosmatesque.

Cosmatesque floor, Santa Maria in Cosmedin

Rome during Unification

UNDER NAPOLEON, Italy had a brief taste of unity, but by 1815 it was once more divided into many small states, and papal rule was restored in Rome. Over the next 50 years, patriots – led by Mazzini, Garibaldi and others – struggled to create an independent, unified Italy. In 1848, Rome was briefly declared a Republic, but Garibaldi's forces were driven out by French troops. The French continued to protect the pope, while the rest of Italy was united as a kingdom under Vittorio Emanuele of Savoy. In 1870, troops stormed the city, and Rome became capital of Italy.

Garibaldi in his distinctive red shirt

EXTENT OF THE CITY

☐ *1870*   ☐ *Today*

Porta Pia

Tricolored flag of the new Italian kingdom

Plumed hat of the Bersaglieri, crack troops from Savoy

Allegory of Italy's Liberty
This patriotic poster from 1890 shows the king; his chief minister, Cavour; Garibaldi; and Mazzini. The woman in red represents Italy.

Vittorio Emanuele II
Vittorio Emanuele, King of Piedmont, became the first King of Italy in 1861.

ROYALISTS STORM PORTA PIA
On September 20, 1870, troops of the kingdom of Italy put an end to the papal domination of Rome. They breached the city walls near Porta Pia; the pope retreated, and Rome was made the Italian capital.

TIMELINE

1751 Piranesi's *Views of Rome* revive interest in Classical ruins

1762 Trevi Fountain is completed

Napoleon Bonaparte

1797 Napoleon captures Rome

1799 Napoleon expelled from Italy by Austrians and Russians

1750		1775		1800

Piranesi etching of Trajan's Forum

1792 Canova creates the Tomb of Pope Clement XIII, St. Peter's

1800–1 Napoleon takes Italy again

1807 Birth of Garibaldi

Garibaldi and Rome

The charismatic leader Giuseppe Garibaldi had taken much of Italy from foreign rule by 1860. Rome still remained a crucial problem. Here he declares "O Roma o morte" (Rome or Death).

Villa Paolina

Giuseppe Verdi

(1813–1901)
Verdi, the opera composer, supported unification and in 1861 became a member of Italy's first national parliament.

Breach in Aurelian Wall

A Freed City

This marble plaque was set up at Porta Pia to commemorate the liberation of Rome.

Victor Emmanuel Monument

A vast monument to Italy's first king (see p74) stands in Piazza Venezia.

· S · P · Q · R ·
VRBE · ITALIAE · VINDICATA
INCOLIS · FELICITER · AVCTIS
GEMINOS · FORNICES · CONDIDIT

1816 Work begins on Piazza del Popolo

Fountain in Piazza del Popolo

1848 Nationalist uprising in Rome. Pope flees and a Republic is formed

1860 Garibaldi and his 1,000 followers take Sicily and Naples

1870 Royalist troops take Rome, completing the unification of Italy

1825	1850

1820 Revolts throughout Italy

1821 Keats dies in Piazza di Spagna

1849 Pope is restored to power, protected by a French garrison

Pope Pius IX

1861 Kingdom of Italy founded with capital in Turin

Modern Rome

World Cup mania

THE FASCIST DICTATOR Mussolini dreamed of recreating the immensity, order and power of the old Roman Empire: "Rome," he said, "must appear wonderful to the whole world." He began to build a grandiose new complex, EUR, in the suburbs, and razed 15 churches and many medieval houses to create space for wide new roads. Fortunately most of the old center has survived, leaving the city with one of Europe's most pictur-esque historic cores. To mark the Holy Year and the new millennium, many crumbling churches, buildings and monuments were given a thorough facelift.

EXTENT OF THE CITY

☐ *1960s*   ☐ *Today*

Mussolini's Plans for Rome
This propaganda poster reflects Mussolini's grandiose projects such as Via dei Fori Imperiali in the Forum area (see p76), and EUR (p267).

Pope John Paul II
John Paul II is the first non-Italian pope since the 1520s. A traditionalist, he exerts a tremendous influence on the lives of the world's Catholics.

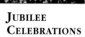

JUBILEE CELEBRATIONS
Jubilee Years are usually celebrated every quarter of a century. Millions of Catholics visited Rome to celebrate the year 2000.

TIMELINE

1915 Italy enters World War I	**1929** Lateran Treaty creates a separate Vatican state **1926** Opposition parties banned	**1944** Allies liberate Rome from Germans	**1946** National referendum establishes Italy as a Republic; King Umberto II exiled

1900	1915	1930	1945

1911 Victor Emmanuel Monument is completed

1922 Fascists march on Rome. Mussolini becomes Prime Minister

Poster for EUR

1940 Italy enters World War II; work begins on EUR zone

Three Tenors Concert (1990)
Combining Italy's love for music and soccer, this opera recital at the Baths of Caracalla was broadcast live during the World Cup.

Poster for La Dolce Vita
In the 1950s and '60s Rome was Europe's Hollywood. Ben-Hur, Quo Vadis? and Cleopatra were made at the Cinecittà studios, as well as Italian movies like Fellini's La Dolce Vita.

Valentino Model
While not as important as Milan for fashion, Rome is still home to some of the industry's leading designers.

City-Center Traffic
Rome's streets are congested, and many buildings have been damaged by pollution. There are plans to close the historic center to traffic.

1960 Olympic Games are held in Rome

1978 Premier Aldo Moro kidnapped, then killed by Red Brigades; Karol Wojtyla is elected Pope John Paul II

1990 Rome hosts soccer World Cup finals

2002 The Euro becomes legal tender

1960	1975	1990	2000	2010

1962 Second Vatican Council brings about Church reforms

1957 Treaty of Rome initiates European Common Market

1981 Assassination attempt on Pope John Paul II in St. Peter's Square

1993 Francesco Rutelli becomes Rome's first elected mayor

2000 Rome enters the 21st century with millions of pilgrims celebrating the Holy Year, known as the Jubilee

ROME AT A GLANCE

FROM ITS EARLY DAYS as a simple settlement of shepherds on the Palatine Hill, Rome grew to rule a vast empire that stretched from northern England to North Africa. Later, after the empire had collapsed, Rome became the center of the Christian world, and artists and architects flocked to work for the popes. The legacy of this history can be seen throughout the city. The following pages are a timesaving summary of the best Rome has to offer. There are sections on churches and temples, museums and galleries, fountains and obelisks, and celebrated visitors and residents. Below are the top attractions no visitor should miss.

ROME'S TOP TOURIST ATTRACTIONS

Capitoline Museums
See pp70–73.

Colosseum
See pp92–5.

Sistine Chapel
See pp244–7.

Spanish Steps
See p134.

Raphael Rooms
See pp242–3.

Trevi Fountain
See p159.

Pantheon
See pp110–11.

Castel Sant'Angelo
See pp248–9.

St. Peter's
See pp230–33.

Roman Forum
See pp78–87.

Piazza Navona
See p120.

Interior of the Pantheon, by Giovanni Paolo Pannini (1691–1765)

Rome's Best: Churches and Temples

As the center of Christianity, Rome has a vast wealth of beautiful and interesting churches. These range from magnificent great basilicas, built to assert the importance of the medieval and Renaissance Catholic church, to smaller, humbler buildings where the first Christians gathered, often in secret. Among the most fascinating early churches are those converted from ancient Roman temples. Additions to these over the years have resulted in some intriguing many-layered buildings. A more detailed historical overview of Rome's churches is on pages 44 to 45.

Pantheon
This monumental 2,000-year-old building is one of the largest surviving temples of ancient Rome.

St. Peter's
At 450 ft (136 m) high, Michelangelo's dome is the tallest in the world. Sadly, the artist died before seeing his work completed.

Santa Maria in Trastevere
Built over a very early Christian foundation, this church is famous for its ornate mosaics.

Vatican

Piazza di Spagna

Piazza della Rotonda

Piazza Navona

Janiculum

Campo de' Fiori

Capito

Trastevere

Santa Cecilia in Trastevere
This statue of Cecilia, showing her as she lay when her tomb was uncovered, was sculpted in 1599 by Stefano Maderno.

Santa Maria in Cosmedin
The decorations in this 6th-century church are 12th century and earlier. A restored painting in the apse shows the Virgin, Child and saints.

Santa Maria Maggiore
Rich mosaics and relics contrast with the sober interior form of Santa Maria Maggiore. Among its treasures are vestments bearing the Borghese coat of arms.

Sant'Andrea al Quirinale
Bernini made maximum use of strong, dynamic curves in this oval interior (1658–70), creating a small masterpiece of the Roman Baroque.

Santa Prassede
Magnificent Byzantine mosaics cover the walls and ceilings of this 9th-century church. This Christ with angels is in the Chapel of St. Zeno.

Santa Croce in Gerusalemme
Saints adorn the façade of Santa Croce. Inside are relics of the Cross, brought from Jerusalem by St. Helena.

Via Veneto

Quirinal

Forum

Palatine

Aventine

Caracalla

Esquiline

Lateran

0 meters 500

0 yards 500

San Clemente
Different archaeological layers lie beneath the 12th-century church. This sarcophagus dates from the 4th century.

San Giovanni in Laterano
The original church was built by Constantine, the first Christian emperor. The Chapel of St. Venantius mosaics include the figure of St. Venantius himself.

Exploring Churches and Temples

THERE ARE MORE CHURCHES in Rome than there are days of the year, so you'll have to be selective. Catholic pilgrims have always been drawn to the seven major basilicas: **St. Peter's**, the heart of the Roman Catholic church; **San Giovanni in Laterano**; **San Paolo fuori le Mura**; **Santa Maria Maggiore**; **Santa Croce in Gerusalemme**; **San Lorenzo fuori le Mura** and **San Sebastiano**. These have a wealth of relics, tombs and magnificent works of art from many different periods. Smaller churches can be equally fascinating, especially those that have preserved their original character.

13th-century fresco by Pietro Cavallini in Santa Cecilia

ANCIENT TEMPLES

ONE PAGAN TEMPLE survives virtually unaltered since it was erected in the 2nd century AD. The **Pantheon**, "Temple of all the Gods," has a domed interior quite different in structure from any other church in Rome. It was reconsecrated as a Christian church in the 7th century.

Other Roman temples have been incorporated into Christian churches at various times. Two of these are in the Forum: **Santi Cosma e Damiano** was established in the Temple of Romulus in 526, while San Lorenzo in Miranda was built onto the ruins of the **Temple of Antoninus and Faustina** in the 11th century. The Baroque façade, built in 1602, looms behind the columns of the temple.

Another church that clearly shows its ancient Roman origins is **Santa Costanza**, built as a mausoleum for Constantine's daughter. It is a round church with some splendid 4th-century mosaics.

EARLY CHRISTIAN AND MEDIEVAL CHURCHES

SOME EARLY BASILICAS – the 5th-century **Santa Maria Maggiore** and **Santa Sabina**, for example – retain much of their original structure. Other, even earlier, churches such as the 4th-century **San Paolo fuori le Mura** and **San Giovanni in Laterano** preserve their original basilica shape. San Paolo was rebuilt after an 1823 fire destroyed the original building, and the San Giovanni of today dates from a 1646 reconstruction by Borromini. Both these churches still have their medieval cloisters.

Santa Maria in Trastevere and **Santa Cecilia in Trastevere** were built over houses where the earliest Christian communities met and worshiped in secret to avoid persecution. One church where the different layers of earlier structures can clearly be seen is **San Clemente**. At its lowest level, it has a Mithraic temple of the 3rd century AD. Other early churches include **Santa Maria in Cosmedin,** with its impressive Romanesque bell tower, and the fortified convent of **Santi Quattro Coronati**. Many Roman churches, most notably **Santa Prassede**, contain fine early Christian and medieval mosaics.

Cloister of San Giovanni in Laterano

The impressive domed interior of the Pantheon, which became a church in 609

UNUSUAL FLOOR PLANS

The design of Rome's first churches was based on the ancient basilica, a rectangular building divided into three naves. Since then, there have been many bold departures from this plan – including round churches, square churches based on the shape of the Greek cross, as in Bramante's plan for St. Peter's and, in the Baroque period, even oval and hexagonal ones.

Pantheon (2nd century)

Santa Costanza (4th century)

RENAISSANCE

The greatest undertaking of the Renaissance popes was the rebuilding of **St. Peter's**. Disagreements on the form it should take meant that, although work started in 1506, it was not completed until well into the 17th century. Fortunately, this did not prevent the building of Michelangelo's great dome. In addition to working on St. Peter's, Michelangelo provided the **Sistine Chapel** with its truly magnificent frescoes.

On a completely different scale, another key work of Renaissance architecture is Bramante's tiny **Tempietto** (1499) on the Janiculum. **Santa Maria della Pace** has a Bramante cloister, some frescoes by Raphael and a charming portico by Pietro da Cortona. Also of interest is Michelangelo's imaginative use of the great vaults of the Roman Baths of Diocletian in the church of **Santa Maria degli Angeli**.

There are other churches worth visiting for the sake of

Michelangelo's dramatic dome crowns St. Peter's interior

their outstanding paintings and sculptures. **Santa Maria del Popolo**, for example, has two great paintings by Caravaggio, the Chigi Chapel designed by Raphael and a series of 15th-century frescoes by Pinturicchio. **San Pietro in Vincoli**, besides having the chains with which St. Peter was bound in prison, boasts Michelangelo's awe-inspiring statue of Moses, while **San Luigi dei Francesi** contains three Caravaggios depicting St. Matthew plus frescoes by Domenichino.

BAROQUE

Interior of Rosati's dome in San Carlo ai Catinari (1620)

The COUNTER-REFORMATION inspired the exuberant, lavish style of such churches as the **Gesù** and **Sant' Ignazio di Loyola**. The best-loved examples of Roman Baroque are the later works associated with Bernini, such as the great colonnade and baldacchino he built for **St. Peter's**. Of the smaller churches he designed, perhaps the finest is **Sant' Andrea al Quirinale**, while **Santa Maria della Vittoria** houses his truly astonishing Cornaro Chapel with its dramatic sculpture, *Ecstasy of St. Teresa*. The late Baroque was not all Bernini, however. You should also look for such churches as **San Carlo ai**

Catinari, with a beautiful dome by Rosato Rosati, and the many churches by Bernini's rival, Borromini. **Sant'Agnese in Agone** and **San Carlo alle Quattro Fontane** are famed for the dramatic concave sur-faces of their façades, while **Sant'Ivo alla Sapienza's** complex structure makes it one of the small-scale Baroque masterpieces.

WHERE TO FIND THE CHURCHES

Bramante's St Peter's (1503)

Sant'Andrea al Quirinale (1658)

Sant'Ivo alla Sapienza (1642)

Rome's Best: Museums and Galleries

T HE MUSEUMS OF ROME are among the richest in the world; the Vatican alone contains incomparable collections of Egyptian, Etruscan, Greek, Roman and Early Christian artifacts, as well as frescoes by Michelangelo and Raphael, priceless manuscripts and jewels. Excavations in the 19th century added treasures from ancient Rome that are now displayed in museums throughout the city. The finest Etruscan collections in the world can be enjoyed in the Villa Giulia. More details on Rome's museums and galleries are given on pages 48 and 49.

Villa Giulia
Etruscan treasures from Rome's early history are displayed in this beautiful Renaissance villa.

Vatican Museums
The galleries and long corridors hold priceless artifacts such as this 9th-century mosaic showing scenes from the life of Christ.

0 meters   500
0 yards   500

Piazza Spagna

Vatican

Piazza della Rotonda

Piazza Navona

Galleria Spada
This collection's strength lies in its 17th- and 18th-century paintings. Earlier works include a Visitation *by Andrea del Sarto (1486–1530).*

Campo de' Fiori

Janiculum

Trastevere

Palazzo Corsini
Included here are works by Caravaggio, Rubens and Van Dyck, as well as a painting of the Baroque sculptor Bernini – a rare portrait by Il Baciccia (1639–1709).

Galleria Doria Pamphilj
Most of the great names of the Renaissance are represented on this gallery's crowded walls. Titian (1485–1576) painted Salomé *early in his career.*

Museo e Galleria Borghese
The ground-floor museum houses ancient Greek and Roman sculpture as well as early Bernini masterpieces, such as his David (1619). Upstairs are paintings by Titian, Rubens and other masters.

Museo Nazionale Romano
This fresco, from Livia's Villa (1st century AD) outside Rome, is one of a huge collection of finds from archaeological sites throughout the city.

Palazzo Barberini
The works of art here date mainly from the 13th to the 16th century. This figure of Providence comes from Pietro da Cortona's The Triumph of Divine Providence (1633–9).

Palazzo Venezia
The highlights of Rome's most important museum of decorative arts are its Byzantine and medieval collections, including this Byzantine enamel of Christ dating from the 13th century.

Via Veneto

Quirinal

Esquiline

pitol

Forum

Palatine

Caracalla

Lateran

entine

Capitoline Museums: Palazzo dei Conservatori
Pietro da Cortona's Rape of the Sabine Women (1629) is one of many Baroque paintings in the picture gallery.

Capitoline Museums: Palazzo Nuovo
Among the sculptures is this head of Giulia Domna (wife of Septimius Severus) from the 2nd century AD.

Exploring Museums and Galleries

ROME'S MUSEUMS and galleries boast two major strengths: Greek and Roman archaeological treasures and paintings and sculpture of the Renaissance and the Baroque. The Vatican Museums have superb collections of both, as do, on a smaller scale, the Capitoline Museums. Fine paintings can also be found scattered throughout Rome in museums, galleries and churches *(see pp44–5)*.

Etruscan clay head, Villa Giulia

ETRUSCAN ARTIFACTS

5th-century BC Etruscan gold plate with inscription, Villa Giulia

THE ETRUSCANS inhabited an area stretching from Florence to Rome from the 8th century BC and ruled Rome from the late 7th century BC *(see pp16–17)*. It was the Etruscan custom to bury the dead along with their possessions, and as a result Etruscan artifacts have been excavated from tombs all over central Italy. Three main collections can be seen in Rome. The **Villa Giulia** has been the home of the Museo Nazionale Etrusco since 1889. The villa, designed by Vignola for Pope Julius III's summer outings, is one of Rome's prettiest Renaissance buildings. Its gardens contain a reconstructed Etruscan temple. Not

all finds here are Etruscan, however; some of the pottery, statuettes and artifacts are relics of the Faliscans, Latins and other tribes who inhabited central Italy before the Romans.

The Gregorian Etruscan Museum in the **Vatican Museums** was opened in 1837 to house Etruscan finds from tombs on church-owned land. The Museo Barracco in the **Piccola Farnesina** has statues from the much-older civilizations of ancient Egypt and Assyria.

ANCIENT ROMAN ART

THE ARCHAEOLOGICAL zone in Rome forms a huge open-air museum of evidence of ancient Roman life, while the porticoes and cloisters of the city's churches are filled with ancient sarcophagi and fragments of statuary. The largest important collection can be seen in the **Museo Nazionale Romano** at the Baths of Diocletian and its new branch Palazzo Massimo. The museum's many ancient artifacts include, most notably, a sarcophagus from Livia's Villa at Prima Porta, just north of Rome. Also on display are some wonderfully well-preserved mosaics. The museum's great collection of Roman statues is now housed in the newly restored **Palazzo Altemps**.

The most important statues are in the **Vatican Museums**, which also have the best of the great Greek works, such as the *Laocoön*, brought to Rome around

Victory banner, Museo della Civiltà Romana

the 1st century AD. It had tremendous influence on the subsequent development of Roman art. Splendid copies of Greek originals can be seen in the **Capitoline Museums**.

In the Forum, occupying two floors of the church of Santa Francesca Romana, **Antiquarium Forense** with restored finds from the excavations. For those who enjoy history, the large-scale model at the **Museo della Civiltà Romana** in EUR gives an excellent idea of what ancient Rome looked like in the 4th century AD.

Centurion's breastplate, Museo della Civiltà Romana

ART GALLERIES

Muses in Raphael's *Parnassus* (1508–11), Vatican Museums

IN THE PAST, many of Rome's great aristocratic families owned magnificent private collections of painting and sculpture. Some of these are still housed in ancestral palazzi that are open to the public. One is the **Galleria Doria Pamphilj**, which has the greatest concentration of paintings of any palazzo in Rome. It's well worth searching through the various rooms to find the pearls of the collection, which include works by Raphael,

Filippo Lippi, Caravaggio, Titian and Claude Lorrain, and a portrait of Pope Innocent X Pamphilj by the Spanish artist Velázquez. The **Galleria Spada** collection, begun by Bernardino Spada in 1632, is still in the fine original gallery built for it. The paintings demonstrate 17th-century Roman taste and include works by Rubens, Guido Reni, Guercino, and Jan Brueghel the Elder. The **Galleria Colonna** houses a collection of art from the same period.

Other old family residences are now showcases for state art collections. The Galleria Nazionale d'Arte Antica is divided between **Palazzo Barberini** and **Palazzo Corsini**. Palazzo Barberini, built between 1625 and 1633 by Bernini and others for the Barberini family, houses paintings from the 13th to the 16th century. It also has objets d'art acquired by the state from various private collections. At some future date, the 17th- and 18th-century paintings exhibited in the Palazzo Corsini, on the south side of the Tiber, will

The Deposition (1604) by Caravaggio, the Vatican

be transferred to join the Palazzo Barberini collection. Another wonderful private collection was that of the Borghese family, also now managed by the state. The **Museo e Galleria Borghese** contains the sculpture collection, including the technically amazing *Apollo and Daphne* by the youthful genius Bernini and the famous statue of Pauline Borghese by Canova. On the first floor is the picture collection with paintings by Titian, Coreggio and others.

The **Capitoline Museums** hold collections that were gifts of the popes to the people of Rome. The Pinacoteca (art gallery) in the **Palazzo dei Conservatori** contains works by Titian, Guercino and Van Dyck. There is an art gallery at the **Vatican Museums**, but lovers of Renaissance art will head straight for the Sistine Chapel and the Raphael Rooms. Rome's main modern art collection is in the **Galleria Nazionale d'Arte Moderna**.

SMALLER MUSEUMS

THE MOST IMPORTANT of the smaller collections is the beautifully laid-out medieval museum in **Palazzo Venezia**, with exhibits ranging from ceramics to sculpture. Rome has a wealth of specialist museums like the **Museum of Musical Instruments**; the **Museo di Roma in Trastevere**, with tableaux showing life in Rome during the last century; and the **Burcardo Theater Museum**.

For those with an interest in the English Romantic poets who lived in Rome in the 19th century, there is the **Keats-Shelley Memorial House**, a museum in the house where John Keats died. Focusing on the French Empire, the **Museo Napoleonico** has relics and paintings

Laocoön (1st century AD) in the Vatican's Pio-Clementine Museum

of Napoleon and his family members, many of whom lived in Rome.

Portrait of Pauline Borghese painted by Kinson (c.1805), now in the Museo Napoleonico

Hellenistic faun, Museo Borghese

Rome's Best: Fountains and Obelisks

ROME HAS SOME of the loveliest fountains in the world. Many of them are the work of the greatest sculptors of the Renaissance and Baroque eras. Some fountains are flamboyant displays, others quiet trickles of water. Many are simply drinking fountains, while a few cascade from the sides of buildings. Obelisks date from far earlier in the city's history. Although some of them were commissioned by Roman emperors, many are even older and were brought to Rome by triumphant conquering armies. A detailed overview of the city's fountains and obelisks is on pages 52 and 53.

Piazza San Pietro
Twin fountains give life to the splendid monumental piazza of St. Peter's. Maderno designed the one on the Vatican side in 1614; the other was later built to match.

Piazza del Popolo
19th-century massive marble lions and fountains surround an ancient obelisk in the center of the piazza.

Vatican

Piazza della Rotonda

Piazza Navona

Fontana dei Quattro Fiumi
The fountain of the four rivers is the work of Bernini. The four figures represent the Ganges, the Plate, the Danube and the Nile.

Janiculum

Campo de' Fiori

Trastevere

Obelisk of Santa Maria sopra Minerva
The Egyptian obelisk, held up by Bernini's marble elephant, dates from the 6th century BC.

Fontana delle Tartarughe
One of Rome's more secret fountains, this jewel of Renaissance sculpture shows youths helping tortoises into a basin.

Fontana della Barcaccia
This elegant 1627 fountain is probably the work of Pietro Bernini, father of the more famous Gian Lorenzo.

Trevi Fountain
The Trevi, inspired by Roman triumphal arches, was designed by Nicola Salvi in 1732. Tradition has it that a coin thrown into the water guarantees a visitor's return to Rome.

0 meters 500

0 yards 500

iazza Spagna   Via Veneto

Quirinal

Esquiline

Capitol

Forum

Palatine

Lateran

Caracalla

Aventine

Fontana delle Naiadi
When this fountain was unveiled in 1901, the realistically sensual bronze nymphs caused a storm of protest.

Obelisk of Piazza San Giovanni in Laterano
The oldest obelisk in Rome dates from the 15th century BC. It came to Rome in AD 357, brought here on the orders of Constantine II.

Piazza della Bocca della Verità Fountain
In this 18th-century fountain, built by Carlo Bizzaccheri for Pope Clement XI, water spills over a craggy rock formation where two Tritons hold aloft a large shell.

Exploring Fountains and Obelisks

Fountain of the Amphorae (1920s)

T HE POPES who restored the ancient Roman aqueducts used to build fountains to commemorate their deeds of munificence. As a result, fountains of all sizes and shapes punctuate the city, drawing grateful crowds on hot summer days. Ancient obelisks provide powerful reminders of the debt Roman civilization owed to the Egyptians. Architects have learned to incorporate them into Roman piazzas in fascinating ways.

FOUNTAINS

T HE TREVI FOUNTAIN is one of the most famous of all. It is a *mostra*, a monumental fountain built to mark the end of an aqueduct – in this case the Acqua Vergine, built by Marcus Agrippa in 19 BC, although the Trevi itself was only completed in 1762. Other *mostre* are the **Fontana dell'Acqua Paola,** built for Pope Paul V in 1612 on the Janiculum, and the **Moses Fountain**, commemorating the opening of the Acqua Felice by Pope Sixtus V in 1587.

Almost all Rome's famous piazzas have fountains. In **Piazza San Pietro** there is a matching pair of powerful fountains. Piazza Navona has Bernini's wonderful Baroque **Fontana dei Quattro Fiumi** (fountain of the four rivers) as its main attraction. The fountain's four figures each represent one of the principal rivers of the four continents then known. To the south of this is the smaller **Fontana del Moro** (the Moor), also by Bernini, showing an Ethiopian struggling with a dolphin. At the north end, Neptune

Fontana dei Cavalli Marini

wrestles with an octopus on a 19th-century fountain. In Piazza Barberini is the magnificent Bernini creation of 1642–3: the **Fontana del Tritone** with its sea god blowing through a shell.

More recently, large piazzas have been redesigned around fountains. Valadier's great design for **Piazza del Popolo** (1816–20) has marble lions and fountains surrounding the

Fountain of the Four Tiaras located behind St Peter's

The Pantheon Fountain

central obelisk plus two more fountains on the east and west sides of the square. The turn of the century saw the opening of the **Fontana delle Naiadi** (nymphs) in Piazza della Repubblica; its earthy figures were a great scandal at the time. The highly original **Fountain of the Amphorae** (map 8 D2) was erected in Piazza dell'Emporio during the 1920s. The same designer, Pietro Lombardi, also created the **Fountain of the Four Tiaras** (map 3 C3) behind the colonnade of St. Peter's.

The city also has a number of smaller, and often very charming fountains. At the foot of the Spanish Steps is the **Fontana della Barcaccia** (the leaking boat) of 1627; the **Fontana delle Tartarughe**

THE TREVI FOUNTAIN

Appropriately for a fountain resembling a stage set, the theatrical Trevi has been the star of many films set in Rome, including romantic films like *Three Coins in a Fountain* and *Roman Holiday*, but also *La Dolce Vita*, Fellini's satirical portrait of Rome in the 1950s. Whatever liberties Anita Ekberg took then, paddling in the fountains of Rome is now forbidden, however tempting it could be in the summer heat.

Anita Ekberg in *La Dolce Vita* (1960)

(the tortoise fountain) has been in the tiny Piazza Mattei since 1581, and by Santa Maria in Domnica is the **Fontana della Navicella** (little boat), created out of an ancient Roman sculpture in the 16th century. In the forecourt of **Santa Sabina** (map 8 D2) water gushes from a huge mask set in an ancient basin. The **Pantheon Fountain** (map 4 F4), from 1575, is by Jacopo della Porta. **Le Quattro Fontane** (four fountains) have stood at the Quirinal hill crossroads since 1593.

Fountains in parks and gardens include the **Galleon Fountain** (1620–21) at the Vatican, and the **Fontana dei Cavalli Marini** (seahorses), of 1791, at Villa Borghese. The somewhat decayed 16th-century terraced gardens of the **Villa d'Este,** with their display of over 500 fountains, are still worth the journey.

Piazza Navona with Fontana dei Fiumi, by Pannini (1691–1765)

time of Augustus and also erected in the Circus Maximus. The slightly smaller **Obelisk of Piazza Montecitorio** was another of Augustus's trophies.

Other obelisks, such as the one at the top of the Spanish Steps, are Roman imitations of Egyptian originals. The **Obelisk of Piazza dell' Esquilino** and the one in **Piazza del Quirinale** (map 5 B4) first stood at the entrance to the Mausoleum of Augustus. When reerected, most obelisks were mounted on decorative bases, often with statues and fountains at their foot. Others became parts of sculptures. Bernini was the creator of the marble elephant balancing the Egyptian **Obelisk of Santa Maria sopra Minerva** on its back, and the **Fontana dei Quattro Fiumi**, its obelisk

from the Circus of Maxentius. Another obelisk was added to the remodeled Pantheon Fountain in 1711. The obelisk in **Piazza San Pietro** is Egyptian but does not have the usual hieroglyphics.

The **Obelisk of Axum** was brought by Mussolini's army from Ethiopia in 1937 as a war trophy. It now stands by the UN Food and Agriculture Organization building near the Circus Maximus.

Wall fountain at Villa d'Este

The Ovato Fountain at Villa d'Este

OBELISKS

THE MOST ANCIENT and tallest of Rome's obelisks is the **Obelisk of Piazza di San Giovanni in Laterano**. Built of red granite, 100 ft (31 m) high, it came from the Temple of Ammon at Thebes, erected in the 15th century BC. It was brought to Rome in AD 357 by the order of Constantine II and put up in the Circus Maximus. In 1587 it was rediscovered, broken into three pieces, and re-erected in the following year. Next in age is the obelisk in **Piazza del Popolo**, from the 12th or 13th century BC. It was brought to Rome in the

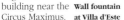

Obelisk in Piazza del Popolo

Celebrated Visitors and Residents

ROME EXERTS a powerful fascination, and foreigners throughout history have succumbed to its charms, often staying for long periods or even taking up permanent residence. The list of famous visitors is almost endless: painters, sculptors and architects from Rome's very earliest days; writers, poets and musicians; and exiles, pilgrims, religious teachers, philosophers, aesthetes and archaeologists – all have passed through. Their orchestral works, operas, paintings, drawings, drama and literary journals testify to Rome's inspirational effect.

Martin Luther *(1483–1546)*
The religious reformer from Germany came to the convent at Santa Maria del Popolo in 1511. His horror at the corruption he saw led to the Reformation.

J.W. von Goethe *(1749–1832)*
The German poet, philosopher, artist, playwright, botanist and courtier lived at 20 Via del Corso, now a museum.

Sant'Ignazio di Loyola
(1491–1556)
He came to Rome from Spain in 1537 and founded the Jesuits near what is now the Gesù, the first Jesuit church.

Queen Christina
(1626–89)
The Swedish queen abdicated in 1654, and came to live in Palazzo Corsini on Via Lungara.

St. Dominic *(1170–1221)*
Founder of the Dominican order, St. Dominic was born in Spain. The order's headquarters were at Santa Sabina on the Aventine.

Vatican

Piazza Popol

Piazz
della Rot

Piazza Navona

Janiculum

Campo de' Fio

Trastevere

Jean Auguste Ingres *(1780–1867)*
The 19th-century French painter, leader of the Neoclassical tradition, lived in Rome from 1806 until 1820. He returned in 1834 as director of the French Academy at Villa Medici.

Pauline Borghese
(1780–1825)
Napoleon's sister was the subject of scandal in 1805, when she posed semi-nude for a statue by Canova, which is now in Museo Borghese.

Via Veneto

The Exiled Stuarts
James Stuart (1688–1766), unsuccessful claimant to the British throne, came to Rome as an exile. He was presented with Palazzo Balestra by Pope Clement XI and died here.

Quirinal

Esquiline

itol

Forum

Lateran

Palatine

Caracalla

Aventine

| 0 meters | 500 |
| 0 yards | 500 |

Lord Byron *(1788–1824)*
Though the English poet's stay in the city was brief, the influence on his work was long-lasting. Stanzas in Childe Harold's Pilgrimage *and* Manfred *were inspired by seeing the Colosseum in moonlight.*

Percy Bysshe Shelley
(1792–1822)
The great English Romantic poet wrote his drama Prometheus Unbound *in the calm of the ruined Baths of Caracalla in 1819.*

Artists and Writers Inspired by Rome

ARTISTS AND WRITERS have been attracted to Rome since Classical times. Many came to work for the emperors; the poets Horace, Virgil and Ovid, for example, all enjoyed the patronage of Emperor Augustus. Later on, especially in the Renaissance and Baroque periods, the greatest artists and architects came to Rome to compete for commissions from the popes. However, patronage was not the only magnet. Since the Renaissance, Rome's Classical past and its picturesque ruins have drawn artists, architects and writers from all over Italy and abroad.

The prolific love poet Ovid (43 BC–AD 17)

Self-portrait by the 18th-century artist Angelica Kauffmann, c.1770

PAINTERS, SCULPTORS AND ARCHITECTS

Diego Velázquez, one of many great 17th-century artists to visit Rome

In the early 16th century, artists and architects were summoned from all parts of Italy to realize the grandiose building projects of the popes. From Urbino came Bramante (1444–1514) and Raphael (1483–1520); from Perugia came Perugino (1450–1523); from Florence came Michelangelo (1475–1564) and many others. They worked in the Vatican, on the new St. Peter's and on the decoration of the Sistine Chapel. Artists were often well rewarded, but they also lived in dangerous times. Florentine sculptor and goldsmith Benvenuto Cellini (1500–71) helped defend Castel Sant' Angelo *(see pp248–9)* during the Sack of Rome (1527) but was later imprisoned there and made a dramatic escape. His memoirs tell the story.

Toward the end of the 16th century, church patronage was generous to the Milanese-born Caravaggio (1571–1610), despite his violent character and unruly life. The Carracci family from Bologna also flourished – especially brothers Annibale (1560–1609) and Agostino (1557–1602).

The work of Gian Lorenzo Bernini (1598–1680) can be seen all over Rome. He succeeded Carlo Maderno (1556–1629) as architect of St. Peter's and created its great bronze baldacchino; the splendid colonnade *(see pp230–31)*; and numerous fountains, churches and sculptures. His rival for the title of leading architect of the Roman Baroque was Francesco Borromini (1599–1667), whose highly original genius can be appreciated in many Roman churches and palazzi.

In the 17th century, it became common for artists from outside Italy to work in Rome. Diego Velázquez (1599–1660), King Philip IV of Spain's court painter, came in 1628 to study the treasures of the Vatican. Rubens (1577–1640) came from Antwerp to study and carry out commissions. The French artists Nicolas Poussin (1594–1665) and Claude Lorrain (1600–82) lived here for many years.

The Classical revival of the 18th century attracted artists to Rome in unprecedented numbers. From Britain came the Scottish architect Robert Adam (1728–92) and the Swiss artist Angelica Kauffmann (1741–1807), who settled here and was buried with honor in Sant'Andrea delle Fratte. After the Baroque excesses, sculpture turned to the simplicity of Neoclassicism. A leader of this movement was Antonio Canova (1757–1821). Sculptors from all over Europe were influenced by him, including the Dane Bertel Thorvaldsen (1770–1844), who lived in Rome for many years.

Claude Lorrain's view of the Forum, painted in Rome in 1632

WRITERS

Dante (1262–1321) visited Rome during his exile from Florence, and in the *Inferno* he describes the great influx of pilgrims for the first Holy Year (1300). The poet Petrarch (1304–74), born in Arezzo, came to the city in much-happier circumstances to be crowned with laurels on the Capitol in 1341. The poet Torquato Tasso (1544–95), from Sorrento, was invited to receive a similar honor, but died soon after his arrival. He is buried in Sant'Onofrio *(see p219)* on the Janiculum.

Torquato Tasso

Two of the first writers from abroad to visit Rome were the French essayist Montaigne (1533–92) and English poet John Milton (1608–74). Then, by the early 18th century, writers seemed to flock to Rome. Edward Gibbon (1737–94) was inspired to write *Decline and Fall of the Roman Empire* when he heard the monks singing the Angelus outside Santa Maria in Aracoeli *(see p69)*. German visitors included J.J. Winckelmann (1717–68),

who wrote influential studies of ancient art, and the poet J.W. von Goethe (1749–1832).

In the Romantic period Rome teemed with English writers: poets Keats, Shelley and Byron, followed by the Brownings and the novelist Charles Dickens. Travel writers in the 19th century included Augustus Hare (1834–1903) and the German historian Ferdinand Gregorovius (1821–91). much of *The Portrait of a Lady* by American Henry James (1843–1916) is set in Rome.

Modern life in Rome is brilliantly captured by the Roman novelist and short-story writer Alberto Moravia (1907–90).

Portrait of the poet John Keats painted by his friend Joseph Severn in 1819

MUSICIANS

Giovanni luigi da Palestrina (1525–94), from the town of that name, became choir-master and organist to the Vatican and composed some of the greatest unaccompanied choral music ever written. In 1770, the 14-year-old Mozart heard Gregorio Allegri's unpublished *Miserere* in the Sistine Chapel and wrote it down from memory. Arcangelo

Corelli (1653–1713), the great violinist and composer of the Baroque age, worked in Rome under the patronage of Cardinal Ottoboni. One of his first commissions was to provide a festival of music for Queen Christina of Sweden.

During the 19th century, the Prix de Rome brought many French musicians to study here at the Villa Medici *(see p135)*. Hector Berlioz (1803–69) owed the inspiration for his popular *Roman Carnival*, the overture to his opera *Benvenuto Cellini*, to his two-year stay in Rome. Georges Bizet (1838–75) and Claude Debussy (1862–1918) were also Prix de Rome winners. Franz Liszt (1811–86), after his 50th year, settled in Rome, took minor orders and became known as Abbé Liszt. He wrote *Fountains of the Villa d'Este* while staying at the villa in Tivoli.

Giacomo Puccini

Twentieth-century musical associations with Rome include the popular works by Ottorino Respighi (1870–1936), *The Fountains of Rome* and *The Pines of Rome*, while Giacomo Puccini (1858–1924) used Roman settings when creating his dramatic tragic opera, *Tosca*.

ROMAN CINEMA

The Cinecittà studios, built in 1937 just outside Rome, are most famous for the films made here in the 1940s – classics of Italian Neorealism such as Roberto Rossellini's *Roma Città Aperta* and Vittorio De Sica's *Sciuscià* and *Ladri di Biciclette*. The director most often linked with Roman cinema is Federico Fellini, through films like *La Dolce Vita* (1960) and *Roma* (1972). However, perhaps the most famous artist associated with Rome is the controversial writer-turned-film-maker Pier Paolo Pasolini (1922–75), widely known for his films *Teorema* (1968) and *Il Decamerone* (1971).

Since the 1950s, Rome and Cinecittà have also been much used for foreign films: from *Ben-Hur* and *Spartacus* in the 1950s through to *The Talented Mr Ripley* and *Gladiator* in the late 1990s.

Pier Paolo Pasolini

ROME THROUGH THE YEAR

THE BEST TIMES to visit Rome are spring and autumn, when the weather is usually warm and sometimes even hot enough to sunbathe and swim at the beaches and lakes outside the city. In the winter months, the weather tends to be gray and extremely rainy, while in high summer, most people (including Romans, who leave the city in droves) find the heat unbearable. Easter and Christmas are obviously very special in Rome, but there are other religious festivals worth seeing at other times in the year, as well as some enjoyable secular events, like the Festa de Noantri in Trastevere and the Flower Festival in Genzano. In villages outside Rome, local celebrations are held to welcome new crops, such as strawberries and beans in the spring, and grapes and truffles in the autumn.

SPRING

EASTER, falling in March or April, marks the official beginning of the tourist season in Rome. Catholics from all over the world flock into the city to make their pilgrimages to the main basilicas and to hear the Pope's Easter Sunday address outside St. Peter's; the less devout come simply to take advantage of the mild weather. Meanwhile, Romans pile into their cars and head for the coast and countryside, so you can expect the roads, beaches and restaurants of the Castelli Romani and Lake Bracciano to be busy.

Temperatures tend to be around 66° F (18° C), but can hit 82° F (28° C), so by mid-May it is usually possible to lunch and dine outside. However, there can still be sudden downpours and temperature swings, so do bring warm clothes and an umbrella. In

Crowds gathering in St. Peter's Square at Easter

April, tubs full of colorful azaleas are arranged on the Spanish Steps and along Via Veneto, and once the roses start to flower in the city's Rose Garden overlooking the Circus Maximus, it is opened to the public.

For two weeks from mid-May, Via dei Coronari is lit by candles, lined with plants and hung with banners for the street's antiques fair, while Via Margutta hosts an outdoor art show. In the first week of May, the International Horse Show is held in the Villa Borghese. Also usually in May, many world-class tennis players flock to Rome to compete in the International Tennis Championships held annually at the Foro Italico.

EVENTS

Festa di Santa Francesca Romana (*March 9*), Santa Francesca Romana. Blessing of the city's cars, buses and trams (*see p87*).
Festa di San Giuseppe (*March 19*), Trionfale area. St. Joseph's (and Father's) Day. Street stalls, food and music.
Good Friday (*March/April*), Colosseum. Procession of the Cross at 9pm led by the pope.
Easter Sunday (*March/April*), St. Peter's Square. Address made by the pope (*see p231*).
Rome's Birthday (*Sunday before April 21*), Piazza del Campidoglio.
Festa della Primavera (*March/April*), Spanish Steps and Trinità dei Monti. Azaleas in the street and concerts.
Art exhibition (*April/May*), Via Margutta (*see p339*).
International Horse Show (*early May*), Villa Borghese (*see p350*).
Antiques Fair (*mid–late May*),Via dei Coronari (*see p324*).
International Tennis Championships (*usually May*), Foro Italico (*see p350*).

International Horse Show in Villa Borghese in May

AVERAGE DAILY HOURS OF SUNSHINE

Hours

(bar chart showing hours of sunshine by month: Jan through Dec)

Jan Feb Mar Apr May Jun Jul Aug Sep Oct Nov Dec

Sunshine Chart
Rome is famous for its light. June is the sunniest month but very dry, and without the occasional shower the bright heat can feel intense. In autumn, Rome's southerly position makes the midday sun enjoyably warm.

SUMMER

IN JUNE, a season of concerts begins, with performances in some of the city's most beautiful palaces, churches and courtyards. In July and August, opera and drama are staged at Ostia Antica *(see pp270–71)* and in various outdoor locations. During the summer there are also contemporary cultural events – film, music of all kinds, dance and theater. On midsummer evenings, there are stalls and amusements on the Tiber embankments by Castel Sant'Angelo, while in the last two weeks of July Trastevere becomes an open-air party, as the Noantri festival is celebrated with trinket stalls, dining in the street and fireworks.

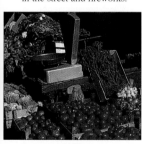

Summer vegetables

The sales *(saldi)* begin in mid-July, and the relatively new Alta Moda Fashion Show is usually held mid- to late July at the Spanish Steps.

Many Romans leave the city at the end of June, when schools close, but since June and July are peak tourist months, hotels, restaurants and cafés and all the main places of interest are packed out. In August, when the

Flower-carpeted streets in Genzano

temperature often soars to over 104° F (40° C), virtually all Romans flee the city for the seaside, meaning many cafés, restaurants and shops close for the entire month.

EVENTS

Flower Festival *(June, the Sunday after Corpus Domini),* Genzano, Castelli Romani, south of Rome. Streets are carpeted with flowers.
Festa di San Giovanni *(June 23–24),* Piazza di Porta San Giovanni. Celebrated with meals of snails in tomato sauce, suckling pig, a fair and fireworks display.
RomaEuropa *(late June–autumn),* mainly in Villa Medici. Films, dance, theater and concerts *(see p341).*
Festa di San Pietro *(June 29),* many churches. Celebrations mark the feast of St. Peter.

Tevere Expo *(end June–mid-July),* along the Tiber. Crafts, food and wine, music and fireworks *(see p339).*
Festa de Noantri *(last two weeks in July),* the streets of Trastevere. Food and entertainment *(see p339 and p341).*
Alta Moda Fashion Show *(usually mid- to late July),* Spanish Steps *(see p339).*
Estate Romana *(July/ August),* Villa Ada, Ostia Antica, in parks by the Tiber. Opera, concerts, drama, dance and film *(see p341).*
Festa della Madonna della Neve *(August 5),* Santa Maria Maggiore. Fourth-century snowfall re-enacted with white flower petals *(see p172).*
Ferragosto *(August 15),* Santa Maria in Trastevere. Midsummer holiday. Almost everything closes down. Celebrations are held for the Feast of the Assumption.

The heat of an August afternoon in front of St. Peter's

AVERAGE MONTHLY RAINFALL

| MM | | | | | | | | | | | | Inches |

Rainfall Chart
Autumn is Rome's rainiest season, with heavy downpours, sometimes lasting for days, especially in November. Rain in summer tends to come in violent – but often extremely refreshing – storms. In winter and early spring, expect a few dull, drizzly days.

FALL

SEPTEMBER AND OCTOBER are the best – and among the most popular – months to visit Rome. The fiery heat of July and August will have cooled a little, but midday can be very hot, and you can still eat and drink outside without feeling chilly until late at night. Visiting Rome in November is not recommended: it is the wettest month of the year, and Roman rainstorms are often very strong and heavy.

At the beginning of October, an artisans' fair is held on Via dell'Orso and adjacent streets, while nearby the antiques galleries of Via dei Coronari hold open house. There are also October antiques fairs in Orvieto and Perugia, two of the loveliest Umbrian hill towns, which are about an hour's drive north of Rome. In November, there's yet another prestigious antiques fair at the papal palace of Viterbo, 40 miles (65 km) north of Rome *(see p271).*

Autumn is, of course, the season of harvest festivals, and it can be fun to head out to the small towns around Rome to sample delicacies such as local cheeses,

A roast chestnut stall in autumn

sausages, chestnuts and mushrooms. Another reason for taking a trip out of Rome is the wine festival in Marino (in the Castelli Romani, south of Rome). There are plenty of opportunities to sample the wines of this region that was once the home to luxurious 16th- and 17th-century country residences but none is renowned particularly for its white wines.

Throughout the autumn and winter, freshly roasted chestnuts can be bought from vendors on street corners, and occasionally there is a stand on Campo de' Fiori where you can sample *vino novello*, the new season's wine. On All Saints and All Souls Days,

which fall on November 1 and 2 respectively, the Romans make pilgrimages to the tombs of relatives who are buried in the cemeteries of Prima Porta and Verano. Chrysanthemums are then traditionally placed on their graves, and for this reason they should definitely not be given as thank-you presents. On a much happier note, the classical concert and opera seasons begin again in October and November. Details of performances can be found in listings magazines such as *Time Out Roma, Trovaroma,* and *Roma c'è (see p340),* in newspapers, such as *La Repubblica (see p367),* and on posters around the city.

EVENTS

Art fair *(September),* Via Margutta *(see p339).*
Crafts fair *(last week September/first week October),* Via dell'Orso, near Piazza Navona *(see p339).*
Marino Wine Festival *(first Sunday in October),* Marino. Celebrations include tastings and street entertainment.
Antiques Fair *(mid-October),* Via dei Coronari *(see p339).*
All Saints and All Souls Days *(November 1, 2),* Prima Porta and Verano cemeteries. Witness the Pope usually celebrating Mass in the extensive Verano cemetary.
Festa di Santa Cecilia *(November 22),* Santa Cecilia in Trastevere and Catacombs of San Callisto.
Vino Novello tasting *(late November),* Campo de' Fiori.

Autumn in the Villa Doria Pamphilj park

AVERAGE MONTHLY TEMPERATURE

Temperature Chart
The chart shows the average minimum and maximum monthly temperatures. July and August can be unbearably hot, making sightseeing a chore. The cooler days of spring and autumn are ideal to visit Rome, but there are some dull and rainy spells.

WINTER

DURING THE WINTER, Rome is bracingly chilly, but the temperature rarely drops below freezing. Not all buildings are centrally heated, so if you are staying in a small hotel bring warm clothes and request extra blankets as soon as you arrive, because they are often in short supply. Warm up in cafés with hot chocolate or a cappuccino.

The run-up to Christmas is great fun in Rome, especially if you have children. Manger scenes, *presepi*, are set up in many churches, piazzas and public places and from mid-December to Twelfth Night,

Rome during one of its rare snowfalls

Market on Piazza Navona

Piazza Navona hosts a market where you can buy manger scenes, decorations and toys.

If you don't have friends in Rome, Christmas can be lonely, since it is such a family event. On New Year's Eve, however, everyone is out on the street to drink sparkling wine and let off fireworks.

La Befana, on January 6, is a traditional holiday when a witch, called La Befana, delivers sweets to children. The Carnival season runs from late January through to February, celebrated largely by children with costume

parties and parades along Via Nazionale, Via Cola di Rienzo and the Pincio. Keep out of the way of teenagers with shaving-cream sprays and water balloons.

EVENTS

Festa della Madonna Immacolata *(December 8)*, Piazza di Spagna. Firemen climb up a ladder to place a wreath on the statue of the Virgin Mary.
Christmas Market *(mid-December – January 6)*, Piazza Navona. Christmas and children's market *(see p120)*.
Nativity scenes *(mid-December – mid-January)*, many churches. Life-size scene in St. Peter's Square, collection at Santi Cosma e Damiano.
Midnight Mass *(December 24)*, at most churches.
Christmas Day *(December 25)*, St. Peter's Square. Blessing by the pope.
New Year's Eve *(December 31)*, all over city. Fireworks displays, furniture thrown out.
La Befana *(January 6)*, all over city. Parties for children.

PUBLIC HOLIDAYS
New Year's Day (Jan 1)
Epiphany (Jan 6)
Easter Monday
Liberation Day (Apr 25)
Labor Day (May 1)
SS Peter and Paul's day (Jun 29)
Ferragosto (Aug 15)
All Saints' Day (Nov 1)
Immaculate Conception (Dec 8)
Christmas Day (Dec 25)
Santo Stefano (Dec 26)

Via Condotti at Christmas

ROME AREA
BY AREA

CAPITOL

THE TEMPLE OF JUPITER on the Capitol, the southern summit of the Capitoline Hill, was the center of the Roman world. Reached by a zig-zagging path up from the Forum, the temple was the scene of all the most sacred religious and political ceremonies. The hill and its temple came to symbolize Rome's authority as *caput mundi*, head of the world, and the concept of a "capital" city is derived from the Capitol. Throughout the city's history, the Capitol (*Campidoglio*) has remained the seat of municipal government. Today's city council, the

Hand of colossal statue in Palazzo dei Conservatori

Comune di Roma, meets in the Renaissance splendor of Palazzo Senatorio. The Capitol also serves as Rome's Wedding Registry Office. Rome's position as a modern capital is seen in the enormous Victor Emmanuel Monument, which blots out the view of the Capitol from Piazza Venezia. The present arrangement of the buildings on the hill dates from the 16th century, when Michelangelo created a beautiful piazza reached by a dramatic flight of steps, the Cordonata. Two of the three buildings around the piazza are now home to the Capitoline Museums.

SIGHTS AT A GLANCE

Churches and Temples
Santa Maria in Aracoeli **7**
Temple of Jupiter **8**
San Marco **12**

Museums and Galleries
Capitoline Museums:
Palazzo Nuovo pp70–71 **1**
Capitoline Museums:
Palazzo dei Conservatori
pp72–3 **2**
Palazzo Venezia
and Museum **11**

Historic Buildings
Roman Insula **5**

Historic Streets and Piazzas
Piazza del Campidoglio **3**
Cordonata **4**
Aracoeli Staircase **6**

Ancient Sites
Tarpeian Rock **9**

Monuments
Victor Emmanuel
Monument **10**

GETTING THERE
All the sights in this area are within walking distance of Piazza Venezia. Bus routes converge here from all parts of the city, as do many thousands of motorists. From Termini station you can catch the 40, 64, or 170; from Piazza Barberini the 63 or 95. From St. Peter's and the Vatican the only buses are the 40, 62 and 64. Piazza Venezia is also a stopping-off point for the 110 tourist bus.

0 meters 200
0 yards 200

N

KEY

Street-by-Street map

SEE ALSO

• **Street Finder**, maps 5, 12

Statue of Marcus Aurelius on Michelangelo's Piazza del Campidoglio

Street by Street: The Capitol and Piazza Venezia

THE CAPITOL, citadel of ancient Rome, is a must stop for every visitor. A broad flight of steps (the Cordonata) leads up to Michelangelo's spectacular Piazza del Campidoglio. This is flanked by the Palazzo Nuovo and the Palazzo dei Conservatori, housing the Capitoline Museums with their fine collections of sculptures and painting. The absence of cars makes the hill a welcome retreat from the squeal of brakes below, but visitors should brave traffic to visit Palazzo Venezia and its museum.

PIAZZA VENEZIA

PIAZZA VENEZIA

PIAZZA VENEZIA

VIA DEL TEATRO DI MARCELLO

Victor Emmanuel Monument
This huge white marble monument to Italy's first king was completed in 1911 ❿

San Marco
The church of the Venetians in Rome has a fine 9th-century apse mosaic ⓬

Palazzo Venezia
The museum's finest exhibits, such as this 13th-century gilded angel decorated with enamel, date from the late Middle Ages ⓫

Roman Insula
This is a ruined apartment block dating from Imperial Rome ❺

Aracoeli Staircase
When it was built in 1348, the staircase became a center for political debate ❻

Cordonata
Michelangelo's great staircase shifted the orientation of the Capitol to the west ❹

KEY

- - -   Suggested route

0 meters	75
0 yards	75

★ **Palazzo dei Conservatori**
Displayed in the courtyard in this part of the Capitoline Museums is a fine series of reliefs from the Temple of Hadrian (see p106) ❷

Santa Maria in Aracoeli
The treasures hidden behind the church's brick façade include this 15th-century fresco of the Funeral of St. Bernardino *by Pinturicchio* ❼

LOCATOR MAP
See Central Rome Map pp12–13

★ **Palazzo Nuovo**
This bust of Augustus in the Hall of the Emperors is one of many fine Classical sculptures in the Capitoline Museums ❶

Palazzo Senatorio was used by the Roman Senate from about the 12th century. It now houses the offices of the mayor.

★ **Piazza del Campidoglio**
Michelangelo designed both the geometric paving and the façades of the buildings ❸

Temple of Jupiter
This artist's impression shows the gold-and-ivory statue of Jupiter that stood in the temple ❽

Tarpeian Rock
In ancient Rome traitors were thrown to their death from this cliff on the Capitol ❾

STAR SIGHTS

★ **Piazza del Campidoglio**

★ **Palazzo dei Conservatori**

★ **Palazzo Nuovo**

Capitoline Museums: Palazzo Nuovo ❶

See pp70–71.

Capitoline Museums: Palazzo dei Conservatori ❷

See pp72–3.

Piazza del Campidoglio ❸

Map 5 A5 & 12 F5. 🚌 See **Getting There** p65.

W HEN EMPEROR Charles V visited Rome in 1536, Pope Paul III Farnese was so embarrassed by the muddy state of the Capitol that he asked Michelangelo to draw up plans for repaving the piazza and for renovating the facades of Palazzo dei Conservatori and Palazzo Senatorio.

Michelangelo proposed adding the Palazzo Nuovo to form a piazza in the shape of a trapezium, embellished with Classical sculptures chosen for their relevance to Rome. Building started in 1546 but progressed so slowly that Michelangelo only lived to oversee the double flight of steps at the entrance of Palazzo Senatorio. The piazza was completed in the 17th

century, the design remaining largely faithful to the original. Pilasters two-stories high and balustrades interspersed with statues link the buildings thematically. The piazza faces west toward St. Peter's, the Christian equivalent of the Capitol. At it center stands a replica of a statue of Marcus Aurelius. The original is in the Palazzo Nuovo *(see pp70–71)*.

Cordonata ❹

Map 5 A5 & 12 F5. 🚌 See **Getting There** p65.

F ROM PIAZZA VENEZIA, the Capitol is approached by a gently rising, subtly widening ramp – the Cordonata. At the foot is a pair of granite Egyptian lions, and a 19th-century monument to Cola di Rienzo is on the left, close to where the 14th-century tyrant was executed. The top of the ramp is guarded by restored Classical statues of the Dioscuri – Castor and Pollux.

Roman *Insula* ❺

Piazza d'Aracoeli. **Map** 5 A5 & 12 F4.
📞 67 10 3819. 🚌 See **Getting There** p65. **Open** by appt only: permit needed (see p367).

T WO THOUSAND YEARS ago the urban poor of Rome used to make their homes in *insulae* – apartment blocks.

A statue of one of the Dioscuri at the top of the Cordonata

These were often badly maintained by landlords and expensive to rent in a city where land costs were high. This 2nd-century AD tenement block, of barrel-vault construction, is the only survivor from that era. The fourth and fifth stories and part of the sixth remain above current ground level.

In the Middle Ages, a section of these upper stories was converted into a church; its bell tower and 14th-century Madonna in a niche are visible from the street.

During the Fascist years, the area was cleared, and three lower floors emerged. Some 380 people may have lived in the tenement, in the squalid conditions described by the 1st-century AD satirical writers Martial and Juvenal. The latter mentions that he had to climb 200 steps to reach his garret.

This *insula* may once have had more stories. The higher you lived, the more dismal the conditions, as the cramped spaces of the building's upper levels testify.

The Cordonata in an 18th-century painting by Antonio Canaletto

Aracoeli Staircase ❻

Piazza d'Aracoeli. **Map** 5 A5 & 12 F4.
🚌 See **Getting There** p65.

THE ARACOELI Staircase contains 124 marble steps (122 if you start from the right) and was completed in 1348, some say in thanks for the passing of the Black Death, but more probably in preparation for the 1350 Holy Year.

The 14th-century tribune-turned-tyrant Cola di Rienzo harangued the masses from the Aracoeli Staircase; 17th-century foreigners slept on the steps, until Prince Caffarelli, who lived on the hill, scared them off by rolling stone-filled barrels down upon them.

Popular belief has it that by climbing the steps on your knees you can win the Italian national lottery. From the top is a good view of Rome, with the domes of Sant' Andrea della Valle and St. Peter's slightly to the right.

Aracoeli Staircase

Santa Maria in Aracoeli ❼

Piazza d'Aracoeli (entrances via Aracoeli Staircase and door behind Palazzo Nuovo). **Map** 5 A5 & 12 F4. 📞 06-679 81 55. 🚌 See **Getting There** p65.
Open 6:30am–noon, 3:15–6pm daily.

DATING FROM AT LEAST the 6th century, the church of Santa Maria in Aracoeli, or St. Mary of the Altar in the Sky, stands on the northern summit of the Capitoline, on the site of the ancient temple

Ceiling commemorating Battle of Lepanto in Santa Maria in Aracoeli

to Juno. Its 22 columns were taken from various ancient buildings; the inscription on the third column to the left explains that it comes *"a cubiculo Augustorum"* – from the bedroom of the emperors.

The church of the Roman senators and people, Santa Maria in Aracoeli has been used to celebrate many triumphs over adversity. Its ceiling, with naval motifs, commemorates the Battle of Lepanto (1571) and was built under Pope Gregory XIII Boncompagni, whose family crest, the dragon, can be seen towards the altar end.

Many other Roman families and individuals are honored by memorials in the church. To the right of the entrance door, the tombstone of archdeacon Giovanni Crivelli, rather than being set into the floor of the church, stands eternally at attention, partly so that the signature "Donatelli" (by Donatello) can be read at eye level.

The frescoes in the first chapel on the right, painted by Pinturicchio in the 1480s in the beautifully clear style of the early Renaissance, relate the life and death of St. Bernardino of Siena. On the left wall, the perspective of *The Burial of the Saint* actually slants to the right, taking into account the position of the viewer standing just outside the chapel.

The church is most famous, however, for an icon with apparently miraculous powers, the *Santo Bambino*, a 15th-century olive-wood figure of the Christ Child which was carved out of a tree from the garden of Gethsemane. Its powers are said to include resurrecting the dead, and it is sometimes summoned to the bedsides of the gravely ill. The original figure was stolen in 1994 but has now been replaced by a replica.

At Christmas the Christ Child is moved to a picturesque crèche (second chapel to the left), but usually it is located in the sacristy, as is the panel of the *Holy Family* from the workshop of Giulio Romano.

The miraculous olive-wood Christ Child at Santa Maria in Aracoeli

Capitoline Museums: Palazzo Nuovo ❶

A COLLECTION of Classical statues has been kept on the Capitoline hill since the Renaissance. The first group of bronze sculptures was given to the city by Pope Sixtus IV in 1471 and more additions were made by Pope Pius V in 1566. The Palazzo Nuovo was designed by Michelangelo as part of the renovation of the Piazza del Campidoglio, and after its completion in 1655, a number of the statues were transferred here. In 1734 Pope Clement XII Corsini decreed that the building be turned into the world's first public museum.

Hall of the Philosophers
The hall contains a rich mix of portraits of Greek politicians, scientists and literary figures. They are Roman copies that decorated the libraries, villas and gardens of the wealthy in ancient times.

MUSEUM GUIDE

The Palazzo Nuovo is devoted chiefly to sculpture, and most of its finest works, such as the Capitoline Venus, are Roman copies of Greek masterpieces. For visitors keen to identify the philosophers and poets of ancient Greece and the rulers of ancient Rome, there are collections of busts assembled in the 18th century. Admission price also includes entry to the Palazzo dei Conservatori opposite. An underground gallery links the two buildings and the Palazzo Senatorio.

Portrait of a Flavian Lady
The woman wears the fanciful and elaborate hairstyle popular among the female aristocracy of the 1st century AD.

Capitoline Venus

First floor

Courtyard

★ **Marcus Aurelius**
This bronze equestrian statue of the emperor dates from the 2nd century AD. It used to stand on a pedestal in the center of the Campidoglio, but has now been restored and is housed in the Palazzo Nuovo. A copy stands on the square.

Ground floor

The façade of Palazzo Nuovo was designed by Michelangelo, but the work was actually finished in 1655 by the brothers Carlo and Girolamo Rainaldi.

Main entrance

STAR SCULPTURES

★ **Marcus Aurelius**

★ **Discobolus**

★ **Dying Galatian**

KEY TO FLOOR PLAN

■ Non-exhibition space

□ Exhibition space

Mosaic of the Doves
This charming, naturalistic mosaic once decorated the floor of Hadrian's Villa at Tivoli (see p269). It shows doves drinking water from a vase.

★ Discobolus
The twisted torso was part of a Greek statue of a discus thrower. An 18th-century French sculptor, Monnot, made the additions that turned him into a wounded warrior.

VISITORS' CHECKLIST

Musei Capitolini, Piazza del Campidoglio. **Map** 5 A5 & 12 F5.
📞 06-6710 2071. 🚌 63, 70, 75, 81, 87, 95, 160, 170, 204, 628, 716 and many other routes to Piazza Venezia.
Open 9:30am–8pm Tue–Sun.
Closed Jan 1, May 1, Dec 25.
Adm charge Entrance ticket is also valid for Palazzo dei Conservatori.
🎫 ♿ 💻 📷 🚻 **NB** The museum is still undergoing some changes.

Red Faun
Found at Tivoli, the famous red marble satyr is a 2nd-century AD version of a Greek original – an example of Hadrian's fondness for all things Greek.

2

Stairs to ground floor

7   8

Stairs to galleries below the Senate and connecting with Palazzo dei Conservatori

Stairs to first floor

★ Dying Galatian
Great compassion is conveyed in this Roman copy of an original Greek work of the 3rd century BC.

Alexander Severus as Hunter
In this marble of the 3rd century AD, the emperor is posed as Perseus, holding up the head of Medusa the Gorgon after he had killed her in her sleep.

Capitoline Museums: Palazzo dei Conservatori **②**

THE PALAZZO DEI CONSERVATORI was the seat of the city's magistrates during the late Middle Ages. Its frescoed halls are still used occasionally for political meetings and the ground floor houses the municipal registry office. The palazzo was built by Giacomo della Porta, who carried out Michelangelo's designs for the Piazza del Campidoglio in the mid-16th century. While much of the palazzo is given over to sculpture, the art galleries on the second floor hold works by Veronese, Guercino, Tintoretto, Rubens, Caravaggio, Van Dyck and Titian.

Façade of Palazzo dei Conservatori
Work began on this Michelangelo design in 1563, the year before his death.

MUSEUM GUIDE

The museum is being reorganized due to restoration, so some objects might move. The rooms on the first floor are remarkable for their original 16th- and 17th-century decoration and Classical statues. The second-floor gallery houses paintings and a collection of porcelain.

Burial and Glory of St. Petronilla
This huge Baroque altarpiece was painted in 1622–3 by Guercino to hang in St. Peter's.

★ St. John the Baptist
Painted in 1595–6, Caravaggio's sensual portrait of the young saint presents a highly unorthodox image of the forerunner of Christ.

Stairs to second floor

Stairs to first floor

Second-floor art gallery

Courtya

Main entrance

The Horatii and Curatii
D'Arpino's fresco was painted in 1613 and depicts a duel taken from early Roman legend.

KEY TO FLOOR PLAN

☐ Garden
■ Non-exhibition space
☐ Undergoing restoration
☐ Exhibition space

Endymion
The youth doomed to sleep forever by the goddess Diana was painted by Pier Francesco Mola (1612–66), who studied under Cavalier d'Arpino.

VISITORS' CHECKLIST

See p71.

STAR EXHIBITS

★ She-Wolf

★ St. John the Baptist by Caravaggio

★ Spinario

Constantine II
The head of a colossal 4th-century AD statue of the emperor has survived, along with a hand and other odd fragments.

Braccio Nuovo

Roman Garden

First floor

Medusa
This bust by Bernini of the mythological Medusa is in Room 5.

★ Spinario
This is a charming bronze sculpture from the 1st century BC of a boy trying to remove a thorn from his foot.

★ She-Wolf
The Etruscan bronze of the wolf dates from the early 5th century BC. The legendary twins Romulus and Remus (see pp16–17) were probably added in the 15th century.

Temple of Jupiter

Via del Tempio di Giove. **Map** 5 A5 & 12 F5. 🚌 *See Getting There p65.*

THE TEMPLE of Jupiter, the most important in ancient Rome, was built in honor of the arch god around 509 BC on the southern summit of the Capitoline Hill. From the few traces that remain, archaeologists have been able to reconstruct the rectangular Greek appearance of the temple as it once stood. In places are remnants of its particularly Roman feature, the podium. Most of this lies beneath the Museo Nuovo wing of the Capitoline Museums *(see pp72–3)*.

By walking around the site, from the podium's south-western corner in Via del Tempio di Giove to its south-eastern corner in Piazzale Caffarelli, visitors can see that the temple was about the same size as the Pantheon.

Ancient coin showing the Temple of Jupiter

Tarpeian Rock

Via di Monte Caprino and Via del Tempio di Giove. **Map** 5 A5 & 12 F5. 🚌 *See Getting There p65.*

THE SOUTHERN TIP of the Capitoline is called the Tarpeian Rock (Rupe Tarpea), after Tarpeia, the young daughter of Spurius Tarpeius, defender of the Capitol in the 8th-century BC Sabine War.

The Sabines, bent on vengeance for the rape of their women by Romulus and

Sabine soldiers crushing the treacherous Tarpeia with their shields

his men, bribed Tarpeia to let them up to the Capitol. As the Augustan historian Livy records, Tarpeia's reward for her treachery was to be what the sabines wore on their shield arms: heavy gold bracelets and jeweled rings.

The Sabines kept to the letter of the bargain if not to its spirit – they repaid Tarpeia not with their jewelry but by crushing her to death between their shields.

Tarpeia was possibly the only casualty of her act of treachery – as the invading warriors met the Roman defenders, the Sabine women leapt between the two opposing armies, and forced them to become reconciled. All traitors and other condemned criminals were subsequently executed by being thrown over the sheer face of the rock.

The place has been considered dangerous and used to be fenced off, but restoration work is now under way.

Victor Emmanuel Monument

Piazza Venezia. **Map** 5 A5 & 12 F4. 🚌 *See Getting There p65.* **Open** 9am–5pm Tue–Sun.

KNOWN AS Il Vittoriano, this monument was begun in 1885 and inaugurated in 1911 in honor of Victor Emmanuel II of Savoy, the first king of a unified Italy. The king is depicted here in a gilt bronze equestrian statue, oversized like the monument itself – the statue is 39 ft (12 m) long.

The edifice contains a museum of the Risorgimento, the events that led to unification *(see pp36–7)*. Built in austere white Brescian marble, the "wedding cake" or "typewriter" (two of the many insulting nicknames given to this unloved white elephant) will never mellow into the ocher tones of surrounding buildings. It is widely held to be the epitome of self-important, insensitive architecture, though the views that it offers are spectacular.

Victor Emmanuel Monument in Piazza Venezia

Palazzo Venezia and Museum ⑪

Via del Plebiscito 118. **Map** 5 A4 &
12 E4. 06-6999 4319 *See
Getting There p65. **Open** 8:30am–
7pm Tue–Sun (last adm: 30 mins
before closing). **Closed** 1 Jan, 1 May,
25 Dec. **Adm charge.**
Temporary exhibitions.

I N ONE OF THE first Renaissance
civic buildings in Rome, this
palazzo has arched windows
and doors that are so
harmonious the
façade was once
attributed to the
great Humanist
architect Leon
Battista Alberti
(1404–72). It
was more
probably
designed by
Giuliano da
Maiano, who
carved the fine doorway to
the piazza.

Pope Paul II

Palazzo Venezia was built in
1455–64 for the Venetian
cardinal Pietro Barbo, who later
became Pope Paul II. It was at
times a papal residence, but
also the Venetian Embassy
before passing into French
hands in 1797. Since 1916 it
has belonged to the state. In
the Fascist era Mussolini used
it as his headquarters, address-
ing crowds from the balcony.

The interior is best seen on
a visit to the Museo del
Palazzo Venezia, Rome's most
underrated museum, which
holds first-class collections of
early Renaissance painting;
painted wood sculptures and
Renaissance chests from
throughout Italy; tapestries
from all over Europe;
majolica; silver; Neapolitan
ceramic figurines; Renaissance
bronzes; arms and armor;
Baroque terra-cotta sculptures
by Bernini, Algardi and others;
and 17th- and 18th-century
Italian paintings. There is a
marble screen from the
Aracoeli convent, which was
destroyed to make way for
the Victor Emmanuel
Monument, and a bust of
Paul II, showing him to rank
with Martin V and Leo X
among the fattest popes. The
building also hosts major
temporary exhibitions.

Palazzo Venezia with Mussolini's balcony in the center

San Marco ⑫

Piazza San Marco 48. **Map** 5 A4 & 12
F4. 06-679 52 05. *See **Getting
There** p65. **Open** 7:30am–12:30pm,
4–7:30pm, Mon–Sat, 8am–1:15pm,
4–7:30pm Sun.

T HE CHURCH of San Marco
was founded in 336 by
Mark, then pope, in honor of
St. Mark the Evangelist. The
relics of Pope Mark lie under
the altar. The church was
restored by Pope
Gregory IV in the 9th
century – the
magnificent
apse mosaics date
from this period.

Further major
rebuilding took
place from
1455–1471, when
Pope Paul II Barbo
made San Marco the
church of the Venetian

**Coat of arms of
Pope Paul II**

community in Rome. The
blue-and-gold coffered ceiling
is decorated with Pope Paul's
heraldic crest, the lion
rampant, recalling the lion of
St. Mark, the patron saint of
Venice. The appearance of the
rest of the interior, with its
colonnades of Sicilian jasper,
was largely the creation of
Filippo Barigioni in the 1740s.
Complemented by an
interesting array of funerary
monuments in the aisles, the
taste is typical of the
late Roman Baroque.

Leon Battista
Alberti, whose name
is also mentioned
tentatively in
connection with
Palazzo Venezia,
may have been the
architect of the
elegant travertine
arcade and loggia
of the façade.

San Marco's apse mosaic of Christ, with Gregory IV on the far left

FORUM

THE FORUM was the center of political, commercial and judicial life in ancient Rome. The largest buildings were the basilicas, where legal cases were heard. According to the playwright Plautus, the area teemed with "lawyers and litigants, bankers and brokers, shopkeepers and strumpets, good-for-nothings waiting for a tip from the rich." As

Figure of barbarian on the Arch of Constantine

Rome's population boomed, the Forum became too small. In 46 BC Julius Caesar built a new one, setting a precedent that was followed by emperors from Augustus to Trajan. In addition to the Imperial Forums, emperors erected triumphal arches to themselves, and just to the east Vespasian built the Colosseum, center of entertainment after the business of the day.

SIGHTS AT A GLANCE

Churches and Temples
Temple of Saturn **5**
Temple of Castor and Pollux **8**
Temple of Vesta **9**
Temple of Antoninus and Faustina **11**
Temple of Romulus and Santi Cosma e Damiano **12**
Santa Francesca Romana **14**
Temple of Venus and Rome **17**

Historic Buildings
Basilica Aemilia **1**
Curia **2**
Basilica Julia **7**

House of the Vestal Virgins **10**
Basilica of Constantine and Maxentius **13**
Trajan's Markets pp88–9 **18**
Torre delle Milizie **20**
Casa dei Cavalieri di Rodi **21**
Mamertine Prison **24**
Colosseum pp92–5 **27**

Museums
Antiquarium Forense **15**

KEY
	Tour of the Forum maps
M	Metro station
i	Tourist information

Arches and Columns
Arch of Septimius Severus **4**
Column of Phocas **6**
Arch of Titus **16**
Trajan's Column **19**
Arch of Constantine **26**

Ancient Sites
Rostra **3**
Forum of Augustus **22**
Forum of Caesar **23**
Forum of Nerva **25**

GETTING THERE
The simplest way is by Metro to Colosseo on line B. The main entrance to the Forum is on Via dei Fori Imperiali, served by buses 75, 85, 87, 117, 175, 186, 810 and 850. It is also a short walk from Piazza Venezia. For Trajan's Markets, the best buses are the 64 and 70 which stop in Via IV Novembre.

SEE ALSO
• *Street Finder*, maps 5, 8, 9, 12

• *Where to Stay* pp294–5

• *Triumphal Arches Walk* pp278–9

View of the Forum with the Colosseum rising behind the bell tower of Santa Francesca Romana

A Tour of the Roman Forum: West

To APPRECIATE THE LAYOUT of the Forum before visiting its confusing patchwork of ruined temples and basilicas, it is best to view the whole area from above, from the back of the Capitol. From there you can make out the Via Sacra (the Sacred Way), the route followed through the Forum by religious and triumphal processions towards the Capitol. Up until the 18th century when archaeological excavations began, the Arch of Septimius Severus and the columns of the Temple of Saturn lay half-buried underground. Excavation of the Forum continues, and the ruins uncovered date from many different periods of Roman history.

The Temple of Vespasian was the point from where Piranesi made this 18th-century engraving of the Forum. Its three columns were then almost completely buried.

Temple of Concord

Portico of the Dii Consentes

Temple of Saturn
The eight surviving columns of this temple stand close by the three columns of the Temple of Vespasian **5**

Rostra
These are the ruins of the platform used for public oratory in the Forum **3**

Basilica Julia
Named after Julius Caesar, who ordered its construction, the basilica housed important law courts **7**

Column of Phocas
One of the very last monuments erected in the Forum, this single column dates from AD 608 **6**

★ **Arch of Septi-
mius Severus**
*A 19th-century
engraving shows
the arch after
the Forum was
first excavated* **④**

Santi Luca e Martina
was an early medieval
church, but was rebuilt
in 1635–64 by Pietro
da Cortona.

The Forum in-
cluded the area
under Via dei Fori
Imperiali. More
parts have now
been made public.

LOCATOR MAP
See Central Rome Map pp12–13

STAR SIGHTS

★ **Arch of
Septimius Severus**

Curia
*This 3rd-century
rebuilding of
the Curia was
greatly restored in
1937* **②**

KEY

- - -	Suggested route

0 meters   75

0 yards   75

Basilica Aemilia
*This large
meeting hall
was razed to
the ground
in the 5th
century AD* **①**

Entrance
to Forum

**The Temple of Julius
Caesar** was erected in
his memory by
Augustus on the spot
where Caesar's body
was cremated after his
assassination in 44 BC.

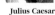
Julius Caesar

**To Roman
Forum: East**
See pp80–81

**Temple of Castor
and Pollux**
*A temple to the twin brothers
(of whom only Pollux was
fathered by Jupiter) stood on
this spot from the 5th century
BC. This section of cornice and
its supporting columns date
from the rebuilding of AD 6* **⑧**

A Tour of the Roman Forum: East

THE EASTERN END of the Roman Forum is dominated by the massive barrel-vaulted ruins of the Basilica of Constantine. To picture the building as it was in the 4th century AD, you must imagine marble columns, floors and statues, as well as glittering tiles of gilt bronze. The remains of the other important buildings are scanty, though the garden and ponds in the center of the House of the Vestal Virgins make it a very attractive spot. The two churches in this part of the Forum cannot be reached from within the archaeological area but are accessible from the road outside.

The Regia was the office of the Pontifex Maximus, the chief priest of ancient Rome.

To Forum entrance

VIA SACRA

Temple of Antoninus and Faustina
The portico of this temple, built in AD 141, has been incorporated into the church of San Lorenzo in Miranda ⑪

An early Iron Age necropolis was found here in 1902. Finds from it, such as this burial urn, are displayed in the Antiquarium.

Temple of Vesta
Partly reconstructed, this tiny temple to the goddess of the hearth was one of ancient Rome's most sacred shrines ⑨

Temple of Romulus
This domed building from the 4th century AD has survived as part of the church of Santi Cosma e Damiano ⑫

★ House of the Vestal Virgins
The priestesses who tended the sacred flame in the Temple of Vesta lived here. The house was a large rectangular building around a central garden ⑩

★ **Basilica of Constantine and Maxentius**
The stark remains of the basilica's huge arches and ceilings give some idea of the original scale and grandeur of the Forum's public buildings ⑬

LOCATOR MAP
See Central Rome Map pp12–13

Santa Francesca Romana
The church takes its name from a saint who cared for the Roman poor in the 15th century ⑭

VIA DEI FORI IMPERIALI

Antiquarium Forense
A small museum houses archaeological finds made in the Forum. They include this frieze of Aeneas and the Founding of Rome from the Basilica Aemilia ⑮

Colonnade surrounding Temple of Venus and Rome

Temple of Venus and Rome
These extensive ruins are of a magnificent temple built here in AD 121 by the Emperor Hadrian, largely to his own design ⑰

VIA SACRA

To the Palatine

Ruined Baths

Arch of Titus
This 19th-century reconstruction shows how the arch may have looked when it spanned the flag-stoned roadway of the Via Sacra ⑯

STAR SIGHTS

★ **Basilica of Constantine**

★ **House of the Vestal Virgins**

KEY

- - - Suggested route

0 meters   75

0 yards   75

Melted coins embedded in the floor of the Basilica Aemilia

Basilica Aemilia **❶**

See Visitors' Checklist.

ORIGINALLY this building was a rectangular colonnaded hall, with a multicolored marble floor and a bronze-tiled roof. It was built by the consuls Marcus Aemilius Lepidus and Marcus Fulvius Nobilor in 179 BC. The two consuls, who were elected annually, exercised supreme power over the Republic.

Basilicas in ancient Rome served no religious purpose; they were meeting halls for politicians, moneylenders and *publicani* (businessmen contracted by the state to collect taxes). A consortium of *publicani* agreed to hand over a specified sum to the state, but its members were allowed to collect as much as they could and keep the difference. This is why tax collectors in the Bible were so loathed.

The basilica was rebuilt many times; it was finally burned down when the Visigoths sacked Rome in AD 410. Business seems to have carried on until the last moment, for the pavement is splashed with tiny lumps of coins that melted in the fire.

Curia **❷**

See Visitors' Checklist.

A MODERN RESTORATION now stands over the ruins of the hall where Rome's Senate (chief council of state) used to meet. The first Curia stood on the site now occupied by the church of Santi Luca e Martina, but after the building was destroyed by fire in 52 BC, Julius Caesar built a new Curia at the edge of the Forum. This was restored by Domitian in AD 94 and, after another fire, rebuilt by Diocletian in the 3rd century. The building you see today is a 1937 restoration of Diocletian's Curia. Inside are two relief panels commissioned by Trajan to decorate the Rostra. One shows Trajan destroying records of unpaid taxes to free citizens from debt; in the other he sits on a throne receiving a mother and child.

The Curia today

Rostra **❸**

See Visitors' Checklist.

Ruins of the Imperial Rostra

SPEECHES WERE delivered from this dais, the most famous – thanks to Shakespeare – being Mark Antony's "Friends, Romans, Countrymen" oration after the assassination of Julius Caesar in 44 BC. Caesar himself had just reorganized the Forum and this speech was made from the newly sited Rostra, which is now in ruins. In the following year the head and hands of Cicero were put on display after he had been put to death by the second Triumvirate (Augustus, Mark Antony and Marcus Lepidus). Fulvia, Mark Antony's wife, stabbed the great orator's tongue with a hairpin. It was also here that Julia, Augustus's daughter, was said to have played the prostitute – one of many scandalous acts that led to her banishment.

The dais took its name from the ships' prows *(rostra)* with which it was decorated. Sheathed in iron (for ramming enemy vessels), these came from ships captured at the Battle of Antium in 338 BC.

ROSTRA
This reconstruction shows the platform for public speaking in the Forum, as it looked in Imperial times.

Honorary statue

Relief panel in balustrade, showing Trajan's acts of charity

Prows of ships *(rostra)*

Arch of Septimius Severus ❹

See Visitors' Checklist.

THIS TRIUMPHAL ARCH, one of the most striking and best-preserved monuments of the Forum, was erected in AD 203 to celebrate the tenth anniversary of the accession of Septimius Severus. The relief panels – largely eroded – celebrate the emperor's victories in Parthia (modern-day Iraq and Iran) and Arabia.

Originally, the inscription along the top of the arch was to Septimius and his two sons, Caracalla and Geta, but after Septimius died, Caracalla murdered Geta and had his brother's name removed. Even so, the holes in which the letters of his name were pegged are still visible.

Barbarian captives, Arch of Severus

During the Middle Ages the central arch, half-buried in earth and debris, was used to shelter a barber's shop.

Triumphal arch of the Emperor Septimius Severus

Temple of Saturn ❺

See Visitors' Checklist.

THE MOST PROMINENT of the ruins in the fenced-off area between the Forum and the Capitoline Hill is the Temple of Saturn. It consists of a high platform, eight columns and a section of entablature. There was a temple dedicated to

Ionic capitals on the surviving columns of the Temple of Saturn

Saturn here as early as 497 BC, but it had to be rebuilt many times and the current remains date only from the 42 BC.

Saturn was the mythical god-king of Italy, said to have presided over a prosperous and peaceful Golden Age from which slavery, private property, crime and war were absent. As such, he appealed particularly to the lower classes and slaves. Every year, between December 17 and December 23, Saturn's reign was remembered in a week of sacrifices and feasting known as the Saturnalia.

As long as the revels lasted, the normal social order was turned upside down. Slaves were permitted to drink and dine with (and sometimes even be served by) their masters. Senators and other high-ranking Romans would abandon the aristocratic togas that they usually wore to distinguish them from the lower classes and put on more democratic, loose-fitting gowns. During the holidays all the law courts and schools in the city were closed. No prisoner could be punished, and no war could be declared.

People also celebrated the Saturnalia in their own homes: they exchanged gifts, in particular special wax dolls and wax tapers, and played lighthearted gambling games, the stakes usually being nuts, a symbol of fruitfulness. Much of the spirit and many of the rituals of the festival have been preserved in the Christian celebration of Christmas.

Column of Phocas ❻

See Visitors' Checklist.

THIS COLUMN, 44 ft (13.5 m) high, is one of the few to have remained upright since the day it was put up. Until 1816, when an inquisitive Englishwoman, Lady Elizabeth Foster, widow of the fifth duke of Devonshire, decided to excavate its pedestal, nobody knew what it was. It turned out to be the youngest of the Forum's monuments, erected in AD 608 in honor of the Byzantine emperor Phocas, who had just paid a visit to Rome. The column may have been placed here as a mark of gratitude to Phocas for giving the Pantheon to the pope *(see pp110–11).*

Slender, fluted Column of Phocas

Remains of the Basilica Julia, a Roman court of civil law

Basilica Julia ❼

See Visitors' Checklist, p82.

THIS IMMENSE basilica, which occupied the area between the Temple of Saturn and the Temple of Castor and Pollux, was begun by Julius Caesar in 54 BC and completed after his death by his great nephew Augustus. It was damaged by fire almost immediately afterward in 9 BC, but was subsequently repaired and dedicated to the emperor's grandsons, Gaius and Lucius.

After numerous sackings and pilferings, only the steps, pavement and column stumps remain. Nevertheless, the ground plan is fairly clear. The basilica had a central hall, measuring 260 ft by 59 ft (82 m by 18 m), surrounded by a double portico. The hall was on three floors, while the outer portico had only two.

The Basilica Julia was the seat of the *centumviri*, a body of 180 magistrates who tried civil law cases. They were split into four chambers of 45 men, and unless a case was particularly complicated, they would all sit separately.

The four courts were, however, divided only by screens or curtains, and the voices of lawyers and cheers and boos of spectators in the upper galleries echoed through the building. Lawyers used to hire crowds of spectators, who would applaud every time the lawyer who was paying them made a point and jeer at his opponents. The clappers and booers must have had a good deal of time on their hands: scratched into the steps are checkerboards where they played dice and other gambling games to while away the time between cases.

TEMPLE OF VESTA
The temple preserved the shape of an original primitive structure made of wooden posts with a thatched roof.

Cella (sacred inner chamber)

Ring of Corinthian columns

Sacred flame

Temple of Castor and Pollux ❽

See Visitors' Checklist, p82.

THE THREE SLENDER fluted columns of this temple form one of the Forum's most beautiful ruins. The first temple here was probably dedicated in 484 BC in honor of the mythical twins and patrons of horsemanship, Castor and Pollux. During the battle of Lake Regillus (499 BC) against the ousted Tarquin kings, the Roman dictator Postumius promised to build a temple to the twins if the Romans were victorious. Some said the twins appeared on the battlefield, helped the Romans to victory and then materialized in the Forum – the temple marks the spot – to announce the news.

The temple, like most buildings in the Forum, was rebuilt many times. The three surviving columns date from the last occasion on which it was rebuilt – by the future Emperor Tiberius after a fire in AD 6. For a long period the temple housed the city's office of weights and measures, and it was also used at times by a number of bankers.

Corinthian columns of the Temple of Castor and Pollux

Temple of Vesta ❾

See Visitors' Checklist, p82.

THE FORUM'S most elegant temple, a circular building originally surrounded by a ring of 20 fine fluted columns, dates from the 4th century AD, though there had been a temple on the site for far longer. It was partially reconstructed in 1930.

The cult of the Vestals was one of the oldest in Rome, and centered on six Vestal Virgins, who were required to keep alight the sacred flame of Vesta, the goddess of the hearth. This responsibility was originally entrusted to the daughters of the king, but it then passed to the Vestals, the only group of women priests in Rome. It was no easy task, as the flame was easily blown out. Any Vestal who allowed the flame to die was whipped by the high priest (Pontifex Maximus) and dismissed.

The girls, who had to belong to noble families, were selected when they were between 6 and 10 years old. They served for 30 years: the first ten were spent learning their duties, the next ten performing them and the final ten teaching novices. They enjoyed high status and financial security, but were compelled to remain virgins. The penalty for transgressing was to be buried alive, although only ten Vestals are recorded as ever having suffered this fate. The men concerned were whipped to death. When Vestals retired, they were free to live the rest of their lives as ordinary citizens. If they wished they could marry, but few ever did.

Another of the Vestals' duties was to guard the Palladium, a sacred statue of the goddess Pallas Athena. The irreverent Emperor Heliogabalus burgled the temple in the 3rd century AD. He thought he had succeeded in stealing the Palladium, but the Vestals had been warned of his intention and had replaced it with a replica.

Central courtyard of the House of the Vestal Virgins

House of the Vestal Virgins ❿

See Visitors' Checklist, p82.

Honorary statue of a Vestal Virgin

As SOON AS a girl became a Vestal she came to live in the House of the Vestal Virgins. Originally this was an enormous complex with about 50 rooms on three stories. The only substantial remains today are some of the rooms around the central courtyard. This space is perhaps the most evocative part of the Forum. Overlooking ponds of water lilies and plump goldfish is a row of eroded, and mostly headless, statues of senior Vestals, dating from the 3rd and 4th centuries AD. The better-preserved examples were transferred to the Museo Nazionale Romano *(see p163)*. On one of the pedestals the inscription has been removed because the Vestal in question suffered some disgrace. It is thought she may have been a certain Claudia, known to have betrayed the cult by converting to Christianity.

Though many of the rooms surrounding the courtyard are well preserved – some even retain flights of steps leading to an upper floor – you are not allowed inside them. If you look into the series of rooms along the south side, however, you might be able to see the remains of a mill,

Restored section of Temple of Vesta

used for grinding the grain with which the Vestals made a special sacrificial cake. The bakery was next door.

Temple of Antoninus and Faustina ⓫

See Visitors' Checklist, p82. **Church open** *10am–noon Thu; ring the bell.*

ONE OF THE FORUM'S oddest sights is the Baroque façade of the church of San Lorenzo in Miranda rising above the porch of a Roman temple. First dedicated in AD 141 by the Emperor Antoninus Pius to his late wife Faustina, the temple was rededicated to them both on the death of the emperor. In the 11th century it became a church because it was thought San Lorenzo (St. Lawrence) had been condemned to death there. The current church dates from 1601.

Temple of Antoninus and Faustina

Temple of Romulus and Santi Cosma e Damiano ⑫

See Visitors' Checklist, p82.
Santi Cosma e Damiano
☎ 06-699 15 40.
Open 9am–1pm, 3–7pm daily.
Crèche closed Mon am.
Adm charge for crèche.

N O ONE IS SURE to whom the so-called Temple of Romulus was dedicated, but it was probably to the son of the Emperor Maxentius's and not to Rome's founder. It is a circular brick building, topped by a cupola, with two rectangular side rooms and a concave porch. The heavy, dull bronze doors are original.

Since the 6th century the temple has acted as a vestibule to the church of Santi Cosma e Damiano, which itself occupies an ancient building – a hall in Vespasian's Forum of Peace. The entrance to the church is on Via dei Fori Imperiali. The beautiful carved figures of its 18th-century Neapolitan *presepio* (crèche or Nativity scene) are back on view now, and the church has a vivid Byzantine apse mosaic with Christ pictured against orange clouds.

Roof of the Temple of Romulus

Basilica of Constantine and Maxentius ⑬

See Visitors' Checklist, p82.

T HE BASILICA'S three vast, coffered barrel vaults are powerful relics of what was the largest building in the Forum. Work began in AD 308 under the Emperor Maxentius. When he was deposed by Constantine after the Battle of the Milvian Bridge in AD 312, work on the massive project continued under the new regime. The building, which like other Roman basilicas was used for the administration of justice and for carrying on business, is often referred to simply as the Basilica of Constantine.

The area covered by the basilica was roughly 330 ft by 215 ft (100 m by 65 m). It was originally designed to have a long nave and aisles running from east to west, but Constantine switched the axis around to create three short broad aisles with the main entrance in the center of the long south wall. The height of the building was 115 ft (35 m). In the apse at the western end, where it could be seen from all over the building, stood a 39 ft (12 m) statue of the emperor, made partly of wood and partly of marble. The giant head, hand and foot are on display in the courtyard of the Palazzo dei Conservatori *(see pp72–3)*. The basilica's roof glittered with gilded tiles until the 7th century, when they were removed and re-used to cover the roof of the old St. Peter's.

The three barrel-vaulted aisles of the basilica were used as law courts.

The octagonal coffers in the vaulted ceiling were originally faced with marble.

The main entrance was added by Constantine in AD 313.

The roof was supported by eight massive Corinthian columns. One now stands in Piazza Santa Maria Maggiore *(see p173).*

Santa Francesca Romana

Piazza di Santa Francesca Romana.
Map 5 B5. 06-679 55 28.
85, 87, 117, 175, 810. 3.
Colosseo. **Open** 9:30am–noon,
3–5pm daily.

EVERY YEAR on March 9, devout Roman drivers try to park as close as possible to this Baroque church with a Romanesque bell tower. The aim of their pilgrimage is to have their vehicles blessed by Santa Francesca Romana, the patron saint of motorists. During the 15th century, Francesca of Trastevere founded a society of pious women devoted to helping the less fortunate. After her canonization in 1608, the church, originally called Santa Maria Nova, was rededicated to Francesca.

Bell tower of Santa Francesca

The most curious sight inside the church is a flagstone with what are reputed to be the imprints of the knees of St. Peter and St. Paul. The story goes that a magician, Simon Magus, decided to prove that his powers were superior to those of the Apostles by levitating himself above the Forum. As Simon was in midair, Peter and Paul fell to their knees and prayed fervently for God to show his divine force. Simon instantly plummeted to his death.

Antiquarium Forense

See Visitors' Checklist, p82.

THE FORMER CONVENT of Santa Francesca Romana now houses a small museum and the offices of those in charge of the excavations of the Forum. The museum is currently being reorganized, and only one or two rooms are open. They contain Iron Age burial urns and graves

Dedication to Titus and Vespasian on the Arch of Titus

and their skeletal occupants, along with some ancient bric-a-brac exhumed from the Forum's drains. Fragments of statues, capitals, friezes and other architectural decoration taken from the Forum's buildings will be on exhibit when the museum reopens.

Frieze of Aeneas in the Antiquarium Forense

Arch of Titus

See Visitors' Checklist, p82.

THIS TRIUMPHAL ARCH was erected in AD 81 by the Emperor Domitian in honor of the victories of his brother, Titus, and his father, Vespasian, in Judea. In AD 68 the Jews, weary of being exploited by unscrupulous Roman officials, rebelled. A bitter war broke out, ending 2 years later in the fall of Jerusalem and the start of Jewish Diaspora.

Although the reliefs inside the arch are badly eroded, you can make out a triumphant procession of Roman soldiers carrying off spoils from the Temple of Jerusalem. The booty includes the altar, silver trumpets and a golden seven-branched menorah.

Temple of Venus and Rome

See Visitors' Checklist, p82.

THE EMPEROR Hadrian designed this temple to occupy what had been the vestibule to Nero's Domus Aurea (*see p175*). Many of the columns have been reerected, and though there is no access, there is a good view as you leave the Forum and also from the upper tiers of the Colosseum. The temple, the largest in Rome, was dedicated to Roma, the personification of the city, and to Venus because she was the mother of Aeneas, father of Romulus and Remus. Each goddess had her own *cella* (shrine). When the architect Apollodorus said that the seated statues in the niches were too big (had they tried to "stand," their heads would have hit the vaults), Hadrian had him put to death.

Statue of goddess   **Porphyry column**

Cross-section of Temple of Venus and Rome

Trajan's Markets ⑱

ORIGINALLY CONSIDERED among the wonders of the Classical world, Trajan's Markets now show only a hint of their former splendor. Emperor Trajan and his architect, Apollodorus of Damascus, built this visionary new complex of 150 shops and offices (probably used for administering the corn ration) in the early 2nd century AD. It was the ancient Roman equivalent of the modern shopping center, selling everything from silks and spices imported from the Middle East to fresh fish, fruit and flowers.

The Markets Today
Above the façade stands the 13th-century Torre delle Milizie, built for defensive purposes.

Cross vaulting

Trajan
The emperor was a benevolent ruler and a successful general.

Main Hall
Twelve shops were built on two floors, and the corn ration was shared out on the upper story. This was a free corn ration given to Roman men to prevent hunger.

Via Biberatica
The main street that runs through the market is named after the drinking inns which once lined it.

Small semicircle of shops

Staircase

TIMELINE

AD 100–112 Building of Trajan's Markets	**472** Invasion by Ricimer the Suevian. Some of his Germanic troops stationed here	**1200s** Torre delle Milizie built on top of the markets	**1572** Convent of Santa Caterina da Siena built over part of markets	**1924** Many medieval houses demolished
AD 100	**AD 500** 1000	1300	1800	1950
AD 117 Death of Trajan **AD 98** Trajan succeeds Nerva as emperor	**552** Byzantine takeover of Rome. Markets occupied and fortified by the army	**1300s** Annibaldi and Caetani families vie for control of the area	**1828** First tentative excavations, but importance of site not recognized	**1911–14** Convent demolished **1930–33** Markets finally excavated

VISITORS' CHECKLIST

Mercati Traianei, Via IV Novembre.
Map 5 B4. 06-679 00 48.
64, 70, 170 and many routes
to Piazza Venezia. **Open** 9am–
5pm Tue–Sun (last adm: 30 mins
before closing). **Closed** Jan 1,
May 1, Dec 25. **Adm charge**.
Newly excavated parts of
Trajan's Markets can be viewed
by prior arrangement.

The Markets in the 16th Century
*This fanciful fresco depicts a gladiatorial combat
taking place in front of the partly buried remains of
Trajan's Markets.*

A Market Shop
*Shops were built with
arched entrances,
their jambs and lintels
creating rectangular
portals and windows.
A wooden mezzanine
was used for storage.*

Upper Corridor
*Shops on this upper level
were thought to have sold
wine and oil, because
storage jars were
discovered here.*

The terrace
over the archway
spanning Via
Biberatica has
a good view of
the Forum
of Trajan
below.

**Wall dividing market area
from Forum of Trajan**

**Large hall with
semidomed ceiling**

Forum of Trajan, built in front of the markets in
AD 107–113, was flanked by the Basilica Ulpia.
The basilica, measuring 558 ft (170 m) by 197 ft
(60 m), is the largest in Rome. A small portion of
the Forum has been excavated; unfortunately,
however, the rest of it remains buried beneath
modern Rome's busy city streets.

MARKET SHOPPING
Shops opened early and closed about
noon. The best ones were decorated
with mosaics of the goods they sold.
Almost all the shopping was done
by men, though women visited the
dressmaker and cobbler. The
tradespeople were almost all
male. In employment records for
the period AD 117 to 193, the
only female shopkeepers
mentioned are three wool-
sellers, two jewelers,
a greengrocer and
a fishwife.

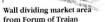

Fish mosaic

Trajan's Markets ⑱

See pp88–9.

Trajan's Column ⑲

Via dei Fori Imperiali. **Map** 5 A4 &
12 F4. *See Visitors' Checklist for
Trajan's Markets, p89.*

Detail of Trajan's Column

THIS ELEGANT marble column
was inaugurated by Trajan
in AD 113, and celebrates his
two campaigns in Dacia
(Romania) in AD 101–103 and
AD 105–106. The column,
base and pedestal are 131 ft
(40 m) tall – precisely the same
height as the spur of the
Quirinal Hill, which was
excavated to make room for
Trajan's Forum. Spiraling up
the column are minutely
detailed scenes from the
campaigns, beginning with the
Romans preparing for war
and ending with the Dacians
being ousted from their
homeland. The column is
pierced with small windows
to illuminate its internal spiral
staircase (closed to the public).
If you wish to see the reliefs in
detail, there is a complete set of
casts in the Museo della Civiltà
Romana at EUR *(see p266).*

When Trajan died in AD 117,
his ashes, and those of his
wife Plotina, were placed in a
golden urn in the column's
hollow base. The column's
survival was largely thanks to
the intervention of Pope
Gregory I ("the Great") who
reigned from 590 to 604. He
was so moved by a relief
showing Trajan helping a
woman whose son had been
killed that he begged God to
release the emperor's soul

from hell. God duly appeared
to the pope to say that Trajan
had been rescued, but asked
him not to pray for the souls
of any more pagans.

According to legend, when
Trajan's ashes were exhumed,
his skull and tongue were not
only intact, but his tongue
told of his release from Hell.
The land around the column
was then declared sacred and
the column spared. The
statue of Trajan remained on
top of the column until 1587,
when it was replaced with
one of St. Peter.

Torre delle Milizie ⑳

Mercati Traianei, Via IV Novembre.
Map 5 B4. *Open by appt only.*

FOR CENTURIES this massive
brick tower was thought to
have been the one in which
Nero stood watching Rome
burn, after he had set it alight
to clear the city's slums. It is
uncertain whether arson was
among Nero's crimes, but it is
certain that he did not watch
the fire from this tower – it
was built in the 13th century.

Casa dei Cavalieri di Rodi ㉑

Piazza del Grillo 1. **Map** 5 B5.
【 06-6710 2634. ▦ 84, 85, 87,
117, 175, 186, 810, 850.
Open by appt only.

Loggia, Casa dei Cavalieri di Rodi

SINCE THE 12TH CENTURY, the
crusading order of the
Knights of St. John, also known
as the Knights of Rhodes (Rodi)
or Malta, have had their prior-
ate in this medieval house
above the Forum of Augustus.
If you are lucky enough to
get inside, ask to see the
beautiful Cappella di San
Giovanni (Chapel of St. John).

Forum of Augustus ㉒

Piazza del Grillo 1. **Map** 5 B5 & 12 F5.
*See Visitors' Checklist for Trajan's
Markets, p89.* **Open** by appt only.

**Podium of the Temple of Mars in
the Forum of Augustus**

THE FORUM of Augustus
was built to celebrate
Augustus's victory over Julius
Caesar's assassins, Brutus and
Cassius, at the Battle of
Philippi in 41 BC. The temple
in its center was dedicated to
Mars the Avenger. The forum
stretched from a high wall at
the foot of the sleazy Suburra
quarter to the edge of the
Forum of Caesar. At least half
of it is now concealed below
Mussolini's Via dei Fori
Imperiali. The temple is easily
identified, with its cracked
steps and four Corinthian
columns. Originally it had a
statue of Mars that looked
very like Augustus. In case
anyone failed to notice the
resemblance, a giant statue of
Augustus himself was placed
against the Suburra wall.

Forum of Caesar ㉓

Via del Carcere Tulliano.
Map 5 A5. 【 06-6996 7850.
▦ 84, 85, 87, 175, 186, 810, 850.
Open by appt only.

THE FIRST of Rome's Imperial
forums was built by Julius
Caesar. He spent a fortune –
most of it booty from his
conquest of Gaul – buying up
and demolishing houses on
the site. The best of these was
a temple dedicated in 46 BC
to the goddess Venus Genetrix,
from whom Caesar claimed
descent. The temple
contained statues of Caesar
and Cleopatra as well as of
Venus. All that remains of this
temple to vanity is a platform

and three Corinthian columns. The forum was enclosed by a double colonnade that sheltered a row of shops, but this burned down in AD 80 and was rebuilt by Domitian and Trajan. Trajan also added the Basilica Argentaria (an important financial exchange) and a heated public lavatory. The forum is only open for visits by appointment, but parts are visible from above in Via dei Fori Imperiali.

Mamertine Prison

Clivo Argentario 1. **Map** 5 A5.
[C] 06-679 29 02. 84, 85, 87, 175, 186, 810, 850. **Open** 9am–noon, 2–5pm daily. **Donation** expected.

19th-century engraving of guards visiting prisoners in the Mamertine

BELOW THE 16th-century church of San Giuseppe dei Falegnami (St. Joseph of the Carpenters) is a dank dungeon in which, according to Christian legend, St. Peter was imprisoned. He is said to have caused a spring to bubble up into the cell, and used the water to baptize his guards.

The prison, also known as Tullianum, was in an old cistern with access to the city's main sewer (the *cloaca maxima*). The lower cell was used for executions, and bodies were thrown into the sewer. Among the enemies of Rome to be executed here was the Gaulish leader Vercingetorix, defeated by Julius Caesar in 52 BC.

17th-century view of the ruined Forum of Nerva

Forum of Nerva

Piazza del Grillo 1 (reached through Forum of Augustus). **Map** 5 B5.
[C] 06-6996 7850. 84, 85, 87, 175, 186, 810, 850. **Open** by appt only.

THE FORUM of Nerva was begun by Nerva's predecessor, Domitian, and completed in AD 97. Little more than a long corridor with a colonnade along the sides and a Temple of Minerva at one end, it was also known as the Forum Transitorium because it lay between the Forum of Peace built by the Emperor Vespasian in AD 70 and the Forum of Augustus. Vespasian's forum is almost completely covered by Via dei Fori Imperiali, as is much of the Forum of Nerva itself. Excavations have unearthed Renaissance shops

Medallion on the Arch of Constantine

and taverns, and part of the forum, including the base of the temple and two columns that were part of the original colonnade. These support a relief of Minerva above a frieze of young girls learning to sew and weave.

Arch of Constantine

Between Via di San Gregorio and Piazza del Colosseo. **Map** 8 F1.
75, 85, 87, 175, 673, 810.
3. [M] Colosseo.

THIS TRIUMPHAL ARCH was dedicated in AD 315 to celebrate Constantine's victory three years before over his co-emperor, Maxentius. Constantine claimed he owed his victory to a vision of Christ, but there is nothing Christian about the arch – in fact, most of the medallions, reliefs and statues were scavenged from earlier monuments. There are statues of Dacian prisoners taken from Trajan's Forum and reliefs of Marcus Aurelius, including one where he distributes bread to the poor. Inside the arch are reliefs of Trajan's victory over the Dacians. These were probably by the artist who worked on Trajan's Column.

Colosseum

See pp92–5.

North side of the Arch of Constantine, facing the Colosseum

Colosseum ㉗

Rome's greatest amphitheater was commissioned by the Emperor Vespasian in AD 72 on the marshy site of a lake in the grounds of Nero's palace, the Domus Aurea (see p175). Deadly gladiatorial combats and wild animal fights were staged free of charge by the emperor and wealthy citizens for public viewing. The Colosseum was built to a practical design, with its 80 arched entrances allowing easy access to 55,000 spectators, but it is also a building of great beauty. The drawing here shows how it looked at the time of its opening in AD 80. It was one of several similar amphitheaters built in the Roman Empire, and some survive at El Djem in North Africa, Nîmes and Arles in France and Verona in northern Italy. Despite being damaged over the years by neglect and theft, it remains a majestic sight.

Outer Wall of the Colosseum
Stone plundered from the façade in the Renaissance was used to build several palaces, bridges and parts of St. Peter's.

The Founder of the Colosseum
Vespasian was a professional soldier who became emperor in AD 69, founding the Flavian dynasty.

The outer walls are made of travertine.

Flora of the Colosseum

By the 19th century, the Colosseum was heavily overgrown. Different micro-climates in various parts of the ruin had created an impressive variety of herbs, grasses and wild flowers. Several botanists were inspired to study and catalog them, and two books were published, one listing 420 different species.

Borage, a herb

The bollards anchored the velarium.

The velarium was a huge awning that shaded spectators from the sun. Supported on poles attached to the upper story of the building, it was then hoisted into position with ropes anchored to bollards outside the stadium.

Timeline

80 Vespasian's son, Titus, stages inaugural festival in the amphitheater. It lasts 100 days.

AD 70		100
72 Emperor Vespasian begins work on the Colosseum	**81–96** Amphitheater completed in reign of Domitian	

Internal Corridors
These were designed to allow the large and often unruly crowd to move freely and to be seated within 10 minutes of arriving at the Colosseum.

The vomitorium was the exit used from each numbered section.

Brick formed the inner walls.

VISITORS' CHECKLIST

Piazza del Colosseo. **Map** 9 A1.
06-6996 7700. 75, 81, 85, 87, 117, 175, 673, 810. 3 to Piazza del Colosseo. Colosseo.
Open 9am–7pm daily (4pm in winter). **Closed** Jan 1, May 1, Dec 25. **Adm charge.** limited.
Beware of unlicensed "gladiators" charging for photographs – negotiate a fee up front.

Corinthian columns

Ionic columns

Doric columns

The podium was a large terrace where the emperor and the wealthy upper classes had their seats.

Entry routes to take the spectators to their seats were reached by means of staircases to the various levels of the amphitheater.

Arched entrances, 80 in total, were all numbered to let in the vast crowds that attended the fights.

Colossus of Nero
The Colosseum may have acquired its name from this huge gilt-bronze statue that stood near the amphitheater.

230 Colosseum restored by Alexander Severus	**404** Gladiatorial combats banned	*A gladiator's shield*	**1200s** Frangipane family turn Colosseum into a fortress			**1870** All vegetation removed
				15th–16th centuries Ruins used as quarry. Travertine blocks recycled by popes		

200	**400**	**1300**	**1500**	**1700**	**1900**

248 Thousandth anniversary celebration of founding of Rome by Romulus and Remus	**442** Building damaged in an earthquake	**523** Wild animal fights banned	**1312** Emperor Henry VII gives Colosseum to the Senate and people of Rome	**1749** Colosseum dedicated to Passion of Jesus	**1893–6** Structure below arena revealed

How Fights were Staged in the Arena

THE EMPERORS HELD shows here that often began with animals performing circus tricks. Then on came the gladiators, who fought one another to the death. When one was killed, attendants dressed as Charon, the mythical ferryman of the dead, carried his body off on a stretcher; sand was raked over the blood to make ready for the next bout. A badly wounded gladiator would surrender his fate to the crowd. The "thumbs up" sign from the emperor meant he could live, "thumbs down" that he die, and the victor became an instant hero. Animals were brought here from as far away as North Africa and the Middle East. The games held in AD 248 to mark the thousandth anniversary of the Rome's founding saw the death of a host of lions, elephants, zebras and elks.

Beneath the Arena
Late 19th-century excavations exposed the network of underground rooms where the animals were kept.

Interior of the Colosseum
The stadium was built in the form of an ellipse, with tiers of seats around a vast central arena.

Emperor's entrance

Emperor's box

Layout of underground passages

Tiers of seats

Consul's box

Consul's entrance

Gladiators' entrance

A complex of rooms, passages and lifts lies beneath the arena.

Dramatic Entrances
Below the sand was a wooden floor through which animals, men and scenery appeared in the arena.

Roman Gladiators
These were usually slaves, prisoners of war or condemned criminals. Most were men, but there were a few female gladiators.

The Colosseum by Antonio Canaletto
This 18th-century view of the Colosseum shows the Meta Sudans fountain (now demolished). Water "sweated" from a metal ball on top of its brick cone.

Metal fencing kept animals penned in, while archers stood by just in case any escaped.

Seating was tiered, and different social classes were segregated.

A winch brought the animal cages up to arena level when they were due to fight.

A ramp and trap door enabled the animal to reach the arena after walking along a corridor.

Cages were actually three-sided elevators that were hoisted to the level where the animals were released.

SEA BATTLES IN THE ARENA

The historian Dion Cassius, writing in the 4th century AD, relates how, 150 years earlier, the Colosseum's arena was flooded to stage a mock sea battle. Scholars now believe that he was mistaken. The spectacle probably took place in the Naumachia of Augustus, a water-filled arena situated across the Tiber in Trastevere.

PALATINE

ACCORDING TO LEGEND, Romulus and Remus were brought up here by a wolf in a cave. Traces of Iron Age huts, dating from the 9th century BC, have been found on the Palatine Hill, providing archaeological support for the area's legendary links with the founding of Rome. The Palatine was a very desirable place to live, becoming home to some of the city's most famous inhabitants. The great orator Cicero had a house here, as did the lyric poet Catullus. Augustus was born on the hill and continued to live here in very modest

Fresco of mask in the House of Augustus

circumstances even when he became emperor. The two buildings identified as the House of Augustus and the House of Livia, his second wife, are among the best preserved. The first emperor's example of frugality was ignored by his successors, Tiberius, Caligula and Domitian, who all built extravagant palaces here. The ruins of Tiberius's palace lie beneath the 16th-century Farnese Gardens. The most extensive ruins are those of the Domus Augustana and Domus Flavia, the two wings of Domitian's palace, and the later extension built by Septimius Severus.

SIGHTS AT A GLANCE

Temples
Temple of Cybele ❻

Historic Buildings
Domus Flavia ❶
Domus Augustana ❸
House of Livia ❺

Ancient Sites
Cryptoporticus ❷
Stadium ❹
Huts of Romulus ❼

Parks and Gardens
Farnese Gardens ❽

SEE ALSO

• *Street Finder*, map 8

GETTING THERE

There are two ways of getting on to the Palatine hill; through either the Roman Forum (from Via dei Fori Imperiali) or through the entrance in Via di San Gregorio. A separate ticket for the Palatine is needed, even if you come from the Forum. The best buses are the 75, 85, 87, 117, 175, 186, 810, 850; all stop in Via dei Fori Imperiali near the main entrance. Tram 3 and Colosseo Metro station *(see p77)* are also handy.

KEY

Tour of the Palatine map

0 meters   200

0 yards   200

Towering ruins of the Palace of Septimius Severus on the Palatine hill

A Tour of the Palatine

SHADED ON ITS LOWER SLOPES with pines, and scattered in spring with wild flowers, the Palatine is the most pleasant and relaxing of the city's ancient sites. You can reach the hill by walking up from the Roman Forum *(see pp76–7)*. The area is dominated by the ruins of the Domus Flavia and the Domus Augustana, two parts of Domitian's huge palace built at the end of the 1st century AD. What you are able to see depends on where excavations are taking place at the time.

Huts of Romulus
These are traces of a 9th-century BC village on the Palatine **7**

To Farnese Gardens
See p101

House of Augustus

Temple of Cybele
Also known as the Temple of the Magna Mater, this was the center of an important fertility cult **6**

★ House of Livia
Many of the wall paintings have survived in the house where Augustus lived with his wife Livia **5**

STAR SIGHTS

★ **Domus Flavia**

★ **House of Livia**

KEY

- - - Suggested route

| 0 meters | 75 |
| 0 yards | 75 |

★ Domus Flavia
This oval fountain was designed to be seen from the dining hall of the palace **1**

Domus Augustana
The Roman emperors lived in this part of the palace, while the Domus Flavia was used for public functions **3**

Cryptoporticus
In this long underground tunnel, built by Nero, the stuccoes that decorated the walls and vault have been replaced with copies ②

LOCATOR MAP
See Central Rome Map pp12–13

Octagonal fountain of the Domus Flavia

The Palatine Museum is inside a former convent, and houses artifacts from ancient Rome.

Stadium
Part of the Imperial palace, this enclosure may have been used by the emperors as a private garden ④

Via San Gregorio entrance

The exedra of the Stadium may have housed a balcony for emperors to view races.

Baths of Septimius Severus

The Palace of Septimius Severus (reigned AD 193–211) was an extension of the Domus Augustana. It projected beyond the hillside, requiring enormous arched supports.

Substructure of palace

Domus Flavia ❶

See Visitors' Checklist.

Marble pavement in the courtyard of the Domus Flavia

IN AD 81, DOMITIAN, the third of the Flavian dynasty of emperors, decided to build a splendid new palace on the Palatine Hill. But the western peak, the Germalus, was covered with houses and temples, while the eastern peak, the Palatium, was very steep. So the emperor's architect, Rabirius, flattened the Palatium and used the soil to fill in the cleft between the two peaks, burying (and thus preserving) a number of Republican-era houses.

The palace had two wings – one official (the Domus Flavia), the other private (the Domus Augustana). It was the main imperial palace for 300 years. At the front of the Domus Flavia, the surviving stubs of columns and fragments of walls trace the shapes of three adjoining rooms. In the first of these, the Basilica, Domitian dispensed his personal brand of justice.

The central Aula Regia was a throne room decorated with 12 black basalt statues. The third room (now covered with corrugated plastic) was the Lararium, a shrine for the household gods known as Lares (usually the owner's ancestors). It may have been used for official ceremonies or by the palace guards.

Fearing assassination, Domitian had the walls of the courtyard covered with shiny marble slabs designed to act as mirrors so that he could see anyone lurking behind him. Ironically, he was assassinated in his bedroom, possibly on the orders of his wife, Domitia. The courtyard is now a pleasant place to pause; the flower beds in the center follow the maze pattern of a sunken fountain pool.

Cryptoporticus ❷

See Visitors' Checklist.

THE CRYPTOPORTICUS, a series of underground corridors, was built by Nero to connect his Domus Aurea *(see p175)* with the palaces of earlier emperors on the Palatine. A branch leading to the Palace of Domitian was added later. Its vaults are decorated with delicate stucco reliefs – copies of originals, now kept in the Palatine's museum.

Domus Augustana ❸

See Visitors' Checklist.

THIS PART of Domitian's palace was called the Domus Augustana because it was the private residence of the "august" emperors. On the upper level, a high brick wall remains, and visitors can make out the shape of its two courtyards. The far better-preserved lower level is closed to the public, though visitors can look down on its sunken courtyard with the geometric foundations of a fountain in its center. Sadly, not visible are the stairs linking the two levels (once lit by sunlight falling on a mirror-paved pool), or the surrounding rooms, paved with colored marble.

Stadium ❹

See Visitors' Checklist.

Stadium viewed from the south

THE STADIUM on the Palatine was laid out at the same time as the Palace of Domitian. It is not clear whether it was a public stadium, a private track for exercising horses or simply a large garden. The alcove in the eastern wall looks as though it may have held a box from which the emperor could have watched races. It is known, however, that the stadium was used for foot races by the Ostrogothic king Theodoric in the 6th century – he added the small oval-shaped enclosure at the southern end of the site.

Remains of the Domus Augustana and the Palace of Septimius Severus

House of Livia ❺

See Visitors' Checklist. If closed, see the custodian.

Fresco in the House of Livia

Tʜɪs ʜᴏᴜsᴇ dating from the 1st century BC is one of the best preserved on the Palatine. It was probably part of the house in which the Emperor Augustus and his second wife, Livia, lived. Compared with later Imperial palaces, it is a modest home. According to Suetonius, the biographer of Rome's early emperors, Augustus slept in the same small bedroom for 40 years on a low bed that had "a very ordinary coverlet." He wore home-made clothes

Detail of floor mosaic

(woven by Livia; his sister, Octavia; and daughter, Julia), but he was vain enough to wear shoes with extremely thick soles to conceal the fact that he was rather short.

The ground level of the Palatine is now above the house, so visitors walk down steps and along a mosaic-paved corridor into a courtyard. Its imitation-marble wall frescoes have been detached in order to preserve them, but they still hang in situ. Though they are very faded, the veining patterns are still visible. Leading off the courtyard are three small reception rooms. The frescoes in the central one include a faded scene of Hermes coming to the rescue of Zeus's beloved Io, who is guarded by the 100-eyed Argos. In the left-hand room are faint frescoes of griffins and other beasts, while the decor in the right-hand room includes colorful landscapes and cityscapes.

Temple of Cybele ❻

See Visitors' Checklist.

Oᴛʜᴇʀ ᴛʜᴀɴ a platform with a few column stumps and capitals, there is little to see of the Temple of Cybele, a popular Roman fertility goddess of Asian origin. The priests of the cult castrated themselves in the belief that the sacrifice of their own fertility would guarantee that of the natural world. The annual festival of Cybele, in early spring, culminated with frenzied eunuch-priests slashing their bodies to offer blood to the goddess, and the ceremonial castration of novice priests.

Statue of the goddess Cybele

Huts of Romulus ❼

See Visitors' Checklist.

Aᴄᴄᴏʀᴅɪɴɢ ᴛᴏ ʟᴇɢᴇɴᴅ, after killing his brother, Remus, Romulus founded a village on the Palatine. In the 1940s a series of holes was found filled with earth lighter in color than the surrounding soil. Archaeologists deduced that these holes must originally have held the supporting poles of three Iron Age huts – the first foundations of Rome (*see pp16–17*).

Farnese Gardens ❽

See Visitors' Checklist.

Iɴ ᴛʜᴇ ᴍɪᴅ-16ᴛʜ century Cardinal Alessandro Farnese, grandson of Pope Paul III, bought the ruins of Tiberius's palace on the Palatine. He filled in the ruined building and had Vignola, architect of the interior of the Gesù church, design a garden. The result was one of the first botanical gardens in Europe, its terraces linked by steps stretching from the House of the Vestal Virgins in the Forum to the Palatine's Germalus peak. The gardeners introduced a number of plants to Italy and Europe, among them *Acacia farnesiana*. Farnese was at the center of a flamboyant set that included a number of courtesans, so the parties here were likely to have been somewhat unholy.

The area was dug up during the excavation of the Palatine and relandscaped afterward. Nevertheless, the tree-lined avenues, rose gardens and glorious views still make it an ideal place to unwind.

Farnese pavilions, relics of the age when the Palatine was a private garden

PIAZZA DELLA ROTONDA

T HE PANTHEON, one of the great buildings in the history of European architecture, has stood at the heart of Rome for nearly 2,000 years. The historic area around it has seen uninterrupted economic and political activity throughout that time. Palazzo di Montecitorio, built for Pope Innocent XII as a papal tribunal in 1694,

Bitter-style apéritif, popular in Roman cafés

is now the Italian parliament and many nearby buildings are government offices. This is also the main financial district of Rome with banking headquarters and the stock exchange. Not many people live here, but in the evenings, Romans stroll in the narrow streets and fill the lively restaurants and cafés that make this a focus for the city's social life.

SIGHTS AT A GLANCE

Churches and Temples
Temple of Hadrian **1**
Sant'Ignazio di Loyola **3**
Gesù pp114–15 **9**
Santa Maria sopra Minerva **11**
Pantheon pp110–11 **13**
Sant'Eustachio **14**
La Maddalena **15**
Santa Maria in
Campo Marzio **18**
San Lorenzo in Lucina **20**

Historic Streets and Piazzas
Piazza di Sant'Ignazio **2**
Via della Gatta **7**

Historic Buildings
Palazzo del Collegio
Romano **4**
Palazzo Doria Pamphilj **6**
Palazzo Altieri **8**
Palazzo Baldassini **17**
Palazzo Borghese **19**
Palazzo di Montecitorio **21**
Palazzo Capranica **24**

Columns, Obelisks
and Statues
Pie' di Marmo **10**
Obelisk of Santa Maria
sopra Minerva **12**
Obelisk of Montecitorio **22**
Column of Marcus Aurelius **23**

Fountains
Fontanella del Facchino **5**

Cafés and Restaurants
Caffè Giolitti **16**

KEY

▢	Street-by-Street map
P	Parking

GETTING THERE
The area has no Metro station, but is about 20 minutes' walk from Spagna or Barberini Metro stops. Buses that stop in Via del Plebiscito include the 46, 64, 70, 186, 492 and 810. Piazza Colonna is served by the 117, 119, 492 and all buses that go up Via del Corso or Piazza S. Silvestro. The only bus that passes through the narrow streets of the area is the 116 electric minibus, which stops right outside the Pantheon.

0 meters 200
0 yards 200

SEE ALSO

- **Street Finder**, maps 4, 5, 12
- **Where to Stay** pp294–5
- **Restaurants** pp310–11

Piazza della Rotonda seen through the granite columns of the Pantheon

Street-by-Street: Piazza della Rotonda

IF YOU WANDER THROUGH this area, sooner or later you will emerge into Piazza della Rotonda, with its jumble of open-air café tables in front of the Pantheon. The refreshing splash of the fountain makes it a welcome resting place. In this warren of narrow streets, it can be hard to imagine just how close you are to some of Rome's finest sights. The magnificent art collection of Palazzo Doria Pamphilj and the Baroque splendor of the Gesù are just a few minutes' walk from the Pantheon. At night there is always a lively buzz of activity as people dine in style or enjoy the coffee and ice creams for which the area is famous.

Temple of Hadrian
The columns of this Roman temple now form the façade of the stock exchange ❶

Piazza di Sant'Ignazio
The square is a rare example of stylish domestic architecture from the early 18th century ❷

La Tazza d'Oro enjoys a reputation for the wonderful coffee consumed on its premises as well as for its freshly ground coffee to take away. *(See p319.)*

Santa Maria sopra Minerva
The rich decoration of Rome's only Gothic church was added in the 19th century ⓫

★ Pantheon
The awe-inspiring interior of Rome's best-preserved ancient temple is only hinted at from the outside ⓭

Obelisk of Santa Maria sopra Minerva
In 1667, Bernini dreamed up the idea of mounting a recently discovered obelisk on the back of a marble elephant ⓬

LOCATOR MAP
See Central Rome Map pp12–13

★ Sant'Ignazio di Loyola
Andrea Pozzo painted this glorious Baroque ceiling (1685) to celebrate St. Ignatius and the Jesuit order ③

Palazzo del Collegio Romano
Up until 1870, the college educated many leading figures in the Catholic Church ④

Fontanella del Facchino
The water in this small 16th-century fountain spurts from a barrel held by a porter ⑤

★ Palazzo Doria Pamphilj
Among the masterpieces in the art gallery of this magnificent family palazzo is this portrait of Pope Innocent X by Velázquez (1650) ⑥

Via della Gatta
The street is named after the statue of a cat ⑦

Palazzo Altieri
This enormous 17th-century palazzo is decorated with the arms of Pope Clement X ⑧

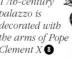

★ Gesù
The design of the first-ever Jesuit church had a great impact on religious architecture ⑨

KEY

- - - Suggested route

| 0 meters | 75 |
| 0 yards | 75 |

Pie' di Marmo
This marble foot is a stray fragment from a gigantic Roman statue ⑩

STAR SIGHTS

★ Pantheon

★ Palazzo Doria Pamphilj

★ Gesù

★ Sant'Ignazio di Loyola

Temple of Hadrian ❶

La Borsa, Piazza di Pietra. **Map** 4 F3 &
12 E2. 🚌 *117, 119, 492 and routes
along Via del Corso or stopping at
Piazza S. Silvestro.* **Closed** *to public.*

THIS TEMPLE honors the
emperor Hadrian as a god,
was dedicated by his son and
successor Antoninus Pius in
AD 145. The remains of
the temple are visible on the
southern side of Piazza di
Pietra, incorporated in a 17th-
century building. This was
originally a papal customs
house, completed by Carlo
Fontana and his son in the
1690s. Today the building
houses the Roman Stock
exchange (La Borsa).

Eleven marble Corinthian
columns 49 ft (15 m) high
stand on a base of *peperino*, a
volcanic rock quarried from
the Alban Hills to the south of
Rome. The columns decorated
the northern flank of the
temple, enclosing its inner
shrine, the *cella*. The *peperino*
wall of the *cella* is still visible
behind the columns, as is part
of the coffered portico ceiling.

A number of reliefs from
the temple representing
conquered Roman provinces
are now in the courtyard of
the Palazzo dei Conservatori
(see pp72–3). They reflect the
mostly peaceful foreign policy
of Hadrian's reign.

Remains of Hadrian's Temple

Piazza di Sant'Ignazio ❷

Map 4 F4 & 12 E3. 🚌 *117, 119, 492
and routes along Via del Corso or
stopping at Piazza S. Silvestro.*

ONE OF THE MAJOR works of
the Roman Rococo, the
piazza (1727–8) is Filippo
Raguzzini's masterpiece. It
offsets the imposing façade of
the church of Sant'Ignazio

Illusionistic ceiling in the crossing of Sant'Ignazio

with the intimacy of the
houses of the bourgeoisie. The
theatrical setting, the curvilinear
design and the playful forms
of its windows, balconies and
balusters mark the piazza as
one of a highly distinct group
of structures. Along with
Palazzo Doria Pamphilj (1731),
the façade of La Maddalena
(1735) and the aristocratic
Spanish Steps (1723), it belongs
to the moment when Rome's
bubbly Rococo triumphed
over conservative Classicism.

Sant'Ignazio di Loyola ❸

Piazza di Sant'Ignazio. **Map** 4 F4 &
12 E3. 🖂 *06-679 44 06.* 🚌 *117, 119,
492 and routes along Via del Corso or
stopping at Piazza S. Silvestro.* **Open**
7:30am–12:30pm, 3–7:15pm daily. 🚹

THE CHURCH was built by
Pope Gregory XV in 1626
in honor of St. Ignatius of
Loyola, founder of the Society
of Jesus and the man who
most embodied the zeal of
the Counter-Reformation.

Together with the Gesù *(see
pp114–15)*, Sant'Ignazio forms
the center of the Jesuit area in
Rome. Its vast interior, lined
with precious stones, marble,
stucco and gilt, creates a
sense of theater. The church
has a Latin-cross plan, with an
apse and many side chapels.

A cupola was planned but
never built, so the space it
would have filled was covered
by a fake perspective painting.
The piers built to uphold the
cupola support the observatory
of the Collegio Romano.

Palazzo del Collegio Romano ❹

Piazza del Collegio Romano. **Map** 5 A4
& 12 E3. 🚌 *117, 119, 492 and routes
along Via del Corso or stopping at Piazza
Venezia.* **Not open** *to the public.*

ON THE SAME BLOCK as the
church of Sant'Ignazio is
the palazzo used by Jesuits as
a college where many future
bishops, cardinals and popes
studied. The college was con-
fiscated in 1870 and turned
into an ordinary school. The
portals bear the coat of arms
of its founder, Pope Gregory
XIII Boncompagni (reigned
from 1572–85). The façade is
also adorned with a bell, two
sundials and a clock. On the
right is a tower
built in 1787 as
a meteorological
observatory. Until
1925 its time
signal regulated
all the clocks in
the city.

**Portal of the
Collegio Romano**

Fontanella del Facchino ❺

Via Lata. **Map** 5 A4 & 12 E3.
🚌 *64, 81, 85, 117, 119, 492 and many other routes.*

IL FACCHINO (the Porter), once in the Corso, now set into the wall of the Banco di Roma, was one of Rome's "talking statues" like Pasquino *(see p124).* Created around 1590, the fountain may have been based on a drawing by painter Jacopino del Conte. The statue of a man holding a barrel probably represents a member of the Università degli Acquaroli (Fraternity of Water Carriers), though it is also said to be of Martin Luther, or of the porter Abbondio Rizzio, who died carrying a barrel.

The Facchino drinking fountain

Palazzo Doria Pamphilj ❻

Piazza del Collegio Romano 2. **Map** 5 A4 & 12 E3. ☎ 06-679 73 23.
🚌 *64, 81, 85, 117, 119, 492 and many other routes.* **Open** 10am–5pm Fri–Wed. **Closed** Jan 1, May 1, Dec 25. **Adm charge.** ♿ 📷 compulsory for private apartments. 🎵 **Concerts** 🌐 www.doriapamphilj.it

PALAZZO DORIA PAMPHILJ is a great island of stone in the heart of Rome, the oldest parts dating from 1435. Through the Corso entrance you can see the 16th-century porticoed courtyard with the coat of arms of the della Rovere family. The Aldobrandini were the next owners. Between 1601 and 1647 the mansion acquired a second courtyard and flanking wings at the expense of a public bath that stood nearby.

When the Pamphilj family took over, they completed the Piazza del Collegio Romano façade and the Via della Gatta wing, a splendid chapel and a theater inaugurated by Queen Christina of Sweden in 1684.

In the first half of the 18th century, Gabriele Valvassori created the gallery above the courtyard and a new façade along the Corso, using the highly decorative style of the period known as the *barocchetto,* which now dominates the building. The stairways and salons, the Mirror Gallery and the picture gallery all radiate a joyous sense of light and space.

The family collection in the Doria Pamphilj gallery has over 400 paintings dating from the 15th to the 18th century, including the famous portrait of Pope Innocent X Pamphilj by Velázquez. There are also important works by Titian, Caravaggio, Lorenzo Lotto, Guercino and Claude Lorrain. The rooms in the private apartment have many of their original furnishings on display including splendid Brussels and Gobelins tapestries.

Via della Gatta ❼

Map 5 A4 & 12 E3. 🚌 *62, 63, 64, 70, 81, 87, 186, 492 & routes along Via del Plebiscito & Corso Vittorio Emanuele II.*

THIS NARROW STREET runs between the Palazzo Doria Pamphilj and the smaller Palazzo Grazioli. The ancient marble sculpture of a cat *(gatta)* that gives the street its name is on the first cornice on the corner of Palazzo Grazioli.

Via della Gatta's marble cat

Palazzo Altieri ❽

Via del Gesù 93. **Map** 4 F4 & 12 E3. 🚌 *46, 62, 63, 64, 70, 81, 87, 186, 492 and routes along Via del Plebiscito and Corso Vittorio Emanuele II.* 🚎 *8.*

THE ALTIERI FAMILY is first mentioned in Rome's history in the 9th century. This palazzo was built by the last male heirs, the brothers Cardinal Giambattista di Lorenzo Altieri and Cardinal Emilio Altieri, later Pope Clement X (reigned 1670–76). Many surrounding houses had to be demolished, but an old woman called Berta refused to leave, so her hovel was incorporated into the building. Its windows are still visible on the west end of the palazzo. Part of the palazzo is occupied by Mirabilia, a ticket agency *(see p340).*

Gesù ❾

See pp114–15.

Caravaggio's *Rest during the Flight into Egypt* in Palazzo Doria Pamphilj

Marble foot from a Roman statue

Pie' di Marmo ⑩

Via di Santo Stefano del Cacco. **Map**
4 F4 & 12 E3. 🚌 *62, 63, 64, 70, 81,
87, 116, 186, 492 and other routes
along Via del Corso, Via del Plebiscito,
and Corso Vittorio Emanuele II.*

I︎T WAS POPULARLY believed in
the Middle Ages that half
the population of ancient Rome
was made up of bronze, gold
and marble statues. Fragments
of these giants, usually gods
or emperors, are scattered over
the city. This piece, a marble
foot (*Pie' di marmo*), comes
from an area dedicated to the
Egyptian gods Isis and Serapis
and was probably part of a
temple statue. Statues were
painted and covered with
jewels and clothes given by the
faithful – a great fire risk with
unattended burning tapers.

Santa Maria sopra Minerva ⑪

Piazza della Minerva 42. **Map** 4 F4 &
12 E3. 📞 *06-679 39 26.* 🚌 *116 and
along Via del Corso, Via del Plebiscito,
and Corso Vittorio Emanuele II.* **Open**
*7am–7pm daily (occasionally closed
Sun pm).* **Cloister open** *9am–12:30pm,
4–6:30pm Mon–Sat.* 🚻 🎵 **Concerts**.

F︎EW OTHER CHURCHES display
such a complete and im-
pressive record of Italian art.
Dating from the 13th century,
the Minerva is one of the few
examples of Gothic architecture in Rome. It was the
traditional stronghold of the
Dominicans, whose anti-
heretical zeal earned them the
nickname of *Domini Canes*
(the hounds of the Lord).

Built on ancient ruins,
supposed to have been the
Temple of Minerva, the
simple T-shaped vaulted
building acquired rich chapels
and works of art by which its

many patrons wished to be
remembered. Note the
Cosmatesque 13th-century
tombs and the exquisite
works of 15th-century Tuscan
and Venetian artists. Native
Roman talent of the period
can be admired in Antoniazzo
Romano's *Annunciation*,
featuring Cardinal Juan de
Torquemada, uncle of the
infamous Spanish Inquisitor.

The more monumental style
of the Roman Renaissance is
well represented in the tombs
of the 16th-century Medici
popes, Leo X and his cousin
Clement VII, and in the richly
decorated Aldobrandini
Chapel. Near the steps of
the choir is the celebrated
sculpture called *Risen Christ*,
started by Michelangelo but
completed by Raffaele da
Montelupo in 1521.

There are also splendid
works of art from the
Baroque period, including a
tomb and a bust by Bernini.
The church is visited not
only for its art, but also
because it contains the
tombs of many famous
Italians: St. Catherine
of Siena, who died here
in 1380; the Venetian
sculptor Andrea
Bregno (died 1506);
the Humanist Cardinal
Pietro Bembo (died
1547); and Fra Angelico,
the Dominican friar and
painter, who died in
Rome in 1455.

Obelisk of Santa Maria sopra Minerva ⑫

Piazza della Minerva. **Map** 4 F4 & 12
D3. 🚌 *116 and routes along Via del
Corso and Corso Vittorio Emanuele II.*

O︎RIGINALLY MEANT to decorate
Palazzo Barberini as a
joke, this exotic elephant and
obelisk sculpture is typical of
Bernini's inexhaustible
imagination. (The elephant was
actually sculpted by Ercole
Ferrata to Bernini's design.)
When the ancient obelisk
was found in the garden of
the monastery of Santa
Maria sopra Minerva, the
friars wanted the monument
erected in their piazza. The
elephant was provided with
its enormous saddlecloth
because of a friar's insis-
tence that the gap under
the animal's abdomen
would undermine its
stability. Bernini knew
better: you need only
look at the Fontana
dei Quattro Fiumi
(see p120) in Piazza
Navona to appreciate
his use of empty
space. The elephant,
an ancient symbol
of intelligence and
piety, was chosen as
the embodiment of
the virtues on which
Christians should
build true wisdom.

Bernini's Egyptian obelisk and marble elephant

Nave of Santa Maria sopra Minerva

Pantheon ⓭

See pp110–11.

Sant'Eustachio ⓮

Piazza Sant'Eustachio. **Map** 4 F4 & 12 D3. 🔴 *06-686 53 34.* 🚌 *116 and along Corso Vittorio Emanuele II.* **Open** *9am–noon, 3:30–7:30pm daily.* 🔲

T HE ORIGINS of this church go back to early Christian times, when it offered relief to the poor. In medieval times many charitable brotherhoods elected Sant'Eustachio as their patron and had chapels here.

The Romanesque bell tower is one of the few surviving remnants of the medieval church, which was totally redecorated in the 17th and 18th centuries.

Nearby is the excellent Caffè Sant'Eustachio *(see p319).*

Bell tower of Sant'Eustachio

La Maddalena ⓯

Piazza della Maddalena. **Map** 4 F3 & 12 D2. 🔴 *06-679 77 96.* 🚌 *116 and many routes along Via del Corso and Corso Vittorio Emanuele II.* **Open** *8am–noon, 5pm–7:30pm daily.* 🔲

S ITUATED IN a small piazza near the Pantheon, the Maddalena's Rococo façade built in 1735, epitomizes the love of light and movement of the late Baroque. Its curves are reminiscent of Borromini's San Carlo alle Quattro Fontane *(see p161).* The façade has been lovingly restored, despite the protests of die-hard Neo-classicists who dismiss its painted stucco as sugar icing.

The small size of the Maddalena did not deter the

The old-fashioned *salone* of the Caffè Giolitti

17th- and 18th-century decorators, who filled the interior with ornament from the floor to the top of the elegant cupola. The organ loft and choir are particularly powerful examples of the Baroque desire to fire the imagination of the faithful.

Many of the paintings and sculptures employ the new Christian imagery of the Counter-Reformation. In the niches of the nave, for example, the statues are personifications of virtues such as Humility and Simplicity. There are also scenes from the life of San Camillo, who died in the adjacent convent in 1614. The church belonged to his followers, the Camillians, a preaching order active in Rome's hospitals. Like the Jesuits, they commissioned works of art to convey the force of their religious message.

La Maddalena's stuccoed façade

Caffè Giolitti ⓰

Via degli Uffici del Vicario 40. **Map** 4 F3 & 12 D2. 🔴 *06-699 12 43.* 🚌 *116 and many routes along Via del Corso and Corso Rinascimento.* **Open** *7am–1am daily.*

F OUNDED IN 1900, the Caffè Giolitti is the heir to the *Belle Époque* cafés that lined the nearby Corso in Rome's first days as capital of the new Italian state. Its *salone* holds tourists in summer and Roman families on weekends and on weekdays is frequented by local workers from a wide range of industries. Its ice creams are especially good.

Palazzo Baldassini ⓱

Via delle Coppelle 35. **Map** 4 F3 & 12 D2. 🚌 *116 and many routes along Via del Corso and Corso Rinascimento.* **Not open** to the public.

M ELCHIORRE BALDASSINI commissioned Antonio da Sangallo the Younger to build his home in Florentine Renaissance style in 1514–20. With its cornices marking the different floors and wrought-iron window grilles, this is one of the best examples of an early 16th-century Roman palazzo. It stands in the part of Rome still known as the Renaissance Quarter, which flourished around the long straight streets such as Via di Ripetta and Via della Scrofa built at the time of Pope Leo X (reigned 1513–21).

Pantheon ⑬

IN THE MIDDLE AGES, the Pantheon, the
Roman temple of "all the gods,"
became a church; in time this magnificent
building with its awe-inspiring domed
interior became a symbol of Rome itself.
The rectangular portico screens the vast
hemispherical dome: only from inside
can its true scale and beauty be
appreciated. The rotunda's height and
diameter are equal: 140 ft (43.3 m).
The opening at the top of the dome, the
oculus, provides the only light. We owe
this marvel of Roman engineering to the
emperor Hadrian (AD 118–125), who
designed it to replace an earlier temple
built by Marcus Agrippa,
son-in-law of Augustus.
The shrines that
now line the wall
of the Pantheon
range from the
Tomb of Raphael to
those of the kings
of modern Italy.

★ Interior of the Dome
*The dome was cast by pouring concrete
mixed with tufa and pumice over a
temporary wooden framework.*

The walls of the drum
supporting the dome
are 19 ft (6 m) thick.

The immense portico is
built on the foundations of
Agrippa's temple.

The portico, enclosed by granite columns

STAR FEATURES

★ **Interior of Dome**

★ **Tomb of Raphael**

Bell Towers
*This 18th-century view
by Bernardo Bellotto
shows Bernini's much-
ridiculed turrets, which
were removed in 1883.*

Floor Patterning
*The marble floor, restored
in 1873, preserves the
original Roman design.*

RAPHAEL AND LA FORNARINA

Raphael, at his own request, was buried here when he died in 1520. He had lived for years with his model, La Fornarina *(see p210)*, seen here in a painting by Giulio Romano, but she was excluded from the ceremony of his burial. To the right of his tomb is a memorial to his fiancée, Maria Bibbiena, niece of the artist's patron, Cardinal Dovizi di Bibbiena.

VISITORS' CHECKLIST

Piazza della Rotonda. **Map** 4 F4 & 12 D3. ☎ 06-68 30 02 30. 🚌 116 and many routes along Via del Corso, Corso del Rinascimento and Corso Vittorio Emanuele II. **Open** 8:30am–7:30pm Mon–Sat, 9am–6pm Sun. **Closed** Jan 1, May 1 & Dec 25. 🚻 ♿ 📷

Relieving Arches
Brick arches embedded in the structure of the wall act as internal buttresses, distributing the weight of the dome.

Oculus

Coffering
Constructing the dome from hollow decorative coffers reduced its weight.

★ **Tomb of Raphael**
The artist's body rests below a Madonna by Lorenzetto (1520).

TIMELINE

27–25 BC Marcus Agrippa builds first Pantheon	*MAGRIPPA* *Inscription on pediment*	**735** Gregory III roofs the Pantheon in lead	**1305–77** While papal seat is in Avignon, Pantheon is used as fortress and poultry market	**1888** Tomb of King Vittorio Emanuele II completed
30 BC	**AD 100**	**600**	**1100**	**1600**
AD 118 Hadrian builds new Pantheon	**609** Pope Boniface IV consecrates Pantheon as church of Santa Maria ad Martyres	**663** Byzantine Emperor Constans II strips gilded tiles from the roof	**1632** Urban VIII melts down bronze from portico for Bernini's baldacchino in St. Peter's	

Bernini's curving southern façade of Palazzo di Montecitorio

Santa Maria in Campo Marzio ⓲

Piazza in Campo Marzio 45. **Map** 4 F3 & 12 D2. 116 and many routes on Via del Corso and Corso Rinascimento. **Closed for renovation.**

A ROUND the courtyard through which you enter the church, there are fascinating remnants of medieval houses, once the property of the original monastery. The church itself was rebuilt in 1685 by Antonio de Rossi, using a square Greek-cross plan with a cupola. Above the altar is a 12th-century painting of the Madonna, which gives the church its name.

Palazzo Borghese ⓳

Largo della Fontanella di Borghese. **Map** 4 F3 & 12 D1. 81, 117, 492, 628. **Closed** to the public.

T HE PALAZZO was acquired in about 1605 by Cardinal Camillo Borghese, just before he became Pope Paul V. Flaminio Ponzio was hired to enlarge the building and give it the grandeur appropriate to the residence of the pope's family. He added a wing overlooking Piazza Borghese and the delightful porticoed courtyard inside. Subsequent enlargements included the building and decoration of a great *nymphaeum* known as the Bath of Venus. For more than two centuries this palazzo housed the Borghese family's renowned collection of paintings, which was bought

by the Italian state in 1902 and transferred to the Galleria Borghese *(see pp260–61)*.

Pope Paul V, who commissioned Palazzo Borghese for his family

San Lorenzo in Lucina ⓴

Via in Lucina 16A. **Map** 4 F3 & 12 E1. 06-687 14 94. 81, 117, 492, 628. **Open** 9am–2pm, 3–7:30pm daily.

T HE CHURCH IS one of Rome's oldest Christian places of worship, and was probably built on a well sacred to Juno, protectress of women. It was rebuilt in the 12th century, and today's external appearance is quite typical of the period featuring a portico with re-used Roman columns crowned by medieval capitals, a plain triangular pediment and a Romanesque bell tower with colored marble inlay.

The interior was totally rebuilt in 1856–8. The old basilical plan was destroyed and the two side naves were replaced

by Baroque chapels. Do not miss the fine busts in the Fonseca Chapel, designed by Bernini, or the *Crucifixion* by Guido Reni above the main altar. There is also a 19th-century monument honoring French painter Nicolas Poussin, who died in Rome in 1655 and was buried in the church.

Palazzo di Montecitorio ㉑

Piazza di Montecitorio. **Map** 4 F3 & 12 E2. 116 and all routes along Via del Corso or stopping at Piazza S. Silvestro. **Open** 10am–5:30pm 1st Sun each month; no bookings. 06-676 01. www.camera.it

T HE PALAZZO's first architect, Bernini, got the job after he presented a silver model of his design to the wife of his patron, Prince Ludovisi. The building was completed in 1694 by Carlo Fontana and became the Papal Tribunal of Justice. In 1871 it was chosen to be Italy's new Chamber of Deputies and by 1927 it had doubled in size with a second grand façade. The 630 members of parliament are elected by a majority system with proportional representation.

The church of San Lorenzo in Lucina

Emperor Augustus's obelisk

Obelisk of Montecitorio ㉒

Piazza di Montecitorio. **Map** 4 F3 & 12 E2. 116 and routes along Via del Corso or to Piazza S. Silvestro.

THE MEASUREMENT of time in ancient Rome was always a rather hit-and-miss affair: for many years the Romans relied on an imported (and therefore inaccurate) sundial, a trophy from the conquest of Sicily. In 10 BC the Emperor Augustus laid out an enormous sundial in the Campus Martius. Its center was roughly in today's Piazza di San Lorenzo in Lucina. The shadow was cast by a huge granite obelisk that he had brought back from Heliopolis in Egypt. Unfortunately this sundial too became inaccurate after only 50 years, possibly due to subsidence.

The obelisk was still in the piazza in the 9th century, but then disappeared until it was rediscovered in the reign of Pope Julius II (1503–13). The pope was intrigued, because Egyptian hieroglyphs, which were thought to hold the key to the wisdom of Adam before the Fall, but it was only under Pope Benedict XIV (reigned 1740–58) that the obelisk was finally unearthed. It was erected in its present location in 1792 by Pope Pius VI.

Column of Marcus Aurelius ㉓

Piazza Colonna. **Map** 5 A3 & 12 E2. 116 and routes along Via del Corso or to Piazza S. Silvestro.

CLEARLY AN IMITATION of the Column of Trajan (see p90), this monument was erected after the death of Marcus Aurelius in AD 180 to commemorate his victories over the barbarian tribes of the Danube. The 80-year lapse between the two works produced a great artistic change: the wars of Marcus Aurelius are rendered in simplified pictures in stronger relief, sacrificing Classical proportions for the sake of clarity and immediacy. The spirit of the work is more akin to the 4th-century Arch of Constantine (see p91) than to Trajan's monument. Gone are the heroic qualities of the Roman soldiers, by now mostly barbarian mercenaries, and a sense of respect for the vanquished. A new emphasis on the supernatural points to the end of the Hellenistic tradition and the beginning of Christianity.

Composed of 28 drums of marble, the column was restored in 1588 by Domenico Fontana on the orders of Pope Sixtus V. The emperor's statue on the summit was replaced by a bronze of St. Paul. The 20 spirals of the low relief chronicle the German war of AD 172–3 and (above) show Sarmatic war of AD 174–5. The column is almost 100 ft (30 m) high and 12 ft (3.7 m) in diameter. An internal spiral staircase leads to the top. The easiest way to appreciate the sculptural work, however, is to visit the Museo della Civiltà Romana at EUR (see p266) and study the casts of the reliefs.

Palazzo Capranica ㉔

Piazza Capranica. **Map** 4 F3 & 12 D2. 116 and routes along Via del Corso or to Piazza S. Silvestro.

Windows of Palazzo Capranica

ONE OF ROME'S small number of surviving 15th-century buildings, the palazzo was commissioned by Cardinal Domenico Capranica both as his family residence and as a college for higher education. Its fortresslike appearance is a patchwork of subsequent additions, not unusual in the late 15th century when Rome was still hovering between medieval and Renaissance taste. The Gothic-looking windows on the right of the building show the cardinal's coat of arms, and the date 1451 is inscribed on the doorway underneath. The palazzo now houses a good restaurant.

Relief of the emperor's campaigns on the Column of Marcus Aurelius

Gesù ⑨

DATING FROM BETWEEN 1568 and 1584, the Gesù was the first Jesuit church to be built in Rome. Its design epitomizes Counter-Reformation Baroque architecture and has been much imitated throughout the Catholic world. The layout proclaims the church's two major functions: a large nave with side pulpits for preaching to great crowds, and a main altar as the centerpiece for the celebration of the mass. The illusionistic decoration in the nave and dome was added a century later. Its message is clear and confident: faithful Catholic worshipers will be joyfully uplifted into the heavens, while Protestants and heretics will be flung into hell's fires.

★ Chapel of Sant'Ignazio
Above its altar is a statue of the saint, framed by gilded lapis lazuli columns. The chapel was built in 1690 to 1700 by Andrea Pozzo, a Jesuit artist.

Triumph of Faith Over Idolatry
This vivid Baroque allegory sculpted by Théudon illustrates the great ambition of Jesuit theology.

ST. IGNATIUS AND THE JESUIT ORDER

The Spanish soldier Ignatius Loyola (1491–1556) joined the Church after being wounded in battle in 1521. He came to Rome in 1537 and founded the Jesuits, sending missionaries and teachers all over the world to win souls for Catholicism.

Main entrance

STAR FEATURES

- ★ Nave Ceiling Decorations

- ★ Chapel of Sant'Ignazio

- ★ Tomb of San Roberto Bellarmino

Allegorical Figures
Antonio Raggi made these stuccoes, which were designed by Il Baciccia to complement the figures on his own nave frescoes.

Madonna della Strada

This 15th-century image, the Madonna of the Road, was originally displayed on the façade of Santa Maria della Strada which once stood on this site.

Monument to San Roberto Bellarmino

Bernini captured the forceful personality of this anti-Protestant theologian, who died in 1621.

The Chapel of St. Francis Xavier

is a memorial to the great missionary who died alone on an island off China in 1552.

Cupola Frescoes

The cupola was completed by della Porta to Vignola's design. The frescoes, by Il Baciccia, feature Old Testament figures.

★ Nave Ceiling Decorations

The figures in Il Baciccia's astonishing fresco of the Triumph of the Name of Jesus *spill out onto the coffered vaulting of the nave.*

TIMELINE

	1540 Founding of the Society of Jesus (the Jesuits)	**1571** Giacomo della Porta's design chosen for the façade	**1696–1700** The Chapel of Sant' Ignazio is designed by Andrea Pozzo, a Jesuit artist	**1773** Pope Clement XIV orders the suppression of the Jesuit order
		1584 Church's consecration		
1500		**1600**		**1700**
1545–63 Council of Trent defines the new Catholic orthodoxy		**1568–71** Vignola builds the church up to the crossing under the patronage of Cardinal Alessandro Farnese	**1670–83** Giovanni Battista Gaulli (Il Baciccia) paints the nave vault, dome and apse	
1556 Ignatius Loyola dies			**1622** Ignatius Loyola is canonized	

PIAZZA NAVONA

THE FOUNDATIONS of the buildings surrounding the elongated oval of Piazza Navona were the ruined grandstands of the vast Stadium of Domitian. The piazza still provides a dramatic spectacle today with the obelisk of the Fontana dei Quattro Fiumi in front of the church of Sant' Agnese in Agone as its focal

Lion on Fontana dei Quattro Fiumi

point. The predominant style of the area is Baroque, many of its finest buildings dating from the reign of Innocent X Pamphilj (1644–55), patron of Bernini and Borromini. Of special interest is the complex of the Chiesa Nuova, headquarters of the Filippini, the order founded by San Filippo Neri, the 16th-century "Apostle of Rome".

SIGHTS AT A GLANCE

Churches and Temples
Sant'Agnese in Agone ④
Santa Maria dell'Anima ⑤
Santa Maria della Pace ⑥
San Luigi dei Francesi ⑦
Sant'Ivo alla Sapienza ⑨
Sant'Andrea della Valle ⑩
Chiesa Nuova ⑮
Oratorio dei Filippini ⑯
San Salvatore in Lauro ⑳

Museums
Palazzo Braschi ⑫
Museo Napoleonico ㉑

Historic Buildings
Palazzo Pamphilj ③
Palazzo Madama ⑧
Palazzo Massimo
alle Colonne ⑪
Torre dell'Orologio ⑰
Palazzo del Banco
di Santo Spirito ⑱
Palazzo Altemps ㉓

Fountains and Statues
Fontana dei Quattro Fiumi ①
Pasquino ⑬

Historic Streets and Piazzas
Piazza Navona ②
Via del Governo Vecchio ⑭
Via dei Coronari ⑲

Restaurants
Hostaria dell'Orso ㉒

SEE ALSO

- *Street Finder*, maps 4, 11, 12
- *Where to Stay* pp294–5
- *Restaurants* pp310–11

GETTING THERE
This central area is within walking distance of many parts of the city and it is easily reached by bus. The principal routes along Corso Vittorio Emanuele II are the 64 from Termini station to St. Peter's and the 46. Corso del Rinascimento, which runs parallel to Piazza Navona, is served by several useful routes, including the 70, 81, 116, 186 and 492.

KEY

	Street-by-Street map
P	Parking
i	Tourist information

0 meters   200
0 yards   200

Piazza Navona, with the Fontana del Moro and church of Sant'Agnese in Agone

Street-by-Street: Piazza Navona

No other piazza in Rome can rival the theatricality of Piazza Navona. Day and night there is always something going on in the pedestrian area around its three flamboyant fountains. The Baroque is also represented in many of the area's churches. To discover an older Rome, walk along Via del Governo Vecchio to admire the façades of its Renaissance buildings and browse in the fascinating antiques shops.

Oratorio dei Filippini
The musical term oratorio comes from this place of informal worship ⑯

Torre dell' Orologio
This clock tower by Borromini (1648) is part of the Convent of the Filippini ⑰

Chiesa Nuova
This church was rebuilt in the late 16th century for the order founded by San Filippo Neri ⑮

To Corso Vittorio Emanuele II

Via del Governo Vecchio
This street preserves a large number of fine Renaissance houses ⑭

Santa Maria della Pace
This medallion shows Pope Sixtus IV who reigned 1471–84 and under whose orders the church was built ⑥

Pasquino
Romans hung satirical verses and dialogues on this weather-beaten statue ⑬

Palazzo Pamphilj
This grand town house was built for Pope Innocent X and his family in the mid-17th century ❸

Palazzo Braschi
A late 18th-century building with a splendid balcony, the palazzo houses the Museo di Roma ⑫

Palazzo Massimo alle Colonne
The magnificent curving colonnade (1536) is by Baldassarre Peruzzi ⑪

STAR SIGHTS

★ Sant'Andrea della Valle

★ San Luigi dei Francesi

★ Piazza Navona

KEY

– – – Suggested route

0 meters	75
0 yards	75

Sant'Agnese in Agone
Borromini's startling concave façade (1657) dominates one side of Piazza Navona ❹

Santa Maria dell'Anima
For four centuries this has been the German church in Rome ❺

Fontana dei Quattro Fiumi
This fountain supporting an Egyptian obelisk was designed by Bernini ❶

Palazzo Madama
A spread-eagled stone lionskin decorates the central doorway of the palazzo, now the Italian Senate ❽

LOCATOR MAP
See Central Rome Map pp12–13

★ San Luigi dei Francesi
An 18th-century statue of St. Louis stands in a niche in the façade ❼

★ Piazza Navona
This unique piazza owes its shape to a Roman racetrack and its stunning decor to the genius of the Roman Baroque ❷

The Fontana del Moro was remodeled in 1653 by Bernini, who designed the central sea god.

Sant'Ivo alla Sapienza
This tiny domed church is one of Borromini's most original creations. He worked on it between 1642 and 1650 ❾

★ Sant'Andrea della Valle
The church, with its grandiose façade by Carlo Rainaldi (1665), has gained fame outside Rome as the setting of the first act of Puccini's Tosca ❿

To Campo de' Fiori

Fontana dei Quattro Fiumi ❶

Piazza Navona. **Map** 4 E4 & 11 C3. 🚌 46, 62, 64, 70, 81, 87, 116, 492, 628.

Built for pope Innocent X Pamphilj, this magnificent fountain in the center of Piazza Navona was unveiled in 1651. The pope's coat of arms, the dove and the olive branch, decorate the pyramid rock formation supporting the Roman obelisk, which once stood in the Circus of Maxentius on the Appian Way. Bernini designed the fountain, which was paid for by means of taxes on bread and other staples. The great rivers – the Ganges, the Danube, the Nile and the Plate – are represented by four giants.

The Nile's veiled head symbolizes the river's unknown source, but there is also a legend that the veil conveys Bernini's dislike for the nearby Sant'Agnese in Agone, designed by his rival

Palazzo Pamphilj, the largest building in Piazza Navona

Borromini. Similarly, the athletic figure of the Plate, cringing with arm upraised, is supposed to express Bernini's fear that the church will collapse. Sadly, these widely believed stories have no basis in fact: Bernini had completed the fountain before Borromini started work on the church.

Piazza Navona ❷

Map 4 E3 & 11 C2. 🚌 46, 62, 64, 70, 81, 87, 116, 492, 628.

Rome's most beautiful Baroque piazza follows the shape of Domitian's Stadium which once stood on this site – some of its arches are still visible below the church of Sant'Agnese in Agone. The *agones* were athletic contests held in the 1st-century stadium, which could seat 33,000 people. The word *Navona* is thought to be a corruption of *in agone*. The piazza's unique appearance

and atmosphere were created in the 17th century with the addition of the Fontana dei Quattro Fiumi. The other fountains date from the previous century but have been altered several times since. The basin of the Fontana di Nettuno, at the northern end, was built by Giacomo della Porta in 1576, while the statues of Neptune and the Nereids date from the 19th century. The Fontana del Moro, at the southern end, was also designed by della Porta, though Bernini altered it later, adding a statue of a Moor fighting a dolphin.

Up until the 19th century, Piazza Navona was flooded during August by stopping the fountain outlets. The rich would splash around in carriages, while street urchins paddled after them. Today, with its numerous shops and cafés, the piazza is a favorite in all seasons. In summer it is busy with street entertainers, while in winter it fills with colorful stands selling toys and candy for the feast of the Befana.

Palazzo Pamphilj ❸

Piazza Navona. **Map** 4 E4 & 11 C3. 🚌 46, 62, 64, 70, 81, 87, 116, 492, 628. **Not open** to the public.

Family dove and olive branch on façade of Palazzo Pamphilj

In 1644 Giovanni Battista Pamphilj became Pope Innocent X. During his 10-year reign, he heaped riches on his own family, especially his domineering sister-in-law, Olimpia Maidalchini. The "talking statue" Pasquino (*see p124*) gave her the nickname "Olim-Pia," Latin for "formerly virtuous." She lived in the grand Palazzo Pamphilj, which has frescoes by Pietro da Cortona and a gallery by Borromini. The building is now the Brazilian embassy and cultural center.

Symbolic figure of the River Ganges in the Fontana dei Quattro Fiumi

Sant'Agnese in Agone ➍

Piazza Navona. **Map** 4 E4 & 11 C3.
☎ 06-329 2326. ▤ 46, 62, 64, 70, 81, 87, 116, 492, 628. **Open** 10am–noon, 4–7pm Tue–Sun. ⛪ ♿

THE CHURCH OF Sant'Agnese in Agone is believed to have been founded on the site of the brothel where, in AD 304, the young St. Agnes was exposed naked to force her to renounce her faith. A marble relief in the crypt shows the miraculous growth of her hair, which fell around her body to protect her modesty. She was martyred on this site and is buried in the catacombs that bear her name along the Via Nomentana *(see p264)*.

Today's church was commissioned by Pope Innocent X in 1652. The first architects were father and son, Girolamo and Carlo Rainaldi, but they were replaced by Borromini in 1653. He stuck more or less to the Rainaldi scheme except for the concave façade designed to emphasize the dome. A statue of St. Agnes on the façade is said to be reassuring the Fontana dei Quattro Fiumi's statue of the River Plate that the church is stable.

Statue of St. Agnes on façade of Sant' Agnese in Agone

Carlo Saraceni's *Miracle of St. Benno and the Keys of Meissen Cathedral*

Santa Maria dell'Anima ➎

Via della Pace 24. **Map** 4 E4 & 11 C2.
☎ 06-682 8181. ▤ 46, 62, 64, 70, 81, 87, 116, 492, 628.
Open 8am–1pm, 2pm–7.30pm daily. ⛪ ♿

POPE ADRIAN VI (reigned 1522–3), son of a ship-builder from Utrecht, was the last non-Italian pope before John Paul II. He would have disapproved of his superb tomb by Baldassarre Peruzzi in Santa Maria dell'Anima. It stands to the right of Giulio Romano's damaged altarpiece and is redolent of the pagan Renaissance spirit the pope had so condemned during his brief, rather gloomy reign, when patronage of the arts ground to a halt. Santa Maria dell'Anima is the German church in Rome and some of its paintings, such as the *Miracle of St. Benno* by Carlo Saraceni (1618), illustrate events connected with the history of Germany.

Santa Maria della Pace ➏

Vicolo dell'Arco della Pace 5. **Map** 4 E3 & 11 C2. ☎ 06-686 1156. ▤ 46, 62, 64, 70, 81, 87, 116, 492, 628. **Open** 10am–6pm daily (to 10pm Sat; to 1pm Sun). ⛪ ♿ 2 steps. Exhibitions, concerts.

A DRUNKEN SOLDIER allegedly pierced the breast of a painted Madonna on this site, causing it to bleed. Pope Sixtus IV della Rovere (reigned 1471–84) placated the Virgin by ordering Baccio Pontelli to build her a church if she would bring the war with Turkey to an end. Peace was restored and the church was named Santa Maria della Pace (St. Mary of Peace).

The cloister was added by Bramante in 1504. As in his famous Tempietto *(see p219)*, he scrupulously followed Classical rules of proportion and achieved a monumental effect in a relatively small space. Pietro da Cortona may have had Bramante's Tempietto in mind when he added the church's charming semicircular portico in 1656. The interior, a short nave ending under an octagonal cupola, houses Raphael's famous frescoes of four *Sybils*, and four *Prophets* by his pupil Timoteo Viti, painted for the banker Agostino Chigi in 1514. Baldassarre Peruzzi also did some work in the church (fresco in the first chapel on the left), as did the architect Antonio da Sangallo the Younger, who designed the second chapel on the right.

San Luigi dei Francesi ❼

Piazza di San Luigi dei Francesi 5.
Map 4 F4 & 12 D2. 📞 *06-688 27 1.*
🚌 *70, 81, 87, 116, 186, 492, 628.*
Open *8:30am–12:30pm, 3:30– 7pm daily.* **Closed** *Thu pm.* 🚪 📷

THE FRENCH national church was founded in 1518, but took until 1589 to complete, with contributions by Giacomo della Porta and Domenico Fontana. The church serves as a last resting place for many illustrious French people, including Chateaubriand's lover Pauline de Beaumont.

Three Caravaggios hang in the fifth chapel on the left, dedicated to St. Matthew. Painted between 1597 and 1602, these were Caravaggio's first great religious works: the *Calling of St. Matthew*, the *Martyrdom of St. Matthew* and *St. Matthew and the Angel*. The first version of this last painting was rejected because of its vivid realism – never before had a saint been shown as a tired old man with dirty feet. All three works display very disquieting realism and highly dramatic use of light.

Caravaggio, whose paintings of St. Matthew hang in San Luigi dei Francesi

Shield linking symbols of France and Rome on facade of San Luigi

Palazzo Madama ❽

Corso del Rinascimento. **Map** 4 F4 & 12 D3. 📞 *06-670 61.* 🚌 *70, 81, 87, 116, 186, 492, 628.*
Open *10am–6pm first Sat of month.*
🖥 *www.senato.it*

THIS 16TH-CENTURY palazzo was built for the Medici family, who had owned a bank here in the previous century. It was the residence of Medici cousins Giovanni and Giuliano, both of whom became popes: Giovanni as Leo X and Giuliano as Clement VII. Caterina de' Medici, Clement VII's niece, also lived here before she was married to Henry, son of King Francis I of France in 1533.

The palazzo takes its name from Madama Margherita of Austria, illegitimate daughter of Emperor Charles V, who married Alessandro de' Medici and, after his death, Ottavio Farnese. Thus part of the art collection of the Florentine Medici famile was inherited by the Roman Farnese family.

The spectacular façade, with its ornate cornice and whimsical roof details, was built in the 17th century by Paolo Maruccelli. Since 1871 the palazzo has been the seat of the Senate, the upper house of the Italian parliament.

Cornice of Palazzo Madama

Sant'Ivo alla Sapienza ❾

Corso del Rinascimento 40. **Map** 4 F4 & 12 D3. 📞 *06-686 49 87*
🚌 *40, 46, 64, 70, 81, 87, 116, 186, 492, 628.* **Open** *10am–4pm Mon–Fri, 10am–1pm Sat, 9am–noon Sun.* 🚪

THE CHURCH's lantern is crowned with a cross on top of a dramatic twisted spiral – a highly distinctive landmark from Rome's roof terraces. No other Baroque church is quite like this one, which is by Borromini. The church is based on a design of astonishing geometrical complexity, with walls that are a breathtaking combination of concave and convex surfaces. It stands in the small courtyard of the Palazzo della Sapienza, seat of the old University of Rome from the 15th century until 1935.

Lantern and spire of Sant'Ivo

Sant'Andrea della Valle ⑩

Piazza Sant'Andrea della Valle. **Map** 4 E4 & 12 D4. 📞 06-686 1339. 🚌 H, 40, 46, 62, 64, 70, 81, 87, 116, 186, 492, 628. 🚋 8. **Open** 7:30am– 12:30pm, 4:30pm–7:30pm daily. ✝

Dome of Sant'Andrea della Valle

THIS CHURCH is the scene of the first act of Puccini's opera *Tosca*, though opera fans will not find the Attavanti chapel, which is a poetic invention. The real church has much to recommend it – the recently restored façade shows the flamboyant Baroque style at its best. Inside, a golden light filters through the high windows, showing off the gilded interior. Here lie the two popes of the Sienese Piccolomini family: on the left of the central nave is the tomb of Pius II, the first Humanist pope (reigned 1458–64); Pope Pius III lies opposite – he reigned for less than a month in 1503.

The church is famous for its beautiful dome, the largest in Rome after St. Peter's. It was built by Carlo Maderno from 1622 to 1625 and was painted with splendid frescoes by Domenichino and Giovanni Lanfranco. The latter's extravagant style, seen in the dome fresco *Glory of Paradise*, won him most of the commission, and the jealous Domenichino is said to have tried to kill him. He failed, but Domenichino's jealousy was unnecessary, as shown by his two beautiful

paintings of scenes from the life of St. Andrew around the apse and altar. In the Strozzi Chapel, built in the style of Michelangelo, the altar has copies of the *Leah and Rachel* by Michelangelo in San Pietro in Vincoli *(see p170).*

Palazzo Massimo alle Colonne ⑪

Corso Vittorio Emanuele II 141. **Map** 4 F4 & 11 C3. 🚌 40, 46, 62, 64, 70, 81, 87, 116, 186, 492, 628. **Chapel open** 7am–noon 16 Mar.

Roman column, Palazzo Massimo

DURING THE LAST two years of his life, Baldassarre Peruzzi built this palazzo for the Massimo family, whose home had been destroyed in the sack of Rome in 1527. Peruzzi displayed great ingenuity in dealing with an awkwardly shaped site. The previous building had stood on the ruined Theater of Domitian, which created a curve in the great processional Via Papalis. Peruzzi's convex colonnaded façade follows the line of the street. His originality is also evident in the small square upper windows, the courtyard and the stuccoed vestibule. The entrance in Piazza de' Massimi has a Renaissance-style frescoed façade. A single column from the theater has been set up in the piazza.

The Massimo family, Quintus Fabius Maximus, traced its origins to the

conqueror of Hannibal in the 3rd century BC, and their proud coat of arms is borne by an infant Hercules. Over the years the family produced many great Humanists; in the 19th century a Massimo negotiated peace with Napoleon. On March 16 each year the family chapel opens to the public to celebrate Paolo Massimo's resurrection from the dead by San Filippo Neri in 1538.

Palazzo Braschi ⑫

Piazza San Pantaleo 10. **Map** 4 E4 & 11 C3. 📞 06-6710 8312. 🚌 40, 46, 62, 64, 70, 81, 87, 116, 186, 492, 628. **Open** 9am–7pm Tue–Sun.

ON ONE SIDE of Piazza San Pantaleo is the last Roman palazzo to be built for the family of a pope. Palazzo Braschi was built in the late 18th century for Pope Pius VI Braschi's nephews by the architect Cosimo Morelli. He gave the building its imposing façade, which looks out on to the piazza.

The palazzo now houses the municipal Museo di Roma. It holds collections of pictures, drawings and everyday objects illustrating life in the city from medieval times until the 19th century.

Angel with raised wing by Ercole Ferrata, flanking the façade of Sant'Andrea della Valle

Pasquino

Piazza di Pasquino. **Map** 4 E4 &
11 C3. 🚌 *40, 46, 62, 64, 70, 81, 87, 116, 492, 628.*

Pasquino, the most famous of Rome's satirical "talking statues"

THIS ROUGH CHUNK of marble is all that remains of a Hellenistic group, probably representing the incident in Homer's *Iliad* in which Menelaus shields the body of the slain Patroclus. For years it lay as a stepping stone in a muddy medieval street until it was erected on this corner in 1501, near the shop of an outspoken cobbler named Pasquino. Freedom of speech was not encouraged in papal Rome, so the cobbler wrote out his satirical comments on current events and attached them to the statue.

Other Romans were quick to follow suit, hanging their maxims and verses on the statue by night to escape punishment. Despite the wrath of the authorities, the sayings of the "talking statue" (renamed Pasquino) were part of popular culture right up until the 19th century. Other statues started to "talk" in the same satirical vein; Pasquino used to conduct dialogues with the statue Marforio in Via del Campidoglio (now in the courtyard of Palazzo Nuovo, *see pp70–71*) and with the Babuino in Via del Babuino *(see p135)*. One of Rome's few English-language cinemas is named after Pasquino *(see p347)*.

Via del Governo Vecchio

Map 4 E4 & 11 B3.
🚌 *40, 46, 62, 64.*

THE STREET TAKES its name from Palazzo del Governo Vecchio, the seat of papal government in the 17th and 18th centuries. Once part of the Via Papalis, which led from the Lateran to St. Peter's, the street is lined with 15th- and 16th-century houses and small workshops. Particularly interesting are those at Nos. 104 and 106. The small palazzo at No. 123 was once thought to have been the home of Bramante.

Opposite is Palazzo del Governo Vecchio. It is also known as Palazzo Nardini, after its founder, whose name is inscribed on the first-floor windows along with the date 1477.

Via del Governo Vecchio

Chiesa Nuova

Piazza della Chiesa Nuova.
Map 4 E4 & 11 B3. 📞 *06-687 52 89.*
🚌 *40, 46, 62, 64.* **Open** 8am–noon, 4.30–7pm daily. 🛉

Façade of the Chiesa Nuova

SAN FILIPPO NERI (St. Philip Neri) is the most appealing of the Counter-Reformation saints. A highly unconventional reformer, he required his noble Roman followers to humble themselves in public. He made aristocratic young men parade through the streets of Rome in rags or even with a fox's tail tied behind them and set noblemen to work as laborers building his church. With the help of Pope Gregory XIII, his church was built in place of an old medieval one, Santa Maria in Vallicella, and it has been known ever since as the Chiesa Nuova (new church).

Begun in 1575 by Matteo da Città di Castello and continued by Martino Longhi the Elder, it was consecrated in 1599, although the façade, by Fausto Rughesi, was finished only in 1606. Against San Filippo's wishes, the interior was decorated after his death; Pietro da Cortona frescoed the nave, dome and apse, taking nearly 20 years. There are also three paintings by Rubens: *Madonna and Angels* above the altar; *Saints Domitilla, Nereus and Achilleus* on the right of the altar; and *Saints Gregory, Maurus and Papias* on the left. San Filippo is buried in his own chapel, to the left of the altar.

Borromini's façade of the Oratorio

Oratorio dei Filippini ⓰

Piazza della Chiesa Nuova. **Map** 4 E4 & 11 B3. 【 06-6880 2662. 🚌 *46, 62, 64.* **Open** *by appt only; call above number.* 🎵 **Concerts.**

W̲ITH THE ADJOINING church and convent, the oratory formed the center of Filippo Neri's religious order, founded in 1575. Its members are commonly known as Filippini. The musical term *oratorio* (a religious text sung by solo voices and chorus) derives from the services held here.

Filippo Neri came to Rome at 18 to work as a tutor. The city was undergoing a period of religious strife and an economic slump after the sack of Rome in 1527. There was also an outbreak of the plague. It was left to newcomers like Neri and Ignazio di Loyola to revive the spiritual life of the city.

Neri formed a brotherhood of laymen who worshiped together and helped pilgrims and the sick *(see Santissima Trinità dei Pellegrini, p147).* He founded the Oratory as a center for religious discourse. Its conspicuous curving brick façade was built by Borromini between 1637 and 1643.

Torre dell' Orologio ⓱

Piazza dell'Orologio. **Map** 4 E4 & 11 B3. 🚌 *40, 46, 62, 64.*

B̲ORROMINI BUILT this clock tower to decorate one corner of the Convent of the Oratorians of San Filippo Neri from 1647 to 1649. It is typical of Borromini in that the front and rear are concave and the

sides convex. The mosaic of the Madonna beneath the clock is by Pietro da Cortona, while on the corner of the building is a small tabernacle to the Madonna flanked by angels in the style of Bernini.

Pietro da Cortona (1596–1669)

Palazzo del Banco di Santo Spirito ⓲

Via del Banco di Santo Spirito. **Map** 4 D4 & 11 A2. 🚌 *40, 46, 62, 64.* **Open** *normal banking hours.*

F̲ORMERLY THE MINT of papal Rome, this palazzo is often referred to as the Antica Zecca (old mint). The upper stories of the façade, built by Antonio da Sangallo the Younger in the 1520s, are in the shape of a Roman triumphal arch. Above the arch stand two Baroque statues symbolizing Charity and Thrift, and in the center of the arch above the main entrance an inscription records the founding of the Banco di Santo Spirito by Pope Paul V Borghese in 1605.

Pope Paul was a very shrewd financier who encouraged Romans to deposit their money at the bank by offering the vast estates of the Hospital of Santo Spirito *(see p226)* as security. The system provided for only the rudimentary banking requirements of the population, but business was brisk as people deposited money here, secure in the knowledge that they could get it out simply by presenting a chit. The hospital coffers also gained from the system. The Banco di Santo Spirito still exists but is now part of the Banca di Roma.

Façade of the Banco di Santo Spirito, built to resemble a Roman arch

Via dei Coronari ⑲

Map 4 D3 & 11 B2. ▦ *40, 46, 62, 64, 70, 81, 87, 116, 186, 280, 492.*

Large numbers of medieval pilgrims making their way to St. Peter's walked along this street to cross over the Tiber at Ponte Sant'Angelo. Of the businesses that sprang up to try to part the pilgrims from their money, the most enduring was the selling of rosaries, and the street is still named after the rosary sellers *(coronari)*. The street followed the course of the ancient Roman Via Recta (straight street), which originally ran from today's Piazza Colonna to the Tiber.

Making one's way through the vast throng of people in Via dei Coronari could be extremely hazardous. In the Holy Year of 1450, some 200 pilgrims died, crushed by the crowds or drowned in the Tiber. Following the tragedy, Pope Nicholas V demolished the Roman triumphal arch that stood at the entrance to Ponte Sant'Angelo. In the late 15th century, Pope Sixtus IV encouraged the building of private houses and palaces along the street.

Although the rosary sellers have been replaced by antiques dealers, the street still has many original buildings from the 15th and 16th centuries. One of the earliest, at Nos. 156–7, is known as the House of Fiammetta, the mistress of Cesare Borgia.

Antiques shop, Via dei Coronari

Cloister, San Salvatore in Lauro

San Salvatore in Lauro ⑳

Piazza San Salvatore in Lauro 15. **Map** 4 E3 & 11 B2. ▌ *06-687 5187.* ▦ *70, 81, 87, 116, 186, 280, 492.* **Open** *4.30–7.30pm daily and some mornings. Call number above to check.* ▐

The church is named "in Lauro" after the laurel grove that grew here in ancient times. The church standing here today was constructed at the end of the 16th century by Ottaviano Mascherino. The belltower and sacristy were 18th-century additions by Nicola Salvi, famous for the Trevi Fountain *(see p159)*.

The church contains the first great altarpiece by the 17th-century artist Pietro da Cortona, *The Birth of Jesus*, in the first chapel to the right.

The adjacent convent of San Giorgio, to the left, has a pretty Renaissance cloister, a frescoed refectory and the monument to Pope Eugenius IV (reigned 1431–47), moved here when the old St. Peter's was pulled down. An extravagant Venetian, Eugenius would willingly spend thousands of ducats on his gold tiara, but requested a "simple, lowly burial place" near his predecessor Pope Eugenius III. His portrait, painted by Salviati, hangs in the refectory.

In 1669 the church became the seat of a pious association, the Confraternity of the Piceni, inhabitants of the Marche region. Fanatically loyal to the pope, the Piceni were traditionally employed as papal soldiers and tax collectors.

Museo Napoleonico ㉑

Piazza di Ponte Umberto 1. **Map** 4 E3 & 11 C1. ▌ *06-6880 6286.* ▦ *70, 81, 87, 116, 186, 280, 492.* **Open** *9am–7pm Tue–Sat, 9am–1pm Sun.* **Closed** *Jan 1, May 1, Dec 25.* **Adm charge.** Ø

This museum contains memorabilia and portraits of Napoleon Bonaparte and his family. Personal relics of Napoleon himself include an Indian shawl he wore during his exile on St. Helena.

After his death in 1821, the pope allowed many of the Bonaparte family to settle in Rome, including his mother Letizia, who lived in Palazzo Misciatelli on Via del Corso, and his sister Pauline who married the Roman Prince Camillo Borghese. The museum has a cast of her right breast, made by Canova in 1805 as a study for his statue of her as a reclining Venus, now in the Museo Borghese *(see p261)*. Portraits and personal effects of other members of the family are on display, including uniforms, court dresses, and a penny-farthing bicycle that belonged to Prince Eugène, the son of Emperor Napoleon III.

The last male of the Roman branch of the family was Napoleon Charles, portrayed in a late 19th-century painting by Guglielmo de Sanctis. The collection was assembled in 1927 by the Counts Primoli, the sons of Charles's sister, Carlotta Bonaparte.

Façade of San Salvatore in Lauro

The palace next door, in Via Zanardelli, houses the Racolta Praz, an impressive selection of over a thousand *objets d'art*, paintings and pieces of furniture. Dating from the 17th and 18th centuries, they were collected by the art historian and literary critic Mario Praz.

Side relief of the Ludovisi Throne, Palazzo Altemps

Entrance to Museo Napoleonico

Hostaria dell'Orso ㉒

Via dei Soldati 25. **Map** 4 E3 & 11 C2.
🚌 70, 81, 87, 116, 186, 204, 280, 492, 628. **Not open** to the public.

THIS ANCIENT INN has a 15th-century portico and loggia built with columns taken from Roman ruins. Legend has it that Dante once stayed here. Luminaries known to have used the inn include the 16th-century French writers Rabelais and Montaigne.

Palazzo Altemps ㉓

Piazza Sant'Apollinare 46. **Map** 4 E3 & 11 C2. 📞 06-683 3659.
🚌 70, 81, 87, 116, 280, 492, 628. **Open** 9am–8pm Tue–Sun. **Adm charge**.

AN EXTRAORDINARY collection of Classical sculpture is housed in this branch of the Museo Nazionale Romano.

Restored as a museum during the 1990s, the palazzo was originally built for Girolamo Riario, nephew of Pope Sixtus IV in 1480. The Riario coat of arms can still be seen in the janitor's room. In the popular uprising that followed the pope's death in 1484, the building was sacked and Girolamo fled the city.

In 1568 the palazzo was bought by Cardinal Marco Sittico Altemps. His family was of German origin – the name is an Italianization of Hohenems – and influential in the church. The palazzo was renovated by Martino Longhi the Elder in the 1570s. He added the great belvedere, crowned with obelisks and a marble unicorn.

The Altemps family were ostentatious collectors; the courtyard and its staircase are lined with ancient sculptures. These form part of the museum's collection, together with the Ludovisi collection of ancient sculptures, which was previously housed in the Museo Nazionale Romano in the Baths of Diocletian *(see p163)*. Located on the ground floor is the Greek statue of Athena Parthenos and the Dionysius group, a Roman copy of the

Greek original. On the first floor, at the far end of the courtyard, visitors can admire the Painted Loggia, dating from 1595. The Ludovisi throne, a Greek original carved in the 5th century BC, is on the same floor. It is decorated with reliefs, one of which shows a young woman rising from the sea, who is thought to represent Aphrodite. In the room which is known as the Salone del Camino is the powerful statue *Galata's Suicide*, a marble copy of a group originally made in bronze. Nearby is the Ludovisi Sarcophagus, dating from the 3rd century AD.

Galata's Suicide in the Palazzo Altemps

PIAZZA DI SPAGNA

BY THE 16th century, the increase in numbers of visiting pilgrims and ecclesiastics was making life in Rome's already congested medieval center unbearable. A new triangle of roads was built (and is still in place today), to help channel pilgrims as quickly as possible from the city's north gate, the Porta del Popolo, to the Vatican. By the 18th century, hotels had sprung up

Lion fountain in Piazza del Popolo

throughout the district. Today this attractive area offers much more: the superb works of Renaissance and Baroque art in Santa Maria del Popolo and Sant' Andrea delle Fratte; the magnificent reliefs of the restored Ara Pacis; art exhibits in the Villa Medici; views of the city from the Spanish Steps and the Pincio Gardens; plus Rome's most famous shopping streets, centered around Via Condotti.

SIGHTS AT A GLANCE

Churches
Sant'Andrea delle Fratte **1**
Trinità dei Monti **10**
All Saints **12**
Santa Maria dei Miracoli and Santa Maria in Montesanto **14**
Santa Maria del Popolo pp138–9 **17**
San Rocco **21**
Santi Ambrogio e Carlo al Corso **22**

Museums and Galleries
Keats-Shelley Memorial House **7**
Casa di Goethe **13**

Historic Buildings
Palazzo di Propaganda Fide **2**
Villa Medici **11**

Arches, Gates and Columns
Colonna dell'Immacolata **3**
Porta del Popolo **18**

Historic Streets and Piazzas
Via Condotti **4**
Piazza di Spagna **6**

Spanish Steps **9**
Piazza del Popolo **16**

Monuments and Tombs
Ara Pacis **19**
Mausoleum of Augustus **20**

Parks and Gardens
Pincio Gardens **15**

Cafés and Restaurants
Caffè Greco **5**
Babington's Tea Rooms **8**

GETTING THERE
For Piazza di Spagna and the shops around Via Condotti, Spagna Metro station on line A is more convenient than the main bus routes along Via del Corso and Via del Tritone. Stay on until Flaminio Metro if you wish to visit Piazza del Popolo. For getting around locally, the 116 and 117 minibuses are very handy.

KEY
■ Street-by-Street map
M Metro station
P Parking
— City Wall
i Tourist information

SEE ALSO
- **Street Finder**, maps 4, 5
- **Where to Stay** pp294–5
- **Restaurants** pp310–11
- **Shops** pp322–37

The Spanish Steps leading up to the church of Trinità dei Monti

Street-by-Street: Piazza di Spagna

THE NETWORK of narrow streets between Piazza di Spagna and Via del Corso is one of the liveliest areas in Rome, drawing throngs of tourists and Romans to its discreet and elegant shops. In the 18th century, the area was full of hotels for frivolous English aristocrats doing the Grand Tour, but there were also artists, writers and composers, who took the city's history and culture more seriously.

Caffè Greco
Busts and portraits recall the café's former artistic patrons ❺

★ **Piazza di Spagna**
For almost three centuries, the square with its curious Barcaccia fountain in the center has been the chief meeting place for visitors to Rome ❻

Via delle Carrozze took its name from the carriages of wealthy tourists that used to queue up here for repairs.

Via Condotti
This shadowy, narrow street has the smartest shops in one of the smartest shopping areas in the world ❹

Bulgari sells very expensive jewellery behind an austere shopfront in Via Condotti.

KEY

– – – Suggested route

Ⓜ Metro station

Trinità dei Monti
This 16th-century church has a spectacular setting and some of the finest views in Rome ❿

Babington's Tea Rooms
English tourists are catered to in the style of the 1890s ❽

Colonna dell'Immacolata
A Roman column supports a statue of the Virgin Mary ❸

LOCATOR MAP
See Central Rome Map pp12–13

Palazzo di Propaganda Fide
This façade (1665) was one of the last works of the great Francesco Borromini ❷

Sant'Andrea delle Fratte
Pasquale Marini painted The Redemption *to decorate the interior of Borromini's high dome in 1691* ❶

★ Keats-Shelley Memorial House
The library is part of the small museum established in the house where the English poet Keats died in 1821 ❼

★ Spanish Steps
Even obscured by crowds, the steps are one of the glories of late Baroque Rome ❾

STAR SIGHTS

★ Piazza di Spagna

★ Keats-Shelley Memorial House

★ Spanish Steps

Sant'Andrea delle Fratte ❶

Via Sant'Andrea delle Fratte 1.
Map 5 A3. ☎ 06-679 31 91. ▣ 116,
117. Ⓜ Spagna. **Open** 6:30am–
12:30pm, 4–7pm daily. ⬆

W HEN SANT'ANDREA delle
Fratte was built in the
12th century, this area was the
northernmost edge of Rome.
Though the church is now
firmly embedded in the city,
its name (*fratte* means
"thickets") recalls its old setting.
   The church was completely
rebuilt in the 17th century,
partly by Borromini. His bell
tower and dome, best viewed
from the higher ground farther
up Via Capo le Case, are
remarkable for the complex
arrangement of concave and
convex surfaces. The bell
tower is particularly fanciful,
with angel caryatids, flaming
torches, and exaggerated

scrolls like semifolded hearts
supporting a spiky crown.
   In 1842, the Virgin Mary
appeared in the church to a
Jewish banker, who promptly
converted to Christianity and
became a missionary. Inside,
the chapel of the Miraculous
Madonna is the first thing
visitors notice. The church is
better known, however, for
the angels that Borromini's
rival, Bernini, carved for the
Ponte Sant'Angelo. Pope
Clement IX declared they
were too lovely to be outside,
so they remained with Bernini's
family until 1729, when they
were moved to the church.

Palazzo di Propaganda Fide ❷

Via di Propaganda 1. **Map** 5 A2.
☎ 06-6987 9299. FAX 06-6988
0246. ▣ 116, 117. Ⓜ Spagna.
Open by appt (via fax).

T HE POWERFUL JESUIT Congregation for the Propagation
of the Faith was
founded in 1622.
Their head-
quarters had to
be a remarkable
building, and
Bernini was
commissioned.
But Innocent X,
who became
pope in 1644,
preferred the
style of Borromini
who was asked
to continue. His
extraordinary
west façade,
completed in
1662, must
have out-
stripped
everyone's expectations. It
is striped with broad
pilasters, between which
the first-floor windows
bend in, and the cent-
ral bay bulges.
   A rigid band divides
its floors, and the
cornice above the con-
vex central bay swerves
inwards. The more you look
at it, the more restless it
seems; a sign perhaps of
the increasing unhappiness
of the architect who
committed suicide in 1667.

**Angel by Bernini,
Sant'Andrea delle Fratte**

Entrance to the Jesuit College

Colonna dell'Immacolata ❸

Piazza Mignanelli. **Map** 5 A2.
▣ 116, 117. Ⓜ Spagna.

I NAUGURATED IN 1857, the
column commemorates
Pope Pius IX's proclamation
of the doctrine of the
Immaculate Conception,
holding that the Virgin Mary
was the only human being
ever to have been born
"without the stain of original
sin." The column itself dates
from ancient Rome but is
crowned with a statue of the
Virgin Mary.
   On December 8 the fire
brigade places a wreath at the
foot of the statue *(see p61).*

**Portrait of Pope Pius IX
(reigned 1846–78)**

Via Condotti ④

Map 5 A2. 🚌 *81, 116, 117, 119, 492 and many routes along Via del Corso or stopping at Piazza S. Silvestro.* Ⓜ *Spagna. See* **Shops and Markets** *pp322–33.*

Named after the conduits that carried water to the Baths of Agrippa near the Pantheon, Via Condotti is now home to the most traditional of Rome's designer clothes shops. Stores selling shoes and other leather goods are also well represented. The street is extremely popular for early evening strolls, when elegant Italians mingle with tourists in shorts and sneakers.

Slightly younger designers such as Laura Biagiotti, Gianfranco Ferrè and the Fendi sisters have shops on the parallel Via Borgognona, while Valentino and Giorgio Armani both have stores on Via Condotti itself. Valentino has a second branch on Via Bocca di Leone, which crosses Via Condotti just below Piazza di Spagna, and Versace also has a shop here. Giorgio Armani has a second store on nearby Via del Babuino, among the discreet art galleries, exclusive antiques shops and furniture stores.

View along Via Condotti towards the Spanish Steps

Caffè Greco ⑤

Via Condotti 86. **Map** 5 A2. 📞 *06-679 17 00.* 🚌 *81, 116, 117, 119, 492.* Ⓜ *Spagna.* **Open** *8am–8:30pm daily.* **Closed** *Jan 1, May 1, 2 weeks in Aug, Dec 25–26.* ♿

This cafe was opened by a Greek (hence *Greco*) in 1760, and throughout the 18th

Caffè Greco, around 240 years old

century it was a favorite meeting place for foreign artists. Writers such as Keats, Byron and Goethe and composers Liszt, Wagner and Bizet all breakfasted and drank here. So, too, did Casanova and mad King Ludwig of Bavaria. Today, locals often stand in the crowded foyer to sip espresso; there are also tables in a cozy back room, against walls studded with the portraits of the café's famous customers.

Piazza di Spagna ⑥

Map 5 A2. 🚌 *116, 117, 119.* Ⓜ *Spagna.*

Shaped like a crooked bow tie and surrounded by tall shuttered houses painted in muted shades of ocher, cream and russet, Piazza di Spagna (Spanish Square) is crowded all day and (in summer) most of the night. The most famous square in Rome, it has long been the haunt of foreign visitors and expatriates.

In the 17th century, Spain's ambassador to the Holy See had his headquarters on the square, and the area around it was deemed to be Spanish territory. Foreigners who unwittingly trespassed were liable to be dragooned into the Spanish army. In the 18th and 19th centuries, Rome was almost as popular with

visitors as it is today, and the square stood at the heart of the city's main hotel district. Some travelers came in search of knowledge and artistic inspiration, but most were more interested in gambling, collecting ancient statues to adorn their family homes and conducting love affairs with Italian women.

Not surprisingly, wealthy travelers attracted hordes of beggars, who often produced tear-jerking letters by scribes who worked in the square.

The Fontana della Barcaccia in the square is the least showy of Rome's Baroque fountains, and it is often completely screened from view by

Pope Urban VIII's arms, with the Barberini bees

people resting on its rim. It was designed either by the famous Gian Lorenzo Bernini or by his father, Pietro. Because the pressure from the aqueduct that feeds the fountain is extremely low, there are no spectacular cascades or spurts of water. Instead, Bernini constructed a leaking boat – *barcaccia* means "useless old boat" – which lies half-submerged in a shallow pool.

The bees and suns that decorate the Fontana della Barcaccia are taken from the family coat of arms of Pope Urban VIII Barberini, who commissioned the fountain.

The Fontana della Barcaccia at the foot of the Spanish Steps

Bust of Shelley by Moses Ezekiel

Keats-Shelley Memorial House ❼

Piazza di Spagna 26. **Map** 5 A2.
📞 06-678 42 35. 🚌 116, 117, 119.
Ⓜ Spagna. **Open** 9am–1pm, 3–6pm
Mon–Fri, 11am–2pm, 3–6pm Sat.
Closed 10 days at Christmas and New
Year. **Adm charge.** 🚫
📷 book in advance. 📷
🌐 www.keats-shelley-house.org

Iℕ ℕOVEMBER 1820 the English
poet John Keats came to
stay with the painter Joseph
Severn in a dusty pink house,
the Casina Rossa, on the
corner of the Spanish Steps.
Suffering from consumption,
Keats had been sent to Rome
by his doctor, in the hope
that the mild, dry climate
would help the young man's
recovery. Depressed because
of scathing criticism of his
work and tormented by his
love for a young girl named
Fanny Brawne, Keats died at
25 the following February.
His death inspired his friend
and fellow poet Percy Bysshe
Shelley to write the poem
"Mourn not for Adonais." In
July 1822 Shelley himself was
drowned in a boating accident
in the Gulf of La Spezia off
the coast of Liguria. Keats,
Shelley and Severn are all
buried in Rome's Protestant
Cemetery (see p205).
In 1906 the house was
bought by an Anglo-American
association and preserved as
a memorial and library to
honor English Romantic

poets. The relics include a
lock of Keats's hair, some
fragments of Shelley's bones
in a tiny urn and a garish
Carnival mask picked up by
Lord Byron as a souvenir of a
trip to Venice. You can visit
the room where Keats died,
though all the original
furniture was burned after his
death, on papal orders.

Babington's Tea Rooms ❽

Piazza di Spagna 23. **Map** 5 A2.
📞 06-678 60 27. 🚌 116, 117, 119.
Ⓜ Spagna. **Open** 9am–8:15pm
daily. **Closed** Dec 25. 🚫

TℍESE AUGUST, old-fashioned
tea rooms were opened in
1896 by two Englishwomen,
Anna Maria and Isabel Cargill
Babington, to serve homesick
British tourists scones, preserves, and pots of Earl Grey
tea. The food remains homey
– shepherd's pie and chicken
supreme for lunch, muffins
and cinnamon toast for tea –
though these days the menu
offers for breakfast pancakes
with maple syrup as well as the
traditional bacon and eggs.

**Purveyors of English breakfasts to
homesick exiles since 1896**

Spanish Steps ❾

Scalinata della Trinità dei Monti,
Piazza di Spagna. **Map** 5 A2. 🚌 116,
117, 119. Ⓜ Spagna.

Iℕ ℂℍE 17TH century the
French owners of Trinità dei
Monti decided to link the
church with Piazza di Spagna
by building a magnificent
new flight of steps. They also
planned to place an equestrian
statue of King Louis XIV at the
top. Pope Alexander VII Chigi
was not very happy at the

The Spanish Steps in spring with azaleas in full bloom

prospect of erecting a statue of a French monarch in the papal city, and the arguments continued until the 1720s, when an Italian architect, Francesco de Sanctis, produced a design that satisfied both parties. The steps, completed in 1726, combine straight sections, curves and terraces to create one of the city's most dramatic and distinctive landmarks.

When the Victorian novelist Charles Dickens visited Rome, he reported that the Spanish Steps were the meeting place for artists' models, who would dress in colorful traditional costumes, hoping to catch the attention of a wealthy artist. The steps are now a popular place to sit, write postcards, take photos, flirt or just watch the passers-by but eating there is no longer allowed.

Trinità dei Monti ⑩

Piazza della Trinità dei Monti.
Map 5 A2. 📞 *06-679 41 79.*
🚌 *116, 117, 119.* Ⓜ *Spagna.*
Open *9am–7pm daily.* ✝

Trinità dei Monti's bell towers

THE VIEWS of Rome from the platform in front of the façade of Trinità dei Monti, with its twin bell towers, are so beautiful that the church itself is often ignored. It is, however, unusual for Rome, for it was founded by the French in 1495, and although it was later badly damaged, there are still traces of attractive late Gothic latticework in the vaults of the transept. The interconnecting side chapels are decorated with Mannerist paintings, including two fine

19th-century engraving of the inner façade of the Villa Medici

works by Daniele da Volterra. A pupil of Michelangelo, Volterra had to paint clothes on the nudes in the *Last Judgment* in the Sistine Chapel, in response to the objections of Pope Pius IV.

Michelangelo's influence is obvious in the muscled bodies shown in the *Deposition* (second chapel on the left). The circles of figures and dancing angels around the Virgin Mary in the *Assumption* (third chapel on the right) have more in common with the graceful style of Raphael.

Villa Medici ⑪

Accademia di Francia a Roma, Viale della Trinità dei Monti 1. **Map** 5 A2.
📞 *06-676 11.* 🚌 *117, 119.*
Ⓜ *Spagna.* **Accademia and gardens open** *10:30am & 11:30am Sat, Sun.*
Exhibitions, concerts.
Adm charge. 📷

SUPERBLY POSITIONED on the Pincio Hill above Piazza di Spagna, this 16th-century villa has kept the name it assumed when Cardinal Ferdinando de' Medici bought it in 1576. From the terrace visitors can look across the city to Castel Sant'Angelo, from where Queen Christina of Sweden is said to have fired the large cannonball that now sits in the basin of the fountain.

The villa is now home to the French Academy, which was founded by Louis XIV in 1666 to give select painters the chance to study in Rome. Nicolas Poussin was one of the first advisers to the Academy, Ingres was a director and ex-students include Fragonard and Boucher.

After 1803, when the French Academy moved to the Villa Medici, musicians were also admitted; both Berlioz and Debussy came to Rome as students of the Academy.

All Saints ⑫

Via del Babuino 153B. **Map** 4 F2.
📞 *06-360 01 881.* 🚌 *117, 119.*
Open *8am–noon Mon–Fri and for services on Sun.* ✝

IN 1816 THE POPE gave English residents and visitors the right to hold Anglican services in Rome, but it wasn't until the early 1880s that they acquired a site to build their own church. The architect was G E Street, best known in Britain for his Neo-Gothic churches and the London Law Courts. All Saints is also built in Victorian Neo-Gothic, and the interior, though splendidly decorated with different colored Italian marbles, has a very English air. Street also designed St-Paul's-within-the-Walls in Via Nazionale, whose interior is a jewel of British Pre-Raphaelite art.

The street on which All Saints stands got its name from the Fontana del Sileno, known as Babuino (baboon) due to the sad condition in which it was found.

Fontana del Sileno, on Via del Babuino since 1957

Casa di Goethe

Via del Corso 18. **Map** 4 F1. 06-32 65 04 12. 95, 117, 119, 490, 495, 628, 926. 2. Flamino.
Open 10am–6pm Wed–Mon. **Adm Charge.**

THE GERMAN POET, dramatist and novelist Johann Wolfgang von Goethe (1749–1832) lived in this house from 1786 until 1788, working on the journal that eventually formed part of his travel book *The Italian Journey.* Rome's noisy street life irritated him, especially during Carnival time. He was a little perturbed by the number of murders in his neighborhood, but Rome energized him and his book became one of the most influential ever written about Italy.

Santa Maria dei Miracoli and Santa Maria in Montesanto

Piazza del Popolo. **Map** 4 F1.
95, 117, 119, 490, 495, 628, 926.
2. Flaminio. **Santa Maria dei Miracoli** 06-361 02 50.
Open 6:30am–1pm, 4–7:30pm Mon–Sat, 8am–1:30pm, 5–7pm Sun & public hols. **Santa Maria in Montesanto**
06-361 0594. **Open** 4–7pm Mon–Sat, 11am–1pm Sun.

THE TWO CHURCHES at the south end of Piazza del Popolo were designed by the architect Carlo Rainaldi (1611–91), proof that he could be as ingenious as his peers, Bernini and Borromini. To provide a focal point for the piazza, the churches had to look

Portrait of Goethe in the Roman countryside by Tischbein (1751–1821)

symmetrical, but the site on the left was narrower. So Rainaldi gave Santa Maria dei Miracoli (on the right) a circular dome and Santa Maria in Montesanto an oval one, cleverly squeezing it into the narrower site; while the sides of the supporting drums that face the piazza are identical.

Pincio Gardens

Il Pincio. **Map** 4 F1. 95, 117, 119, 490, 495, 628, 926. 2.
Flaminio.

THE PINCIO GARDENS lie above Piazza del Popolo, on a hillside that has been so skillfully terraced and richly planted with trees that, from below, the zigzagging road climbing to the gardens is virtually invisible. In ancient Roman times, there magnificent gardens on the Pincio hill, but the present gardens were designed in the early 19th century by Giuseppe Valadier (who also redesigned the Piazza

The Pincio Gardens water clock

del Popolo). The broad avenues, lined with umbrella pines, palm trees and evergreen oaks, soon became a fashionable place to stroll, and even this century such diverse characters as Gandhi and Mussolini, Richard Strauss and King Farouk of Egypt patronized the Casina Valadier, an exclusive café and restaurant on the grounds.

From the Pincio's main square, Piazzale Napoleone I, the panoramic views of Rome stretch from the Monte Mario to the Janiculum. For full effect, approach the gardens from the grounds of Villa Borghese *(see pp258–9)* above the Pincio or along Viale della Trinità dei Monti.

The twin churches of Santa Maria di Montesanto (left) and Santa Maria dei Miracoli in a 19th-century view of Piazza del Popolo

The panorama is particularly beautiful at sunset, the traditional time for tourists to take a stroll in the gardens.

One of the most striking features of the park itself is an Egyptian-style obelisk that Emperor Hadrian erected on the tomb of his favorite, the beautiful male slave Antinous. After the slave's premature death (according to some accounts he died saving the emperor's life), Hadrian deified him.

The 19th-century water clock on Via dell'Orologio was designed by a Dominican monk. It was displayed at the Paris Exhibition of 1889.

The Casina Valadier restaurant in the Pincio Gardens

Piazza del Popolo **⑯**

Map 4 F1. 95, 117, 119, 490, 495, 926. 2. **M** Flaminio.

A VAST COBBLED OVAL standing at the apex of the triangle of roads known as the Trident, Piazza del Popolo forms a grand symmetrical antechamber to the heart of Rome. Twin Neoclassical façades stand on either side of the Porta del Popolo; an Egyptian obelisk rises in the center; and the matching domes and porticoes of Santa Maria dei Miracoli and Santa Maria di Montesanto flank the beginning of Via del Corso.

Although it is now one of the most unified squares in Rome, Piazza del Popolo evolved gradually over the centuries. In 1589 the great town-planning pope, Sixtus V, had the obelisk erected in the center by Domenico Fontana.

Traditional carnival band in Piazza del Popolo

Over 3,000 years old, the obelisk was originally brought to Rome by Augustus to adorn the Circus Maximus after the conquest of Egypt. Almost a century later Pope Alexander VII commissioned Carlo Rainaldi to build the twin Santa Marias.

In the 19th century the piazza was turned into a grandiose oval by Giuseppe Valadier, the designer of the Pincio Gardens. He also encased Santa Maria del Popolo in a Neoclassical shell to make its south façade fit in better with the overall appearance of the piazza.

In contrast to the piazza's air of ordered rationalism, many of the events staged here were barbaric. In the 18th and 19th centuries, public executions were held in Piazza del Popolo, often as part of the celebration of Carnival. Condemned men were sometimes hammered to death by repeated blows to the temples. The last time a criminal was executed in this way was in 1826, even though the guillotine had by then been adopted as a more scientific means of execution.

The riderless horse races from the piazza down Via del Corso were scarcely more humane: the performance of the runners was enhanced by feeding the horses stimulants, wrapping them in nail-studded ropes and letting off fireworks at their heels.

Santa Maria del Popolo **⑰**

See pp138–9.

Porta del Popolo **⑱**

Between Piazzale Flaminio and Piazza del Popolo. **Map** 4 F1. 95, 117, 119, 490, 495, 926. 2. **M** Flaminio.

THE VIA FLAMINIA, built in 220 BC to connect Rome with Italy's Adriatic coast, enters the city at Porta del Popolo, a grand 16th-century gate built on the orders of Pope Pius IV Medici. The architect, Nanni di Baccio Bigio, modeled it on a Roman triumphal arch. The outer face has statues of St. Peter and St. Paul on either side and a huge Medici coat of arms above.

A century later, Pope Alexander VII commissioned Bernini to decorate the inner face to celebrate the arrival in Rome of Queen Christina of Sweden. Lesser visitors were often held up while Customs officers rifled their luggage. The only way to speed things up was with a bribe.

Porta del Popolo's central arch

Santa Maria del Popolo ⓱

ONE OF ROME'S greatest stores of artistic treasures, this early Renaissance church was commissioned by Pope Sixtus IV della Rovere in 1472. Among the artists who worked on the building were Andrea Bregno and Pinturicchio. Later additions were made by Bramante and Bernini. Many illustrious families have chapels here, all decorated with appropriate splendor. The Della Rovere Chapel has delightful Pinturicchio frescoes; the Cerasi Chapel has two Caravaggio masterpieces, the *Conversion of St. Paul* and the *Crucifixion of St. Peter*, but the finest of all is the Chigi Chapel designed by Raphael for his patron, the banker Agostino Chigi. The most striking of the church's many Renaissance tombs are the two by Andrea Sansovino behind the main altar.

★ Chigi Chapel
Raphael designed this chapel, which has an altarpiece by Sebastiano del Piombo. Niches on either side of the altar house sculptures by Bernini and Lorenzetto. Mosaics in the dome show God as creator of the seven heavenly bodies.

Kneeling Skeleton
This floor mosaic of the figure of death was added to the Chigi Chapel in the 17th century.

NERO'S GHOST

Nero lived on in the imagination of the people long after the fall of the Roman Empire. In the Middle Ages, a legend arose that a walnut tree growing here on the spot where his ashes were buried was haunted by the emperor. Ravens roosting in the tree were thought to be demons tormenting him for his hideous crimes. When the first church was built here in 1099 by Pope Paschal II, the tree was cut down, supposedly putting an end to the supernatural events that had terrified local people.

Entrance

Cybo
Chapel

Della Rovere Chapel
Pinturicchio painted the frescoes in the lunettes and the Nativity above the altar from 1490.

STAR FEATURES

★ **Chigi Chapel**

★ **Caravaggio Paintings in Cerasi Chapel**

★ **Delphic Sibyl**

VISITORS' CHECKLIST

Piazza del Popolo 12. **Map** 4 F1.
📞 06-361 08 36. 🚌 95, 117, 119, 490, 495, 926. 🚋 2. Ⓜ Flaminio. **Open** 7:30am–noon, 4–7pm Mon–Sat, 7:30am–1:30pm, 4:30–7:30pm Sun. 🚻

★ Caravaggio Paintings in Cerasi Chapel

One of two Caravaggios in the Cerasi Chapel, The Crucifixion of St. Peter *uses dramatic fore-shortening to highlight the sheer effort involved in turning the saint's crucifix upside down.*

The altarpiece of *The Assumption* is by Annibale Carracci (1540–1609).

Stained Glass

In 1509, French artist Guillaume de Marcillat was invited to provide Rome's first two stained-glass windows.

The Tomb of Ascanio Sforza, who died in 1505, is by Andrea Sansovino.

★ Delphic Sibyl

This is one of a series of frescoes by Pinturicchio, some Classical and others biblical, painted from 1508–10 to decorate the apse ceiling.

The altar houses the 13th-century painting known as the *Madonna del Popolo.*

The Tomb of Giovanni della Rovere (1483) is by pupils of Andrea Bregno.

TIMELINE

	1213–27 Church enlarged under Gregory IX	*Pinturicchio (c.1454–1513)*	**1485–9** Della Rovere Chapel painted by Pinturicchio	**1513–16** Raphael designs and executes Chigi Chapel
1090	**1200**	**1300**	**1400**	**1500**
1099 Paschal II builds chapel over tombs of the Domitia family (which included Nero) in honour of the Madonna		*Pope Paschal II (reigned 1099–1118)*	**1472–8** Sixtus IV builds church (one of the first Renaissance churches in Rome) **1473** Main altar built	**1530–34** Chigi Chapel altarpiece built by Sebastiano del Piombo

Ara Pacis ⑲

Via di Ripetta. **Map** 4 F2.
☎ 06-3600 3471.
🚌 70, 81, 117, 119, 186, 628.
Closed for restoration.

Rᴇᴄᴏɴsᴛʀᴜᴄᴛᴇᴅ at great expense over a period of many years, the Ara Pacis (Altar of Peace) is one of the most significant monuments of ancient Rome. It celebrates the peace created throughout the Mediterranean area by Emperor Augustus after his victorious campaigns in Gaul

Frieze on south wall showing a procession with the family of Augustus

Marcus Agrippa (right)

and Spain. The monument was commissioned by the Senate in 13 BC and completed four years later. It was positioned so that the shadow of the huge obelisk sundial on Campus Martius (*see p113*) would fall upon it on Augustus' birthday. It is a square enclosure on a low platform with the altar in the center. All the surfaces are decorated with magnificent friezes and reliefs carved in Carrara marble, most likely by Greek craftsmen. The reliefs on the north and south walls depict a procession that took place on July 4 in 13 BC;

in which the members of the emperor's family can be can be identified, ranked by their position in the succession. The heir apparent at the time was Marcus Agrippa, husband of Augustus' daughter, Julia. All the portraits in the relief are carved with extraordinarily effective realism, even the innocent toddler clinging to his mother's skirts.

The tale of the rediscovery of the Ara Pacis dates back to the 16th century, when the first panels were unearthed. One section ended up in Paris, another in Florence. Other discoveries were made in the late 19th century,

when archaeologists finally realized just what they had found. What we see today has all been pieced together since 1938, in part original, in part facsimile. In 1999 work began to organize further the whole archeological area.

Livia *(right)*, Augustus's second wife and mother of Tiberius, with an unidentified family member

South wall

East wall

The altar was used once a year for a sacrifice on the anniversary of the monument's inauguration.

West wall

North wall

An acanthus frieze runs around the lower half of the outside wall.

Augustus's young grandson, Lucius

Mausoleum of Augustus ⑳

Piazza Augusto Imperatore.
Map 4 F2. 🚌 *81, 117, 492, 628, 926.* **Open** *by appt only: permit needed* (see p367).

Now just a weedy mound, ringed with cypresses and sadly strewn with litter, this was once the most prestigious burial place in Rome. Augustus had the mausoleum built in 28 BC, the year he became sole ruler, as a tomb for himself and his descendants. The circular building was 285 ft (87 m) in diameter with two obelisks (now in Piazza del Quirinale and Piazza dell' Esquilino) at the entrance.

Inside were four concentric passageways (linked by corridors) where the urns containing the ashes of the imperial family were placed. The first to be buried here was Augustus's favorite nephew, Marcellus, who had married Julia, the emperor's daughter. He died in 23 BC, possibly poisoned by Augustus's second wife, Livia, who felt that her son Tiberius would make a more reliable emperor. When Augustus died in AD 14, his ashes were placed in the mausoleum, Tiberius duly became emperor and dynastic poisonings continued to fill the family vault with urns.

This sinister monument was later used as a medieval fortress, a vineyard, a private garden and, even, in the 18th century, as an auditorium and a theater.

Augustus, the first Roman emperor

***Madonna, San Rocco and Sant'Antonio with Victims of the Plague* by Il Baciccia (1639–1709)**

San Rocco ㉑

Largo San Rocco 1. **Map** 4 F2. 📞 *06-689 64 16.* 🚌 *81, 117, 492, 628, 926.* **Open** *7:30– 9am, 4:30–7:45pm Mon–Sat, 9am–1pm, 5–8pm Sun.* **Closed** *Aug 17–31.* ✝

This church, with a restrained Neoclassical façade by Giuseppe Valadier, the designer of Piazza del Popolo, began life as the chapel of a 16th-century hospital with beds for 50 men – San Rocco was a healer of the plague-stricken. A maternity wing was added for the wives of Tiber bargemen to save them from having to give birth in the insanitary conditions of a boat. The hospital came to be used by unmarried mothers, and one section was set aside for women who wished to be unknown. They were even permitted to wear a veil for the duration of their stay. Unwanted children were sent to an orphanage, and if any mothers or children died they were buried in anonymous graves. The hospital was abandoned at the turn of the 20th century and demolished in the 1930s during the excavation of the Mausoleum of Augustus.

In the church sacristy has an interesting Baroque altarpiece (c.1660) by Il Baciccia, the artist who decorated the ceiling of the Gesù *(see pp114–15).*

Santi Ambrogio e Carlo al Corso ㉒

Via del Corso 437. **Map** 4 F2. 📞 *06-687 83 35.* 🚌 *81, 117, 492, 628, 926.* **Open** *7am–7pm daily. Ring porter's door to left of church if closed.* 🚫

This church belonged to the Lombard community in Rome and is dedicated to two canonized bishops of Milan, Lombardy's capital. In 1471, Pope Sixtus IV gave the Lombards a church that they dedicated to Sant'Ambrogio, who died in 397. Then in 1610, when Carlo Borromeo was canonized, the church was rebuilt in his honor. Most of the new church was the work of father and son Onorio and Martino Longhi, but the fine dome is by Pietro da Cortona. The altarpiece by Carlo Maratta (1625–1713) is *Gloria dei Santi Ambrogio e Carlo.* An ambulatory leads behind the altar to a chapel housing the the heart of San Carlo in a richly decorated reliquary.

Statue of San Carlo by Attilio Selva (1888–1970) behind the apse of Santi Ambrogio e Carlo

CAMPO DE' FIORI

BETWEEN Corso Vittorio Emanuele II and the Tiber, the city displays many distinct personalities. The open-air market of Campo de' Fiori preserves the lively bohemian atmosphere of the medieval inns that once flourished here, while the area also contains Renaissance palazzi, such as Palazzo Farnese and Palazzo Spada, where powerful Roman families built

18th-century Madonna in Campo de' Fiori

their fortresslike houses near the route of papal processions. Close by, overlooking the picturesque Tiber Island, lies the former Jewish Ghetto, where many traces of daily life from past centuries can still be seen. The Portico of Octavia and the Theater of Marcellus are spectacular examples of the city's many-layered history, built up over the half-ruined remains of ancient Rome.

SIGHTS AT A GLANCE

Churches and Temples
Santissima Trinità dei Pellegrini ❺
Santa Maria dell'Orazione e Morte ❼
San Girolamo della Carità ❾
Sant'Eligio degli Orefici ❿
Santa Maria in Monserrato ⓫
San Carlo ai Catinari ⓲
Santa Maria in Campitelli ⓴
San Nicola in Carcere ㉑
San Giovanni dei Fiorentini ㉙

Museums and Galleries
Palazzo Spada ❻
Piccola Farnesina ⓮
Burcardo Theatre Museum ⓯

Historic Buildings
Palazzo Pio Righetti ❷
Palazzo del Monte di Pietà ❸
Palazzo Farnese ❽
Palazzo Ricci ⓬
Palazzo della Cancelleria ⓭
Casa di Lorenzo Manilio ㉕
Palazzo Cenci ㉖

Fountains
Fontana delle Tartarughe ⓳

Historic Streets and Piazzas
Campo de' Fiori ❶
Tiber Island ㉗
Ghetto and Synagogue ㉔
Via Giulia ㉘

Famous Theaters
Teatro Argentina ⓰

Ancient Sites
Sotterranei di San Paolo alla Regola ❹
Area Sacra dell'Argentina ⓱
Theatre of Marcellus ㉒
Portico of Octavia ㉓

GETTING THERE
Only bus 116 can manage the narrow streets around Campo de' Fiori, but many routes, including the 40, 46, 62 and 64, and tram 8, converge on Largo Argentina. This is a useful starting point for exploring the area. Only the 40, 46, 62 and 64 run the full length of Corso Vittorio Emanuele II while 23 and 280 travel along Lungotevere.

SEE ALSO

• **Street Finder**, maps 4, 8, 11, 12

• **Where to Stay** pp294–5

• **Restaurants** pp310–11

• **Via Giulia Walk** pp276–7

0 meters 300
0 yards 300

KEY

☐ Street-by-Street map

P Parking

Fruit stalls surrounding the statue of Giordano Bruno in the Campo de' Fiori market

Street-by-Street: Campo de' Fiori

THIS FASCINATING PART of Renaissance Rome is also an exciting area for shopping and nightlife, centered on the market square of Campo de' Fiori. Its stalls supply many nearby restaurants, and young people shop for clothes in Via dei Giubbonari. Popular restaurants keep the area alive late into the night, when overcrowding and drunks can become problems. By day there are great buildings to admire, though few are open to the public. Two exceptions are the Piccola Farnesina, with its collection of Classical statues, and Palazzo Spada, home to many important paintings.

Sant'Eligio degli Orefici
A small Renaissance church designed by Raphael is concealed behind a later façade ❿

Palazzo Ricci
Painted Classical scenes were a favorite form of decoration for the façades of Renaissance houses ⓬

San Girolamo della Carità
The chief attraction of this church is Borromini's fabulous Spada Chapel ❾

Santa Maria in Monserrato
This church, which has strong connections with Spain, houses a Bernini bust of Cardinal Pedro Foix de Montoya ⓫

Santa Maria dell'Orazione e Morte
A pair of dramatic winged skulls flank the doorway to this church dedicated to the burial of the dead ❼

KEY

– – – Suggested route

0 meters   75
0 yards   75

Palazzo Farnese
Michelangelo and other great artists helped create this monumental Renaissance palazzo ❽

Palazzo della Cancelleria
The papal administration ran the affairs of the church from this vast building ⓭

Piccola Farnesina
This plaque honors Giovanni Barracco. His sculpture collection is housed in the palazzo ⓮

LOCATOR MAP
See Central Rome Map pp12–13

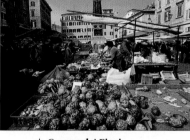

★ Campo de' Fiori
This colorful market makes Piazza Campo de' Fiori one of Rome's most entertaining squares ❶

Palazzo Pio Righetti
Heraldic eagles stare down from the pediments of the palazzo's windows ❷

Palazzo del Monte di Pietà
This was a papal institution, where the poor pawned their possessions in order to borrow small sums of money ❸

Sotterranei di San Paolo alla Regola
Remains of a Roman house have survived in the basement of an old palace ❹

★ Palazzo Spada
The picture gallery houses a collection started by two wonderfully eccentric 17th-century cardinals ❻

Santissima Trinità dei Pellegrini
The principal role of this church was one of charity, looking after poor pilgrims arriving in Rome ❺

STAR SIGHTS

★ Campo de' Fiori

★ Palazzo Spada

Campo de' Fiori ●

Piazza Campo de' Fiori. **Map** 4 E4 & 11 C4. ▭ 116 and routes to Largo di Torre Argentina or Corso Vittorio Emanuele II. See **Markets** p338.

T HE CAMPO DE' FIORI (field of flowers), once a meadow, occupies the site of the open space facing the Theater of Pompey. Cardinals and noblemen used to rub shoulders with fishmongers and foreigners in the piazza's market, thus it was one of the liveliest areas of medieval and Renaissance Rome. Today's market retains much of the traditional atmosphere.

In the center of the square is a statue of the philosopher Giordano Bruno, burnt at the stake for heresy here in 1600. The hooded figure is a grim reminder of the executions that were held here.

The piazza was surrounded by inns for pilgrims and other travelers. Many of these were once owned by the successful 15th-century courtesan Vannozza Catanei, mistress of Pope Alexander VI Borgia. On the corner between the piazza and Via del Pellegrino is Catanei's shield, which she had decorated with her own coat of arms and those of her husband and her lover, the Borgia pope.

Market stalls in Campo de' Fiori

Palazzo Pio Righetti ❷

Piazza del Biscione 89. **Map** 4 E5 & 11 C4. ▭ 116 and routes to Largo Torre Argentina or Corso Vittorio Emanuele II. **Not open** to the public.

T HE VAST 17th-century Palazzo Pio Righetti was built over the ruined Theater

Window pediment with heraldic lion and pine cones, Palazzo Pio Righetti

of Pompey. The windows of the palazzo are decorated with lions and pine cones from the coat of arms of the Pio da Carpi family who lived here.

The curve of the Theater of Pompey, completed in 55 BC, is followed by Via di Grotta Pinta. Rome's first permanent theater was built of stone and concrete, and in the basement of the Pancrazio restaurant, you can see early examples of *opus reticulatum* – small square blocks of tufa (porous rock) set diagonally as a facing for a concrete wall.

Palazzo del Monte di Pietà ❸

Piazza del Monte di Pietà 33. **Map** 4 E5 & 11 C4. ▮ 06-54 451. ▭ 116 and routes to Largo di Torre Argentina or Corso Vittorio Emanuele II. ▯ 8. **Chapel open** only by appt. Call above number between 8:30am and 1:30pm.

T HE MONTE, as it is known, is a public institution founded in 1539 by Pope Paul III Farnese as a pawnshop to staunch the usury then rampant in the city. The building still has offices and auction rooms for the sale of unredeemed goods.

The stars with diagonal bands on the huge central plaque decorating the façade are the coat of arms of Pope Clement VIII Aldobrandini, added when Carlo Maderno enlarged the palace in the 17th century. The clock on the left was added later.

Within, the chapel is a jewel of Baroque architecture, adorned with gilded stucco, marble paneling and reliefs. The decoration makes a perfect setting for the sculptures by Domenico Guidi – a bust of San Carlo Borromeo and a

relief of the *Pietà*. There are also splendid reliefs by Giovanni Battista Théudon and Pierre Legros of biblical scenes illustrating the charitable nature of the institution.

Relief by Théudon of *Joseph Lending Grain to the Egyptians* in Palazzo del Monte di Pietà

Sotterranei di San Paolo alla Regola ❹

Via di San Paolo alla Regola. **Map** 11 C5. ▮ 06-67 10 38 19. ▣ 06-689 2115. ▭ 23, 116, 280 and routes to Largo di Torre Argentina. ▯ 8. **Adm** by request in advance via fax.

A N OLD PALACE hides the perfectly conserved re-mains of an ancient Roman house, dating from the 2nd–3rd centuries. Restoration works are being carried out in order to open this site to the public, but at present it is only possible to visit by special arrangement.

A ramp leads down well below today's street level, to reveal the locations of shops of the time. One level above is the Stanza della Colonna, at one time an open courtyard, with traces of frescoes and mosaics on its walls.

Guido Reni's *Holy Trinity*, in Santissima Trinità dei Pellegrini

Santissima Trinità dei Pellegrini ❺

Piazza della Trinità dei Pellegrini. **Map** 4 E5 & 11 C5. 06-686 84 51. 23, 116, 280 and routes to Largo di Torre Argentina. 8. **Open** 11am–1pm Sun.

THE CHURCH WAS donated in the 16th century to a charitable organization founded by San Filippo Neri to care for the poor and sick, in particular the thousands of paupers who flocked in pilgrimage to Rome during the special holy years known as Jubilees.

The 18th-century façade has niches with statues of the Evangelists by Bernardino Ludovisi. The interior, with Corinthian columns, ends in a horseshoe vault and apse, dominated by Guido Reni's striking altarpiece titled *Holy Trinity* (1625). The frescoes in the lantern are also by Reni.

Other interesting paintings include *St. Gregory the Great Freeing Souls from Purgatory*, by Baldassarre Croce (third chapel to the left); Cavalier d'Arpino's *Virgin and Saints* (second chapel to the left); and a painting by Borgognone (1677) showing the Virgin and recently canonized saints, including San Carlo Borromeo and San Filippo Neri. In the sacristy are depictions of the nobility washing the feet of pilgrims, a custom that was started by San Filippo.

Palazzo Spada ❻

Piazza Capo di Ferro 13. **Map** 2 F5. 06-686 11 58 (Palazzo) or 06-32 8 10 (Galleria). 23, 116, 280 and routes to Largo di Torre Argentina. 8. **Galleria Spada Open** 9am–7pm Tue–Sat, 9am–1pm Sun. **Closed** Jan 1, May 1, Dec 25. **Adm charge.** W www.galleriaborghese.it.

THIS MAJESTIC PALAZZO, built around 1550 for Cardinal Capo di Ferro, has an elegant stuccoed courtyard and a façade decorated with reliefs evoking Rome's glorious past

Cardinal Bernardino Spada, who lived here in the 17th century with his brother, Virginio (also a cardinal), hired architects Bernini and Borromini to work on the building. The brothers' whimsical delight in false perspectives resulted in a colonnaded gallery by Borromini that appears four times longer than it really is.

The cardinals also amassed a superb private collection of paintings, which is now on display in the Galleria Spada. The collection features a wide range of artists, including Rubens, Dürer and Guido Reni. The most important works on display include *The Visitation* by Andrea del Sarto (1486–1530), *Cain and Abel* by Giovanni Lanfranco (1582–1647) and *The Death of Dido* by Guercino (1591–1666).

Santa Maria dell'Orazione e Morte ❼

Via Giulia. **Map** 4 E5 & 11 B4. 06-6880 2715. 23, 116, 280. **Open** 4–6:30pm Sun.

A PIOUS CONFRATERNITY was formed here in the 16th century to collect the bodies of the unknown dead and give them a Christian burial. The theme of death is stressed in this church, dedicated to St. Mary of Prayer and Death. The doors and windows of Ferdinando Fuga's dramatic Baroque façade are decorated with

winged skulls. Above the central entrance is a *clepsydra* (an ancient hourglass) – symbolic of death.

Offertory box in Santa Maria dell'Orazione e Morte

Palazzo Farnese ❽

Piazza Farnese. **Map** 4 E5 & 11 B4. 23, 116, 280 and routes to Corso Vittorio Emanuele II. **Not open** to the public.

THE PROTOTYPE for many princely palaces, the imposing Palazzo Farnese was originally built for Cardinal Alessandro Farnese (who became Pope Paul III in 1534). He commissioned the greatest artists to work on it, starting with Antonio da Sangallo the Younger as architect in 1517. Michelangelo, who took over after him, contributed the great cornice and central window of the main façade, and the third level of the courtyard.

Michelangelo had a plan for the Farnese gardens to be connected by a bridge to the Farnese home in Trastevere, Villa Farnesina (see pp220–21). The elegant arch spanning Via Giulia belongs to this sadly unrealized scheme. The palazzo was completed in 1589, on a less ambitious scale, by Giacomo della Porta. It is now the home of the French Embassy, which moved in as early as 1635.

Majestic façade of Palazzo Farnese

Spada Chapel in San Girolamo

San Girolamo della Carità **❾**

Via di Monserrato 62A.
Map 4 E5 & 11 B4.
📞 06-687 9786.
🚌 23, 40, 46, 62, 64, 116, 280.
Open 10:30–11:30am Sun. 🈳

THE CHURCH was built on the site of the home of San Filippo Neri, the 16th-century saint from Tuscany who renewed Rome's spiritual and cultural life with his friendly, open approach to religion. He would have loved the frolicking putti shown surrounding his statue in his chapel, reminding him of the Roman urchins he had cared for during his lifetime.

The breathtaking Spada Chapel was designed by Borromini and is unique both

as a work of art and as an illustration of the spirit of the Baroque age. All architectural elements are concealed so that the space of the chapel's interior is defined solely by decorative marblework and statues. Veined jasper and precious multicolored marbles are sculpted to imitate flowery damask and velvet hangings. Even the altar rail is a long swag of jasper drapery held up by a pair of kneeling angels with wooden wings.

Although there are memorials to former members of the Spada family, oddly, there is no indication as to which of the Spadas was responsible for endowing the chapel. It was probably art lover Cardinal Virginio Spada, a follower of San Filippo Neri.

Sant'Eligio degli Orefici **❿**

Via di Sant'Eligio 8A.
Map 4 D4 & 11 B4. 📞 06-686 8260.
🚌 23, 40, 46, 62, 64, 116, 280.
Open 10am–1pm Mon, Tue, Thu & Fri. Ring bell at No. 7. Telephone booking preferred. **Closed** Aug. 🈳

THE NAME of the church records the fact that it was commissioned by a rich corporation of goldsmiths (orefici) in the early 16th century. The original design was by Raphael, who, like his master, Bramante, had acquired a sense of the grandiose from the remains of Roman antiquity. The influence of some of Bramante's works, such as the choir of Santa Maria del Popolo (see pp138–9), is evident in the simple way the arches and pilasters define the structure of the walls.

The cupola of Sant' Eligio is attributed to Baldassarre Peruzzi, while the façade was added in the early 17th century by Flaminio Ponzio. Among the various 16th-century painters who decorated the interior was Taddeo Zuccari, who worked on Palazzo Farnese (see p147).

Santa Maria in Monserrato **⓫**

Via di Monserrato. **Map** 4 E4 & 11 B3. 📞 06-686 5865. 🚌 23, 40, 46, 62, 64, 116, 280. **Open** for mass only, 10am–1pm Sun. **Closed** to the public, except by special permission: call the above number. 🈳

An early bust by Bernini of Cardinal Pedro Foix de Montoya

THE ORIGINS of the Spanish national church in Rome go back to 1506, when a hospice for Spanish pilgrims was begun by a brotherhood of the Virgin of Montserrat in Catalonia. Inside is Annibale Carracci's painting *San Diego de Alcalà* and, in the third chapel on the left, a copy of a Sansovino statue of St. James. Some beautiful 15th-century tombs by Andrea Bregno and Luigi Capponi are in the court-yard and side chapels. Don't miss Bernini's bust of Pedro Foix de Montoya, the church's benefactor, in the annex.

***San Diego* by Annibale Carracci**

Statue of San Filippo Neri by Pierre Legros

Palazzo Ricci @

Piazza de' Ricci. **Map** 4 D4 & 11 B4.
🚌 23, 40, 46, 62, 64, 65, 116, 280, 870. **Not open** to the public.

Palazzo Ricci was famous for its frescoed façade – now rather faded – originally painted in the 16th century by Polidoro da Caravaggio, a follower of Raphael.

In Renaissance Rome it was common to commission artists to decorate the outsides of houses with heroes of Classical antiquity. A fresco by a leading artist such as Polidoro, reputedly the inventor of this style of painting, was a conspicuous status symbol, in the nobility's attempts to outshine each other with their palazzi.

Palazzo della Cancelleria @

Piazza della Cancelleria.
Map 4 E4 & 11 C3.
📞 06-6989 3491. 🚌 40, 46, 62, 64, 70, 81, 87, 116, 492.
Open by appointment.

This palazzo, a supreme example of the confident architecture of the Early Renaissance, was begun in 1485. It was financed partly with the gambling winnings of Cardinal Raffaele Riario. Roses, the emblem of the Riario family, adorn the vaults and capitals of the beautiful Doric courtyard. The palazzo's interior was decorated after the Sack of Rome in 1527. Giorgio Vasari boasted that he had completed work on one enormous room in just 100 days; Michelangelo allegedly retorted: "It looks like it." Other Mannerist artists, Perin del Vaga and Francesco Salviati, frescoed the rooms of the cardinal in charge of the Papal Chancellery, the office that gave the palazzo its name when it was installed here by Pope Leo X. On the right of the main entrance is the unobtrusive and rather quaint church of San Lorenzo in Damaso, founded by Pope

Part of the frescoed façade of Palazzo Ricci

Damasus (reigned 366–384). It was reconstructed in 1495 and although Bernini made alterations to the transept and apse in 1638, it was later restored to its 15th-century lines. Its porticoes housed libraries that held the first Papal Archives.

Piccola Farnesina @

Corso Vittorio Emanuele II 166.
Map 4 E4 & 11 C3.
📞 06-6880 6848.
🚌 40, 46, 62, 64, 70, 81, 87, 116, 492. Call for opening times.
Adm charge. 🚫

This delightful miniature palazzo acquired its name from the lilies decorating its cornices. These were mistakenly identified as part of the Farnese family crest. In fact, they were part of the coat of arms of a French clergyman, Thomas Le Roy, for whom the palazzo was built in 1523.

The entrance is in a new façade, built to overlook Corso Vittorio Emanuele II when the road was constructed at the turn of the century. The original façade on the left of today's entrance is attributed to Antonio da Sangallo the Younger. Note the asymmetrical arrangement of its windows and ledges. The elegant central courtyard also retains its original appearance. The Piccola Farnesina now houses the Museo Barracco, a collection of ancient sculpture assembled during the last century by the politician Barone Giovanni Barracco. A bust of the baron

Lily on façade of the Piccola Farnesina

can be seen in the courtyard. The collection includes an ancient Egyptian relief of the scribe Nofer, some Assyrian artifacts and, among the Etruscan exhibits, a delicate ceramic female head. On the first floor is the Greek collection with a head of Apollo.

Inner courtyard, Piccola Farnesina

Burcardo Theater Museum @

Via del Sudario 44. **Map** 4 F4 & 12 D4. 📞 06-681 9471. 🚌 40, 46, 62, 64, 70, 81, 186, 492.
🚇 8. **Museum and Library Open** 9am–1:30pm Mon–Fri.
Closed Aug. 🎭

This late 15th-century house belonged to Johannes Burckhardt, chamberlain to Pope Alexander VI Borgia and author of a diary of Rome under the Borgias. His house now holds Rome's most complete collection of theater literature, plus Chinese puppets and comic masks from the various regions of Italy.

Teatro Argentina 🔟

Largo di Torre Argentina 56. **Map** 4
F4 & 12 D4. **[** 06-6880 4601.
▦ *40, 46, 62, 64, 70, 81, 87, 186,
492, 810.* ▦ *8. **Plays** performed
Oct–Jun. See **Entertainment**
pp346–7.* **W** www.teatrodiroma.it

ONE OF ROME'S most
important theaters was
founded by the powerful
Sforza Cesarini family in 1732,
though the façade dates from
a century later. Many famous
operas, including those of
Verdi, were first performed
here. In 1816, the theater
saw the ill-fated début of
Rossini's *Barber of Seville*,
during which the composer
insulted the unappreciative
audience, who then pursued
him, enraged, through the
streets of Rome.

Detail of façade, Teatro Argentina

Area Sacra dell'Argentina 🔟

Largo di Torre Argentina. **Map** 4 F4 &
12 D4. ▦ *40, 46, 62, 64, 70, 81,
87, 186, 492, 810.* ▦ *8.*
Open *by appt only: permit needed
(see p367).*

THE REMAINS of four temples
were discovered here
during rebuilding in the 1920s.
Dating from the Republican
era, they are among the oldest
to have been found in Rome.
They are known as A, B, C
and D. The oldest (temple C)
dates from the early 3rd
century BC. It was placed on
a high platform preceded by
an altar and is typical of Italic
as opposed to the Greek plans.
Temple A is from later in the
3rd century BC. In medieval
times the small church of San
Nicola de' Cesarini was built
over its podium. The remains
of its two apses are still visible.

San Carlo at Prayer by Guido Reni

The north column stumps
belonged to a great portico,
the Hecatostylum (portico of
100 columns). In Imperial
times two marble lavatories
were built here – the remains
of one are visible behind
temple A. Behind temples B
and C are remains of a great
platform of tufa blocks. These
have been identified as part of
the Curia of Pompey – a rectangular building with a statue
of Pompey – where the Senate
met and Julius Caesar was
murdered on 15 March 44 BC.

**Area Sacra, with circular ruins of
temple B in the foreground**

San Carlo ai Catinari 🔟

Piazza B Cairoli. **Map** 4 F5 & 12 D4.
[06-6880 3554. ▦ *see Area
Sacra.* ▦ *8.* **Open** *7:30am–noon,
5–7pm daily.* **✝**

IN 1620, ROME'S Milanese
congregation decided to
honour Cardinal Carlo
Borromeo with this great

church. It was called "ai
Catinari" on account of the
bowl-makers' *(catinari)*
shops in the area. The
solemn travertine façade
was completed in 1638 by
the Roman architect Soria.
The 16th-century basilican
plan is flanked by chapels.
The St. Cecilia chapel was
designed and decorated by
Antonio Gherardi, who
added a family portrait.
  The church's paintings and
frescoes by Pietro da Cortona
and Guido Reni are confident,
mature works of the Counter-
Reformation, depicting the
life and acts of the recently
canonized San Carlo. Make
sure you also see the ornate
crucifix, inlaid with marble,
glass and mother-of-pearl, by
the 16th-century sculptor
Algardi on the sacristy altar.

Sacristy altar, San Carlo ai Catinari

Fontana delle Tartarughe 🔟

Piazza Mattei. **Map** 4 F5 & 12 D4.
▦ *46, 62, 63, 64, 70, 87, 186,
492, 810.* ▦ *8.*

THE DELIGHTFUL Fontana
delle Tartarughe –
tartarughe are tortoises – was
commissioned by the Mattei
family to decorate "their"
piazza between 1581 and
1588. The design was by
Giacomo della Porta, but the
fountain owes much of its
charm to the four bronze
youths each resting one foot
on the head of a dolphin,
sculpted by Taddeo Landini.
Nearly a century later an

Della Porta's graceful Fontana delle Tartarughe

unknown sculptor added the struggling tortoises to complete the composition.

Santa Maria in Campitelli ⑳

Piazza di Campitelli 9. **Map** 4 F5 & 12 E5. ⚫ 06-6880 3978. 🚌 40, 46, 62, 63, 64, 70, 87, 186, 780, 810. **Open** 7:30am–noon, 4–7pm daily. 🔒 ♿

I N 17TH-CENTURY ROME the plague could still strike fiercely and there were no reliable, effective remedies. Many Romans simply prayed for a cure to a sacred medieval icon of the Virgin, the Madonna del Portico. When a particularly lethal outbreak of plague abated in 1656, popular gratitude was so strong that a new church was built to house the icon.

Lavish altar tabernacle in Santa Maria in Campitelli

The church, designed by a pupil of Bernini, Carlo Rainaldi, was completed in 1667. The main elements of the lively Baroque façade are the graceful columns, symbolizing the supporters of the true faith.

Inside the church stands a fabulously ornate, gilded altar tabernacle with spiral columns which was designed by Giovanni Antonio de Rossi to contain the image of the Virgin. The side chapels are decorated by some of Rome's finest Baroque painters: Sebastiano Conca, Giovanni Battista Gaulli (known as Il Baciccia) and Luca Giordano

Façade and medieval bell tower of San Nicola in Carcere

San Nicola in Carcere ㉑

Via del Teatro di Marcello 46. **Map** 5 A5 & 12 E5. ⚫ 06-6830 7198. 🚌 44, 63, 81, 95, 160, 170, 628, 780, 781. **Open** 7:30am–noon, 4–7pm Mon–Sat, 10am–12:30pm Sun. **Closed** Aug. 🔒

T HE MEDIEVAL CHURCH of San Nicola in Carcere stands on the site of three Roman temples of the Republican era which were converted into a prison *(carcere)* in the Middle Ages. The temples of Juno, Spes and Janus faced a city gate leading from the Forum Holitorium, the city's vegetable and oil market, to the road down to the port on the Tiber. The columns embedded in the walls of the church belonged to two flanking temples whose platforms are now marked by

grass lawns. The church was rebuilt in 1599 and restored in the 19th century, but the bell tower and Roman columns are part of the original design.

The Theater of Marcellus by Thomas Hartley Cromek (1809–73)

Theater of Marcellus ㉒

Via del Teatro di Marcello. **Map** 4 A5 & 12 E5. ⚫ 06-6710 3819. 🚌 44, 63, 81, 95, 160, 170, 628, 780, 781. **Closed** for restoration. Phone above number for information.

T HE CURVED OUTER WALL of this vast amphitheater has supported generations of Roman buildings. It was built by Emperor Augustus (27 BC–AD 14), who dedicated it to Marcellus, his nephew and son-in-law, who had died aged 19 in 23 BC.

The Middle Ages were a turbulent time of invasions and local conflicts *(see p28)* and by the 13th century the theatre had been converted into the fortress of the Savelli family. In the 16th century Baldassarre Peruzzi built a great palace on the theater ruins for the Orsini family, including a garden facing the Tiber. The lower arches were later occupied by humble dwellings and workshops.

Close to the theater stand three beautiful Corinthian columns and a section of frieze. These are from the Temple of Apollo, which housed many great works of art that the Romans had plundered from Greece in the 2nd century BC.

Portico of Octavia ㉓

Via del Portico d'Ottavia. **Map** 4 F5 &
12 E5. 46, 62, 63, 64, 70, 87,
186, 780, 810.

BUILT IN HONOR of Octavia
(the sister of Augustus and
the abandoned wife of Mark
Antony), this is the only surviving portico of what used to be
the monumental piazza of
Circus Flaminius. The rectangular portico enclosed temples
dedicated to Jupiter and Juno,
decorated with bronze statues.
The part we see today is the
great central atrium originally
covered by marble facings.
In the Middle Ages a great
fish market and a church,
Sant'Angelo in Pescheria,
were built in the ruins of the
portico. Because the church
was associated with the fishing
activities of the nearby river
port, aquatic flora and fauna
feature in many of its inlays.
Links with the Tiber are also
apparent in the stucco façade
on the adjacent Fishmonger's
Oratory, built in 1689. The
church has a fresco of the
Madonna and angels by the
school of Benozzo Gozzoli.

Narrow lane in the Jewish Ghetto

Ghetto and Synagogue ㉔

Synagogue, Lungotevere dei Cenci.
Map 4 F5 & 12 E5. 06-6840 0661.
23, 63, 280, 780 and routes to
Largo di Torre Argentina. 8.
Open 9am–4:30pm (Oct–Apr),
9am–7:30pm (May–Sep) Mon–Thu,
9am–1:30pm Fri, 9am–12:30pm Sun.
Closed on Jewish public hols. **Adm
charge.** Ghetto, main
street is Via del Portico d'Ottavia.

THE FIRST Jews came to Rome
as traders in the 2nd century BC and there has been a
Jewish community in Rome

Synagogue overlooking the Tiber

ever since. Jews were much
appreciated for their financial
and medical skills during the
time of the Roman Empire.
Systematic persecution began
in the 16th century. From July
25, 1556 all Rome's Jews were
forced to live inside a high-
walled enclosure, erected on
the orders of Pope Paul IV. The
Ghetto was in an unhealthy
part of Rome. Inhabitants were
only allowed out during the
day, and on Sundays they
were driven into the Church
of Sant'Angelo in Pescheria to
listen to Christian sermons – a
practice abolished only in 1848.
Persecution started again in
1943 with the German occupation. Although many Jews
were helped to escape or
hidden by Roman citizens,
thousands were deported to
German concentration camps.
Today many Jews still live
in the former Ghetto and the
medieval streets retain much
of their old character. The
imposing Synagogue on
Lungotevere was completed
in 1904. It houses a Jewish
museum which describes the
history of the community
through plans, torahs and
other artifacts.

Casa di Lorenzo Manilio ㉕

Via del Portico d'Ottavia 1D.
Map 4 F5 & 12 D5. 46, 62, 63,
64, 70, 87, 186, 780, 810.
Not open to the public.

BEFORE THE RENAISSANCE, most
Romans had only vague
ideas of their city's past, but
the 15th-century revival of
interest in the philosophy and
arts of antiquity, inspired
some to build houses to recall
the splendor of ancient Rome.
In 1468 a certain Lorenzo
Manilio built a great house for
his family, decorating it with

an elegant Classical plaque.
The Latin inscription dates the
building according to the ancient Roman method – 2,221
years after the foundation of
the city – and mentions the
owner's name. Original reliefs
are embedded in the façades
as well as a fragment of an
ancient sarcophagus. The
Piazza Costaguti façade's
windows are inscribed *Ave
Roma* (Hail Rome).

Balcony of Palazzo Cenci

Palazzo Cenci ㉖

Vicolo dei Cenci. **Map** 4 F5 & 12 D5.
See Ghetto. **Not open** to the
public.

PALAZZO CENCI belonged to
the family of Beatrice
Cenci, who was accused,
together with her brothers and
stepmother, of witchcraft and
the murder of her tyrannical
father. She was condemned to
death and beheaded at Ponte
Sant'Angelo in 1599.

**Row of Roman busts decorating
the Casa di Lorenzo Manilio**

Tiber Island, with Ponte Cestio linking it to Trastevere

Most of the original medieval palazzo has been demolished, and the building you see today dates back to the 1570s, though its rather forbidding appearance seems medieval. Heraldic half-moons decorate the main façade on Via del Progresso while pretty balconies open on the opposite side where a medieval arch joins the palace to Palazzetto Cenci, designed by Martino Longhi the Elder. Inside is a traditional courtyard with an Ionic-style loggia; many of the rooms retain the original 16th-century decoration that the unfortunate Beatrice would have known as a child.

Tiber Island ㉗

Isola Tiberina. **Map** 8 D1 & 12 D5.
🚌 *23, 63, 280, 780.* 🚋 *8.*

IN ANCIENT TIMES the island, which lay opposite the city's port, had large structures of white travertine at either end built to resemble the stern and prow of a ship.

Since 293 BC, when a temple was dedicated here to Aesculapius, the god of healing and protector against the plague, the island has been associated with the sick and there is still a hospital here.

San Bartolomeo all'Isola, the church in the island's central piazza, was built on the ruins of the Temple of Aesculapius in the 10th century. Its Romanesque bell tower is clearly visible from across the river.

From the Ghetto area you can reach the island by a footbridge, the Ponte Fabricio. The oldest original bridge over the Tiber still in use, it was built in 62 BC. In medieval times the Pierleoni,

and then the Caetani, two powerful families, controlled this strategic point by means of a tower, still in situ. The other bridge to the island, the Ponte Cestio, is inscribed with the names of the Byzantine emperors associated with its restoration in AD 370.

Via Giulia ㉘

Map 4 D4 & 11 A3. 🚌 *23, 116, 280, 870.*

THIS PICTURESQUE street was laid out by Bramante for Pope Julius II della Rovere. Lined with 16th–18th-century aristocratic palazzi, as well as fine churches and antique shops, Via Giulia makes a fascinating walk *(see pp276–7).*

Mask fountain in Via Giulia

San Giovanni dei Fiorentini ㉙

Via Acciaioli 2. **Map** 4 D4 & 11 A2.
📞 *06-6889 2059.* 🚌 *23, 40, 46, 62, 64, 116, 280, 870.* **Open** *9am–1pm, 4–7pm daily.* ⛪

THE CHURCH of St. John of the Florentines was built for the large Florentine community living in this area. Pope Leo X wanted it to be an expression of the cultural superiority of Florence over Rome. Started in the early 16th century, the church took over a century to build. The principal architect was Antonio da Sangallo the Younger, but many others contributed before Carlo Maderno's elongated cupola was finally completed in 1620. The present façade was added in the 18th century.

The church was decorated mainly by Tuscan artists. One interesting exception is the 15th-century statue of San Giovannino by the Sicilian Mino del Reame in a niche above the sacristy. The spectacular high altar houses a marble group by Antonio Raggi, the *Baptism of Christ.* The altar itself is by Borromini, who is buried in the church along with Carlo Maderno.

This and San Lorenzo in Lucina *(see p112)* are the only churches in Rome which admit animals: the faithful can bring their pets, and an Easter lamb-blessing takes place.

Antonio Raggi's *Baptism of Christ* in San Giovanni dei Fiorentini

QUIRINAL

ONE OF THE original seven hills of Rome, the Quirinal was a mainly residential area in Imperial times. To the east of the hill were the vast Baths of Diocletian, still standing in front of Rome's main train station. Abandoned in the Middle Ages, the district returned to favor in the late 16th century. The prime site

1st-century BC stucco in the Museo Nazionale Romano

was taken by the popes for Palazzo del Quirinale. Great families such as the Colonna and the Aldobrandini had their palazzi lower down the hill. With the end of papal rule in 1870, the surrounding area, especially Via Nazionale, was redeveloped as the Quirinal became the residence of the kings of Italy, then of the President.

SIGHTS AT A GLANCE

Churches
Santi Apostoli **4**
San Marcello al Corso **5**
Santa Maria in Trivio **7**
Santi Vincenzo e Anastasio **9**
Sant'Andrea al Quirinale **11**
San Carlo alle Quattro Fontane **12**
Santa Maria degli Angeli **15**
Santa Maria dei Monti **20**
Sant'Agata dei Goti **21**
Santi Domenico e Sisto **23**

Museums and Galleries
Accademia Nazionale di San Luca **8**
Museo Nazionale Romano (Palazzo Massimo) **16**

Museo delle Paste Alimentari **10**
Palazzo delle Esposizioni **19**

Historic Piazzas
Piazza della Repubblica **18**

Historic Buildings
Palazzo del Quirinale **2**
Palazzo Colonna **3**
Baths of Diocletian **17**

Fountains and Statues
Castor and Pollux **1**
Trevi Fountain **6**
Le Quattro Fontane **13**
Moses Fountain **14**

Parks and Gardens
Villa Aldobrandini **22**

GETTING THERE
The area has Metro stops at Repubblica and Cavour. Buses include the 40 (only one stop), 64 and 70 along Via Nazionale and the 71, 116T and 117, which go through the Traforo Umberto I tunnel. Many buses run along Via del Tritone but there is no bus to the top of the Quirinal. You have to walk up Via XXIV Maggio.

KEY
■ Street-by-Street map
M Metro station
P Parking
i Tourist information

0 meters 300
0 yards 300

SEE ALSO
- *Street Finder*, maps 5, 6, 12
- *Where to Stay* pp294–5
- *Restaurants* pp310–11
- *Bernini Walk* pp282–3

Fontana delle Naiadi in Piazza della Repubblica

Street-by-Street: The Quirinal Hill

E̲ᴠᴇɴ ᴛʜᴏᴜɢʜ Palazzo del Quirinale is closed to the public, it is well worth walking up the hill to the palace to see the giant Roman statues of Castor and Pollux in the piazza and enjoy fine views of the city below. Come down the hill by way of the narrow streets and stairways that lead to one of Rome's unforgettable sights, the Trevi Fountain. Many small churches lie hidden away in the back streets. Towards Piazza Venezia there are grand palazzi, including that of the Colonna, one of Rome's most ancient and powerful families.

Santa Maria in Via is famous for its medieval well and miraculous 13th-century icon of the Madonna.

Santa Maria in Trivio
The attractive façade of this tiny church conceals a rich Baroque interior ❼

Accademia Nazionale di San Luca
The art academy has works by famous former members, such as Canova and Angelica Kauffmann ❽

Santi Vincenzo e Anastasio
The grand façade of this small Baroque church is on a corner facing the Trevi Fountain ❾

★ **Trevi Fountain**
Rome's grandest and best-known fountain almost fills the tiny Piazza di Trevi ❻

San Marcello al Corso
This stark Crucifixion *by Van Dyck hangs in the sacristy of the church* ❺

Palazzo Odescalchi has a Bernini façade from 1664, with a balustrade and richly decorated cornice. The building faces Santi Apostoli.

Museo delle Cere, a wax museum opened in 1953, places its emphasis on horror.

To Piazza Venezia

Museo delle Paste Alimentari
All worth knowing about pasta is explained in this museum ⑩

LOCATOR MAP
See Central Rome Map pp12–13

Palazzo del Quirinale
The old papal palace is now the home of the president of Italy. Palace guards in colorful dress uniform can often be seen outside ②

Castor and Pollux
The statues are grouped with an obelisk and a fountain ①

Piazza della Pilotta is dominated by the imposing façade of the Gregorian University.

Santi Apostoli
The figures of Christ and the Apostles on the balustrade were added by Carlo Rainaldi in 1681 ④

Palazzo Colonna
One of the art gallery's finest old masters is Annibale Carracci's The Bean Eater ③

STAR SIGHT

★ **Trevi Fountain**

KEY

— — — Suggested route

| 0 meters | 75 |
| 0 yards | 75 |

Castor and Pollux ❶

Piazza del Quirinale. **Map** 5 B4.
🚌 H, 40, 64, 70, 170 and many routes along Via del Tritone.

Quirinal fountain and obelisk with Roman statues of Castor and Pollux

Castor and pollux – the patrons of horsemanship – and their prancing horses stand in splendor in the Piazza del Quirinale. Over 18 ft (5.5 m) high, these statues are huge Roman copies of 5th-century BC Greek originals. They once stood at the entrance to the nearby Baths of Constantine. Pope Sixtus V had them restored and placed here in 1588. Formerly known as the "horse tamers," they gave the square its familiar name of Monte Cavallo (Horse Hill).

The obelisk that stands between them was brought here in 1786 from the Mausoleum of Augustus. In 1818 the composition was completed by the addition of a massive granite basin, once a cattle trough in the Forum.

Palazzo del Quirinale ❷

Piazza del Quirinale. **Map** 5 B3.
📞 06-469 91. 🚌 H, 40, 64, 70, 170 and many routes along Via del Tritone. **Open** 8:30am– 12:30pm Sun. **Closed** Aug & public holds. **Adm charge**.
🌐 www.quirinale.it

By the 1500s, the Vatican had a reputation as an un-healthy location because of the high incidence of malaria, so

Pope Gregory XIII chose this superb site on the highest of Rome's seven hills as a papal summer residence. Work began in 1574. Piazza del Quirinale has buildings on three sides, while the fourth is open, with a splendid view of the city. Many great arch-itects worked on the palace before it assumed its present form in the 1730s. Domenico Fontana designed the main façade; Carlo Maderno, the huge chapel and Bernini the narrow wing running the length of Via del Quirinale.

Following the unification of Italy in 1870, it became the official residence of the king; then in 1947 of the president of the republic. A Changing of the Guard ceremony takes place in front of the palace at 4pm daily.

Palazzo del Quirinale, official residence of the President of Italy

Palazzo Colonna ❸

Via della Pilotta 17. **Map** 5 A4 & 12 F3. 📞 06-679 43 62. 🚌 H, 40, 64, 70, 170 and many routes to Piazza Venezia. **Open** 9am–1pm Sat only (last adm: noon). **Closed** Aug & public hols. **Adm charge**. 🚫

Pope martin v Colonna (reigned 1417–31) began building the palazzo, but most of the structure dates from the 18th century. The art gallery, built by Antonio del Grande between 1654 and 1665, is the only part open to the public. The pictures are numbered but unlabeled, so pick up a guide on the way in. Go up the stairs

Canova's monument to Pope Clement XIV in Santi Apostoli, with figures of Humility and Modesty

and through the antechamber leading to a series of three gleaming marble rooms with prominent yellow columns, the Colonna family emblem (*colonna* means "column").

The ceiling frescoes celebrate Marcantonio Colonna's victory over the Turks at the Battle of Lepanto (1571). On the walls are 16th- to 18th-century paintings, including Annibale Carracci's *The Bean Eater* (*see p157*). The room of landscape paintings, many by Poussin's brother-in-law, Gaspare Dughet, reflects the 18th-century taste of Cardinal Girolamo Colonna. Beyond is a room with a ceiling fresco, the *Apotheosis of Martin V.* The throne room has a chair reserved for visiting popes and a copy of Pisanello's portrait of Martin V. The gallery also offers a fine view of the private palace garden, site of the ruined Temple of Serapis.

Santi Apostoli ❹

Piazza dei Santi Apostoli. **Map** 5 A4 & 12 F3. 📞 06-679 40 85. 🚌 H, 40, 64, 70, 170 and many other routes to Piazza Venezia. **Open** 7am–noon, 4pm–7pm daily. 🛐

The original 6th-century church on this site was rebuilt in the 15th century by Popes Martin V Colonna and

Sixtus IV della Rovere, whose
oak-tree crest decorates the
capitals of the late
15th-century portico.
Inside the portico on
the left is Canova's 1807
memorial to the engraver
Giovanni Volpato. The church
itself contains a much larger
monument by Canova, his
Tomb of Clement XIV (1789).

The Baroque interior by
Francesco and Carlo Fontana
was completed in 1714. Note
the 3D effect of Giovanni
Odazzi's painted *Rebel Angels*,
who appear to be really
falling from the sky. A huge
18th-century altarpiece by
Domenico Muratori shows the
martyrdom of the Apostles
James and Philip, whose
tombs are in the crypt.

Detail of Triton and "sea-horse" at Rome's grandest fountain, the Trevi

San Marcello al Corso ❺

Piazza San Marcello 5. **Map** 5 A4 &
12 F3. ☎ *06-69 93 01.* 🚌 *62, 63, 81,
85, 95, 117, 119, 160, 175, 492, 628.*
Open *7am–noon, 4–7pm Mon–Sat,
8:30am–noon, 4–7pm Sun.* ✝

THIS CHURCH was originally
one of the first places of
Christian worship in Rome,
which were known as *tituli*.
A later Romanesque building

burned down in 1519, and was
rebuilt by Jacopo Sansovino
with a single nave and many
richly decorated private
chapels on either side. The
imposing travertine façade
was designed by Fontana in
late Baroque style.

The third chapel on the
right has fine frescoes of the
Virgin Mary by Francesco
Salviati. The decoration of the
next chapel was interrupted
by the Sack of Rome in 1527.
Raphael's follower Perin del
Vaga fled, leaving the ceiling
frescoes to be completed by

Daniele da Volterra and
Pellegrino Tibaldi when
peace returned to the city.
In the nave stands a splendid
Venetian-style double tomb
by Sansovino, a memorial to
Cardinal Giovanni Michiel
(victim of a Borgia poisoning
in 1503) and his nephew,
Bishop Antonio Orso.

Trevi Fountain ❻

Fontana di Trevi. **Map** 5 A3 & 12 F2.
🚌 *52, 53, 61, 62, 63, 71, 80, 95, 116,
119 and many other routes along Via
del Corso and Via del Tritone.*

MOST VISITORS gathering
around the coin-filled
fountain assume that it has
always been here, but by the
standards of the Eternal City,
the Trevi is a fairly recent
creation. Nicola Salvi's
theatrical design for Rome's
largest and most famous
fountain *(see p52)* was completed only in 1762. The
central figures are Neptune,
flanked by two Tritons. One
struggles to master a very
unruly "sea-horse", the other
leads a far more docile animal.
These symbolize the two
contrasting moods of the sea.

The site originally marked
the terminal of the Aqua
Virgo aqueduct built in 19
BC. One of the first-story
reliefs shows a young girl
(the legendary virgin after
whom the aqueduct was
named) pointing to the spring
from which the water flows.

Chapel in San Marcello al Corso, decorated by Francesco Salviati

Façade of Santa Maria in Trivio

Santa Maria in Trivio ⑦

Piazza dei Crociferi 49. **Map** 5 A3 & 12 F2. 06-678 96 45. 52, 53, 61, 62, 63, 71, 80, 95, 116, 119. **Open** 8am–noon, 3:30–7:30pm daily.

I⸱T HAS BEEN SAID that Italian architecture is one of façades, and nowhere is this clearer than in the 1570s façade of Santa Maria in Trivio, delightfully attached to the building behind it. Note the false windows. There is illusion inside, too, particularly in the ceiling frescoes, which show scenes from the New Testament by Antonio Gherardi (1644–1702).

The name of the tiny church probably means "St. Mary-at-the-meeting-of-three-roads."

Accademia Nazionale di San Luca ⑧

Piazza dell'Accademia di San Luca 77. **Map** 5 A3 & 12 F2. 06-679 88 50. 52, 53, 61, 62, 63, 71, 80, 95, 116, 119 and many other routes along Via del Corso and Via del Tritone. **Open** 9am–1:30pm Mon–Sat.

S⸱T LUKE IS supposed to have been a painter, hence the name of Rome's academy of fine arts. Appropriately, the gallery contains a painting of *St. Luke Painting a Portrait of the Virgin* by Raphael and his followers. The academy's heyday was in the 17th and 18th centuries, when many

members gave their work to the collection. Canova donated a model for his famous marble group, the *Three Graces*.

Of particular interest are three fascinating self-portraits painted by women: the 17th-century Italian Lavinia Fontana; the 18th-century Swiss Angelica Kauffmann, whose painting is copied from a portrait of her by Joshua Reynolds; and Elisabeth Vigée-Lebrun, the French painter of the years before the 1789 Revolution.

Santi Vincenzo e Anastasio ⑨

Vicolo dei Modelli 73. **Map** 5 A3 & 12 F2. 06-678 30 98. 52, 53, 61, 62, 63, 71, 80, 95, 116, 119. **Open** 7:30am–12:30pm, 4–7pm daily.

O⸱VERLOOKING the Trevi Fountain is one of the most over-the-top Baroque façades in Rome. Its thickets of columns are crowned by the huge coat of arms of Cardinal Raimondo Mazzarino, who commissioned Martino Longhi the Younger to build the church in 1650. The female

bust above the door is of one of the cardinal's famous nieces, either Louis XIV's first love, Maria Mancini (1639–1715), or her younger sister, Ortensia. In the apse, memorial plaques record the popes whose *praecordia* (a part of the heart) are enshrined behind the wall. This gruesome tradition was started at the end of the 16th century by Pope Sixtus V and continued until Pius X stopped it in the early 20th century.

Museo delle Paste Alimentari ⑩

Piazza Scanderberg 117. **Map** 5 A3 & 12 F2. 06-699 11 19. 52, 53, 61, 62, 63, 71, 80, 95, 116, 119. **Open** 9:30am–5:30pm daily. **Closed** public hols.

T⸱HE ROLE OF PASTA in Italian cuisine cannot be exaggerated, and this entertaining museum presents everything there is to know about the beloved staple. Its rooms focus on various aspects, such as the history of pasta, how it is made and the background of the different shapes, while others exhibit photography and art with a pasta theme.

Self-portrait by Lavinia Fontana in the Accademia Nazionale di San Luca

Interior of Bernini's oval Sant'Andrea al Quirinale

Sant'Andrea al Quirinale ⓫

Via del Quirinale 29. **Map** 5 B3.
⚞ 06-4890 3187. ⛟ 116, 117 and routes to Via del Tritone. **Open** 9am–noon, 4–7pm Wed–Mon (closed in the afternoon in August). **Gratuity** expected by sacristan for showing St. Stanislas's rooms. ⛨ Ø

KNOWN AS the "Pearl of the Baroque" because of its beautiful roseate marble interior, Sant'Andrea was designed by Bernini and executed by his assistants between 1658 and 1670. It was built for the Jesuits, hence the many IHS emblems (*Iesus Hominum Salvator* – Jesus Saviour of Mankind).

The site for the church was wide but shallow, so Bernini pointed the long axis of his oval plan not towards the altar, but towards the sides; he then leads the eye round to the altar end. Here he ordered works of art in various media which function not in isolation, but together. The crucified St. Andrew (Sant' Andrea) of the altarpiece looks up at a stucco version of himself, who in turn ascends towards the lantern and the Holy Spirit.

Do not miss the rooms of St. Stanislas Kostka in the adjacent convent. The quarters of the Jesuit novice, who died in 1568 aged 19, reflect not his own spartan taste, but the richer style of the 17th-century Jesuits. The Polish saint has been brilliantly immortalized in marble by Pierre Legros (1666–1719).

San Carlo alle Quattro Fontane ⓬

Via del Quirinale 23. **Map** 5 B3.
⚞ 06-488 32 61. ⛟ 116, 117 and many routes to Piazza Barberini. Ⓜ Barberini. **Open** 10am–1pm daily; 3–7pm Mon–Fri. ⛨

IN 1634, the Spanish Trinitarians, an order whose role was to pay the ransom of Christian hostages to the Arabs, commissioned Borromini to design a church and convent at the Quattro Fontane cross-roads. The church, so small it would fit inside one of the piers of St. Peter's, is also known as "San Carlino".

Although dedicated to Carlo Borromeo, the 16th-century Milanese cardinal canonized in 1620, San Carlo is as much a monument to Borromini. Both the façade and interior employ bold curves that give light and life to a small, cramped site. The oval dome and tiny lantern are particularly ingenious. The undulating lines of the façade are decorated with angels and a statue of San Carlo. Finished in 1667, the façade is one of Borromini's very last works.

There are further delights in the playful inverted shapes in the cloister and the stucco work in the refectory (now the sacristy), which houses a painting of San Carlo by Orazio Borgianni (1611).

In a small room off the sacristy hangs a portrait of Borromini himself wearing the Trinitarian cross. Borromini committed suicide in 1667, and in the crypt (which may soon be opened to the public) a small curved chapel reserved for him remains empty.

Dome of San Carlo alle Quattro Fontane, lit by concealed windows

Fountain of Strength (or Juno)

Le Quattro Fontane **⑬**

Intersection of Via delle Quattro Fontane and Via del Quirinale. **Map** 5 B3. 🚌 *Routes to Piazza Barberini or Via Nazionale.* Ⓜ *Barberini.*

THESE FOUR small fountains are attached to the corners of the buildings at the intersection of two narrow, busy streets. They date from the great redevelopment of Rome in the reign of Sixtus V (1585–90). Each fountain has a statue of a reclining deity. The river god accompanied by the she-wolf is clearly the Tiber; the other male figure may be the Arno. The female figures represent Strength and Fidelity or the goddesses Juno and Diana.

The crossroads is at the highest point of the Quirinal hill and commands splendid views of three distant landmark obelisks: those placed by Sixtus V in front of Santa Maria Maggiore and Trinità dei Monti, and the one that stands in Piazza del Quirinale.

Moses Fountain **⑭**

Fontana dell'Acqua Felice, Piazza San Bernardo. **Map** 5 C2. 🚌 *36, 60, 61, 62, 84, 175, 492.* Ⓜ *Repubblica.*

OFFICIALLY KNOWN as the Fontana dell'Acqua Felice, this fountain owes its popular name to the grotesque statue of Moses in the central niche. The massive structure with its three elegant arches was designed by Domenico Fontana to mark the terminal of the Acqua Felice aqueduct, so called because it was one of the many great improvements commissioned by Felice Peretti, Pope Sixtus V. Completed in 1587, it brought clean piped water to this quarter of Rome for the first time.

The notorious statue of Moses striking water from the rock is larger than life and the proportions of the body are obviously wrong. Sculpted either by Prospero Bresciano or Leonardo Sormani, it is a clumsy attempt at recreating the awesome appearance of Michelangelo's Moses in the church of San Pietro in Vincoli *(see p170)*. As soon as it was unveiled, it was said to be frowning at having been brought into the world by such an inept sculptor.

Fontana's Moses Fountain

The side reliefs also illustrate water stories from the Old Testament: Aaron leading the Israelites to water and Joshua pointing the army towards the Red Sea. The fountain's four lions are copies of Egyptian originals (now in the Vatican Museums), which Sixtus V had put there for public "convenience" and "delight".

Gold coin with head of the Emperor Diocletian (AD 285–305)

Santa Maria degli Angeli **⑮**

Piazza della Repubblica. **Map** 5 C3. 📞 *06-488 0812.* 🚌 *36, 60, 61, 62, 64, 84, 90, 116, 170, 492, 910.* Ⓜ *Repubblica, Termini.* **Open** *7am–6pm daily.* 🚻 ♿ 🚹

PARTS OF THE RUINED Baths of Diocletian *(right)* provided building material and setting for this church, constructed by Michelangelo in 1563. The church was so altered in the 18th century that it has lost most of its original character.

An exhibition in the sacristy gives a detailed account of Michelangelo's original design.

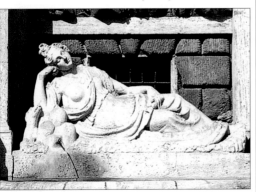

Fidelity (or Diana) with her attendant dog, one of the Quattro Fontane

Museo Nazionale Romano (Palazzo Massimo) ⑯

Part of the Museo Nazionale Romano in the Baths of Diocletian

Palazzo Massimo, Largo di Villa Peretti 1. **Map** 6 D3. 06-3996 7700. 36, 38, 40, 64, 86, 170, 175, H and other routes to Piazza dei Cinquecento. Ⓜ Repubblica, Termini. **Open** 9am–7pm Tue–Sun. **Closed** Jan 1, May 1, Dec 25. **Adm charge** (the biglietto cumulativo gives entry to the museum's five branches).

Founded in 1889, the Museo Nazionale Romano holds most of the antiquities found in Rome since 1870 as well as pre-existing collections, and is one of the world's leading museums of Classical art. It now has five branches: its original site, occupying part of the Baths of Diocletian; the Palazzo Massimo; the Palazzo Altemps (see 127); the Aula Ottagona (near the Baths of Diocletian); and Crypta Balbi in Via delle Botteghe Oscure 31, excavated from the foyer of Augustean Balbus' Theater and housing findings from medieval Rome.

The Palazzo Massimo, built in 1883–7 on the site of a villa which belonged to Sixtus V, used to be a Jesuit college. In 1981–97 it was restored to house a significant proportion of the museum's collections. The exhibits, contained on four floors, are originals dating from the 2nd century BC to the end of 4th century AD.

The basement contains an excellent display of ancient coins, precious artifacts and the only mummified child to be found in the ancient city. The ground floor is devoted to Roman statuary, with funeral monuments in Room 2 and Emperor Augustus in Pontifex Maximus guise in Room 5. Upstairs there are statues from Nero's summer villa in Anzio and Roman copies of famous Greek originals, such as the Discobolos Ex-Lancellotti. The real joy of the museum, however, is on the second floor, where entire rooms of wall paintings have been brought from various villas excavated in and around Rome. A guided tour of the wall paintings is necessary: you can book this at the museum entrance. The most incredible frescoes are from Livia's Villa at Prima Porta. her triclinium (dining room) was decorated with an

abundance of trees, plants and fruit, painted in a totally naturalistic style to fool guests that they were eating alfresco, rather than indoors. Other marvels include rooms brought from the first Villa Farnesina: the children's room has a predominantly white design, while the adults' bedroom is red, complete with erotic paintings. Equally impressive is the museum's diplay of mosaics on the same floor.

Baths of Diocletian ⑰

Terme di Diocleziano, Piazza della Repubblica. **Map** 6 D3. 06-3996 7700. 36, 60, 61, 62, 84, 90. Ⓜ Repubblica, Termini. **Open** 9am–7pm Tue–Sun.

Built in AD 298–306 under the infamous Emperor Diocletian, who murdered thousands of Christians, the baths (see pp22–3) were the most extensive in Rome and could accommodate up to 3,000 bathers at a time.

Part of the Museo Nazionale Romano, the complex houses a vast collection of Roman statues and inscriptions and incorporates a former Carthusian monastery which has a beautiful cloister designed by Michelangelo.

One of the Quattro Aurighe mosaics, Museo Nazionale Romano

Piazza della Repubblica ⑱

Map 5 C3. 36, 60, 61, 62, 64, 84, 90, 170, 175, 492, 646, 910. Ⓜ Repubblica.

Romans often refer to the piazza by its old name, Piazza Esedra, which it was given because it follows the shape of an *exedra* (a semicircular recess) that was part of the Baths of Diocletian. The piazza was part of the redevelopment program undertaken when Rome became capital of a unified Italy. Under its sweeping 19th-century colonnades were once elegant shops, but they have been replaced by banks, travel agencies and cafés.

In the middle of the piazza stands the Fontana delle Naiadi. Mario Rutelli's four naked bronze nymphs caused something of a scandal when they were unveiled in 1901. Each reclines on an aquatic creature symbolizing water in its various forms: a sea-horse for the oceans, a water snake for rivers, a swan for lakes and a curious frilled lizard for subterranean streams. The middle figure, added in 1911, is of the sea god Glaucus, who represents man victorious over hostile nature.

Piazza della Repubblica and the Fontana delle Naiadi

Palazzo delle Esposizioni ⑲

Via Nazionale 194 (second entrance in Via Milano). **Map** 5 B4. 06-474 59 03. 40, 60, 64, 70, 116T, 170. **Open** 10am–9pm Wed–Mon (last adm: 8:30pm). **Closed** Jan 1, May 1, Dec 25. **Adm charge.** ∅ from Via Piacenza entrance only. **Concerts, lectures, films.** See **Entertainment** pp346–7. W www.palaexpo.com

Façade of the Palazzo delle Esposizioni

This somewhat grandiose building, with wide steps, Corinthian columns and statues, was designed as an exhibition center by the architect Pio Piacentini and built by the city of Rome in 1882 during the reign of Umberto I. The main entrance looks like a triumphal arch.

The Palazzo is still used to house exhibitions today and the exhibition space has recently been modernized. The exhibitions are changed every three months, and include a variety of sculpture and paintings. Live performances, films and lectures also take place here. Foreign films are usually shown in the original language.

Santa Maria dei Monti ⑳

Via Madonna dei Monti 41. **Map** 5 B4. 06-48 55 31. 75, 84, 117. Ⓜ Cavour. **Open** 7am–noon, 5–7:30pm Mon–Sat, 8:30am–1pm, 5–7:30pm Sun.

Designed by Giacomo della Porta, this church, dating from 1580, has a particularly splendid dome. Over the high altar is a stunning medieval painting of the Madonna, patroness of this quarter of Rome. The altar in the left transept houses the tomb and effigy of the unworldly French saint Benoît-Joseph Labre, who died here in 1783, having spent his life as a solitary pilgrim. He slept rough in the ruins of the Colosseum, gave away any charitable gifts he received and came regularly to Santa Maria dei Monti to worship. His faith could not sustain his body: when he was only in his mid-thirties, he collapsed and died outside the church. The foul rags he wore are preserved as relics.

One of the bronze nymphs of the fountain in Piazza della Repubblica

Sant'Agata dei Goti ㉑

Via Mazzarino 16 and Via Panisperna.
Map 5 B4. **06-488 80 61.**
40, 60, 64, 70, 71, 117, 170.
Open 7–9am, 4–7pm Mon–Sat,
8:30am–noon, 4–7pm Sun.

T HE GOTHS who gave their
name to this church (*Goti*
are Goths) occupied Rome in
the 6th century AD. They were
Aryan heretics who denied the
divinity of Christ. The church
was founded between AD 462
and 470, shortly before the
main Gothic invasions, and the
beautiful granite columns date
from this period. The main altar
has a well-preserved 12th-cen-
tury Cosmatesque tabernacle,
but the most delightful part of
the church is the charming
18th-century courtyard built
around an ivy-draped well.

Villa Aldobrandini ㉒

Via Panisperna. Entrance to gardens:
Via Mazzarino 1. **Map** 5 B4.
40, 60, 64, 70, 71, 117, 170.
Gardens open dawn–dusk daily.
Villa not open to the public.

B UILT IN the 16th century for
the dukes of Urbino and
acquired for his family by Pope
Clement VIII Aldobrandini
(reigned 1592–1605), the
villa is now government
property and houses an
international law library.

The villa itself, decorated
with the family's six-starred
coat of arms, is closed to the
public, but the gardens and
terraces, hidden behind a
high wall that runs along Via
Nazionale, can be reached
through an iron gate in Via
Mazzarino. Steps lead up past
2nd-century AD ruins into the
recently renovated gardens,
highly recommended as an
oasis of tranquillity in the
center of the city. Gravel
paths lead between formal
lawns and clearly marked
specimen trees, and benches
are provided for the weary.
Since the garden is raised
some 30 ft (10 m) above street
level, the views are excellent.

18th-century courtyard of Sant'Agata dei Goti

Santi Domenico e Sisto ㉓

Largo Angelicum 1. **Map** 5 B4.
06-670 21. 40, 60, 64, 70,
71, 117, 170. **Open** by appt only.
Closed Jul–Sep.

Chapel in Santi Domenico e Sisto

T HIS CHURCH has a tall,
slender Baroque façade
rising above a steep flight of
steps. This divides into two
curving flights that sweep up
to the terrace in front of the
entrance. The pediment of the
façade is crowned by eight
flaming candlesticks.

The interior has a vaulted
ceiling with a large
fresco, *The Apotheosis of
St. Dominic,* by
Domenico Canuti
(1620–84). The
first chapel on
the right was
decorated by
Bernini, who
may also have
designed the
sculpture of Mary
Magdalene
meeting the
risen Christ in
the Garden of
Gethsemane.
This fine marble
group was
executed by

Façade of Santi Domenico e Sisto

Antonio Raggi (1649). Above
the altar is a 15th-century
terra-cotta plaque of the
Virgin and Child. On the left
over a side altar is a large
painting of the Madonna from
the same period, attributed to
Benozzo Gozzoli (1420–97),
a pupil of Fra Angelico.

ESQUILINE

THE ESQUILINE is the largest and highest of Rome's seven hills. In Imperial Rome the western slopes over-looking the Forum housed the crowded slums of the Suburra. On the eastern side there were a few villas belonging to wealthy citizens like Maecenas, patron of the arts and adviser to Augustus. The essential charac-ter of the place has persisted through two millennia; it is still one of the poorer quarters

Michelangelo's *Rachel* **in San Pietro in Vincoli**

of the city. The area is now heavily built up, except for a rather seedy park on the Colle Oppio, a smaller hill to the south of the Esquiline, where you can see the remains of the Baths of Titus, the Baths of Trajan and Nero's Domus Aurea. The area's main interest, however, lies in its churches. Many of these were founded on the sites of private houses where Christians met to worship secretly in the days when the religion was banned.

SIGHTS AT A GLANCE

Churches
San Martino ai Monti **1**
San Pietro in Vincoli **2**
Santa Pudenziana **3**
Santa Maria Maggiore pp172–3 **4**
Santa Prassede **5**
Santa Bibiana **7**

Museums
Museo Nazionale d'Arte Orientale **9**

Historic Piazzas
Piazza Vittorio Emanuele II **8**

Ancient Sites
Auditorium of Maecenas **10**
Domus Aurea **12**
Sette Sale **11**

Arches
Arch of Gallienus **6**

GETTING THERE
This area is close to Termini station and has several other Metro stops: Vittorio Emanuele and Manzoni on line A, Cavour and Colosseo on line B. Bus routes here are a little confusing. Among the most useful are the 16, 75 and 714 from Stazione Termini and the 84. Tram 3 runs along Via Labicana.

SEE ALSO

KEY

	Street-by-Street map
FS	Railroad station
M	Metro station
P	Parking
i	Tourist information

0 meters   300
0 yards   300

Southern façade of Santa Maria Maggiore by night

Street-by-Street: The Esquiline Hill

THE SIGHT that draws most people to this unkempt part of Rome is the great basilica of Santa Maria Maggiore. But it is also well worth searching out some of the smaller churches on the Esquiline: Santa Pudenziana and Santa Prassede, with their celebrated mosaics, and San Pietro in Vincoli, home to one of Michelangelo's most famous sculptures. To the south, in the Colle Oppio park, are the scattered remains of the Baths of Trajan.

Santa Pudenziana
The apse of this ancient church has a magnificent 4th-century mosaic of Christ surrounded by the Apostles ❸

Piazza dell'Esquilino
was furnished in 1587 with an obelisk by Pope Sixtus V. This helped to guide pilgrims coming from the north to the important church of Santa Maria Maggiore.

To the Colosseum

PIAZZA DI SAN PIETRO IN VINCOLI

★ San Pietro in Vincoli
This church's treasures include Michelangelo's Moses *and the chains that bound St. Peter* ❷

Th
Baths
Trajan (A
109) were th
first to be built
the massive scale lat
used in the Baths
Diocletian and of Caracall

VIA CAVOUR

DELL PI

VIA DEI QUATTRO CANT

VIA SFORZA

VIA GIOVANNI LANZA

PIAZZA S
MARTINO A

VIA IN SELCI

VIALE DEL MONTE OPP

★ Santa Maria Maggiore
This imposing rear façade was added by Baroque architect Carlo Rainaldi in 1673. Santa Maria's interior is one of the most richly decorated in Rome ❹

LOCATOR MAP
See Central Rome Map pp12–13

The Tomb of Pius V (died 1572) by Domenico Fontana stands in this less well-known Sistine Chapel, under the northeast dome of Santa Maria Maggiore.

Arch of Gallienus
This was built in the 3rd century AD to replace an entrance in the old Servian Wall ❻

To Vittorio Emanuele Metro

★ Santa Prassede
The 9th-century mosaics in the Chapel of San Zeno are among the finest in Rome ❺

The Torre dei Capocci, a restored medieval tower, is one of the area's most distinctive landmarks.

San Martino ai Monti
The frescoes include 17th-century Roman landscapes and scenes from the life of Elijah by Gaspare Dughet ❶

KEY

- - - - Suggested route

0 meters 75

0 yards 75

STAR SIGHTS

★ Santa Maria Maggiore

★ San Pietro in Vincoli

★ Santa Prassede

San Martino ai Monti ❶

Viale del Monte Oppio 28. **Map** 6 D5.
📞 06-487 3166. 🚌 16, 714.
Ⓜ Cavour, Vittorio Emanuele.
Open 7:30am–noon, 4:30–6:30pm
Mon–Sat, 8am–12:30pm,
4:30–7:30pm Sun. ⛪ ♿

**Fresco of old San Giovanni in
Laterano in San Martino ai Monti**

CHRISTIANS have been
worshipping on the site
of this church since the 3rd
century, when they used to
meet in the house of a man
named Equitius. In the 4th
century, after Constantine had
legalized Christianity, Pope
Sylvester I built a church, one
of very few things he did
during his pontificate. In fact
he was so insignificant that
in the 5th century a more
exciting life was fabricated
for him – which included
tales of him converting
Constantine, curing him of
leprosy and forcing him to
close all pagan temples.
Pope Sylvester's fictional life
was further enhanced in the
8th century, with the forgery
of a document in which
Constantine offered him
the Imperial crown.

Pope Sylvester's church
was replaced in about
AD 500 by St. Symmachus,
rebuilt in the 9th century
and then transformed
completely in the 1630s. The
only immediate signs of its
age are the ancient Corinthian
columns dividing the nave
and aisles. The most
interesting interior features
are a series of frescoed
landscapes of the countryside
around Rome (*campagna
romana*) by the 17th-century

French artist Gaspare Dughet,
Poussin's brother-in-law, in
the right aisle. The frescoes
by Filippo Gagliardi, at either
end of the left aisle, show old
St. Peter's and the interior of
San Giovanni in Laterano
before Borromini's redesign.
If you can find the sacristan,
you can go beneath the church
to see the remains of
Equitius's house.

San Pietro in Vincoli ❷

Piazza di San Pietro in Vincoli 4A.
Map 5 C5. 📞 06-488 28 65. 🚌
75, 84, 117. Ⓜ Cavour, Colosseo.
Open 7am–12.30pm, 3.30–7pm
(Oct–Mar: 6pm) daily. ⛪ ♿ 📷

ACCORDING TO TRADITION, the
two chains (*vincoli*) used
to shackle St. Peter while he
was being held in the depths

Michelangelo's *Moses* in San Pietro

Reliquary with St Peter's chains

of the Mamertine Prison (*see
p91*) were subsequently taken
to Constantinople. In the 5th
century, Empress Eudoxia
deposited one in a church in
Constantinople and sent the
other to her daughter Eudoxia
in Rome. She in turn gave hers
to Pope Leo I, who had this
church built to house it. Some
years later the second chain
was brought to Rome,
where it linked miraculously
with its partner.

The chains are still here,
displayed below the high
altar, but the church is now
best known for Michelangelo's
Tomb of Pope Julius II. When
it was commissioned in 1505,
Michelangelo spent 8 months
searching for perfect blocks
of marble at Carrara in
Tuscany, but Pope Julius
became more interested in
the building of a new St.
Peter's and the project
was laid aside. After the
pope's death in 1513,
Michelangelo resumed
work on the tomb, but
had only finished the
statues of *Moses* and
The Dying Slaves when Pope
Paul III persuaded him to
start work on the Sistine
Chapel's *Last Judgment*.
Michelangelo had planned
a vast monument with
over 40 statues, but the
tomb that was built –
mainly by his pupils –
is simply a façade with
six niches for statues.
The Dying Slaves are in
Paris and Florence, but
the tremendous bearded
Moses is here. The horns
on Moses' head should
really be beams of light
– they are the result of
the Hebrew original from
the Old Testament being
wrongly translated.

Santa Pudenziana ❸

Via Urbana 160.
Map 5 C4. ☎ 06-481 4622.
🚌 16, 75, 84, 105, 714.
Ⓜ Cavour.
Open 8am–6pm daily. ✝

CHURCHES tend to be dedicated to existing saints, but in this case, the church, through a linguistic accident, created a brand new saint. In the 1st century AD a Roman senator called Pudens lived on this site, and, according to legend, allowed St. Peter to lodge with him. In the 2nd century a bath house was built on this site and in the 4th century a church was established inside the baths, known as the *Ecclesia Pudentiana* (the church of Pudens). In time it was assumed that "Pudentiana" was a woman's name and a life was created for her – she became the sister of Prassede and was credited with caring for Christian victims of persecution. In 1969 both saints were declared invalid, though their churches both kept their names.

The 19th-century façade of the church retains an 11th-century frieze depicting both Prassede and Pudenziana dressed as crowned Byzantine empresses. The apse has a remarkable 4th-century mosaic, clearly influenced by Classical pagan art in its use of subtle colors. The Apostles are represented as Roman senators in togas but a clumsy attempt at restoration in the 16th century destroyed two of the Apostles and left other figures without legs.

Apse mosaics in Santa Prassede, showing the saint with St. Paul

Santa Maria Maggiore ❹

See pp172–3.

Santa Prassede ❺

Via Santa Prassede 9A. **Map** 6 D4.
☎ 06-488 24 56. 🚌 16, 70, 71, 75, 714. Ⓜ Vittorio Emanuele.
Open 7am–noon, 4pm–6:30pm daily. ✝ ♿

THE CHURCH was founded by Pope Paschal II in the 9th century, on the site of a 2nd-century oratory. Although the interior has been altered and rebuilt, the structure of the original design of the 9th-century church is clearly visible. Its three naves are separated by rows of granite columns. In the central nave, there is a round stone slab covering the well where, according to the legend, St. Prassede would have buried the remains of 2,000 martyrs.

Artists from Byzantium decorated the church with glittering, jewel-colored mosaics. Those in the apse and choir depict stylized white-robed elders, the haloed elect looking down from the gold and blue walls of heaven, spindly legged lambs, feather-mop palm trees and bright red poppies.

In the apse, Santa Prassede and Santa Pudenziana stand on either side of Christ, with the fatherly arms of St. Paul and St. Peter on their shoulders. Beautiful mosaics of saints, the Virgin and Christ and the Apostles also cover the walls and vault of the Chapel of St. Zeno, built as a mausoleum for Pope Paschal's mother, Theodora. Part of a column brought back from Jerusalem, allegedly the one to which Christ was bound and flogged, also stands here.

11th-century frieze and medallions on the façade of Santa Pudenziana

Santa Maria Maggiore ❹

O F ALL THE GREAT Roman basilicas, Santa
Maria has the most successful blend
of different architectural styles. Its colonnaded triple nave is part of the original
5th-century building. The Cosmatesque
marble floor and delightful Romanesque
bell tower, with its blue ceramic roundels,
are medieval. The Renaissance saw a new
coffered ceiling, and the Baroque gave
the church twin domes and its imposing
front and rear façades. The mosaics are
Santa Maria's most
famous feature. From
the 5th century come
the biblical scenes
in the nave and the
spectacular mosaics
on the triumphal
arch. Medieval high-
lights include a 13th-
century enthroned
Christ in the loggia.

★ Cappella Paolina
*Flaminio Ponzio designed this
richly decorated chapel (1611)
for Pope Paul V Borghese.*

**Obelisk in Piazza
dell'Esquilino**
*The Egyptian obelisk
was erected by Pope
Sixtus V in 1587
as a landmark
for pilgrims.*

LEGEND OF THE SNOW

In 356, Pope Liberius had a
dream in which the Virgin
told him to build a church
on the spot where he found
snow. When it fell on the
Esquiline, on the morning of
August 5 in the middle of a
baking Roman summer, he
naturally obeyed. The miracle
of the snow is commemorated
each year by a service
during which thousands of
white petals float down from
the ceiling of Santa Maria.
Originally roses
were used, but
nowadays the
petals are more
usually taken
from dahlias.

Coffered Ceiling
*The gilded ceiling, possibly
by Giuliano da Sangallo,
was a gift of Alexander VI
Borgia at the end of the 15th
century. The gold is said
to be the first brought from
America by Columbus.*

TIMELINE

356 Virgin appears to
Pope Liberius

432–40 Sixtus III
completes church

420 Probable
founding date

1075 Pope Gregory
VII kidnapped by
opponents while
reading Christmas
mass in Santa Maria

*Pope Gregory
VII*

1347 Cola di Rienzo
crowned Tribune of
Rome in Santa Maria

1288–92
Nicholas IV
adds apse
and transepts

1673 Carlo
Rainaldi
rebuilds apse

1743 Ferdinando
Fuga adds main
façade on orders
of Benedict XIV

*Coat of arms
of Gregory VII*

300 AD	600	900	1200	1500	1800

★ **Coronation of the Virgin Mosaic**
This is the central image of a series of wonderful apse mosaics of the Virgin by Jacopo Torriti (1295).

Baldacchino *(1740s)*
Its columns of red porphyry and bronze were the work of Ferdinando Fuga.

★ **Tomb of Cardinal Rodriguez**
The Gothic tomb (1299) contains magnificent Cosmatesque marblework.

★ **Cappella Sistina**
This Sistine Chapel was built for Pope Sixtus V (1584–87) by Domenico Fontana and houses the pope's tomb.

Column in Piazza Santa Maria Maggiore
A bronze of the Virgin and Child was added to this ancient marble column in 1615. The column came from the Basilica of Constantine in the Forum.

STAR FEATURES

★ **Cappella Sistina**

★ **Coronation of the Virgin Mosaic**

★ **Cappella Paolina**

★ **Tomb of Cardinal Rodriguez**

Arch erected in memory of Emperor Gallienus

Arch of Gallienus ❻

Via Carlo Alberto. **Map** 6 D4. 🚌 *16, 71, 714.* Ⓜ *Vittorio Emanuele.*

SQUASHED between two buildings just off Via Carlo Alberto is the central arch of an originally three-arched gate erected in memory of Emperor Gallienus, who was assassinated by his Illyrian officers in AD 262. It was built on the site of the old Esquiline Gate in the Servian Wall, parts of which are visible nearby.

Santa Bibiana ❼

Via Giovanni Giolitti 154. **Map** 6 F4. 🕻 *06-446 1021.* 🚌 *71.* 🚊 *5, 14.* Ⓜ *Vittorio Emanuele.* **Open** *7:30–11am, 4:30–7:30pm daily.* ✝ ♿

THE DECEPTIVELY simple façade of Santa Bibiana was Bernini's first foray into architecture. It is a clean, economic design with superimposed pilasters and deeply shadowed archways. The church itself was built on the site of the palace belonging to Bibiana's family. This is where the saint was buried

after being flogged to death with leaded cords during the brief persecution of the Christians that took place in the reign of Julian the Apostate (361–3). Just inside the church is a small column against which Bibiana is said to have been whipped. Her remains, along with those of her mother Dafrosa and her sister Demetria, who also suffered martyrdom, are preserved in an alabaster urn below the altar. In a niche above the altar stands a statue of Santa Bibiana by Bernini – the first fully clothed figure he ever sculpted. He depicts her standing beside a column, holding the cords with which she was whipped, apparently on the verge of a deadly swoon.

Early sculpture by Bernini of the martyr Santa Bibiana (1626)

Piazza Vittorio Emanuele II ❽

Map 6 E5. 🚌 *4, 9, 71.* 🚊 *5, 14.* Ⓜ *Vittorio Emanuele. See **Markets** p338.*

PIAZZA VITTORIO, as it is called for short, was once one of the city's main open-air food markets, though now it has moved around the corner to new, covered premises. The arcaded square was built in the urban development undertaken after the unification of Italy in 1870. It was named after Italy's first king, but there is nothing regal about its appearance today.

However, the garden area in the centre of the square has recently been restored. It contains a number of mysterious ruins, including a large mound, part of a Roman fountain from the 3rd century AD and the Porta Magica, a curious 17th-century doorway inscribed with alchemical signs and formulae.

Museo Nazionale d'Arte Orientale ❾

Via Merulana 248. **Map** 6 D5. 🕻 *06-487 4415.* 🚌 *16, 70, 71, 714.* Ⓜ *Vittorio Emanuele.* **Open** *9am–2pm Mon, Wed, Fri, Sat; 9am–7:30pm Tue, Thu, Sun.* **Closed** *1st & 3rd Mon of month.* **Adm charge.** ♿

THE MUSEUM occupies part of the late 19th-century Palazzo Brancaccio, home of the Italian Institute of the Middle and Far East since 1957. The collection ranges from prehistoric Iranian ceramics, sculpture from Afghanistan, Nepal, Kashmir and India to 18th-century Tibetan paintings on vellum. From the Far East there are collections of Japanese screen paintings and Chinese jade.

The most unusual exhibits are the finds from the Italian excavation of the ancient civilization of

4th-century relief from Kashmir

Nepalese Bodhisattva in the Museo Nazionale d'Arte Orientale

Swat in northeast Pakistan. This fascinating Gandhara culture lasted from the 3rd century BC to about the 10th century AD. Its wonderfully exotic, sensual reliefs show an unusual combination of Hellenistic, Buddhist and Hindu influences.

Auditorium of Maecenas ⑩

Largo Leopardi. **Map** 6 D5.
📞 06-487 3262. 🚌 16, 714.
Ⓜ Vittorio Emanuele. **Open**
9am–7pm (9am–5pm Oct–Mar)
Tue–Sat; 9am–1:30pm Sun. Ⓟ ♿

Maecenas, fop, gourmet and patron of the arts, was also an astute adviser and colleague of the Emperor Augustus. Fabulously rich, he created a fantastic villa and gardens on the Esquiline hill, most of which has long disappeared beneath the modern city. The partially reconstructed auditorium, isolated on a traffic island, is all that remains.

Inside, a semicircle of tiered seats suggests that it may have been a place for readings and performances. If it was, then Maecenas would have been entertained here by his protégés, the lyric poet Horace and Virgil, author of the *Aeneid,* reading their latest works. However, water ducts have also been discovered and it may well have been a *nympheum* – a kind of summerhouse – with

fountains. Traces of frescoes remain on the walls: you can make out garden scenes and a procession of miniature figures – including one of a characteristically drunken Dionysus (the Greek god of wine) being propped upright by a satyr.

Sette Sale ⑪

Via delle Terme di Traiano. **Map** 5 C5.
📞 06-6710 3819.
🚌 85, 87, 117, 186, 810, 850.
🚋 3. Ⓜ Colosseo. **Open** only by request; call in advance.

Not far from Nero's Domus Aurea is the cistern of the Sette Sale. It was built here to supply the enormous quantities of water needed for the Baths of Trajan. These were built for Emperor Trajan in AD 104 on parts of the Domus Aurea damaged by a fire.

A set of stairs leads down into the cistern, well below street level. There is not much to see here now, but a walk through the huge, echoing cistern where light rays illuminate the watery surfaces is still an evocative experience. The nine sections, 98 ft (30 m) long and 16 ft (5 m) wide, had a capacity of 8 million litres.

Domus Aurea ⑫

Via della Domus Aurea. **Map** 5 C5.
📞 06-3996 7700. 🚌 85, 87, 117, 186, 810, 850. 🚋 3. Ⓜ Colosseo.
Open 9am–7pm daily. Advance booking required: call the above number (listen for Domus Aurea). 🎧

After allegedly setting fire to Rome in AD 64, Nero decided to build himself an outrageous new palace. The Domus Aurea (sometimes called Nero's Golden House) occupied part of the Palatine and most of the Celian and Esquiline hills – an area approximately 25 times the size of the Colosseum. The vestibule on the Palatine side of the complex contained a colossal gilded statue of Nero. There was an artificial lake, with gardens and woods

where imported wild beasts were allowed to roam free. According to Suetonius in his life of Nero, the palace walls were adorned with gold and mother-of-pearl, rooms were designed with ceilings that showered guests with flowers or perfumes, the dining hall rotated and the baths were fed with both sulphurous water and sea water.

Tacitus described Nero's debauched garden parties, with banquets served on barges and lakeside brothels serviced by aristocratic women, though as Nero killed himself in AD 68, he did not have long to enjoy his new home.

Nero's successors, anxious to distance themselves from the monster-emperor, did their utmost to erase all traces of the palace. Vespasian drained the lake and built the Colosseum (see pp92–5) in its place, Titus and Trajan each erected a complex of baths over the palace, and Hadrian placed the Temple of Venus and Rome (see p87) over the vestibule.

Rooms from one wing of the palace have survived, buried beneath the ruins of the Baths of Trajan on the Oppian hill. Recent excavations have revealed large frescoes and mosaics which are thought to be a panorama of Rome from a bird's-eye perspective. Hopefully more areas will open to the public when considered safe from landslides.

Frescoed room in the ruins of the Domus Aurea

LATERAN

IN THE MIDDLE AGES the Lateran Palace was the residence of the popes, and the basilica of San Giovanni beside it rivaled St. Peter's in splendor. After the return of the popes from Avignon at the end of the 14th century, the area declined in importance. Pilgrims still continued to visit San Giovanni and Santa

Cherub from San Giovanni in Laterano

Croce in Gerusalemme, but the area remained sparsely inhabited. Ancient convents slumbered amid gardens and vineyards until Rome became capital of Italy in 1870 and a network of residential streets was laid out here to house the influx of newcomers. The main sites of archaeological interest are the Aurelian Wall and the ruins of the Aqueduct of Nero.

SIGHTS AT A GLANCE

Churches
San Giovanni in Laterano pp182–3 ❶
Santa Croce
in Gerusalemme ❺
Santi Quattro Coronati ⓫
San Clemente pp186–7 ⓬
Santo Stefano Rotondo ⓭

Shrines
Scala Santa and Sancta
Sanctorum ❷

Arches and Gates
Porta Asinaria ❸
Porta Maggiore ❼

Ancient Sites
Amphiteatrum Castrense ❹
Baker's Tomb ❽
Aqueduct of Nero and
the Freedmen's Tombs ❾

Museums
Museum of Musical
Instruments ❻
Museo Storico della
Liberazione di Roma ❿

SEE ALSO

• **Street Finder**, maps 6, 9, 10

• **Restaurants** pp310–11

• **Mosaics Walk** pp280–81

GETTING THERE
San Giovanni Metro station on line A is just outside the city wall, but handy for many of the sights in the area. The 16, 81, 85, 87 and 186 are among the many buses to Piazza di San Giovanni in Laterano. This can also be reached by the 3 tram. This is slow, but its route makes it useful for exploring this part of Rome.

KEY

	Street-by-Street map
—	City Wall
M	Metro station
P	Parking
i	Tourist information

15th-century apse fresco in Santa Croce in Gerusalemme

Street-by-Street: Piazza di San Giovanni

Both the basilica of San Giovanni and the Lateran Palace look out over a huge open area, the Piazza di San Giovanni, laid out at the end of the 16th century with an Egyptian obelisk, the oldest in Rome, in the center. Sadly, the traffic streaming in and out of the city through Porta San Giovanni tends to detract from its grandeur. Across the square is the building housing the Scala Santa (the Holy Staircase), one of the most revered relics in Rome and the goal for many pilgrims. The area is also a venue for political rallies, and the feast of St. John on June 23 is celebrated with a fair at which Romans consume roast *porchetta* (see p59).

The Chapel of Santa Rufina, originally the portico of the baptistry, has a 5th-century mosaic of spiraling foliage in the apse.

VIA DI SANTO STEFANO ROTONDO

VIA DELL'AMBA ARADAM

VIA DEI LATERANI

The Cloister of San Giovanni fortunately survived the two fires that destroyed the early basilica. A 13th-century masterpiece of mosaic work, the cloister now houses fragments from the medieval basilica.

Piazza di San Giovanni in Laterano boasts an ancient obelisk and parts of Nero's Aqueduct. This 18th-century painting by Canaletto shows how the piazza once looked.

Star Sights

★ **San Giovanni in Laterano**

Key

- - - Suggested route

| 0 meters | 75 |
| 0 yards | 75 |

The Chapel of San Venanzio is decorated with a series of 7th-century mosaics on a gold background. This detail from the apse shows one of the angels beside the central figure of Christ. San Venanzio was an accomplished 6th-century Latin poet.

LOCATOR MAP
See Central Rome Map pp12–13

The Lateran Palace, residence of the popes until 1309, was rebuilt by Domenico Fontana in 1586.

★ **San Giovanni in Laterano**
Borromini's interior dates from the 17th century, but the grand façade by Alessandro Galilei, with its giant statues of Christ and the Apostles, was added in 1735 ❶

PIAZZA DI SAN GIOVANNI IN LATERANO

VIA D. FONTANA

PIAZZA DI PORTA SAN GIOVANNI

Scala Santa
This door at the top of the holy stair-case leads to the Sancta Sanctorum ❷

The Triclinio Leoniano is a piece of wall and a mosaic from the dining hall of 8th-century Pope Leo III.

Porta Asinaria
This minor gateway, no longer in use, is as old as the Aurelian Wall, dating back to the 3rd century AD ❸

San Giovanni in Laterano ❶

See pp182–3.

Scala Santa and Sancta Sanctorum ❷

Piazza di San Giovanni in Laterano 14. **Map** 9 C1. ☎ 06-772 6641. 🚌 16, 81, 85, 87, 186 and other routes to Piazza di San Giovanni in Laterano. 🚊 3. Ⓜ *San Giovanni.* **Open** 6:30am–noon, 3–6pm (to 6:30pm in summer). ✝

Devout Christians climbing the Scala Santa on their knees

Oᴺ ᴛʜᴇ ᴇᴀꜱᴛ ꜱɪᴅᴇ of Piazza di San Giovanni in Laterano, a building designed by Domenico Fontana (1589) houses two surviving parts of the old Lateran Palace. One is the Sancta Sanctorum, the other the holy staircase, the Scala Santa. The 28 steps, said to be those that Christ ascended in Pontius Pilate's house during his trial, are supposed to have been brought from Jerusalem by St. Helena, mother of the Emperor Constantine. This belief, however, cannot be traced back any earlier than the 7th century.

The steps were moved to their present site by Pope Sixtus V (reigned 1585–90) when the old Lateran Palace was destroyed. No foot may touch the holy steps, so they are covered by wooden boards. They may be climbed only by the faithful on their knees, a penance that is performed especially on Good Friday. In the vestibule

are various 19th-century sculptures, including an *Ecce Homo* by Giosuè Meli (1874).

The Scala Santa and two side stairways lead to the Chapel of St. Lawrence or Sancta Sanctorum (Holy of Holies), built by Pope Nicholas III in 1278. Decorated with fine Cosmatesque marblework, the chapel contains many important relics, the most precious being an image of Jesus – the *Acheiropoeton,* or "picture painted without hands," said to be the work of St. Luke, assisted by an angel. The image was taken on procession in medieval times to ward off plagues.

On the walls and in the vault, restoration work has revealed 13th-century frescoes which for 500 years had been covered by later paintings. The frescoes, representing the legends of St. Nicholas, St. Lawrence, St. Agnes and St. Paul, show signs of the style that would characterize the frescoes of Giotto in Assisi, made a few years later.

Porta Asinaria ❸

Between Piazza di Porta San Giovanni and Piazzale Appio. **Map** 10 D2. 🚌 16, 81, 85, 87. 🚊 3. Ⓜ *San Giovanni. See **Markets** p339.*

Tʜᴇ ᴘᴏʀᴛᴀ ᴀꜱɪɴᴀʀɪᴀ (Gate of the Donkeys) is one of the minor gateways in the Aurelian Wall *(see p196).* Twin circular

Porta Asinaria from inside the wall

towers were added and a small enclosure built around the entrance; the remains are still visible today. From outside the walls visitors can see the gate's white travertine façade and two rows of small windows, giving light to two corridors built into the wall above the gateway. In AD 546 treacherous barbarian soldiers serving in the Roman army opened this gate to the hordes of the Goth Totila, who mercilessly looted the city. In 1084 the Holy Roman Emperor Henry IV entered Rome via Porta Asinaria with the antipope Guibert to oust Pope Gregory VII. The gateway was badly damaged in the conflicts that followed.

The area close to the gate, especially in the Via Sannio, is the home of a popular flea-market *(see p339).*

Amphiteatrum Castrense ❹

Between Piazza di Santa Croce in Gerusalemme and Viale Castrense. **Map** 10 E1. 🚌 649. 🚊 3. **Not open** to the public.

Columns and bricked-up arches of the Amphiteatrum Castrense

Tʜɪꜱ ꜱᴍᴀʟʟ 3rd-century amphitheater was used for games and baiting animals. It owes its preservation to the fact that it was incorporated into the Aurelian Wall *(see p196),* which included several existing high buildings in its fortifications. The graceful arches framed by brick semicolumns were blocked up. The amphitheater is best seen from outside the walls, where there is also a very good view of the bell tower of Santa Croce in Gerusalemme.

Discovery and Triumph of the Cross, attributed to Antoniazzo Romano, in Santa Croce in Gerusalemme

Santa Croce in Gerusalemme ❺

Piazza di Santa Croce in Gerusalemme 12. **Map** 10 E1. **[** 06-701 47 69. **[=]** 16, 81, 649, 810. **[=]** 3. **Open** 7am–7pm daily. **[=] [=]**

EMPEROR CONSTANTINE'S mother, St. Helena, founded this church in AD 320 on the grounds of her private palace. Although the church stood at the edge of the city, the relics of the Crucifixion that St. Helena had brought back from Jerusalem made it a center of pilgrimage. Most

18th-century statue of St Helena on the façade of Santa Croce

important were the pieces of Christ's Cross (*croce* means "cross") and part of Pontius Pilate's inscription in Latin, Hebrew and Greek: "Jesus of Nazareth King of the Jews."

In the crypt is a Roman statue of Juno, found at Ostia (*see pp270–71*); it was transformed into a statue of St. Helena by replacing the head and arms and adding a cross. The 15th-century apse fresco shows the medieval legends that arose around the Cross. Helena is shown holding it over a dead youth and restoring him to life. Another episode shows its recovery from the Persians by the Byzantine Emperor Heraclitus after a bloody battle. In the center of the apse is a magnificent tomb by Jacopo Sansovino made for Cardinal Quiñones, Emperor Charles V's confessor (died 1540).

Museum of Musical Instruments ❻

Museo degli Strumenti Musicali, Piazza di Santa Croce in Gerusalemme. **Map** 10 E1. **[** 06-701 47 96. **[=]** 16, 81, 649, 810. **[=]** 3. **Open** 8:30am–7:30pm Tue–Sun. **Closed** Jan 1, Dec 25. **Adm charge.** **[=]**

ONE OF ROME'S lesser-known museums, this building stands on the site of the Sessorianum, the great

Imperial villa belonging to Empress St. Helena, later included in the Aurelian Wall. Opened in 1974, the museum has a collection of over 3,000 instruments from all over the world. It includes instruments typical of the various regions of Italy, and wind, string and percussion instruments of all ages (including Egyptian, Greek and Roman). There are also sections dedicated to church and military music.

The greater part of the collection is composed of Baroque instruments: do not miss the gorgeous Barberini harp, remarkably well preserved, on the first floor in Room 13. There are spinets, harpsichords and clavichords of many different kinds, plus one of the first pianos ever made, dating from 1722.

Art Nouveau entrance to the Museum of Musical Instruments

San Giovanni in Laterano ❶

EARLY IN THE 4th century, the Laterani family were disgraced and their land taken by Emperor Constantine to build Rome's first Christian basilica. Today's church retains the original shape, but has been destroyed by fire twice and rebuilt several times. Borromini undertook the last major rebuild of the interior in 1646, and the main façade is an 18th-century addition. Before the pope's move to Avignon in 1309, the adjoining Lateran Palace was the official papal residence, and until 1870 all popes were crowned in the church. The pope is the Bishop of Rome and here in the city's main cathedral he celebrates Maundy Thursday mass and attends the annual blessing of the people.

Cappella di San Venanzio
This chapel is attached to the baptistry and is decorated with 7th-century mosaics.

Entrance to museum

Apse

Papal Altar
Only the Pope can celebrate mass at this altar. The Gothic baldacchino, decorated with frescoes, dates from the 14th century.

★ **Cloisters**
Built by the Vassalletto family in about 1220, the cloisters are remarkable for their twisted twin columns and inlaid marble mosaics.

TIMELINE

AD 313 Constantine gives Laterani site to Pope Melchiades for a church		**1144** Church dedicated to San Giovanni in Laterano		**1646** Borromini rebuilds interior
314–18 Five-aisled basilica church is built	**896** Church damaged in earthquake	**1309** Papacy moves to Avignon	**1377** Return of popes from Avignon	

AD 300	800	1000	1400

324 Basilica consecrated by Pope Sylvester I and dedicated to the Redeemer	**904–911** Church rebuilt under Pope Sergius III	**1300** First Holy Year proclaimed	**1360** Church burnt down for second time	**1586** Domenico Fontana builds north façade
		1308 Church destroyed by fire		**1730–40** Alessandro Galilei constructs main façade

★ Baptistry
Though much restored, the domed baptistry dates back to Constantine's time. It assumed its present octagonal shape in AD 432 and the design has served as the model for baptistries throughout the Christian world.

VISITORS' CHECKLIST

Piazza di San Giovanni in Laterano 4. **Map** 9 C2.
06-6988 6452. 16, 81, 85, 87, 186, 650, 850 and other routes to Piazza San Giovanni.
San Giovanni. 3. **Church, Cloister open** 7am–7pm daily. **Museum open** 9am–1pm Sat and first Sun of month. **Baptistry open** 7:30am–1pm, 3:30–6:30pm daily. **Adm charge** for museum and cloister.

STAR FEATURES

★ Baptistry
★ Cloisters

North Façade
This was added by Domenico Fontana in 1586. The pope gives his blessing from the upper loggia.

The original Lateran Palace was almost destroyed by the fire of 1308 which devastated San Giovanni. Pope Sixtus V commissioned Fontana to replace it in 1586.

Statues of Christ and the Apostles

Boniface VIII Fresco
This fragment showing the pope proclaiming the Holy Year of 1300 is attributed to Giotto.

A side door is opened every Holy Year.

The main entrance's bronze doors originally came from the Curia *(see p82)*.

TRIAL OF A CORPSE
Fear of rival factions led the early popes to extraordinary lengths. An absurd case took place at the Lateran Palace in 897 when Pope Stephen VI tried the corpse of his predecessor, Formosus, for disloyalty to the Church. The corpse was found guilty, its right hand was mutilated and it was thrown into the Tiber.

Pope Formosus

Corsini Chapel
This chapel was built in the 1730s for Pope Clement XII. The altarpiece is a mosaic copy of Guido Reni's painting of Sant'Andrea Corsini.

Porta Maggiore ●

Piazza di Porta Maggiore. **Map** 6 F5.
🚋 *105*. 🚊 *3, 5, 14, 19.*

ORIGINALLY the two arches of Porta Maggiore were not part of the city wall but part of an aqueduct built for the Emperor Claudius in AD 52. They carried the water of the Aqua Claudia over the Via Labicana and Via Prenestina, two of ancient Rome's main southbound roads. You can still see the original roadway beneath the gate. In the large slabs of basalt – a hard volcanic rock used in all old Roman roads – are the great ruts created by generations of cartwheels. On top of the arches, separate conduits carried the water of two aqueducts, the Aqua Claudia, and its offshoot, the Aqueduct of Nero. They bear inscriptions from the time of the Emperors Claudius, Vespasian and Titus, who restored them in the years AD 71 and AD 81, respectively. In all, six aqueducts from different water sources entered the city at Porta Maggiore.

The Aqua Claudia was 43 miles (68 km) long, with more than 9 miles (15 km) above ground. Its majestic arches are a strong feature of the Roman countryside, and a brand of mineral water still bears its name. Some arches of the Aqua Claudia were bricked up when it was joined to the 3rd-century Aurelian Wall *(see p196)*.

Porta Maggiore, a city gate formed by the arches of an aqueduct

Relief showing breadmaking on the tomb of the baker Eurysaces

Baker's Tomb ●

Piazzale Labicano. **Map** 6 F5. 🚋 *105*.
🚊 *3, 5, 14, 19.*

IN THE MIDDLE of the tram junction near Porta Maggiore stands the tomb of the rich baker Eurysaces and his wife, Atistia, built in 30 BC. Roman custom forbade burials within city walls, and the roads leading out of cities became lined with tombs and monuments for the middle and upper classes. This tomb is shaped like a baking oven: a low-relief frieze at the top shows Eurysaces presiding over his slaves in the various phases of breadmaking. The inscription proudly asserts his origins and reveals him as a freed slave, probably of Greek origin. Many men like him saved money from their meager slave salaries to earn their freedom and set up businesses, becoming the backbone of Rome's economy.

Aqueduct of Nero and the Freedmen's Tombs ●

Intersection of Via Statilia and Via di Santa Croce in Gerusalemme.
Map 10 D1. 🚋 *105, 649.* 🚊 *3, 5, 14, 19.* **Open** *by appt only: permit needed* (see p367).

THE AQUEDUCT was built for Nero in the 1st century AD as an extension of the Aqua Claudia. to supply Nero's Golden House *(see p175)*. It was later extended to the Imperial residences on the Palatine. Partly incorporated into later buildings, the imposing arches make their way via the Lateran to the Celian Hill. Along the first section of the aqueduct, in Via Statilia, is a small tomb in the shape of a house, dating from the 1st century BC, and bearing the names and likenesses of a group of freed slaves. Their name, Statilii, indicates that they had been freed by the Statilii, the family of Claudius's notorious wife, Messalina. Servants of families often pooled funds in this way to pay for a dignified burial in a common resting place.

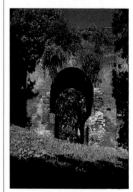

Relief on the Tomb of the Statilii freedmen

Well-preserved section of Nero's Aqueduct near San Giovanni

Museo Storico della Liberazione di Roma ⑩

Via Tasso 145. **Map** 9 C1. 🔲 06-700 3866. Ⓜ Manzoni, San Giovanni. 🚎 3. **Open** 4–7pm Tue, Thu & Fri; 9.30am–12.30pm Sat & Sun.

THIS SMALL museum, dedicated to the resistance to 1943–44 Nazi occupation of Rome, is housed in the ex-prison of the Gestapo. The makeshift cells with bricked-up windows and bloodstained walls linger in the mind.

Santi Quattro Coronati ⑪

Via dei Santi Quattro Coronati 20. **Map** 9 B1. 🔲 06-7047 5427. 🚎 85, 117, 850. 🚎 3. **Open** 8am–noon, 4–6pm daily. ✝ ♿

Cloister of Santi Quattro Coronati

THE NAME of this fortified convent (Four Crowned Saints) refers to four Christian soldiers martyred after they refused to worship a pagan god. For centuries it was the bastion of the pope's residence, the Lateran Palace. Its high apse still looms over the houses below, while a Carolingian tower dominates the entrance. Erected in the 4th century AD, it was rebuilt after the invading Normans set fire to the neighborhood in 1084. Hidden within is the garden of the delightful inner cloister (admission on request), one of the earliest of its kind, built around 1220.

The remains of medieval frescoes can be seen in the Chapel of Santa Barbara, but the convent's main feature is the Chapel of St. Sylvester – its remarkable frescoes (1246) recount the legend of the conversion to Christianity of the Emperor Constantine by Pope Sylvester I (reigned 314–35), then living as a hermit on Monte Soratte, north of Rome.

Stricken by the plague, Constantine is prescribed a bath in children's blood, to the horror of the matrons of Rome. Unable to bring himself to obey, Constantine is visited in a dream by St. Peter and St. Paul. They advise him to find Sylvester, who cures him and baptizes him. The final scene shows the emperor kneeling before the pope. The implied idea of the pope as heir to the Roman Empire would affect the whole course of medieval European history.

San Clemente ⑫

See pp186–7.

Santo Stefano Rotondo ⑬

Via di Santo Stefano Rotondo 7. **Map** 9 B2. 🔲 06-42 11 99. 🚎 81, 117, 673. **Open** 2–4:15pm Mon; 9am–1pm, 2–4:15pm Tue–Sat (summer: 3:30–6pm daily). **Closed** public hols. 📷

ONE OF ROME'S earliest Christian churches, Santo Stefano Rotondo was built between 468 and 483. It has an unusual circular plan with

Distinctive circular outline of Santo Stefano Rotondo

four chapels in the shape of a cross. The round inner area was surrounded by concentric corridors with 22 Ionic supporting columns. The high drum in the center is 72 ft (22 m) high and just as wide. It is lit by 22 high windows, a few of them restored or blocked by restorations carried out under Pope Nicholas V (reigned 1447–55), who consulted the Florentine architect Leon Battista Alberti. The archway in the center may have been added during this period.

In the 16th century the church walls were frescoed by Niccolò Pomarancio, with particularly gruesome illustrations of the martyrdom of innumerable saints. Some of the medieval decor remains in the chapels: in the first chapel to the left of the entrance is a 7th-century mosaic of Christ with San Primo and San Feliciano.

Fresco of St Sylvester and Constantine in Santi Quattro Coronati

San Clemente ⓬

SAN CLEMENTE PROVIDES an opportunity to travel back through three layers of history. At street level, there is a 12th-century church; underneath this lies a 4th-century church; and below that are ancient Roman buildings, including a Temple of Mithras. Mithraism, an all-male fertility cult imported from Persia in the 1st century BC, was a rival to Christianity during the age of Imperial Rome.

The upper levels are dedicated to St. Clement, the fourth pope, who was exiled to the Crimea and martyred by being tied to an anchor and drowned. His life is illustrated in some of the frescoes in the 4th-century church. The site was taken over in the 17th century by Irish Dominicans, who still continue the excavating work begun by Father Mullooly in 1857.

Entrance to the church is through a door in Via di San Giovanni in Laterano.

Paschal Candlestick
This 12th-century spiraling candlestick, striped with glittering mosaic, is a magnificent example of Cosmati work.

18th-Century Façade
Twelfth-century columns were used in the arcade.

★ Cappella di Santa Caterina
The restored frescoes by the 15th-century Florentine artist, Masolino da Panicale, show scenes from the life of the martyred St. Catherine of Alexandria.

12th-century church

4th-century church

Piscina
This deep pit was discovered in 1967. It could have been used as a font or fountain.

1st–3rd-century temple and buildings

TIMELINE

2nd century Site possibly used for secret Christian worship	**867** Reputed transfer of remains of San Clemente to Rome	**1108** New church built over 4th-century church	**1857** Original 4th-century church rediscovered by Father Mullooly
Late 2nd century Temple of Mithras built			

AD 10	500	1000	1500	1900

90–99 Papacy of St. Clement	**4th century** First church built over courtyard of earlier Roman building	**1667** Church and convent given to Irish Dominicans	
AD 64 Nero's fire destroys area	**1084** Church destroyed during Norman invasion led by Robert Guiscard	**1861** Church is excavated. Roman ruins discovered	

★ Apse Mosaic
The 12th-century Triumph of the Cross *includes beautifully detailed animals and acanthus leaves.*

Schola Cantorum
The 6th-century enclosure for the choir was retained for the new church, built in 1108.

★ Triclinium and Altar of Mithras
The altar, with a relief of Mithras slaying the bull, stands in the triclinium, *a room used for ritual banquets.*

Temple of Mithras

★ 11th-Century Frescoes
Commissioned by the de Rapiza family, one shows the story of a boy found alive in St. Clement's tomb beneath the Black Sea.

Catacomb
Discovered in 1938 and dating from the 5th or 6th century, it contains 16 wall tombs known as loculi.

VISITORS' CHECKLIST

Via di San Giovanni in Laterano.
Map 9 B1. 06-7045 1018.
85, 87, 117, 186, 810, 850.
3. Colosseo. **Open** 9am–12:30pm, 3pm–6pm daily (Sun opening at 10am); last adm: 30 mins before closing. **Adm charge** to excavations.

STAR FEATURES

★ **Apse Mosaic**

★ **Cappella di Santa Caterina**

★ **11th-Century Frescoes**

★ **Triclinium and Altar of Mithras**

IOVINVS ALVMNVS

CARACALLA

THE CELIAN HILL overlooking the Colosseum takes its name from Caelius Vibenna, the legendary hero of Rome's struggle with the Tarquins *(see pp16–17)*. In Imperial Rome, this was a fashionable place to live, and some of its vanished splendor is still apparent in the vast ruins of the Baths of Caracalla. Today, thanks to

Capital from ruins of Baths of Caracalla

the Archaeological Zone established at the turn of the century, it is a delightfully peaceful area, a green wedge stretching from the Aurelian Wall to the heart of the city. Through it runs the cobbled Via di Porta San Sebastiano, part of the old Via Appia. It leads to Porta San Sebastiano, one of the best-preserved gates in the ancient city wall.

SIGHTS AT A GLANCE

Churches
Santi Giovanni e Paolo **1**
San Gregorio Magno **2**
Santa Maria in Domnica **4**
San Sisto Vecchio **6**
Santi Nereo e Achilleo **7**
San Cesareo **8**
San Giovanni a Porta Latina **9**
San Giovanni in Oleo **10**
Santa Balbina **16**

Arches and Gates
Arch of Dolabella **3**
Arch of Drusus **13**
Aurelian Wall and
Porta San Sebastiano **14**
Sangallo Bastion **15**

Historic Buildings
Obelisk of Axum **17**
Baths of Caracalla **18**

Tombs
Columbarium of
Pomponius Hylas **11**
Tomb of the Scipios **12**

Parks and Gardens
Villa Celimontana **5**

GETTING THERE
Circo Massimo Metro station is handy if you are visiting the churches and parks on the Celian Hill. For the Baths of Caracalla and other sights closer to Porta San Sebastiano, take the 628 along Viale delle Terme di Caracalla.

SEE ALSO

• *Street Finder*, maps 8, 9

• *Where to Stay* pp294–5

• *Restaurants* pp310–11

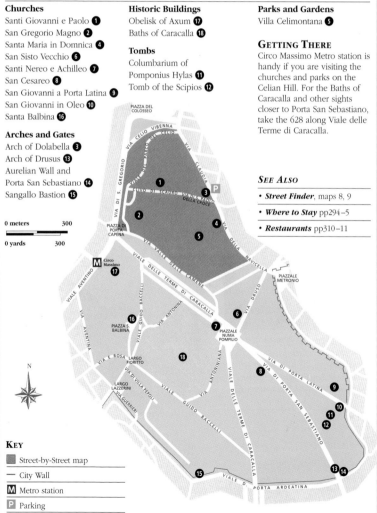

0 meters 300
0 yards 300

KEY
▨ Street-by-Street map
— City Wall
Ⓜ Metro station
🅿 Parking

Mosaic of an athlete from the Baths of Caracalla

Street-by-Street: The Celian Hill

IN THE COURSE OF A MORNING exploring the green slopes of the Celian Hill, you will see a fascinating assortment of archaeological remains and beautiful churches. A good starting point is the church of San Gregorio Magno, from where the Clivo di Scauro leads up to the top of the hill. The steep narrow street passes the ancient porticoed church of Santi Giovanni e Paolo, with its beautiful Romanesque bell tower soaring above the surrounding medieval monastery buildings. Of the parks on the hill, the best-kept and most peaceful is the Villa Celimontana, with its formal walks and avenues. It is a good place for a picnic, because few bars or restaurants are nearby.

Clivo di Scauro, the Roman *Clivus Scauri*, leads up to Santi Giovanni e Paolo, passing under the flying buttresses that support the church.

La Vignola is a delightful Renaissance pavilion, reconstructed here in 1911 after it had been demolished during the creation of the Archaeological Zone around the Baths of Caracalla.

To Circo Massimo Metro

San Gregorio Magno
A monastery and a chapel were founded here by Pope Gregory the Great at the end of the 6th century ❷

★ Santi Giovanni e Paolo
The nave of the church, lit by a blaze of chandeliers, has been restored many times and assumed its present appearance in the 18th century ❶

★ Villa Celimontana
The delightful 16th-century villa built for the Mattei family is now the center of a public park ❺

Trams passing over the Celian Hill from the Colosseum rumble up a picturesque narrow track through the Parco del Celio.

LOCATOR MAP
See Central Rome Map pp12–13

Ruins of the Temple of Claudius are visible over a large area of the Celian hill. These travertine blocks have been incorporated in the base of the bell tower of Santi Giovanni e Paolo.

The gateway of San Tommaso in Formis is decorated with a wonderful 13th-century mosaic showing Christ with two freed slaves, one white, one black.

Arch of Dolabella
Built in the 1st century AD, probably as an entrance to the city, this archway was later incorporated in Nero's aqueduct to the Palatine ③

★ **Santa Maria in Domnica**
This church is famed for its 9th-century mosaics. These Apostles appear on the triumphal arch above the apse, flanking a medallion containing the figure of Christ ④

STAR SIGHTS

★ **Santi Giovanni e Paolo**

★ **Santa Maria in Domnica**

★ **Villa Celimontana**

KEY

- - -	Suggested route

0 meters 75

0 yards 75

Santi Giovanni e Paolo ❶

Piazza Santi Giovanni e Paolo 13.
Map 9 A1. 📞 *06-772 711.*
🚌 *75, 81, 117, 175, 673.* 🚊 *3.*
Ⓜ *Colosseo or Circo Massimo.*
Open *8:30am–noon,
3:30pm–6:30pm Mon–Sat,
8:30am–12:45pm, 3:30pm–7pm Sun.
For timetable for Roman House, call
06-721 6601.* ✝ ♿ *church only.*

S ANTI GIOVANNI E PAOLO is
dedicated to two martyred
Roman officers whose house
stood on this site. Giovanni
(John) and Paolo (Paul) had
served the first Christian
emperor, Constantine. When
they were later called to arms
by the pagan emperor Julian
the Apostate, they refused
and were beheaded in their
own house in AD 362.

Built toward the end of the
4th century, the church
retains many elements of its
original structure. The Ionic
portico dates from the 12th
century, and the apse and bell
tower were added by
Nicholas Breakspeare, the
only English pope, who
reigned as Adrian IV
(1154–59). The base of the
superb 13th-century,
Romanesque bell
tower was part
of the Temple
of Claudius that stood
on this site.

The interior,
remodelled in 1718,
has granite piers and
columns. A tomb slab in the
nave marks the burial place of
the martyrs, whose relics are
preserved in an urn under the
high altar. In a tiny room near
the altar, a magnificent 13th-
century fresco depicts the
figure of Christ flanked by his
Apostles (ask the sacristan to
unlock the door for you).

Excavations beneath the
church have revealed two 2nd-
and 3rd-century Roman houses,
used as a Christian burial place.
These are well worth a visit.
The two-storey construction,
with 20 rooms and a labyrinth
of corridors, has well-preserved
pagan and Christian paintings.
The arches to the left of the
church were part of a 3rd-
century street of shops.

Fresco of Christ and the Apostles in Santi Giovanni e Paolo

San Gregorio Magno ❷

Piazza di San Gregorio. **Map** 8 F2.
📞 *06-700 8227.* 🚌 *75, 81, 117, 175,
673.* 🚊 *30b.* Ⓜ *Circo Massimo.*
Open *8:30am–12:30pm, 1:45–6:30pm
daily.* ✝

Façade of San Gregorio Magno

T O THE ENGLISH, this is one
of the most important
churches in Rome, for it was
from here that St. Augustine
was sent on his mission to
convert England to Christianity.
The church was founded in AD
575 by San Gregorio Magno (St.
Gregory the Great), who turned
his family home on this site into
a monastery. It was rebuilt in
medieval times and restored in
1629–33 by Giovanni Battista
Soria. The church is reached via
a flight of steps from the street.

The forecourt contains some
interesting tombs. To the left
is that of Sir Edward Carne,
who came to Rome several
times between 1529 and 1533
as King Henry VIII's envoy to
gain the pope's consent to the
annulment of Henry's marriage
to Catherine of Aragon.

The interior, remodeled in the mid-
18th century, is Baroque, apart
for the fine mosaic floor and
some ancient columns. At the
end of the right aisle is the
chapel of St. Gregory. Leading
off it, another small chapel, believed to have been the saint's
own cell, houses his episcopal
throne – a Roman chair of
sculpted marble. The Salviati
Chapel on the left contains a
picture of the Virgin said to
have spoken to St. Gregory.

Outside, amid the cypresses
to the left of the church, stand
three small chapels, dedicated
to St. Andrew, St. Barbara and
St. Sylvia (Gregory the Great's
mother). Recently restored,
they contain frescoes by
Domenichino and Guido Reni.

**Marble throne of Gregory the Great
from the 1st century BC**

Arch of Dolabella ❸

Via di San Paolo della Croce.
Map 9 A2. 🚌 *81, 117, 673.*
🚃 *3.* Ⓜ *Colosseo.*

T HE ARCH was built in AD 10
by consuls Caius Junius
Silanus and Cornelius
Dolabella, possibly on the
site of one of the old Servian
Wall's gateways. It was made
of travertine blocks and later
used to support Nero's
extension of the Claudian
aqueduct, built to supply the
Imperial palace on the
Palatine hill.

The restored Arch of Dolabella

Santa Maria in Domnica ❹

Piazza della Navicella 12.
Map 9 A2. 🄲 *06-700 1519.*
🚌 *81, 117, 673.* 🚃 *3.* Ⓜ *Colosseo.*
Open *9am–noon, 3:30–6pm (winter),
4–7pm (summer) daily.* 🚻 ⚿

T HE CHURCH overlooks the
Piazza della Navicella
(little boat) and takes its name
from the 16th-century fountain.

Dating from the 7th century,
the church was made from an
ancient stone galley, which
was probably a temple
offering of a Roman traveler
for his safe return to the city.
In the 16th century Pope Leo
X added the portico and the
coffered ceiling.
    In the apse behind the
modern altar is a superb 9th-
century mosaic commissioned
by Pope Paschal I. Wearing
the square halo of the living,
the Pope appears at the feet of
the Virgin and Child. The
Virgin, surrounded by a throng
of angels, holds a handkerchief
in the manner of a fashionable
lady at a Byzantine court.

Villa Celimontana ❺

Piazza della Navicella. **Map** 9 A2.
🚌 *81, 117, 673.* **Park open**
7am–dusk daily.

T HE DUKES OF MATTEI bought
this land in 1553 and transformed the vineyards that covered the hillside into a formal
garden. As well as palms and
other exotic trees, the garden
has its own Egyptian obelisk.
Villa Mattei, built in the 1580s
and now known as Villa
Celimontana, houses the Italian
Geographical Society.
    The Mattei family used to
open the park to the public
on the day of the Visit of the
Seven Churches, an annual
event instituted by San Filippo
Neri in 1552. Starting from the
Chiesa Nuova *(see p124),*
Romans went on foot to the
city's seven major churches
and, on reaching Villa Mattei,

were given bread, wine, salami,
cheese, an egg and two apples.
The garden, now owned by
the city of Rome, still makes
an ideal place for a picnic. In
summer it hosts an excellent
jazz festival *(see p344).*

Park of Villa Celimontana

San Sisto Vecchio ❻

Piazzale Numa Pompilio 8.
Map 9 A3. 🄲 *06-7720 5174.*
🚌 *160, 628, 671, 714.* **Open** *by
appt only.* 🚫

T HIS SMALL CHURCH is of great
historical interest, for it
was granted to St. Dominic in
1219 by Pope Honorius III.
The founder of the Dominican
order soon moved his own
headquarters to Santa Sabina
(see p204), San Sisto becoming
the first home of the order of
Dominican nuns. The church
with its 13th-century bell
tower and frescoes, is also a
popular place for weddings.

Apse mosaic of the Virgin and Child in Santa Maria in Domnica

Santi Nereo e Achilleo ➐

Via delle Terme di Caracalla 28. **Map** 9 A3. **☎** 06-575 7996. **🚌** 160, 628, 671, 714. **Open** Apr–Oct: 10am–noon, 4–6pm Wed–Mon. &

ACCORDING to legend, St. Peter, after escaping from prison, was fleeing the city when he lost a bandage from his wounds. The original church was founded here in the 4th century on the spot where the bandage fell, but later it was rededicated to the 1st-century martyrs St. Nereus and St. Achilleus.

Detail of mosaic, Santi Nereo e Achilleo

Restored at the end of the 16th century, the church has retained many medieval features, including some fine 9th-century mosaics on the triumphal arch. A magnificent pulpit rests on an enormous porphyry pedestal that was found nearby in the Baths of Caracalla. The walls of the side naves are decorated with a series of rather grisly 16th-century frescoes by Niccolò Pomarancio, showing in clinical detail how each of the Apostles was martyred.

Fresco by Niccolò Pomarancio of the *Martyrdom of St Simon* in Santi Nereo e Achilleo

San Cesareo ➑

Via di Porta San Sebastiano. **Map** 9 A3. **☎** 06-58 23 01 40. **🚌** 218, 628. **Open** 10am–noon Sun & by appt.

THIS SPLENDID old church, built over Roman ruins of the 2nd century AD, has been closed since 1988. You can still admire Giacomo della Porta's fine Renaissance façade, but by phoning ahead to book a visit, you can also see Cosmatesque mosaic work and carving to rival that of any church in Rome. The episcopal throne, altar and pulpit are decorated with delightful birds and beasts. The church was restored in the 16th century by Pope Clement VIII, whose coat of arms decorates the ceiling.

San Giovanni a Porta Latina ➒

Via di San Giovanni a Porta Latina. **Map** 9 B3. **☎** 06-7049 1777. **🚌** 218, 360, 628. **Open** 8am–12:30pm, 3–6:30pm daily. ✝ &

THE CHURCH of "St. John at the Latin Gate" was founded in the 5th century, rebuilt in 720 and restored in 1191. This is one of the most picturesque of the old Roman churches. Classical columns support the medieval portico, and the 12th-century bell tower is superb. A tall cedar tree shades an ancient well standing in the forecourt. The interior has recently been restored, but it preserves the rare simplicity of its early origins, with ancient columns of varying styles lining the aisles. Traces of early medieval frescoes can still be seen. There are 12th-century frescoes showing 46 different biblical scenes from both the Old and New Testaments, which are among the finest of their kind in Rome.

Fresco, San Giovanni a Porta Latina

San Giovanni in Oleo ➓

Via di Porta Latina. **Map** 9 C4. **🚌** 628. **Adm** ask at S. Giovanni a Porta Latina.

Frieze of San Giovanni in Oleo

THE NAME of this charming octagonal Renaissance chapel means "St. John in Oil." The tiny building marks the spot where, according to legend, St. John was boiled in oil – and came out unscathed, or even refreshed. An earlier chapel is said to have existed on the site; the present one was built in the early 16th century. The design has been attributed to Baldassare Peruzzi or Antonio da Sangallo the Younger. It was restored by Borromini, who altered the roof, crowning it with a cross supported by a sphere decorated with roses. He also added a terra-cotta frieze of roses and palm leaves. The wall paintings inside the chapel include one of St. John in a cauldron of boiling oil.

Niches for funerary urns in the Columbarium of Pomponius Hylas

Columbarium of Pomponius Hylas ⓫

Via di Porta Latina 10. **Map** 9 B4.
🚌 *218, 360, 628.* **Open** *by appt only: permit needed (see p 367).*

Kᴺᴼᶦᴺ ᴬˢ a columbarium because it resembles a dovecote (*columba* is the Latin word for dove), this kind of vaulted tomb was normally built by rich Romans to house the cremated remains of their freedmen. Many similar tombs have been uncovered in this part of Rome, which up until the 3rd century AD lay outside the city wall. This one, ex-cavated in 1831, dates from the 1st century AD. An in-scription informs us that it

is the Tomb of Pomponius Hylas and his wife, Pomponia Vitalinis. Above her name is a "V," which indicates that she was still living when the inscription was made. The tomb was probably a commercial venture. Niches in the interior walls of the columbarium were sold to people who could not afford to build vaults of their own.

Tomb of the Scipios ⓬

Via di Porta San Sebastiano 9.
Map 9 B4. 📞 *06-6710 3819.*
🚌 *218, 360, 628.* **Open** *by appt. Call above number.*

Tʜᴇ ꜱᴄɪᴘɪᴏꜱ were a family of conquering generals. Southern Italy, Corsica, Algeria, Spain and Asia Minor all fell to their victorious Roman armies. The most famous of these generals was Publius Cornelius Scipio Africanus, who defeated the great Carthaginian general Hannibal at the Battle of Zama in 202 BC *(see p21).* Scipio Africanus himself was not buried here in the family tomb, but at Liternum near Naples, where he owned a favorite villa.

The Tomb of the Scipios was discovered in 1780. It

contained various sarcophagi, statues and niches with terra-cotta burial urns. Many of the originals have now been moved to the Vatican Museums, and copies stand in their place.

The earliest sarcophagus was that of Cornelius Scipio Barbatus, consul in 298 BC, for whom the tomb was built. Members of his illustrious family continued to be buried here up to the middle of the 2nd century BC. Excavations in the area have revealed a columbarium similar to that of Pomponius Hylas, a Christian catacomb and a three-story house dating from the 3rd century AD, which was built over the Tomb of the Scipios.

Arch of Drusus ⓭

Via di Porta San Sebastiano.
Map 9 B4. 🚌 *218, 360.*

Arch of Drusus, part of the Aqua Antoniniana aqueduct

Oɴᴄᴇ ᴍɪꜱᴛᴀᴋᴇɴʟʏ identified as a triumphal arch, the Arch of Drusus merely supported the branch aque-duct that supplied the Baths of Caracalla. It was built in the 3rd century AD and so had no connection with Drusus, a stepson of the Emperor Augustus. Monumental in size, it supported the aqueduct across the important main route, Via Appia. The arch still spans right over the old cobbled road, just 160 ft (50 m) short of the well-known gateway Porta San Sebastiano.

Mosaic inscription in the Columbarium of Pomponius Hylas

Fortified gateway of Porta San Sebastiano

Aurelian Wall and Porta San Sebastiano ⑭

Museo delle Mura, Via di Porta San Sebastiano 18. **Map** 9 B4. 🚌 *218, 360.* 📞 *06-7047 5284.* **Open** *9am–7pm Tue–Sun (Oct–Mar closes 5pm Sun); last adm: 30 mins before closing).* **Closed** *public hols.* **Adm charge.**

Most of the Aurelian Wall, begun by the emperor Aurelian (AD 270–75) and completed by his successor, Probus (AD 276–82), has survived. Aurelian ordered its construction as a defense against marauding Germanic tribes, whose raids were penetrating deeper and deeper into Italy. Some 11 miles (18 km) round, with 18 gates and 381 towers, the wall took in all the seven hills of Rome. It was raised to almost twice its original height by Maxentius (AD 306–12).

The wall continued to be Rome's main defense until 1870, when it was breached by Italian artillery just by Porta Pia, close to today's British Embassy. Many of the gates are still in use, and although the city has spread, most of its noteworthy historical and cultural sights still lie within the walls.

Porta San Sebastiano, the gate that leads to the Via Appia Antica *(see p284)* is the largest and best-preserved gateway in the Aurelian Wall. It was rebuilt by Emperor Honorius in the 5th century AD. Originally the Porta Appia, in Christian times it gradually became known as

the Porta San Sebastiano, because the Via Appia led to the Basilica and Catacombs of San Sebastiano, which were popular places of pilgrimage.

It was at this gate that the last triumphal procession to enter the city by the Appian Way was received in state – that of Marcantonio Colonna after the victory of Lepanto over the Turkish fleet in 1571. Today the gate's towers house a museum containing prints and models illustrating the walls' history. From here you can take a short walk along the restored walls. The views are spectacular, especially out over the Via Appia.

Sangallo Bastion ⑮

Viale di Porta Ardeatina. **Map** 9 A4. 🚌 *160.* **Closed** *for restoration.*

Pope Paul III Farnese

Haunted by the memory of the Sack of Rome in 1527 and fearing attack by the Turks, Pope Paul III asked Antonio

da Sangallo the Younger to reinforce the Aurelian Wall. Work on the huge projecting bastion began in 1537. For the moment its massive bulk can only be admired from outside.

Santa Balbina ⑯

Piazza di Santa Balbina 8. **Map** 8 F3. 📞 *06-578 0207.* 🚌 *160.* 🚊 *3.* Ⓜ *Circo Massimo.* **Open** *8am–6pm daily.* ⛪

Overlooking the Baths of Caracalla, this isolated church framed by cypresses is dedicated to Santa Balbina, a 2nd-century virgin martyr. Dating back to the 4th century, this is one of the city's oldest churches. Inside stands the magnificent sculpted and inlaid tomb of Cardinal Stefanus de Surdis, signed by Giovanni di Cosma (1303).

Obelisk of Axum ⑰

Viale delle Terme di Caracalla. **Map** 8 F2. 🚌 *60, 75, 81, 160, 628, 673.* 🚊 *3.* Ⓜ *Circo Massimo.*

Obelisk of Axum

The 4th century Obelisk of Axum was looted from Ethiopia by Mussolini and stands in front of a building commissioned by him to house the Ministry of Italian Africa. The building, completed in 1952, now houses the Food and Agriculture Organization of the United Nations.

Baths of Caracalla ⑱

Viale delle Terme di Caracalla 52.
Map 9 A3. ☎ *06-575 8626.* 🚌 *160, 628.* 🚃 *3.* Ⓜ *Circo Massimo.*
Open *9am–1hr before sunset Tue–Sun; 9am–2pm Mon.* **Closed** *Jan 1, May 1, Dec 25.* **Adm charge.** 📷 🚻 ♿

COMPLETED by Emperor Caracalla in AD 217, the baths functioned for about 300 years, until the "plumbing" was destroyed by invading Goths. Over 1,600 bathers at a time could enjoy the facilities. A Roman bath was a serious business, beginning with a sort of Turkish bath, followed by a spell in the *caldarium*, a large, hot room with pools of water to moisten the atmosphere. Then came the lukewarm *tepidarium*, a visit to the large central meeting place, known as the *frigidarium*, and finally a plunge into the *natatio*, an open-air swimming pool. For the rich,

Fragment of mosaic pavement

this was followed by a rubdown with scented woolen cloths. In addition to the baths, there were spaces for exercise, libraries, art galleries and gardens – creating a true leisure center. Most of the rich marble decorations of the baths were removed by the Farnese family in the 16th century to adorn the interior of Palazzo Farnese *(see p147).* Until

recently, open-air operas were staged here – the vocal exertions of the performers are now thought to pose a threat to the structure of this ancient monument.

Part of one of the gymnasia in the Baths of Caracalla

KEY

- ▢ Caldarium (very hot)
- ▢ Tepidarium (lukewarm)
- ▢ Frigidarium (cold)
- ▢ Natatio (pool)
- ▢ Garden

Conference and meeting rooms

Original front entrance

Changing rooms

Gymnasia

Storage room for oils and perfumes

Greek and Latin libraries

Water tanks

Stadium

Gymnasium

Conference and meeting room

AVENTINE

THIS IS ONE of the most peaceful areas within the walls of the city. Although it is largely residential, there are some unique historic sights. From the top of the Aventine Hill, crowned by the magnificent basilica of Santa Sabina, there are exceptional views across the river to Trastevere and St. Peter's. At the

Mask fountain in courtyard of Santa Sabina

foot of the hill, ancient Rome is preserved in the two small Temples of the Forum Boarium and the Circus Maximus. The liveliest streets are in Testaccio, with its many stores, restaurants and clubs, while to the south, beside Rome's solitary pyramid, the Protestant Cemetery is a lovely oasis of calm.

SIGHTS AT A GLANCE

Churches and Temples
Santa Maria in Cosmedin **1**
San Giorgio in Velabro **3**
San Teodoro **4**
Santa Maria della Consolazione **5**
San Giovanni Decollato **6**
Temples of the Forum Boarium **8**
Santa Sabina **9**
Santi Bonifacio e Alessio **10**
San Saba **15**

Historic Buildings
Casa dei Crescenzi **7**

Arches
Arch of Janus **2**

Historic Streets and Piazzas
Piazza dei Cavalieri di Malta **11**

Ancient Sites
Monte Testaccio **12**
Circus Maximus **16**

Monuments and Tombs
Protestant Cemetery **13**
Pyramid of Caius Cestius **14**

GETTING THERE
The quickest way is by Metro line B to Piramide or Circo Massimo. For a more interesting trip, take tram 3. Several buses go down from Piazza Venezia, including 81, 160 and 628, while 23 and 280 run along Via Marmorata to Piramide.

KEY

	Street-by-Street map
—	City Wall
M	Metro station
P	Parking

SEE ALSO

- *Street Finder*, maps 7, 8, 12
- *Where to Stay* pp294–5
- *Restaurants* pp310–11

Pines and orange trees on the Aventine hill with dome of St. Peter's in the distance

Street-by-Street: Piazza della Bocca della Verità

THE AREA ATTRACTS VISITORS eager to place their hands inside the Bocca della Verità (the Mouth of Truth) in the portico of Santa Maria in Cosmedin. There are many other sights to see in this quiet corner of the city beside the Tiber, which was the site of ancient Rome's first port and its busy cattle market. Substantial Classical remains include two small temples from the Republican age and the Arch of Janus from the later Empire. In the 6th century the area became home to a Greek community from Byzantium, who founded the churches of San Giorgio in Velabro and Santa Maria in Cosmedin.

Sant'Omobono, a late 16th-century church, now stands in isolation in the middle of an important archaeological site. The remains of sacrificial altars and two temples from the 6th century BC have been discovered.

Casa dei Crescenzi
This 11th-century building used columns and capitals from ancient Roman temples ❼

Ponte Rotto, as this forlorn ruined arch in the Tiber is called, means simply "broken bridge." Built in the 2nd century BC, its original name was Pons Aemilius.

★ **Temples of the Forum Boarium**
The tiny round Temple of Hercules and its neighbor, the Temple of Portunus, are the best preserved of Rome's Republican temples ❽

KEY

- - -   Suggested route

0 meters   75

0 yards   75

STAR SIGHTS

★ **Santa Maria in Cosmedin**

★ **Temples of the Forum Boarium**

★ **Santa Maria in Cosmedin**
This medieval church has a mosaic floor and a Gothic altar canopy ❶

Santa Maria della Consolazione
This 16th-century church used to serve a hospital nearby **5**

San Teodoro
The 15th-century portal of this ancient round church is decorated with the arms of Pope Nicholas V **4**

LOCATOR MAP
See Central Rome Map pp12–13

San Giovanni Decollato
The plain Renaissance façade was completed in about 1504 **6**

San Giorgio in Velabro
The simple 12th-century portico of Ionic columns was destroyed by a bomb in 1993 but has been restored **3**

Arch of Janus
This square structure with arches on each side dates from the 4th century AD **2**

The Arco degli Argentari, dedicated to the Emperor Septimius Severus in AD 204, is decorated with scenes of religion and war.

The Fontana dei Tritoni by Carlo Bizzaccheri was built here in 1715. The style shows the powerful influence of Bernini.

VIA DEI FIENILI

VIA DI SAN TEODORO

DECOLLATO

A DELLA
A DELLA
ERITÀ

VIA DEI CERCHI

A GRECA

**Bocca della Verità at
Santa Maria in Cosmedin**

Santa Maria in Cosmedin **❶**

Piazza della Bocca della Verità 18.
Map 8 E1. **(** 06-678 1419. 🚌 *23,
44, 81, 95, 160, 170, 280, 628, 715,
716.* **Open** *winter: 9am–5pm daily;
summer: 9am–6pm daily.* 🔶 🔶 🔶

THIS BEAUTIFUL unadorned
church was built in the
6th century on the site of the
ancient city's food market.
The elegant Romanesque bell
tower and portico were added
during the 12th century. In the
19th century a Baroque façade
was removed and the church
restored to its original
simplicity. It contains many
fine examples of Cosmati work,
in particular the mosaic
pavement, the raised choir, the
bishop's throne and the canopy
over the main altar.

Set into the wall of the
portico is the Bocca della Verità
(Mouth of Truth). This may
have been a drain cover
dating from before the 4th
century BC. Medieval tradition
had it that the formidable jaws
would snap shut over the
hands of those who told lies –
a useful trick for testing the
faithfulness of spouses.

Arch of Janus **❷**

Via del Velabro. **Map** 8 E1. 🚌 *23,
44, 63, 81, 95, 160, 170, 280, 628,
715, 716, 780.*

PROBABLY DATING from the
reign of Constantine, this
imposing four-faced marble
arch stood at the crossroads
on the edge of the Forum
Boarium, near the ancient

docks. Merchants did business
in its shade. On the keystones
above the four arches you can
see small figures of the
goddesses Roma, Juno, Ceres
and Minerva. In medieval times
the arch formed the base of a
tower fortress. It was restored
to its original shape in 1827.

San Giorgio in Velabro **❸**

Via del Velabro 19. **Map** 8 E1.
(06-6920 4534. 🚌 *23, 44,
63, 81, 95, 160, 170, 280, 628,
715, 716, 780.* **Open** *10am–
12:30pm, 4–6:30pm daily.*

**San Giorgio in Velabro after its
restoration in 1999**

IN THE HOLLOW of the street
named after the Velabrum,
the swamp where Romulus
and Remus are said to have
been found by the she-wolf,
is a small church dedicated to
St. George, whose bones lie
under the altar.

The 7th-century basilica has
suffered over the centuries
from periodic floods, and in
1993 a bomb caused exten-

sive damage to the front of
the church. Careful restoration
has, however, returned it to
its original appearance.

A double row of assorted
granite and marble columns
(taken from ancient Roman
temples) divides the triple
nave. The austerity of the
cool grey interior is relieved
by golden frescoes in the
apse (attributed to Pietro
Cavallini, 1295). The facade
and the bell tower date from
the 12th century.

San Teodoro **❹**

Via di San Teodoro 7. **Map** 8 E1.
(06-678 6624. 🚌 *23, 44, 81,
95, 160, 170, 280, 628, 715, 716.*
Closed for restoration.

IF YOU HAPPEN to be in the
area on a Sunday morning,
you will find this small round
6th-century church at the foot
of the Palatine a truly delightful place to visit for a weekly
mass. Inside, the 6th-century
mosaics in the apse are breathtaking, as is the Florentine
cupola (1454). The fetching
outer courtyard was designed
by Carlo Fontana in 1705.

**The church of San Teodoro, one
of Rome's hidden treasures**

The Arch of Janus, where cattle dealers sheltered from the midday sun

Façade of Santa Maria della Consolazione

Santa Maria della Consolazione ❺

Piazza della Consolazione 84.
Map 5 A5. 🕿 06-678 4654.
🚌 23, 44, 63, 81, 95, 160, 170, 280, 628, 715, 716, 780.
Open 8am–noon, 3:30–6pm daily.
🚻 ♿

THE CHURCH STANDS near the foot of the Tarpeian Rock, the site of public executions since the Sabine War *(see p74)*.

In 1385, Giordanello degli Alberini, a condemned nobleman, paid two gold florins for an image of the Virgin Mary to be placed here, to provide some consolation to prisoners in their final moments. From this came the name of the church built here in 1470. It was reconstructed between 1583 and 1606 by Martino Longhi, who provided the early Baroque façade.

The church's 11 side chapels are owned by noble families and local crafts guild members. In the presbytery is the famed image of Mary attributed to Antoniazzo Romano.

San Giovanni Decollato ❻

Via di San Giovanni Decollato 22.
Map 8 E1. 🕿 06-699 0728.
🚌 23, 44, 63, 81, 95, 160, 170, 280, 628, 715, 716, 780. **Open** by appt only. Fax 06-679 1890.

THE MAIN ALTAR is dominated by Giorgio Vasari's *Beheading of St. John* (1553), from which the church takes its name, San Giovanni Decollato. In 1490, Pope Innocent VIII gave this church site to a very specialized Florentine fraternal order. Clad in black robes and hoods, their task was to encourage condemned prisoners to repent and to give them a decent burial after they had been hanged. In the cloisters are seven manholes (one is reserved for women), which received the bodies.

The oratory contains a cycle of frescoes describing the life of St. John the Baptist, by the leading Florentine Mannerists Jacopino del Conte and Francesco Salviati. In style, the figures resemble some of those in the Sistine Chapel.

Casa dei Crescenzi ❼

Via Luigi Petroselli. **Map** 8 E1.
🚌 23, 44, 63, 81, 95, 160, 170, 280, 628, 715, 716, 780.

STUDDED WITH archaeological fragments, the house is what remains of a 11th-century tower fortress. The powerful Crescenzi family built it to keep an eye on the docks of Rome (today the site of the Anagrafe or Public Records Office) and on the bridge where they collected a toll.

Ancient Roman fragments in the Casa dei Crescenzi

Temples of the Forum Boarium ❽

Piazza della Bocca della Verità. **Map** 8 E1. 🚌 44, 81, 95, 160, 170, 628.

Temple of Portunus

THESE MIRACULOUSLY well preserved Republican temples, set in a grassy enclave under the umbrella pines beside the Tiber, are particularly appealing by moonlight. They date from the 2nd century BC and were saved for posterity when they were reconsecrated as Christian churches in the Middle Ages. They offer rare examples of combined elements from Greek and Roman architecture.

The rectangular temple (formerly known as the Temple of Fortuna Virilis) was in fact dedicated to Portunus, the god of rivers and ports – a reference to the nearby port of ancient Rome. Set on a podium, the temple has four Ionic travertine columns fluted at the front and 12 pilasters, embedded in the tufa wall of the *cella* – the room that housed the image of the god. Nearby is the small circular Temple of Hercules. It is often referred to as the Temple of Vesta because of its similarity to the one in the Forum.

Luminous interior of Santa Sabina

Santa Sabina ⑨

Piazza Pietro d'Illiria 1.
Map 8 E2. **(** *06-579 40600.*
🚌 *23, 280, 716.* Ⓜ *Circo Massimo.*
Open *6.30am–12.45pm, 3.30–7pm
daily.* ♿

Hᴵᴳʜ ᴏɴ the Aventine stands an early Christian basilica, founded by Peter of Illyria in AD 425 and restored to its original simplicity in the early 20th century. Light filters through 9th-century windows upon a wide nave framed by white Corinthian columns supporting an arcade decorated with a marble frieze. Over the main door is a 5th-century blue and gold mosaic dedicatory inscription. The pulpit, carved choir and bishop's throne date from the 9th century.

The church was given to the Dominicans in the 13th century and in the nave is the magnificent mosaic tombstone of one of the first leaders of the order, Muñoz de Zamora (died 1300).

The side portico has 5th-century paneled doors carved from cypress wood, representing scenes from the Bible, including one of the earliest Crucifixions in existence.

Santi Bonifacio e Alessio ⑩

Piazza di Sant'Alessio 23. **Map** 8 D2.
(*06-574 34 46.* 🚌 *23, 280, 716.*
Ⓜ *Circo Massimo.* **Open** *8am–8pm
daily.* ♿

Tʜᴱ ᴄʜᴜʀᴄʜ is dedicated to two early Christian martyrs, whose remains lie under the main altar. Legend has it that Alessio, son of a rich senator living on the site, fled East to avoid an impending marriage and become a pilgrim. Returning home after many years, he died as a servant, unrecognized, under the stairs of the family entrance hall, clutching the manuscript of his story for posterity.

The original 5th-century church has undergone many changes over time. Noteworthy are the 18th-century façade with its five arches, the restored Cosmati doorway and sidewalk, and the magnificent Romanesque five-story belltower (1217).

An 18th-century Baroque chapel by Andrea Bergondi houses part of the famous staircase. Other relics include the well from Alessio's family home and the glowing Byzantine Madonna of the Intercession brought from Damascus to Rome at the end of the 10th century.

Piazza dei Cavalieri di Malta ⑪

Map 8 D2. 🚌 *23, 280, 716.*
Ⓜ *Circo Massimo.*

Sᴜʀʀᴏᴜɴᴅᴇᴅ ʙʏ cypress trees, this ornate walled piazza decorated with obelisks and military trophies was designed by Piranesi in 1765. It is named after the Order of the Knights of Malta (Cavalieri di Malta), whose priory (at No. 3) is famous for the bronze keyhole through which there is a miniature view of St. Peter's, framed by a tree-lined avenue. The priory church, Santa Maria del Priorato, was restored in Neoclassical style by Piranesi in the 18th century. To visit the church, ask permission in person at the Order's building at 48 Via Condotti. At the southwest corner of the square is Sant'Anselmo, the international Benedictine church, where Gregorian chant may be heard on Sundays *(see p342)*.

Doorway of the Priory of the Knights of Malta

Monte Testaccio ⑫

Via Galvani. **Map** 8 D4. Ⓜ *Piramide.*
🚌 *23, 95, 673.* 🚋 *3.* **Open** *by appt
only (see p367).*

Fʀᴏᴍ ᴀʙᴏᴜᴛ 140 BC to AD 250 this hill was created by dumping millions of *testae* (hence Testaccio) – pieces of the amphorae used to carry goods to nearby warehouses. The full archaeological significance of this 118-ft (36-m) high artificial hill was not realized until the late 18th century.

Façade of Santi Bonifacio e Alessio

Protestant Cemetery ⑬

Cimitero Acattolico, Via Caio Cestio 6.
Map 8 D4. ☎ 06-574 1900.
🚌 23, 95, 280. 🚊 3.
Ⓜ Piramide. **Open** 9am–5.30pm
(Oct–Mar: 4.30pm) Tue–Sun.
Donation expected. 🚻

THE PEACE of this well-tended cemetery beneath the Aurelian Wall is profoundly moving. Non-Catholics, mainly English and German, have been buried here since 1738.

In the oldest part are the graves of John Keats (died 1821 – his epitaph reads: "Here lies One Whose Name was writ in Water"), and his friend Joseph Severn (died 1879); not far away are the ashes of Percy Bysshe Shelley (died 1822). Goethe's son Julius is also buried here.

Tombstone of John Keats

Pyramid of Caius Cestius ⑭

Piazzale Ostiense. **Map** 8 E4. 🚌 23, 95, 280. 🚊 3. Ⓜ Piramide.

Detail of carving on sarcophagus in the portico of San Saba

San Saba ⑮

Via di San Saba.
Map 8 F3. ☎ 06-574 3352.
🚌 75, 175, 673. 🚊 3.
Open 7am–noon, 4–6.30pm daily. 🚻

TUCKED AWAY in a residential street on the Little Aventine hill, San Saba began life as an oratory for Palestinian monks fleeing from Arab invasions in the 7th century. The existing church dates from the 10th century and has undergone much restoration. The portico houses a fascinating collection of archaeological remains.

The church has three naves in the Greek style and a short fourth 11th-century nave to the left with vestiges of 13th-century frescoes of the life of St. Nicholas of Bari. Particularly intriguing is a scene of three naked young ladies lying in bed, who are saved from

Reconstruction of the Circus Maximus in its heyday

penury by the gift of a bag of gold from St. Nicholas, the future Santa Claus. The beautiful marble inlay in the main door, the floor and the remains of the choir are all 13th-century Cosmati work.

Circus Maximus ⑯

Via del Circo Massimo.
Map 8 F2. 🚌 81, 160, 628, 715.
🚊 3. Ⓜ Circo Massimo.

WHAT WAS ONCE ancient Rome's largest stadium is today little more than a long grassy esplanade. Set in the valley between the Palatine and Aventine hills, the Circus Maximus was continually embellished and expanded from the 4th century BC until AD 549 when the last races were held. The grandstands held some 300,000 spectators, cheering wildly at the horse and chariot races, athletic contests and animal fights, and betting furiously throughout.

The Circus had a central dividing barrier (spina) with seven large egg-shaped objects on it used for counting the laps of a race. These were joined in 33 BC by seven bronze dolphins that served a similar purpose. In 10 BC Augustus built the Imperial box under the Palatine and decorated the spina with the obelisk that now stands in the center of Piazza del Popolo (see p137). A second obelisk, which was added in the 4th century by Constantine II, is now in Piazza di San Giovanni in Laterano (see pp178–9).

CAIUS CESTIUS, a wealthy praetor (senior Roman magistrate), died in 12 BC. His one claim to fame is his tomb, an imposing pyramid faced in white marble set in the Aurelian Wall near Porta San Paolo. It stands 118 ft (36 m) high and, according to an inscription, took 330 days to build. Unmistakable as a landmark, it must have looked almost as incongruous when it was built as it does today.

Memorial pyramid of Caius Cestius

TRASTEVERE

THE PROUD and aggressively independent inhabitants of Trastevere, the area "across the Tiber", consider themselves the most authentic Romans. In one of the most picturesque old quarters of the city, it is still possible to glimpse scenes of everyday life that seem to belong to bygone centuries. There are, however, signs that much of the earthy, proletarian character of the place may soon be destroyed by the proliferation of fashionable restau-

Romanesque bell tower

rants, clubs and boutiques. Some of Rome's most fascinating medieval churches lie hidden away in the patchwork of narrow, cobbled backstreets, the only clue to their location an occasional glimpse of a Romanesque bell tower. Santa Cecilia was built on the site of the martyrdom of the patron saint of music, San Francesco a Ripa commemorates St. Francis of Assisi's visit to Rome, and Santa Maria in Trastevere is the traditional center of the spiritual and social life of the area.

SIGHTS AT A GLANCE

Churches
Santa Maria della Scala ❸
Santa Maria in Trastevere
pp212–13 ❺
San Crisogono ❻
Santa Cecilia in Trastevere ❽
San Francesco a Ripa ❿

Museums and Galleries
Sant'Egidio and Museo
di Roma in Trastevere ❹

Historic Buildings
Casa della Fornarina ❶
Caserma dei Vigili della
VII Coorte ❼
San Michele a Ripa Grande ❾

Bridges
Ponte Sisto ❷

Parks and Gardens
Villa Sciarra ⓫

SEE ALSO

- **Street Finder**, maps 4, 7, 8, 11
- **Where to Stay** pp294–5
- **Restaurants** pp310–11
- **Tiber Walk** pp274–5

KEY

▨	Street-by-Street map
—	City Wall
P	Parking
ℹ	Tourist information

GETTING THERE
The most convenient way is to take tram 8 which starts from Largo di Torre Argentina, crosses the river and runs along the broad, busy Viale di Trastevere. The H bus follows the same route but starts at Stazione Termini. From the Vatican it is best to take a 23 or 280 along Lungotevere.

0 meters	300
0 yards	300

A typical *vicolo* (narrow alleyway) between the densely packed buildings of Trastevere

Street-by-Street: Trastevere

ALL YEAR ROUND TRASTEVERE is a major attraction both for its restaurants, clubs and cinemas, and for its picturesque maze of narrow cobbled alleyways. On summer evenings the streets are packed with jostling groups of pleasure seekers, especially during the noisy local festival, the Festa de Noantri *(see p59)*. Everywhere café and restaurant tables spill out over pavements, especially around Piazza di Santa Maria in Trastevere and outside the pizzerias along Viale di Trastevere. There are also kiosks selling slices of watermelon and *grattachecca*, a mixture of syrup and grated ice. It is usually easier to appreciate the antique charm of Trastevere's narrow streets in the more tranquil atmosphere of the early morning.

Casa della Fornarina
Raphael's beautiful mistress is said to have lived here. There is now a flourishing restaurant in the back garden ❶

Santa Maria dei Sette Dolori
This church (1643) is a minor work by Borromini.

Santa Maria della Scala
The church's unassuming façade conceals a rich Baroque interior ❸

Sant'Egidio and Museo del Folklore
This 17th-century fresco of Sant' Egidio by Pomarancio decorates the left-hand chapel in the church. The convent next door is a museum of Roman life and customs ❹

★ Santa Maria in Trastevere
The church is famous for its mosaics by Pietro Cavallini but it also has earlier works such as this mosaic of the prophet Isaiah to the left of the apse ❺

STAR SIGHT
★ Santa Maria in Trastevere

KEY

- - - Suggested route

0 meters   75

0 yards   75

The fountain of Piazza di Santa Maria in Trastevere by Carlo Fontana (1692) is a popular meeting place. At night it is floodlit and dozens of young people sit on the steps around its octagonal base.

Ponte Sisto
This bridge was built on the orders of Sixtus IV in 1474 to link Trastevere to central Rome ❷

LOCATOR MAP
See Central Rome Map pp12–13

Piazza Belli is named after Giuseppe Gioacchino Belli (1791–1863), who wrote satirical sonnets in Roman dialect rather than academic Italian. At the centre of the piazza stands a statue of the poet (1913).

Vicolo del Piede is one of the picturesque narrow streets lined with restaurant tables leading off Piazza di Santa Maria in Trastevere.

The Torre degli Anguillara (13th century) is the only survivor of the many medieval towers that once dominated the Trastevere skyline.

Caserma dei Vigili della VII Coorte
The courtyard of this antique Roman fire station still stands ❼

San Crisogono
The Romanesque bell tower dates from the early 12th century. The plain portico is a later addition (1626), but is in keeping with the spirit of this ancient church ❻

Casa della Fornarina ❶

Via di Santa Dorotea 20. **Map** 4 D5 & 11 B5. 🚌 23, 280. *See Restaurants p316.*

NOT MUCH is known about Raphael's model and lover, La Fornarina, yet over the centuries she has acquired a name, Margherita, and even a biography. Her father was a Sienese baker (*la fornarina* means the baker's girl) and his shop was here in Trastevere near Raphael's frescoes in the Villa Farnesina *(see pp220–21).*

Margherita earned a reputation as a "fallen woman" and Raphael, wishing to be absolved before dying, turned her away from his deathbed. After his death she took refuge in the convent of Santa Apollonia in Trastevere.

She is assumed to have been the model for Raphael's famous portrait *La Donna Velata* in the Palazzo Pitti in Florence.

Ponte Sisto ❷

Map 4 E5 & 11 B5. 🚌 23, 280.

NAMED AFTER Pope Sixtus IV della Rovere (reigned 1471–84), who commissioned it, this bridge was built by Baccio Pontelli to replace an ancient Roman bridge. The enterprising pope also built the Sistine Chapel *(see pp244–7)*, the Hospital of Santo Spirito *(see p226)* and restored many churches and monuments. This put him in great financial difficulties and he had to sell personal collections in order to finance his projects.

Another method of financing projects was to levy a tax on the city's prostitutes. Several popes are known to have re-sorted to this un-popular form of taxation.

Pope Sixtus IV

Gilded Baroque altar of Santa Maria della Scala

Santa Maria della Scala ❸

Piazza della Scala 23. **Map** 4 D5 & 11 B5. 📞 06-580 62 33. 🚌 23, 280. **Church open** 7am–12:30pm, 3:30–7pm daily. 🚻

THIS CHURCH belongs to a time of great building activity that lasted about 30 years from the end of the 16th to the early 17th century. Its rather simple façade contrasts with a rich interior decorated with multicoloured marbles and a number of spirited Baroque altars and reliefs.

Sant'Egidio and Museo di Roma in Trastevere ❹

Piazza Sant'Egidio 1. **Map** 7 C1. 🚌 H, 23, 280. 📺 8. **Church** 📞 06-58 56 61. *Not open to the public.* **Museo di Roma in Trastevere** 📞 06-581 6563. **Open** 10am–8pm Tue–Sun. ♿

BUILT IN 1630, Sant'Egidio was the church of the adjoining Carmelite convent, one of many founded in the area to shelter the poor and destitute. The convent is now a folklore museum, containing a wealth of material relating to the festivals, pastimes, superstitions and customs of the Romans when they lived under papal rule.

There are old paintings and prints of the city and tableaux showing scenes of everyday life in 18th- and 19th-century Rome, including reconstructions of shops and a tavern.

The museum also has manuscripts by the much-loved poets Belli and Trilussa who wrote in local dialect.

Watercolour of public scribe (1880) in the Museo di Roma in Trastevere

Santa Maria in Trastevere ❺

See pp212–13.

San Crisogono ❻

Piazza Sonnino 44. **Map** 7 C1. 📞 06-581 82 25. 🚌 H, 23, 280, 780. 📺 8. **Open** 7–11:30am, 4:15–7:30pm, Mon–Sat; 8:30am–1pm, 4:15–7:30pm Sun. **Adm charge** for excavations. 🚻 ♿

THIS CHURCH was built on the site of one of the city's oldest *tituli* (private houses used for Christian worship). An 8th-century church with 11th-century frescoes can still be seen beneath the present church. This dates from the early 12th century, a period of intense building activity in Rome. San Crisogono was decorated by

Apse mosaic in San Crisogono

Pietro Cavallini – the apse mosaic by his school remains.

Most of the columns were taken from previous buildings, including the great porphyry ones of the triumphal arch. The mosaic floor is the result of recycling precious marble from various Roman ruins.

Caserma dei Vigili della VII Coorte **❼**

Via della VII Coorte.
Map 7 C1. 📞 *06-6710 3819.*
🚌 *H, 23, 280, 780.* 🚃 *8.*
Open *by appt.*

NOT ALL ROMAN RUINS are Imperial villas or grand temples; one that illustrates the daily life of a busy city is the barracks of the guards of the VII Coorte, the Roman fire brigade. It was built under Augustus' reign, in the 1st century AD, and the excavated courtyard is where the men would rest while waiting for an alarm.

Santa Cecilia in Trastevere **❽**

Piazza di Santa Cecilia. **Map** 8 D1.
📞 *06-589 9289.* 🚌 *H, 23, 44, 280.*
🚃 *8.* **Open** *9:30am–12:30pm,*
4–7pm daily. **Adm charge**
for excavations. *Cavallini fresco*
can be seen 10–11:30am Tue & Thu;
11:30am–noon Sun.

ST. CECILIA, ARISTOCRAT and patron saint of music, was martyred here in AD 230. After an attempt at scalding her to death, she was beheaded. A church was founded – perhaps in the 4th century – on the site of her house. (The house, beneath the church with the remains of a Roman tannery, is well worth a visit.). Her body turned up in the Catacombs of San Callisto (see p265) and was buried here in the 9th century by Pope Paschal I, who rebuilt the church. A fine apse mosaic survives from this period.

The altar canopy by Arnolfo di Cambio and the fresco of *The Last Judgment* by Pietro Cavallini, reached through the adjoining convent, date from the 13th century, one of the few periods when Rome had

Detail of 13th-century fresco by Pietro Cavallini in Santa Cecilia

a distinctive artistic style of its own. In front of the altar is a statue of St. Cecilia by Stefano Maderno, who used her miraculously preserved remains as a model when she was briefly disinterred in 1599.

San Michele a Ripa Grande **❾**

Via di San Michele. **Map** 8 D2.
📞 *06-584 31.* 🚌 *23, 44, 75, 280.*
Open *for special exhibitions only.*

THIS HUGE, IMPOSING complex, now housing the Ministry of Culture, stretches 985 ft (300 m) along the river Tiber. It was built on the initiative of Pope Innocent XII and contained a home for the elderly, a boys' reform school, a woollen mill

and various chapels. Today contemporary exhibitions are often held here.

San Francesco a Ripa **❿**

Piazza San Francesco d'Assisi 88.
Map 7 C2. 📞 *06-581 9020.*
🚌 *H, 23, 44, 75, 280.* 🚃 *8.*
Open *8am–noon, 4–7pm Mon–Sat,*
7am–1pm, 4–7:30pm Sun. 🚻 ♿

ST FRANCIS OF ASSISI lived here in a hospice when he visited Rome in 1219 and his stone pillow and crucifix are preserved in his cell. The church was rebuilt by his follower, the nobleman Rodolfo Anguillara, who is portrayed on his tombstone wearing the Franciscan habit.

Entirely rebuilt in the 1680s by Cardinal Pallavicini, the church is rich in sculptures. Particularly flamboyant are the 18th-century Rospigliosi and Pallavicini monuments in the transept chapel.

The Paluzzi-Albertoni chapel (fourth on the left, along the nave) contains Bernini's breathtaking *Ecstasy of Beata Ludovica Albertoni.*

Villa Sciarra **⓫**

Via Calandrelli 35. **Map** 7 B2. 🚌 *44,*
75. **Park open** *9am–sunset daily.*
House closed for restoration. ♿

IN ROMAN TIMES the site of this small, attractive public park was a nymph's sanctuary. It is especially picturesque in spring when its wisterias are in full bloom. The paths through the park are decorated with Romantic follies, fountains and statues, and there are splendid views over the bastions of the Janiculum.

Bernini's *Ecstasy of Beata Ludovica Albertoni* (1674) in San Francesco a Ripa

Santa Maria in Trastevere ⑤

PROBABLY THE FIRST official Christian place of worship to be built in Rome, this basilica became the focus of devotion to the Virgin Mary. According to legend, the church was founded by Pope Callixtus I in the 3rd century, when Christianity was still a minority cult. Today's church is largely a 12th-century building, remarkable for its mosaics, in particular those by Pietro Cavallini. The 22 granite columns in the nave were taken from the ruins of ancient Roman buildings. Despite some 18th-century Baroque additions, Santa Maria has retained its medieval character. This friendly church has strong links with the local community.

Piazza Santa Maria in Trastevere
The piazza in front of the church is the traditional heart of Trastevere. Today it is surrounded by lively bars and restaurants. Carlo Fontana built the octagonal fountain in the late 17th century.

The floor, relaid in the 1870s, is a re-creation of the Cosmatesque mosaic floor of the 13th century.

The bell tower was built in the 12th century. At the top is a small mosaic of the Virgin.

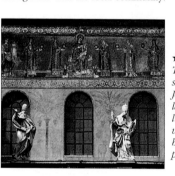

★ Façade Mosaics
The 12th-century mosaic shows Mary feeding the baby Jesus and ten women holding lamps. Eight of the lamps are lit, symbolizing virginity; the veiled women whose lamps have gone out are probably widows.

STAR FEATURES

★ **Cavallini Mosaics**

★ **Façade Mosaics**

MODEST DONORS

Many of Rome's mosaics include a portrait of the pope or cardinal responsible for the building of the church. Often the portrait is dwarfed by the rest of the picture, which glorifies the saint to whom the church is dedicated. On the façade of Santa Maria, two tiny unidentified figures kneel at the Virgin's feet. Were they to stand up, the men would barely reach her knees.

Façade mosaic, detail

The portico was remodeled in 1702 by Carlo Fontana. Statues of four popes decorate the balustrade above.

Front entrance

15th-century wall tabernacle by Mino del Reame

Apse Mosaic
The 12th-century mosaic in the basin of the apse shows the Coronation of the Virgin. She sits on Christ's right hand, surrounded by saints.

VISITORS' CHECKLIST

Piazza Santa Maria in Trastevere.
Map 7 C1. ☎ 06-581 4802.
🚌 H & 780 to Piazza S. Sonnino
23 & 280 along Lungotevere
Sanzio. 🚋 8.
Open 7am–8pm daily.
✝ 6pm daily. ♿ 🚻

★ Cavallini Mosaics
The details in the six mosaics of the Life of the Virgin (1291) display a touching realism.

Madonna della Clemenza
The life-size icon probably dates from the 7th century. A replica is displayed above the altar of the Cappella Altemps.

Tomb of Cardinal Pietro Stefaneschi
The last of his line, Pietro Stefaneschi died in 1417. His tomb is by an otherwise unknown sculptor called Paolo.

TIMELINE

30 BC	AD 200	1150	1400	1650	1900
	AD 217–22 Church founded by Pope Callixtus I	*Pope Innocent II*	**1291** Pietro Cavallini adds mosaics of scenes from the life of the Virgin for his patron, Bertoldo Stefaneschi	**1617** Domenichino designs coffered ceiling with octagonal panel of the Assumption of the Virgin	
38 BC Jet of mineral oil spouts from the ground on this site. Later interpreted as a portent of the coming of Christ		**c1138** Pope Innocent II starts rebuilding the church	**1580** Martino Longhi the Elder restores church and builds family chapel for Cardinal Marco Sittico Altemps	**1702** Pope Clement XI has portico rebuilt **1866–77** Church restored by Virginio Vespignani	

JANICULUM

OVERLOOKING THE TIBER
on the Trastevere
side of the river, the
Janiculum Hill has often
played its part in the
defense of the city. The
last occasion was in
1849, when Garibaldi
held off attacking French
troops. The park at the
top of the hill is filled with
monuments to Garibaldi
and his men. A popular
place for walks, the park
provides a welcome escape from the
densely packed streets of Trastevere.

**Puppets in the park at the
top of the Janiculum hill**

Visitors will often find puppet
shows and other entertainment
and activities for children.
In medieval times, most of
the hill was occupied by
monasteries and con-
vents. Bramante built his
miniature masterpiece, the
Tempietto, in the convent of
San Pietro in Montorio. The
Renaissance also saw the
development of the river-
side area along Via della
Lungara, where the rich
and powerful built large beautiful
houses such as the Villa Farnesina.

SIGHTS AT A GLANCE

Churches and Temples
Sant'Onofrio ❻
San Pietro in Montorio ❼
Tempietto ❽

Museums and Galleries
Palazzo Corsini and Galleria
Nazionale d'Arte Antica ❷

Historic Buildings
Villa Farnesina
pp220–21 ❶

Fountains
Fontana dell'Acqua
Paola ❾

Monuments
Garibaldi Monument ❺

Arches and Gates
Porta Settimiana ❸

Parks and Gardens
Botanical Gardens ❹

SEE ALSO

GETTING THERE

The Janiculum (Il Gianicolo) is
not the easiest part of Rome to
reach by public transport. It
can be approached either
from the Vatican area *(see
p223)* or from Trastevere
(see p207). There is only one
bus, the 870, that goes up to
the top of the hill, but the 44
will take you from Piazza
Venezia to Via Giacinto Carini
from where you start your walk
up. For sights along Via della
Lungara, take the 23 or 280,
which go along Lungotevere.

| 0 meters | 300 |
| 0 yards | 300 |

KEY

▢ Tour of the Janiculum map

– City Wall

The staircase fountain in the Botanical Gardens

A Tour of the Janiculum

THE LONG HIKE to the top of the Janiculum is rewarded by wonderful views over the city. The park's monuments include a lighthouse and statues of Garibaldi and his wife Anita. There is also a cannon which is fired at noon each day. In Via della Lungara, between the Janiculum and the Tiber, stand Palazzo Corsini with its national art collection and the Villa Farnesina, decorated by Raphael for his friend and patron, the fabulously wealthy banker Agostino Chigi.

Tasso's Oak is a memorial to the poet Torquato Tasso, who liked to sit here in the days before he died in 1595. The tree was struck by lightning in 1843.

The Manfredi Lighthouse, built in 1911, was a gift to the city of Rome from Italians in Argentina.

The Monument to Anita Garibaldi by Mario Rutelli was erected in 1932. The great patriot's Brazilian wife lies buried beneath the statue.

The view from Villa Lante, a beautiful Renaissance summer residence, gives a magnificent panorama of the whole city.

ROMA O MORTE

Garibaldi Monument
The inscription on the base of the equestrian statue says "Rome or Death" ➎

Botanical Gardens
These were established in 1883 when part of the grounds of Palazzo Corsini was given to the University of Rome ④

★ Palazzo Corsini
This 15th-century triptych by Fra Angelico hangs in the Galleria Nazionale d'Arte Antica ②

LOCATOR MAP
See Central Rome Map pp12–13

★ Villa Farnesina
The suburban villa of the banker Agostino Chigi is celebrated for its frescoes by Raphael, Baldassarre Peruzzi and other Renaissance masters ①

Porta Settimiana
Looking through this Renaissance gateway from Via della Lungara, you catch a glimpse of Trastevere's warren of narrow streets ③

KEY

– – – Suggested route

0 meters	75
0 yards	75

STAR SIGHTS

★ Villa Farnesina

★ Palazzo Corsini and Galleria Nazionale d'Arte Antica

Villa Farnesina ❶

See pp220–21.

Palazzo Corsini and Galleria Nazionale d'Arte Antica ❷

Via della Lungara 10. **Map** 4 D5 & 11 A5. **☎** 06-6880 2323. **🚌** 23, 280. **Open** 9am–7pm Tue–Fri, 9am–2pm Sat, 9am–1pm Sun & public hols. **Closed** Jan 1, May 1, Aug 15 & Dec 25. **Adm charge**. ⊘ 🖗 & 🖳 W www.galleriaborghese.it

Queen Christina's bedroom in the Palazzo Corsini

T HE HISTORY of Palazzo Corsini is intimately en-twined with that of Rome. Built for Cardinal Domenico Riario in 1510–12, it has boasted among its many distinguished guests Bramante, the young Michelangelo, Erasmus and Queen Christina of Sweden, who died here in 1689. The old palazzo was completely re-built for Cardinal Neri Corsini by Ferdinando Fuga in 1736. As Via della Lungara is too narrow for a good frontal view, Fuga designed the façade so it could be seen from an angle.

Palazzo Corsini now houses the Galleria Nazionale d'Arte Antica, also known as Galleria Corsini. This outstanding collection includes paintings by Rubens, Van Dyck, Murillo, Caravaggio and Guido Reni, as well as 17th- and 18th-century Italian regional art. The palazzo is also home to the Accademia dei Lincei, a

learned society founded in 1603, which once included Galileo among its members.

In 1797 Palazzo Corsini was the backdrop to momentous events: French General Duphot (the fiancé of Napoleon's sister Pauline) was killed here in a skirmish between papal troops and Republicans. The consequent French occupation of the city and the deportation of Pope Pius VI led to the proclamation of a short-lived Roman Republic (1798–9).

Porta Settimiana ❸

Between Via della Scala and Via della Lungara. **Map** 4 D5 & 11 B5. **🚌** 23, 280.

T HIS GATE was built in 1498 by Pope Alexander VI Borgia to replace a minor passageway in the Aurelian Wall. The Porta Settimiana marks the start of Via della Lungara, a long straight road built in the early 16th century.

Botanical Gardens ❹

Largo Cristina di Svezia 24, off Via Corsini. **Map** 4 D5. **☎** 06-4991 7106. **🚌** 23, 280. **Open** Apr–Sep: 9:30am–6:30pm Tue–Sat (Oct–Mar: 5:30pm). **Closed** public hols and Aug. **Adm charge** 🖗 (phone to book).

S EQUOIAS, PALM TREES and splendid collections of orchids and bromeliads are housed in Rome's Botanical Gardens *(Orto Botanico)*. These tranquil gardens contain more than 7,000 plant species from all over the world.

Indigenous and exotic species are grouped to illustrate their botanical families and their adaptation to different climates and ecosystems. There are also plants such as the gingko that have survived virtually unchanged from earlier eras. The gardens were originally part of the Palazzo Corsini but since 1983 have belonged to the University of Rome.

Garibaldi Monument ❺

Piazzale Giuseppe Garibaldi. **Map** 3 C5. **🚌** 870.

Base of the Garibaldi Monument

T HIS HUGE equestrian statue is part of a park that commemorates the heroic events witnessed on the Janiculum when the French army attacked the city in 1849. Garibaldi's Republicans fended off the greatly superior French forces for weeks, until the Italians were overwhelmed. Garibaldi and his men escaped. The monument, erected in 1895, was the work of Emilio Gallori. Around the pedestal are four smaller sculptures in bronze showing battle scenes and allegorical figures.

Steps and tiered fountains at the Botanical Gardens

Courtyard of Sant'Onofrio

Sant'Onofrio ❻

Piazza di Sant'Onofrio 2. **Map** 3 C4.
☎ 06-686 44 98. ████ 870. **Open**
10am–4pm Mon–Sat (Sun for mass
only). **Closed** Aug, except Saint's
feast day on Aug 12. **☎ Museum
open** by appt only. **☎** 06-682 8121.

BEATO NICOLA da Forca
Palena, whose tombstone
guards the entrance, founded
this church in 1419 in honor
of the hermit Sant'Onofrio. It
retains the flavor of the 15th
century in the simple shapes
of the portico and the cloister.
In the early 17th century the
portico was decorated with
frescoes by Domenichino.

The monastery next to the
church houses a small museum
dedicated to the 16th-century
poet Torquato Tasso, who
died here in one of the cells.

San Pietro in Montorio ❼

Piazza San Pietro in Montorio 2.
Map 7 B1. **☎** 06-581 39 40. ████ 44,
75. **Open** 7:30am–noon, 4–6pm
daily. If closed, ring bell at door to
right of church. **☎**

SAN PIETRO IN MONTORIO – the
church of St. Peter on the
Golden Hill – was founded in
the Middle Ages near the spot
where St. Peter was presumed
to have been crucified. It was
rebuilt by order of Ferdinand
and Isabella of Spain at the
end of the 15th century and
decorated by outstanding
artists of the Renaissance.

The façade is typical of a
time when clean, geometric
shapes derived from Classical
architecture were in vogue.
The single nave ends in a
deep apse that once contained

Raphael's *Transfiguration*,
now in the Vatican. Two wide
chapels, one on either side of
the nave, were decorated by
some of Michelangelo's most
famous pupils. The left chapel
was designed by one of the
few artists Michelangelo
admired, Daniele da Volterra,
who was also responsible for
the altar painting, *The Baptism
of Christ*. The chapel on the
right was the work of Giorgio
Vasari, who included a self-
portrait (in black, on the left)
in his biblical altar painting,
The Conversion of St. Paul.

The first chapel to the right
of the entrance contains the
powerful *Flagellation*, by
Venetian artist Sebastiano del
Piombo (1518); Michelangelo
is said to have provided the
original drawings. Work by
Bernini and his followers can
be seen in the second chapel
on the left and in the flanking
De Raymondi tombs.

Tempietto ❽

Piazza San Pietro in Montorio (in courtyard). **Map** 7 B1. **☎** 06-581 3940.
████ 44, 75. **Open** 9:30am–12:30pm,
2–4pm (summer 4–6pm) Tue–Sun.
See **The History of Rome** pp30–31.

AROUND 1502 BRAMANTE com-
pleted what many consider
to be the first true Renaissance building in Rome – the
Tempietto. The name means
simply "little temple." Its
circular shape echoes early
Christian *martyria*,
chapels built on
the site of a saint's
martyrdom. This
was believed to be
the place where St.
Peter was crucified.

Bramante chose
the Doric order for
the 16 columns
surrounding the
domed chapel.
Above the columns
is a Classical frieze
and a delicate
balustrade. Though
the scale of the
Tempietto is tiny,
Bramante's masterly
use of Classical
proportions creates
a satisfyingly
harmonious whole.

The Tempietto illustrates the
great Renaissance dream that
Rome would relive its ancient
glory.

Fontana dell'Acqua Paola ❾

Via Garibaldi. **Map** 7 B1. ████ 44, 75.

Fontana dell'Acqua Paola

THIS MONUMENTAL FOUNTAIN
commemorates the
reopening in 1612 of an
aqueduct originally built by
Emperor Trajan in AD 109.
The aqueduct was renamed
the Acqua Paola after Paul V,
the Borghese pope who
ordered its restoration. When
it was first built, the fountain
had five small basins, but in
1690 Carlo Fontana altered the
design, adding the huge basin
you can see today. Despite
many laws intended to deter
them, generations of Romans
used this convenient pool of
fresh water for bathing and
washing their vegetables.

Bramante's round chapel, the Tempietto

Villa Farnesina ❶

THE WEALTHY SIENESE BANKER Agostino Chigi, who had established the headquarters of his far-flung financial empire in Rome, commissioned the villa in 1508 from his compatriot Baldassarre Peruzzi. The simple, harmonious design, with a central block and projecting wings, made this one of the earliest true Renaissance villas. The decoration was carried out between 1510 and 1519, and this has recently been restored. Peruzzi frescoed some of the interiors himself. Later, Sebastiano del Piombo, Raphael and his pupils added more elaborate works. The frescoes illustrate Classical myths, and the vault of the main hall, the Sala di Galatea, is adorned with scenes showing the position of the stars at the time of Chigi's birth. Artists, poets, princes, cardinals and the pope himself were entertained here in style by their wealthy host. In 1577 the villa was bought by Cardinal Alessandro Farnese. Since then, it has been known as the Villa Farnesina.

North Façade
The Loggia of Cupid and Psyche looks out on formal gardens that were used for parties and putting on plays.

Entrance

The Wedding of Alexander and Roxanne by Sodoma
Cherubs are shown helping the bride Roxanne prepare for her marriage.

★ **Triumph of Galatea by Raphael**
The beautiful sea nymph Galatea was one of the 50 daughters of the god Nereus.

The Gabinetto delle Stampe
sometimes holds exhibitions of rare prints.

Frescoes in the Room of Galatea
Perseus beheads Medusa in a scene from one of Peruzzi's series of mythological frescoes.

THE ARCHITECT

Baldassarre Peruzzi, painter and architect, arrived in Rome from Siena in 1503, at age 20, becoming Bramante's chief assistant. His architectural designs were typical of Classicism, but his painting owes more to Gothic influences – his figurework is highly stylized. On Raphael's death, he became Head of Works at St. Peter's but was captured in the Sack of Rome *(see p31)*, exiled to Siena until 1535 and died in 1536.

Baldassarre Peruzzi

★ Salone delle Prospettive
Peruzzi's frescoes create the illusion of looking out at views of 16th-century Rome through a marble colonnade.

Fresco from the Salone delle Prospettive
This scene shows the Torre delle Milizie (see p90) as it looked in the 1500s.

★ Loggia of Cupid and Psyche
The model for the figure on the left in Raphael's painting of The Three Graces was Agostino Chigi's mistress, the courtesan Imperia.

Lunette in the Room of Galatea
Once thought to be by Michelangelo, this giant monochrome head is the work of Peruzzi.

STAR FEATURES

★ **Triumph of Galatea by Raphael**

★ **Loggia of Cupid and Psyche**

★ **Salone delle Prospettive**

VATICAN

As THE SITE where St. Peter was martyred and buried, the Vatican became the residence of the popes who succeeded him. Decisions reached here have shaped the destiny of Europe, and the great basilica of St. Peter's draws pilgrims from all over the Christian world. The papal palaces beside St. Peter's house the Vatican Museums. With the added attractions of Michelangelo's Sistine Chapel and the Raphael Rooms, their wonderful

Nuns in St. Peter's Square

collections of Classical sculpture make them the finest museums in Rome. The Vatican's position as a state within a state was guaranteed by the Lateran Treaty of 1929, marked by the building of a new road, the Via della Conciliazione. This leads from St. Peter's to Castel Sant' Angelo, a monument to a far grimmer past. Built originally as the Emperor Hadrian's mausoleum, this papal fortress and prison has witnessed many fierce battles for control of the city.

SIGHTS AT A GLANCE

Churches and Temples
St. Peter's pp230–33 **1**
Santo Spirito in Sassia **4**
Santa Maria in Traspontina **9**

Museums and Galleries
Vatican Museums pp234–47 **2**

Historic Buildings
Hospital of Santo Spirito **5**
Palazzo del Commendatore **6**
Palazzo dei Convertendi **7**
Palazzo dei Penitenzieri **8**

Palazzo Torlonia **12**
Castel Sant'Angelo pp248–9 **13**
Palazzo di Giustizia **14**

Gates
Porta Santo Spirito **3**

Historic Streets and Piazzas
The Borgo **10**
Vatican Corridor **11**

GETTING THERE
The quickest way to reach the area is by Metro line A to Ottaviano S. Pietro. The 40 and 64 buses run regularly from Piazza dei Cinquecento, in front of Termini station, although the 62 is the only bus which runs along Via della Conciliazione. Other routes that serve the area include the 81 and 492, which stop in Piazza del Risorgimento. There is also a regular shuttle bus between St. Peter's and the Vatican Museums.

| 0 meters | | 400 |
| 0 yards | | 400 |

KEY

- Tour of the Vatican map
- --- City Wall
- P Parking
- i Tourist information

N

SEE ALSO

- **Street Finder**, maps 3, 4
- **Where to Stay** pp294–5
- **Restaurants** pp310–11

Dome of St. Peter's dominating the Vatican skyline

A Tour of the Vatican

THE VATICAN, a center of power for Catholics all over the world and a sovereign state since February 1929, is ruled by the pope. About 1,000 people live here, staffing the Vatican's facilities. There are a post office and shops, Radio Vatican, broadcasting to the world in over 20 languages; a daily newspaper *(l'Osservatore Romano)*; Vatican offices; and a publishing house.

The Madonna of Guadalupe shows the miraculous image of the Madonna which appeared on the cloak of a Mexican Indian in 1531.

Papal heliport

The Grotto of Lourdes is a replica of the grotto in the southwest of France, where in 1858 the Virgin appeared to St. Bernadette.

The Vatican Railway Station, opened in 1930, connects with the line from Rome to Viterbo, but is now used only for freight.

Radio Vatican is broadcast from this tower, part of the Leonine Wall built in 847.

The Papal Audience Chamber, by Pier Luigi Nervi, was opened in 1971. It seats up to 12,000.

The information office gives details of tours of the Vatican Gardens.

★ **St. Peter's**
The Chapel of St. Peter is in the Grottoes under the basilica. The rich marble decoration was added by Clement VIII at the end of the 16th century ❶

Piazza San Pietro was laid out by Bernini between 1656 and 1667. The narrow space in front of the church opens out into an enormous ellipse flanked by colonnades.

The obelisk was erected here in 1586 with the help of 150 horses and 47 winches.

STAR SIGHTS

★ **St. Peter's**

★ **Vatican Museums**

The Eagle Fountain was built to celebrate the arrival of water from the Acqua Paola aqueduct at the Vatican. The eagle is the Borghese crest.

LOCATOR MAP
See Central Rome Map pp12–13

The Casina of Pius IV is a delightful summerhouse in the Vatican Gardens built by Pirro Ligorio in the mid-16th century.

Entrance to Vatican Museums

★ Vatican Museums
Raphael's Madonna of Foligno *(1513) is just one of the Vatican's many Renaissance masterpieces* ❷

The Galleon Fountain is a perfect scale model of a 17th-century ship in lead, brass and copper. It was made by a Flemish artist for Pope Paul V.

The Cortile della Pigna is mostly the work of Bramante. The niche for the pine cone, once a Roman fountain, was added by Pirro Ligorio in 1562.

To Via della Conciliazione

KEY

- - - Suggested route

0 meters 75
0 yards 75

St. Peter's ❶

See pp230–33.

Vatican Museums ❷

See pp234–47.

Porta Santo Spirito ❸

Via dei Penitenzieri. **Map** 3 C3. 🚌 *23, 34, 46, 62, 64, 98, 870, 881, 982.*

THIS GATE stands at what was the southern limit of the "Leonine City," the area enclosed within walls by Pope Leo IV as a defense against the Saracens who had sacked Rome in AD 845. The walls measure 2 miles (3 km) in circumference.

Work on the walls started in 846. Pope Leo supervised the huge army of laborers personally, and thanks to his encouragement, the job was completed in 4 years. He then led a solemn procession to consecrate his massive feat of construction.

Since the time of Pope Leo, the walls have needed much reinforcement and repair. The gateway visible today at Porta Santo Spirito was built by the architect Antonio da Sangallo the Younger in 1543–4. It is framed by two huge bastions that were added in 1564 by

Pope Pius IV Medici. Sadly, Sangallo's design for a monumental entrance to the Vatican was never completed; the principal columns come to an end somewhat abruptly in a modern covering of cement.

Santo Spirito in Sassia ❹

Via dei Penitenzieri. **Map** 3 C3. 📞 *06-687 9310.* 🚌 *23, 34, 46, 62, 64, 98, 870, 881, 982.* **Open** *7am–12:30pm, 3–7pm daily.* ✝ ♿

Nave of Santo Spirito in Sassia

BUILT ON THE SITE of a church erected by King Ine of Wessex, who died in Rome in the 8th century, the church is the work of Antonio da Sangallo the Younger. It was rebuilt (1538–44) after the

Sack of Rome had left it in ruins in 1527. The façade was added under Pope Sixtus V (1585–90). The nave and side chapels are decorated with a series of light, lively frescoes. The pretty bell tower is earlier, dating from the reign of Sixtus IV (1471–84). It was probably the work of the pope's architect Baccio Pontelli, who also built the nearby Hospital of Santo Spirito, and the Ponte Sisto *(see p210)* farther down the River Tiber.

Sixtus V's arms over door of Santo Spirito

Hospital of Santo Spirito ❺

Borgo Santo Spirito 2. **Map** 3 C3. 🚌 *23, 34 46, 62, 64, 98, 870, 881, 982.* **Octagonal chapel open** *8:30am–2pm daily.*

THE OLDEST HOSPITAL in Rome, this is said to have been founded as a result of a nightmare experienced by Pope Innocent III (1198–1216). In the dream, an angel showed him the bodies of Rome's unwanted babies dredged up from the Tiber River in fishing nets. As a result the pope hastened to build a hospice for sick paupers.

Fresco of an angel in the octagonal chapel of the Hospital of Santo Spirito

In 1475 the hospital was reorganized by Pope Sixtus IV to care for poor pilgrims expected for the Holy Year. Sixtus's hospital was a radical building. Cloisters divided the different types of patient; one area is still reserved for orphans and their nurses.

Unwanted infants were passed through a revolving barrel-like contraption called the *rota*, still visible to the left of the central entrance in Borgo Santo Spirito to guarantee anonymity. Martin Luther, who visited in 1511, was shocked by the number of abandoned children he saw, believing them to be "the sons of the pope himself."

In the center, under the hospital's conspicuous drum, is an octagonal chapel, where mass was said for patients. This room can be visited while the rest of the building still functions as a hospital.

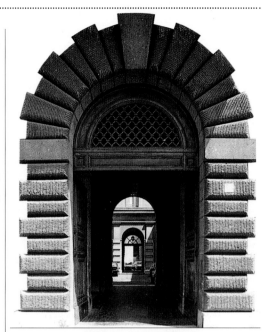

Rusticated doorway of the Palazzo dei Convertendi

The *rota* of Santo Spirito, where mothers left unwanted babies

Palazzo del Commendatore ❻

Borgo Santo Spirito 3. **Map** 3 C3.
🚌 23, 34, 46, 62, 64, 98, 881, 982.
Courtyard only open to the public.

A S DIRECTOR of the Hospital of Santo Spirito, the Commendatore not only ran the hospital, he was also responsible for its estates and revenues. This important post was originally given to members of the pope's family.

The palazzo, built next door to the hospital, has a spacious 16th-century frescoed loggia appropriate to the dignity and sobriety of its owners. The frescoes represent the story of the founding of the Hospital of Santo Spirito. To the left of the entrance is the Spezieria, or Pharmacy. This still has the wheel used for grinding the bark of the cinchona tree to produce the drug quinine, first introduced here in 1632 by Jesuits from Peru as a cure for malaria.

Above the courtyard is a splendid clock (1827). The dial is divided into six; it was not until 1846 that the familiar division of the day into two periods of 12 hours was introduced in Rome by Pope Pius IX.

Palazzo dei Convertendi ❼

Via della Conciliazione 43.
Map 3 C3. 🚌 23, 34, 62, 64.
Not open to the public.

W ITH THE BUILDING of Via della Conciliazione in the 1930s, Palazzo dei Convertendi was taken down and later moved to this new site nearby. The house, which is partly attributed to the architect Bramante, is where the artist Raphael died in 1520.

Palazzo dei Penitenzieri ❽

Via della Conciliazione 33.
Map 3 C3. 📞 06-682 8121.
🚌 23, 34, 62, 64. **Open** for visits 3:30–6:30pm Mon, Thu (fax to 06-6880 2298). **Adm charge** for groups. See **Where to Stay** p295.

Della Rovere arms

T HE PALAZZO owes its name to the fact that the place was once home to the confessors *(penitenzieri)* of St. Peter's. Now the Hotel Columbus, it was originally built by Cardinal Domenico della Rovere in 1480, the palazzo still bears the family's coat of arms, the oak tree (*rovere* means oak), on its graceful courtyard wellhead. On the cardinal's death, the palazzo was acquired by Pope Julius II della Rovere's favorite, Cardinal Francesco Alidosi. Suspected of treason, the cardinal was murdered in 1511 by the pope's nephew, the duke of Urbino, who also took possession of his palazzo. A few of the rooms still contain beautiful frescoes.

View of the Tiber and the Borgo between Castel Sant'Angelo and St. Peter's by Gaspare Vanvitelli (1653–1736)

Santa Maria in Traspontina 9

Via della Conciliazione 14.
Map 3 C3. **(** 06-6880 6451.
🚌 23, 34, 62, 64.
Open 6:30am–noon, 4–7pm daily.
⛪ ♿

The façade of the Carmelite church of Santa Maria in Traspontina

THE CHURCH occupies the site of an ancient Roman pyramid, believed in the Middle Ages to have been the Tomb of Romulus. The pyramid was destroyed by Pope Alexander VI Borgia, but representations of it survive in the bronze doors at the entrance to St. Peter's and in a Giotto triptych in the Vatican Pinacoteca *(see p240)*.

The present church was begun in 1566 to replace an earlier one which had been in the line of fire of the cannons defending Castel Sant'Angelo during the Sack of Rome in 1527. The papal artillery officers insisted that the dome of the new church should be as low as possible, so it was built without a supporting drum. The first chapel to the right is dedicated to the gunners' patron saint, Santa Barbara, and is decorated with warlike motifs. In the third chapel on the left are two columns, said to be those to which St. Peter and Paul were bound before martyrdom.

The Borgo 10

Map 3 C3. 🚌 23, 34, 40, 62.

THE WORD BORGO derives from the German *burg*, meaning town. Rome's Borgo is where the first pilgrims to St. Peter's were housed in hostels and hospices, often for quite lengthy periods. The first of these foreign colonies, called "schools," was founded in AD 725 by a Saxon, King Ine of Wessex, who wished to live a life of penance and to be buried near the Tomb of St. Peter. These days hotels and

hostels have made the Borgo a colony of international pilgrims once again. Much of the area's character was destroyed by redevelopment in the 1930s, but it is still enjoyable to explore the old narrow streets on either side of Via della Conciliazione.

Vatican Corridor 11

Castel Sant'Angelo to the Vatican.
Map 3 C3. 🚌 23, 34, 40, 62.

Clement VII, who used the Vatican Corridor to evade capture in 1527

LOCALLY KNOWN as the Passetto (small corridor), this long passageway was built into the fortifications during medieval times. Meant to link the Vatican with the fortress of Castel Sant'Angelo, it constituted a fortified escape route which could also be used to control the strategic Borgo area. Arrows and other missiles could be fired from its bastions on to the streets and houses below. The corridor was used in 1494 by Pope Alexander VI Borgia when Rome was invaded by King Charles VIII of France. In 1527 it enabled Pope Clement VII to take refuge in Castel Sant'Angelo, as the troops commanded by the Constable of Bourbon began the Sack of Rome.

Palazzo Torlonia ⑫

Via della Conciliazione 30. **Map** 3 C3.
🚌 *23, 34, 40, 62, 64.* **Not open** to the public.

Palazzo Torlonia (1496), unaffected by changes to the surrounding area

THE PALAZZO was built in the late 15th century by the wealthy Cardinal Adriano Castellesi, in a style closely resembling Palazzo della Cancelleria *(see p149).* The cardinal was a much-traveled rogue, who collected vast revenues from the bishopric of Bath and Wells which he was given

Pope Leo X

by his friend King Henry VII of England. In return he gave Henry his palazzo for use as the seat of the English ambassador to the Holy See. Castellesi was finally stripped of his cardinalate by Pope Leo X Medici and disappeared from history.

Since then the palazzo has had many owners and tenants. In the 17th century it was rented for a time by Queen Christina of Sweden. The Torlonia family, who acquired the building in 1820, owed its fortune to the financial genius of shopkeeper-turned-banker Giovanni Torlonia. He lent money to the impoverished Roman nobility and bought up their property during the Napoleonic Wars.

Castel Sant'Angelo ⑬

See pp248–9.

Palazzo di Giustizia ⑭

Piazza Cavour. **Map** 4 E3. 🚌 *34, 49, 70, 87, 186, 280, 492, 913, 926, 990.* **Not open** to the public.

THE MONUMENTAL Palazzo di Giustizia (Palace of Justice) was built between 1889 and 1910 to house the national law courts. Its riverside façade is crowned with a bronze chariot and fronted by giant statues of the great men of Italian law.

The building was supposed to embody the new order replacing the injustices of papal rule, but it has never endeared itself to the Romans. It was soon dubbed the Palazzaccio (roughly, "the ugly old palazzo") both for its appearance and for the nature of its business. By the 1970s the building was collapsing under its own weight, but it has now been restored.

The ornate travertine façade of the Palazzo di Giustizia

St. Peter's ●

THE CENTER of the Roman Catholic faith, St. Peter's draws pilgrims from all over the world. Few are disappointed when they enter the sumptuously decorated basilica beneath Michelangelo's vast dome.

A shrine was erected on the site of St. Peter's tomb in the 2nd century, and the first great basilica, ordered by the Emperor Constantine, was completed around AD 349. By the 15th century it was falling down, so in 1506 Pope Julius II laid the first stone of a new church. It took more than a century to build, and all the great architects of the Roman Renaissance and Baroque had a hand in its design.

★ **Dome of St. Peter's**
Designed by Michelangelo, though not finished in his lifetime, the spectacular cupola, 448 ft (136.5 m) high, gives unity to the majestic interior of the basilica.

The nave's total length is 715 ft (218 m).

Papal Altar
The present altar dates from the reign of Clement VIII (1592–1605). The plain slab of marble found in the Forum of Nerva stands under Bernini's baldacchino, over-looking the well of the confessio, the crypt where St. Peter's body is reputedly buried.

Baldacchino
This magnificent canopy of gilded bronze, supported on spiral columns 66 ft (20 m) high, was designed by Bernini in the 17th century.

TIMELINE

AD 61 Burial of St. Peter		**1506** Julius II lays first stone	**1547** Michelangelo named as chief architect of St. Peter's		**1626** New basilica of St. Peter's consecrated
	324 Constantine builds basilica	**1452** Nicholas V plans restoration		**1593** Dome completed	

AD 60	800	1500	1550	1600	

	200 Altar built marking grave of St. Peter	**1503** Pope Julius II chooses Bramante as architect for new basilica	**1538** Antonio da Sangallo the Younger made director of works	**1606** Carlo Maderno extends basilica	**1614** Maderno finishes the façade
800 Charlemagne crowned Holy Roman Emperor in St. Peter's			**1514** Raphael director of works	**1564** Death of Michelangelo	

★ **View from the Dome**
The superb symmetry of Bernini's colonnade can be appreciated from the dome.

The two minor cupolas at the corners of the transept are by Vignola.

Pope Urban VIII's Keys
At the base of the columns of the baldacchino, the coat of arms of Pope Urban VIII features the keys to the Kingdom of Heaven.

Façade by Carlo Maderno (1614)

Stairs to the dome

Filarete Door
Finished in 1445, Antonio Averulino's bronze door came from the original basilica.

Entrances

Piazza San Pietro
On Sundays and religious occasions the pope blesses the crowds from his balcony above the square.

STAR FEATURES

★ **Dome of St. Peter's**

★ **View from the Dome**

A Guided Tour of St. Peter's

T HE VAST BASILICA'S 615-ft (187-m) long, marble-encrusted interior contains 11 chapels and 45 altars in addition to a wealth of precious works of art. Some were salvaged from the original basilica and others commissioned from late Renaissance and Baroque artists, but much of the elaborate decoration is owed to Bernini's work in the mid-17th century. The two side aisles are 250 ft (76 m) long and converge under Michelangelo's enormous dome. The central focus of the building is the Papal Altar beneath Bernini's great baldacchino, filling the space between four massive piers which support the dome. From the basilica you can visit the Grottoes, the Treasury and St. Peter's Sacristy, or climb up to the terrace for panoramic views.

⑤ **Baldacchino by Bernini**
Commissioned by Pope Urban VIII in 1624, the extravagant Baroque canopy dominates the nave and crowns the Papal Altar, at which only the pope may celebrate mass.

Bernini's Monument to Urban VIII

④ **Throne of St. Peter in Glory**
In the domed apse, look up to the window above Bernini's Baroque sculpture of 1656–65. It lights the image of the Holy Spirit, shown as a dove amid clouds, rays of sunlight and flights of angels.

Entrance to Treasury and Sacristy

HISTORICAL PLAN OF THE BASILICA OF ST. PETER'S

St. Peter was buried in AD 64 in a necropolis near his crucifixion site at the Circus of Nero. Constantine built a basilica on the burial site in AD 324. In the 15th century the old church was found to be unsafe and had to be demolished. It was rebuilt in the 16th and 17th centuries. By 1614 the façade was ready, and in 1626 the new church was consecrated.

KEY

▓	Circus of Nero
▓	Constantinian
▓	Renaissance
▓	Baroque

Entrance to Necropolis

③ **Monument to Pope Alexander VII**
Bernini's last work was finished in 1678 and is in an alcove on the left of the transept. The pope sits among the figures of Truth, Justice, Charity and Prudence.

② **Monument to Leo XI**
On the left beneath the aisle arch is Alessandro Algardi's white marble 1650 monument to Leo XI, whose reign as pope lasted only 27 days.

KEY

 Tour route

⑥ Angelo della Navicella

A fragment of Giotto's beautiful 13th-century mosaic, salvaged from the old basilica, is now in the Grottoes. A later copy of the entire mosaic of Jesus and St. Peter fishing on Lake Tiberias decorates the atrium.

⑦ St. Peter

Until recently this famous 13th-century statue, now attributed to Arnolfo di Cambio, was thought to be a late Roman work. Situated at the end of the nave, it is sculpted in bronze with a delicate filigree halo.

Entrance to Grottoes

The Tabernacle by Bernini is made of gilt bronze in the shape of a temple.

Chapel of St. Sebastian

Stuart Monument by Canova

The Porta Santa (Holy Door) is opened only in Holy Years. The Pope knocks on it with a bronze hammer, it is unlocked and remains open throughout the Holy Year.

⑧ Pietà

This famous marble sculpture was finished in 1499 when Michelangelo was only 25. It stands in a chapel to one side of the nave, protected by glass since being damaged in 1972.

Filarete Door

Navicella Mosaic

Atrium by Carlo Maderno

① Tomb of Maria Clementina Sobieski

Near the entrance is Filippo Barigioni's sentimentally expressive 18th-century monument to Maria Clementina, the wife of James Stuart, the Old Pretender.

Vatican Museums ②

THE BUILDINGS that house one of the world's most important art collections were originally papal palaces built for such Renaissance popes as Sixtus IV, Innocent VIII and Julius II. The long courtyards and galleries, linking Innocent VIII's Belvedere Palace to the other buildings, are by Donato Bramante and were commissioned for Julius II in 1503. Most of the later additions to the buildings were made in the 18th century, when priceless works of art accumulated by earlier popes were first put on display. This complex of museums also houses the Sistine Chapel and the Raphael Rooms, which should not be missed.

★ Atrium of the Four Gates
Built by Camporese in 1792–3, this vast domed edifice was the original entrance to the Vatican Museums.

The Belvedere Palace was commissioned in the late 15th century by Pope Innocent VIII.

★ Cortile della Pigna
This huge bronze pine cone, part of an ancient Roman fountain, once stood in the courtyard of old St. Peter's. Its niche was designed by Pirro Ligorio.

Cortile della Biblioteca

Cortile del Belvedere

Apartment of Pius V

Sistine Chapel

Borgia Tower

Borgia Apartment

Raphael Loggia

Cortile di San Damaso

STAR FEATURES

★ Cortile della Pigna

★ Atrium of the Four Gates

★ Bramante Stairway

Spiral Ramp

The spectacular stairway leading down from the museums to the street was designed by Giuseppe Momo in 1932.

Entrance

VISITORS' CHECKLIST

Città del Vaticano. Entrance in Viale Vaticano. **Map** 3 B2. ☎ 06-6988 3333. 🚌 49 to entrance, 23, 81, 492, 990 to Piazza del Risorgimento or 62 to St. Peter's. Ⓜ Cipro Musei Vaticani, Ottaviano S. Pietro. **Open** 8:45am–3:45pm (last admission 2:20pm) Mon–Fri (Nov–Feb: to 12:20pm); 8:45am–1:45pm (last admission 2:20pm) Sat and last Sun of each month. **Closed** public & relig hols. Special permit needed for Raphael Loggia, Vatican library, Lapidary Gallery & Vatican Archives. **Adm charge**, free last Sun of month. ♿ special routes. 📷 **Temporary exhibitions, lectures.** 🍴 🚻 📷 🎁 Vatican Gardens: 06-6988 4466. 🌐 www.vatican.va

Simonetti Stairway

Built in the 1780s with a vaulted ceiling, the stairs were part of the conversion of the Belvedere Palace into the Pio-Clementine Museum.

Cortile Ottagonale

The inner court of the Belvedere Palace was given its octagonal shape in 1773.

Braccio Nuovo

★ Bramante Stairway

Pope Julius II built the spiral staircase within a square tower as an entrance to the palace. The staircase could be ridden up on horseback in case of emergency.

TIMELINE

1000	1500	1600	1700	1800
1198 Innocent III creates papal palace	**1503** Bramante lays out Belvedere Courtyard **1509** Raphael begins work on Rooms	**1655** Bernini designs Scala Regia	**1756** Foundation of Christian Museum	**1800–23** Chiaramonti Museum founded **1837** Etruscan Museum founded
1473 Pope Sixtus IV builds Sistine Chapel	**1503–13** Pope Julius II starts Classical sculpture collection	*Bramante (1444–1514)*	**1758** Museum of Pagan Antiquities founded **1776–84** Pius VI enlarges museum	**1822** Braccio Nuovo is opened **1970** Pope Paul VI opens Gregorian Museum of Pagan Antiquities

Exploring the Vatican Museums

FOUR CENTURIES of papal patronage and connoisseurship have resulted in one of the world's great collections of Classical and Renaissance art. The Vatican houses many of the great archaeological finds of central Italy, including the *Laocoön* group, discovered in 1506 on the Esquiline; the *Apollo del Belvedere*; and the Etruscan bronze known as the *Mars of Todi*. During the Renaissance, parts of the museums were decorated with wonderful frescoes commissioned for the Sistine Chapel, the Raphael Rooms and the Borgia Apartment.

Mars of Todi

Gallery of the Candelabra
Once an open loggia (courtyard gallery), this gallery of Greek and Roman sculpture has a view of the Vatican Gardens.

Room of the Big

Gallery of Tapestries

Etruscan Museum

Siege of Malta
The Gallery of Maps is an important record of 16th-century history and cartography.

Upper floor

Raphael Loggia

Modern Religious Art

Sistine Chapel

Raphael Rooms

GALLERY GUIDE
Visitors have to follow a one-way system. It is best to concentrate on a single collection or to choose one of the four suggested itineraries. These are color-coded so that you can follow them throughout the museums. Routes vary in length from 90 minutes to 5 hours. If you are planning a long visit, make sure you allow plenty of time for resting. Conserve your stamina for the Sistine Chapel and the Raphael Rooms; they are 20 to 30 minutes' walk from the entrance, not counting any viewing time along the way.

Sala dei Misteri
This is one of the rooms of the Borgia Apartment, richly decorated with Pinturicchio frescoes.

Gregorian Profane Museum

Pio-Christian Museum

Pinacoteca

Greek Cross Room

Stairs up

Stairs down

Braccio Nuovo

Egyptian Museum

Vatican Library

Lapidary Gallery

Lower floor

Chiaramonti Museum

Pio-Clementine Museum

Entrance

Round Room

St Jerome
Leonardo da Vinci's unfinished work, lost then rediscovered in the 19th century, shows the artist's mastery of anatomy.

Room of the Busts
This contains portraits of emperors and other notable Romans.

Laocoön
This 1st-century AD marble group depicts the Trojan priest Laocoön and his sons struggling with two serpents.

Room of the Animals
Roman mosaics, like these delightful ducks, decorate the walls and floor of this room of animal sculpture.

Apollo del Belvedere
This Roman copy of a Greek statue of the sun god Apollo perfectly embodies the ideals of Classical beauty.

KEY TO FLOOR PLAN

- Egyptian and Assyrian art
- Greek and Roman art
- Etruscan and Italic art
- Early Christian and medieval art
- 15th- to 19th-century art
- Modern Religious art
- Non-exhibition space
- Open by special permit only

Exploring the Vatican's Collections

THE VATICAN'S GREATEST TREASURES are its Greek and Roman antiquities. These have been on display since the 18th century. The 19th century saw the addition of exciting discoveries from Etruscan tombs and excavations in Egypt. In the Pinacoteca (art gallery) there is a small, choice collection of painting, including works by Raphael, Titian and Leonardo. Works by great painters and sculptors are also displayed throughout the older parts of the museums in the form of sumptuous decorations commissioned by the Renaissance popes.

Coloured bas-relief from an Egyptian tomb (c2400 BC)

EGYPTIAN AND ASSYRIAN ART

THE EGYPTIAN COLLECTION contains finds from 19th- and 20th-century excavations in Egypt and statues that were brought to Rome in Imperial times. There are also Roman imitations of Egyptian art from Hadrian's Villa *(see p269)* and from the Campus Martius district of ancient Rome. Egyptian-style statuary from Hadrian's Villa was used to decorate the Greek Cross Room, the entrance to the new wing built in 1780 by Michelangelo Simonetti.

The genuine Egyptian works, exhibited on the lower floor of the Belvedere Palace, include statues, mummies, mummy cases and funerary artifacts. There is also a large collection of documents written on papyrus, the paper the ancient Egyptians made from reeds. Among the main treasures is a colossal granite statue of Queen Tuia, the mother of Rameses II, found on the site of the Horti Sallustiani gardens

(see p251) in 1714. The statue, which dates from the 13th century BC, may have been brought to Rome by the Emperor Caligula (reigned AD 37–41), who had an unhealthy interest in pharaohs and in his own mother, Agrippina.

Also noteworthy are the head of a statue of Montuhotep IV (21st century BC); the beautiful mummy case of Queen Hetep-heret-es; and the tomb of Iri, the guardian of the Pyramid of Cheops (22nd century BC).

The Assyrian Stairway is decorated with fragments of reliefs from the palaces of the Kings of Nineveh (8th century BC). These depict the military exploits of King Sennacherib and his son, Sargon II, and show scenes from Assyrian and Chaldean mythology.

ETRUSCAN AND OTHER PRE-ROMAN ART

THIS COLLECTION comprises artifacts from pre-Roman civilizations in Etruria and Latium, from Neolithic times to the 1st century BC, when these ancient populations were assimilated into the Roman state. Among the finest objects in the Gregorian Etruscan Museum are those from the Regolini-Galassi tomb, excavated in 1836 at the necropolis of Cerveteri *(see p271)*. The tomb was found intact and yielded numerous everyday household objects, plus a throne, a bed and a funeral cart, all cast in bronze, dating from the 7th century BC. Beautiful black vases, delightful terra-cotta figurines and such bronze statues as the famous *Mars of Todi*, displayed in the Room of the Bronzes, show the Etruscans to have been a highly civilized, sophisticated people.

A number of Greek vases also found in Etruscan tombs are on display in the Vase Collection. The Room of the Italiot Vases contains only vases produced locally in the Greek cities of Southern Italy and in Etruria itself. These date from the 3rd to the 1st century BC.

Etruscan gold clasp (*fibula*) from the 7th century BC

Head of an athlete in mosaic from the Baths of Caracalla

GREEK AND ROMAN ART

T HE GREATER PART of the Vatican Museums is dedicated to Greek and Roman art. Exhibits line connecting corridors and vestibules; walls and floors display fine mosaics; and famous sculptures decorate the main courtyards.

The first serious organization of the collection took place in the reign of Julius II (1503–13) around Bramante's Belvedere Courtyard. The prize pieces form the nucleus of the 18th-century Pio-Clementine Museum. In the pavilions of the Octagonal Courtyard and in the surrounding rooms are sculptures considered among the greatest achievements of Western art. The *Apoxyomenos* (an athlete wiping his body after a race) and the *Apollo del Belvedere* are high-quality Roman copies of Greek originals of about 320 BC. The magnificent *Laocoön*, sculpted by three artists from Rhodes, had long been known to exist from a description by Pliny the Elder. It was rediscovered near the ruins of the Domus Aurea *(see p175)* in 1506. Classical works such as these had a profound influence on Michelangelo and other Renaissance artists.

The much smaller Chiaramonti Museum, named after Pope Pius

VII Chiaramonti, was laid out by Canova in the early 19th century. It includes a striking colossal head of the goddess Athene. The Braccio Nuovo, an extension of the Chiaramonti, decorated with Roman floor mosaics, contains a statue of Augustus from the villa of his wife, Livia, at Prima Porta. Its pose is based on the famous *Doryphoros* by the Greek sculptor Polyclitus, a Roman copy of which can be seen on display nearby.

Exhibits in the Vase Rooms range from the Greek geometric style (8th century BC) to black-figure vases from Corinth, such as the famous vase by Exekias, with Achilles and Ajax playing a game similar to checkers (530 BC), and to the later red-figure type, such as the *kylix* (a wide shallow cup) with Oedipus and the Sphinx from the 5th century BC. A stairway links this section to the Gallery of the Candelabra and the Room of the Biga (a two-horse chariot). The horses and harness were added in the 18th century.

The Gregorian Profane Museum, housed in a new wing, charts the evolution of Roman art from dependence upon Greek models to a recognizably Roman style.

The *Doryphoros* or spear-carrier, a Roman copy in marble of an original Greek bronze

Original Greek works here include large marble fragments from the Parthenon in Athens. There is also a Roman copy of *Athene and Marsyas* by Myron, which was part of the decoration of the Parthenon. Totally Roman in character are two reliefs known as the Rilievi della Cancelleria, because they were discovered beneath the Palazzo della Cancelleria *(see p149)* in the 1930s. They show military parades of the Emperor Vespasian and his son, Domitian. This section also has fine Roman floor mosaics. There are two from the Baths of Caracalla *(see p197)*, depicting athletes and referees. They date from the 3rd century AD. Most striking of all is a mosaic that creates the impression of an unswept floor, covered with debris after a meal. Away from the main Classical collections, in one of the rooms of the Vatican Library, is the *Aldobrandini Wedding*, a beautiful Roman fresco of a bride being prepared for her marriage, dating from the 1st century AD.

Marble relief of the Emperor Vespasian

Floor mosaic from the Baths of Otricoli in Umbria, in the Chiaramonti Museum

Detail from Giotto's *Stefaneschi Triptych*

EARLY CHRISTIAN AND MEDIEVAL ART

THE MAIN COLLECTION of early Christian antiquities is in the Pio-Christian Museum, founded in the last century by Pope Pius IX and formerly housed in the Lateran Palace. It contains inscriptions and sculpture from catacombs and early Christian basilicas. The sculpture consists chiefly of reliefs decorating sarcophagi, though the most striking work is a free-standing 4th-century statue of the *Good Shepherd*. The sculpture's chief appeal lies in the way it blends biblical episodes with pagan mythology. Christianity adopted Classical images so that its doctrines could be understood in clear visual terms. The idealized pastoral figure of the shepherd, for example, became Christ himself, while bearded philosophers turned into the Apostles. At the same time, Christianity laid claim to be the spiritual and cultural heir of the Roman Empire.

The first two rooms of the Pinacoteca are dedicated to late medieval art, featuring wooden panels tempera-painted that served as altarpieces. The outstanding work is Giotto's altarpiece dating from about 1300, known as the *Stefaneschi Triptych*. It expresses much the same theme as the early Christian works: the continuity between the Classical world of the Roman Empire and the new order of Christian Europe. The crucifixion of St. Peter takes place between two landmarks of ancient Rome, the Pyramid of Caius Cestius *(see p205)*, and the pyramid known in the Middle Ages as the Tomb of Romulus, which stood near the Vatican. The triptych, which decorated the main altar of old St Peter's, includes portraits of Pope St. Celestine V (reigned 1294–6), and of the donor, Cardinal Jacopo Stefaneschi, shown offering the triptych to St. Peter.

The Vatican Library has a number of medieval treasures exhibited rather haphazardly in showcases; these include woven and embroidered cloths, reliquaries, enamels and icons. One of the aims of the 18th-century reorganization of the Vatican collections was to glorify Christian works by contrasting them with earlier pagan creations. In the long Lapidary Gallery, over 3,000 stone tablets with Christian and pagan inscriptions are displayed on opposite walls. The world's greatest collection of its kind, it may be visited only with special permission.

15TH- TO 19TH-CENTURY ART

THE RENAISSANCE POPES, many of whom were cultured connoisseurs of the arts, considered it their duty to sponsor the leading painters, sculptors and goldsmiths of

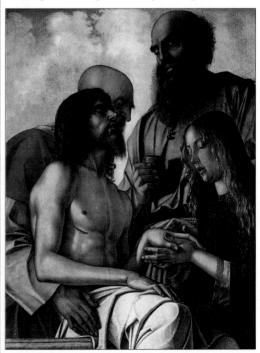

***Pietà* by the Venetian artist Giovanni Bellini (1430–1516)**

RAPHAEL'S LAST PAINTING

When Raphael died in 1520, the *Transfiguration* was found in his studio, almost complete. The wonderful luminous work was placed at the head of the bier where the great artist's body lay. It depicts the episode in the Gospels in which Christ took three of the Apostles to the top of a mountain, where He appeared to them in divine glory. In the detail shown here, Christ floats above the ground in a halo of ethereal light.

the age. The galleries around the Cortile del Belvedere were all decorated by great artists between the 16th and the 19th century. The Gallery of Tapestries is hung with tapestries woven in Brussels to designs by students of Raphael; the Apartment of Pope Pius V has beautiful 15th-century Flemish tapestries; and the Gallery of Maps is frescoed with 16th-century maps of ancient and contemporary Italy. When you visit the Raphael Rooms *(see pp242–3)*, be sure to also visit the nearby Room of the Chiaroscuri and Pope Nicholas V's tiny private chapel, frescoed by Fra Angelico between 1447 and 1451. Similarly, before reaching the Sistine Chapel *(see pp244–7)*, visit the Borgia Apartment, frescoed in a decorative, flowery style by Pinturicchio and his students in the 1490s. The contrast with Michelangelo's Sistine Chapel ceiling, begun in 1508, could hardly be greater. Another set of fascinating frescoes decorates the Loggia of Raphael, but this requires special permission to visit.

Many important works by Renaissance masters are displayed in the Pinacoteca (art gallery). Highlights among the works by 15th-century painters are a fine *Pietà* by the Venetian Giovanni Bellini and Leonardo da Vinci's unfinished *St. Jerome*. Of the

great 16th-century works, do not miss the fine altarpiece by Titian, the *Crucifixion of St. Peter* by Guido Reni, the *Deposition* by Caravaggio and the *Communion of St. Jerome* by Domenichino. Raphael has a whole room dedicated to his work. It contains the beautiful *Madonna of Foligno* and the *Transfiguration*, as well as eight tapestries made to his designs.

Lunette of the *Adoration of the Magi* by Pinturicchio in the Room of the Mysteries in the Borgia Apartment

MODERN RELIGIOUS ART

MODERN ARTISTS exhibited in the Vatican Museums face daunting competition from the great works of the past. Few modern works are displayed conspicuously, the exceptions being Momo's spiral staircase of 1932, which greets visitors as they enter the museums, and Giò Pomodoro's abstract sculpture in the center of the Cortile della Pigna.

In 1973, a contemporary art collection was inaugurated by Pope Paul VI. Housed in the Borgia Apartment, it includes over 800 exhibits by modern artists from all over the world, donated by collectors or the artists themselves. Works in a great variety of media show many contrasting approaches to religious subjects. There are paintings, drawings, engravings and sculptures by 19th- and 20th-century artists, as well as mosaics, stained glass, ceramics and tapestries. Well-known modern painters such as Georges Braque, Paul Klee, Edvard Munch and Graham Sutherland are also represented, and there are drawings by Henry Moore, ceramics by Picasso and stained glass by Fernand Léger. Projects for modern church ornaments include Matisse's decorations for the church of St. Paul de Vence, Luigi Fontana's models for the bronze doors of Milan cathedral and Emilio Greco's panels for the doors of Orvieto cathedral.

***Town with Gothic Cathedral* by Paul Klee (1879–1940)**

Raphael Rooms

Pope Julius II's private apartments were built above those of his hated predecessor, Alexander VI, one of the Borgias, who died in 1503. Julius was impressed with Raphael's work and chose him to redecorate the four

Detail from *The Expulsion of Heliodorus from the Temple*, showing Pope Julius II watching the scene from his litter

rooms *(stanze)*. Raphael and his pupils began the task in 1508, replacing existing works by several better-known artists, including Raphael's own teacher, Perugino. The work took over 16 years, and Raphael himself died before its completion. The frescoes express the religious and philosophical ideals of the Renaissance. They quickly established Raphael's reputation as an artist in Rome, putting him on a par with Michelangelo, then working on the ceiling of the Sistine Chapel.

Cortile del Belvedere

KEY TO FLOORPLAN

① Hall of Constantine
② Room of Heliodorus
③ Room of the Segnatura
④ Room of the Fire in the Borgo

HALL OF CONSTANTINE ①

The frescoes in this room were started in 1517, 3 years before Raphael's death, but Raphael himself probably had little hand in their execution. As a result, they are not held in the same high regard as those in the other rooms. The work was completed in 1525, during the reign of Pope Clement VII, by Giulio Romano and two other former pupils of Raphael, Giovanni Francesco Penni and Raffaellino del Colle.

The theme of the decoration is the triumph of Christianity over paganism. The four major frescoes show scenes from the life of Constantine and include his *Vision of the Cross* and his victory over his rival Maxentius at *The Battle of the Milvian Bridge*, for which Raphael had provided a preparatory sketch. In both *The Baptism of Constantine* and *The Donation of Constantine*, the figure of Pope Sylvester *(see p170)* was given the features of Clement VII.

ROOM OF HELIODORUS ②

This private antechamber was decorated by Raphael between 1512 and 1514. The main frescoes show the miraculous protection granted to all the Church's ministers, doctrines and property. The room's name refers to the fresco on the right, *The Expulsion of Heliodorus from the Temple*. This shows a story from Jewish history, in which a thief called Heliodorus is felled

Swiss guards waiting with papal chair in *The Mass at Bolsena*

by a horseman as he tries to make off with the treasure from the Temple of Jerusalem. The scene is witnessed by the pope, borne on a litter by courtiers. The incident is also a thinly veiled reference to Julius II's success in driving foreign armies out of Italy. In *The Meeting of Leo I and Attila*, Raphael pays a similar compliment to the pope's political skill. Pope Leo was originally given the face of Julius II, but after his death, Raphael substituted the features of Julius's successor, Leo X.

The Mass at Bolsena depicts a miracle that occurred in 1263. A priest

The Battle of the Milvian Bridge, completed by one of Raphael's assistants

The Liberation of St. Peter, a three-part composition, shows the saint asleep in his cell in the middle section, led out of prison by an angel on the right, while, on the left, the prison guards cower in terror.

who doubted that the bread and wine really were the body and blood of Christ suddenly saw the host bleed while he was celebrating mass. Julius II appears in this fresco, accompanied by a colorful group of Swiss guards.

Julius appears again as St. Peter in *The Liberation of St. Peter*. This fresco is remarkable for its dramatic lighting effects, achieved despite the painting's awkward shape and its position above a window.

ROOM OF THE SEGNATURA ③

THE NAME is derived from a special council that met in this room to sign official documents. The frescoes here were completed between 1508 and 1511. The scheme Raphael followed was dictated by Pope Julius II. It reflects the Humanist belief that there could be perfect harmony between Classical culture and Christianity in their mutual search for truth.

The Dispute over the Holy Sacrament, the first fresco completed by Raphael for Pope Julius, represents the triumph of religion and spiritual truth. The consecrated host is shown at the center of the painting. This links the group of learned scholars, who discuss its significance, to the Holy Trinity and the saints floating on clouds up above.

On the opposite wall, *The School of Athens (see p30)* is a bustling scene

centered around the debate on the search for truth between Greek philosophers Plato and Aristotle. It also features portraits of many of Raphael's contemporaries, including Leonardo da Vinci, Bramante and Michelangelo. The other works include a portrait of the bearded Pope Julius II, who in 1511 vowed not to shave until he had rid Italy of all usurpers.

ROOM OF THE *FIRE IN THE BORGO* ④

THIS WAS ORIGINALLY the dining room, but when the decoration was completed under Pope Leo X, it became a music room. All the frescoes exalt the reigning pope by depicting events in the lives of his namesakes, the 9th-century popes Leo III and IV. The main frescoes were finished by two of Raphael's assistants between 1514 and 1517, following their

master's own plans. The most famous, *The Fire in the Borgo*, was painted from Raphael's designs and reflects his maturity as an artist. It celebrates the miracle that took place in 847, when Pope Leo IV extinguished a fire raging in the Borgo *(see p228)* by making the sign of the cross. The incident is likened to the flight of Aeneas from Troy described by Virgil. The figure of Aeneas appears in the foreground carrying his father on his back. This borrowing of an event from Classical legend shows Raphael's new willingness to experiment. Sadly, his pupils did not always follow his designs faithfully, and this, combined with poor restoration, has spoiled the work.

Detail from *The Fire in the Borgo*, showing Aeneas, the Trojan hero, with his father on his back, fleeing from the fire

The Dispute over the Holy Sacrament, the first fresco completed in the Rooms

Sistine Chapel: The Walls

THE MASSIVE WALLS of the Sistine Chapel, the main chapel in the Vatican Palace, were frescoed by some of the finest artists of the 15th and 16th centuries. The 12 paintings on the side walls, by artists including Perugino, Ghirlandaio, Botticelli and Signorelli, show parallel episodes from the life of Moses and of Christ. The decoration of the chapel walls was completed between 1534 and 1541 by Michelangelo, who added the great altar wall fresco, *The Last Judgment.*

KEY TO THE FRESCOES: ARTISTS AND SUBJECTS

The Last Judgment

☐ Perugino   ☐ Botticelli   ☐ Ghirlandaio

☐ Rosselli   ☐ Signorelli   ☐ Michelangelo

1 Baptism of Christ in the Jordan
2 Temptations of Christ
3 Calling of St Peter and St Andrew
4 Sermon on the Mount
5 Handing over the Keys to St Peter
6 Last Supper

7 Moses's Journey into Egypt
8 Moses Receiving the Call
9 Crossing of the Red Sea
10 Adoration of the Golden Calf
11 Punishment of the Rebels
12 Last Days of Moses

THE LAST JUDGMENT BY MICHELANGELO

REVEALED IN 1993 after a year's restoration, *The Last Judgment* is considered to be the masterpiece of Michelangelo's mature years. It was commissioned by Pope Paul III Farnese, and required the removal of some earlier frescoes and two windows over the altar. A new wall was erected which slanted inwards to stop dust settling on it. Michelangelo worked alone on the fresco for seven years, until its completion in 1541.

The painting depicts the souls of the dead rising up to face the wrath of God, a subject that is rarely used for an altar decoration. The pope chose it as a warning to Catholics to adhere to their faith in the turmoil of the Reformation. In fact the work conveys the artist's own tormented attitude to his faith. It offers neither the certainties of Christian orthodoxy, nor the ordered view of Classicism.

In a dynamic, emotional composition, the figures are caught in a vortex of motion. The dead are torn from their graves and hauled up to face Christ the Judge, whose athletic, muscular figure is the focus of all the painting's movement.

Christ shows little sympathy for the agitated saints around him, clutching the instruments of their martyrdom. Neither is any pity shown for the damned, hurled down to the demons in hell. Here Charon, pushing people off his boat into the depths of Hades, and the infernal judge Minos, are taken from Dante's *Inferno.* Minos has ass's ears, and is a portrait of courtier Biagio da Cesena, who had objected to the nude figures in the fresco. Michelangelo's self-portrait is on the skin held by the martyr St. Bartholomew.

Souls meeting the wrath of Christ in Michelangelo's *Last Judgment*

WALL FRESCOES

Detail from Botticelli's fresco
Temptations of Christ

W HEN THE Sistine Chapel was built, the papacy was a strong political power with vast accumulated wealth. In 1475 Pope Sixtus IV was able to summon some of the greatest painters of his day to decorate the chapel. Among the artists employed were Perugino, who was Raphael's master and is often credited with overseeing the project, Sandro Botticelli, Domenico Ghirlandaio, Cosimo Rosselli and Luca Signorelli. Their work on the chapel's frescoes took from 1481 to 1483.

Although frequently overlooked by visitors who concentrate on Michelangelo's work, the frescoes along the side walls of the chapel include some of the finest works of 15th-century Italian art. The two cycles of frescoes represent scenes from the lives of Moses and Christ. Above them in the spaces between the windows are portraits of the earliest popes, painted by various artists, including Botticelli.

The fresco cycles start at the altar end of the chapel, with the story of Christ on the right-hand wall and that of Moses on the left. Originally there were two paintings, *The Birth of Christ* and *The Finding of Moses*, on the wall behind the altar, but these were both destroyed to make way for Michelangelo's *The Last Judgment*.

The final paintings of the two cycles are also lost. They were on the entrance wall, which collapsed during the 16th century. When the wall was restored, they were replaced with poor substitutes.

As was customary at the time, each fresco contains a series of scenes, linked thematically to the central episode. Hidden meanings and symbols connect each painting with its counterpart on the opposite wall, and there are also many allusions to contemporary events.

The elaborate architectural details in the frescoes include familiar Roman monuments. The Arch of Constantine (*see p91*) provides the backdrop for the *Punishment of the Rebels* by Botticelli, the fifth panel in the cycle of Moses, in which the artist himself appears as the last figure but one on the right. Two similar arches appear in the painting opposite, Perugino's *Handing over the Keys to St. Peter*.

Moses was both spiritual and temporal leader of his people. He called down the wrath of God on those who challenged his decisions, thus

The crowd of onlookers in the *Calling of St Peter and St Andrew* by Ghirlandaio

setting a precedent for the power exercised by the pope. In *Handing over the Keys to St. Peter*, Christ confers spiritual

and temporal authority on St. Peter by giving him the keys to the Kingdoms of Heaven and Earth. The golden-domed building in the center of the vast piazza represents both the Temple of Jerusalem and the Church, as founded by Peter, the first pope. The fifth figure on the right is thought to be a self-portrait by Perugino.

Botticelli's *Temptations of Christ* includes a view of the

The central episode in Botticelli's *Punishment of the Rebels*

Hospital of Santo Spirito, rebuilt in 1475 by Sixtus IV (*see p226*). Here the devil is disguised in the habit of a Franciscan monk. Portraits of both Botticelli and Filippino Lippi are visible in the left hand corner. A portrait of the pope's nephew, Girolamo Riario, appears in the painting of the *Crossing of the Red Sea* by Rosselli, in which the sea is literally red. This painting also commemorates the papal victory at Campomorto in 1482.

Perugino's *Handing over the Keys to St Peter*

Sistine Chapel: The Ceiling

MICHELANGELO FRESCOED the ceiling for Pope Julius II between 1508 and 1512, working on specially designed scaffolding. The main panels, which chart the Creation of the World and Fall of Man, are surrounded by subjects from the Old and New Testaments – except for the Classical Sibyls who are said to have foreseen the birth of Christ. In the 1980s the ceiling was restored revealing colors of an unsuspected vibrancy.

Libyan Sibyl
The pagan prophetess reaches for the Book of Knowledge. Like most female figures Michelangelo painted, the beautiful Libyan Sibyl was probably modelled on a man.

Illusionistic architecture

Creation of the Sun and Moon
Michelangelo depicts God as a dynamic but terrifying figure commanding the sun to shed light on the earth.

KEY TO CEILING PANELS

GENESIS: 1 God Dividing Light from Darkness; **2** Creation of the Sun and Moon; **3** Separating Waters from Land; **4** Creation of Adam; **5** Creation of Eve; **6** Original Sin; **7** Sacrifice of Noah; **8** The Deluge; **9** Drunkenness of Noah.

ANCESTORS OF CHRIST: 10 Solomon with his Mother; **11** Parents of Jesse; **12** Rehoboam with Mother; **13** Asa with Parents; **14** Uzziah with Parents; **15** Hezekiah with Parents; **16** Zerubbabel with Parents; **17** Josiah with Parents.

PROPHETS: 18 Jonah; **19** Jeremiah; **20** Daniel; **21** Ezekiel; **22** Isaiah; **23** Joel; **24** Zechariah.

SIBYLS: 25 Libyan Sibyl; **26** Persian Sibyl; **27** Cumaean Sibyl; **28** Erythrean Sibyl; **29** Delphic Sibyl.

OLD TESTAMENT SCENES OF SALVATION: 30 Punishment of Haman; **31** Moses and the Brazen Serpent; **32** David and Goliath; **33** Judith and Holofernes.

Original Sin
This shows Adam and Eve tasting the forbidden fruit from the Tree of Knowledge, and their expulsion from Paradise. Michelangelo represents Satan as a snake with the body of a woman.

The Ignudi are athletic male nudes whose significance is uncertain.

The lunettes are devoted to frescoes of the ancestors of Christ, like Hezekiah.

RESTORATION OF THE SISTINE CEILING

Restorers used computers, photography and spectrum analysis to inspect the fresco before cleaning began. They were therefore able to detect and remove the changes previous restorers had made to Michelangelo's original work. Analysis showed that the ceiling had been cleaned with materials ranging from bread to retsina wine. The restoration then revealed the familiarly

A restorer cleaning the Libyan Sibyl

dusky, eggshell-cracked figures to have creamy skins, lustrous hair and to be dressed in brightly colored, luscious robes: "a Benetton Michelangelo" mocked one critic, claiming that a layer of varnish which the artist had added to darken the colors had been removed. However, after examining the work, most experts agreed that the new colors probably matched those painted by Michelangelo.

Castel Sant'Angelo ⓭

THE MASSIVE FORTRESS of Castel Sant'Angelo takes its name from the vision that Pope Gregory the Great had of the Archangel Michael on this site. It began in AD 139 as Emperor Hadrian's mausoleum. Since then it has had many roles: as part of Emperor Aurelian's city wall, as a medieval citadel and prison and as the residence of the popes in times of political unrest. From the dank cells in the lower levels to the fine apartments of the Renaissance popes above, a 58-room museum covers all aspects of the castle's history.

Mausoleum of Hadrian
This artist's impression shows the tomb before Aurelian fortified its walls in AD 270 to 275.

Courtyard of Honor
Piles of stone cannonballs decorate the courtyard, once the castle's ammunition store.

The Treasury was probably the original site of Hadrian's burial chamber.

Hall of the Columns

Loggia of Paul III

Hall of the Library

PROTECTING THE POPE

The Vatican Corridor leads from the Vatican Palace to Castel Sant'Angelo. It was built in 1277 to provide an escape route when the pope was in danger. The pentagonal ramparts built around the castle during the 17th century improved its defenses in times of siege.

The Rooms of Clement VIII are inscribed with the family crest of the Aldobrandini pope (1592–1605).

The spiral ramp was the entrance to the mausoleum.

The Hall of Justice is decorated with a fresco of *The Angel of Justice* by Domenico Zaga (1545).

▪ Walls and fortifications
☐ Vatican Corridor

★ **View from Terrace**
The castle's terrace, scene of the last act of Puccini's Tosca, *offers splendid views in every direction.*

The Chamber of the Urns housed the ashes of members of Hadrian's family.

VISITORS' CHECKLIST

Lungotevere Castello 50 (entrance through gardens to the right of building).
Map 4 D3 & 11 A1. 06-3996 7600. 23, 34, 62 to Lungotevere Vaticano; 34, 49, 87, 280, 492, 926, 990 to Piazza Cavour. **Open** 9am–8pm (last admission 7pm) Tue–Sun. **Closed** Jan 1, Dec 25. **Adm charge**.
Exhibitions.

Bronze Angel
The gigantic statue of the Archangel Michael is by the 18th-century Flemish sculptor Pieter Verschaffelt.

The Round Hall houses the original model from which Verschaffelt's angel was cast.

★ **Sala Paolina**
The illusionistic frescoes by Perin del Vaga and Pellegrino Tibaldi (1546–8) include one of a courtier entering the room through a painted door.

Hall of Apollo
The room is frescoed with scenes from mythology attributed to the pupils of Perin del Vaga (1548).

Ventilation shaft

★ **Staircase of Alexander VI**
This staircase cuts right through the heart of the building.

Bridge

TIMELINE

AD 139 Mausoleum completed by Antoninus Pius	**590** Legendary date of appearance of Archangel Michael above the castle	**1493** Pope Alexander VI restores Vatican Corridor	*Façade of Castel Sant'Angelo*
		1390 Pope Boniface IX remodels the castle	
AD 100	**500**	**1000**	**1500**
271 Tomb is incorporated into Aurelian Wall and fortified		**1527** Castle withstands siege during Sack of Rome	**1557** Ramparts built to protect the castle
AD 130 Hadrian begins family mausoleum	*Cannonballs in the Courtyard of Honor*	**1542–9** Sala Paolina and apartments built for Pope Paul III	**1870** Castle used as barracks and military prison

VIA VENETO

Film director Federico Fellini

IN IMPERIAL ROME, this was a suburb where rich families owned luxurious villas and gardens. Ruins from this era can be seen in the excavations in Piazza Sallustio, named after the most extensive gardens in the area, the Horti Sallustiani. After the Sack of Rome in the 5th century, the area reverted to open countryside. Not until the 17th century did it recover its lost splendor, with the building of Palazzo Barberini and the now-vanished Villa Ludovisi.

When Rome became capital of Italy in 1870, the Ludovisi sold their land for development. They kept a plot for a new house, but tax on the profits from the sale was so high that they had to sell that, too. By 1900, Via Veneto had become a street with smart modern hotels and cafés. It featured prominently in Fellini's 1960 film *La Dolce Vita*, a scathing satire on the lives of film stars and the idle rich, but since then it has lost its position as the meeting place of the famous.

SIGHTS AT A GLANCE

Churches and Temples
Santa Maria della Concezione ❸
Santa Susanna ❼
Santa Maria della Vittoria ❽

Historic Buildings
Casino dell'Aurora ❷
Palazzo Barberini ❻

Famous Streets
Via Veneto ❶

Fountains
Fontana delle Api ❹
Fontana del Tritone ❺

SEE ALSO

- *Street Finder*, map 5
- *Where to Stay* pp294–5
- *Restaurants* pp310–11

0 meters   200
0 yards   200

N

GETTING THERE

This is one of the easiest parts of Rome to reach by public transportation. Barberini and Repubblica Metro stations on line A are very handy, and Stazione Termini is only 10 to 15 minutes' walk away. The Via Veneto itself starts at Piazza Barberini, well served by buses from all parts of the city. The 95 goes the whole length of Via Veneto to Porta Pinciana. Other useful routes include the 52, 53, 63, 80, 116 and 119.

KEY

	Street-by-Street map
—	City Wall
M	Metro station
P	Parking

The onset of autumn in Via Veneto

Street-by-Street: Via Veneto

THE STREETS AROUND VIA VENETO, though within the walls of ancient Rome, contain little dating from before the unification of Italy in 1870. With its hotels, restaurants, bars and travel agencies, the area is the center of 20th-century tourism in the way that Piazza di Spagna was the hub of the tourist trade in the Rome of the 18th-century Grand Tour. However, glimpses of the old city can be seen among the modern streets. These include Santa Maria della Concezione, the church of the Capuchin friars, whose convent once stood in its own gardens. In the 17th century Palazzo Barberini was built here for the powerful papal family. Bernini's Fontana del Tritone and Fontana delle Api have stood in Piazza Barberini since it was the meeting place of cart tracks entering the city from surrounding vineyards.

Casino dell'Aurora
A pavilion is all that remains of the great Ludovisi estate that once occupied most of this quarter of Rome ❷

Santa Maria della Concezione
This church is best known for the macabre collection of bones in its crypt ❸

Fontana delle Api
Bernini's drinking fountain is decorated with bees, emblem of his Barberini patrons ❹

Fontana del Tritone
Bernini's muscular sea god has been spouting water skywards for 350 years ❺

★ Palazzo Barberini
Pietro da Cortona worked on his spectacular ceiling fresco The Triumph of Divine Providence *between 1633 and 1639* ❻

The Porta Pinciana was built in AD 403. Only the central arch of white travertine is original.

LOCATOR MAP
See Central Rome Map pp12–13

Via Veneto
Built during the redevelopment of Rome at the end of the 19th century, this street of smart hotels and spacious pavement cafés enjoyed its heyday during the 1950s and 1960s ❶

Santa Susanna
This church is dedicated to a martyr executed during Diocletian's persecution of Christians in the 3rd century AD ❼

Star Sights

★ Santa Maria della Vittoria

★ Palazzo Barberini

Key

━ ━ ━ Suggested route

0 meters   75
0 yards   75

★ Santa Maria della Vittoria
The highlight of this Baroque church is the Cornaro Chapel, designed to resemble a theater. The center of the stage is occupied by Bernini's thrilling sculpture of the Ecstasy of St. Teresa ❽

Pavement café in Via Veneto

Via Veneto ❶

Map 5 B1. 🚌 *52, 53, 63, 80, 95, 116, 119 and many routes to Piazza Barberini.* Ⓜ *Barberini.*

VIA VENETO descends in a lazy curve from the Porta Pinciana to Piazza Barberini, lined in its upper reaches with exuberant late 19th-century hotels and canopied sidewalk cafés. It was laid out in 1879 over a large estate sold by the Ludovisi family in the great building boom of Rome's first years as capital of Italy. Palazzo Margherita, intended to be the new Ludovisi family palazzo, was completed in 1890. It now houses the American embassy.

In the 1960s this was the most glamorous street in Rome, its cafés patronized by film stars and plagued by the paparazzi. Most of the people drinking in the cafés today are tourists, as film stars now seem to prefer the livelier Bohemian atmosphere of Trastevere.

Palazzo Margherita, the US embassy

Casino dell'Aurora ❷

Via Lombardia 46. **Map** 5 B2. 📞 *06-48 39 42.* 📠 *06-4201 0745.* 🚌 *52, 53, 63, 80, 95, 116, 119.* Ⓜ *Barberini.* **Open** *by appt only. Call above number, then fax.*

THE CASINO (a stately country residence) was a summer-house on the grounds of the Ludovisi palace. It was built by Cardinal Ludovisi in the 17th century, and frescoed by Guercino. The ceiling fresco creates the impression that the Casino has no roof but lies open to a cloudy sky, across which horses pull the carriage of Aurora, the goddess of dawn, from the darkness of night toward the light of day.

Santa Maria della Concezione ❸

Via Veneto 27. **Map** 5 B2. 📞 *06-487 1185.* 🚌 *52, 53, 61, 62, 63, 80, 95, 116, 119, 175.* Ⓜ *Barberini.* **Open** *7am–noon, 3–7pm daily.* **Crypt open** *9am–noon, 3–6pm Fri–Wed.* **Donation** *expected.* ⛪

POPE URBAN VIII's brother, Antonio Barberini was a cardinal and a Capuchin friar. In 1626 he founded this plain, unassuming church at what is now the foot of the Via Veneto. When he died, he was buried not, like most cardinals, in a grand marble sarcophagus, but below a simple flag-stone close to the altar, with the bleak epitaph in Latin: "Here lies dust, ashes, nothing."

The grim reality of death is illustrated even more graphically in the crypt beneath the church, where generations of Capuchin friars decorated the walls of the five vaulted chapels with the bones and skulls of their departed brethren. In all, some 4,000 skeletons were used over about 100 years to create this macabre *memento mori* started in the late 17th century. Some of the bones are wired together to form Christian symbols such as crowns of thorns, sacred hearts and crucifixes. There are also some complete skeletons, including one of a Barberini princess who died as a child. At the exit, an inscription in Latin reads: "What you are, we used to be. What we are, you will be." **Pope Urban VIII**

Fontana delle Api ❹

Piazza Barberini. **Map** 5 B2. 🚌 *52, 53, 61, 62, 63, 80, 95, 116, 119, 175.* Ⓜ *Barberini.*

THE FOUNTAIN of the bees – *api* are bees, symbol of the Barberini family – is one of Bernini's more modest works. Tucked away in a corner of Piazza Barberini, it is quite easy to miss. Dating from 1644, it pays homage to Pope Urban VIII Barberini, and features rather crablike bees that appear to be sipping the water as it dribbles down into the basin. A Latin inscription informs us that the water is for the use of the public and their animals.

Bernini's Fontana delle Api

Fontana del Tritone ❺

Piazza Barberini. **Map** 5 B3. 🚌 *52, 53, 61, 62, 63, 80, 95, 116, 119, 175.* Ⓜ *Barberini.*

IN THE CENTER of busy Piazza Barberini is one of Bernini's liveliest fountains, the Triton Fountain. It was created for Pope Urban VIII Barberini in 1642, shortly after the completion of his palace on the ridge above. Acrobatic dolphins stand on their heads, twisting their tails together to support a huge scallop shell on which the sea god Triton kneels, blowing a spindly column of water up into the air through a conch shell. Entwined artistically among the dolphins' tails are the papal tiara, the keys of St. Peter and the Barberini coat of arms.

The Triton and his conch shell in Bernini's Fontana del Tritone

Palazzo Barberini ❻

Via delle Quattro Fontane 13. **Map** 5 B3. **【** 06-328 10. **🚌** 52, 53, 61, 62, 63, 80, 95, 116, 175, 492, 590. **Ⓜ** Barberini. **Open** 9am–7pm Tue–Thu, Sun, 9am–10pm Fri, Sat (last adm 30 mins before closing). **Closed** public holidays. **Adm charge**. 🚻 📷 🔼 ♿ 🔳 www.galleriaborghese.it

WHEN MAFFEI BARBERINI became Pope Urban VIII in 1623, he decided to build a grand palace for his family on the fringes of the city, overlooking a ruined temple. The architect, Carlo Maderno, designed it as a typical rural villa, with wings extending into the surrounding gardens. Maderno died in 1629 and Bernini took over, assisted by Borromini. The peculiar pediments on some of the top-floor windows, and the oval staircase inside, are almost certainly by Borromini.

Of the many sumptuously decorated rooms, the most striking is the Gran Salone, with a dazzling illusionistic ceiling fresco by Pietro da Cortona. The palazzo also houses paintings from the 13th to the 16th centuries, part of the Galleria Nazionale d'Arte

Antica, with important works by Filippo Lippi, El Greco and Caravaggio. There is also a Holbein portrait of King Henry VIII of England dressed for his wedding to Anne of Cleves. Of greater local significance are Guido Reni's *Beatrice Cenci*, the young woman executed for planning her father's murder *(see p152)*, and *La Fornarina*, traditionally identified as a portrait of Raphael's mistress, but not necessarily painted by him.

Santa Susanna ❼

Via XX Settembre 14. **Map** 5 C2. **【** 06-4201 4554. **🚌** 60, 61, 62, 84, 175, 492, 910. **Ⓜ** Repubblica. **Open** 9am–noon, 4–7pm daily. 🚻

Façade of Santa Susanna

SANTA SUSANNA'S most striking feature is its vigorous Baroque facade by Carlo Maderno, finished in 1603. Christians have worshiped on the site since at least the 4th century. In the nave, there are four huge frescoes by Baldassarre Croce (1558–1628), painted to resemble tapestries. These depict scenes from the life of Susanna, an obscure Roman saint who was martyred here, and the rather better-known life of the Old Testament Susanna, who was spotted bathing in her husband's garden by two lecherous judges.

Santa Susanna is the Catholic church for Americans in Rome and holds services in English every day.

Santa Maria della Vittoria ❽

Via XX Settembre 17. **Map** 5 C2. **【** 06-4274 0571. **🚌** 60, 61, 62, 84, 175, 492, 910. **Ⓜ** Repubblica. **Open** 8:30–11am, 3–6pm Mon–Sat, 8:45–10am, 3–6pm Sun. 🚻 📷

SANTA MARIA della Vittoria is an intimate Baroque church with a lavishly decorated candlelit interior. It contains one of Bernini's most ambitious sculptural works, the *Ecstasy of St. Teresa* (1646), centerpiece of the Cornaro Chapel, built to resemble a miniature theater. It even has an audience: sculptures of the chapel's benefactor, Cardinal Federico Cornaro, and his ancestors sit in boxes, as if watching and discussing the scene played out in front of them.

Visitors may be shocked or thrilled by the apparently physical nature of St. Teresa's ecstasy. She lies on a cloud, her mouth half-open and her eyelids closed, with rippling drapery covering her body. Looking over her with a smile, which from different angles can appear either tender or cruel, is a curly-haired angel holding an arrow with which he is about to pierce the saint's body for a second time. The marble figures are framed and illuminated by rays of divine light cast out of bronze.

Bernini's astonishing *Ecstasy of St. Teresa*

FARTHER AFIELD

THE MORE INQUISITIVE visitor to Rome may wish to try a few excursions to the large parks and some of the more isolated churches on the outskirts of the city. With a day to spare, you can explore the villas of Tivoli and the ruins of the ancient Roman port of Ostia. Traditional haunts of

Dish (3rd century BC) in Villa Giulia

the Grand Tour *(see p130)*, such as the catacombs and the ruined aqueducts of Parco Appio Claudio, still offer glimpses of the rapidly vanishing Campagna, the country-side around Rome. More modern sights include the suburb of EUR, built in the Fascist era, and the memo-rial at the Fosse Ardeatine.

SIGHTS AT A GLANCE

Towns and Areas
EUR ⑭
Tivoli ⑱

Historic Roads
Via Appia Antica ⑧

Churches
Santa Costanza ⑤
Sant'Agnese fuori le Mura ⑥
San Lorenzo fuori le Mura ⑦
San Paolo fuori le Mura ⑮

Museums and Galleries
Museo e Galleria Borghese pp260–61 ②
Villa Giulia pp262–3 ③
Galleria Comunale d'Arte Moderna ④
Centrale Montemartini ⑯

Ancient Sites
Hadrian's Villa ㉑
Ostia Antica ㉒

Parks and Gardens
Villa Borghese ①
Villa Doria Pamphilj ⑰
Villa d'Este ⑲
Villa Gregoriana ⑳

Tombs and Catacombs
Catacombs of San Callisto ⑨
Catacombs of San Sebastiano ⑩
Catacombs of Domitilla ⑪
Fosse Ardeatine ⑫
Tomb of Cecilia Metella ⑬

SIGHTS OUTSIDE ROME

N

KEY

Main sightseeing areas

Highway

0 kilometers 2

0 miles 1

SIGHTS OUTSIDE THE CENTRE

Caryatids beside the canal of the Canopus at Hadrian's Villa

Villa Borghese ❶

Map 2 E5. 🚌 *52, 53, 88, 95, 116, 490, 495.* 🚋 *3, 19.* **Park open** *dawn to sunset.* **Bioparco** Viale del Giardino Zoologico. **Map** 2 E4.
📞 *06-360 8211.* 🚌 *52.* 🚋 *3, 19.* **Open** *daily Mar–Oct: 9:30am–6pm; Nov–Feb: 9:30am– 5pm (last adm 1hr before closing).* **Closed** *Jan 1.*
♿ 🚻 🛒 📷 🌐 www.bioparco.it
Galleria Nazionale d'Arte Moderna Viale delle Belle Arti 131. **Map** 2 D4. 📞 *06-322 981.*
🚋 *3, 19.* **Open** *9am–7:30pm Tue–Sun.* **Closed** *May 1.*
♿ 📷 🚻 🛒 📷

British School at Rome, designed by Edwin Lutyens in 1911

T HE VILLA and its park were designed in 1605 for Cardinal Scipione Borghese, nephew of Pope Paul V. The park was the first of its kind in Rome. It contained 400 newly-planted pine trees, garden sculpture by Bernini's father, Pietro, and dramatic waterworks built by Giovanni Fontana. The layout of the formal gardens was imitated by other prominent Roman families at Villa Ludovisi and Villa Doria Pamphilj, but the cardinal's 18th-century successors preferred a more natural-looking park.

In the early 19th century Prince Camillo Borghese assembled the family's magnificent art collection in the Casino Borghese, now the home of the Galleria and Museo Borghese.

In 1901 the park became the property of the Italian state. Within its 4-mile (6-km) circumference there are now museums and galleries, foreign academies and schools of archaeology, a zoo, a riding school, a grassy amphitheatre, an artificial lake, an aviary and an array of summerhouses, fountains, Neo-Classical statuary and exotic follies.

There are several ways into the park, including a monumental entrance on Piazzale Flaminio, built for Prince Camillo Borghese in 1825 by Luigi Canina. Other conveniently-sited entrances are at Porta Pinciana at the end of Via Veneto and from the Pincio Gardens *(see p136).* The main attraction of Italian gardens in hot weather is shade, so the long avenues are lined with hedges and trees. Piazza di Siena, a pleasantly open, grass-covered amphitheatre surrounded by tall umbrella pines, was the inspiration for Ottorino Respighi's famous symphonic poem *The Pines of Rome,* written in 1924. Near Piazza di Siena are the so-called Casina di Raffaello, said to have been owned by Raphael, and the

Statue of the English poet Byron by Thorvaldsen

18th-century Palazzetto dell'Orologio. These were summerhouses from which people enjoyed the beautiful vistas across the park. Many buildings in the park were originally surrounded by formal gardens: the Casino Borghese and the nearby 17th-century Casino della Meridiana and its aviary *(uccelliera)* have both kept their geometrical flowerbeds. Throughout the park the intersections of paths and avenues are marked by fountains and statues. West of Piazza di Siena is the Fontana dei Cavalli

Marini (the Fountain of the Seahorses) added during the villa's 18th-century remodeling. Walking through the park you will encounter statues of Byron, Goethe and Victor Hugo, and a gloomy equestrian King Umberto I.

Dotted about the park are picturesque temples made to look like ruins, including a circular Temple of Diana between Piazza di Siena and Porta Pinciana, and a Temple of Faustina, wife of Emperor Antoninus Pius, on the hill north of Piazza di Siena. The nearby medieval-looking Fortezzuola by Canina contains the works of the sculptor Pietro Canonica, who lived in the building and died there in 1959. In the garden stands Canonica's *Monument to the Alpino and his Mule,* which honors the humblest

Neo-Classical Temple of Diana

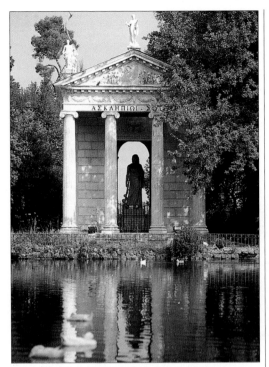

Ionic temple dedicated to Aesculapius, built on the lake island

by Edwin Lutyens, with a façade adapted from the upper west portico of St. Paul's Cathedral in London. Originally a School of Archaeology, it is now a research institute for classical studies, history and the visual arts. Nearby statues include Simon Bolivar and other liberators of Latin America, and the Persian poet Firdusi.

In the northeastern corner of the park lie the Museo Zoologico and a small re-developed Zoo, known as the Bioparco, where the emphasis is on conservation. Nearby the pretty 16th-century Villa Giulia houses a world-famous collection of Etruscan and other pre-Roman remains.

Bioparco symbol

Another Renaissance building of importance is the Palazzina of Pius IV, close to the Via Flaminia entrance. Designed by the architect Vignola in 1552, it later became an elegant apartment for Pius IV's nephew Carlo Borromeo. It now houses the Italian Embassy to the Holy See.

protagonists in Italy's alpine battles against Austria in World War I.

In the center of the park is the Giardino del Lago, its main entrance marked by an 18th-century copy of the Arch of Septimius Severus.

The garden has an artificial lake complete with an Ionic Temple to Aesculapius, the god of health, by the 18th-century architect Antonio Asprucci. Rowing boats and ducks make the lake a favorite with children, banana trees and bamboo grow around the shore, and clearings are studded with sculptures.

Surrounded by flowerbeds south of the lake is the Art Nouveau Fontana dei Fauni, one of the garden's prettiest sculptures. In a clearing close to the entrance on Viale Pietro Canonica are the original Tritons of the Fontana del Moro in Piazza Navona *(see p120)* – they were moved here and replaced by copies in the 19th century.

From the northwest the park is entered by the Viale delle Belle Arti, where the Galleria Nazionale d'Arte Moderna houses a good collection of 19th- and 20th-century paintings. The Art Nouveau character of the area dates from the International Exhibition held here in 1911, for which pavilions were built by many nations, the most impressive being the British School at Rome,

Museo e Galleria Borghese ❷

See pp260–61.

Villa Giulia ❸

See pp262–3.

A stone lion guarding the ornate entrance to the Zoo

Museo e Galleria Borghese ❷

THE VILLA AND PARK were laid out by Cardinal Scipione Borghese, favorite nephew of Paul V, who had the house designed for pleasure and entertainment. The hedonistic cardinal was also an extravagant patron of the arts and he commissioned sculptures from the young Bernini which rank among his most famous works. Scipione also opened his pleasure park to the public. Today the villa houses the superb private Borghese collection of sculptures and paintings in the Museo and Galleria Borghese.

MUSEUM GUIDE

The museum is divided into two sections: the sculpture collection (Museo Borghese) occupies the entire ground floor and the picture gallery (Galleria Borghese) is on the upper floor. The Galleria Borghese has reopened to the public after extensive restoration work.

Façade of the Villa Borghese
This painting (1613) by the villa's Flemish architect Jan van Santen shows the highly ornate façade of the original design.

★ Rape of Proserpine
One of Bernini's finest works shows Pluto (Hades) abducting his bride. The sculptor's amazing skill with marble can be seen clearly in the twisting figures.

4

5

6

7

8

Sleeping Hermaphrodite

Dated around 150 BC, this is a bronze Roman copy of the Greek original by Polycles. The head and mattress were added by Andrea Bergondi in the 17th century.

The Egyptian Room
Frescoes show episodes in Egyptian history and Egyptian motifs.

TIMELINE

1613 15-year-old Bernini sculpts *Aeneas and Anchises*	**Early 1800s** Statues and reliefs are considered too ornate and stripped from the villa's façade	**1809** Much of the collection is sold by Prince Camillo Borghese to France and goes to Louvre	**1902** Villa, grounds and collection bought by the state
1621–5 Bernini sculpts *Pluto and Persephone*			
1625	**1725**	**1825**	
1622–5 Bernini sculpts *Apollo and Daphne*		**1805** Canova sculpts the semi-nude, reclining Pauline Borghese	**Early 1900s** Balustrade round the forecourt is bought by Lord Astor for the Cliveden estate in England
1613–15 The Flemish architect Jan van Santen designs and builds Villa Borghese			

Daphne's fingers turning into leaves

★ Apollo and Daphne
Bernini's most famous masterpiece depicts the nymph Daphne fleeing the sun god Apollo at the moment of Daphne's dramatic transformation into a tree.

Rear entrance

David is captured the moment before he slew Goliath in the sculpture by Bernini, who modeled his face on his own.

VISITORS' CHECKLIST

Villa Borghese, Piazzale Scipione Borghese 5. Map 2 F5.
(06-328 10 (reservations).
FAX 06-3265 1329. 🚌 52, 53, 116, 910 to Via Pinciana. 🚋 3, 19 to Viale delle Belle Arti.
Open 9am–7pm Tue–Sun.
Closed Jan 1, May 1, Dec 25.
Adm charge. Advance booking recommended weekdays and obligatory Sat & Sun.
📷 🎥 🚫 ⬛ 🔲
Ⓦ www.galleriaborghese.it

★ Galleria Borghese
The gallery has old master paintings, such as Titian's Sacred and Profane Love *(detail) dating from 1514.*

★ Pauline Borghese
Napoleon's sister Pauline posed as Venus for this sculpture. Once the statue was finished, her husband locked it away, even from its sculptor Canova.

Front entrance

Gladiator Mosaic
The floor is decorated with the fragments of a 4th-century AD mosaic from a villa in Torrenova.

KEY TO FLOOR PLAN
☐ Exhibition space
▨ Non-exhibition space

STAR SCULPTURES

★ Pauline Borghese by Canova

★ Apollo and Daphne by Bernini

★ Rape of Proserpine by Bernini

★ Galleria Borghese

Villa Giulia ❸

THIS VILLA was built as a country retreat for Pope Julius III, and was designed for entertaining rather than as a permanent home. It once housed an impressive collection of statues – 160 boatloads were sent to the Vatican after the pope died in 1555. The villa, gardens, pavilions and fountains were designed by exceptional architects: Vignola (designer of the Gesù), Vasari and the sculptor Ammannati. Michelangelo also contributed. The villa's main features are its façade, the court-yard and garden and the *nymphaeum*. Since 1889 Villa Giulia has housed the Museo Nazionale Etrusco, with its out-standing collection of pre-Roman antiquities from central Italy.

★ Ficoroni Cist
Engraved and beautifully illustrated, this fine bronze marriage coffer dates from the 4th century BC.

Chigi Oinochoe
Battle and hunting scenes adorn this Corinthian vase from the 6th century BC.

★ Husband and Wife Sarcophagus
This 6th-century BC masterpiece, from Cerveteri, shows a dead couple at the eternal banquet.

MUSEUM GUIDE
This is the most important Etruscan museum in Italy, housing artifacts from most of the major excavations in Tuscany and Lazio. Rooms 1–10 and 23–34 are arranged by site and include Vulci, Todi, Veio and Cerveteri, while private collections are in rooms 11–22.

Votive Offering
The religious Etruscans made artifacts, such as this model of a boy feeding a bird, in their gods' honor.

TIMELINE

1550 Work begins on Villa Giulia under Pope Julius III	**1655** Queen Christina of Sweden stays in villa as Vatican guest	**1889** Etruscan museum founded **Late 1700s** First large-scale studies of Etruscan artifacts	**1919** Castellani private collection donated to museum	

1550	1650	1750	1850	1950

Late 1500s First, chance finds of Etruscan artifacts raise some scholastic interest		**1908** Barberini private collection bought by the state	**1972** Pesciotti private collection bought by the state
1555 Villa completed	*Corner decoration of bronze chariot used to burn incense*		

Façade
The villa's façade dates from 1552–3. The entrance is designed in the form of a triumphal arch.

VISITORS' CHECKLIST

Piazzale di Villa Giulia 9.
Map 1 C4. [06-322 6571
*(information), 06-328 10
(reservations).* 📧 52, 926 to
*Viale Bruno Buozzi, 88, 95, 490,
495 to Viale Washington.*
🚃 3, 19 to Piazza Thorwaldsen.
Open 9am–7pm Tue–Sun (last
entry 30 mins before closing
time). **Closed** Jan 1, May 1,
Dec 25. **Adm charge.**
✏ with seven days' notice.
🎧 🅿 🚻 ♿ **Concerts** in the
courtyard in July. **Lectures.**

★ **Reconstruction
of an Etruscan Temple**
*Count Adolfo Cozza built the Temple
of Alatri here in 1891. He based his
design on the accounts of Vitruvius
and 19th-century excavations.*

Nymphaeum
*Literally, the "area
dedicated to the
nymphs," this is a
sunken courtyard
decorated with
Classical mosaics,
statues and fountains.*

STAR EXHIBITS

★ **Husband and Wife
Sarcophagus**

★ **Ficoroni Cist**

★ **Reconstruction of
an Etruscan Temple**

Main entrance

**Faliscan Crater
of the Dawn**
*This ornate vase,
painted in the free
style of the 4th century
BC, shows Dawn
rising in a chariot.*

KEY TO FLOOR PLAN

☐ Ground floor

☐ First floor

☐ Non-exhibition space

Galleria Comunale d'Arte Moderna ❹

Via Reggio Emilia 54. **Map** 6 E1.
☎ 06-6710 7900. 🚍 36, 60, 84, 90.
Open 9am–6:30pm Tue–Sun.
Adm charge. 🏛 🖥 **Branch** Via
Francesco Crispi 24. **Map** 5 B2.
☎ 06-474 2848. **Open** 9am–6:30pm
Tue–Sat, 9:30am–1:30pm Sun. **Adm**
charge. 🏛 ♿ via Via Zucchelli 7.

THE GALLERY has two
branches. The restored
Peroni beer factory on Via
Reggio Emilia holds temporary
exhibitions and post-1950
contemporary art. The branch
on Via Francesco Crispi has
the permanent collection of
pre-1950 art. Most paintings
date from the 19th century
and include works by Rodin,
Ximenes, Balla and Guttuso.

Interior of Santa Costanza

Santa Costanza ❺

Via Nomentana 349. ☎ 06-861 0840.
🚍 36, 60, 84, 90. **Open** 9am–noon,
4–6pm Tue–Sat, 4–6pm Sun, 9am–
noon Mon. **Adm charge**. ♿ 📷

THE ROUND CHURCH of Santa
Costanza was first built as
a mausoleum for Emperor
Constantine's daughters
Constantia and Helena, in the
early 4th century. The dome
and its drum are supported
by a circular arcade resting on
12 magnificent pairs of granite
columns. The ambulatory that
runs around the outside of
the central arcade has a barrel-

Part of the 4th-century mosaic in the ambulatory of Santa Costanza

vaulted ceiling decorated with
wonderful 4th-century mosaics
of flora and fauna and
charming scenes of a Roman
grape harvest. In a niche on
the far side of the church from
the entrance is a replica of
Constantia's ornately carved
porphyry sarcophagus. The
original was moved to the
Vatican Museums in 1790.

Constantia's sanctity
is debatable – she was
described by the historian
Marcellinus as a fury
incarnate, constantly goading
her equally unpleasant
husband Hannibalianus to
violence. Her canonization
was probably the result of
some confusion with a saintly
nun of the same name.

Sant'Agnese fuori le Mura ❻

Via Nomentana 349. ☎ 06-861 0840.
🚍 36, 60, 84, 90.
Open 9am–noon, 4–6pm Tue–Sat,
4–6pm Sun, 9am–noon Mon.
Adm charge to catacombs. ♿ 📷

THE CHURCH OF Sant'Agnese
stands among a group of
early Christian buildings which
includes the ruins of a covered

cemetery, some extensive
catacombs and the crypt
where the 13-year-old martyr
St. Agnes was buried in
AD 304. Agnes was exposed
naked by order of Emperor
Diocletian, furious that she
should have rejected the
advances of a young man at
his court, but her hair
miraculously grew to protect
her modesty *(see p121)*.

The church is said to have
been built at the request of
the Emperor Constantine's
daughter, Constantia, after
she had prayed at the Tomb
of St. Agnes for delivery
from leprosy.

Though much altered over
the centuries, the form and
much of the structure of the
4th-century basilica remain
intact. In the 7th-century apse
mosaic St. Agnes appears as a
bejeweled Byzantine empress
in a stole of gold and a violet
robe. According to tradition
she appeared like this 8 days
after her death holding a white
lamb. Every year on January
21 two lambs are blessed
on the church altar and a
vestment called the *pallium* is
woven from their wool. Every
newly appointed archbishop
is sent a *pallium* by the pope.

Apse mosaic in Sant'Agnese, showing the saint flanked by two popes

Cloister, San Lorenzo fuori le Mura

San Lorenzo fuori le Mura ⓿

Piazzale del Verano 3. █ 06-49 15 11. ▥ 71, 492. ▤ 3, 19. **Open** 7:30am–12:30pm, 3–7pm (7:30pm in summer) daily. ♿

JUST OUTSIDE the eastern wall of the city stands the church of San Lorenzo. Roasted slowly to death in AD 258, San Lorenzo was one of the most revered of Rome's early Christian martyrs. The first basilica erected over his burial place by Constantine was largely rebuilt in 576 by Pope Pelagius II. Close by stood a 5th-century church dedicated to the Virgin Mary. The intriguing two-level church we see today is the result of these two churches being knocked into one. This process, started in the 8th century, was completed in the 13th century by Pope Honorius III, when the nave, the portico and much of the decoration were added. The remains of San Lorenzo are in the choir of the 6th-century church (beneath the 13th-century high altar).

Romanesque bell tower of San Lorenzo

Via Appia Antica ❽

▥ 118, 218, 660. See **Walks** pp284–5.

THE FIRST PART of the Via Appia was built in 312 BC by the Censor Appius Claudius Caecus. When it was extended to the ports of Benevento, Taranto and Brindisi in 190 BC, the road became Rome's link with its expanding empire in the East. It was the route of the funeral processions of the dictator Sulla (78 BC) and Emperor Augustus (AD 14) and it was along this road that St. Paul was led a prisoner to Rome in AD 56.

Gradually abandoned during the Middle Ages, the road was restored in the mid-16th century by Pope Pius IV. It is lined with ruined family tombs and the collective burial places known as columbaria. Beneath the fields on either side lies a vast maze of catacombs. Today the road starts at Porta San Sebastiano (see p196). Major Christian sights include the church of Domine Quo Vadis?, built where St. Peter is said to have met Christ while fleeing from Rome, and the Catacombs of San Callisto and San Sebastiano. The tombs lining the road include those of Cecilia Metella (see p266) and Romulus (son of Emperor Maxentius) who died in AD 309. The ancient Villa dei Quintili is nearby, at Via Appia Nuova 1092 (call 06-481 5576).

Catacombs of San Callisto ❾

Via Appia Antica 126. █ 06-513 01 51. ▥ 118, 218, 660. **Open** 8:30am–noon, 2:30–5:30pm (Oct–Mar: 5pm) Thu–Tue. **Closed** Feb; Jan 1, Easter Sun & Dec 25. **Adm charge**. ▯ ∅ ▮ ▯ ▯ ▯ W www.catacombe.roma.it

IN BURYING their dead in underground cemeteries outside the city walls, the early Christians were obeying the laws of the time: it was not because of persecution. So many saints were buried that the catacombs became shrines and places of pilgrimage.

The vast Catacombs of San Callisto are on four different

levels and only partly explored. The rooms and connecting passageways are hewn out of volcanic tufa. The dead were placed in niches, known as *loculi*, which held two or three bodies. The most important rooms were decorated with stucco and frescoes. The area that can be visited includes the Crypt of the Popes, where many of the early popes were buried, and the Crypt of Santa Cecilia, where the saint's body was discovered in 820 before being moved to her church in Trastevere (see p211).

Catacombs of San Sebastiano ❿

Via Appia Antica 136. █ 06-788 7035. ▥ 118, 218, 660. **Open** 8:30am–noon, 2:30–5:30pm (Oct–Mar: 5pm) Mon–Sat. **Closed** Nov. **Adm charge**. ▯ ▮ ▯ W www.catacombe.roma.it

THE 17TH-CENTURY church of San Sebastiano, above the catacombs, occupies the site of a basilica. Preserved at the entrance to the catacombs is the *triclia*, a building that once stood above ground and was used by mourners for taking funeral refreshments. Its walls are covered with graffiti invoking St. Peter and St. Paul, whose remains may have been moved here during one of the periods of persecution.

Cypresses lining part of the Roman Via Appia Antica

Catacombs of Domitilla ⓫

Via delle Sette Chiese 282.
📞 06-511 0342. 🚍 218, 716.
Open 8:30am–noon, 2:30pm–
5:30pm (Oct–Mar: 5pm) Wed–Mon.
Closed Jan. **Adm charge.** 🚫 📷

THIS NETWORK of catacombs is the largest in Rome. Many of the tombs from the 1st and 2nd centuries AD have no Christian connection. In the burial chambers there are frescoes of both Classical and Christian scenes, including one of the earliest depictions of Christ as the *Good Shepherd*. Above the catacombs stands the basilica of Santi Nereo e Achilleo. After rebuilding and restoration, little remains of the original 4th-century church.

Bronze entrance gates to the Fosse Ardeatine by Mirko Basaldella

Fosse Ardeatine ⓬

Via Ardeatina 174. 📞 06-513 6742.
🚍 218, 716. **Open** 8:15am–5pm
daily. **Closed** public hols.

ON THE EVENING of March 24 1944, Nazi forces took 335 prisoners to this abandoned quarry south of Rome and shot them at point blank range. The execution was in response to a bomb attack that had killed 32 German soldiers. The victims included various political prisoners, 73 Jews and ten other civilians, among them a priest and a 14-year-old boy. The Germans blew up the tunnels where the massacre had taken place, but a local peasant had witnessed the scene and later helped find

the corpses. The site is now a memorial to the values of the Resistance against the Nazi occupation, which gave birth to the modern Italian Republic. A forbidding bunker-like monument houses the rows of identical tombs containing the victims.

Beside it is a museum of the Resistance. Interesting works of modern sculpture include *The Martyrs*, by Francesco Coccia, and the gates shaped like a wall of thorns by Mirko Basaldella.

Tomb of Cecilia Metella ⓭

Via Appia Antica, km 3.
📞 06-3996 7700. 🚍 118, 660.
Open 9am–1 hour before sunset daily.

ONE OF THE most famous landmarks on the Via Appia Antica is the huge drum-shaped tomb built for the noblewoman Cecilia Metella. Her father and husband were rich patricians and successful generals of late Republican Rome, but hardly anything is known about the woman herself. Byron muses over her unknown destiny in his poem *Childe Harold*.

In 1302 Pope Boniface VIII donated the tomb to his family, the Caetani. They incorporated it in a fortified castle that blocked the Via Appia, allowing them to control the traffic on the road and exact high tolls.

The marble facing of the tomb was pillaged by another pope, Sixtus V, at the end of the 16th century.

Fragments of marble relief on the Tomb of Cecilia Metella

EUR's Palazzo della Civiltà del Lavoro, the "Square Colosseum"

EUR ⓮

🚍 170, 671, 714 and other routes.
Ⓜ EUR Fermi, EUR Palasport.
Museo della Civiltà Romana Piazza
G. Agnelli 10. 📞 06-592 6041.
Open 9am–6:15pm Tue–Sat,
9am–1pm Sun and public hols. **Closed**
Jan 1, May 1, Dec 25. **Adm charge**.

THE ESPOSIZIONE Universale di Roma (EUR), a suburb south of the city, was built for an international exhibition, a kind of "Work Olympics", that was planned for 1942, but never took place because of the war. The architecture was intended to glorify Fascism and the style of the public buildings is very overblown and rhetorical. The eerie shape of the Palazzo della Civiltà del Lavoro (the Palace of the Civilization of Work) is an unmistakable landmark for people arriving from Fiumicino airport.

The scheme was completed in the 1950s. In terms of town planning, EUR has been quite successful and people still flock to live here. The great marble halls house several government offices and museums. The Museo della Civiltà Romana displays a vast scale model of Rome at the time of Constantine and casts of the reliefs on Trajan's Column. These are highly recommended and make the museum well worth a visit.

To the south is a lake and park, and the huge domed Palazzo dello Sport built for the 1960 Olympics.

San Paolo fuori le Mura ⑮

Via Ostiense 186. ⓒ 06-541 0341.
🚌 23, 128, 170, 670, 707, 761,
769. Ⓜ San Paolo. **Open** 7am–7pm
daily (summer), 7am–6:30pm daily
(winter). **Cloister closed** 1–3pm
daily. 🚻 ♿ 🏛

Today's church is a faithful reconstruction of the great 4th-century basilica destroyed by fire on July 15, 1823. Few fragments of the original church survived. The triumphal arch over the nave is decorated on one side with restored 5th-century mosaics. On the other side are mosaics by Pietro Cavallini, originally on the façade. The splendid Venetian apse mosaics (1220) depict Christ with St. Peter, St. Andrew, St. Paul and St. Luke.

The fine marble canopy over the high altar is signed by the sculptor Arnolfo di Cambio (1285) "together with his part-ner Pietro", who may have been Pietro Cavallini. Below the altar is the *confessio*, the tomb of St. Paul. To the right is an impressive Paschal candlestick by Nicolò di Angelo and Pietro Vassalletto.

The cloister of San Paolo, with its pairs of colorful inlaid

19th-century mosaic on façade of San Paolo fuori le Mura

columns supporting the arcade, was spared completely by the fire. Completed around 1214, it is considered one of the most beautiful in Rome.

Centrale Montemartini ⑯

Via Ostiense 106. ⓒ 06-574 8042
🚌 23, 769. **Open** 9:30am–7pm
Tue–Sun. **Closed** public hols.
Adm charge. 🚻 ♿ 🖥 🛍

An enormous old industrial site has been restored to house the ACEA art centre. Originally, the building was used as Rome's first power station and its two huge generators still occupy the central machine room creating quite an intriguing contrast to the exhibitions. On display are Roman statues and artifacts belonging to the Capitoline Museums (*see pp70–73*). Many of the statues were discovered during excavations in the late 19th and early 20th centuries but were kept in storage until fairly recently.

Casino del Bel Respiro, summer residence in Villa Doria Pamphilj

Villa Doria Pamphilj ⑰

Via di San Pancrazio. 🚌 31, 44, 75,
710, 870. **Park open** dawn–dusk
daily.

One of Rome's largest public parks, the Villa Doria Pamphilj was laid out in the mid-17th century for Prince Camillo Pamphilj. His uncle Pope Innocent X paid for the magnificent summer residence, the Casino del Bel Respiro, fountains and summerhouses, some of which still survive.

Statue in Centrale Montemartini, former power plant turned art center

Day Trips around Rome

Tivoli, a favorite place to escape the heat of the Roman summer

Tivoli 🔟

Town is 20 miles (31 km) northeast of Rome. **FS** *from Tiburtina.* 🚌 *COTRAL from Ponte Mammolo (on Metro line B).*

Tivoli has been a popular summer resort since the days of the Roman Republic. Among the famous men who owned villas here were the poets Catullus and Horace, Caesar's assassins Brutus and Cassius and the Emperors Trajan and Hadrian. Tivoli's main attractions were its clean air and beautiful location on the slopes of the Tiburtini hills, its healthy sulphur springs and the waterfalls of the Aniene – the Emperor Augustus said these had cured him of insomnia.

The Romans' luxurious lifestyle was revived in Renaissance times by the owners of the Villa d'Este, the town's most famous sight.

Detail of Fontana dell'Organo at Villa d'Este

In the Middle Ages, Tivoli suffered frequent invasions since its position made it an ideal base for an advance on Rome. In 1461, Pope Pius II built a fortress here, the Rocca Pia, declaring: "It is easier to regain Rome while possessing Tivoli, than to regain Tivoli while possessing Rome."

After suffering heavy bomb damage in 1944, Tivoli's main buildings and churches were speedily restored. The town's cobbled streets are still lined with medieval houses. The Duomo (cathedral) houses a beautiful 13th-century life-size wooden group representing the *Deposition from the Cross.*

Villa d'Este 🔟

Piazza Trento 1, Tivoli.
📞 *0774-31 2070.* 🚌 *COTRAL from Ponte Mammolo (on Metro line B).* **Open** *8:30am–1 hr before sunset Tue–Sun.* **Closed** *Jan 1, May 1, Dec 25.* **Adm charge.** 🔲

The villa occupies the site of an old Benedictine convent. In the 16th century, the estate was developed by Cardinal Ippolito d'Este, son of Lucrezia Borgia. A palace was designed by Pirro Ligorio to make the most of its hilltop situation, but the villa's fame rests more on the terraced gardens and fountains laid out by Ligorio and Giacomo della Porta.

The gardens have suffered from neglect, but the grottoes and fountains still give a vivid impression of the great luxury which the princes of the church enjoyed. From the great loggia of the palace you descend through the shrub-lined paths to the Grotto of Diana and Bernini's Fontana del Bicchierone. Below to the right is the Rometta (little Rome), a model of Tiber Island with allegorical figures and the legendary she-wolf.

The Rometta is at one end of the Viale delle Cento Fontane, 100 fountains in the shape of grotesques, obelisks, ships and the eagles of the d'Este coat of arms, now overgrown with moss. Other fountains have also lost much of their former glory. The Fontana dell'Organo was a water organ, in which the force of the water pumped air through the pipes, but it has long been silent. The garden's lowest level has flower beds and fountains as well as some splendid views out over the plain below.

Terrace of 100 Fountains in the gardens of Villa d'Este

Villa Gregoriana 🔟

Largo Massimo, Tivoli. **FS** 🚌 *Tivoli, then short walk.* **Open** *9:30am–1 hr before sunset daily (summer), 9:30am–6:30pm (winter).* **Adm charge.**

The main attractions of this steeply sloping wooded park are the waterfalls and grottoes created over the centuries by the River Aniene. The park is named after Pope Gregory XVI, who in the 1830s ordered the building of a tunnel to eradicate flooding. This created a new waterfall, the Grande Cascata, which plunges 525 ft (160 m) into the valley behind the town.

The Canopus, extensively restored, with replicas of its original caryatids lining the bank of the canal

Hadrian's Villa ㉑

Villa Adriana, Via Tiburtina. Site is 6 km (4 miles) southwest of Tivoli.
🅒 0774-53 02 03. 🄵🅂 Tivoli, then local bus No. 4. 🚌 COTRAL from Ponte Mammolo (on Metro line B).
Open 9am–1 hr before sunset daily. **Closed** Jan 1, May 1, Dec 25. **Adm charge.** ▫️ ▫️ ▫️

Built as a private summer retreat between AD 118 and 134, Hadrian's Villa was a vast open-air museum of the finest architecture of the Roman world. The grounds of the Imperial palace covered an area of 300 acres (120 hectares) and were filled with full-scale reproductions of the emperor's favorite buildings from Greece and Egypt. Although excavations began here in the 16th century, many of the ruins lying scattered in the surrounding fields have yet to be identified with any certainty. The grounds of the villa make

a very picturesque site for a picnic, with scattered fragments of columns lying among olive trees and cypresses.

For an idea of how the whole complex would have looked in its heyday, study the scale model in the building beside the parking area. Important buildings have signs, and several have been partially restored or reconstructed. One of the most impressive is the Maritime Theater. This is a round pool with an island in the middle, surrounded by columns. The island, reached by means of a swing bridge, was probably Hadrian's private studio, where he withdrew from the cares of the Empire to indulge in his favorite pastimes, painting and architecture. There were also theaters; Greek and Latin libraries; two bathhouses; extensive housing for guests and the palace staff; and formal gardens with fountains, statues and pools.

Hadrian was a lover of Greek philosophy as well as architecture. One part of the gardens is thought to have been Hadrian's reproduction of the Grove of Academe, where Plato lectured to his students.

Fragment of marble mosaic pavement in the Imperial palace

Hadrian also had a replica of the Stoà Poikile, a beautiful painted colonnade in Athens, from which the Stoic philosophers took their name. Hadrian's Poikile enclosed a piazza with a central pool. The area known as the Hall of the Philosophers near the Poikile was probably a library.

The most ambitious of Hadrian's replicas was the Canopus, a sanctuary of the god Serapis near Alexandria. For this a canal 130 yd (119 m) long was dug and Egyptian statues were imported to decorate the temple and its grounds. This impressive piece of engineering has been restored, and the banks of the canal are lined with caryatids.

Another picturesque spot in the grounds is the Vale of Tempe, the legendary haunt of the goddess Diana, with a stream representing the river Peneios. Below ground, the

Pair of Ionic columns in the vaulted baths of Hadrian's Villa

emperor built a fanciful re-creation of the underworld, Hades, reached through many underground tunnels which linked the various parts of the villa.

Plundered by barbarians who camped here in the 6th and 8th centuries, the villa fell into disrepair. Its marble was burned to make lime for cement, and Renaissance antiquarians contributed further to its destruction. Statues unearthed in the grounds are displayed in museums around Europe. The Vatican's Egyptian Collection (see p238) has many fine works that were found here.

Ostia Antica ㉒

Viale dei Romagnoli 717. Site is 16 miles
(25 km) southwest of Rome.
C 06-5635 8099. **FAX** 06-565 1500.
M *Piramide, then train from Porta
San Paolo station.*
Excavations and museum open
9am–1 hour before sunset.
Closed *Jan 1, May 1, Dec 25.*
Adm charge. 🚻 💻 ♿

IN REPUBLICAN TIMES Ostia was
Rome's main commercial
port and a military base
defending the coastline and
the mouth of the Tiber. The
port continued to flourish
under the Empire, despite the
development of Portus, a new
port slightly to the northwest,
in the 2nd century AD. Ostia's
decline began in the 4th
century, when a reduction in
trade was combined with the
gradual silting up of the
harbor. Then malaria became
endemic in the area, and the
city, whose population may
have been nearly 100,000 at its
peak, was totally abandoned.

Buried for centuries by
sand, the city is remarkably
well preserved. The site is
less spectacular than Pompei
or Herculaneum because
Ostia died a gradual death,
but it gives a more complete
picture of life under the
Roman Empire. People of all
social classes and from all
over the Mediterranean lived
and worked here.

Visitors can understand the
layout of Ostia's streets almost
at a glance. The main road
through the town, the
Decumanus Maximus, would
have been filled with hurrying
slaves and citizens, avoiding
the jostling carriages and
carts, while tradesmen
pursued their business under

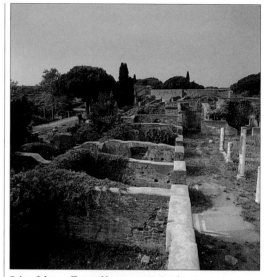

Ruins of shops, offices and houses near Ostia's theater

the porticoes lining the street.
The floor plans of the public
buildings along the road are
very clear. Many were bathhouses, such as the Baths
of the Cisiarii (carters)
and the grander Baths
of Neptune, named after
their fine black-and-white
floor mosaics. Beside the
restored theater, three large
masks, originally part of
the decoration of the stage,
have been mounted on
large blocks of tufa. Beneath
the great brick arches that
supported the semicircular
tiers of seats were taverns
and shops. Classical plays
are put on here now in
the summer.

The Tiber's course has
changed considerably since
Ostia was the port of Rome. It
once flowed past just to the
north of Piazzale delle

**Mask decorating
the theater**

Corporazioni, the square
behind the theater. The
corporations were the guilds
of the various trades involved
in fitting out and
supplying ships:
tanners and rope
makers, ship-
builders and
timber merchants,
ships' chandlers
and corn weighers.
There were some
60 or 70 offices
around the square.
Mosaics showing
scenes of everyday
life in the port and
the names and
symbols of the
corporations can
still be seen.
There were also offices used
by ship-owners and their
agents from places as far
away as Tunisia and the
south of France, Sardinia and
Egypt. In one office,
belonging to a merchant from
the town of Sabratha in North
Africa, there is a delightful
mosaic of an elephant.

The main cargo coming into
Rome was grain from Africa.
Much of this was distributed
free to prevent social unrest.
Although only men received
this *annona,* or corn ration,
at times over 300,000 were
eligible. In the center of the
square was a temple, probably

Mural from Ostia of merchant ship being loaded with grain

dedicated to Ceres, goddess of the harvest. Among the buildings excavated are many large warehouses in which grain was stored before it was shipped on to Rome.

The Decumanus leads to the Forum and the city's principal temple, erected by Hadrian in the 2nd century AD and dedicated to Jove, Juno and Minerva. In this rather romantic, lonely spot, it is hard to imagine the Forum as a bustling center where justice was dispensed and officials

Floor mosaic of Nereid and sea monster in the House of the Dioscuri

Detail of floor mosaic in the Piazzale delle Corporazioni

met to discuss the city's affairs. In the 18th century it was used as a sheepfold.

Away from the main street are the buildings where Ostia's inhabitants lived. The great majority lived in rented apartments in blocks three or four stories high, known as *insulae*. These varied widely in their comfort and decor. The House of Diana was one of the more elegant ones, with a balcony around the second floor, a private bath-house and a central courtyard with a cistern where tenants came to get their water. Around the ground floor of the block were shops, taverns and bars selling snacks and drinks. In the bar at the House of Diana you can see the marble counter used by customers buying their sausages and hot wine sweetened with honey.

For the wealthy there were detached houses *(domus)* such as the House of the Dioscuri, which has fine colored mosaics, and the House of Cupid and Psyche, named after a charming statue found there. This is now in the site's Museo Ostiense, near the Forum, along with other sculptures.

Among the houses and shops there are other buildings, including a laundry and the firemen's barracks.

Various religions are practiced in Ostia. There are no fewer than 18 temples dedicated to the Persian god Mithras, as well as a Jewish synagogue dating from the 1st century AD and a Christian basilica. A plaque records the death of St. Augustine's mother in a hotel here in Ostia in AD 387.

ALSO WORTH SEEING

Anagni FS *from Termini (c.50 min).* Picturesque hill town with papal palace and famous Romanesque cathedral.

Bracciano FS *from Termini or Tiburtina (c.90 min).* 🚌 *from Lepanto, on Metro line A (bus c.90 min).* Volcanic lake with villages and wooded hills. Nice for walks or a visit to Orsini Castle. Swimming in summer.

Cerveteri FS *from Termini, Tiburtina or Ostiense to Cerveteri-Ladispoli, then local bus (c.70 min).* 🚌 *from Via Lepanto, on Metro line A (bus c.80 min).* One of the greatest Etruscan cities. Necropolis with complete streets and houses.

Nemi 🚌 *from Anagnina, on Metro line A (bus c.60 min).* Charming village at volcanic lake in the Castelli Romani. Famous for its wine and strawberries.

Palestrina 🚌 *from Anagnina, on Metro line A (bus c.70 min).* Impressive Roman sanctuary to goddess Fortuna. Museum and the Mosaic of the Nile.

Pompei FS *to Naples, then change to local train (c.170 min).* 🚌 *Special bus tours from tourist agents.* Excavations of the wealthy and bustling Roman city where the busy daily life was put to a sudden end by the eruption of Vesuvius in AD 79.

Subiaco 🚌 *from Ponte Mammolo, on Metro line B (bus c.120 min).* Birthplace of St. Benedict. Two monasteries to visit.

Tarquinia FS *from Termini or Ostiense (c.180 min).* 🚌 *from Via Lepanto, on Metro line A. Change at Civitavecchia (c.150 min).* Outstanding collection of Etruscan objects and frescoes from Tarquinia's necropolis.

Viterbo FS *from Termini (c.90 min) or train from Roma Nord, Piazzale Flaminio, on Metro line A (c.120 min).* 🚌 *from Saxa Rubra reached by the train above (bus c.90 min).* Medieval quarter, papal palace and archaeological museum within 13th-century walls.

SIX GUIDED WALKS

Bernini angel on Ponte Sant'Angelo

ROME IS an excellent city for walking. The distances between major sights in the historic center can easily be covered on foot, and many streets have been pedestrianized. When you get tired, there are plenty of pavement cafés in wonderful settings, such as Piazza Navona and Campo de' Fiori. If you are interested in archaeology, then try a walk across the Forum *(see pp76–87)* and over the Palatine *(see pp96–101)* to take you away from the roaring traffic of modern Rome into a different world of scattered ruins and shady pine trees.

The first of the six suggested walks takes in picturesque quarters on either side of the Tiber, the river that has played such an important part in the city's development. The second walk, along the perfectly straight Via Giulia, gives a vivid impression of the Renaissance city. The next three walks each follow a particular theme. For visitors who wish to savor the glory of ancient Rome, there is a walk taking in the surviving triumphal arches of the emperors. For those who prefer the Middle Ages, there is a tour of early Christian churches with well-preserved mosaics, and for those who enjoy the Roman Baroque, there is a walk concentrating on Bernini's contribution to the city's appearance.

The Romans were famous for their straight roads. The final walk is outside the central sightseeing area, along the best-known Roman road, the Via Appia Antica, parts of which remain after more than 2,000 years of use.

CHOOSING A WALK

Bernini
(pp282–3)

Via Giulia
(pp276–7)

The Six Walks
The routes of the first five walks are marked on the larger map, which also shows the main sightseeing areas of Rome. The smaller inset map shows the location of the Via Appia walk in relation to the central area.

Mosaics
(pp280–81)

Tiber
(pp274–5)

N

KEY

- - Walk routes

— City Wall

0 kilometers   1

0 miles   0.5

Triumphal Arches
(pp278–9)

Via Appia Antica
(pp284–5)

Pedestrians strolling across Ponte Sant'Angelo

A Two-Hour Walk by the River Tiber

ROME OWES ITS VERY EXISTENCE to the Tiber; the city grew up around an easy fording point where a market place developed. The river could also be a hazard; shallow and torrent-like, it flooded the city every winter up to 1870, when work began on the massive Lungotevere embankments that run along both sides of the river. These provide many fine views from points along their avenues of plane trees. The walk also explores the neighbourhoods along the riverside, in particular the Jewish Ghetto and Trastevere, which have preserved much of their character from earlier periods in the colourful history of Rome.

From the old port of Rome to Via dei Funari

Starting from the church of Santa Maria in Cosmedin ① (see p202), cross the piazza to the Temples of the Forum Boarium ② (see p203). This was the cattle market that stood near the city's river port. The river here has preserved two less obvious structures from ancient Rome: the mouth of the Cloaca Maxima ③, the city's great sewer, and one arch of a ruined bridge, known as the Ponte Rotto ④. In Via Petroselli stands the rather extraordinary medieval Casa dei Crescenzi ⑤ (see p203), decorated with fragments of Roman temples. Passing the modern Anagrafe (public records office) ⑥, built on the site of the old Roman port, you come to San Nicola in Carcere ⑦ (see p151).

You are now in the Foro Olitorio, Rome's ancient vegetable market. To the east stand the ruins of a Roman portico and the medieval house of the Pierleoni family. Head for the massive Theatre

Santa Maria in Cosmedin ①

of Marcellus ⑧ (see p151), and look for the three Corinthian columns of the Temple of Apollo beside it. Turn into Piazza Campitelli and walk up to Santa Maria in Campitelli ⑨ (see p151). The church honours a miraculous image of the Virgin credited with halting the plague in 1656. The 16th-century piazza was the home of Flaminio Ponzio, its architect, who lived at No. 6. Take Via dei Delfini to Piazza Margana where you should look up at the 14th-century tower of the Margani family ⑩. Retrace your steps, then go up Via dei Funari (Street of the Ropemakers) to the 16th-century façade of Santa Caterina dei Funari ⑪.

The Ghetto

From Piazza Lovatelli take Via Sant'Angelo in Pescheria, which

leads to the ruined Portico of Octavia ⑫ (see p152) in the Jewish Ghetto (see p152). The Roman portico, once Rome's fish market, houses the church of Sant'Angelo in Pescheria. Find the marble plaque on the façade: fish longer than this slab were given to the city's *conservatori* (governors). Turn into the Ghetto: two column stumps belonging to the Portico stand in front of a patched-up doorway made of fragments of Roman sculpture. The cramped buildings and streets around Via del Portico

Arch of the Ponte Rotto ④

Main altar of Santa Maria in Campitelli ⑨

d'Ottavia are typical of old Rome: see the Casa di Lorenzo Manilio ⑬ *(see p152)*, and turn down Via del Progresso, past Palazzo Cenci ⑭ *(see p152)*, towards the river. On Lungotevere walk past the Synagogue ⑮ *(see p152)* to the small church of San Gregorio ⑯. Here stood the Ghetto's gates, which were locked at sundown.

Across the river to Trastevere

Crossing to Tiber Island *(see p153)* by Ponte Fabricio, with its two ancient

Classical relief of Medusa above the doorway of Palazzo Cenci ⑭

much of the spirit of old Trastevere. Walk up to the start of Viale di Trastevere at Piazza Belli. After crossing the road look back

Santa Maria in Trastevere, don't miss the old-fashioned chemist's shop at No. 7. The piazza itself, in front of the magnificent church of Santa Maria in Trastevere *(see pp212–13)*, has a cheerful atmosphere, and the fountain steps are a favourite meeting place. Go back a little way to Via del Moro. This leads to Piazza Trilussa, dominated by the fountain of the Acqua Paola ㉓, where you emerge on to the bank of the river again. Note the lifelike statue, near the fountain, of Roman poet Trilussa, who wrote in the local dialect. From Ponte Sisto ㉔ *(see p210)*, look back to Tiber Island and, beyond it, to the medieval bell tower of Santa Maria in Cosmedin, set against the pine trees on the summit of the Palatine.

The western tip of Tiber Island

stone heads on the parapet, you can enjoy a good view of the river in both directions. On the island itself, you should not miss the Pierleoni Tower ⑰ or the church of San Bartolomeo all'Isola ⑱.

Trastevere

As you cross into Trastevere, you can see the medieval house of the powerful Mattei family ⑲, with its fragments of ancient sculpture. Beyond it, Piazza in Piscinula and the surrounding streets retain

KEY

- - Walk route

🔆 Good viewing point

at the medieval tower of the Anguillara ⑳ and the statue honouring the poet Gioacchino Belli ㉑ *(see p209)*. As you go down Via della Lungaretta to Piazza

Piazza in Piscinula, old Trastevere

TIPS FOR WALKERS

Starting point: *Piazza della Bocca della Verità.*

Length: *3.5 km (2 miles).*

Getting there: *The 23, 44, 81, 160, 280, 628, 715 and 716 buses stop near Santa Maria in Cosmedin.*

Best time for walk: *This walk can be very romantic in the evening, but is enjoyable at any time.*

Stopping-off points: *Piazza Campitelli and Piazza Margana have typical Roman restaurants, and Via del Portico d'Ottavia has restaurants and a bakery. Tiber Island has a bar and the famous Sora Lella restaurant (see p314). In Viale Trastevere there are bars and pizzerias of all kinds. Piazza Santa Maria in Trastevere has lively bars and restaurants with outdoor tables.*

0 meters   250

0 yards   250

A One-Hour Walk along Via Giulia

LAID OUT BY BRAMANTE for Pope Julius II in the early 16th century, Via Giulia was one of the first Renaissance streets to slice through Rome's jumble of medieval alleys. The original plan included new law courts in a central piazza, but this project was abandoned for lack of cash. The street now is dominated by antiques shops and furniture restorers. On summer evenings hundreds of oil lamps light the street while cloisters and courtyards provide romantic settings for a special season of concerts.

Baroque capital on the façade of Sant'Eligio degli Orefici ⑦

From Lungotevere to Largo della Moretta

Starting from Lungotevere dei Tebaldi ① at the eastern end of Via Giulia, you will see ahead of you an archway ② spanning the road. This was the start of Michelangelo's unrealized project linking Palazzo Farnese and its gardens *(see p147)* with the Villa Farnesina *(see pp220–21)* on the other side of the river.

Just before you reach the archway, you will see to your left the curious Fontana del Mascherone ③, in which an ancient grotesque mask and granite basin were combined to create a Baroque fountain.

Beyond the Farnese archway on the left is the lively Baroque façade of the church of Santa Maria dell'Orazione e Morte ④ *(see p147)*. A bit farther along on the same side of the road stands Palazzo Falconieri ⑤, enlarged by Borromini in 1650. Note its two stone falcons glowering at each other across the width of the façade. On the other side of the road, you pass the yellowish façade of Santa Caterina da Siena ⑥, church of the Sienese colony in Rome, which has pretty 18th-century reliefs. The figures of Romulus and Remus symbolize Rome

Relief of Romulus and Remus on Santa Caterina da Siena ⑥

and Siena – there is a legend that the city of Siena was founded by the less fortunate of the twins. After passing the short street that leads down to Sant'Eligio degli Orefici ⑦ *(see p148)* and the façade of Palazzo Ricci ⑧ *(see p149)*, you come to an area of half-demolished buildings around the ruined church of San Filippo Neri ⑨, called Vicolo della Moretta. If you look to the left down to the river, you

Fontana del Mascherone ③

can see Ponte Mazzini and the huge prison of Regina Coeli on the other side of the Tiber. At this point you may like to make a small detour to the right to the beginning of Via del Pellegrino, where there is an inscription ⑩ defining the *pomerium*, or boundary, of the city in the time of the Emperor Claudius.

From Largo della Moretta to the Sofas of Via Giulia

Farther on, facing the narrow Vicolo del Malpasso, are the imposing prisons, the Carceri

Nuove ⑪, built by Pope Innocent X Pamphilj in 1655. When first opened, they were a model of humane treatment of prisoners, but they were replaced by the Regina Coeli prison across the river at the end of the 19th century. The buildings now house offices of the Ministry of Justice and a small Museum of Crime.

At the corner of Via del Gonfalone, a small side street running down to the river,

KEY

- ▬ ▬ Walk route
- ※ Good viewing point

0 meters	250
0 yards	250

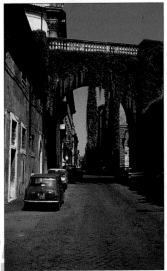

Farnese archway across Via Giulia, built to a design by Michelangelo ②

the traditional distribution of bread to the poor that took place on the saint's feast day.

On the corner there are more travertine blocks belonging to the foundations of Julius II's projected law courts, known because of their curious shape as the "Sofas of Via Giulia."

The Florentine Quarter

Your next stop should be the imposing Palazzo Sacchetti at No. 66 ⑮. Originally this was the house of Antonio da Sangallo the Younger, the architect of Palazzo Farnese, but it was greatly enlarged by later owners. The porticoed courtyard houses a 15th-century Madonna and a striking Roman relief of the 3rd century AD. Just opposite Palazzo Sacchetti is the beautiful late Renaissance portal of Palazzo Donarelli ⑯. The 16th-century house at No. 93 is richly decorated with stuccoes and coats of arms ⑰. No. 85 is another typical Renaissance palazzo with a heavily rusticated ground floor ⑱. There is a tradition

you can see part of the foundations of Julius II's planned law courts. Just down the street stands the small Oratorio di Santa Lucia del Gonfalone ⑫, which is often used for concerts.

The next interesting façade is Carlo Rainaldi's 17th-century Santa Maria del Suffragio ⑬ on the left. On the same side is San Biagio degli Armeni ⑭, the Armenian church in Rome. It is often referred to by local people as San Biagio della Pagnotta (of the loaf of bread). The nickname originates from

Plaque honouring Antonio da Sangallo on Palazzo Sacchetti ⑮

that, like many houses of the period, it once belonged to Raphael. Palazzo Clarelli ⑲ was built by Antonio da Sangallo the Younger as his own house. The inscription above the doorway bears the name of Duke Cosimo II de' Medici, whose family later bought the palazzo.

This whole area used to be inhabited by a flourishing Florentine colony, which had its own water-mills built on pontoons along the Tiber. Their national church is San Giovanni dei Fiorentini ⑳ (see p153), the final great landmark at the end of Via Giulia. Many Florentine artists and architects had a hand in its design, including Sangallo and Jacopo Sansovino.

Coat of arms of Pope Paul III Farnese on the façade of Via Giulia No. 93 ⑰

Detail on the side of the door of Santa Maria del Suffragio ⑬

TIPS FOR WALKERS

Starting point: Lungotevere dei Tebaldi, by Ponte Sisto.
Length: 1,100 yds (1 km).
Getting there: The 116 goes to and along Via Giulia, or you can take 46, 62 or 64 to Corso Vittorio Emanuele II, then walk down Via dei Pettinari, or take a 23 or 280 along Lungotevere.
Best time for walk: On summer evenings, oil lamps light the street. At Christmas, there are crèches on display in many shop windows.
Stopping-off points: There are bars in Via Giulia, at Nos. 21 and 84. Campo de' Fiori has better bars, with outdoor tables, and a wide choice of places to eat. These include a fried fish restaurant in Piazza Santa Barbara dei Librai (closed Sun).

A 90-Minute Tour of Rome's Triumphal Arches

ROME'S GREATEST GIFT to architecture was the arch, and the Roman people's highest tribute to its victorious generals was the triumphal arch. In Imperial times, arches were erected to honor an emperor's campaign victories almost as a matter of course, promoting his personal cult and ensuring his subsequent deification. Spectacular processions passed through these arches. Conquering generals, cheered by rapturous crowds, rode in their chariots to the Capitol, accompanied by their legions bearing spoils from their campaigns.

Part of the Via Sacra, once spanned by the Arch of Augustus ③

Arches of the Forum

This walk through the Forum and around the base of the Palatine takes in Rome's three great surviving triumphal arches and two arches of more

Relief of barbarian captives on the Arch of Septimius Severus ①

humble design that were used simply as places of business. It starts from the Arch of

TIPS FOR WALKERS

Starting point: The Roman Forum, entrance Largo Romolo e Remo, on Via dei Fori Imperiali.
Length: 2.5 km (1.5 miles).
Getting there: The nearest Metro station is Colosseo on line B. Buses 84, 85, 87, 117, 175, 186, 810, 850 stop in Via dei Fori Imperiali, near the Forum entrance.
Best time for walk: Any time of day during Forum opening hours (see p82) is suitable.
Stopping-off points: Several bars and restaurants overlook the Colosseum. There is a small bar in Via dei Cerchi and a smarter one behind San Giorgio in Velabro, in Piazza San Giovanni Decollato (closed Sun). For a meal, try Alvaro al Circo Massimo (closed Mon) in Via di San Teodoro.

Emperor Septimius Severus ① and his sons Geta and Caracalla (see p83) in the Forum. Erected in AD 203, it celebrates a successful campaign in the Middle East. Eight years later, when Caracalla had his brother killed, all mention of Geta was removed from the inscription.

Look up at the reliefs showing phases of the campaigns. Set in tiers, they are probably the sculptural counterparts of the paintings illustrating the general's feats that were borne aloft in the triumphal procession. On the right, the inhabitants of a fortified city surrender to the Romans' siege machines. Below are smaller friezes showing the triumphal procession itself.

Heading east, make your way through the Forum to the ruins of the Temple of Julius Caesar ②. The temple was built by Augustus in 29 BC, on the site where Caesar's body was cremated after Mark Antony's famous funerary oration. A nearby sign marks the ruins of one of the arches dedicated to Augustus ③, spanning the Via Sacra between the Temple of Castor and Pollux ④ (see p84) and the Temple of Caesar. This arch, erected after Augustus had defeated Mark Antony and Cleopatra, was finally demolished in 1545, and its

Capital from Temple of Castor and Pollux ④

materials were used in the new St. Peter's. From here, proceed uphill towards the elegant Arch of Titus ⑤ (see p87). Compared with Septimius Severus's arch, it shows an earlier, simpler style. Look up at the beautiful lettering of the inscription before

KEY

— Walk route

※ Good viewing point

Ⓜ Metro station

0 meters   250

0 yards   250

Arch of Titus in a 19th-century watercolor by the English artist Thomas Hartley Cromek ⑤

Arches of Domitian's extension to the Claudian Aqueduct ⑨

Four-sided Arch of Janus in the Forum Boarium ⑬

excavated in the 18th and 19th centuries. Many of the carts that passed through the arch would have been carrying building materials quarried from the Forum's many ruined monuments.

Arch of Constantine

Leave the Forum by heading down the hill towards the Colosseum ⑥ *(see pp92–5)* and the nearby Arch of Constantine ⑦ *(see p91)*. This arch, hastily built to commemorate the emperor's victory over his rival Maxentius in AD 312, is a patchwork of reliefs from different periods. Stand on the Via di San Gregorio side and compare you examine the inner bas-reliefs. These show Roman legionaries carrying the spoils looted from the conquest of Jerusalem, heralds holding plaques with the names of vanquished peoples and cities, and Titus riding in triumph in his chariot.

The medieval Frangipane family turned the Colosseum into a vast impregnable stronghold and incorporated the Arch of Titus into their fortifications. Notice the wheelmarks scratched on the inside walls of the arch by generations of carts; they indicate the steady rise in the level of the Forum floor before it was eventually

the earlier panels at the top (AD 180–193) with the hectic battle scenes just above the smaller arches, sculpted in AD 315. In the curious dwarf-like soldiers, you can see the transition from Classicism to a cruder medieval style of sculpture.

Now take Via di San Gregorio, which runs the length of the valley between the Palatine and Celian hills. This was the ancient route taken by most triumphal processions. Passing the entrance to the Palatine ⑧ and the well-preserved arches of the Claudian Aqueduct ⑨ on the right, you come to Piazza di Porta Capena ⑩, named after the gate that stood here to mark the beginning of the Via Appia *(see p284)*. After rounding the back of the Palatine, follow Via dei Cerchi, which runs alongside the grassy area that preserves, in an oval outline, all that remains of the Circus Maximus ⑪ *(see p205)*.

Arches of the Forum Boarium

When you reach the church of Sant'Anastasia ⑫, turn right up Via di San Teodoro, then first left down Via del Velabro. Straddling the street is the four-sided Arch of Janus ⑬ *(see p202)*, erected in the 3rd century AD. This is not a triumphal arch but a covered area where merchants could take shelter from the sun or rain when discussing business. Like the Arch of Titus, it became part of a fortress built by the Frangipane family during the Middle Ages.

Tucked away beside the nearby church of San Giorgio in Velabro ⑭ *(see p202)* is what looks like a large rectangular doorway. This is the Arco degli Argentari, or Moneychangers' Arch ⑮. Look up at the inscription, which says that it was erected by local silversmiths in honor of Septimius Severus and his family in AD 204. As in the emperor's triumphal arch, the name of Geta has been obliterated by his brother and murderer, Caracalla. Geta's figure has also been removed from among the portraits on the panels inside the arch. Triumph in Imperial Rome could be very short-lived.

A Three-Hour Tour of Rome's Best Mosaics

IN IMITATION of the audience chambers of Imperial palaces, Rome's early Christian churches were decorated with brilliant mosaics. These were pieced together from cubes of marble, colored stone and fragments of glass. To create a golden background, gold leaf was placed between pieces of glass. These were then heated so that they fused. The glorious colors and subjects portrayed gave the faithful a glimpse of the heavenly court of the King of Kings. This walk concentrates on a few of the churches decorated in this wonderful medium.

Apse mosaic in the Chapel of Santa Rufina ③

San Giovanni

Start from Piazza di Porta San Giovanni, where you can visit the heavily restored mosaic of the Triclinio Leoniano *(see p179)*. Originally in the banqueting hall of Pope Leo III (reigned 795–816) ①, showing Christ among the Apostles. On the left are Pope Sylvester and the Emperor Constantine, on the right, Pope Leo and Charlemagne, just before he was crowned Holy Roman Emperor in AD 800. Inside the basilica of San Giovanni in Laterano ② *(see pp182–3)*, the 13th-century apse mosaic shows Christ as he appeared miraculously during the consecration of the church. In the panels by the windows, look for the small figures of two Franciscan friars; these are the artists Jacopo Torriti *(left)* and Jacopo de

Obelisk and side façade of San Giovanni in Laterano ②

Camerino *(right)*. Leave by the exit on the right near the splendid 16th-century organ and head for the octagonal Baptistry of San Giovanni ③, where the Chapel of Santa Rufina has a beautiful apse mosaic dating from the 5th century. In the neighboring Chapel of San Venanzio there are golden 7th-century mosaics, showing the strong influence of the Eastern Church at this time.

Santo Stefano Rotondo to San Clemente

Leave the piazza by the narrow road that leads to the round church of Santo Stefano Rotondo ④ *(see p185)*. One of its chapels contains a 7th-century Byzantine mosaic honoring two martyrs buried here. Farther on, in Piazza della Navicella, is the church of Santa Maria in Domnica ⑤ *(see p193)*. It houses the superb mosaics commissioned by Pope Paschal I, who gave new impetus to Rome's mosaic production in the 9th century. He is represented kneeling beside the Virgin. On leaving the church, notice the façade of San Tommaso in Formis ⑥, which has a charming mosaic of Christ flanked by two freed slaves, one black and one white, dating from the 13th

Ceiling mosaic, Baptistry of San Giovanni ③

acanthus leaves. San Clemente also has a fine 12th-century Cosmatesque mosaic floor.

The Colle Oppio

Passing the old entrance to the church, cross Via Labicana and walk up the hill to the small Colle Oppio park ⑨. This has fine views of the Colosseum and contains the ruins of the Domus Aurea ⑩ *(see p175)* and the Baths of

Interior of Baptistry of San Giovanni ③

century. From here, head up the steep hill, past the forbidding apse of Santi Quattro Coronati ⑦ *(see p185)*, to the fascinating church of San Clemente ⑧ *(see pp186–7)*. Its 12th-century apse mosaic shows the cross set in a swirling pattern of

Trajan ⑪. Across the park lie San Martino ai Monti ⑫ *(see p170)*, which has a 6th-century mosaic portrait of Pope St. Sylvester near the crypt, and Santa Prassede ⑬ *(see p171)*. Here the Chapel of St. Zeno contains the most important Byzantine mosaics in Rome, reminiscent of the fabulous mosaics of Ravenna. Pope Paschal I erected the chapel as a mausoleum for his

14th-century façade mosaics by Filippo Rusuti. Inside, the 5th-century mosaics in the nave depict Old Testament stories, while the triumphal arch has scenes relating to the birth of Christ, including one of the Magi wearing striped stockings. In the apse is a *Coronation of the Virgin* by Jacopo Torriti (1295).

On leaving Santa Maria, pass the obelisk ⑮ in the piazza behind the church and go downhill to Via Urbana and Santa Pudenziana ⑯ *(see p171)*. The figures in the apse mosaic, one of the oldest in Rome (AD 390), are remarkable for their naturalism. The two women with crowns are traditionally identified as Santa Prassede and Santa Pudenziana. When you leave the church, you can either retrace your steps to Santa Maria Maggiore or walk down Via Urbana to Via Cavour Metro station.

Mosaic saint in Santa Prassede ⑬

11th-century frieze above the doorway of Santa Pudenziana ⑯

PIAZZA DI S. GIOVANNI IN LATERANO

PIAZZA DI PORTA S. GIOVANNI

San Giovanni Ⓜ

N

mother, Theodora. The apse and triumphal arch of the church itself also have fine mosaics. When you move on to Santa Maria Maggiore ⑭ *(see pp172–3)*, go to the column in the center of the piazza in front of the church to see the beautiful

KEY

– – Walk route

— City Wall

☆ Good viewing point

Ⓜ Metro station

0 meters   250

0 yards   250

TIPS FOR WALKERS

Starting point: *Piazza di Porta San Giovanni.*

Length: *2 miles (3.5 km).*

Getting there: *The nearest Metro station is San Giovanni, on line A, in Piazzale Appio, just outside Porta San Giovanni. The 16, 81, 85, 87, 650 and 850 buses and the 3 tram stop in front of San Giovanni in Laterano, while 117, 218 and 650 stop around the corner on Piazza San Giovanni in Laterano.*

Best time for walk: *Go in the morning, in order to appreciate the mosaics in the best light.*

Stopping-off points: *The bars and restaurants in Piazza del Colosseo are popular with tourists. In the Parco del Colle Oppio there is a café kiosk with tables. There are several bars around Santa Maria Maggiore, some with outdoor tables.*

A Two-Hour Walk around Bernini's Rome

GIAN LORENZO BERNINI (1598–1680) is the artist who probably left the strongest personal mark on the appearance of the city of Rome. Favorite architect, sculptor and town planner to three successive popes, he turned Rome into a uniquely Baroque city. This walk traces his enormous influence on the development and appearance of the center of Rome. It starts from the busy Largo di Santa Susanna just north of Termini station, at the church of Santa Maria della Vittoria.

Façade of Santa Maria in Via ⑬

Quirinale. The long wing of the Palazzo del Quirinale ⑦ *(see p158)*, nicknamed the Manica Lunga (long sleeve), is by Bernini. On the other side of the road is the façade of Sant'Andrea al Quirinale ⑧ *(see p161)*, one of Bernini's greatest churches. When you reach the Piazza del Quirinale ⑨, note the doorway of the palazzo, attributed to Bernini. From the piazza, go down the

composer Donizetti lived at No. 77 and turn into Via di Santa Maria in Via, where the church ⑬ has a fine Baroque

Bernini's Fontana del Tritone ②

Through Piazza Barberini
Santa Maria della Vittoria ① *(see p255)* houses the Cornaro Chapel, the setting for one of Bernini's most revolutionary and controversial sculptures, the *Ecstasy of St. Teresa* (1646). From here take Via Barberini to Piazza Barberini. In its center is Bernini's dramatic Fontana del Tritone ② *(see p254)* and at one side stands the more modest Fontana delle Api ③ *(see p254)*. As you go up Via delle Quattro Fontane, you catch a glimpse of Palazzo Barberini ④ *(see p255)* built by Bernini and several other artists for Pope Urban VIII. The gateway and cornices are decorated with the bees that made up part of the Barberini family crest. Next make your way to the crossroads, decorated by Le Quattro Fontane ⑤ *(see p162)*, to enjoy the splendid views in all four directions.

Passing the diminutive San Carlo alle Quattro Fontane ⑥ *(see p161)*, built by Bernini's rival Borromini, take Via del

stairs to Via della Dataria, and into Vicolo Scanderbeg which leads to a small piazza with the same name ⑩. Scanderbeg was the nickname of the Albanian prince Giorgio Castriota (1403–68), the "Terror of the Turks." His portrait is preserved on the house where he lived.

The Trevi Fountain
Go along the narrow Vicolo dei Modelli ⑪, where male models waited to be chosen by artists, then turn toward the Trevi Fountain ⑫ *(see p159)*. Its energy is clearly inspired by Bernini's work, a tribute to his lasting influence on Roman taste. Leave the piazza along Via delle Muratte where the

Neptune Fountain at the north end of Piazza Navona ⑱

façade by Bernini's follower
Carlo Rainaldi. At the top of
this street, turn left down to
Via del Corso. On the other
side of the road, you will see
the towering Column of
Marcus Aurelius ⑭ *(see p113)*
in Piazza Colonna. Beyond
this is Palazzo Montecitorio ⑮,
begun in 1650 by Bernini and
now the home of the Italian
parliament *(see p112)*.

Pantheon to Piazza Navona
Via in Aquiro leads you to the
Pantheon ⑯ *(see pp110–11)*.
Refusing Pope Urban VIII's
request for him to redecorate

Statue of the river Nile from the Fontana dei Quattro Fiumi

Quattro Fiumi *(see p120)*, was
by Bernini, though the figures
symbolic of the four rivers
were sculpted by other artists.
The central figure in the
Fontana del Moro, however, is
by Bernini himself. Bernini's
contemporaries were fascinated
by the innovative use of
shells, rocks and other natural
forms in his fountains, and his
expert handling of water to
create constant movement.

An extended walk
More energetic walkers may
like to head toward the river
to see the Ponte Sant'Angelo
and its Bernini angels, and
then on to St. Peter's *(see
pp230–33)* where they
can admire Bernini's great
colonnaded piazza in front
of the church, the papal
tombs, his altar decorations
and the bronze baldacchino.

the dome,
Bernini said that
although St. Peter's
had a hundred defects,
the Pantheon did not have
any. From the Pantheon,
make a small detour to Piazza
della Minerva where you can
see the bizarre Bernini obelisk,
supported by a small elephant,
by the church of Santa Maria
sopra Minerva ⑰ *(see p108)*.
Then retrace your steps and
take Salita dei Crescenzi to

Angel on Ponte Sant'Angelo

reach the fabulous Piazza
Navona ⑱ *(see p120)* which
was remodeled by Bernini for
Pope Innocent X Pamphilj.
The design for the central
fountain, the Fontana dei

KEY

— Walk route

🔆 Good viewing point

Ⓜ Metro station

0 meters	250
0 yards	250

TIPS FOR WALKERS

Starting point: Largo di
Santa Susanna.
Length: 3.5 km (2 miles).
Getting there: Take Metro line A
to Repubblica or any bus to
Termini, then walk. Buses 61,
62, 175 and 492 stop in Via
Barberini.
Best time for walk: Go either
between 9am and noon for good
lighting conditions in the churches,
or between 4pm and 7pm.
Stopping-off points: The
Piazza Barberini and Fontana di
Trevi areas have lots of bars and
pizzerias. The many elegant cafés
en route include the famous
Caffè Giolitti (see p109) and
outdoor cafés and restaurants
are plentiful around Piazza della
Rotonda and Piazza Navona.

A 90-Minute Walk along the Via Appia Antica

LINED WITH CYPRESSES AND PINES as it was when the ancient Romans came here by torchlight to bury their dead, the Via Appia is wonderfully atmospheric. The fields are strewn with ruined tombs set against the picturesque background of the Alban hills to the south. Although the marble or travertine stone facings of most tombs have been plundered, a few statues and reliefs survive or have been replaced by copies.

Tomb of Sixtus Pompeus the Righteous ⑨

Capo di Bove

Start from the Tomb of Cecilia Metella ① *(see p266).* In the Middle Ages this area acquired the name Capo di Bove (ox head) from the frieze of festoons and ox heads still visible on the tomb. On the other side of the road you can see the ruined Gothic church of San Nicola ②, which, like the Tomb of Cecilia Metella, was part of the medieval fortress of the Caetani family.

Proceed to the crossroads ③, where there are still many original Roman paving slabs, huge blocks of extremely durable volcanic basalt. Just

Gothic windows in the church of San Nicola ②

on both sides of the Appia, are other tombs, some still capped with the remains of the medieval towers that were built over them. On the right after passing some private villas, you come to a military zone around the Forte Appio ⑤, one of a series of forts built around the city in the 19th century. On the left, a little further on, stand the ruins of the Tomb of Marcus Servilius ⑥, showing fragments of reliefs excavated in 1808 by the Neo-Classical sculptor Antonio Canova. He was one of the first to work on the principle that excavated tombs and their inscriptions and reliefs should be allowed to remain in situ. On the other side of the road stands a tomb with a relief of a man, naked except for a short cape, known as the

The ruined church of San Nicola ②

past the next turning (Via Capo di Bove), you will see on your left the nucleus of a great mausoleum overgrown with ivy, known as the Torre di Capo di Bove ④. Beyond it,

"Heroic Relief" ⑦. On the left of the road are the ruins of the so-called Tomb of Seneca ⑧. The great moralist Seneca owned a villa near here, where he committed suicide in AD 65 on the orders of Nero.

The next major tomb is that of the family of Sixtus Pompeus the Righteous, a freed slave of the 1st century AD ⑨. The verse inscription records the father's sadness at having to bury his own children, who died young.

Artist's impression of how the mausoleums and tombs lining the Via Appia looked in the 2nd century AD

Section of the Via Appia Antica, showing original Roman paving stones

From Via dei Lugari to Via di Tor Carbone

Just past Via dei Lugari on the right, screened by trees, is the Tomb of Pope St. Urban (reigned 222–230) ⑩. Set back from the road on the left stands a large ruined podium, probably part of a Temple of Jupiter ⑪. The next stretch was excavated by the architect Luigi Canina early in the 19th century. On the right is the Tomb of Caius Licinius ⑫, followed by a smaller Doric tomb ⑬ and the imposing Tomb of Hilarius Fuscus ⑭, with five portrait busts in relief of members of his family. Next comes the Tomb of Tiberius Claudius Secondinus ⑮, where a group of freedmen of the Imperial household were buried in the 2nd century AD.

Passing a large ruined columbarium, you reach the Tomb of Quintus Apuleius ⑯ and the reconstructed Tomb of the Rabirii freed slaves (1st century BC) ⑰. This has a frieze of three half-length figures above an inscription.

The figure on the right is a priestess of Isis. Behind her you can see the outline of a *sistrum*, the metal rattle used at ceremonies of the cult.

The majority of the tombs are little more than shapeless stacks of eroded brickwork. Two exceptions in the last stretch of this walk are the Tomb of the Festoons ⑱, with its reconstructed frieze of festive putti, and the Tomb of the Frontispiece ⑲, which has a copy of a relief with four portraits. The two central figures are holding hands.

When you reach Via di Tor Carbone, the Via Appia still stretches out ahead of you in a straight line and, if you wish to extend your walk, there are many more tombs and ruined villas to visit along the way.

KEY

– – Walk route

꧁ Good viewing point

0 meters	250
0 yards	250

TIPS FOR WALKERS

Starting point: Tomb of Cecilia Metella.
Length: 3 km (2 miles).
Getting there: Taking a taxi is the easiest way to reach the tomb. Alternatively, take the 118 from Piazzale Ostiense or the 660 from Colli Albani on Metro Line A.
Best time for walk: Go fairly early, before it becomes too hot.
Stopping-off points: There is a bar near the church of Domine Quo Vadis?, before the start of the walk, but it is advisable to bring your own refreshment. There are also several well-established restaurants on the first stretch of the Appia, including the Cecilia Metella, Via Appia Antica 129, tel 06-513 67 43 (closed Mon).

Figure on the Tomb of the Heroic Relief ⑦

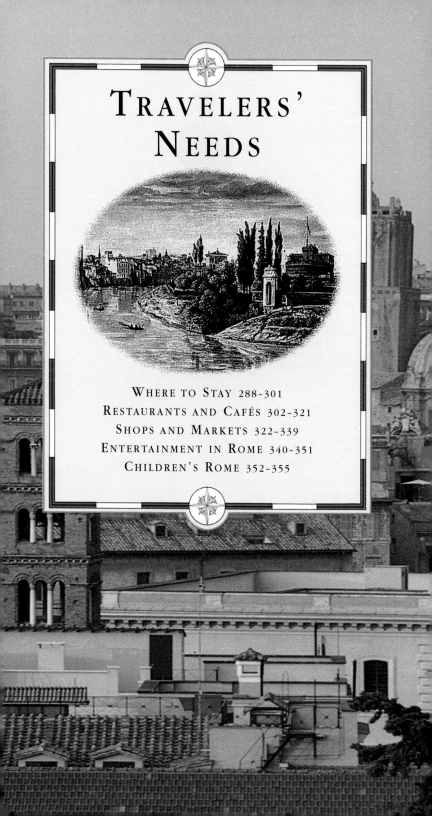

TRAVELERS'
NEEDS

WHERE TO STAY

ROME HAS BEEN a major tourist center since the Middle Ages, when pilgrims from all over Europe came to visit the home of Catholicism and its relic-packed churches. The nostalgic can still sleep in a 15th-century hotel or stay around the Campo de' Fiori market, where visiting ecclesiastics were entertained by courtesans in the Renaissance era. Those who prefer their history a little less raffish can stay in an ex-monastery, convent or a still-functioning religious house. Romantics can sleep in the house once occupied by Keats, while the celebrity-conscious can stay in former palaces graced by VIPs of the past and present. Rome offers the full range of accommodations, mainly in historical buildings. *Pensione* (guest-house) is no longer an official category, but in practice many places retain the name and more personal character that has made them so popular with travelers. Other possibilities include hostels, residential hotels and accommodations with kitchens.

Porter at the Majestic Hotel

The 72 hotels we have selected are listed in the *Choosing a Hotel* chart *(pp294–5)*, organized *(pp296–301)* according to their price category and area.

WHERE TO LOOK

AROUND the Spanish Steps and Piazza di Spagna lies the traditional heartland of foreign visitors, with some of the most exclusive smaller hotels. Similar places can be found all over the center, to the west of Via del Corso.

While moderately priced accommodations are rare in central Rome, the advantages of staying right on the doorstep of the city's many ancient sights cannot be over-estimated; you can walk to the major areas of interest and easily return at midday for a shower, meal and siesta.

If the less expensive hotels we have recommended in the center are full, try the Borgo – close to the Vatican – or the lively quarter of Trastevere.

Those in search of glamour should head for Via Veneto, which has many grand and luxurious hotels.

If you're looking for a peaceful retreat, try the area around the Aventine or one of the high-class hotels next to the Villa Borghese park.

Although many of the streets immediately around Termini Station are somewhat seedy, the area is nonetheless a convenient stopover for travelers. There's also a concentration of cheap hotels, with some decent (if basic) ones among them. The hotels recommended lie in a fairly safe area on the east side of the station. The approach to the center from Termini has a number of good hotels that are particularly suitable for the business traveler.

HOTEL PRICES

ALTHOUGH ROME MAY still offer less expensive accommodation than other large cities like London or New York, rates for comparable establishments have caught up. Prices are set by the state, and hotels must display the official rate on the door of each room. VAT (*IVA* in Italian) is usually included and has been taken into account in the price categories on page 291.

Hotels in Rome generally have low and high season rates, so it is often advisable to double-check when booking, as you may be quoted the higher rate – even in the winter months before and after Christmas, when competition is less strong. Discounts for long-term visitors and groups are often negotiable.

Rooms without a bathroom can cost about 30 percent less. Single travelers will find few bargains: though it

The Verdi Room in Via Veneto's Majestic Hotel *(see p301)*

The Plaza Minerva *(see p296)*

is possible to find a single room for 60 percent of the price of a double, on the average you'll pay 70 percent, and occasionally up to 90 percent.

HIDDEN EXTRAS

E VEN IF the price of your room includes service, you are often still expected to give a tip at for room service or for bellboys.

Hotels will often add hefty surcharges to international phone calls and may charge extra for parking and air conditioning. The cost of drinks in minibars can be high – you can buy a cheaper supply from local shops.

FACILITIES

H OTEL STANDARDS have improved of late – you can expect air-conditioning and some bathrooms with hair dryers in middle-range establishments and direct-dial phones in middle-to-lower price rooms, although budget travelers staying in cheaper hotels shouldn't expect much more than a clean room.

Because most hotels occupy historic buildings, room sizes can vary dramatically even within the same establishment (and this is often reflected in the

The Portoghesi Hotel *(see p297)*

pricing), so don't be afraid to ask to see your room before you check in. For the same reason, swimming pools are few and far between, but roof terraces or gardens are common across the range.

First-class hotels will usually have some degree of soundproofing; otherwise, noise levels can be dreadful, in which case ask for a room facing away from the road. The chart on pages 294 to 295 indicates which hotels have a quiet location – this covers both peaceful neighborhoods and certain quiet streets in busy areas.

Parking in central Rome is a problem, though a few hotels have a limited number of parking spaces of their own.

Business visitors to the capital are well provided for, with hotel facilities ranging from fax machines to meeting and conference rooms *(see pp294–5)*.

MAKING RESERVATIONS

T HE ITALIAN postal service tends to be unreliable, so it is safer to reserve by phone or fax. You should do this at least two months in advance if you want a particular hotel in May, June, September or October; Easter and Christmas are also busy.

If a deposit is required, you can pay by credit card or international money order. Under Italian law a reservation is valid as soon as the deposit is paid, so you're likely to lose money if you cancel. If you arrive by train, people may approach you at the station with offers of accommodations. They can be of some use if you are looking for a budget hotel, but you should exercise the usual caution. A better bet if you have not reserved a room anywhere in advance is to head for one of the tourist board offices. Here, staff will reserve you a room within your price range.

Villa San Pio garden *(see p299)*

CHECKING IN AND OUT

I TALIAN HOTELIERS are legally obliged to register you with the police, which is the reason they always ask for your passport. They usually hold on to it for a few hours, but you will need it if you are going to change money. Everyone in Italy is supposed to carry with them some sort of identification.

In some of Rome's cheaper *pensioni,* do not be surprised if you are asked to pay in advance. To speed up the checking-out process, mention in advance if you intend to pay by credit card.

The Locarno *(see p297)*

TOURIST BOARDS

P ROVINCIAL and state tourist boards can provide advice on accommodations. There is also a free booking service.

Rome Provincial Tourist Board (APT)
Via Parigi 5, 00185. *06-48 89 9253.*
Open *9am–7pm Mon–Sat.*
Closed *Sun.*

Leonardo da Vinci Airport, Fiumicino, 00054. *06-6595 4471 or 06-6595 6074.*
Open *8:15am–7pm Mon–Sat.*

Termini Station, Piazza dei Cinquecento, 00185 *06-4890 6300.* **Open** *8am–9pm daily.*

Hotel Reservation
06-699 1000.
Open *7am–10pm daily.*

The reception area of the Regina Hotel Baglioni *(see p301)*

DISABLED TRAVELERS

Provision for the disabled is very poor. Small hotels that occupy parts of buildings sometimes offer only rooms that must be reached via several flights of stairs, while certain establishments can accommodate disabled guests only on the ground floor or have only one or two rooms that are appropriate. Ramps, wide doorways and bathroom handrails are rare.

Our entries for wheelchair access in the listings below rely on the establishments' own assessments; any specific requirements should be checked before reserving.

There is a private organization, Associazione Nazionale degli Handicappati at Corso Vittorio 154, which advises disabled travelers. They can be contacted on 06-6821 9168, 9:30am–5pm Mon–Fri.

TRAVELING WITH CHILDREN

Italians love children, and they are usually welcome across the range of hotels. Facilities, however, tend to be unimpressive. Most hotels can provide cribs or small beds, but highchairs, children's meals and babysitting services are rare. However, many establishments – especially smaller, family-run ones – go out of their way to be helpful.

Many hotels do not have any special rates for children, especially in high season, and charge a standard rate if you require an extra bed in a room, whether for a baby or an adult; this can add anything from a few euros to 40 percent on to the price of a double room. For a family with older children, two-room suites are sometimes to be found. For hotels providing children's facilities, see Choosing a Hotel *(pp294–5)*.

BED & BREAKFAST

A fairly new option for visitors to Rome is bed & breakfast accommodation. Roman hosts offer their spare rooms to visitors, generally for a much lower price than an equivalent hotel room. Contact the **Bed & Breakfast Association of Rome** for a good selection of rooms and apartments, or **Rome Bed & Breakfast**, based in the US.

Bed & Breakfast Association of Rome
Via A. Pacinotti 73.
📞 06-553 02248. 📠 06-553 02259.
@ info@b-b.rm.it
w www.b-b.rm.it

Rome Bed & Breakfast
📞 1-619-531 1179.
📠 1-619-531 1686.
w www.romebandb.com

RESIDENTIAL HOTELS

If you want the comfort and privacy of your own apartment coupled with the services of a hotel, you could opt to stay in a *residenza*. Prices range from around €250 to over €3,000 for a week in a two-bedded room, though some *residenze* are available only for two-week or monthly lets. A full list is available from tourist board offices *(see p289)*. These are some of the most central:

Residence Babuino
Via del Babuino 172, 00187.
📞 & 📠 06-361 1663.

Di Ripetta
Via di Ripetta 231, 00186.
📞 06-323 1144.
📠 06-320 3959.
@ info@ripetta.it
w www.ripetta.it

In Trastevere
Vicolo Moroni 35–36, 00153.
📞 & 📠 06-581 2768.

Vittoria
Via Vittoria 60-64, 00187.
📞 & 📠 06-679 7533.

RELIGIOUS INSTITUTIONS

If you do not mind an early curfew, quite a few religious institutions take in paying guests. You do not have to be a practicing Catholic to stay in one of these, but be sure to reserve well in advance since all of the following places cater to groups of students and pilgrims. **Domus Mariae** and **Istituto Madri Pie** are near the Vatican; **Congregazione Suore dello Spirito Santo** is farther out of town, 4 miles (6 km) west of the center. Prices are near those of the cheapest hotels.

Domus Mariae
Via Aurelia 481, 00165.
📞 06-662 3138. 📠 06-663 8823.

The Gregoriana *(see p297)*

Residence Madri Pie
Via A. de Gasperi 4, 00165.
📞 06-63 19 67. FAX 06-63 19 89.

Congregazione Suore dello Spirito Santo
Via della Pineta Sacchetti 227, 00168.
📞 06-305 3101. FAX 06-305 3125.

Facade of the Excelsior *(see p301)*

BUDGET ACCOMMODATIONS

EVEN IF YOU ARE TRAVELING on a shoestring, it is possible to find a clean, decent room in Rome. Dormitory accommodations can be found at rock-bottom prices in simple establishments, such as the **Ottaviano.** Youth hostels are a good option – and not just for the young. The **Ostello del Foro Italico** provides bed, breakfast and shower at a very reasonable price.

Women can get single, double or triple rooms at the **Young Women's Christian Association** (YWCA). Its location near Termini Station is convenient but somewhat unsafe, so take care if arriving at night. Those wishing to book budget accommodations are advised to contact the organization in advance. Advance bookings are not always accepted.

HOSTEL AND DORMITORY ADDRESSES

Ottaviano
Via Ottaviano 6, 00192.
📞 06-39 73 72 53.
@ gi.costantini@agora.stm.it
W www.pensioneottaviano.com

Associazione Italiana Alberghi per la Gioventù
(Youth Hostels Association)
Via Cavour 44, 00184.
📞 06-487 1152.
FAX 06-488 0492.
W www.hostels-aig.org

Ostello del Foro Italico
Viale delle Olimpiadi 61, 00194.
📞 06-323 6267.
FAX 06-324 2613.
W www.hostels-aig.org

YWCA
Via C. Balbo 4, 00184.
📞 06-488 3917.
FAX 06-487 1028.

CAMPING

MOST CAMPSITES are located quite far out of town – suitable for an occasional excursion into Rome – with the exception of **Flaminio**, near the Olympic Village, which is only 4 miles (6 km) north of the center.

Flaminio
Via Flaminia Nuova 821, 00191.
📞 06-333 2604.
FAX 06-333 0653.
W www.villageflaminio.com

The pool in the Aldrovandi Palace garden *(see p301)*

Rome's Best: Hotels

Roman hotels range from frescoed palaces and *fin-de-siècle* bastions of faded glamor to family-run guesthouses. Most are within easy reach of restaurants, shops and transport. Whatever the price level, all the hotels shown on this map have something special to offer, whether it is a chic location, or a roof terrace with soaring views across the city. The only drawback is that these places and the others listed on pages 294–301 are exceptions to the many unremarkable hotels in the city, so you should book well in advance. The hotels shown here are the best in their particular style or price range.

Hotel Raphaël

Sole al Pantheon
The writers Jean Paul Sartre and Simone de Beauvoir stayed in this superbly located – and recently refurbished – 15th-century palazzo. (See p296.)

0 meters   500

0 yards   500

Raphael
Full of antiques and art, the Raphael offers a central location. (See p297.)

Vatican

Piazza
Spag

Pi
d
Rot

Piazza
Navona

Campo
de' Fiori

Janiculum

Campo de' Fiori
Central Rome's best bargain offers small, well-furnished rooms and terrific views from the sixth-floor roof terrace. (See p298.)

Trastever

Crowne Plaza Minerva
Smart, post-modern interiors grace this international standard hotel. (See p296.)

Sant'Anselmo
To be sure of getting a room you need to book well in advance at this peacefully located Roman villa. An added bonus is the lovely secluded garden. (See p299.)

Hassler
Luxurious suites and an air of faded grandeur remind visitors of the Hassler's heyday. The roof-top restaurant is Rome's most famous. (See p298.)

Hotel Eden
One of the oldest and most exclusive hotels in Rome, the Eden offers elegant decor and truly innovative cuisine. (See p301.)

Carriage
The serene atmosphere makes this city-center hotel a special haven. (See p297.)

Via Veneto

St. Regis Grand
Good service and extensive facilities are the main features of this old-fashioned, luxury hotel. (See p299.)

Quirinal

pitol

Esquiline

Forum

Palatine

Caracalla

Lateran

ntine

Scalinata di Spagna
The prized location at the top of the Spanish Steps, and a large private terrace, make this hotel a popular choice with visitors. (See p298.)

Inghilterra
Sip a cocktail in the Inghilterra's club-like bar, once frequented by Ernest Hemingway. (See p298.)

Choosing a Hotel

THE 72 HOTELS listed in the following pages have all been inspected and assessed. This chart includes some of the features that may affect your hotel choice. The hotels are listed alphabetically within their price category. For more detailed information, see pages 296 to 301.

		Number of Rooms	Large Rooms	Business Facilities	Hotel Parking	Recommended Restaurant	Close to Shops and Restaurants	Quiet Location	24-Hour Room Service
FORUM (see p296)									
Lancelot	€€€	60				●		■	
Forum	€€€€€	76		■					●
PIAZZA DELLA ROTONDA (see p296)									
Abruzzi	€€	25					●		
Mimosa	€€	11					●	■	
Santa Chiara	€€€€	98		■			●		
Colonna Palace	€€€€€	110	●				●		
Grand Hotel de la Minerve	€€€€€	134	●	■		■	●	■	
Nazionale	€€€€€	84	●	■			●		
Sole al Pantheon	€€€€€	25					●		
PIAZZA NAVONA (see p296)									
Navona	€€€	21					●	■	
Due Torri	€€€€	26					●	■	
Genio	€€€€€	65					●		
Portoghesi	€€€€€	28					●	■	
Raphael	€€€€€	70					●	■	
PIAZZA DI SPAGNA (see p297)									
Jonella	€	4					●		
Margutta	€€	24					●	■	
Suisse	€€	12	●				●	■	
Condotti	€€€€	16	●				●		
Homs	€€€€	48					●	■	
Locarno	€€€€	48		■	●		●		
Dei Borgognoni	€€€€€	50		■	●		●	■	
Carriage	€€€€€	24	●				●		
Gregoriana	€€€€€	19					●	■	●
Hassler	€€€€€	100	●	■	●	■	●		
D' Inghilterra	€€€€€	98		■			●	■	
Manfredi	€€€€€	18		■			●	■	
Mozart	€€€€€	56					●	■	
Piazza di Spagna	€€€€€	17	●				●		
Hotel de Russie	€€€€€	129		■		■	●		●
Scalinata di Spagna	€€€€€	16					●		●
Valadier	€€€€€	49		■		■	●	■	●
CAMPO DE' FIORI (see p298)									
Della Lunetta	€€	35					●	■	
Piccolo	€€	15					●		
Rinascimento	€€	19			●		●	■	
Smeraldo	€€	50					●		
Campo de' Fiori	€€€	27					●		
Pomezia	€€€	25					●		
Sole	€€€	58		■	●		●		
Teatro di Pompeo	€€€€	12		■	●		●	■	

Price categories for a double room per night, including breakfast, tax and service:
€ under €65
€€ €65–€99
€€€ €100–€149
€€€€ €150–€199
€€€€€ over €200.

HOTEL PARKING
Car parking facilities attached to the hotel or in the hotel complex.

CLOSE TO SHOPS AND RESTAURANTS
Within a 5-minute walk of a good area for shops, bars, cafés and restaurants.

BUSINESS FACILITIES
Message-taking service, fax machine for guest use, desk and telephone in each room and a meeting room that is available within the hotel.

		NUMBER OF ROOMS	LARGE ROOMS	BUSINESS FACILITIES	HOTEL PARKING	RECOMMENDED RESTAURANT	CLOSE TO SHOPS AND RESTAURANTS	QUIET LOCATION	24-HOUR ROOM SERVICE
QUIRINAL *(see p299)*									
Hotel des Artistes	€€€€	32	●				●	■	
St Regis Grand	€€€€€	170	●	■	■				●
TERMINI *(see p299)*									
Katty	€	17							
Restivo	€	6							
Cervia	€€	28							
Giuliana	€€€	11	●				●		
Canada	€€€€	70	●	■					
Venezia	€€€€	61	●				●		
AVENTINE *(see p299)*									
Aventino	€€€	23	●	■				■	
Sant'Anselmo	€€€€	46		■				■	
Villa San Pio	€€€€	84	●	■	●			■	
Domus Aventina	€€€€€	26	●	■				■	●
TRASTEVERE *(see p300)*									
Carmel	€€	11							
San Francesco	€€€€	24	●	■			●		
VATICAN *(see p300)*									
Alimandi	€€€	35			●			■	
Amalia	€€€€	30					●		
Columbus	€€€€	92		■	●				
Atlante Star	€€€€€	62	●	■	●	■	●		●
Hotel dei Mellini	€€€€€	80		■	●			■	●
VIA VENETO *(see p300)*									
Alexandra	€€€€	45					●		
Barocco	€€€€	32		■			●		
Oxford	€€€€	56		■					
La Residenza	€€€€	26	●		●		●		
Bernini Bristol	€€€€€	127	●	■			●		●
Eden	€€€€€	121	●	■		■	●	■	●
Excelsior	€€€€€	327	●	■	●		●		●
Imperiale	€€€€€	95		■			●		●
Majestic	€€€€€	100			●	■	●		●
Regina Hotel Baglioni	€€€€€	151	●	■	●		●		
Victoria	€€€€€	113		■			●	■	●
VILLA BORGHESE *(see p301)*									
Villa Borghese	€€€€	31			●				●
Aldrovandi Palace	€€€€€	137		■	●	■		■	●
Lord Byron	€€€€€	37		■				■	●

FORUM

Lancelot

Via Capo D'Africa 47, 00184. **Map** 9
A1. **C** *06-70 45 0615.* **FAX** *06-7045
0640.* **W** www.lancelothotel.com
Rooms: 60.
AE, DC, MC, V, JCB. €€€

In a quiet street, close to the
Colosseum, this family-run hotel
offers tastefully furnished rooms,
some with terraces and views.
Public rooms have a slightly retro
feel, while special features include
a cool courtyard bar and a
restaurant with vegetarian dishes.

Forum

Via Tor de' Conti 25, 00184. **Map** 5 B5.
C *06-679 2446.* **FAX** *06-678 6479.*
W www.hotelforum.com
Rooms: 76. AE,
DC, MC, V, JCB. €€€€€

Occupying a palace built out of
materials from the ruins of the
nearby Imperial Fora, the Forum is
an old-fashioned hotel. It features
mellow wood-paneled public
rooms, and a sunny roof terrace
restaurant giving wonderful views
over the archaeological center.

PIAZZA DELLA ROTONDA

Abruzzi

Piazza della Rotonda 69, 00186.
Map 4 F4 & 12 D3. **C** *06-679 2021.*
Rooms: 25. 1 €€

The Abruzzi provides clean, basic
rooms with terra-cotta-tiled floors
in an ochre-colored palazzo overlooking the Pantheon. The rooms
at the back, while not the best, are
quiet. No breakfast is served.

Mimosa

Via di Santa Chiara 61, 00186. **Map**
4 F4 & 12 D3. **C** *06-68 80 17 53.*
FAX *06-683 35 57.* **W** www.hotel
mimosa.net **Rooms**: 11. 1
€€

A clean, if slightly basic, family-run
hotel near the Pantheon. Rooms are
cool, and the five communal
bathrooms are immaculate. The
hotel is popular with student
groups, so reserve well ahead.

Santa Chiara

Via di Santa Chiara 21, 00186.
Map 4 F4 & 12 D3. **C** *06-687 2979.*
FAX *06-687 3144.*
W www.albergosantachiara.com

Rooms: 96.
AE, DC, MC, V, JCB.
€€€€

Conveniently located in the historic
center, the Santa Chiara occupies
an apricot-washed palazzo. Public
rooms are cool, particularly the
marble reception area. Bedrooms
are carpeted and well furnished.

Colonna Palace

Piazza di Montecitorio 12, 00186.
Map 4 F3 & 12 E2. **C** *06-675 191.*
FAX *06-679 4496.* **W** www.itihotels.it
Rooms: 104. AE, DC, MC, V.
€€€€€

The Colonna Palace stands on the
same piazza as Italy's Chamber of
Deputies, and so the area attracts
politicians as well as tourists.
Bedrooms are spacious, though
the bathrooms are small. Breakfast
is served in a basement room
livened up by frescoes. There are
lovely views from the impressive
roof garden, where a Jacuzzi has
been installed.

Grand Hotel de la Minerve

Piazza della Minerva 69, 00186. **Map**
4 F4 & 12 D3. **C** *06-69 5201.* **FAX** *06-
679 4165.* **@** minerva@pronet.it
Rooms: 134.
AE, DC, MC, V, JCB. €€€€€

Occupying Palazzo Fonseca
behind the Pantheon, this is one
of Rome's newest luxury hotels.
The interior was designed by Post-
Modern architect Portoghesi, and
its centerpiece is the lounge,
canopied in semi-translucent
Venetian glass and presided over
by a statue of Minerva. The large
bedrooms are decorated in shades
of beige and coral. Views from the
roof terrace are magnificent,
stretching over the Pantheon,
St. Peter's and the Janiculum Hill.

Nazionale

Piazza di Montecitorio 131, 00186.
Map 4 F3 & 12 E2. **C** *06-69 50 01.*
FAX *06-678 6677.* **W** www.
nazionaleroma.it **Rooms**: 84.
AE, DC, MC, V. €€€€€

Home to Robert de Niro while
making *Godfather II*, the Nazionale
is usually frequented by tourists,
businesspeople and politicians – it
stands right on the corner of the
Chamber of Deputies. Public
rooms are comfortable, particularly
the lounge, with its brocade sofas
and flower arrangements. Some of
the rooms are huge, and most are
partially furnished with French
and Italian antiques.

Sole al Pantheon

Via del Pantheon 63, 00186.
Map 4 F4 & 12 D3. **C** *06-678 0441.*
FAX *06-6994 0689.* **@** hotsole@
flashnet.it **Rooms**: 25.
AE, DC, MC, V.
€€€€€

A hotel since 1467, the Sole
boasts an illustrious list of former
guests – from Renaissance writer
Ariosto to Jean-Paul Sartre and
Simone de Beauvoir. It is easy to
explain its attraction: its location
opposite the Pantheon is
unbeatable, and though it has
been modernized (60 per cent
of the rooms now have Jacuzzis),
there are still bedrooms with
painted, paneled ceilings.

PIAZZA NAVONA

Navona

Via dei Sediari 8, 00186. **Map** 4 F4 &
12 D3. **C** *06-686 4203.* **FAX** *06-6880
3802.* **@** navona@posta2000.com
Rooms: 21. 15.
€€€

Run largely by the owners'
Australian son-in-law, the Navona
has very basic bedrooms most
of which have bathrooms. The
restaurant opens for groups of
15 or more. A superb location
– across from Piazza Navona
and five minutes' stroll from the
Pantheon – means you may have
to book well in advance.

Due Torri

Vicolo del Leonetto 23, 00186.
Map 4 E3 & 11 C1. **C** *06-687 6983.*
FAX *06-686 5442.* **W** www.hotel
duetorriroma.com **Rooms**: 26. 1
AE, DC,
MC, V. €€€€

This amiable hotel is a short
walk from Piazza Navona, tucked
into an alleyway in the artisans'
district of the old town.
Bedrooms vary: some are stylish,
others plain. The lounge is both
elegant and homey, with looped-
back drapes, statuettes, an
immense gilt-framed mirror
and pink velvet sofas.

Genio

Via Zanardelli 28, 00186. **Map** 4 E3 &
11 C2. **C** *06-683 3781.* **FAX** *06-6830
7246.* **@** leonardi@travel.it
Rooms: 65. 1 AE, DC, MC, V, JCB.
€€€€€

On a fairly busy road just behind
Piazza Navona, the Genio's
bedrooms are ordinary, though
comfortable. It has a roof terrace
where you can picnic.

Portoghesi

Via dei Portoghesi 1, 00186.
Map 4 E3 & 11 C2. 📞 06-686 4231.
FAX 06-687 6976. W www.hotel
portoghesiroma.com *Rooms*: 28.
🛏 1 🔄 TV 🗎 🎵 🔊 📻 *MC, V.*
€€€€€

Ideally located on a cobbled street
a brief walk from Piazza Navona,
the Portoghesi is a simple hotel,
with slightly dated bedrooms. The
public rooms, however, are elegant,
and there is a roof terrace looking
out to the dome of the Portuguese
community's church next door.

Raphael

Largo Febo 2, 00186. **Map** 4 E3 &
11 C2. 📞 06-68 28 31. FAX 06-687
8993. W www.raphaelhotel.com
Rooms: 70. 🛏 1 TV 🍽 🔄 🗎
🔄 🍽 🍴 🎵 *AE, DC, MC, V,*
JCB. €€€€€

The Raphael, just off Piazza
Navona, is curtained with ivy. The
big reception lounge has the air
of an exhibition hall, being full of
antique statues, modern sculpture
and even a painted sled. There is
a restaurant in the basement
whose outstanding feature is an
ornate wine cabinet. Bedrooms
have parquet floors, marbled
walls and 18th-century-style
furniture. The top-floor rooms
offer terrific views.

PIAZZA DI SPAGNA

Jonella

Via della Croce 41, 00187.
Map 4 F2. 📞 06-679 7966.
FAX 06-446 2368. *Rooms*: 4.
1 🔄 €

The Jonella occupies an orange-
colored palazzo on one of the
most attractive shopping streets in
the Piazza di Spagna area. The
decor is somewhat ordinary, but
the location and low prices make
this place worth considering. The
owner occasionally pops out to
shop, so it's best to call with the
precise time of your arrival.

Margutta

Via Laurina 34, 00187. **Map** 4 F1.
📞 06-322 3674. FAX 06-320 0395.
Rooms: 24. 🛏 🔄 🔄 *AE, DC,*
MC, V. €€

The Margutta is on a quiet
cobbled street just below the
Piazza del Popolo. The scruffy
facade and old-fashioned grubby seats in
the lobby are forgotten as soon as
you get into your room, which has
white walls and green wrought-
iron bedsteads and candleholders.
If you wish to stay in one of the

three attic rooms that share a
pretty roof terrace, be sure to
book well in advance.

Suisse

Via Gregoriana 54–56, 00187.
Map 5 A2 & 12 F1. 📞 06-678 3649.
FAX 06-678 1258. *Rooms*: 12. 🛏 12.
1 🔄 🔄 €€

Occupying the third floor of a dusty
palazzo, the Suisse is a pleasant
small hotel with friendly staff.
Chinese prints hang along the
corridors and in the rooms, which
also have polished floors, molded
ceilings and marble-topped
dressers and tables.

Condotti

Via Mario de' Fiori 37, 00187.
Map 5 A2 & 12 F1.
📞 06-679 4661. FAX 06-679 0457.
W www.hotelcondotti.com
Rooms: 16. 🛏 1 TV 🍽 🗎 🚶
🔄 🍴 📻 *AE, DC, MC, V, JCB.*
€€€€

Close to Piazza di Spagna and in
the heart of the designer shopping
district, the Condotti is a comfortable, inviting hotel with its own
ambience and style. Rooms are
medium to large and well
decorated. One room has its
own small terrace, and three
others share one.

Homs

Via della Vite 71–72, 00187.
Map 5 A3 & 12 F1. 📞 06-679 2976.
FAX 06-678 0482. *Rooms*: 48. 🛏 1
🔄 TV 🍽 🔄 🛏 🔊 🍴 📻 *AE,*
DC, MC, V. €€€€

On one of the quieter, less
pretentious shopping streets in
the Piazza di Spagna area, the
Homs has basic rooms with
dark-green carpets, white walls
and white bathrooms. The
breakfast room opens out on to
a pleasant terrace.

Locarno

Via della Penna 22, 00186. **Map** 4 F1.
📞 06-361 0841. FAX 06-321 5249.
W www.hotellocarno.com
Rooms: 68. 🛏 🛏 🔄 TV 🍽 🗎
🔊 🔄 📻 🔊 🍴 🍴 *AE,*
DC, MC, V. €€€€

Situated on a small, busy side-
street near the Tiber, a brief
walk from Piazza del Popolo,
the Locarno is an attractive 1920s
hotel with an Art Nouveau door
and swags of lilac growing across
its façade. Old-fashioned touches
remain, such as a grandfather
clock and a marble-topped bar
of polished wood. Outside, there
is a patio packed with greenery
and kept cool by a tiny fountain.

Dei Borgognoni

Via del Bufalo 126, 00187. **Map** 5 A3
& 12 F1. 📞 06-6994 1505.
FAX 06-6994 1501. W www.hotel
borgognoni.it *Rooms*: 50. 🛏 1 🔄
TV 🍽 🗎 🔄 🔄 📻 🔊 🍴 *AE,*
DC, MC, V, JCB. €€€€€

This elegant hotel is just off Piazza
San Silvestro, five minutes from
the Spanish Steps. In the public
rooms, a modern style is coupled
with traditional oil paintings. The
bedrooms – some with terraces –
are beautifully understated.

Carriage

Via delle Carrozze 36, 00187. **Map** 5
A2. 📞 06-699 0124. FAX 06-678
8279. @ hotel.carriage@alfanet.it
Rooms: 24. 🛏 1 TV 🍽 🗎
🔄 *AE, DC, MC, V, JCB.* €€€€€

Situated on a street where the
nobility used to park their carriages,
this hotel's elegance is immediately
evident in the reception area, with
its paneling, candelabra and gilt-
framed mirrors. The rooms are a
serene shade of blue, with some
antique furniture. Two rooms
open on to the charming, leafy,
terra-cotta-tiled public terrace; two
have their own private terrace.

Gregoriana

Via Gregoriana 18, 00187.
Map 5 A2 & 12 F1. 📞 06-679 4269.
FAX 06-678 4258. *Rooms*: 19.
🛏 1 🔄 TV 🗎 🚶 🔄 🔊 🍴 🍴
€€€€€

The Gregoriana is a stylish hotel,
situated close to the Spanish Steps
on a tree-lined, quiet street of
elegant palazzi. The rooms are
all the same: black lacquer
doors, terra-cotta-colored carpets,
flowery wallpaper and 1920s
drawings on the walls. There are
no public rooms, so breakfast and
drinks are served in the bedrooms.

Hassler

Piazza Trinità dei Monti 6, 00187.
Map 5 A2. 📞 06-69 9340. FAX 06-
678 9991. W www.hasslerroma.com
Rooms: 100. 🛏 1 🔄 TV 🍽 🌿
🗎 🔊 🔄 🔊 🍴 🍴 🍴
AE, DC, MC, V, JCB. €€€€€

Standing at the top of the Spanish
Steps, with magnificent views
of Rome from its roof terrace,
restaurant *(see p313)* and suites,
the Hassler was once host to
royalty and the glitterati of Europe
and America. Its *dolce vita* days
are over, but the lounges and
bedrooms lit by Venetian glass
chandeliers, the wood-paneled bar
and the marble bathrooms retain
the air of a more extravagant era.

D' Inghilterra

Via Bocca di Leone 14, 00187.
Map 5 A2. 06-69 9811.
FAX 06-6992 2243. **W** www.hotel
dinghilterra.it *Rooms*: 98.
AE, DC, MC, V. €€€€€

Liszt and Hemingway are among
the writers, artists and musicians
who have stayed here. In Rome's
designer shopping area and close
to the Spanish Steps, it is a
desirable place to stay. The
bedrooms are individually
decorated and furnished. The bar
could have been lifted straight
from a London gentlemen's club,
and the restaurant's walls, painted
with garden views and sky-
frescoed ceiling, create the illusion
of dining in the open.

Manfredi

Via Margutta 61, 00187. **Map** 5 A2.
06-320 7676. **FAX** 06-320 7736.
W www.hmanfredi.com *Rooms*: 18.
AE, MC, V, JCB.
€€€€€

This pretty hotel is excellently
located, just off Piazza di Spagna,
on a cobbled street of art galleries
and antiques shops. The reception
area and bar/breakfast room are
paved with marble and decorated
in soft pastels. The comfortable
bedrooms are all soundproofed
with pale fabric wallcoverings and
coordinated furnishings.

Mozart

Via dei Greci 23b, 00187. **Map** 4 F2.
06-3600 1915. **FAX** 06-3600 1735.
W www.hotelmozart.com
Rooms: 56.
AE, DC, MC, V, JCB.
€€€€€

Located on a cobbled street
between Piazza del Popolo and
Piazza di Spagna, the Mozart is
immediately appealing. Decor is
attractively worn and includes a
Venetian mirror. There is a breakfast room, as well as a bar-café,
which opens off the stone-flagged
reception. Rooms have ceramic-
tiled or parquet floors, and bathrooms tend to be small, most
having only a shower.

Piazza di Spagna

Via Mario de' Fiori 61, 00187.
Map 5 A2 & 12 F1. 06-679 6412.
FAX 06-679 0654. **W** www.hotelpiazza
dispagna.it *Rooms*: 17.
AE, MC, V.
€€€€€

Close to the designer boutiques of
Via Condotti, this attractive, small

hotel has simple but good-sized
rooms with tiled floors, and a
couple of bathrooms with Jacuzzis.
The breakfast room and bar are
tiny, so most residents decide to
take breakfast in their own rooms.

Hotel de Russie

Via del Babuino 9, 00187. **Map** 4 F1.
06-32 88 81. **FAX** 06-3288 8888.
W www.rfhotels.com *Rooms*: 129.
AE, DC, JCB, MC, V.
€€€€€

A recent addition to Rocco Forte's
empire, this historic hotel, once
frequented by Cocteau and Picasso,
has reopened on its original site.
Apart from the breathtaking views,
understated luxury is the keynote
here, with muted colors and
unobtrusive efficiency. The hotel
facilities include fine terrace cafés, an
excellent restaurant and access to
the Russie's secret garden on the
slopes of the Pincio hill.

Scalinata di Spagna

Piazza Trinità dei Monti 17, 00187.
Map 5 A2. 06-679 3006.
FAX 06-6994 0598. **W** www.hotel
scalinata.com *Rooms*: 16.
AE,
DC, MC, V. €€€€€

This hotel occupies a small 18th-
century villa at the top of the
Spanish Steps. Breakfast is served
at a communal table under the gaze
of a parrot. Some of the rooms
retain their old paneled ceilings.
Reserve far in advance if you want
to stay in one of the rooms that
open out on to the large terrace.

Valadier

Via della Fontanella 15, 00187. **Map**
4 F1. 06-361 1998. **FAX** 06-320
1558. **W** www.hotelvaladier.com
Rooms: 49. AE, DC,
MC, V, JCB. €€€€€

Slickly decorated with shiny wood
and marble, the Valadier styles
itself as an intimate hideaway for
those on a romantic visit to Rome.
Public rooms are tailor-made for
seduction, with low sofas, marble
floors and oriental rugs.

CAMPO DE' FIORI

Della Lunetta

Piazza del Paradiso 68, 00186.
Map 4 E4 & 11 C4. 06-686 1080.
FAX 06-689 2028. *Rooms*: 35. 25.
€€

Located on a tiny crumbling
piazza, this little hotel offers neat,

simple rooms and a courtyard. It is
popular with large groups of
students and can be very noisy.
No breakfast is served.

Piccolo

Via dei Chiavari 32, 00186. **Map** 4 E4
& 11 C4. 06-6880 2560.
Rooms: 15. 1
AE, MC, V. €€

Close to Piazza Campo de' Fiori,
the Piccolo is a family-run hotel at
the lowest end of the price range.
There is, however, nothing cheap
about the atmosphere: cool and
serene, featuring clean, simple
rooms of various sizes. The
Piccolo also has a separate,
bar/breakfast room.

Rinascimento

Via del Pellegrino 122, 00186. **Map** 4
E4 & 11 B3. 06-687 4813.
FAX 06-683 3518. htlrinascimento@
iol.it *Rooms*: 19. TV
AE, MC, V.
€€

With an appealing location in the
Campo de' Fiori district, close to
artisans' workshops and a variety
of trattorias, the Rinascimento is
housed in an old palazzo with
stone arched windows. The
bedrooms tend to be slightly worn
with rather cramped bathrooms.

Smeraldo

Vicolo dei Chiodaroli 11, 00186.
Map 4 F5 & 12 D4. 06-687 5929.
FAX 06-6880 5495. **W** www.hotel
smeradoroma.com *Rooms*: 50.
29. TV
AE, MC, V. €€

Situated in the heart of the
bustling Campo de' Fiori quarter,
the Smeraldo offers an oasis of
serenity, with clean, simple rooms
in an ocher-washed building with
shutters over the windows.

Campo de' Fiori

Via del Biscione 6, 00186. **Map** 4 E4
& 11 C4. 06-6880 6865. **FAX** 06-
687 6003. framar1@ inwind.it
Rooms: 27. 13.
MC, V. €€€

This mid-range hotel occupies a
well-kept house, just off the noisy
Campo de' Fiori market square.
You enter the tiny reception area
along a passageway in which
mirrors repeat a series of columns
into an illusory suggestion of
infinity. The small bedrooms have
beams and paisley furnishings or
sky-painted ceilings, lacy walls
and frilly bedcovers.

On the sixth floor, a split-level
roof garden gives vertiginous
but aesthetically rewarding views

over such landmarks as the Pantheon, the Victor Emmanuel monument and St. Peter's.

Pomezia

Via dei Chiavari 12, 00186. **Map** 4 E4 & 12 D4. **☎** 06-686 1371. **@** h.pomezia@libero.it **Rooms**: 25. 🛏 18. 🚻 ▦ 📺 ⌇ AE, DC, MC, V. €€€€

In the heart of the lively Campo de' Fiori district, the Pomezia has spotless, simply decorated rooms and a bar in the reception area to welcome weary arrivals.

Sole

Via del Biscione 76, 00186. **Map** 4 E4 & 11 C4. **☎** 06-6880 6873. **FAX** 06-689 3787. **W** www.solealbiscione.it **Rooms**: 58. 🛏 33. 🚻 ▦ ⌇ 🅿 🅟 🅰 €€€

Possibly the oldest hotel in Rome, this pleasing establishment is in a palazzo just off the central Campo de' Fiori. Rooms are furnished in a slightly haphazard way, but with some character. There are small sitting areas and a leafy, sunny terrace with a drinks-and-snack machine. No breakfast is served.

Teatro di Pompeo

Largo del Pallaro 8, 00186. **Map** 4 E4 & 11 C4. **☎** 06-6830 0170. **FAX** 06-6880 5531. **@** hotel.teatrodipompeo@tiscalinet.it **Rooms**: 12. 🛏 🚻 ▦ 📺 ⌇ ▦ 🅰 🚻 AE, DC, MC, V. €€€€

This small hotel sits over the ruins of the first permanent theater in the city, which was completed in 55 BC. You can eat breakfast among the original theater arches, and the bar has a terra-cotta floor and marble tables.

QUIRINAL

Hotel des Artistes

Via Villafranca 20, 00185. **Map** 6 D3. **☎** 06-445 4365. **FAX** 06-446 2368. **W** www.hoteldesartistes.com **Rooms**: 32. 🛏 🚻 ▦ 24 📺 ▦ ⌇ 🅰 AE, DC, JCB, MC, V. €€€€

On a quiet side street close to shops and tourist attractions, this hotel has been recently renovated. Its rooms are comfortable and reasonably priced and the staff are friendly and helpful.

St. Regis Grand

Via V. E. Orlando 3, 00185. **Map** 5 C2. **☎** 06-47 091. **FAX** 06-474 7307. **W** www.stregis.com/grandrome

Rooms: 170. 🛏 🚻 ▦ 24 📺 ⌇ ▦ ⌇ 🅰 ▦ 🚻 📺 🅰 AE, DC, MC, V, JCB. €€€€€

To step into the Grand is to enter another world. Cherubs cavort over the reception area; flowers and fruit are carved on the walls of the lounge, and rich pastel rugs lie on the parquet floor. Facilities include a sauna, beauty salon, hairdresser, and a restaurant renowned as one of the most beautiful in the country. The standard of bedrooms varies, but you might find yourself in an antique bed reading by the light of a genuine Venetian lamp.

TERMINI

Katty

Via Palestro 35, 00185. **Map** 6 E2. **☎ & FAX** 06-444 1216. **Rooms**: 17. 🛏 11. 🚻 ▦ ⌇ MC, V. €

The Katty has clean, basic rooms, some with an occasional piece of antique furniture. It is very popular with British and American students, so either reserve in advance or turn up early, ideally between 8 and 9am. No breakfast is served.

Restivo

Via Palestro 55, 00185. **Map** 6 E2. **☎** 06-446 2172. **FAX** 06-445 2629. **Rooms**: 6. 🚻 ▦ €

The Restivo has six immaculately maintained bedrooms. The owner keeps a hall full of gifts and postcards from grateful guests who often return again and again.

Cervia

Via Palestro 55, 00185. **Map** 6 E2. **☎** 06-49 10 57. **FAX** 06-49 10 56. **@** hotelcervia@wnt.it **Rooms**: 28. 🛏 11. 🚻 ▦ ⌇ AE, DC, MC, V. €€

The Cervia is a hotel housed in the same palazzo as the Restivo. Some of the rooms have been refurbished with sponge-painted walls and private bathrooms, and these are excellent value. The rest are a bit more basic. The public areas are immaculate, and there is a pleasant bar/breakfast room.

Giuliana

Via Agostino Depretis 70, 00185. **Map** 5 C3. **☎** 06-488 0795. **FAX** 06-482 4287. **W** www.hotelgiuliana.it **Rooms**: 11. 🛏 11. 🚻 ▦ 🚻 ⌇ AE, DC, JCB, MC, V. €€€

A Santacroce husband and English wife team run this small, welcoming hotel close to the bustle of the Via Nazionale and the Basilica of Santa Maria Maggiore. Rooms are simple but spacious.

Canada

Via Vicenza 58, 00185. **Map** 6 E2. **☎** 06-445 7770. **FAX** 06-445 0749. **W** www.hotelcanadaroma.com **Rooms**: 70. 🛏 🚻 ▦ 📺 ▦ 🚻 ⌇ 🅰 🚻 AE, DC, MC, V. €€€€

Behind Termini Station, the Canada is an above-average mid-range hotel. Rooms are very comfortable, and there is a pleasant lounge with attractive cane seats and sofas. The service is courteous.

Venezia

Via Varese 18, 00185. **Map** 6 E2. **☎** 06-445 7101. **FAX** 06-495 7687. **W** www.hotelvenezia.com **Rooms**: 61. 🛏 🚻 ▦ 📺 ▦ 🚻 ⌇ AE, DC, MC, V, JCB. €€€€

One of the nicer mid-size hotels near Termini station, the Venezia is pleasantly decorated with antique furniture and Murano glass chandeliers in the public areas. The bedrooms are light and airy with smart bathrooms.

AVENTINE

Aventino

Via San Domenico 10, 00153. **Map** 8 D2. **☎** 06-578 3214. **FAX** 06-544 1112. **W** www.aventinohotels.com **Rooms**: 23. 🛏 🚻 ▦ 🚻 ⌇ 🚻 ⌇ AE, DC, MC, V. €€€

Run by the owners of Villa San Pio and Sant'Anselmo, the Aventino is more modest, with large but fairly simple rooms. However, its lush garden location is gorgeous, and the breakfast room has a magnificent armoire and stained glass.

Sant'Anselmo

Piazza di Sant'Anselmo 2, 00153. **Map** 8 D2. **☎** 06-574 3547. **FAX** 06-578 3604. **W** www.aventinohotels.com **Rooms**: 46. 🛏 🚻 ▦ 🚻 ⌇ 🅰 AE, DC, MC, V. €€€€

This pretty villa, in the gardens of the peaceful Aventine, is quite near the Colosseum. The entrance hall ceiling is stenciled with flowers; there are chandeliers and corridors with floors of inlaid marble. The lounge looks out on to the hotel's garden. Reserve well in advance.

Villa San Pio

Via di San Melania 19, 00153. **Map** 8 E3. **☎** 06-578 3214. **FAX** 06-57 4112. **W** www.aventinohotels.com **Rooms**: 84. 🛏 🚻 ▦ 🚻 🅰 ⌇ ▦ 🅟 🅰 🚻 ⌇ AE, DC, MC, V. €€€€

The Villa San Pio is set in a garden graced with statues. The entrance hall is furnished with velvet and brocade chairs and an 18th-century Venetian tapestry. Some rooms have flower-stenciled furniture.

Domus Aventina

Via di Santa Prisca 11B, 00153. **Map** 8 E2. **[** 06-574 6135. **FAX** 06-5730 0044. **W** www.domus-aventina.com **Rooms:** 26. 🛏 **1** 🛗 **24** **TV** **Y** 📶 🍴 🗄 🛗 **🗗** 🛗 AE, DC, MC, V, JCB. €€€€€

This immaculate hotel occupies a 14th-century convent at the foot of the Aventine Hill. Rooms are large and simply decorated in pastel tones. There are wonderful views of the Celian Hill from many of the rooms and from the huge terrace.

TRASTEVERE

Carmel

Via Mameli 11, 00153. **Map** 7 C2. **[** 06-580 9921. **FAX** 06-581 8853. **@** hotelcarmel@hotmail.com **Rooms:** 11. 🛏 11. **1** 🛗 €€

The Carmel's most appealing feature is a terrace with its leafy canopy. A couple of rooms open off the terrace. All ten rooms are spotless, and most have bathrooms. It is essential to book in advance.

San Francesco

Via Jacopa de Settesoli 7, 00193. **Map** 4 E2. **[** 06-5830 0051. **FAX** 06-5833 3413. **W** www.hotelsanfran cesco.net **Rooms:** 24. 🛏 **1** 🛗 **24** **TV** 📶 🗄 🛗 🗗 🛗 🛗 **Y** 🗐 AE, DC, JCB, MC, V. €€€€

The rooms here are furnished with traditional Roman elegance. Special attractions include rooftop terrace views and a chance to linger over coffee looking out on a small 15th-century cloister.

VATICAN

Alimandi

Via Tunisi 8, 00192. **Map** 3 B2. **[** 06-3972 3941. **FAX** 06-3972 3943. **W** www.alimandi.org **Rooms:** 35. 🛏 **1** 🛗 **TV** 🛗 **P** 🗗 **Y** 📶 AE, DC, MC, V. €€€

On a quietish street just below the entrance to the Vatican Museums, the Alimandi is a simple *pensione* at the cheap end of its price range – hence its popularity with young travelers. Rooms are clean and adequate. Its outstanding feature is the lovely, large roof terrace. A courtesy bus service to and from Fiumicino airport is available.

Amalia

Via Germanico 66, 00192. **Map** 3 C2. **[** 06-3972 3354. **FAX** 06-3972 3365. **W** www.hotelamalia.com **Rooms:** 30. 🛏 25. **1** **TV** 📶 **Y** 🗐 AE, DC, MC, V, JCB. €€€€

Situated between the Ottaviano Metro station and the Vatican, the Amalia attracts mainly Italian guests. It has spotless rooms ranged on three floors and a lounge with bar.

Columbus

Via della Conciliazione 33, 00193. **Map** 3 C3. **[** 06-686 5435. **FAX** 06-686 4874. **W** www.hotel columbus.net **Rooms:** 92. 🛏 **1** 🛗 **TV** **Y** 📶 🗄 🛗 🗗 🛗 **P** 🛗 🍴 🗐 AE, DC, MC, V, JCB. €€€€

Perfect for anyone wishing to stay near the Vatican, the Columbus occupies an austere former monastery. Heavy wrought-iron light fixtures hang in the reception hall; the magnificent upper lounge has a beamed ceiling and terra-cotta floor; the function room (the old refectory) has kept its frescoes; and there is a walled terrace garden.

Atlante Star

Via Vitelleschi 34, 00193. **Map** 3 C2. **[** 06-687 3233. **FAX** 06-687 2300. **W** www.atlantehotels.com **Rooms:** 62. 🛏 **1** 🛗 **24** **TV** **Y** 📶 📶 🗄 🛗 🗗 🛗 🐕 **P** 🛗 **Y** 🍴 🗐 AE, DC, MC, V, JCB. €€€€€

This hotel is a good option for business travelers needing on-site office facilities. The rooftop restaurant has views of St. Peter's, but both service and atmosphere leave much to be desired. Double rooms are modest in size, and singles can be cramped, some of them with only a shower. Avoid street-facing rooms since they can be noisy.

Hotel dei Mellini

Via Muzio Clementi 81, 00193. **Map** 4 E2. **[** 06-32 47 71. **FAX** 06-3247 7801. **W** www. hotelmellini.com **Rooms:** 80. 🛏 **1** 🛗 **24** **TV** **Y** 📶 📶 🗄 🛗 🗗 🛗 **P** 🛗 🍴 **Y** 🗐 AE, DC, MC, V. €€€€€

Opened in 1996 in a converted late 19th-century building, this hotel has all the modern comfort you could wish for but still feels charming and welcoming. It is located in a quiet residential area near Castel Sant'Angelo and only a short walk across the river from Via Condotti. The reception staff are very helpful and there is a small but nice bar in the lobby and a roof terrace.

VIA VENETO

Alexandra

Via Veneto 18, 00187. **Map** 5 B2. **[** 06-488 1943. **FAX** 06-487 1804. **@** alexandra@venere.it **Rooms:** 45. 🛏 **1** 🛗 **TV** **Y** 🗄 🛗 🗗 🛗 🛗 AE, DC, MC, V, JCB. €€€€

One of the less expensive hotels on the upscale Via Veneto, the Alexandra has a pleasant conservatory-style breakfast room and a lounge decorated with chintz and brocade. All the bedrooms are unique; some furnished with antiques, some with splash-painted walls. Traffic noise is audible in some rooms.

Barocco

Via della Purificazione 14, 00187. **Map** 5 B3. **[** 06-487 2001. **FAX** 06-48 59 94. **W** www. hotelbarocco.it **Rooms:** 32. 🛏 **1** 🛗 **TV** **Y** 🗄 🛗 🗗 🛗 🛗 **Y** 🍴 🗐 AE, DC, MC, V, JCB. €€€€

Occupying a restored palazzo at the bottom of Via Veneto, the Barocco is ideal for anyone who prefers a small hotel. Bedrooms are pleasant with unobtrusive décor, and some have working areas. There are two small lounges (one with a bar) and a restaurant.

Oxford

Via Boncompagni 89, 00187. **Map** 5 C1. **[** 06-420 3601. **FAX** 06-4281 5349. **W** www.hoteloxford.com **Rooms:** 56. 🛏 **1** **TV** **Y** 🗄 🛗 🗗 🛗 **Y** 🍴 🗐 AE, DC, MC, V, JCB. €€€€

On a quiet road off Piazza Fiume, about ten minutes' walk from Via Veneto, the Oxford has stylish public rooms: squashy sofas and modern pictures in the reception area; striped sofas and abstract art in the bar. The bedrooms are more dated, with hessian-covered walls and candlewick bedspreads.

La Residenza

Via Emilia 22–24, 00187. **Map** 5 B2. **[** 06-488 0789. **FAX** 06-48 57 21. **@** hotel.la.residenza@venere.it **Rooms:** 26. 🛏 **1** 🛗 **TV** **Y** 🗄 **P** 🛗 **Y** 🍴 🗐 AE, MC, V. €€€€

The Residenza is an elegant hotel that occupies a villa on a quiet road off Via Veneto. There is a canopied terrace with pine furniture, and a terra-cotta-tiled roof garden with potted plants. The bedrooms are comfortable and well-equipped.

Bernini Bristol

Piazza Barberini 23, 00187. **Map** 5 B3.
☎ 06-488 3051. FAX 06-482 4266.
W www.sinahotels.it **Rooms**: 127.
AE, DC, MC, V, JCB.
€€€€€

This unprepossessing brick building overlooks a busy piazza that has Bernini's Triton fountain as its centerpiece. The marble-laden hotel is comfortable, with a roof garden, but the decor is uninspiring and the atmosphere more conducive to work than pleasure. The central location and secretarial facilities ensure a steady stream of business visitors.

Eden

Via Ludovisi 49, 00187. **Map** 5 B2.
☎ 06-47 81 21. FAX 06-482 1584.
W www.hotel-eden.it
Rooms: 121.
AE, DC, MC, V, JCB. €€€€€

Historically one of Rome's most illustrious hotels, the Eden has recently been restored to pristine condition. The roof garden is stunning, giving every justification for the hotel's name. La Terrazza restaurant (see p317) nestles on the roof like a beacon of refinement.

Excelsior

Via Veneto 125, 00187. **Map** 5 B1.
☎ 06-47 081. FAX 06-482 6205.
@ reso70excelsiorrome@westin.com
Rooms: 327.
AE, DC, MC, V, JCB.
€€€€€

Exotically sculpted balconies supported by statues set the tone for this extravagant hotel, which houses boutiques, saunas, a restaurant and a famous piano bar. Public rooms are sumptuous, with marble walls and floors, rich carpets and brocade furnishings – and the corridors are paneled with silk or imitation marble. The bedrooms are elegant and spacious, with chandeliers, painted and gilded wooden paneling and ornate, marble bathrooms.

Imperiale

Via Veneto 24, 00187. **Map** 5 B2.
☎ 06-482 6351. FAX 06-474 2583.
W www.loanimperiale.com
Rooms: 95.
AE, DC, MC, V. €€€€

One of the more reasonably priced Via Veneto hotels, the Imperiale lacks the panache of its more glamorous neighbors, but the friendly staff make for a relaxed atmosphere. The bar is quite pleasant, and the bedrooms are well decorated, with pretty coordinating furnishings and small marble bathrooms.

Majestic

Via Veneto 50, 00187. **Map** 5 B2.
☎ 06-42 14 41. FAX 06-488 0984.
W www.hotelmajestic.com
Rooms: 100.
AE, DC, MC, V, JCB. €€€€€

Founded in 1889, the Majestic is the oldest of Via Veneto's hotels. Since its five-year refurbishment, it has played host to international stars such as Pavarotti and Sylvester Stallone. Most of the furniture and much of the decor in the public rooms are original, down to the startling gilded lime-green lounge. Bedrooms and corridors are decorated in a bold, bright style, particularly on the fifth floor, where carpets with a zig-zag pattern provide the background to chintz and brocade.

Regina Hotel Baglioni

Via Veneto 72, 00187. **Map** 5 B2.
☎ 06-42 11 11. FAX 06-4201 2130.
@ regina.roma@baglionihotels.com
Rooms: 151.
AE, DC, MC, V. €€€€€

The exuberance of the Baglioni's exterior – it is painted vanilla and strawberry pink and decorated with grimacing masks – continues in the reception area, where a wrought-iron staircase is guarded by the statue of a sea god. The bedrooms are painted in vivid shades of coral, aqua and blue, and many are very spacious. Double glazing in the rooms overlooking Via Veneto cuts down on some of the noise, but light sleepers might prefer a room at the back of the hotel.

Victoria

Via Campania 41, 00187. **Map** 5 B1.
☎ 06-47 39 31. FAX 06-487 1890.
@ hotel.victoria@flashnet.it
Rooms: 113.
AE, DC, MC, V. €€€€€

Situated on a quiet road at the top of Via Veneto and overlooking the walls abutting the Porta Pinciana, the Victoria prides itself on being a "hotel for individuals," keeping its personal touch by refusing large group reservations. It is renowned for good service. There are stylish public rooms and an attractive roof terrace, but the bedrooms are rather uninspired.

VILLA BORGHESE

Villa Borghese

Via Pinciana 31, 00198. **Map** 2 F5.
☎ 06-854 9648. FAX 06-841 4100.
@ hotel.villaborghese@tiscalinet.it
Rooms: 31.
AE, DC, MC, V, JCB. €€€€

This immediately likable hotel occupies a villa close to Villa Borghese. Although the hotel is on a rather busy main road, the atmosphere is pleasant: more that of a private home than a hotel. Public rooms include an intimate old-fashioned bar and a lounge with comfortable sofas. There is a courtyard sheltered by a pretty ivy-covered pergola. The rooms are on the small side but they are tastefully decorated.

Aldrovandi Palace

Via Aldrovandi 15, 00197. **Map** 2 E4.
☎ 06-322 3993. FAX 06-322 1435.
W www.aldrovandi.com
Rooms: 137.
AE, DC, MC, V, JCB.
€€€€€

Among the most restful luxury hotels in the city, the Aldrovandi is situated just outside the center of Rome on a fairly busy road overlooking Villa Borghese. The reception lounge is elegant and decorated with rich soft furnishings, carpets and chandeliers. The real highlight of the hotel, however, is the sunny garden with its attractive swimming pool, which is over-looked by an airy restaurant.

Lord Byron

Via de Notaris 5, 00197. **Map** 2 D4.
☎ 06-322 0404. FAX 06-322 0405.
W www.lordbyronhotel.com
Rooms: 37.
AE, DC, MC, V. €€€€€

This refined small hotel is housed in a dazzling white building in the residential district of Parioli. It was originally a monastery, but there is nothing ascetic about its rooms today. The lounge is lavishly furnished with antiques and tapestry-seated chairs, and the tiny sitting room has large sofas and old-fashioned portraits. The restaurant is decorated with plenty of chintz and fresh flowers and serves some of the best food in Rome. All the bedrooms have tapestry and floral soft furnishings with marble coffee tables and are provided with a full decanter of port, which comes with the compliments of the management.

For key to symbols see p291

RESTAURANTS AND CAFES

I N ROME, eating out can be both a joy and an entertainment. On warm summer evenings tables flow out onto every conceivable open space, and diners dedicate long hours to the popular social activity of people watching (and of being noticed and admired themselves) in a confusion of passers-by, street performers, rose sellers and traffic. Although Romans have always loved to linger at the table, the lavish feasts of ancient Rome have been scaled down and today's cooking is based on simplicity, freshness and good quality local raw ingredients in

Waiter at Alberto Ciarla (see p316)

what is essentially a seasonal cuisine. Fast food is gradually arriving, but it is fundamentally alien to the Roman temperament and way of life.

The 66 restaurants reviewed in this chapter have been selected from the best that Rome can offer across all price ranges. The chart on pages 310 and 311 will help narrow down your selection, and the map on page 308 shows the highlights of the list. The section *Light Meals and Snacks*, featured on pages 318 to 321, has details of recommended cafés, pizzerias, wine bars and other places for more casual eating.

WHERE TO FIND GOOD RESTAURANTS

E VERY AREA of the city has its own culinary delights. True Roman cooking can be found in the old slaughterhouse area of Testaccio and in the Jewish quarter (the Ghetto) near Campo de' Fiori. Around the university, in San Lorenzo, northeast of the city center, you will find lots of cheap pizzerias and *trattorias*.

Near Termini station there's a good selection of African – particularly Ethiopian and Eritrean – restaurants. For dining outdoors, which often means in beautifully secluded piazzas or in impressively ancient parts of the city, try the restaurants in the narrow streets of Trastevere (the old

artists' quarter); around Campo de' Fiori, or along the old Via Appia Antica.

TYPES OF RESTAURANTS

I N GENERAL, a *trattoria* is an unassuming family-run establishment with good home cooking, while a *ristorante* is more elegant and thus more expensive.

Many eating places – where paper tablecloths give a clue to low prices – simply have no name. They offer an open doorway and,

Fresh artichokes, a Roman speciality

more often than not, excellent basic home cooking. Some of them offer a great deal more, and your chances of finding authentic Roman cooking are higher in the best of these establishments than in more expensive restaurants.

There will probably be times when you do not want a full restaurant meal, and Rome offers a huge variety of places for more casual eating (*see pp318–21*). One type of place offering snacks or more substantial dishes is the *enoteca*, which

doubles as a well-stocked wine shop for browsers and connoisseurs.

Other places for a sit-down, informal lunch or dinner are *birrerie*, which are not only for beer drinkers but also offer pizzas or even four-course meals.

There is always plenty of interesting take-out food for sale – *pizza rustica* or *pizza al taglio* (pizza by the slice) is available all over the city. For full-size pizzas, choose places with wood stoves (*forno a legna*) for better results than from electric ovens. Other take-out foods such as whole roast chickens, potatoes, *pomodori al riso* (tomatoes stuffed with rice) or *supplì* (fried rice croquettes) can be had from *rosticcerie*. A self-service *tavola calda* will serve an impressive array of hot food and is ideal for lunch.

VEGETARIAN FOOD

P URELY VEGETARIAN restaurants are few and far between in Rome, but everywhere you will find pasta or rice dishes (*risotto*) using interesting combinations of vegetables, salads, artichokes cooked in different ways or vegetables stuffed and then baked in the oven. Most menus are very adaptable.

The interior of Relais le Jardin (see p317)

THE PRICE OF A MEAL

WHAT YOU PAY will clearly depend on your choice of establishment. In a *tavola calda*, or Roman pizzeria, for example, you can still eat for as little as €8 a head. A local *trattoria* costs perhaps €15, whereas in a smarter restaurant expect to pay around €25 and up. Bottled wine, as opposed to a jug or carafe of house wine *(vino della casa)*, commands higher prices but should offer a more interesting range of tastes *(see p306)*. House wine can be a hit-or-miss affair.

READING THE MENU

NOT EVERY restaurant automatically provides a menu – the waiter will often tell you the day's specialities *(piatti del giorno)*, usually not mentioned on the standard menu but almost always worth ordering. If you are not sure about these, you can always ask for *la lista* (the menu) and then allow yourself to be guided.

A meal could begin with *antipasti* (appetizers) or *primi piatti* – the latter consisting of *pasta asciutta* (pasta with some kind of sauce), *pasta in brodo* (clear broth with pasta in it), *pasta al forno* (baked pasta), risotto or a substantial soup. You then move on to the *secondi*, the main meat or fish course, for which you will usually need to order vegetables *(contorni)* separately if you would like them. Afterward you have a choice of *formaggi* (cheeses), *frutta* (fruit) or *dolci* (desserts).

One of many Trastevere cafés

Outdoor café life in the piazza outside Santa Maria in Trastevere

Romans do not usually eat cheese as well as a sweet dish. Strong espresso coffee and perhaps a liqueur *(amaro* or *digestivo)* rounds off the meal *(see p307)*. You may want to skip the first course, or you may prefer to choose a salad or vegetable dish or substitute the main course with an *antipasto*. Pasta alone tends not to be seen as a full meal.

OPENING TIMES

RESTAURANTS are generally open from about noon to 3pm and from 8 to 11pm or much later. The busiest times tend to be 9 to 9:30pm for dinner and 1 to 1:30pm for lunch. Dinner is generally the preferred time for more relaxed eating, particularly in summer, when it begins and ends late as the heat of the day subsides. Bars are open all day, often from the early hours, serving all kinds of drinks (alcohol can be sold at any time of day) and snacks. The quietest month is August, when many restaurant owners take their annual vacation (shown by *Chiuso per Ferie* signs).

RESERVING A TABLE

MAKING A RESERVATION *(prenotazione)* is generally advisable, especially for Sunday lunch and often for Saturday evening. Also, check the weekly closing day: many places are closed on Monday, and Sunday evening can also be difficult for reservations.

In summer try to reserve a shady table outside, since air-conditioning is not universal, and indoors the atmosphere may be stuffy.

WHEELCHAIR ACCESS

ROME is slowly adapting to the needs of those in wheelchairs, but a call to the restaurant in advance will help secure the right table.

TAKING CHILDREN ALONG

CHILDREN are very welcome, particularly in family-run places. You can usually order half-portions (but expect to pay more than half), or just ask for an extra plate. Highchairs *(seggioloni)* may also be available in some establishments.

USING THE LISTINGS

Key to symbols in the listings on pp312 to 317.

- 🍽️ fixed-price menus
- 🚭 nonsmoking area
- Ⓥ vegetarian dishes
- 🧒 child portions and sometimes highchairs
- ♿ wheelchair access
- 👔 jacket and tie required
- 🎵 live music
- ▦ tables outside
- ▽ exceptional wine list
- ★ highly recommended
- 💳 credit cards accepted
- *AE* American Express
- *DC* Diners Club
- *MC* MasterCard/Access
- *V* VISA
- *JCB* Japanese Credit Bureau

Price categories for a three-course meal for one, including a half bottle of house wine, cover charge, tax and service:
- € up to €25
- €€ €25–€45
- €€€ €45–€65
- €€€€ €65–€80
- €€€€€ over €80

What to Eat in Rome

Bulb of fresh garlic

THE TRADITIONAL *cucina romanesca* has always relied on local markets full of fresh seasonal vegetables, fruit, cheese and meat from the nearby countryside, plus seafood from the Mediterranean. As in the rest of Italy, pasta is an important part of the menu; one popular dish is the famous *spaghetti alla carbonara*, which was devised in Rome. Many genuinely Roman meat dishes are based on the so-called *quinto quarto* (fifth quarter) – head, innards, tail, pig's feet and so on. Highly flavored with olive oil, herbs, bacon *(pancetta)* or pig's cheek *(guanciale)*, they become a culinary delight. Fish from the Mediterranean is excellent. In season, mushrooms and artichokes may be served in dozens of different ways. *Mesticanza* is also good in season: it is a fresh mix of salad leaves, including the peppery *rughetta* (arugula) and *puntarelle* (curly endive shoots, often served with anchovy dressing). For dessert, be sure to try Italian ice cream or puddings such as the classic *tiramisù*.

Maritozzi alla Panna
These soft buns with raisins and candied peel are filled with whipped cream.

Fresh basil

Anchovies

Artichoke hearts

Roasted peppers

Baby octopus

Antipasto
Italian appetizers may include olives, cured meats, seafood and grilled or preserved vegetables.

Bruschetta
Toasted bread is rubbed with salt, garlic and olive oil; tomato can be added.

Supplì
Fried rice croquettes stuffed with mozzarella make a tasty snack.

Olive Oil and Vinegar
Always on the table, these are for dressing salads and flavoring antipasti.

Filetti di Baccalà
A Jewish speciality, deep-fried cod fillets are a typical Roman snack or first course.

Risotto alla Romana
Liver, sweetbreads, Marsala and Romano cheese are used to make this risotto.

TYPICAL ITALIAN PASTA

Penne rigate (quills)

Farfalle (butterflies)

Fusilli (spirals)

Conchigliette (shells)

Cappelletti (small hats)

Bucatini all'Amatriciana
Pasta tubes are served with bacon, tomatoes and onion, with grated Romano on top.

Spaghetti alla Carbonara
Chopped bacon, eggs and cheese are used to prepare this famous local dish.

Gnocchi alla Romana
Small semolina dumplings are served with tomatoes or with butter.

Fiori di Zucca e Carciofi Fritti
Squash blossoms in batter and whole artichokes deep-fried are popular antipasti.

Coda alla Vaccinara
A traditional Roman dish made from braised oxtail with celery and tomatoes.

Saltimbocca alla Romana
Veal with Parma ham and sage, this tasty dish is also served rolled and skewered.

Fave al Guanciale
Fresh springtime broad beans are simmered with bacon and onion.

Parmesan

Italian Cheeses
Parmesan is the best-known Italian cheese, but Rome's classic is pecorino Romano, made from ewe's milk. The mature, hard version is often used grated, but fresh Romano can be eaten as a dessert cheese. Mild buffalo-milk mozzarella is the classic one for pizza.

Mozzarella

Crostata di Ricotta
This Roman cheesecake is filled with ricotta, Marsala and lemon.

Tiramisù
Mascarpone cheese, coffee and chocolate are combined for this wonderful dessert.

What to Drink in Rome

Roman mosaic showing bird and vines

ITALY IS ONE OF Europe's most significant wine-producing countries, keeping up a tradition started in the hills around Rome over 2,000 years ago. Today, wine is usually drunk with meals as a matter of course, and knowing the difference between *rosso* (red) and *bianco* (white) may be all the vocabulary you need to get by. Beer is widely available too, as well as good selections of apéritifs and digestifs. Rome's drinking water, another debt to the ancient Romans, is particularly good, fresh and sweet, and in abundant supply.

The vineyards of Frascati, southeast of Rome

WHITE WINE

Orvieto   **Frascati**

VINES THRIVE in the warm climate of Lazio, the region around Rome, producing abundant supplies of inexpensive dry white wine for the city's cafés and restaurants. It is usually sold by the carafe. Of local bottled wines, Frascati is the best known, but Caste lli Romani, Marino, Colli Albani and Velletri are very similar in style. All are made from one grape variety, the Trebbiano, though better quality versions contain a dash of Malvasia for perfume and flavor. Other central Italian whites worth trying are Orvieto and Verdicchio. Quality white wines from all over Italy, including fine whites from Friuli in the northeast, are widely available in Rome.

Calcaia comes from Barberani, a reliable producer of Orvieto.

Bigi produce good quality Orvieto, especially the single-vineyard Torricella.

Casal Pilozzo is an easy-drinking white wine from Frascati producers, Colli di Catone. Choose the youngest vintage.

Colle Gaio, with its rich, fruity flavour, stands out among the dry white Frascatis.

WINE TYPE	GOOD VINTAGES	GOOD PRODUCERS
WHITE WINE		
Friuli (Pinot Bianco, Chardonnay, Pinot Grigio, Sauvignon)	The most recent	Gravner, Jermann, Puiatti, Schiopetto, Volpe Pasini
Orvieto/ Orvieto Classico	The most recent	Antinori, Barberani, Bigi, Il Palazzone
RED WINE		
Chianti/ Chianti Classico/ Chianti Rufina	95, 88, 85	Antinori, Castello di Ama, Castello di Cacchiano, Castello di Volpaia, Felsina Berardenga, Fontodi, Frescobaldi, Isole e Olena, Il Palazzino, Riecine, Rocca delle Macie, Ruffino, Vecchie Terre di Montefili, Villa Cafaggio
Brunello di Montalcino/ Vino Nobile di Montepulciano	95, 88, 85	Altesino, Avignonesi, Biondi Santi, Caparzo, Case Basse, Lisini, Il Poggione, Poliziano, Villa Banfi
Barolo/ Barbaresco	95, 89, 88, 85 82, 78	Aldo Conterno, Altare, Ceretto, Clerico, Gaja, Giacomo Conterno, Giacosa, Mascarello, Ratti, Voerzio

RED WINE

THOUGH SOME local red wine is made, most of the bottled red wine in Rome comes from other parts of Italy. Tuscany and Piedmont produce very good everyday drinking wines as well as top-grade ones like Barolo. Price should reflect quality – try Dolcetto, Rosso di Montalcino or Montepulciano, all affordable reds.

Tuscan table wine   Barolo

READING THE LABEL

ITALY has a two-tier system for labeling quality wine. DOC *(denominazione di origine controllata)* means you can be sure the wine is from the region declared on the label and is made from designated grape varieties. A higher classification – DOCG *(denominazione di origine controllata e garantita)* – is given to top wines such as the reds Barolo, Barbaresco, Chianti Classico and Brunello di Montalcino.

Chianti Classico

DRINKING WATER

Unlike many Mediterranean cities, Rome benefits from a constant supply of fresh drinking water, piped down from the hills through a system of pipes and aqueducts that has changed little from ancient Roman times. Only if there is a sign saying *acqua non potabile* is the water not safe to drink.

One of Rome's many fresh water drinking fountains

Coffee is almost more important to Roman life than wine. For strong black coffee, have expresso at any time of day. Try milky cappuccino for breakfast or mid-afternoon or, for extra milk, caffè latte.

Montepulciano d'Abruzzo, a rich and juicy red wine, is always a good choice. It is produced in the Abruzzi region.

Torre Ercolana is produced in small quantities and is generally regarded as one of Lazio's best red wines. It is made from Cesanese and Cabernet grapes and requires at least five years' aging.

Chianti Classico Riserva is older and stronger than a normal Chianti Classico.

APÉRITIFS AND OTHER DRINKS

BITTER, herb-flavored drinks like Martini, Campari or Aperol are the most popular apéritifs. (Ask for an *analcolico* if you prefer a non-alcoholic one.) Italians drink their apéritifs neat or with ice and soda. Strong, herby after-dinner drinks, known as *digestivi* or *amari*, are worth trying if you need to settle your stomach. Italian brandy and grappa can be very fiery. Italian beer, popular with pizza, is made in lager style.

Campari

SOFT DRINKS

ITALIAN FRUIT juices are good and most bars squeeze fresh orange juice *(spremuta di arancia)* on the spot. Iced coffee and fruit-flavored tea, such as peach, are popular.

Refrigerated storage for wine and beer

Espresso   **Cappuccino**

Caffè latte

Rome's Best: Restaurants and Cafés

ROME IS NOT particularly known for luxury restaurants, but more for atmospheric places where the focus is on the social side of dining and on regional cooking. An amazing variety can be found. Many places specialize, priding themselves on being the best of their kind – whether they offer superb espresso, or traditional foods like deep-fried salted cod *(baccalà)*. Other restaurants can offer beautiful settings or are the best places to see and be seen. This selection shows some of the many highlights of a city where eating is taken very seriously.

Caffè Giolitti
This historic ice cream shop serves a variety of flavors, to eat in or take away. (See p320.)

Camponeschi
This stylish restaurant offers elegantly prepared dishes and outdoor tables on Piazza Farnese. (See p314.)

Filetti di Baccalà
This small, crowded place serves tasty fried fillets of cod – one of Rome's most traditional dishes – and offers a truly Roman experience. (See p320.)

Alberto Ciarla
Fish dominate the exquisite dishes as well as the decor in this elegant restaurant. (See p316.)

Piperno
For over a century, traditional Roman Jewish cooking has been the speciality of Piperno, in the heart of the Jewish Ghetto. (See p314.)

Vatican

Piazza Navona

Campo de' Fiori

Janiculum

Trastevere

Babington's Tea Rooms
This old-fashioned, genteel establishment at the foot of the Spanish Steps serves English tea and cakes. (See p320.)

La Terrazza
Gloriously situated in the roof garden of Hotel Eden, La Terrazza offers some of the finest cuisine in Rome, with views to match. (See p317.)

Caffè Greco
Famous as the haunt of writers, artists and intellectuals in the 19th century, this café still retains the faded grandeur shown in this painting. (See p320.)

Piazza di Spagna

Via Veneto

Piazza della Rotonda

Quirinal

Capitol

Esquiline

Forum

Palatine

Caracalla *Lateran*

Aventine

| 0 meters | 500 |
| 0 yards | 500 |

Sora Lella
This Roman trattoria is famous for its setting on the Isola Tiberina and for the fashionable crowd which it attracts. (See p314.)

Tazza d'Oro
This figure graces the façade of Tazza d'Oro, where you will find some of the best espresso in Rome. (See p320.)

Choosing a Restaurant

THE RESTAURANTS in this guide have been selected for their good value or exceptional food. This chart highlights some of the factors that may influence your choice. Entries are alphabetical within price category. For more details on the restaurants, see pages 312 to 317. Information on cafés and wine bars is on pages 318 to 321.

	Price	Fixed Price Menu	Vegetarian Dishes	Tables Outside	Seafood Specialities	Late Opening	Air-Conditioning	Attractive Setting
PIAZZA DELLA ROTONDA (see p312)								
Il Buco	€			●		●	▪	
Da Gino	€							
Il Bacaro	€€	●		●	▪	●	▪	
Le Due Colonne	€€	●	▪		▪	●	▪	
Myosotis	€€		▪	●			▪	
Vecchia Locanda	€€	●	▪	●		●	▪	●
Enoteca Capranica	€€€	●	▪			▪		●
Sangallo	€€€	●					▪	
La Rosetta ★	€€€€			●		●	▪	
El Toulà	€€€€	●	▪		▪		▪	
PIAZZA NAVONA (see p312)								
La Taverna	€	●		●	▪		▪	●
La Campana	€€							
Osteria dell'Antiquario	€€			●			▪	●
Il Convivio ★	€€€€	●			▪		▪	
Papà Giovanni	€€€€		▪			●	▪	
PIAZZA DI SPAGNA (see p313)								
Al 34	€	●	▪	●	▪		▪	
Birreria Viennese	€	●		●		●	▪	
Mario alle Vite	€			●			▪	
Nino	€€							
Porto di Ripetta	€€€	●			▪		▪	
Hassler Roof Restaurant	€€€€€						▪	●
CAMPO DE' FIORI (see p313)								
Monserrato	€€			●			▪	
Il Drappo	€€	●		●		●	▪	
Dal Pompiere	€€						▪	
Sora Lella	€€	●					▪	
Piperno	€€€	●	▪	●	▪		▪	
Vecchia Roma	€€€		▪	●	▪	●	▪	●
Camponeschi	€€€€			●	▪	●	▪	●
QUIRINAL (see p314)								
Colline Emiliane	€€						▪	
Hasekura	€€	●	▪				▪	
Il Posto Accanto	€€		▪		▪		▪	
Quadrifoglio	€€					●	▪	
Al Moro	€€€			●	▪	●	▪	
TERMINI (see p314)								
Coriolano	€€€		▪		▪		▪	
ESQUILINE (see p314)								
Cicilardone	€€					●	▪	
La Gallina Bianca	€€			●			▪	
Trattoria Monti	€€						▪	
Agata e Romeo ★	€€€€	●					▪	

Price categories for a three-course meal for one, half a bottle of house wine, and all unavoidable extra charges such as cover, service, tax:
€ up to €25
€€ €25–€45
€€€ €45–€65
€€€€ €65–€80
€€€€€ over €80.

★ Means highly recommended.

FIXED PRICE MENU
Restaurant offering *menu turistico* (tourist menu): usually three or four courses without wine or coffee, for a set price.
VEGETARIAN DISHES
Restaurant specializing in seafood or fish or serving good seafood selection.
LATE OPENING
Last orders on or after 11:30pm.
ATTRACTIVE SETTING
Restaurant set in a pretty piazza or having a garden terrace or a lovely view.

	FIXED PRICE MENU	VEGETARIAN DISHES	TABLES OUTSIDE	SEAFOOD SPECIALITIES	LATE OPENING	AIR-CONDITIONING	ATTRACTIVE SETTING
LATERAN *(see p315)*							
Alfredo a Via Gabi	€		●			■	
Cannavota	€€			■		■	
Charly's Saucière	€€				●	■	
AVENTINE *(see p315)*							
Court Delicati	€	■					
Luna Piena	€	■	●			■	
Perilli a Testaccio	€€					■	
Checchino dal 1887 ★	€€€			●	●	■	
TRASTEVERE *(see p316)*							
Da Lucia	€		●				
Asinocotto	€€	■		■			
La Cornucopia	€€	●	●	■		■	●
Da Paris	€€		●	■		■	●
Romolo nel Giardino della Fornarina	€€		●		●		●
Alberto Ciarla ★	€€€	●	●	■	●	■	
JANICULUM *(see p316)*							
Antico Arco ★	€€					●	■
VATICAN *(see p316)*							
San Luigi	€€	●	■	●		●	■
Taverna Angelica	€€					■	
Les Etoiles	€€€€			●	■		■
VIA VENETO *(see p317)*							
Giovanni	€€			■		■	
Tullio	€€			■		■	
Andrea	€€€	■		■		■	
George's ★	€€€		●		●	■	●
Le Sans Souci ★	€€€€€	■		■	●	■	
La Terrazza ★	€€€€€	■	●	■	●	■	●
VILLA BORGHESE *(see p317)*							
Al Ceppo	€€	■	●	■		■	
Relais la Piscine ★	€€€€	●	●	■		■	●
Relais le Jardin	€€€€€			■		■	

Piazza della Rotonda

Il Buco

Via di Sant'Ignazio 8. **Map** 4 F4 & 12 E3. 06-679 3298, 06-678 4467. **Open** 12:30–4pm, 7pm–midnight Tue–Sun. **Closed** Aug, Christmas. AE, DC, MC, V.

Much has happened since the tiny *buco* (hole) opened in 1891 – the small *osteria* has become a large restaurant, yet the calm atmosphere, unfailing courtesy and formidable Tuscan menu remain. From the traditional *crostini* (liver pâté canapés), robust *ribollita* (thick vegetable soup) and huge Florentine steaks, to the final *tozzetti* (almond biscuits) with *vin santo* (dessert wine), this is a truly Tuscan experience.

Da Gino

Vicolo Rosini 4 (Piazza del Parlamento). **Map** 4 F3 & 12 D1. 06-687 3434. **Open** 1–3pm, 8–10:30pm Mon–Sat. **Closed** Aug.

Journalists, politicians and the initiated scramble for a seat under the kitsch, frescoed pergola of this ancient, ultra-Roman *trattoria* to feast on traditional daily dishes: *gnocchi* and *osso buco* (Thursdays), *baccalà* (Fridays), tripe (Saturdays), plus classic sturdy soups, dutifully executed Roman standards and delectable homemade *tiramisù*.

Il Bacaro

Via degli Spagnoli. **Map** 12 D2. 06-686 4110. **Open** 12:30–2:30pm, 8–11:30pm Mon–Fri, 8–11:30pm Sat. **Closed** 3 weeks Jan. DC, MC, V, JCB.

Located in the historic center of the city, near the Pantheon, this tiny restaurant serves meals cooked in a minute kitchen. The menu is based on meat and fish dishes and includes such main courses as fillet steak in a red wine sauce. The superb desserts include an excellent chocolate mousse.

Le Due Colonne

Via del Seminario 122. **Map** 4 F4 & 12 D3. 06-678 1449. **Open** 11:30am–3:30pm, 6:30–11:30pm daily. AE, DC, MC, V, JCB.

Evocative of ancient Rome, the decor of this restaurant includes two imperial columns, from which it gets it name, and an ancient fountain.

The cuisine is rich in Mediterranean flavors, with most dishes cooked on the spot. The seafood dishes, such as *calamari* stuffed with onions and hard-boiled eggs and giant shrimp with *pachino* tomatoes, are particularly good.

Myosotis

Vicolo della Vaccarella 3–5. **Map** 12 D2. 06-686 5554. **Open** 12:30–3pm, 7:30–11:30pm Mon–Sat. **Closed** 2 wks Aug. AE, DC, MC, V.

Situated in a tiny street near the Pantheon, Myosotis has emerged as a foodie temple for those who want to keep an eye on their pockets. An imaginative approach and the freshest ingredients mean that whatever choice you make is a good one, from the house *antipasti* (mozzarella, ricotta and stuffed pimentos) to the *frittura di paranza* (lighly fried fish and seafood).

Vecchia Locanda

Vicolo Sinibaldi 2. **Map** 4 F4 & 12 D3. 06-6880 2831. **Open** 12:30–3pm, 7–11:30pm Mon–Sat. **Closed** 1 wk mid-Aug, Christmas. V AE, DC, MC, V.

Visit this small family-run Ligurian restaurant in summer, when tables line the secluded arched street. Everything shows extreme care – including the impeccable service. An imaginative combination of herbs and vegetables characterizes the menu: *risotto* with zucchini blossoms, *porcini* crêpes, stuffed truffled rabbit and lots of fresh fish. There is a good selection of French and regional wines.

Enoteca Capranica

Piazza Capranica 99–100. **Map** 12 D2. 06-6994 0992. **Open** 12:30–3pm, 7:30–10:30pm Mon–Fri, 7:30–10:30pm Sat. **Closed** possibly Aug (check). AE, DC, V, JCB.

Housed in part of the impressive 15th-century Palazzo Capranica *(see p113)*, the Enoteca Capranica offers an extensive menu, mostly bases around seafood and vegetable dishes. Starters include lobster and mango salad, while exotic main courses include *risotto con zuca e tartufo* (risotto with pumpkin and truffel) and *spigola al sale* (sea bass in a salt crust).

Sangallo

Vicolo della Vaccarella 11. **Map** 4 F3 & 12 D2. 06-686 5549. **Open** 7:30–11pm Mon–Sat. **Closed** 2 weeks Aug. AE, DC, MC, V.

This elegant fish restaurant has an interesting menu complemented by an impressive wine list. Antipasti include *crostini con calamaretti al radicchio* (baby squid and radicchio on toast). First courses such as *fettucelle con gamberi, pomodori e pecorino* (pasta with shrimp, tomatoes and pecorino cheese) are prepared delicately and simply. Ask about the specialty of the day.

La Rosetta

Via della Rosetta 9. **Map** 4 F4 & 12 D2. 06-6830 8841. **Open** 7:45–11:45pm Mon–Sat, 1–3pm Mon–Fri. **Closed** 3 weeks Aug, Christmas. ★ AE, DC, MC, V, JCB.

Despite the exorbitant prices, people flock nightly (having reserved in advance) for a seat in this elegant restaurant. Fresh fish and seafood brought in daily from Sicily and cooked in the simplest ways, achieve close to culinary perfection. The enthusiastic service and top quality wines, particularly the Sicilian whites, available do justice to the cuisine.

El Toulà

Via della Lupa 29B. **Map** 4 F3 & 12 D1. 06-687 3498. **Open** 1–3pm, 8–11pm Tue–Fri, 8–11pm Mon, Sat. **Closed** Aug, Christmas. V AE, DC, MC, V, JCB.

El Toulà is justly renowned as one of the most exclusive, traditional and luxurious restaurants in Rome. The Venetian-inspired cooking is serious and professional, with forays into the best classic international cuisine. In dignified, formal surroundings, the service is exemplary and the selection of wines superb.

Piazza Navona

La Taverna

Via del Banco di Santo Spirito 58. **Map** 4 D3 & 11 A2. 06-686 4116. **FAX** 06-686 4116. **Open** noon–3pm, 7pm–11pm Tue–Sun. AE, DC, MC, V, JCB.

Tourists and local residents mingle in Giovanni's crowded Roman *trattoria* to enjoy the family atmosphere and traditional regional cooking. Particularly appreciated are the *rigatoni all'amatriciana; coda alla vaccinara* and, on Thursday, Friday and Saturday, respectively, *gnocchi, baccalà* and tripe.

La Campana

Vicolo della Campana 18. **Map** 12 D1. **(06-686 7820. Open** 12:30–3pm, 7:30–11:30pm Tue–Sun. **Closed** Aug. 🚹 🈳 AE, DC, MC, V. €€

The Campana, reputedly Rome's oldest restaurant, was already in business when Michelangelo was a lad. There is something timeless about the brisk, friendly service provided by experienced waiters while tourists and locals alike pore over the extensive menu. Specialties include *vignarola* (traditional vegetable and bean soup), pasta with fresh anchovies, *frittura mista* (fried cheese, vegetables and brains) and, for die-hard Roman cuisine lovers, *coda alla vaccinara* (stewed ox-tail).

Osteria dell'Antiquario

Piazzetta San Simeone 27. **Map** 4 E3 & 11 B2. **(06-687 9694. FAX** 06-6880 5381. **Open** 12:30–2:30pm, 8–11pm Tue–Sat, 8–11pm Mon. **Closed** 2 wks Aug, 2 wks Jan. 🚹 🈳 AE, DC, MC, V. €€€

In the comfort of the elegantly restructured rooms of an old antiques shop, Giorgio Nisti offers an unusual menu dictated by the whims of the chef and the daily market. The largely traditional dishes are creatively adapted to contemporary health-conscious tastes. There is an impressive choice of regional, French and California wines.

Il Convivio

Vicolo dei Soldati 28. **Map** 4 E3 & 11 C2. **(06-686 9432. Open** 1–2:30pm, 8–10:30pm Tue–Sat, 8–10:30pm Mon. **Closed** 1 week Aug. 🍴 🈳 ★ 🈳 🈳 🈳 AE, DC, MC, V, JCB. €€€€€

An air of sophisticated tranquillity pervades this intimate restaurant, one of the very best specializing in modern creative cookery. Its young chef, one of the three brother/owners from the Marches, creates both subtle and unusual combinations of flavors and the highly personalized menu evolves with the seasons. The wine list is extensive and the service discreet.

Papà Giovanni

Via dei Sediari 4. **Map** 4 F4 & 12 D3. **(06-686 5308. Open** 1–2:30pm, 7:30–11pm Mon–Sat. 🈳 🈳 🈳 🈳 MC, V. €€€€€

Nearly 60 years have passed since Papà Giovanni first sold his country wines in Rome; the bottles lining the walls are testimony to the past and to the superb cellar of Giovanni's son, Renato Sentuti.

Here diners sample the best of the new lighter Roman cuisine. Classics such as *cacio e pepe*, salt cod and tripe, are offered alongside exotic salads and truffled dishes. Desserts include ricotta soufflé with strawberry sauce, hot chocolate profiteroles and exquisite sorbets.

PIAZZA DI SPAGNA

Al 34

Via Mario de' Fiori 34. **Map** 5 A2. **(06-679 5091. Open** 12:30–3pm, 7–11pm Tue–Sun. **Closed** 3 weeks Aug. 🈳 🈳 🍴 🈳 AE, DC, MC, V. €

This busy, bustling restaurant is an ideal choice if you're in a hurry, as the service is speedy and efficient. Predominantly featuring southern Italian cooking, the extensive menu offers an esoteric selection, particularly where vegetables and herbs are served with pasta, meat and fish. Given its size and location, the prices are reasonable.

Birreria Viennese

Via della Croce 21. **Map** 5 A2. **(06-679 5569. Open** 10am–midnight daily. 🈳 AE, DC, MC, V. €

The stained-glass entrance leads to a long crowded room where, for more than 60 years, traditional beers and Austrian specialties have been sampled. Try sausages, goulash, *Wienerschnitzel*, sauer-kraut or the massive *piatto di legno della Transilvania* (wooden platter heaped with delights, for two). Wine is available, and the service is helpful and courteous.

Mario alla Vite 🖉

Via della Vite 55. **Map** 5 A3 & 12 E1. **(06-678 3818. Open** noon–3pm, 7–11pm Mon–Sat. **Closed** Aug. 🈳 🚹 🈳 AE, DC, MC, V. €

Despite an exclusive address, Mario has kept prices reasonable, and his food is still simple, honest Tuscan fare. Elbow-to-elbow dining, haphazard service and noisy confusion seem inevitable. Nevertheless, the food is worth it – traditional *fagioli al fiasco* (cannellini beans in oil), *ribollita* (thick vegetable soup), Florentine steaks and delicious pastries are the attractions, along with a wide selection of wines.

Nino

Via Borgognona 11. **Map** 5 A2 & 12 E1. **(06-679 5676. Open** 12:30–3pm, 7:30–11pm Mon–Sat. 🚹 🈳 AE, DC, JCB, MC, V. €€€

A reliable restaurant, located among the fancy shops around Piazza di Spagna, Nino has been popular since it opened in 1934. The menu features mostly Tuscan food, so there is always a hearty soup as well as game and other standards such as *bistecca alla fiorentina* (grilled T-bone steak). The desserts are all home-made.

Porto di Ripetta

Via di Ripetta 250. **Map** 4 F2. **(06-361 2376. Open** 12:45–2:30pm, 8–11pm Mon–Fri, 8–11pm Sat. **Closed** Aug. 🍴 🚹 🍴 🈳 🈳 AE, DC, MC, V, JCB. €€€€

The fame of this restaurant depends largely on the genius of chef Maria Romani. With the fish that arrives daily from her native Marches, she creates inspired combinations such as fish and broad bean soup or giant prawns with artichokes. It is expensive but worth it; the fixed price menu is much cheaper. There's a selection of excellent wines to choose from.

Hassler Roof Restaurant

Piazza Trinità dei Monti 6. **Map** 5 A2. **(06-6993 4726. Open** 7:30–11am, noon–2:30pm, 7:30–10:30pm Mon–Sat, 7:30–11am, 12:30–3pm, 7:30–10pm Sun. 🍴 🚹 🈳 🈳 🈳 AE, DC, MC, V, JCB. €€€€€

Perched on the sixth floor of the Hotel Hassler, overlooking the Spanish Steps, this roof restaurant commands a breathtaking view of Rome. Come for the gargantuan but pricey Sunday brunch. The wine list is excellent, the hovering waiter attentive but discreet. In the evening, when prices are higher, there is piano music.

CAMPO DE' FIORI

Monserrato

Via Monserrato 96. **Map** 4 D4. **(06-687 3386. Open** 12:30–3pm, 7:30–11:30pm Tue–Sun. **Closed** 2 wks Aug. 🈳 🈳 AE, DC, MC, V. €€

Monserrato is one of the safest bets in the city centre. It serves reliably good food, cooked with imaginative touches, throughout the year. The *gnocchi veraci* (gnocchi with clams) is a good starter, and the *rombo al forno con patate* (oven-cooked turbot with potatoes) is an excellent main course. Various fish dishes are served, with ingredients depending on the season.

For key to symbols *see p303*

Il Drappo

Vicolo del Malpasso 9. **Map** 4 D4 & 11 B3. 📞 06-687 7365. **Open** 8pm–midnight Mon–Sat. **Closed** Jan 1, Easter, 2 wks Aug, Dec 25. 🔧 🍴 🏮 🖥 🍷 AE, DC, MC, V, JCB. €€€

A small, intimate restaurant with ceiling drapes (hence the name), plants and candlelight, Il Drappo provides an authentic taste of Sardinia – traditional dishes imbued with flashes of culinary creativity. Everything is evocative of the island, particularly the *seada* (sweet cheese-filled ravioli) for dessert Try the *mirto* liqueur at the end.

Dal Pompiere

Via S. M. dei Calderari 38. **Map** 4 F5 & 12 D5. 📞 06-686 8377. **Open** 12:30–3pm, 7:30–11pm Mon–Sat. **Closed** Aug. 🍷 🧒 🖥 AE, MC, V. €€

In the heart of the Jewish Ghetto, Dal Pompiere occupies the first floor of the 16th-century Palazzo Cenci-Bolognetti. Under its frescoed open-beamed ceilings, in an authentically retro atmosphere, all the classic dishes of the substantial Roman cuisine are expertly served: among them fried zucchini flowers with anchovies, *rigatoni con la pajata* and spring lamb.

Sora Lella

Via Ponte Quattro Capi 16, Isola Tiberina. **Map** 8 D1. 📞 06-686 1601. **Open** 1–2:30pm, 8–11pm Mon–Sat. **Closed** Aug. 🖥 AE, DC, MC, V. €€

Founded by the exuberant Roman actress Sora Lella, this small, bright *trattoria* is a well-known place to people watch. Sora Lella is now run by Lella's son, Aldo. Dishes are based on traditional Roman cuisine, but prices are very high for an essentially simple style of cooking. Go instead for the beautiful location on the Isola Tiberina, the often glamorous clientele and the good service.

Piperno

Via Monte de' Cenci 9. **Map** 4 F5 & 12 D5. 📞 06-686 1113. **Open** 12:45–2:30pm, 8–10:30pm Tue–Sat, 12:30–3pm Sun. **Closed** Easter, Aug, Christmas. 🔧 🧒 🍴 🖥 AE, DC, MC, V. €€€

Piperno, in the heart of the old Jewish Ghetto, has been famed for over a century for its traditional Jewish/Roman dishes. Despite the competition, the restaurant is still unbeaten for lightly fried zucchini flowers, vegetable *fritto misto*, *carciofi alla giudia*, tripe and

superb fish, served in plain surroundings. Service is familiarly attentive and timely. The house wine is excellent Frascati. Reserve well in advance.

Vecchia Roma

Piazza Campitelli 18. **Map** 4 F5 & 12 E5. 📞 06-686 4604. **Open** 1–3:30pm, 8–11pm Thu–Tue. **Closed** 2 weeks Aug. 🔽 🖥 🏮 🍷 🖥 AE, DC. €€€

Set in a quiet, atmospheric piazza, this is one of the best places for a summer evening. Reliable Roman cooking is offered, with tempting antipasti, simply cooked fish and grilled meats, plus a connoisseur's wine list. Specialties are summer salads and, in winter, numerous variations of polenta. Added pleasures are the 18th-century interior and the excellent service.

Camponeschi

Piazza Farnese 50. **Map** 4 E5 & 11 C4. 📞 06-687 4927. **Open** 8pm–12:30am Mon–Sat. **Closed** 10 days Aug. 🖥 🖥 AE, DC, MC, V. €€€€

Camponeschi is set in one of the most attractive piazzas in Rome, especially beautiful in summer, so reserving in advance is necessary. The extensive menu includes modern and regional Italian cooking, creative Mediterranean fish and meat dishes, soufflés and refined French specialties.

QUIRINAL

Colline Emiliane

Via degli Avignonesi 22. **Map** 5 B3. 📞 06-481 7538. **Open** 12:45–2:45pm, 7:45–10:45pm Sat–Thu. **Closed** Aug. 🔧 🖥 MC, V, JCB. €€

Regional dishes are the hallmarks of this small family *trattoria*: one unpretentious room presenting a haven from the nearby bustle of Via del Tritone. Enjoy food typical of the province of Emilia Romagna – salamis and cold meats, homemade pastas (*tagliatelle, tortellini*), boiled meats with *salsa verde* (spinach, anchovy and onion sauce) and Emilian wines.

Hasekura

Via dei Serpenti 27. **Map** 5 B4. 📞 06-48 36 48. **Open** noon–2pm, 7–10:30pm Mon–Sat. **Closed** Aug. 🍴 📋 🔽 🖥 AE, DC, JCB, MC, V. €€

While Hasekura is not the most characteristic-looking Japanese

restaurant in Rome, it is the one that exiles recommend. The lunch menu is good value (with delicious, melt-in-the-mouth tempura) and Ito, the master chef, makes excellent sushi and sashimi (slices of raw fish). Fine sake and Japanese beer, and friendly service. Booking advisable.

Il Posto Accanto

Via del Boschetto 36 A. **Map** 5 B4. 📞 06-474 3002. **Open** 1–3pm Mon–Fri, 8–11pm Mon–Sat. **Closed** Aug. 🔽 🧒 🔧 🖥 AE, DC, MC, V. €€

Tiny, intimate and pleasant, this family-run restaurant owes its success to a carefully chosen short menu revolving around homemade pasta (excellent *tagliolini con asparagi* and *ravioli con zenzero* – ginger), simply prepared fish and meat, top-quality vegetables and familiar desserts (*tiramisù*), often prepared within sight of the lucky diners. There is a range of wines, as well as good grappas.

Quadrifoglio

Via del Boschetto 19. **Map** 5 B4. 📞 06-482 6096. **Open** 7–11pm Mon–Sat. **Closed** Aug. 🧒 🔧 🖥 AE, DC, JCB, MC, V. €€

Chef Pino Forlenza prepares authentic dishes from Naples, Campania and the tip of Africa, tailored to modern tastes with carefully selected raw ingredients. These are delivered with courteous service. Most of the wines are from Campania, too.

Al Moro

Vicolo delle Bollette 13. **Map** 5 A3 & 12 F2. 📞 06-678 3495. **Open** 1–3:30pm, 8–11:30pm Mon–Sat. **Closed** Aug. 🖥 🔽 V. €€€

Franco Romagnoli's *trattoria* is a reliable choice for traditional Roman cooking, using fresh local ingredients. Noisy and crowded, its closely packed tables do not encourage intimate dining. Classic dishes are served: *bucatini all'amatriciana*, *spaghetti alla Moro* (special *carbonara*), fried vegetables, excellent *baccalà alla Moro* (salt cod), tripe and *abbacchio* (lamb). The wine list is vast.

TERMINI

Coriolano

Via Ancona 14. **Map** 6 D1. 📞 06-4424 9863. **Open** 12:30–3pm, 7:30–11pm daily. **Closed** 3 weeks Aug. 🔽 🧒 🍷 🖥 AE, MC, V. €€€

This small restaurant aims at perfection with its lacy tablecloths and crystal glasses. The Italian menu changes with the seasons and uses only the freshest of raw ingredients, including fish. Specialties include homemade *ravioli di ricotta e spinaci*, *capretto* (kid) and chocolate *zuppa del contadino*.

ESQUILINE

Cicilardone

Via Farini 12. **Map** 6 D4.
C 06-48 35 49. **Open** noon–3pm Tue –Sat, 8pm–midnight Mon–Sat. **Closed** mid 2 weeks Aug. ⑩❶
🖪 *AE, DC, MC, V.* €€

Ring at Cicilardone's door and your host – Domenico Lucia – will greet you like an old friend and converse about the gastronomic delights from the region of Basilicata. Try the *menu di assaggini* – a number of dishes to give you an idea of the regional taste, including traditional pastas and hot chocolate profiteroles. There is a selection of some unusual southern wines.

La Gallina Bianca

Via Antonio Rosmini 9. **Map** 6 D4.
C 06-474 3777. **Open** noon–3pm, 6pm–midnight daily. 🔁🏠🔁
🖪 V 🖪 *AE, DC, MC, V.* €€

For all its ersatz rustic atmosphere, this popular restuarant-pizzaria is renowned for its wide-ranging menu which offers everything from large salads to various pasta dishes and deep-fried fare. However, the best option is to imitate local afficionados and to order a pizza (cooked in a wood-fired oven) or a platter of grilled meats with vegetables.

Trattoria Monti

Via di San Vito 19. **Map** 6 D4.
C 06-446 6573. **Open** 12:30–3pm, 7:30–11pm Tue–Sat, 12:30–3pm Sun. **Closed** Easter, Aug, 2 wks Dec–Jan.
🔁🔁🖪 *AE, DC, MC, V.* €€

This small unpretentious local *trattoria* serves delicate, creative regional dishes from the Marches region. Franca Camerucci cooks, while her husband, Mario, is an attentive waiter and expert sommelier. Specialties include fried stuffed olives, artichokes and *ciauscolo* (salami); *tortello al rosso d'uova* (fresh pasta stuffed with ricotta, spinach and tomato); and *tacchino all'aceto balsamico* (turkey braised in balsamic vinegar). There is a good Verdicchio house wine and a commendable wine list.

Agata e Romeo

Via Carlo Alberto 45. **Map** 6 D4.
C 06-446 6115. **Open** 1–3pm, 8–11pm Mon–Sat. **Closed** 2 weeks Jan, 2 weeks Aug. ⑩❶🖪🖪★
🖪 *AE, DC, MC, V, JCB.* €€€€

One of the newer *trattoria*-turned-restaurants, its increasing prices sadly reflect recent popular acclaim. Nevertheless, Agata's skill in producing a changing menu of predominantly Roman and southern Italian dishes, and Romeo's impeccable service and range of carefully chosen wines, are hard to beat. Well-spaced, elegantly set tables are ideal for tranquil eating. The *menu degustazione* is recommended.

LATERAN

Alfredo a Via Gabi

Via Gabi 36. **Map** 10 D3.
C 06-7720 6792. **Open** 12:30–3pm, 7:30–11pm Wed–Mon. **Closed** Aug.
🔁 *AE, DC, MC, V.* €€

This is a spacious local *trattoria* with a pavement pergola for outdoor eating. Specialties from Rome and the Marches – served in ample portions – include *tonnarelli ai sapori di bosco* (pasta with mushrooms), excellent *porcini* (in season), *straccetti all'ortica* (meat in nettle sauce), and *panna cotta* (rich *crème caramel*) with fruit or chocolate. Service is cheerful and friendly.

Cannavota

Piazza San Giovanni in Laterano 20. **Map** 9 C1. **C** 06-7720 5007. **Open** 12:30–3pm, 7:45–11pm Thu–Tue. **Closed** Aug 1–20.
🖪 *AE, DC, MC, V.* €€

Join the enthusiastic regulars who crowd this friendly restaurant if you are feeling especially hungry. Portions are generous, the cooking is traditional Italian and the service is swift. Seafood – shrimp, in particular – is excellent, but meat is also featured on the menu.

Charly's Saucière

Via San Giovanni in Laterano 270. **Map** 9 B1. **C** 06-7049 5666. **Open** 12:45–2:15pm, 7:45–11:15pm Tue–Fri, 8pm–midnight Mon, Sat. **Closed** 2 weeks Aug. 🖪 🖪 *AE, MC, V, JCB.* €€

An old-style, unsurprising and well-established French restaurant, this has scarcely altered over the years and is especially warm and intimate on a winter evening. Diners choose from French and Swiss fare: pâtés, onion soup,

cheese soufflé, fondues, *rösti*, steaks in a variety of sauces, and crêpes, accompanied by a small but careful selection of wines. The service is always highly professional and attentive.

AVENTINE

Court Delicati

Via Aventino 39. **Map** 8 E3. **C** 06-574 6108. **Open** noon–2:45pm, 7:30–11pm Tue–Sun. **Closed** Aug.
🖪 V 🖪 *AE, DC, MC, V.* €

This excellent Chinese restaurant has gained in popularity owing to the various Indonesian and Thai specialties it offers alongside the more traditional fare of pancake rolls and steamed dumplings. Thus the more adventurous can try out *nasi-goreng*, or the incredibly hot *tomyam* soup. The restaurant is much patronized by workers from the nearby UN Food and Agriculture Organization building and the reasonable mark-ups on beer and wine add to the wallet-friendly experience.

Luna Piena

Via Luca della Robbia 15–17.
Map 8 D3. **C** 06-575 0279.
Open 7–11:30pm Mon–Sat, 12:30–3pm Mon, Thu–Sun.
Closed mid-Jun–mid-Jul. 🖪 🖪
🔁 V 🖪 *AE, DC, JCB, MC, V.* €

The success of Luna Piena derives from its simple Mediterranean classics made from ingredients bought at the local Testaccio market. The menu varies according to the season, with the day's specials chalked up on a board at the door. The place for a traditional *pasta alla carbonara* and *saltimbocca alla Romana* (veal and Parma ham cooked with sage and wine).

Perilli a Testaccio

Via Marmorata 39. **Map** 8 D3.
C 06-574 2415. **Open** 12:30–3pm, 7:30–11pm Thu–Tue.
Closed Aug. 🖪 🖪 *AE, DC, MC, V.* €€

In the heart of Testaccio, this archetypal Roman *trattoria* is always packed with hungry regulars (and the occasional famous face). On offer are giant-size quantities of robust traditional fare – *rigatoni alla pajata* (pasta with veal intestines), *spaghetti alla carbonara* (served in king-size bowls), *coda alla vaccinara*, *carciofi alla romana*. Everything is efficiently served. Ignore the noise and awful murals and enjoy yourself.

For key to symbols *see p303*

Checchino dal 1887

Via di Monte Testaccio 30.
Map 8 D4. 06-574 6318.
Open 12:30–3pm, 8–11:30pm
Tue–Sat. **Closed** Aug, 1 week at
Christmas. ★
AE, DC, MC, V, JCB. €€€

Checchino specializes in dishes
using the *quinto quarto* (offal,
intestines, tripe and tail), originally
discarded by the old slaughterhouse opposite. Ninetta Mariani
and her two sommelier sons offer
traditional *rigatoni alla pajata*,
coda alla vaccinara, *crostata di
ricotta*, a superb cheese tray and
an extraordinary wine selection.
Carved into the artificial Monte
de' Cocci (made from broken
amphoras), its cool, natural wine
cellar deserves a special visit.

TRASTEVERE

Da Lucia

Vicolo del Mattonato 2. **Map** 7 B1.
06-580 3601. **Open** 12:30–3:30pm,
7:30–11pm Tue–Sun. **Closed** 2 weeks
Aug, 1 week Christmas. €

Head for this popular well-worn
trattoria off Via Garibaldi to enjoy
genuine Roman cooking. You will
not be disappointed by the *pasta e
ceci*, *baccalà*, *pollo con i peperoni*
(chicken with peppers), boiled
meats and, incongruously,
Milanese risotto. However the
service is take it or leave it, and
the choice of wine basic. The
outdoor tables make a more
attractive dining area in summer.

Asinocotto

Via dei Vascellari 48. **Map** 8 D1.
06-589 8985. **Open** 8–11pm
Tue–Sun. **Closed** 3 wks Jan.
AE, DC, JCB, MC, V. €€

Young cook Giuliano Brenna has
brought imaginative cooking to
Trastevere with this casually
elegant restaurant. The menu
changes according to the season,
with three or four well-chosen
antipasti, firsts, main courses and
desserts, plus several daily
specials. The eggplant, arugula
and nettle *ravioli* are a dream,
though fresh fish is also served
with cool imagination: the seabass
with black truffles is excellent.
Sweets are successfully tempting
and the wine cellar well stocked.

La Cornucopia

Piazza in Piscinula 18. **Map** 8 D1.
06-580 0380. **Open** noon–3pm,
7–11pm Wed–Mon. AE,
DC, JCB, MC, V. €€

La Cornucopia it is recommended
for its candlelight, elegant place
settings and, in summer,
comfortable tables outside in the
piazza. The dishes are largely
Mediterranean, with good
antipasti, unusual pasta, simply
cooked fish such as *spigola al
vapore* (steamed sea bass) and
selected meats.

Da Paris

Piazza San Calisto 7A. **Map** 7 C1.
06-581 5378. **Open** 12:30–3pm,
7:30–11pm Tue–Sat, 12:30–3pm Sun.
Closed Aug. AE, DC, MC,
V, JCB. €€

This classic Roman/Jewish
restaurant is a firm favorite with
choosy diners in Trastevere. Jole
Cappellanti's homemade pasta
and traditional dishes are a must
and include *minestra di arzilla*
(ray) and *trippa* (tripe) *alla
romana*. The *fritto misto vegetale*
is extraordinary, the fish fresh.
There are good desserts and the
owner's personal choice of wines.

Romolo nel Giardino della Fornarina

Via Porta Settimiana 8.
Map 4 D5 & 11 B5. 06-581 8284.
Open noon–3pm, 7:30–11pm
Tue–Sun. **Closed** Aug.
AE, DC, MC, V. €€
See p210.

A Roman institution, this was said
to have been the home of La
Fornarina, Raphael's celebrated
mistress and model. Its atmosphere
is best enjoyed on a summer
evening. Eat out by candlelight in
the walled courtyard, to the
accompaniment of a melancholy
guitar. The food is Roman,
including fried *mozzarella alla
Fornarina* and *cervella e carciofi*
(brains and artichokes).

Alberto Ciarla

Piazza San Cosimato 40. **Map** 7 C1.
06-581 8668. **Open** 8pm–
midnight Mon–Sat. ★ AE, DC, MC, V, JCB.
€€€

This is the quintessential restaurant for fish lovers – at least, those
who are prepared to splash out.
The elegant, dramatically dark
decor is lit by candlelight. Perfectly executed dishes fluctuate
between the traditional and the
inventive, always with an eye to
what's best in the market, ranging
from the simple to the elaborately
creative. A few innovatory meat
dished can be had. Ciarla, who is
president of the Italian sommeliers,
provides an exceptional wine list,
including many fine French and
Californian wines.

JANICULUM

Antico Arco

Piazzale Aurelio 7. **Map** 7 A1.
06-581 5274. **Open** 7:30pm–
midnight Mon–Sat, 12:30–3pm Sun.
★ AE, DC, JCB, MC, V.
€€

Since changing managment a few
years ago, the Anitco Arco has
become one of Rome's best places
to eat innovative food and drink
excellent wines without spending
a fortune. Choose from a long list
of interesting wines from all over
Italy and France (with a few
dozen labels available by the
glass). The menu is based on
classic Mediterranean dishes using
seasonal ingredients, but they
have been "revisited" and given
a modern twist. The low-key
but elegant decor makes it
suitable for an intimate meal as
well as convivial dining.

VATICAN

San Luigi

Via Mocenigo 10. **Map** 3 B2.
06-3972 0704.
Open noon–3:30pm, 7pm–midnight
Mon–Sat. AE, DC, JCB,
MC, V. €€

If you have just spent hours in
the Vatican Museums, the pleasure
of a relaxing restaurant with
19th-century decor and soft music
will soothe your aching limbs.
A fixed menu is offered at lunch
and a choice of traditional Roman
and creative dishes in the evening.
Pastas and desserts are particularly
successful. There is a choice of
good French and Italian wines.

Taverna Angelica

Piazza A. Capponi 6.
Map 3 C2. 06-687 4514.
Open 7:30pm–12:30am daily.
Closed 1 wk Aug.
AE, MC, V. €€

The elegantly minimalist
restaurant near St. Peter's,
serves excellent fish with a
nouvelle touch, but also offers other
inventive dishes which include
pasta and meats served with
imaginative sauces and *contorni*.

Les Etoiles

Via Vitelleschi 34. **Map** 3 C2.
06-689 3434. **Open** 12:30–
2:30pm, 7:30–10:30pm daily.
AE, DC, MC, V,
JCB. €€€€

Located at the top of the Atlante Star hotel (see p300), this rooftop restaurant was completely renovated in 1992, and now includes free valet parking and a separate entrance with a lift leading directly to the restaurant levels. The restaurant and its terraces offer panoramic views of the Rome skyline, including St. Peter's. Speciality dishes include shrimps served with exotic fruits, quail's eggs on a bed of rocket with mustard dressing, and *tagliolini* (pasta) with clams and *finferli* (mushrooms).

VIA VENETO

Giovanni

Via Marche 64. **Map** 5 B1.
📞 06-482 1834. **Open** 12:30–3pm, 7:30–11pm Sun–Thu, 12:30–3pm Fri. **Closed** Aug, Christmas.
💳 AE, DC, JCB, MC, V. €€

A throng of satisfied regulars crowd this classic, well-established restaurant near Via Veneto. The efficient, reliable service is hard to beat. The place is run along traditional lines by the Sbrega family, with a strong regional influence from Lazio and the Marches. They serve such fresh pasta dishes as *tagliolini all'amatriciana*, vegetable soups, boned chicken with rice, unbeatable roast lamb, *osso buco*, fresh fish and *millefeuilles*. The house wines are of very good quality.

Tullio

Via San Nicola da Tolentino 26. **Map** 5 B2. 📞 06-474 5560. **Open** 12:30–3pm, 7:30–11pm Mon–Sat. **Closed** Aug. ♿
💳 AE, DC, MC, V, JCB. €€

This genuine Tuscan restaurant is frequented by an enthusiastic clientele for its generous helpings and fair prices. Typical dishes include *porcini* mushrooms in every possible form, *pappardelle al sugo di lepre* (fresh pasta with wild hare sauce), grilled meat and fish and Florentine steaks – served in agreeable surroundings by courteous, speedy waiters.

Andrea

Via Sardegna 28. **Map** 5 C1.
📞 06-482 1891, 06-474 0557.
Open 12:30–3pm, 7:30–11pm Mon–Fri, 7:45–11pm Sat.
Closed 2 weeks Aug, Christmas.
🍽 💳 AE, DC, MC, V, JCB. €€€

This congenial, refined restaurant offers a superb array of *antipasti*, ranging from humble but delicious *suppli* (rice croquettes) to regal lobster dishes (such as *insalata catalana*). Try not to be completely seduced by the starters, however; leave room for the impressive seasonal first and second courses and for the delicious desserts. There is an extensive choice of French and Italian wines.

George's

Via Marche 7. **Map** 5 B2.
📞 06-4208 4575. **Open** 12:30–3pm, 7:30–11:30pm (piano bar 2am) Mon–Sat. **Closed** Aug.
🍽 💳 AE, DC, MC, V, JCB. €€€

Visit this slightly tarnished survivor from the *dolce vita* era for its nostalgic air of luxurious elegance. The softly illuminated rooms, garden terrace, tinkling piano music and impeccable service provide the perfect foil for George's tempting and expertly prepared international dishes. There is also a good selection of French and Italian wines on offer.

Le Sans Souci

Via Sicilia 20–24. **Map** 5 C1.
📞 06-4201 4510. **Open** 8pm–midnight Tue–Sun. **Closed** Aug.
💳 AE, DC, MC, V, JCB. €€€€€

This restaurant has overcome a glitzy fame to emerge as a sound exponent of elaborate French and Italian cuisine. The decor is black and gold throughout, with 17th-century gilt mirrors and chandeliers. In the sophisticated anteroom you can drink a leisurely apéritif and consult the menu and magnificent wine list. The service is eagerly efficient.

La Terrazza

Via Ludovisi 49. **Map** 5 B2.
📞 06-47 81 2752. **Open** noon–2:30pm, 7:30–10:30pm Mon–Sat. **Closed** 2 weeks Aug, Dec 25–Jan 6.
💳 AE, DC, MC, V, JCB. €€€€€

Positioned in the roof garden of the Eden Hotel (see p301) this spacious establishment has gained a reputation in its own right. The menu is traditional Italian – in this case a guarantee of quality – and the kitchen is just about as spotless as spotless gets. As you might expect from its location, the views of the city are peerless.

VILLA BORGHESE

Al Ceppo

Via Panama 2. **Map** 2 F3.
📞 06-841 9696. **Open** 1–3pm, 7:45–11pm Tue –Sun. **Closed** 2 weeks Aug. 💳 AE, DC, MC, V. €€

Over 35 years, two sisters from the Marches, Cristina and Marisella Milozzi, have won an affectionate following of regulars in this exclusive, notoriously diffident area of Rome. Patrons are attracted by the consistently reliable food and the hospitable yet refined family atmosphere. The strictly seasonal menu concentrates on traditional dishes with a touch of invention, as well as excellent grilled meats, homemade desserts and Italian wines.

Relais la Piscine dell'Aldrovandi Palace Hotel

Via G Mangili 6. **Map** 2 D4.
📞 06-321 6126. **Open** 12:30–3pm, 7:30–11pm daily. 💳 AE, DC, MC, V. €€€€

The autonomous restaurant of the Aldrovandi Palace Hotel is especially beautiful in summer, when tables are set on the terrace by the pool. Jean Luc Frenat, the young Breton chef, produces an excellent, typically Mediterranean nouvelle cuisine, using prime meat and fish, vegetables and herbs. This is accompanied by meticulous service, wonderful desserts and a decent wine list. Business lunches are a specialty.

Relais le Jardin dell'Hotel Lord Byron

Via Giuseppe de Notaris 5. **Map** 2 D4.
📞 06-322 0404. **Open** 12:30–2:30pm, 8–10:30pm Mon–Sat.
May be closed Aug. Call to check.
💳 AE, DC, MC, V, JCB. €€€€€

This restaurant is located in the quiet, exclusive and green area of Parioli. Diners who come here are undaunted by the top prices, high-class surroundings, impeccable service and *haute cuisine*. The chef tends to draw predominantly on traditional Italian regional cooking, with creative combinations of fruit, herbs and vegetables as partners to a variety of meats and fish. The desserts and pastries are homemade and the list of French, Italian and Californian wines is comprehensive.

For key to symbols see p303

Light Meals and Snacks

Where should you go for a casual bite to eat? Rome has the ability to satisfy the all-important stomach at most hours of the day and night. A network of *gelaterie, pasticcerie*, pizzerias, wine bars, *rosticcerie* and *tavole calde* mean that many varieties of good food and drink are always just around the corner.

Start with a classic breakfast at your local stand-up bar: cappuccino and a hot *cornetto* (similar to a croissant). A heavy morning's sightseeing may leave you ready for an apéritif in one of Rome's elegant 19th-century bars, followed by lunch at a wine bar or Roman-style fast-food place. In the afternoon, there are plenty of opportunities for coffee and cakes at a *pasticceria*, while the late-night bars, especially those with tables outside, are a source of entertainment. Here you can sip a drink or linger over the final ice cream of the day.

Pizzerias

Roman pizzerias are the natural choice for informal eating: they are noisy, convivial and fun. However, most open only in the evening. Look out for the *Forno a Legna* (wood-burning oven) sign – electric ovens simply don't produce the same results. In the best pizzerias you sit in view of the vast marble slabs where the *pizzaioli* flatten the dough and whip the pizzas in and out of the oven on long-handled peels. The turnover is quick, so you may not be encouraged to linger.

The running order is straightforward: you might have a *bruschetta* (toasted tomato or garlic bread) to start, some *supplì* (fried rice balls) or some fried zucchini flowers Alternatively, try some *filetti di baccalà* (battered cod filets), or a plate of cannellini beans in oil. Follow this with a *calzone* (folded-over pizza) or the classic Roman pizza – round, thin and crunchy – with various toppings: *napoletana* (tomatoes, anchovies, mozzarella), *margherita* (without anchovies), *capricciosa* (ham, artichokes, eggs, olives) and anything else the *pizzaiolo* fancies. Draft beer is the classic thing to drink, but wine is always available. You should expect to pay around 10 euros a head for a meal.

The most representative Roman pizzerias, from all points of view, are **Da Baffetto,** which can be located by looking for the line outside, and its offspring, **La Montecarlo**. **Remo** in Testaccio and **Dar Poeta** and **Ivo** in Trastevere, where tables line the road in summer, are also typically Roman. Another popular place not to be missed is **Panattoni**, where a huge variety of customers patiently line up for a sidewalk seat on Viale Trastevere in summer or clamor for one of the marble-topped tables (from which the restaurant gets its well known nickname "the mortuary") inside. For slick interiors and high-rise pizza, try **'Gusto** or **PizzaRè**, but be prepared to queue.

Enoteche (Wine Bars)

Enoteche offer a fine selection of wines from Italy and around the world. They are usually run by experts, eager to share their knowledge about the best combinations of wine and food. Some *enoteche* are simply shops for browsing. Others, like **Achilli al Parlamento** and **Bevitoria Navona**, offer the traditional *mescita* – wine and champagne tasting by the glass, accompanied by snacks and canapés. Their prices are reasonable: about €2 for a glass on tap, €3 upward for a quality wine, to about €4 for champagne. **Vineria Reggio** in Campo de' Fiori is a typical spot for *mescita*, especially at night. Here professionals, local bright young things and tourists meet for an apéritif or gather round a table to share a bottle. Nearby, **Il Goccetto** and **L'Angolo Divino** serve excellent wines and good food.

For more substantial food for as little as €13 a head, try the bistro- or restaurant-style *enoteche*, open from lunch until late. Particularly recommended are the innovative **Cul de Sac**, **Trimani Wine Bar**, the tiny **Il Tajut** serving specialties from Friuli and **Cavour 313**.

Birrerie (Beer Houses)

Roman *birrerie* had their heyday in the early years of the 20th century and many have closed but, thanks to their popularity with Italian teenagers, they are undergoing something of a revival. Many British- and Irish-style pubs have opened all over the city. At German-style beer houses you can still enjoy beer and substantial snacks in traditional wood-paneled rooms. The permanently crowded **Fratelli Tempera**, serving classic beer-drinkers' fare, is worth a visit for its authentic turn-of-the-century air of decadence. Another place that attracts Italians and foreigners alike is the **Birreria Viennese/Wiener Bierhaus,** with its excellent Transylvanian specialties, which come heaped generously on wooden plates. If you eat here or at the **L'Oasi della Birra**, you'll spend about €20–€25. Elsewhere will be cheaper if you want to concentrate on drinking.

Fast Food

Rome has plenty of home spun fast-food options for when you need something quick and inexpensive to eat. Slices of freshly baked pizza are available for €1 or €2 from *pizza al taglio* shops. Many of these places also sell spit-roasted chickens, *supplì* and other traditional pizzeria fare. *Rosticcerie* offer deliciously tasty roast chicken and potatoes, as well as ready-made pasta dishes, cooked vegetables, salads and desserts – useful for picnics or for making a complete take-out meal. For a similarly speedy but sit-down snack, bars with a *tavola calda* (hot table) have the same kind of selection, especially at lunch; one of the largest and most popular is **Brek** at Largo Argentina. **Le Pain Quotidien** in Via Tomacelli offers good salads and delicious pastries; it is popular at lunchtime.

Most *alimentari* (grocery shops) will make you up a *panino* (filled roll). Especially delicious are **Paladini's** hot plain pizza pockets stuffed with choices from the shop's counters; here you can also have a glass of wine. Try one of the region's specialties if you see the sign *Porchetta*: whole aromatic roast pig with crackling, sliced into *rosette* (rolls) or thick country-bread sandwiches – there is a good stall selling these at the tram stop in Viale Carlo Felice opposite San Giovanni in Laterano. At the hole-in-the-wall **Er Buchetto** you can even sit down in relative comfort with a glass of wine. For a really typical Roman snack, make a late-afternoon detour to **Filetti di Baccalà**, which serves, as the name suggests, fried cod fillets.

BARS, CAFÉS AND TEA ROOMS

ROMAN BARS are the city's lifeline: they are places to meet, eat, drink, buy supplies of milk and coffee, make phone calls or use the bathroom. Some of them are small, stand-up, basic one-counter bars for grabbing a quick *cornetto* and cappuccino; others are quite luxurious affairs doubling as cake shops, ice cream parlors, tea rooms or *tavola calda*, or all of these in one. Most open early at around 7:30am, and

close late, particularly on weekends, at around midnight or 2am. In summer, tables cover the available outdoor space, and the fight for a place in the shade begins. Traditionally elegant – and pricey – bars for people-watching are the conveniently located **Rosati** and **Doney**, as well as **Caffè Greco**, the 19th-century haunt of artists, writers and composers *(see p133)*, and the carefully restored **La Caffettiera** at the Pantheon. Other popular and well-established bars are **Antico Caffè della Pace** and **Caffè Flores** (with piano music), both recommended for late-night drinks, as is **Zodiaco** on Monte Mario for its panoramic views.

Earlier in the day, Rome's favored meeting places are its tea rooms. **Babington's** *(see p134)* is the place to go for an expensive cup of tea and cakes in genteel surround-ings; **Dolci e Doni** is more relaxed. Try a *gran caffè speciale* at the counters of **Sant'Eustachio** or one of Rome's best espressos at **Tazza d'Oro**. **Ciampini al Café du Jardin**, with its garden setting and rooftop views, is unbeatable in summer, particularly at the apéritif hour, as is the **Bar Parnaso** in Parioli.

Museum cafés in Rome are gradually becoming the norm and it is worth visiting the one at the Capitoline Museums for its breathtaking views. The café of the **Palazzo delle Esposizioni** *(see p164)* is open throughout the day and serves a good selection of snacks and drinks. A self-service restaurant is on the second floor.

PASTICCERIE (PASTRY SHOPS)

ON SUNDAY mornings you'll often see Romans emerging from the local *pasticceria* with a beautifully wrapped package. This can contain dainty individual pastries, whole cakes or tarts, traditional Easter *colombe* (doves) or Christmas *panettoni* (huge cakes with raisins and candied peel) all

for consumption by large gatherings of friends, relatives or family after lunch. The window displays of Rome's cake shops are often fantastic. These, and the aroma of brewing coffee, might tempt you in for a hot *cornetto* or a brioche in the early morning, a midday *pizzetta* or savory tart, or a choux pastry or fruit tart later in the afternoon.

GELATERIE (ICE CREAM PARLORS)

ICE CREAM *(gelato)* is one of summer's particular delights, and nowhere more so than in Rome. In the *gelaterie* the choice is endless – water ices made with a phenomenal variety of fruit; lemon and coffee *granite* (crushed ice); as well as more exotic ice cream specialties such as rice, *zuppa inglese* (English trifle), *zabaglione, tiramisù* and After Eight.

Choose as many varieties as the size of your cone or cup will hold, topped with cream *(panna)*, and then go for a stroll or take a break and enjoy an ornate creation with all the trimmings served to you at a table. *Gelaterie* are open all day until late at night, when they become evening entertainment.

Tre Scalini in Piazza Navona is a famous spot for enjoying the expensive yet so heavenly chocolate *tartufo*, while a summer evening in EUR, especially with children, nearly always ends in a trip to **Giolitti**, known historically for ice cream; try also the strategically placed, crowded original parlor near the Pantheon *(see p109)*. Real fans of ice cream should not miss **San Crispino**, which offers homemade delicacies made with the best ingredients.

Adults may prefer to pick their nighttime treat at **Chalet del Lago**, again in EUR, while sitting beside the lake. If you happen across a small kiosk bearing the sign *Grattachecche* (most likely in Trastevere and Testaccio), try one of Rome's oldest traditions – ice grated on the spot and enlivened with a variety of classic flavorings.

DIRECTORY

CAPITOL

Bars, Cafés and Tea Rooms
Caffè Capitolino
Piazzale Caffarelli.
Map 5 A5 & 12 F5.

FORUM

Pizzerias
Alle Carrette
Via della Carrette 19,
off Via della Madonna
dei Monti. **Map** 5 B5.

PIAZZA DELLA ROTONDA

Pizzerias
Barroccio
Via dei Pastini 13.
Map 4 F4 & 12 D2.

Er Faciolaro
Via dei Pastini 123.
Map 4 F4 & 12 D2.

Wine Bars
Achilli al Parlamento
Via dei Prefetti 15.
Map 4 F3 & 12 D1.

Corsi
Via del Gesù 88.
Map 4 F4 & 12 E3.

Spiriti
Via di Sant'Eustachio 5.
Map 4 F4 & 12 D3.

Bars, Cafés and Tea Rooms
La Caffettiera
Piazza di Pietra 65.
Map 4 F3 & 12 E2.

Ciampini
Piazza S. Lorenzo in
Lucina 29.
Map 4 F3 & 12 D1.

Sant'Eustachio
Piazza Sant'Eustachio 82.
Map 4 F4 & 12 D3.

Tazza d'Oro
Via degli Orfani 82/84.
Map 4 F4 & 12 D2.

Teichner
Piazza S. Lorenzo in
Lucina 15.
Map 4 F3 & 12 E1.

Ice Cream Parlors
Fiocco di Neve
Via del Pantheon 51.
Map 4 F4 & 12 D2.

Giolitti
Via degli Uffici del Vicario
40. **Map** 4 F3 & 12 D2.

PIAZZA NAVONA

Pizzerias
Da Baffetto
Via del Governo Vecchio
114. **Map** 4 E4 & 11 B3.

Corallo
Via del Corallo 10.
Map 4 E4 & 11 B3.

La Montecarlo
Vicolo Savelli 12/13.
Map 4 E4 & 11 C3.

Wine Bars
Bevitoria Navona
Piazza Navona 72.
Map 4 E4 & 11 C2.

Cul de Sac
Piazza Pasquino 73.
Map 4 E4 & 11 C3.

Fast Food
Paladini
Via del Governo Vecchio
28/29. **Map** 4 E4 & 11 B3.

Bars, Cafés and Tea Rooms
Antico Caffè della Pace
Via della Pace 5.
Map 4 E4 & 11 C3.

Pastry Shops
Bella Napoli
Corso Vittorio Emanuele II
246. **Map** 4 E4 & 11 B3.

Ice Cream Parlors
Tre Scalini
Piazza Navona 28.
Map 4 E4 & 11 C3.

PIAZZA DI SPAGNA

Pizzerias
PizzaRé
Via di Ripetta 14.
Map 4 F1.

'Gusto
Piazza Augusto Imperatore
9. **Map** 4 F2.

Wine Bars
Antica Enoteca di Via
delle Croce
Via della Croce 76B.
Map 5 A2.

Buccone
Via di Ripetta 19.
Map 4 F1.

Beer Houses
Birreria Viennese/
Wiener Bierhaus
Via della Croce 21.
Map 5 A2.

Fast Food
Difronte a
Via della Croce 38.
Map 4 F2.

Le Pain Quotidien
Via Tomacelli 24/25.
Map 12 D1.

Bars, Cafés and Tea Rooms
Babington's Tea Rooms
Piazza di Spagna 23.
Map 5 A2.

Caffè Greco
Via Condotti 86.
Map 5 A2.

Café Notegen
Via del Babuino 159.
Map 4 F2.

Ciampini al Café
du Jardin
Viale Trinità dei Monti.
Map 5 A2.

Dolci e Doni
Via delle Carrozze 85.
Map 4 F2.

Mercedes Café
Via delle Convertite 19.
Map 12 E1.

Rosati
Piazza del Popolo 5.
Map 4 F1.

CAMPO DE' FIORI

Wine Bars
Bottega del Vino
da Bleve
Via Santa Maria del Pianto
9A/11.
Map 4 F5 & 12 D5.

Il Goccetto
Via dei Banchi Vecchi 14.
Map 4 D4 & 11 B3.

L'Angolo Divino
Via dei Balestrari 12.
Map 4 E5 & 11 C4.

Vineria Reggio
Piazza Campo de' Fiori 15.
Map 4 E4 & 11 C4.

Fast Food
Brek
Largo Argentina 1.
Map 4 F4 & 12 D4.

Filetti di Baccalà
Largo dei Librari 88.
Map 4 E5 & 11 C4.

Forno Campo de'
Fiori
Piazza Campo
de' Fiori 22.
Map 4 E4 & 11 C4.

Bars, Cafés and Tea Rooms
Alberto Pica
Via della Seggiola 12.
Map 4 F5 & 12 D5.

Bernasconi
Piazza Cairoli 16.
Map 12 D4.

Pastry Stores
La Dolceroma
Via del Portico
d'Ottavia 20B.
Map 4 F5 & 12 E5.

Boccione
Via del Portico
d'Ottavia 1.
Map 4 F5 & 12 E5.

QUIRINAL

Pizzerias
Est! Est! Est!
Via Genova 32.
Map 5 C4.

I Rioni
Via dei SS. Quattro
Coronati 24.
Map 9 B1.

Wine Bars
Cavour 313
Via Cavour 313.
Map 5 B5.

Beer Houses
Fratelli Tempera
Via San Marcello 19.
Map 5 A4 & 12 F3.

The Albert
Via del Traforo 132.
Map 5 B3.

Fast Food
Er Buchetto
Via Viminale 2.
Map 5 C3.

McDonald's
Piazza della
Repubblica 40.
Map 5 C3.

Nadia e Davide
Via Milano 33.
Map 5 B4.

**Bars, Cafés and
Tea Rooms**
Caffeteria Nazionale
Via Nazionale 26–27.
Map 5 C3.

News Café
Via della Stamperia 72.
Map 5 A3 & 12 F1.

**Palazzo delle
Esposizioni**
Via Milano 9.
Map 5 B4.

Pastry Shops
Dagnino
Via Vittorio Emanuele
Orlando 75.
Map 5 C2.

Ice Cream Parlors
San Crispino
Via della Panetteria 42.
Map 5 A3 & 12 F2.

TERMINI

Pizzerias
La Bruschetta
Via Ancona 35.
Map 6 D1.

Formula Uno
Via degli Equi 13.
Map 6 F4.

Le Maschere
Via degli Umbri 16.
Map 6 F4.

Wine Bars
Trimani Wine Bar
Via Cernaia 37B.
Map 6 D2.

ESQUILINE

Beer Houses
The Fiddler's Elbow
Via dell'Olmata 43.
Map 6 D4.

Ice Cream Parlors
Palazzo del Freddo
Via Principe Eugenio
65/67. **Map** 6 E5.

LATERAN

Fast Food
Porchetta Stall
Viale Carlo Felice.
Map 10 D1.

Ice Cream Parlors
Premiate Gelaterie
Fantasia
Via La Spezia 100/102.
Map 10 E1.

AVENTINE

Pizzerias
Remo
Piazza Santa Maria
Liberatrice 44. **Map** 8 D3.

Fast Food
Di Pietro
Piazza Porta San Paolo
6A–9. **Map** 8 E4.

Volpetti Più
Via Alessandro Volta 8.
Map 8 D3.

Beer Houses
L'Oasi della Birra
Piazza Testaccio 41.
Map 8 D3.

TRASTEVERE

Pizzerias
Da Vittorio
Via di S. Cosimato 14a.
Map 7 C1.

Dar Poeta
Vicolol del Bologna 45
Map 4 E5 & 11 B5.

Ivo
Via di San Francesco
a Ripa 158. **Map** 7 C1.

Panattoni
Viale Trastevere 53.
Map 7 C1.

Ar Popi Popi
Via delle Fratte di
Trastevere 45. **Map** 7 C1.

Wine Bars
Il Cantiniere di Santa
Dorotea
Via di S. Dorotea 9.
Map 4 D5 & 11 B5.

Ferrara
Piazza Trilussa 41.
Map 7 C1.

Fast Food
Frontoni
Viale Trastevere 52.
Map 7 C1.

**Bars, Cafés and
Tea Rooms**
Sala da Tè Trastè
Via della Lungaretta 76.
Map 7 C1.

Pastry Shops
Valzani
Via del Moro 37B.
Map 7 C1.

Ice Cream Parlors
La Fonte della Salute
Via Cardinale Marmaggi
2–4. **Map** 7 C1.

Sacchetti
Piazza San Cosimato 62.
Map 7 C1.

VATICAN

Pizzerias
Pizzeria San Marco
Via Tacito 29. **Map** 4 D2.

Il Tempio della Pizza
Viale Giulio Cesare 91.
Map 3 C1.

Wine Bars
Il Simposio di Piero
Costantini
Piazza Cavour 16.
Map 4 E2.

Beer Houses
Cantina Tirolese
Via Vitelleschi 23.
Map 3 C2.

Ice Cream Parlours
Pellacchia
Via Cola di Rienzo 105.
Map 4 D2.

VIA VENETO

Wine Bars
Semidivino
Via Alessandria 230.
Map 6 D1.

**Bars, Cafés and
Tea Rooms**
Doney
Via Veneto 145.
Map 5 B2.

EUR

Wine Bars
Le Cave des Amis
Piazzale Ardigò 26–29.

**Bars, Cafés and
Tea Rooms**
Chalet del Lago
Lake, EUR.

Ice Cream Parlors
Giolitti
Casina dei Tre Laghi,
Viale Oceania 90.

FURTHER AFIELD

Pizzerias
Al Forno della Soffitta
Via dei Villini 1e.
Map 6 E1.

Wine Bars
Guerrini
Viale Regina Margherita
205/207.

Il Tajut
Via Albenga 44.
Map 10 E3.

**Bars, Cafés and
Tea Rooms**
Caffè Parnaso
Piazza delle Muse 22.
Map 2 E2.

Duse
Via Eleonora Duse 1E.
Map 2 F2.

Mondi
Via Flaminia 468.
Map 6 D1.

San Filippo
Via di Villa San
Filippo 8/10.
Map 2 F2.

Zodiaco
Viale Parco Mellini 90.

Pastry Shops
Euclide
Via Filippo Civinini 119.
Map 2 D3.

SHOPS AND MARKETS

Stylish window display

ROME HAS BEEN a thriving center for design and cosmopolitan shopping since ancient times. In the heyday of the Empire the finest craftsmen were drawn to Rome, and artifacts and produce of all kinds, including gold, furs, wine and slaves, were imported from far-flung corners of the Empire to service the needs of the wealthy Roman population. Shopping in Rome today in many ways reflects this diverse tradition. Italian designers have an international reputation for their luxuriously chic style in fashion, knitwear and leather goods (especially shoes and handbags) as well as in interior design, fabrics, ceramics and glass. The artisan-craftsman tradition is strong and the love of good design filters through into the smallest items. Rome is not a city for bargains (although it is often better value than Florence or Milan), but the joys of window shopping here will offer plenty of compensation.

BEST BUYS

LEATHER GOODS of all kinds, including shoes and bags, are a strong point. Ready-to-wear Italian designer clothes are not cheap, but they are certainly less expensive than in other countries. Armani jeans are a good example *(see p327)*. You are also likely to find designer lighting fixtures, for example, at lower prices here. Both modern and traditional Italian ceramics and handicrafts can be very beautifully made and, if you have time to wander around the back streets, really unusual and individual gifts can often be found.

SALES

SALE TIME *(saldi)* is from mid-July to mid-September and the period from just before Christmas to the first week in March. Top designers *(see p326)* slash prices by half, but their clothes are still very expensive even then. Good bargains can be found in the young designer-wear shops *(see p327)* and good-quality large shoe sizes are sold off very cheaply (most Italians have small feet). Both of the Cesari shops *(see p327 and p333)* are well known for their sales. In general, though, sales in Rome do not offer huge discounts.

Both the original and the sale price should be quoted on each reduced item. *Liquidazioni* (closing-down sales) are usually genuine and can sometimes be worth investigating. However, other signs in shop windows such as *vendite promozionali* (special introductory prices) and *sconti* (discounts) are often only lures to get you into the shop. The sign on the door saying *entrata libera* means "browsers welcome."

Antiques at Acanto *(see p336)*

WHEN TO SHOP

SHOPS ARE GENERALLY open from 9am to 1pm and from 3:30pm to 7:30pm (4pm to 8pm in the summer months). Some of the shops in the center stay open all day from 10am to 7:30pm.

Most shops are closed on Sunday (except immediately before Christmas). Shops are also closed on Monday morning, apart from most food shops, which close on Thursday afternoons in winter and Saturday afternoons in high summer.

August brings the city to a virtual standstill as Roman families escape the heat to the sea or the mountains, but this is gradually changing, with Romans taking shorter summer vacations. Most shops close for at least 2 weeks around 15 August, the national holiday.

Flower stalls in Piazza Campo de' Fiori *(see p338)*

SHOPPING ETIQUETTE

APART FROM a few department stores, most Roman shops are small, specializing in just one field. Browsing at leisure may at first seem daunting if you are used to large shopping centers. Customers will almost always receive better attention if they dress smartly – the emphasis on *fare una bella figura* (making a good impression) is taken seriously.

Sizes are not always uniform, so it is wise to try clothes on if possible before buying, since refunds and exchanges are not usually given.

Stylish leather gloves on display

HOW TO PAY

MOST SHOPS now accept all the major credit cards, whose signs are displayed on the shop window. Some will also accept foreign currency, though the exchange rate may not be good. When you make a purchase you are bound by Italian law to leave the shop with a *scontrino fiscale* (receipt). You can try asking for a discount if paying cash and you may be lucky, though many shops have a *prezzi fissi* (fixed prices) sign.

VAT EXEMPTION

VALUE ADDED TAX – VAT (IVA in Italy) – ranges from 12 percent on clothing to 35 percent on luxury items such as jewelry and furs. Marked or advertised prices normally include the IVA. It is possible for non-European Union

One of many designer shops around Piazza di Spagna

citizens to obtain an IVA refund for individual purchases that exceed about 160 euros, but be prepared for a long and bureaucratic process. The simplest method is to shop at a place displaying the "Euro Free Tax" sign.

Present your passport when you make your purchase, and fill in a form from the shop; the shop then deducts the IVA, gives you a copy of the form, and sends their copy to the Euro Free Tax Organization in Milan which will then deal with the paperwork.

If you wish to buy something from a shop which is not part of the "Euro Free Tax" scheme, you must get the Italian customs to stamp the vendor's receipt at your departure, showing them the purchased article, and then post the stamped receipt back to the shop, who should then send you a refund.

Mercato delle Stampe *(see p338)*

DEPARTMENT STORES AND SHOPPING CENTERS

DEPARTMENT STORES, known as *grandi magazzini*, are few and far between in Rome. **La Rinascente** and **Coin** are good for ready-to-wear clothes, household linens and haberdashery, and have well-stocked perfume counters. La Rinascente gives 10 percent discount to tourists on perfumes and cosmetics if you show your passport. The **Oviesse** and **Upim** chain stores offer moderately priced medium-quality clothes and household goods.

Another alternative for the zealous shopper is to head for one of Rome's two shopping centers. **Cinecittà Due Centro Commerciale**, built in 1988, offers around 100 shops plus bars, banks

Bargains in Via Sannio *(see p339)*

and restaurants within easy reach of the center by Metro (line A to Cinecittà).

Cinecittà Due Centro Commerciale
Viale Palmiro Togliatti 2.
[06-722 09 10.

Coin
Piazzale Appio 7. **Map** 10 D2.
[06-708 00 20.

Via Cola di Rienzo 173.
Map 3 C2.
[06-3600 4298.

La Rinascente
Via del Corso 189.
Map 5 A3 & 12 E2.
[06-679 76 91.

Piazza Fiume.
Map 6 D1.
[06-884 12 31.

Oviesse
Viale Trastevere 62.
Map 7 C2.
[06-5833 3633.

Via Appia Nuova 181–5.
Map 10 D2.
[06-702 32 14.

Upim
Via del Tritone 172.
Map 5 A3.
[06-678 33 36.

Via Nazionale 211.
Map 5 C3.
[06-48 45 02.

Piazza Santa Maria Maggiore.
Map 6 D4.
[06-446 55 79.

Rome's Best: Shopping Streets and Markets

THE MOST INTERESTING shops in Rome are in the old center, so shopping is easy to combine with sightseeing. The shops are often housed in medieval or Renaissance buildings and their window displays can be exquisite. Just like shopkeepers in past centuries, traders tend to specialize in one type of merchandise. Street names often refer to the old tradesmen: locksmiths in Via dei Chiavari, leather jerkin makers in Via dei Giubbonari and chairs in Via dei Sediari. Today, antique merchants have taken over from the rosary sellers on Via dei Coronari. The top names in fashion and modern design dominate the Via Condotti area, and the artisan-craftsman tradition is still strong around Campo de' Fiori and Piazza Navona.

Via dei Coronari
Art Nouveau and antiques enthusiasts will love browsing in the shops that line this charming street just northwest of Piazza Navona. But be prepared for high prices as most of the items are imported.

Via Cola di Rienzo
Situated close to the Vatican Museums, this long wide street has the finest food shops and is also good for clothes, books and gifts.

Vatican

Piazza Navona

Via del Pellegrino
Bookshops and art shops abound here next to working artisans in the historic center. Do not miss the mirror-lined alley near Campo de' Fiori.

Janiculum

Campo de' Fiori

Trastevere

Via dei Cappellari
This narrow, medieval street is a great place for watching furniture restorers and other artisans plying their crafts in the open air.

Porta Portese
You can buy anything from antiques to a tin whistle at Trastevere's Sunday morning flea market. (See p339.)

Via Margutta
Upscale antique shops mix with genteel restaurants on this peaceful, cobbled street.

Via del Babuino
This street is renowned for designer furniture, lighting and glass, as well as interesting antique and fashion shops.

N

za di
gna

e inset
map

Via Veneto

Quirinal

zza
ella
tonda

Capitol

Forum

Esquiline

Palatine

Caracalla

Lateran

entine

DESIGNER SHOPPING
All the well-known stars of the Italian fashion scene, plus exclusive jewelers, gift shops, shoe designers and tailors, are concentrated in this cluster of chic and stylish shopping streets by the Spanish Steps *(see pp326–31).* Romans love to stroll here in the early evening.

MISSONI

GIORGIO ARMANI

PIAZZA DI SPAGNA

VIA CONDOTTI

PRADA

GUCCI

D&G

valentino

VIA DEL CORSO

VIA BORGOGNONA

FENDI

VIA FRATTINA

MaxMara

Via Borgognona
Crowds flock here to buy, or just gaze at, high-fashion clothes, shoes, leather bags and other accessories.

0 meters	500
0 yards	500

Testaccio Market
A visual feast of fruit and vegetables greets the eye in this lively market. (See p338.)

Men's and Women's Fashion

ITALY IS ONE of the leading lights in high-class fashion, or *alta moda*. Many of the most famous designers are based in Milan, but Rome is home to a cluster of sophisticated and internationally distinguished fashion houses. There is also a wonderful selection of *alta moda* shops. Boutiques displaying an eclectic mix of designer goods are next door to prestigious showrooms devoted to single collections. But even those unable to splurge on genuine designer wear will delight in a stroll down the glittering streets that radiate out from the Piazza di Spagna, where the window displays are not merely creative but truly spectacular.

Custom-made fashions are beyond most budgets, but designers also offer ready-to-wear alternatives in their boutiques. While not cheap, these provide style at a price far less than that of a tailor-made garment.

WOMEN'S HIGH FASHION

ROME'S MOST famous designer internationally is probably **Valentino**. However, one of the first houses to make a name for Roman fashion was **Sorelle Fontana**. This was *the* salon to be dressed by during the 1950s heyday of Rome's *dolce vita*. Sorelle Fontana has been dressing high society since the 1930s and stocks a wide selection of ready-to-wear clothes and accessories.

Fendi occupies a large tract of the fashion street Via Borgognona. Fendi made its name with high-fashion furs, then branched out into leather goods, accessories and ready-to-wear, collaborating with Karl Lagerfeld, who designed the coveted double-F logo that emblazons its very collectible products. Third-generation family members design the younger, less expensive Fendissime line.

For well over a decade, **Laura Biagiotti** has reigned as Rome's queen of discreet, conservative couture. From her headquarters in a castle just outside Rome, she designs a range of timelessly elegant knitwear and silk separates for women who don't want to sacrifice style for comfort. She is famous for her use of cashmere and white as well as her creative use of fabrics and quality of finish. Her flagship showroom in Via Borgognona stocks her complete collection, which now includes hosiery,

perfumes, swimwear and leather goods. Her scarves make wonderful presents and are often reduced in price during sales; other items from previous collections are available in the shop all year round at very good discounts. Meanwhile, in nearby Via Borgognona, there is the temple to the creations of **Gianfranco Ferrè**.

Other internationally known Rome-based designers include **Renato Balestra**, who produces tailored suits and glamorous evening-wear and **Roberto Capucci**, who uses wonderful textures and fabrics in classy suits. **Mila Schön's** specialty is dramatic eveningwear.

Milan's miraculous fashion house **Prada** has an alluring branch on Via Condotti, featuring clothes, shoes and accessories in unmistakable style. Other luminaries of Italian fashion who have shops in Rome include **Giorgio Armani**, **Gianni**

Versace, **Trussardi** and **Dolce & Gabbana**.

A rising star in ready-to-wear is **Roberto Cavalli**, whose design team produces some coolly imaginative and stylish collections.

If you're looking for clothes from more unconventional designers, **Gente** is the place to go – its Roman showrooms have exclusive rights to the original couture collections of avant-garde stylists such as Dolce & Gabbana, Moschino and Jean Paul Gaultier.

MaxMara also has a number of branches here. Chic suits and separates are the mainstays of this popular label. The quality of fabric and finish is superb, and, with suits available for around €500, its prices are much lower than those of other *alta moda* designers' ready-to-wear lines.

MEN'S TAILORS AND DESIGNER WEAR

ITALIAN MEN are every bit as fashion conscious as the women, and there is no shortage of choice in Rome for the well-dressed man Suits generally begin at around €620, jackets €415 and trousers €155.

Most of the "star" designers of women's *alta moda* have a shop for men, like **Valentino Uomo**, **Gianfranco Ferrè** and **Versus by Versace**. The designs are generally less dramatic than the women's, with the accent on understated sophistication and casual sportiness. Valentino's distinctive monogrammed accessories are relatively affordable.

VALENTINO

One of the high priests of Italian fashion, **Valentino Garavani** opened the doors of his Roman atelier in 1959 to a distinguished clientele that included Sophia Loren, Audrey Hepburn and Jackie Kennedy, and has never looked back. He has created some of the most dramatic and flattering evening dresses of the last three decades. In the 1970s, he began designing ready-to-wear lines for both men and women alongside his *alta moda* collections, and you can now find his very distinctive "V" logo on a wide range of accessories. Valentino's headquarters are in a huge palazzo in Piazza Mignanelli, and he also has a separate ready-to-wear boutique nearby (see p330).

Battistoni is probably the most prestigious designer concentrating on menswear. Giorgio Battistoni and family's fine custom-made shirts and suits have been in demand with film stars and high society for 50 years. **Etro** sells classically cut clothes and accessories for men and women in exotic Italian-designed printed fabrics. **Ermenegildo Zenga** is housed in a Baroque palazzo setting offers elegant ready-to-wear, and the master tailor Gaetano will also make to measure. **Davide Cenci** has been a mecca those in search of the English country gentle-man look since 1926. **Brioni** offers traditional tailor-made and their own ready-to-wear men's clothing, **Trussardi** sells beautifully tailored classics and **Testa** has impeccably tailored suits that appeal to the younger set, while **Enzo Ceci** is popular for ready-to-wear *alta moda* designs. **Degli Effetti** stocks more avant-garde designers, such as Romeo Gigli and Jean Paul Gaultier.

Young Designer Wear

There is a huge choice for the young. Top designers Valentino and Armani offer their leading fashions trans-lated into more affordable lines at **Valentino Sport** and **Emporio Armani** (Armani jeans are a very good buy at about €52). Fendi has its Fendissime line, and Max-Mara's Penny Black label can be found in its **Max & Co** branches. Targeted at the younger set, these are good places to pick up stylish, sporty numbers.

Timberland is another very popular casual label. Average prices are in the region of €52 for a shirt, €210 for raincoats, €415 for suits.

Energie is a big hit and has some of the best window displays in Rome. Teenagers flock here for jeans and T-shirts, both the shop's own and other labels. Trussardi's casual line is found at **T'Store**, and **Aria**, **Diesel** and **Box 233** are also very popular

these days. **Eventi** represents the more avant-garde styles – *dark*, as they call it here – fusing Gothic, New Age and punk influences, which can result in some outrageous window creations. For women, Via del Governo Vecchio is a place to head for. **Arsenale**, **Luna e L'altra** and **Maga Morgana** offer some trendy unconventional designer clothes in a pleasant, friendly atmosphere.

High Street Fashion

Rome is not a good place to look for everyday wear, since there is a distinct lack of mid-price shops bridging the huge gap between the dazzlingly priced *alta moda* designer exclusives and the ultracheap goods sold in markets (see pp338–9). Lower-budget shops do exist, but quality is often poor. If you have the stamina, you may find a bargain along Via del Corso, Via del Tritone, Via Nazionale, Via Cavour, Via Cola di Rienzo, Via Ottaviano or Via dei Giubbonari.

The most convenient places to shop are department stores such as La Rinascente, Coin and Upim (see p323). They may not sound exciting, but you can browse at leisure and find attractive things. It is also worth trying shops mentioned under "Young Designer Wear" – particularly the *alta moda* designers' cheaper lines, such as **Emporio Armani** and **Max & Co**. At **Discount System** you can find end-of-season designer labels at 50 percent less than the boutique prices. And while you don't need to come to Rome to shop at **Benetton**, there are many shops here which sell the authentic garments in their universal colors.

Knitwear

Knitwear is a particular strength in Italian design, and in Rome there are plenty of specialist shops. **Laura Biagiotti** is celebrated for her luxurious cashmere separates, and **Missoni Sport** and **Missoni Uomo/Donna** for

spectacular kaleidoscopic patterns and colors.

Krizia no longer has a shop in Rome, however, its sophisticated knitwear is available from **Liz**.

Choses de Cachemire has cashmere cardigans, pullovers and knitted suits. Other shops, such as the **Luisa Spagnoli** outlets, offer a wider selection, including lower-priced items.

Lingerie

This is another Italian specialty excelling in both style and quality, with lines such as La Perla exported world-wide. Lingerie is traditionally sold in leading household linen shops (see p333) – **Cesari**, for example, has its own complete range. There are also boutiques specializing in lingerie and swimwear.

Liberti has a range of swim-wear that's ideal for Italian beaches, as well as lingerie and women's night attire. **Brighenti** is said to be where film stars go for their lingerie. **Schostal** has more traditional underwear, with a very good men's section.

Secondhand Clothes

Those who are willing to browse will find a wide variety of secondhand clothes, whether inspired by a collector's interest in vintage clothes or a low budget. Apart from Via Sannio and Porta Portese markets (see p339), which have many secondhand clothes stalls, the mecca is Via del Governo Vecchio. Among the best shops in this ancient street near Piazza Navona is **Mado**, which has mostly 1920s dresses and some hats and jewelry.

Le Gallinelle offers a marvelous selection of second-hand and vintage clothes as well as their own line. At **Via dei Chiavari 40** you can find smart clothes dating from the 1920s on-ward, and owner Solange also does some dressmaking on the premises and sells at reasonable prices. Via del Pellegrino is also a good street for shops selling second-hand clothes.

Shoes and Accessories

ITALY'S LEATHER INDUSTRY is renowned all over the world, and shoes, bags and belts are a good buy in Rome. Accessories in general are not just an afterthought but an integral part of an outfit for the well-dressed Roman. The choice of stylish jewellery, scarves, ties and other accessories is excellent.

SHOES

ROME IS FULL of shoe shops, ranging from high-quality stores in the Via Condotti area (where prices tend to start at €155) to the more economical shops around the Trevi fountain, and every big market has its bargain shoe stalls on its fringes.

Probably the best-known shop is **Ferragamo** – one of the world's top shoe shops. It stocks classic yet fashion-conscious shoes, as well as women's clothing and leather goods – the silk signature scarves are quite a feature.

Fratelli Rossetti is a close contender for the number one position. Founded by brothers Renzo and Renato over 30 years ago, this company produces classic men's shoes and beautiful, dressy low-heeled shoes for women that reflect the most up-to-the minute trends. Along with **Campanile** in Via Condotti it represents the epitome of elegance. Its prices, of course, are sky-high but why not buy something small, and at least you'll have the bag! **Bruno Magli**, Bologna's well-known star, has dressy patent-leather pumps and other classic styles. **Barrilà** near Piazza di Spagna sells trendy women's shoes.

Rome's own **Raphael Salato** has three extremely elegant, high-priced shops: his shoes are genuine master-pieces of craftsmanship, and many are made of intricately embroidered leather.

Carlotto Rio is one of the more long-lived shoe shops in Rome, having been in business for over a decade, but it can't compete with **Domus**, which opened in 1938. Carlotto Rio sells made-to-measure footwear for both men and women, particularly shoes for special occasions, and also makes bags to customers specifications. Domus sells a selection of high-quality footwear, spe-cializing in classic shoes for women. They also stock a limited range of bags. **De Bach** has colorful shoe styles for women.

Via Frattina also has several more great shoes shops such as **Pollini**, which makes boots and bags for both men and women in trendy and imaginative styles. Native designer **Fausto Santini** stocks original, stylish, colorful designs for younger people. More moderate prices can be found at **Cervone**, which specializes in highly colorful women's shoes. **Borini** stocks simple and elegant, low-heeled designs. The **Mr Boots** chain of shops stocks a wide range of trendy boots and casual shoes for men and women, while **Dominici** sells witty, smart and affordable footwear for women.

LEATHER BAGS AND ACCESSORIES

THE MOST FAMOUS of Rome's leather shops is the super-trendy **Gucci**, a dandy's paradise selling shoes, suit-cases, handbags, wallets, belts and other accessories. It has a fashion boutique for men and women and is well known for its silk ties and scarves. **Fendi** also has exquisite leather goods as well as some lower-priced lines in synthetic materials and a range of gift items. Although their famous "stripe" line leather-finished syn-thetic handbags cost as much as €130 (and their all-leather ones start at €155), at least they are cheaper to buy here than abroad. **Skin** and **Ginocchi**, both situated in the Via Sistina area, are also quite pricey. Located a short walk to the south of Skin and Ginocchi, near the Trevi Fountain, is **La Sella**. It sells all things leather, including a range of shoes, bags, purses and belts.

Mandarina Duck's brightly colored fabric bags and line of luggage are very much in fashion and make an attractive (and vegetarian) alternative to the more traditional leather styles. For sleek, utterly fashionable handbags, try **Furla**.

For a more unusual men's present, try **La Cravatta** in Trastevere. In addition to their selection of classy hand-made ties, they also manufacture ties to meet customers speci-fications. You can choose the design, material, length, and the shape of tie to create the perfect gift.

CLASSIC JEWELRY

WHAT CARTIER is to Paris, Tiffany & Co. is to New York and Asprey's is to London, **Bulgari** is to Rome. This internationally revered jeweler's has passers-by glued to the windows gazing at its large fat gemstones. These "windows" are rather curious small boxes inserted into a wall with one or two pieces of jewelry in each of them, which adds to the feeling of looking at precious items in a case at a museum. Bulgari's watches, especially the men's, are popular and very elegant, as are the famous mesh necklaces. It specializes in large, colorful stones in High Renaissance-style settings but also produces a selection of contemporary designs. This was one of Andy Warhol's favorite shops, and it is definitely the most palatial shop on Via Condotti. Inside, the shop's atmosphere is one of almost religious awe and contemplation.

Buccellati is an offshoot of the famous Florentine dynasty, which was begun by Mario Buccellati in the 1920s and patronized by the poet Gabriele D'Annunzio.

Its delicately engraved designs are inspired by the Italian Renaissance, and are real classics displaying superb craftsmanship. **Ansuini** designs are fashionable yet classic, with strong, imaginative themes being introduced for each new collection. **Massoni**, founded in 1790, is one of Rome's oldest jewelry houses. Its refined one-of-a-kind pieces and brooches are quite outstanding.

At **Moroni Gioielli** you will also find imaginative, unique pieces of the highest-quality workmanship. **Petochi**, which was jeweler to the former Italian monarchy (1861–1946), the House of Savoy, has both traditional and contemporary styles on display.

Peroso is an old-fashioned shop that has been going since 1891 and specializes in antique jewelry and silver-ware. **Boncompagni Sturni** sells traditional designs with the emphasis on quality and craftsmanship. You have to ring the bell to be admitted to both of these shops, and they are extremely expensive.

COSTUME JEWELRY

FOR LESS conventional tastes, there are several shops selling innovative, avant-garde pieces, often using semi-precious metals and stones. **Via dei Coronari 193** is worth trying.

Tempi Moderni has an interesting collection of Art Deco and Liberty period jewelry. You can also find some nice pieces from the 1920s and 1930s in Cose Così (*see p336*).

Bozart is the place for trendy, flashy costume jewelry. **Siragusa** puts beautiful 3rd- and 4th-century BC beads and coins into handmade gold chains, in a museum-like shop just off the Piazza di Spagna.

TRADITIONAL GOLDSMITHS AND SILVERSMITHS

THE MAINSTAY of Rome's jewelry industry is still the traditional artisan goldsmith and silversmith, working to order in tiny studio workshops. These are concentrated in the old Jewish Ghetto area, by the Tiber river, Campo de' Fiori, Ponte Sisto near Via Giulia, and Montepietà (which is also where the pawnbrokers live).

Artisan jewelry can also be found in Via dei Coronari, Via dell'Orso and Via del Pellegrino. The jewelers create individual pieces to their own designs and have often learned their profession from their parents and grand-parents. They also do repair work, or take old gold jewelry, melt it down and make it into something to suit you.

Gioie d'Arte produces some traditional artisan jewelry and always works to customers' commissions.

GLOVES, HATS AND HOSIERY

IF YOU'RE LOOKING for top quality, you will find an expensive line of gloves and scarves at **Merola**. **Di Cori** and **Sermoneta** stock every imaginable kind of glove.

To find smart leather gloves to match your new shoes and handbags, whatever their color, make a visit to **Settimio Mieli**, which is sure to have something suitable, and at a reasonable price.

Catello d'Auria specializes in gloves and hosiery. **Borsalino** is a good place to go for all sorts of hats, including its namesake. **Calza e Calze** has the best range of hosiery in Rome – the friendly staff will serve you with almost any color or pattern of tights and stockings that you could wish for.

SIZE CHART

For Australian sizes follow British and American convention.

Children's clothing

Italian	2-3	4-5	6-7	8-9	10-11	12	14	14+ (years)
British	2-3	4-5	6-7	8-9	10-11	12	14	14+ (years)
American	2-3	4-5	6-6x	7-8	10		12	14	16 (size)

Children's shoes

Italian	24	25½	27	28	29	30	32	33	34
British	7	8	9	10	11	12	13	1	2
American	7½	8½	9½	10½	11½	12½	13½	1½	2½

Women's dresses, coats and skirts

Italian	38	40	42	44	46	48	50
British	8	10	12	14	16	18	20
American	6	8	10	12	14	16	18

Women's blouses and sweaters

Italian	81	84	87	90	93	96	99 (cms)
British	31	32	34	36	38	40	42 (inches)
American	6	8	10	12	14	16	18 (size)

Women's shoes

Italian	36	37	38	39	40	41
British	3	4	5	6	7	8
American	5	6	7	8	9	10

Men's suits

Italian	44	46	48	50	52	54	56	58 (size)
British	34	36	38	40	42	44	46	48 (inches)
American	34	36	38	40	42	44	46	48 (inches)

Men's shirts (collar size)

Italian	36	38	39	41	42	43	44	45 (cms)
British	14	15	15½	16	16½	17	17½	18 (inches)
American	14	15	15½	16	16½	17	17½	18 (inches)

Men's shoes

Italian	39	40	41	42	43	44	45	46
British	6	7	7½	8	9	10	11	12
American	7	7½	8	8½	9½	10½	11	11½

DIRECTORY

WOMEN'S HIGH FASHION

Dolce & Gabbana
Via Condotti 51.
Map 5 A2.
[06-678 2990.

Fendi
Via Borgognona 36–39.
Map 5 A2.
[06-69 6661.

Genny
Piazza di Spagna 27.
Map 5 A2.
[06-679 6074.

Gente
Via del Babuino 80.
Map 4 F1.
[06-320 7671.
Also: Via Frattina 69.
Map 5 A2.
[06-678 9132.

Gianni Versace
Via Bocca di Leone 26.
Map 5 A2.
[06-678 0521.

Giorgio Armani
Via Condotti 77.
Map 5 A2.
[06-699 1461.
Also: Via del Babuino 140.
Map 4 F1.
[06-3600 2197.

Laura Biagiotti
Via Borgognona 43–44.
Map 5 A2.
[06-679 1205.

Max & Co
Via Condotti 46.
Map 5 A2.
[06-678 7946.

MaxMara
Via Frattina 28.
Map 5 A2.
[06-679 3638.

Prada
Via Condotti 92–95.
Map 5 A2.
[06-679 0897.

Renato Balestra
Via Sistina 67. **Map** 5 A2.
[06-679 5537.

Roberto Capucci
Via Gregoriana 56.
Map 5 A2.
[06-679 5180.

Roberto Cavalli
Via Borgognona 7A.
Map 5 A2.
[06-6938 0130.

Sorelle Fontana
Salita S. Sebastianello 5.
Map 5 A2.
[06-6992 2156.

Trussardi
Via Condotti 49–50.
Map 5 A2.
[06-679 2151.

Valentino
Via Condotti 13.
Map 5 A2.
[06-678 3656.

MEN'S TAILORS AND DESIGNER WEAR

Battistoni
Via Condotti 61.
Map 5 A2.
[06-678 6827.

Brioni
Via Barberini 79.
Map 5 A2.
[06-678 3635.

Davide Cenci
Via Campo Marzio 1–7.
Map 4 F3 & 12 D2.
[06-679 1650.

Degli Effetti
Piazza Capranica 79.
Map 4 F3 & 12 D2.
[06-679 0202.

Enzo Ceci
Via della Vite 52.
Map 5 A3 & 12 E1.
[06-679 8882.

Ermenegildo Zegna
Via Borgognona 7E.
Map 5 A2.
[06-678 9143.

Etro
Via del Babuino 102.
Map 5 A2.
[06-678 8257.

Gianfranco Ferrè
Via Borgognona 6.
Map 5 A2.
[06-679 7445.

Testa
Via Borgognona 13.
Map 5 A2.
[06-679 6174.

Also: Via Frattina 104.
Map 5 A2.
[06-679 1296.

Trussardi
See Women's High Fashion.

Valentino
Via Bocca di Leone 15.
Map 5 A2.
[06-679 5862.

Versus by Versace
Via Borgognona 34.
Map 5 A2.

YOUNG DESIGNER WEAR

Aria
Via Nazionale 239.
Map 5 C3.
[06-48 4421.

Arsenale
Via del Governo Vecchio 64.
Map 4 E4 & 11 B3.
[06-686 1380.

Box 233
Via Nazionale 233.
Map 5 C3.
[06-481 4518.

Diesel
Via del Corso 186.
Map 4 F3 & 12 E1.
[06-678 3933.

Emporio Armani
Via del Babuino 140.
Map 4 F1.
[06-3600 2197.

Energie
Via del Corso 486–487.
Map 4 F2.
[06-322 7046.

Eventi
Via dei Serpenti 134.
Map 5 B4.
[06-48 49 60.

Luna e L'Altra
Via del Governo Vecchio 105.
Map 4 E4 & 11 B3.
[06-6880 4995.

Maga Morgana
Via del Governo Vecchio 27.
Map 4 E4 & 11 C3.
[06-687 9995.

Max & Co
Via Nazionale 56. **Map** 5 C3. [06-4890 3110.

Also: Via Appia Nuova 201–203. **Map** 10 D2.
[06-701 4413.

Timberland
Via del Babuino 75. **Map** 4 F1. [06-3600 0836.

T'Store
Via del Corso 477.
Map 4 F2.
[06-322 6057.

Valentino
Via del Babuino 61.
Map 4 F1.
[06-3600 1906.

HIGH STREET FASHION

Benetton
Via Cesare Battisti 129.
Map 5 A4 & 12 F3.
[06-6992 4010.

Discount System
Via Viminale 35.
Map 5 C3.
[06-482 3917.

Emporio Armani
See Young Designer Wear.

Max & Co
See Young Designer Wear.

Onyx
Via del Corso 330. **Map** 4 F2. [06-699 321.

KNITWEAR

Choses de Cachemire
Via del Babuino 105.
Map 4 F1.
[06-679 8488.

Laura Biagiotti
See Women's High Fashion.

Liz
Via Appia Nuova 90.
Map 10 D2.
[06-700 3609.

Luisa Spagnoli
Via del Tritone 30.
Map 5 A3 & B3 & 12 F1.
[06-6992 2769.
Also: Via Vittorio Veneto 130.
Map 5 B1.
[06-4201 1281.
Also: Via Frattina 84B.
Map 5 A2.
[06-699 1706.

Missoni Sport
Via del Babuino 96A–97.
Map 4 F1.
06-679 7971.

Missoni Uomo/Donna
Piazza di Spagna 78.
Map 5 A2.
06-679 2555.

LINGERIE

Brighenti
Via Frattina 7–8.
Map 5 A2.
06-679 1484.

Cesari
Via del Babuino 195.
Map 5 B3.
06-361 3451.

Liberti
Via del Tritone 101.
Map 12 F1.
06-488 2246.

Schostal
Via del Corso 158.
Map 4 F3 & 12 E1.
06-679 1240.

SECOND-HAND CLOTHES

Le Gallinelle
Via del Boschetto 76.
Map 5 B4.
06-488 1017.

Mado
Via del Governo Vecchio
89A. **Map** 4 E4 & 11 B3.
06-687 5028.

SHOES

Barrilà
Via del Babuino 33A.
Map 4 F1.
06-3600 1726.

Borini
Via dei Pettinari 86–87.
Map 4 E5 & 11 C5.
06-687 5670.

Bruno Magli
Via Vittorio Veneto 70A.
Map 5 B2.
06-4201 1671.

Campanile
Via Condotti 58.
Map 5 A2.
06-678 3041.

Carlotto Rio
Via dell'Arco della
Ciambella 8. **Map** 12 D3.
06-687 2308.

Cervone
Via del Corso 99.
Map 4 F2.
06-678 3522.

De Bach
Via del Babuino 123.
Map 4 F1.
06-678 3384.

Dominici
Via del Corso 14.
Map 12 E1.
06-361 0591.

Domus
Via Belsiana 52.
Map 4 F2.
06-678 9083.

Fausto Santini
Via Frattina 120.
Map 5 A2.
06-678 4114.

Ferragamo
Via Condotti 73–74.
Map 5 A2.
06-679 1565.
Also: Via Condotti 66.
Map 5 A2.
06-678 1130.

Fratelli Rossetti
Via Borgognona 5A.
Map 5 A2.
06-678 2676.

Furla
Via del Corso 481.
Map 4 F3.
06-3600 3619.

Mr Boots
Piazza Re di Roma 10.
Map 10 D3.
06-7720 8672.
Also: Via A Brunetti 2.
Map 4 F1.
06-321 5733.

Pollini
Via Frattina 22–24.
Map 5 A2 & 12 E1.
06-678 9028.

Raphael Salato
Via Veneto 149.
Map 5 B1.
06-482 1816.

LEATHER GOODS

La Cravatta
Via di Santa Cecilia 12.
Map 8 D1.
06-581 6676.

Fendi
See Women's High Fashion.

Ginocchi
Via Sistina 35.
Map 5 B2.
06-488 3925.

Gucci
Via Condotti 8. **Map** 5 A2.
06-678 9340.

Mandarina Duck
Via di Propaganda 1.
Map 5 A2.
06-6994 0320.

La Sella
Via del Lavatore 56.
Map 5 A3 & 12 F1.
06-679 6654.

Skin
Via Capo la Case 44.
Map 5 A3 & 12 F1.
06-678 5531.

CLASSIC JEWELRY

Ansuini
Via del Babuino 150D.
Map 4 F1.
06-322 1072.

Boncompagni
Via del Babuino 115.
Map 4 F1.
06-678 3239.

Buccellati
Via Condotti 31.
Map 5 A2.
06-679 0329.

Bulgari
Via Condotti 10.
Map 5 A2.
06-679 3876.

Massoni
Largo Carlo Goldoni 48.
Map 4 F2 & 12 E1.
06-678 2679.

Moroni Gioielli
Via Belsiana 32A.
Map 4 F2.
06-678 0466.

Peroso
Via Sistina 29A.
Map 5 B3.
06-474 7952.

Petochi
Piazza di Spagna 23.
Map 5 A2.
06-679 1128.

COSTUME JEWELRY

Bozart
Via Bocca di Leone 4.
Map 5 A2.
06-678 1026.

Siragusa
Via delle Carrozze 64.
Map 5 A2.
06-679 7085.

Tempi Moderni
Via del Governo Vecchio
108. **Map** 4 E4 & 11 B3.
06-687 7007.

Via dei Coronari 193
Via dei Coronari 193.
Map 4 E3 & 11 B2.
06-6880 1503.

TRADITIONAL GOLDSMITHS AND SILVERSMITHS

Gioie d'Arte
Via de' Gigli d'Oro 10.
Map 4 E3 & 11 C2.
06-687 7524.

GLOVES, HATS AND HOSIERY

Borsalino
Piazza del Popolo 20.
Map 4 F1.
06-3265 0838.

Calza e Calze
Via della Croce 78.
Map 4 F2.
06-678 4281.

Catello d'Auria
Via dei Due Macelli 55.
Map 5 A2 & 12 F1.
06-679 3364.

Di Cori
Piazza di Spagna 53.
Map 5 A2.
06-678 4439.

Merola
Via del Corso 143.
Map 4 F3 & 12 E1.
06-679 1961.

Sermoneta
Piazza di Spagna 61.
Map 5 A2.
06-679 1960.

Settimio Mieli
Via San Claudio 70.
Map 5 A3 & 12 E2.
06-687 5979.

Interior Design

ITALIAN DESIGN belongs to a long-established tradition based on the skills of the master craftsperson, and some firms have a history going back hundreds of years. Rome's stylish interior design shops are worth seeking out, even if it is only to look around and enjoy the ambience. You might well pick up some design ideas for your home, as well as find some interesting or unusual things to buy.

FURNITURE

ALTHOUGH THERE is no distinct area of Rome that is renowned for its furniture shops, most of the top shops are located to the north of the city center.

Take a look at **Studio Punto Tre** if you want something different: it is packed with strangely painted chests of drawers, Egyptian-style artifacts and small items that would make good presents.

Myricae dazzles with its sensible prices and its covetable Tuscan wrought iron and Venetian painted furniture in sun-drenched or delicate hues.

Spazio Sette, near Largo Argentina, is worth visiting for the building itself. The shop has a spectacular showroom on three levels in the Palazzo Lazzaroni, a former cardinal's palace. It is one of Rome's premier home furnishing shops, and, apart from furniture, it stocks items that would make interesting gifts. The furniture – modern, laminated, stack-up chairs and so forth, plus vases, glass, bowls, and kitchen equipment – is jumbled together in a fascinating display.

Nearby, on Via dei Chaivari, is **Paola Agostara**, another shop that stocks an impressive cornucopia of household objects. Items ranging from hand-painted furniture to glasswear from Eastern Europe are on sale here, along with a collection of designer fabrics and furniture by Paola Agostara herself.

Stildomus, situated approx-imately half an hour's drive out of the center of the city, has a showroom displaying mainly very fine modern wood furniture.

LIGHTING FIXTURES

LIGHTING FIXTURES are one of the most popular and more easily transportable items to buy, and there are several superb showrooms in Rome that are worth a visit.

Flos is a merger of two design houses whose Roman showroom displays its lights as if they were museum exhibits. The design style is typically minimalist – plenty of black and white, chrome and steel.

Nearby **Artemide** is, like Flos, a design house in its own right and is similarly well-known abroad. Its showroom in Rome is elegant, with expensive, high-tech lighting design. **Borghini** sells less famous names, and so is more economical.

Paolo Marj is a sculptor working in mixed media such as glass, wood and plastics to create lamps that are original works of art in themselves. Also on sale are a variety of original sculptures by the artist.

Italian lighting and other electrical equipment are designed for 220–240 volts. If you are going to use an item in countries with lower voltage, always ask the shop whether the product needs a transformer, because this can depend on the model.

Lighting fixtures generally take screw bulbs, although some designer models can be ordered with fittings for bayonet bulbs.

KITCHENS AND BATHROOMS

ALTHOUGH YOU won't be able to take one home with you, you may like to take a look at the ultramodern high-tech kitchen designs in Rome.

For an overview of the latest smart, steel designs, visit **Arclinea**, near Ponte Garibaldi, for its select display of state-of-the-art kitchens.

Italian bathroom shops concentrate almost entirely on modern design. **Odorisio** has a selection of about 15 bathroom sets from about nine different Italian manufacturers. Some of the examples in its showroom are luxuriously decadent. **Ravasini**, nearby, sells very decorative floral fixtures with some matching accessories. **Andreucci** also has a bath-room shop stocking all the latest styles.

TILES

THE ITALIAN ceramic tile tradition is an ancient one. A great variety of tiles is displayed in kitchen and bathroom showrooms, but there are also a number of specialty shops.

The most beautiful and the most expensive of these is **Farnese**, looking ancient Roman in style with its mosaic tables. Di Donato uses old-fashioned methods to design and produce the tiles – hence the cost. He is influenced by Roman and Pompeiian art but also produces modern one-of-a-kind designs.

Ceramiche Musa specializes in modern tiles with decorative floral and ancient Roman motifs, which are popular with visitors.

GLASS

DECORATIVE GLASS objects are popular to buy in Rome. **Murano Più,** just behind Piazza Navona, sells Murano and other glass items at reasonable prices. This shop is one of the few that opens on Sundays – which can be useful for vistors on short trips to Rome.

Archimede Seguso also specializes in Murano glass but includes smaller pieces and also offers a range of gift-sized items.

Arteque is a very beautiful shop, which has a more traditional flavor.

For less expensive gifts, try **Stilvetro**. It is the ideal place for pasta bowls, glass, and ceramics.

An added advantage is that shipment abroad can usually be arranged at any of these glass establishments so you are able make your purchases without worrying about the heart-stopping hassle of transporting it home without damaging your gifts.

FABRICS

BEAUTIFUL FABRICS and wallpapers to order are offered by **Il Sigillo** who has a rich assortment of samples.

At **Emporio Triestino** you can find all manner of beautiful fabrics, including those by the most famous designer names.

If you are looking for worthwhile bargains, take a wander around the old Jewish quarter that runs from Largo Argentina down to the Tiber; the area contains numerous cheaper fabric shops, such as **Paganini**. During sale times, remnants of fabrics (*scampoli*) are always sold cheaply, and you could find just the right fabric for just the right price.

HOUSEHOLD LINEN AND KITCHENWARE

A SELECTION of lovely sheets can be found at **Frette**. If you enjoy designer kitchenware, don't miss **C.u.c.i.n.a.** tucked away in No. 65 Via Mario de Fiori. It stocks kitchen utensils from all over the world, as well as pots and pans in both rustic and high-tech styles and countless space-saving accessories.

Culti specializes in stainless steel designs and other minimalist lines for bathroom and kitchen fittings and furnishings.

The Roman pizzeria '**Gusto** (*see p320*) also offers an interesting range of kitchen utensils and essentials in its ground-floor shop.

Finally, for the budget conscious, there is also **Salvoni**, whose basement is well stocked with cut-price gift ideas. Here, you will find an extraordinary arrary of household and kitchenware, including silver, china and crystal items.

DIRECTORY

FURNITURE

Myricae
Piazza del
Parlamento 38–39.
📞 06-687 3742.
Also: Via Campo Marzio
11. **Map** 4 F3 & 12 D1.
📞 06-689 2485.

Palo Agostara
Via del Chiavari 8.
Map 4 E4 & 11 C4.
📞 06-689 3377.

Spazio Sette
Via dei Barbieri 7.
Map 4 F5 & 12 D4.
📞 06-6880 4261.

Stildomus
Via Laurentina km. 27.
📞 06-914 5144.

Studio Punto Tre
Via Giulia 145.
Map 4 E4 & 11 B4.
📞 06-686 4321.

LIGHTING FIXTURES

Artemide
Via Margutta 107–108.
Map 4 F1.
📞 06-3600 1802.

Borghini
Via Belsiana 87–89.
Map 4 F2.
📞 06-679 0629.

Flos
Via del Babuino 84.
Map 5 A2.
📞 06-320 7631.

Paolo Marj
Piazza del Fico 21a.
Map 11 B3.
📞 06-6880 7707.

KITCHENS AND BATHROOMS

Andreucci
Via Po 39.
Map 2 F5.
📞 06-884 8147.

Arclinea
Lungotevere
dei Cenci 4b.
Map 4 F5 & 12 D5.
📞 06-686 5104.

Odorisio
Via Tomacelli 150.
Map 4 F2.
📞 06-687 8235.

Ravasini
Via di Ripetta 71.
Map 4 F2.
📞 06-322 7096.

TILES

Farnese
Piazza Farnese 52.
Map 4 E5 & 11 C4.
📞 06-687 4792.

Ceramiche Musa
Via Campo Marzio 39.
Map 4 F3 & 12 D1.
📞 06-687 1242.

GLASS

Archimede Seguso
Via dei Due Macelli 56.
Map 5 A2.
📞 06-679 1781.

Arteque
Via Giulia 13.
Map 4 D4 & 11 A3.
📞 06-687 7388.

Murano Più
Corso Rinascimento 43.
Map 4 E3.
📞 06-6880 8038.

Stilvetro
Via Frattina 56.
Map 5 A2.
📞 06-679 0258.

FABRICS

Emporio Triestino
Corso Vittorio Emanuele 9.
Map 12 D4.
📞 06-679 2773.

Paganini
Via delle Botteghe
Oscure 51.
Map 4 F5 & 12 E4.
📞 06-678 6831.

Il Sigillo
Via Laurina 15.
Map 4 F1.
📞 06-361 3247.

HOUSEHOLD AND KITCHENWARE

C.u.c.i.n.a.
Via Mario de' Fiori 65.
Map 5 A2.
📞 06-679 1275.

Culti
Via Francesco Crispi 45–47.
Map 5 B2.
📞 06-679 0272.

Frette
Piazza di Spagna 10.
Map 5 A2.
📞 06-679 0673.

'Gusto
Piazza Augusto
Imperatore 9.
Map 4 F2.

Salvoni
Via Arenula 38.
Map 4 F5.
📞 06-6880 6770.

Books and Gifts

ROME OFFERS A HUGE SELECTION for gift buying. You will find products from all over Italy as well as locally produced artisanwares. Seeking out the smaller shops can be an adventure in itself, as many are in attractive parts of the city that you might not otherwise visit.

Some of the artisan ceramics are very unusual; there are also beautiful books on Italian art and architecture, plus wonderful paper products. Food gifts and drinks are always welcome – especially if they are something really special, such as 20-year-old balsamic vinegar. In addition to the usual souvenirs, there is an abundance of religious artifacts – for obvious reasons – and Michelangelo masterpieces are the most popular icons for T-shirts, statuettes and postcards.

BOOKSHOPS

ROME IS RICH in bookshops, from the encyclopedic to the very specialized. Italian books, both hardcover and softcover, are generally very attractive but also tend to be quite expensive.

Rizzoli, one of Rome's largest bookshops, has a wide selection on art and cookery, among other subjects, and many books in English and other foreign languages. **Feltrinelli** has three shops in the capital. The most central is situated in Largo Argentina and offers a wide selection of contemporary literature. There is also an excellent **Feltrinelli International** bookshop in Via Emanuele Orlando, which sells foreign books and magazines.

Milanese **Franco Maria Ricci** offers very beautiful art books, as well as its own glossy magazine, *FMR*. **Libreria Godel** is also good for browsing – it carries books on Rome, great postcards, art calendars and secondhand art books.

Remainder has half-price bargains and sells games for children, too. There are also many discount bargains as well as secondhand book stalls in Via delle Terme di Diocleziano and in Largo della Fontanella di Borghese.

MULTIMEDIA AND MUSIC

ROME'S BIGGEST music shop is **Ricordi**. In addition to records, cassettes and CDs, it sells musical instruments and musical scores in its four central outlets. By contrast, **Discoteca Frattina** is quite a small, handy music shop that also sells videocassettes.

STATIONERY AND PAPERCRAFT

A WIDE SELECTION of pretty marbled notebooks, attractive writing paper, files and boxes in various sizes are on offer at **Laboratorio Scatole**. **Pineider**, stationery suppliers to the Roman gentry, will print sets of exquisite visiting cards for you. For excellent paper articles and gifts, also try **Fabriano**. Just as classy, though less traditional, **Vertecchi** is filled with original paper gifts. These include boxes of every imaginable size and shape, paper napkins and tablecloths, wrapping paper and a dazzling range of Christmas decorations.

ARTISAN HANDICRAFTS AND DESIGN

DOMENICO and Lavinia Sarti's **Bottega Artigiana** nearby is a small shop with ceramics made by the couple in their Anzio studio. You can buy vases and urns in unglazed terra-cotta and attractive terra-cotta light fixtures. **Arti e Mestieri** is the workshop of a friendly mother and daughter who make original articles in wood and terra-cotta.

If you are more interested in contemporary design, visit the **Palazzo dell'Esposizioni** *(see p164)*, where a wide range of objects by famous designers is available.

For a really original gift, go to **Opificio Romano**, a workshop that reproduces ancient Roman and Pompeian mosaics, where they will re-create any design you choose to order.

SOUVENIRS AND RELIGIOUS ARTIFACTS

MOST OF the tobacco shops in central Rome sell postcards, stamps and a variety of souvenirs, and many cheap and sometimes appealingly kitsch souvenirs are sold by the mobile stalls around the major tourist attractions.

Bookshops near the main basilicas, such as **Libreria Belardetti**, sell souvenirs and religious mementos. Other shops specialize in religious articles for both the clergy and the layperson. Facing the Vatican gates in Via di Porta Angelica are several shops, such as **Al Pellegrino Cattolico**, selling mementos to visitors and tourists.

FOOD

ONE OF THE unusual things about shopping in Rome is the absence of large-scale supermarkets in the center. It has been local government policy to keep them out in order to protect the little *alimentari*, or delicatessens. There are hundreds of these, not on the main shopping streets, but in small side streets running off them or in the "village" districts, such as Monti, Trastevere, the Ghetto, Borgo and Campo de' Fiori. They are often crammed from floor to ceiling with all the irresistible delicacies that are typical of Italy.

Here you can buy, the day before your departure, your supply of parmesan and pecorino Romano cheese *(see p305)*, Parma ham or prosciutto di montagna, attractive bottles of dark-green extra-virgin unfiltered olive oil, dried porcini mushrooms and sun-dried tomatoes to take home (but check Customs restrictions first). Food is by no means cheap, and most of the above are considered luxury items.

Pietro Franchi is without doubt the most exclusive delicatessen in the city, and its windows are a visual feast of seafood platters, pâtés, cheeses and cold meats. Next door is the famous coffee shop **Castroni**, which has Rome's largest selection of imported products from all over the world. It also stocks Italian olive oils, balsamic vinegars, honeys and preserves and, of course, coffee.

Via della Croce deserves a special mention for its good selection of well-stocked *alimentari* like **Fratelli Fabbi**, while over in Testaccio, Volpetti sells an excellent range of regional hams, cheeses, breads, pies and pasta.

Cheese lovers can usually find plenty of Italian varieties in any of the many small *alimentari* dotted around the city. However, it is also well worth trying the local cow, sheep and buffalo milk cheeses that are sold at the **Cisternino Cooperativa fra Produttori di Latte di Lazio**. There are several branches, but the most central is situated near Piazza Campo de' Fiori.

Boxes of chocolates and traditional confectionery and cakes such as *torrone* and *panettone* can generally be bought from good-quality bars. **L'Albero del Pane** sells wonderful wholemeal and rye flour breads and other health foods.

WINE

WINE IS GENERALLY sold in *alimentari* and supermarkets. There are also many specialty shops (look for the sign *Enoteca*) with a huge stock of wines and spirits. They invariably have a bar where they serve wine and light snacks or canapés. Here you can find Italian wines, and usually local wines, mostly white, from the nearby Frascati, Colli Albani and Marino vineyards, on tap. One of the best is **Enoteca Buccone**, in an old coachhouse. Another well-known one is **Antica Enoteca**, which has an old-world feeling to it. **Enoteca del Corso** is more modern, with a good selection of Italian grappa and jars of marinated fruits. **Enoteca Corsi** in Via del Gesù is also worth a visit.

Art and Antiques

R OME'S ART and antiques shops range from exclusive establishments to contemporary art galleries. In response to a fashion for collecting early 20th-century artifacts, new dealers and galleries are springing up throughout Rome – Venini's Murano glass is popular, as are lighting and furniture. Many more sell general bric-a-brac and jewelry. Copies of antique prints can be picked up for a fraction of the original's price. Rome is not good for bargain antiques, but it is worth looking in shops along Via dei Cappellari and Via del Pellegrino or going to the Porta Portese Sunday market *(see p339)*.

ANTIQUES AND OLD MASTER PAINTINGS

T HERE ARE antiques shops dotted all over the center of Rome, though the cream tend to be concentrated in distinct areas. Discreet haggling in the shops is accepted practice, but even if you get a reduction in price, make sure the dealer provides you with the relevant export documents.

The famous Via del Babuino and to a lesser extent Via Margutta, which is more famous for its art galleries, are home to around 30 of Rome's grandest showrooms for antique furniture, Old Master paintings and objets d'art. **Lampronti** is owned by top dealer Cesare Lampronti. Aided and complemented by his partner, Carlo Peruzzi, he sells 16th- to 18th-century European paintings, with an emphasis on Roman and Italian works.

Amedeo di Castro, apparently no relation to the other four di Castros on this street, is a fourth-generation dealer in bas-relief sculptures and exquisite furniture from the 18th and early 19th centuries.

Via Giulia *(see p153)* has over 20 high-quality antiques shops to choose from. Definitely worth a visit is **Antichita Cipriani**, which is a temple to owner Paola Cipriani's love of simply elegant Neo-classical furniture and paintings. She also sells the occasional modern piece. Another shop not to miss on Via Giulia is **Antiquariato Valligiano**. This is the only place in Rome where you can find 19th-century Italian country furniture – a rustic antidote for those overpowered by the grandiose Baroque.

Via Monserrato, running parallel, is worth scouring for slightly lower quality pieces at more attainable prices.

The area just to the north of the Via Giulia is also a good potential hunting ground. **Mario Prilli**, on Via Banchi Nuovi, is tiny, but don't let that deter you. With every space occupied by a wide variety of antiques, this fascinating shop is worth a look even if you are only browsing.

Via dei Coronari is almost exclusively devoted to antiques, with over 40 shops lining both sides of this picturesque street. Quality is very high – as are the prices. It is a good place for Baroque and Empire elaborately inlaid vases, secretaries and consoles.

Ad Antiqua Domus is a treasure trove of antique Italian furniture. Pieces dating from ancient Rome through to the 19th century are on sale.

L'Art Nouveau specializes in high-quality Art Nouveau (usually called *Liberty* here). The **Art Deco Gallery** sells furniture and sculpture from that period.

Piero Tagoni has a superb collection of lighting fixtures from the Baroque through to Art Deco periods. **Antichità Arredamenti** also specializes in Italian light fittings and candlesticks.

Slightly farther away lies Via della Stelletta, which is home to a handful of unusual and fascinating shops. **Acanto** is an inexpensively priced Aladdin's cave with an eclectic mix of objets d'art. It is the perfect place to search for religious memorabilia, Italian curiosities and prints.

Bilenchi is yet another specialist, but in exquisite, turn-of-the-century lamps.

Another relatively undiscovered area is Via del Boschetto and Via Panisperna. Shops around here tend to specialize in early 20th-century artifacts, with some English Victorian pieces thrown in.

Tad is a great place to come and browse, with a large collection of weird and original design items from all around the world.

Of course there are many perennial favorites apart from these streets. The best way to discover them is through word of mouth or just by chance as you stroll along. **Cose Così**, in the north of the city, is a shop full of decorative pieces from 1800 to 1940 (watches, silver, glass, frames, vases and jewelry), while **Galleria dei Cosmati** is one of the oldest antique shops in Rome, and definitely one of the largest. It offers an impressive collection of European antiques.

Anticaja e Petrella has an eccentric collection of used junk and printed ephemera stored under Sant'Andrea della Valle *(see p123)*.

MODERN ART

R OME IS RICH in avant-garde galleries exhibiting paintings by recognized modern masters through to the up-and-coming generation of young, mainly Italian, artists.

Rome's art galleries are usually open 10am to 1pm and 5 to 8pm Tuesday to Saturday. Some open only in the afternoon; others also stay open on Monday afternoon. The best times to visit are in the afternoons and early evenings.

As with Rome's antiques shops, the art galleries tend to be concentrated in a couple of distinct areas. The largest of these covers the triangle area between Via del Babuino and Via di Ripetta and adjoining streets, known locally as the Trident.

The pioneering **Agenzia d'Arte Moderna**, founded in 1913, promoted Futurism from the start and other modern art movements as well. There are works by Burri and Kounellis always on display.

Sperone, under the owner-directorship of Gian Enzo Sperone, shows works by American artists like Ray Smith, Julio Galan and Jonathan Lasker. Also included are Italian artists like Gallo, Bianchi, Dessi, Paladino and Merzi.

One of this area's highlights is the Via Margutta art fair *(see p339)*, which usually takes place around Christmas and in springtime.

Via Giulia and its surroundings is the next area to investigate: **Galleria Giulia** is a gallery-cum-bookshop with works by artists such as Argeles, Boille, Cano, Cascella, Echaurren, Erba and Lionni, as well as by Bauhaus artists and German Expressionists.

Fabio Sargentini at **L'Attico** follows the latest trends in Italian art from Del Giudice to Corsini and Fabiani.

Other more innovative ventures in the city centre include: **Galleria Bonomo** (owned by Alessandra Bonomo), which spotlights young Italian and foreign painters, such as Schifano, Boetti, Twombly, Nunzio, Tremlett, LeWitt and Dokoupil.

In a stupendous villa situated quite a way out of Rome, **Mauro Vigneti** specializes in both Italian and international artists who are working in the city. Fortunately, he has also opened a showroom in the Monti District.

ANTIQUE PRINTS AND PHOTOGRAPHS

THE JUSTIFIABLY celebrated **Nardecchia**, named after its erudite owner, Plinio, is the cream of Rome's print dealers. Look for originals by the 18th-century engraver

Piranesi and views of the city and ancient Roman life.

Another Roman institution, **Casali**, has been trading for over 100 years. The family now runs two shops specializing in 16th- to 19th-century drawings and engravings of Roman scenes ranging from museum-standard Piranesi down to relatively inexpensive and delightfully decorative floral scenes by unknowns.

The Florence-based **Alinari** family is renowned for its sepia photographs of Italy from 1890 onward, including shots of Rome a century ago. At its Roman outlet, prices of photographs from the original plates start at around €16 and mounted prints at €260. Larger sizes can be mounted on wood or board.

Another place definitely worth heading for in search of that perfect print of old Rome and some enjoyable, relaxing, and maybe persuasive, browsing is the **Mercato delle Stampe** *(see p338)*.

Outdoor Markets

ROME'S OUTDOOR MARKETS are essential to visit if you are interested in experiencing the exuberance and vitality for which Romans are renowned. The markets are wonderfully vivid visually too, as Italian stallholders and vendors have raised the display of even the humblest vegetable to an art form.

The city is dotted with popular, small outdoor food markets, and there are several fascinating well-established ones near the center, along with the most famous flea market over in Trastevere.

It is important to keep your wits about you in all these markets, because pickpockets work with lightning speed in the bustling crowds. However, Roman markets provide such a vibrant source of entertainment, it would be a shame to let such caveats deter you from joining in.

The street fairs that take place throughout the year offer various pleaures and also normally sell a good variety of local produce, handicrafts and clothes. Seasonal fairs also occur, especially around Christmas, when you can stock up on Italian specialties and gifts.

Campo de' Fiori

Piazza Campo de' Fiori. **Map** 4 E4 & 11 C4. 📟 40, 46, 62, 64, 70, 81, 116, 492, 628. 🚋 8. **Open** 7am–1:30pm Mon–Sat. See p146.

Right in the heart of the old city, Rome's most picturesque market is also its most historical. Its name, Campo de' Fiori, which translates as "field of flowers," sometimes misleads people into expecting a flower market. In fact, the name is said to derive from Campus Florae (Flora's square) – Flora being the lover of the great Roman general Pompey. A market has actually been held in this beautiful piazza for many centuries.

Every morning except Sunday, the piazza is transformed by an array of stalls selling fruit and vegetables, meat, poultry and fish. One or two stalls specialize in legumes, rice, dried fruit and nuts, and there are also flower stalls situated near the fountain. But the huge open baskets of broccoli and spinach, chopped vegetables and freshly prepared green salad mixes are the main attraction for visitors. They provide a real visual display as well as an edible feast.

The excellent delicatessen's on the square and bread shops nearby complement the market. They make it a great place to stock up for an impromptu picnic if the weather turns out fine and you are tempted to do some alfresco dining in one of Rome's many attractive parks. The market gets extremely busy on Saturdays, so be prepared to fight your way through the crowds.

Mercato delle Stampe

Largo della Fontanella di Borghese. **Map** 4 F3 & 12 D1. 📟 81, 116, 117, 492, 628. **Open** 7am–1pm Mon–Sat.

This market is a veritable haven for lovers of old prints, books (both genuine antiquarian and less costly secondhand), magazines and other printed ephemera. The quality varies, but it is a good deal more specialized than the *banche*, or stalls, near Termini station which are a more obvious tourist trap. Italian-speaking collectors can enjoy a field day leafing through back issues of specialty magazines. Other visitors might prefer the wonderful selection of illustrated art books and old prints of Rome. It is a good place to pick up that Piranesi print of your favorite Roman vista, ruin or church – but be prepared to bargain hard.

Mercato dei Fiori

Via Trionfale. **Map** 3 B1. Ⓜ Ottaviano S. Pietro. 📟 23, 51, 30, 490. **Open** 10:30am–1pm Tue.

Essentially a trade market, the Flower Market, just north of Via Andrea Doria, is open to the public only on Tuesdays. Housed in a covered hall, it has two floors brimming over with cut flowers upstairs and all kinds of potted plants on the lower floor. Anyone who has an interest in flowers will enjoy this wonderful array of Mediterranean blooms, which are for sale at giveaway prices.

Mercato Andrea Doria

Via Andrea Doria. **Map** 3 B1. Ⓜ Ottaviano S. Pietro. 📟 23, 70, 490. **Open** 7am–1:30pm Mon–Sat.

The market used to stretch the whole length of this wide avenue. It has now been reorganized onto a huge square of open ground between Via Santamaura and Via Tunisi. Apart from the magnificent displays of fruit and vegetables, it has numerous stalls selling meat, poultry, fish and groceries, as well as an interesting clothes and shoe section. Situated northwest of the Vatican Museums, it is a little off the normal beaten track and has remained very much a Roman market that caters to the needs of the large local population.

Nuovo Mercato Esquilino

Via Principe Amedeo. **Map** 6 E5. Ⓜ Vittorio Emanuele. 📟 105. **Open** 7am–2pm Mon–Sat. See p174.

Bustling Piazza Vittorio was, until recently, perhaps the most Roman of the city's larger markets.

Now renamed, it has moved to new covered premises, but it is still the place where bargain-hunting *popolari*, Rome's bustling shoppers, buy their food. Stallholders offer cheap prices if you buy by the kilo, but watch out for bad fruit.

Lately it has become more international and now features African and Asian food stalls, which cater to the area's many ethnic groups. Definitely a place to go to to capture the atmosphere of a traditional but changing city.

Mercato di Testaccio

Piazza Testaccio. **Map** 8 D3. Ⓜ Piramide. 📟 23, 75, 280. 🚋 3. **Open** 7:30am–1:30pm Mon–Sat.

The covered market at Testaccio occupies the central area of the Testaccio piazza. The few cheap clothing and shoe stalls skirting the outside are unremarkable, but the inside is well worth a visit. Lined with butchers, grocers and fishsellers, the whole central area is given over to fruit and vegetables – a theater-set array of seductive colors and textures. Very popular with local residents, it offers super-fresh, high-quality produce and reasonable prices. Much of this market's charm for visitors lies in its compact size and relaxed, friendly atmosphere.

Porta Portese

Via Portuense & Via Ippolito Nievo.
Map 7 C3. 🚌 H, 23, 44, 75. 🚋 3, 8.
Open 6:30am–2pm Sun.

The *mercato delle pulci*, or flea market, is relatively new in Roman terms. Established shortly after the end of World War II, it is said to have grown out of the thriving black market that operated at Tor di Nona opposite Castel Sant' Angelo during those lean years. Stall holders from as far away as Naples start setting up shop in the early hours of the morning – if you happen to be strolling in that direction after a late night on the town in Trastevere, it is well worth pausing just to watch.

Anything and everything seems to be for sale, piled high on stalls in carefully arranged disorder – clothes, shoes, bags, luggage, camping equipment, linen, towels, pots, pans, kitchen utensils, plants, pets, spare parts, cassettes and CDs, old LPs and 78s.

Furniture stalls tend to be concentrated around Piazza Ippolito Nievo along with what they call "antiques," though you may have to sort through an awful lot of junk before finding a real one. And then you will have to bargain for it. The technique is to offer them half the asked price and then walk away. Many go just to haggle but usually end up buying something anyway.

There are also secondhand clothes – leather or sheepskin coats and jackets go for €10 – with many of the Via Sannio stall holders relocating here for the Sunday trade. The stretch along Via Ippolito Nievo is often monopolized by "*i Russi di Porta Portese*," immigrant Russian stallholders selling icons (authenticity uncertain), lace, other ethnic handicrafts, old cameras and binoculars. A must if you have a Sunday morning to spare.

Mercato di Via Sannio

Via Sannio. **Map** 9 C2. Ⓜ *San Giovanni.* 🚌 16, 81, 87. **Open** 8am–1pm Mon–Fri & 8am–6pm Sat.

In the 1960s and 1970s this used to be Italy's answer to Carnaby Street or Soho. Today, at first glance, it seems not to have anything very special to offer. Random stalls sell inexpensive casual clothes, shoes, bags, belts, jewelry, toys, kitchen utensils and music cassettes. However, toward the end of the street is a large covered section that extends back to the Aurelian Wall *(see p196)*. Here visitors will find many stalls piled high with secondhand clothes at very low prices for those who like to

rummage for bargains. There is also a section that sells military-style goods plus camping and fishing equipment.

Some of these stalls move their wares to Porta Portese on Sunday morning.

Local Markets

Generally open 7am–1pm Mon–Sat.

Piazza delle Coppelle (map 4 F3 & 12 D2), near the Pantheon, is probably the most picturesque of all the outdoor food markets around the city. A tiny market devoted to food and fruit and

flowers, it offers a charming splash of color in the heart of the city.

Piazza San Cosimato (map 7 C1) in Trastevere hosts another lively local market selling tempting cheeses and salami.

There is a fairly big market on **Via Alessandria** (map 6 D1) in Nomentana, and other smaller ones in **Via della Pace** (map 4 E4 & 11 C3) near Piazza Navona, and in **Via Balbo** (map 5 C4) and **Via Milazzo** (map 6 E3) near Termini Station. You can also visit the trade market, the **Mercato Generale** (map 8 D5), in Via Ostiense, which is open to the public after 8am.

STREET FAIRS

A special and interesting feature of shopping in Rome is the street fair.

The **Tevere Expo** exhibition starts each year between mid-June and mid-July on both sides of the river bank between the Sant'Angelo and Cavour bridges. Its stalls display Italian regional arts and crafts and also sell pasta, jam, olive oil, wines and liqueurs. Some items are cheaper than in the shops. The exhibition opens in the evening (6pm–1am). The entrance fee occasionally includes a ferry trip across the Tiber.

There are two antiques fairs, both known as the **Fiera dell'Antiquariato**, that take place in Via dei Coronari. The first starts in the second half of May, 10am to 1pm and 4pm to 11pm daily. It makes a memorable scene at night, when lighted torches line the carpeted street. The second goes along Via dell'Orso as well and normally occurs in mid-October (or late September), Monday to Thursday from 3–11pm and Friday and Saturday from 10am–11pm. Stalls sell leatherwork, jewelry and gifts.

The **Via Margutta Art Fair** usually takes place around Christmas and in springtime. Set in one of the most charming and exclusive streets of the city, it is an event not to be missed – although it is more

for browsing because prices are very high. The utterly glamorous **Spanish Steps Alta Moda Fashion Show** is a fairly new event and does not have a set date. The seating space is filled by invitation only. However, the public can squeeze in the back to enjoy this display of Italian designer fashion. So far it has been held mid- to late July.

The traditional **Christmas Fair** held in Piazza Navona from mid-December until January 6 is now rather low-key but still fascinating for those who have never seen it. Stalls selling clay statues for nativity scenes and sweets that look like pieces of coal are the main attraction.

Natale Oggi is a well-established event taking place near Christmas in the Fiera di Roma at EUR, and it is worth visiting to have a look at the special Italian Christmas treats.

Via Giulia hosts art fairs now and then, plus open evenings when the antiques and art galleries stay open late offering food and wine to all visitors.

Every year Trastevere hosts its very own carnival, the **Festa de Noantri**, in late July, when Viale Trastevere is overrun with the typical *porchetta* stalls *(see p341)*, party lights, gift stalls and people.

The details given here may change, so check the local listings, the tourist office or ring the tourist call center *(see p359)*.

ENTERTAINMENT IN ROME

THERE'S A PARTICULAR excitement attached to Roman entertainment. Football and opera, for example, are both worth experiencing for sheer atmosphere alone, whether or not you are a fan. The jazz scene is especially good, with international stars appearing alongside local talent. And concerts and films take on an added dimension when performances take place beneath the stars in the many open-air arenas spread across the city. Unexpectedly, given the general shutdown among shops and restaurants, the summer remains Rome's liveliest time for live music and other cultural events. Rome's many graceful Renaissance squares, vast parks, villa gardens, Classical ruins and other open spaces host various major arts festivals. If you prefer sports, or want to try out some Roman nightclubs, there's plenty to choose from.

Gregory Peck and Audrey Hepburn in *Roman Holiday*

WHAT'S HAPPENING

A GOOD SOURCE of information about what's on is *Trovaroma*, the weekly Thursday supplement to *La Repubblica* newspaper. It has a day-by-day rundown of what's on and where, and covers music, exhibitions, theater, movies,

Lester Bowie at Alpheus *(see p344)*

guided tours, restaurants and children's entertainment. The weekly listings magazine, *Roma c'è*, has an English section covering the "Week in Rome" and *Time Out Roma* makes an occasional appearance. Daily newspapers like *Il Messaggero*, *Il Manifesto* and *La Repubblica* usually list that evening's entertainment.

The magazine, *Wanted in Rome*, found at Via Veneto newsstands or at English book-shops, provides less detailed listings in English. Also worth getting hold of is *L'Evento*, available from the APT *(see p359)*, which gives details in English of classical music, festivals, theater and exhibitions in the city and surroundings. Up-to-date information can also be found on various websites.

Punctuality is not what Italians are renowned for, so don't be surprised if some events start slightly later than advertised in listings.

RESERVING TICKETS

R ESERVING in advance is not part of Italian lifestyle, though this is slowly changing. Two agencies that will reserve tickets for some performances for you (for a small fee) are **Orbis** and **Box Office**. Many theaters do not accept telephone reservations – you have to visit the box office. They will charge you a *prevendita* supplement (about 10 per cent of the normal price) for any tickets sold in advance. A theater ticket can cost anything between €8 and €52.

Tickets for classical concerts are usually sold on the spot, and are sometimes for that night only, an arrangement that favors the last-minute decision to go. Opera is the exception. Tickets are sold months in advance, with just a few held back until two days before the performance. It is usually easier (and also

One of the many stages at Alpheus

cheaper) to get tickets for the open-air summer performances.

The **Teatro dell'Opera** box office *(see p343)* handles sales for both summer and winter seasons, and they have a high-tech reservation system, with a computer that color-codes unsold seats.

Tickets for most big rock and jazz events can be bought at **Orbis**, **Prontospettacolo**, **Mirabilia** and at larger record shops, such as **Rinascita**.

Remember that if you are trying to get a ticket for a particular performance that has already sold out, you are unlikely to be able to obtain one from unofficial

Member of contemporary dance group Momix *(see p343)*

sources – there are few ticket scalpers in Rome, except at major football matches, such as important finals.

DISCOUNT TICKETS

THEATERS and concert venues tend not to offer discounts on tickets, even when left-over seats are in abundance. Movie theaters, however, offer people over 60 and disabled people a 30 percent reduction on weekdays. Many also have cheaper ticket prices for weekday afternoon screenings and for all shows on Wednesday. Some clubs at the beach resorts, such as Fregene, offer reductions: watch for *due per uno* coupons in local bars; they allow two people entrance for the price of one.

FACILITIES FOR THE DISABLED

FEW ROMAN venues provide easy access for people with restricted mobility, and any disabled visitors and their companions are likely to find the lack of provision for them very frustrating.

The situation does improve a little in summer, however, when a great many performances in the city are held in the open air. The classical concerts held in the beautiful gardens of Villa Giulia *(see pp262–3)* have wheelchair access.

For more general information on provisions for the disabled, see page 359.

The Teatro dell'Opera *(see p342)*

Summer night outdoor performance among Roman ruins

OPEN-AIR ENTERTAINMENT

OPEN-AIR OPERA, movies, classical music and jazz concerts fill the calendar from late June until the end of September. These performances outdoors can be wonderful, with spectacular settings and enthusiastic audiences. Some of them are grand affairs, but small events may be just as evocative – a guitar recital in the cloisters of Santa Maria della Pace *(see p121)*, for example, or jazz in the beautiful gardens of Villa Celimontana *(see p193)*.

Singers performing the *Barber of Seville*

Some movie theaters roll back their ceilings in summer for open-air screenings or else move to outdoor arenas, and there are also annual open-air movie festivals. The Cineporto along the Tiber and the Festival di Massenzio offer films, food and small exhibitions in July and August. Theater, too, moves outside in summer. Greek and Roman plays are staged at Ostia Antica *(see p270)* and other shows take place at the Anfiteatro del Tasso *(see p347)*.

Rome's most important autumn performing arts festival is RomaEuropa, with occasional performances in the grounds of the Villa Medici. There are other, smaller festivals, but times and venues change from year to year, so it is best to consult

listings in newspapers, magazines or websites *(see p340)* or watch for posters around the city for the most recent information. More traditional is Trastevere's community festival, Festa de Noantri *(see p59)*, with music, fireworks and processions. This religious festival begins on the Saturday after July 16, but celebrations continue into August. The Festa dell'Unità, run by the DS (the former Communist Party), but not limited to politics, is generally held in September. The celebration includes games, stalls, food and drink.

Finally, if you like your entertainment less structured, and more leisurely, you can always do as the Romans tend to do and take part in the *passeggiata* (early-evening stroll) – the city's favorite spots are Piazza Navona *(see p120)* and along Via del Corso.

TICKET AGENCIES

Box Office
Via del Corso 506 (inside Ricordi Record Shop). **Map** 4 F2 & 12 E1.
Tickets for classical music, rock, pop and jazz concerts and some sporting events.
〔 06-320 2790.

Orbis
Piazza dell'Esquilino 37.
Map 6 D4. **〔** 06-482 7403.

USEFUL WEBSITES

W www.tkts.it
W www.romapreview.com
W www.romaturismo.it
W www.pierreci.it

Classical Music and Dance

CLASSICAL CONCERTS take place in a surprising number of venues: tickets for opera premieres may be hard to get, but those for soloists, groups or orchestras playing in gardens, churches, villas or ancient ruins are more available. World-renowned soloists and orchestras make appearances throughout the year; past visitors have included Luciano Pavarotti and Placido Domingo, the Berlin Philharmonic and prima ballerina Sylvie Guillem.

Programs are generally international in scope, but some festivals are dedicated to one of Italy's very own, such as Palestrina, the great 16th-century master of polyphonic church music, or Arcangelo Corelli, inventor of the Baroque *concerto grosso*.

MUSIC IN CHURCHES

ONE OF ROME'S main attractions for classical music is the rich repertoire that can be heard in the city's churches. Always sacred in theme (by decree of Pope John Paul II), music is mainly performed as concerts rather than during services.

Programs are posted around the city and outside the churches. You will often find very good musicians playing in the main churches, while the smaller, out-of-the-way churches frequently have young musicians and amateur choirs as well.

St. Peter's *(see p230)* hosts one major RAI (national broadcasting company) concert on December 5 attended by the pope and free for the general public. It has two established choirs. The Coro della Cappella Giulia sing at the 10:30am mass and 5pm vespers on Sunday. The Coro della Cappella Sistina sing whenever the pope celebrates mass here, as on June 29 (St. Peter's and St. Paul's day).

Important choral masses also take place on January 25 in **San Paolo fuori le Mura** *(see p267)*, when the Pope attends; on June 24 in **San Giovanni in Laterano** *(p182)*; and on December 31 at the **Gesù** *(pp114–5)*, where the *Te Deum* is sung. The church of **Sant'Ignazio di Loyola** *(p106)* is another favorite venue for choral concerts.

Plain song and Gregorian chant can be heard in **Sant' Anselmo** *(p204)* every Sunday (Oct–Jul) at the 8:30am mass

and 7:15pm vespers. Easter and Christmas are great times for cheap but chilly concerts.

ORCHESTRAL, CHAMBER AND CHORAL MUSIC

WITHOUT DOUBT the arts event of the decade was the opening of the new Renzo Piano-designed auditorium on the Via Flaminia in spring 2002. Up to then the **Auditorium di Santa Cecilia** and the **Teatro dell' Opera** were Rome's main auditoriums, with their own resident orchestras and choirs. The Orchestra e Coro dell' Accademia di Santa Cecilia is the top orchestra, but both offer interestingly varied seasons that include visiting groups and soloists from all over the world. It remains to be seen how the Santa Cecilia fares in its new home.

The season at the **Teatro Olimpico** usually offers good chamber music, some orchestral concerts and ballet, with at least one concert a week.

Although a variety of classical concerts take place at the **Accademia Filarmonica Romana**, the emphasis is on chamber and choral music, with an internationally renowned series of concerts running from mid-October to mid-May. Performances take place in the Sala Casella, which seats around 180.

Ticket prices for classical concerts vary depending on performers and venue. The **Auditorium del Foro Italico** sells tickets for most concerts for under €15; a ticket for the **Teatro Olimpico** costs between €15 and €25, but

seats for an important concert at **Teatro dell'Opera** may cost as much as €80.

The Associazione Musicale Romana, dedicated to Renaissance and Baroque music, sponsors three annual festivals in the **Palazzo della Cancelleria** *(see p149):* the Festival Internazionale di Cembalo (harpsichord festival) in March; Musica al Palazzo in May; and the Festival Internazionale di Organo in September. Classical music fans should also watch out for performances by the Orchestra di Roma e del Lazio at **Teatro Argentina** or **Teatro Valle** *(see p347).*

It is always worth checking which musicians are due to be playing at the **Teatro Ghione**, the **Oratorio del Gonfalone** and especially the **Aula Magna dell' Università La Sapienza**, which has one of the most innovative programmes of classical and contemporary music.

OPEN-AIR SUMMER CONCERTS

IN THE SUMMER, music lovers can enjoy concerts in cloisters, palazzo courtyards and ancient ruins. Concerts can be one-time events or part of a festival, regular fixtures or impromptu. Do as the Romans do: wait until the last moment and keep an eye on the posters and listings pages *(see p340).*

Open-air opera and dance once had their home in the majestic Baths of Caracalla, but this venue is seldom used. Classical concerts are often part of festivals like RomaEuropa *(see p341),* but there are also a number of open-air festivals and concert series dedicated specifically to classical music. Among the more interesting of these is the Stagione Estiva dell'Orchestra dell'Accademia di Santa Cecilia held at the Ninfeo *(nympheum)* on the grounds of **Villa Giulia** *(see p263).* Also listed as the Concerti a Villa Giulia, the concerts take place in July, and tickets are about €12.

The Associazione Musicale Romana organizes Serenate in Chiostro – a lively and varied program of concerts during July in the cloisters of **Santa Maria della Pace** *(see p121)*, with tickets at reasonable prices. The Concerti del Tempietto are a real summer treat, with concerts held almost every evening from July to September in the **Area Archeologica del Teatro di Marcello** *(see p151)* or in the park of the Villa Torlonia.

Festival Villa Pamphilj in Musica, in July, is a series of concerts in the gardens of **Villa Doria Pamphilj** *(see p267)*. Programs range from comic opera to jazz and 20th-century classical music.

Brass bands can be heard in the **Pincio Gardens** *(see p136)* on Sunday mornings from the end of April until mid-July – they usually strike up at around 10:30am.

CONTEMPORARY MUSIC

THE **Auditorium di Santa Cecilia** and the Accademia Filarmonica Romana (usually at the **Teatro Olimpico**) often include modern pieces in their programs but these are less popular than the classics; there is no set venue with a regular contemporary program.

International names appear on festival programs and at one-off concerts at the **Aula Magna dell'Università La Sapienza**. The most interesting contemporary music festival is organized by the Nuova Consonanza in autumn. Modern Italian composers are performed in the Rassegna Nuova Musica Italiana concert series two or three times a year. Also worth keeping an eye out for are performances by scholars of the French Academy at **Villa Medici** *(see p135)*.

OPERA

ITALY AND OPERA are to many people synonymous. Critics will tell you (justifiably) that Rome's opera is not up to the standard of that at Milan's La Scala, or Naples's San Carlo. But that doesn't mean it is not worth visiting – world-class singers do appear here *(see p38)*, mainly in premieres or solo recitals. However you judge the quality of the per-formances, the surroundings in which they take place are often incomparable. In summer, the visual spectacle of *Aida*, performed in the open air, is simply magnificent.

The season starts late at **Teatro dell'Opera**, between November and January. In recent years, programs have concentrated on the great popular operas rather than on staging experimental productions. Tickets range from €13 to €130.

Until recently the Teatro dell'Opera would move outdoors in July and August, to stage opera and ballet in the ancient baths of Caracalla. This tradition has now stopped as the vibrations were deemed to be a threat to the structural integrity of the Baths.

BALLET AND DANCE

OPPORTUNITIES to watch ballet or contemporary dance are fairly limited in Rome. The opera house's resident company, Corpo di Ballo del Teatro dell'Opera di Roma, performs the great classics as well as Roland Petit–style modern choreo-graphies. Performances are staged at **Teatro dell'Opera**.

Contemporary dance is most likely found during the summer festivals, but foreign companies often perform at **Teatro Olimpico** as well. American modern dance groups of the Moses Pendleton school – Pilobolus, Momix, ISO and Daniel Ezralow – are popular visitors. **Teatro del Vascello** is another venue noted for experimental dance perform-ances. In summer and autumn, outdoor performances are organized during the **RomaEuropa Festival**.

DIRECTORY

For information about festivals and open-air concerts, see Trovaroma or similar listings (see pp340 & 359).

ORCHESTRAL, CHAMBER AND CHORAL MUSIC

Accademia Filar-monica Romana
Via Flaminia 118. **Map 1** A1. C 06-320 1752.
W www.filarmonica romana.org

Auditorium di Santa Cecilia
Via della Conciliazione 4.
Map 3 C3.

C 06-6880 1044 (for information);
C 06-3938 7297 (for credit card sales).
W www.santacecilia.it

Aula Magna dell' Università La Sapienza
Piazzale Aldo Moro 5.
C 06-361 0051.
W www.concertiiuc.it

Oratorio del Gonfalone
Via del Gonfalone 32A.
Map 4 D4 & 11 A3.
C 06-687 5952.

Sant'Anselmo
Piazza Cavalieri di Malta 5. **Map 8** D2.
C 06-579 11.

Teatro Olimpico
Piazza Gentile da Fabriano 17.
C 06-326 5991.

Teatro dell'Opera
Piazza Beniamino Gigli 1.
Map 5 C3.
C 06-4816 0287.
W www.opera.roma.it

Teatro Ghione
Via delle Fornaci 37.
Map 3 B4.
C 06-637 2294.

OPERA

Teatro dell'Opera
Piazza Beniamino Gigli 1.
Map 5 C3.
C 06-4816 0287.

BALLET AND DANCE

RomaEuropa Festival
Via XX Settembre 3.
C 06-4890 4024.

Teatro dell'Opera
Piazza Beniamino Gigli 1.
Map 5 C3.
C 06-4816 0287.

Teatro Olimpico
Piazza Gentile da Fabriano 17.
C 06-326 5991.

Teatro del Vascello
Via G Carini 72.
Map 7 A2.
C 06-588 1021.

Rock, Jazz, Folk and World Music

Rome's non-classical music scene is unpredictable and subject to vast seasonal changes, but there is a huge variety of music at the many clubs and stadiums, with visiting foreign and home-grown stars. Recent years have seen the emergence of many new Italian bands who are well worth seeing. Summer months bring excellent open-air rock, jazz and world music festivals.

The music sections of *Trovaroma, Time Out Roma* or *Roma c'è (see p340)* give a good idea of what's on, and ticket agencies at Orbis and Ricordi will have info on the latest tours. For smaller venues you might need to buy a *tessera* (monthly or annual membership card) costing anything from €2 to €11, which often includes the entrance fee for smaller bands.

ROCK MUSIC

Big-name rock concerts are held in sports venues at the **Palaeur**, **Palacisalfa** and the legendary **Stadio Olimpico**. Testaccio's **Villaggio Globale** at the Ex-Mattatoio (a converted abattoir) is another large-scale venue for concerts and other events, while farther out is the **Palaghiaccio**. Entrance for top names can cost above €25, but there are plenty of opportunities for smaller pockets. If you are in Rome for May 1st, join the crowds at the massive open-air concert which is usually held at Piazza San Giovanni. Bands also play for free during the European Festival of Music celebrations on and around June 21st. For all mega-concerts it is always a good idea to turn up an hour or so before the act gets under way to be sure of a good place.

Rome has various lively clubs playing rock music, each attracting its own loyal clientele. **Horus** is the place to head for if you want to see US and English outfits that are just breaking big internationally.

One of the city's most interesting venues is **Forte Prenestino**, a former prison taken over by squatters a few years ago and turned into a social center with a characteristically alternative feel. It now hosts rock concerts, debates and art exhibitions. In the center of town is the enterprising **Akab-Cave** which usually has

a season full of interesting rock and ethnic fixtures. Meanwhile, **Radio Londra Caffè** and **Il Locale**, with its low entrance fee and central location, are places where many up-and-coming Roman bands and soloists cut their teeth.

Discos often double as live music venues too, and so check to see if there are any mid-week surprises at **Piper** or weekend concerts at **Black Out** and the slightly more alternative **Ex-Magazzini Generali**.

JAZZ

Rome's taste for jazz has developed over the years as a result of visits from American and other foreign musicians. Miles Davis played one of his last concerts here and other jazz gurus such as Pat Metheny, Michael Brecker, Sonny Rollins and Joe Zawinul's Syndicate are all frequent visitors.

The best musicians play at **Alexanderplatz** or **La Palma**, which also hosts short festivals. Trastevere's **Big Mama** club is one of the city's legendary addresses for important names, offering punters everything from trad r'n'b to progressive jazz and rock. It is also worth checking out what's on at **Café Renault** and **Gregory's**. **Alpheus** is unique in offering separate concert halls and interesting festivals featuring high-quality ensembles. Otherwise check local listings to see what's on at **Caffè**

Latino or **Caffè Caruso**. Some of Rome's so-called disco-pubs, like **The Four XXXX**, also showcase formidable new talent.

If you want to mix music with your meal, then try **'Gusto**, a slick pizzeria / restaurant in the city-center with live jazz on most nights. If Creole cuisine is more to your taste, then book a table in advance at Alexanderplatz.

Local names to look out for include pianist Antonello Salis, who mingles jazz and Caribbean rhythms, and respected soul-singer Fulvio Tomaino. Other leading lights on the blues scene are Roberto Gatto and Maurizio Gianmarco, frequent visitors at Big Mama.

The Roman summer abounds in jazz. The principal event is the Alexanderplatz Jazz Image festival in June and July with nightly al fresco performances at the Villa Celimontana park, just behind the Colosseum. Tickets cost around €8 and are available at the park itself. Other annual fixtures are the smaller festivals which take place in October and in the nearby towns of Ciampino and Tivoli in spring and early summer.

FOLK MUSIC

Since the sad demise of Rome's historic Folkstudio, there is no single venue for folk aficionados in the city, though those prepared to scour the listings may uncover a country evening at **Four Green Fields**, an interesting acoustic set at **Caffè Latino** or a soulful soloist at **Il Locale**.

Traditional Roman folk music has been more or less reduced to tourist-diluted serenades at outdoor restaurants; besides, young locals tend to favor the folk music of other regions and countries. Many new bands from various parts of Italy, such as Mau Mau, Almamegretta and Agricantus, have found success by drawing on regional rhythms and singing in dialect.

Italians' love of all things Irish also means that strains of the fiddle and drum can be heard in many of the Irish pubs dotted throughout the city. If you have to choose one, then make it the Guinness-enriched **Fiddler's Elbow** near Santa Maria Maggiore.

WORLD MUSIC

AS CAPITAL of a Latin country which has strong links with other Mediterranean cultures, Rome is a place where world music flourishes. Whether you are looking for South American salsa, African rhythms or Arab cadences, you are unlikely to be disappointed.

Latin American music is no passing fad, as the well-established festivals, dance-schools and sell-out tours by the likes of Brazilian mega-star Caetano Veloso testify. Many venues offer opportunities to enjoy Latin American music throughout the year: **Speedy Gonzales** offers Mexican food, salsa and mixed, commercial fare, while **Arriba Arriba**, a newcomer to the scene, serves up a choice menu of strictly spicy Latin rhythms. Check too what's on at **Café Caruso** in Testaccio. Or head off to **Barrio Latino**, where you can enjoy a cocktail or two along with the Brazilian music.

But it is summer when Latin American music really comes into its own. The two-month Fiesta festival at the **Ippodromo delle Capannelle** has become by far the most popular feature of the many Roman Summer events, clocking up over one million ticket sales.

If your tastes are more African, there's also an excellent June–July festival which takes place at Villa Ada, a large park north of the city center, where fans gather each evening to appreciate the talents of names like Angelique Kidjo and South African pianist Abdullah Ibrahim.

World music is also well-served at the aptly-named **Villaggio Globale**. For a more eclectic experience, try **Lettere Caffè**, Rome's first literary café, which offers world music on Fridays with performances of anything from Australian aborigine to Greek syrtaki sounds.

DIRECTORY

Akab-Cave
Via Monte Testaccio 69.
Map 8 D4.
06-578 2390.

Alexanderplatz
Via Ostia 9.
Map 3 B1.
06-3974 2171.

Alpheus
Via del Commercio 36–8.
Map 8 D5.
06-574 7826.

Arriba Arriba
Via delle Capannelle 104.
06-721 3772.

Barrio Latino
Via B. Alimena (east of city, along Via Prenestina).
06-723 0460.

Big Mama
Vicolo San Francesco a Ripa 18.
Map 7 C2.
06-581 2551.

Black Out
Via Saturnia 18.
Map 9 C3.
06-7049 6791.

Caffè Caruso
Via di Monte Testaccio 36.
Map 8 D4.
06-574 5019.

Caffè Latino
Via di Monte Testaccio 96.
Map 8 D4.
06-5728 8556.

Café Renault
Via Nazionale 183. **Map** 5 B4.
06-4782 4452.

Ex-Magazzini Generali
Via dei Magazzini Generali 8 bis. **Map** 8 D5.
06-575 8040.

Fiddler's Elbow
Via dell'Olmata 43. **Map** 6 D4.
06-487 2110.

Fonclea
Via Crescenzio 82A.
Map 3 C2.
06-689 6302.

Forte Prenestino
Via F. Delpino (east of city, along Via Prenestina).
06-2180 7855.

Four Green Fields
Via Morin 40. **Map** 3 B1.
06-372 5091.

Four XXXX Pub
Via Galvani 29. **Map** 8 D4.
06-575 7296.

Gregory's
Via Gregoriana 54D.
Map 5 A2.
06-679 6386.

'Gusto
Piazza Augusto Imperatore 9. **Map** 4 F2.
06-322 6273.

Horus Club
Corso Sempione 21 (near Monte Sacro).
06-8680 1410.

Ippodromo delle Capannelle
Via Appia Nuova 1245 (km.12).
06-718 3143.

Lettere Caffè
Via San Francesco a Ripa 100.
Map 7 C1.
06-5833 4379.

Il Locale
Vicolo del Fico 3.
Map 11 B2.
06-687 9075.

Orbis
Piazza Esquilino 37.
Map 6 D4.
06-482 7403.

Palacisalfa
Via dell'Oceano Atlantico 271d, EUR.
06-5728 8024.

Palaeur
Viale dell'Umanesimo, EUR.
06-3976 0420.

Palaghiaccio
Via Appia Nuova (km 19).
06-592 2100.

La Palma
Via dei Mirri 35 (to the southeast of Stazione Tiburtina).
06-4359 9029.

Radio Londra Caffè
Via di Monte Testaccio 65b. **Map** 8 D4.
06-575 0044.

Ricordi
Via del Corso 506.
Map 5 A4 & 12 F3.
06-361 2370.

Speedy Gonzales
Via Libetta 13 (to the south of Stazione Ostiense).
06-5728 7338.

Stadio Olimpico
Viale dei Gladiatori (northwest of city center, across the Tiber by Monte Mario).

Villagio Globale
Ex-Mattatoio, Lungotevere Testaccio. **Map** 8 D4.
06-5730 0329.

Movies and Theater

MOVIEGOING IS A POPULAR pastime in Rome, with around 40 films playing on an average weekday; theater-goers, however, have far less choice.

The great majority of Roman movie theaters are *prima visione* (first run) and show the latest international films in dubbed versions. The smaller art theaters are more likely to show subtitled versions of foreign films.

Theater productions are performed in Italian whether the plays are national classics or by foreign playwrights. The main theaters offer a selection by great Italian playwrights. There are also performances of traditional cabaret, avant-garde theater and dance theater. Theater tickets cost between €8 and €50 and can generally be bought in advance only by visiting the theater box office in person, or through agencies such as **Gesman** and **Box Office** (*see p341*).

MOVIES (*PRIMA VISIONE*)

THERE ARE OVER 80 *prima visione* movie theaters in the city. The best for decor and comfort are the **Fiamma** (two screens), **Barberini** (three screens) and **Rivoli**.

Foreign films are usually dubbed. Films in the original language are shown at the **Quirinetta** (daily) and on Mondays at the **Nuovo Olimpia** and **Alcazar**.

Tickets for new films generally cost around €7, but a few theaters listed as *prima visione* charge less, namely **Farnese** and **Cinema Roma**. Senior citizens and disabled people are normally entitled to a 30 percent reduction on weekdays. Tickets are reduced in many movie theaters on weekday afternoons and Wednesdays. Check the newspaper or listings magazines such as *Trovaroma* or *Roma c'è* for details (*see p340*).

ART MOVIE THEATERS

THERE ARE TWO main types of art movie theaters in Rome: the *cine-clubs* and the *cinema d'essai*. Both are good for older classics and new foreign films, as well as films by some of the contemporary Italian directors. The *d'essai* theaters now and then show films in the original language (indicated by *v.o.* for *versione originale* in the listings). Try the **Azzurro Scipioni** (one of the few to remain open all summer), **Filmstudio** or

Nanni Moretti's **Nuovo Sacher**. Some of the smaller theaters are called *cine-clubs* and require membership.

The multimedia arts center **Palazzo delle Esposizioni** shows international films in the Sala Rossellini (prior reservations advised).

Cartoons and children's favorites are shown at **Dei Piccoli**. The evening showings for adults, often in the original language, are listed as Dei Piccoli Sera.

The **Tibur**, a small theater with a varied program, is one of the few places where students get a reduction.

ENGLISH-LANGUAGE FILMS

IN ADDITION TO occasional undubbed showings of British, American and Australasian films in art theaters and the **Quirinetta**, Rome has its own English-language movie theater, the **Pasquino**, in Trastevere. Titles change every few days (tickets cost around €6).

SUMMER MOVIES

SOME ROMAN movie theaters have retractable ceilings used in summer, while other theaters close for the summer. The **Nuovo Sacher** has an outdoor arena that is used for summer screenings. Rome also has various summer movie festivals: Cineporto and Massenzio to name but two. These show several films nightly from 9pm until the

small hours, with food and drinks on sale and often live music during the intervals. Cineporto (nightly, Jul–Sept) is held in the Parco della Farnesina, but Massenzio moves around (see listings).

Sci-fi enthusiasts should enjoy the Fantafestival (early Jun), a science fiction, fantasy and horror film festival. The Venezia a Roma event (Sept) gives film buffs the chance to see movies presented at the summer Venice Film Festival.

The listings pages (*see p340*) have details on retrospectives or avant-garde film programs at the **Azzurro Scipioni** and the open-air arts festivals, like Roma-Europa (*see p341*) and Festa dell'Unità (*see p341*).

MAINSTREAM THEATER

THE BACKBONE of Rome's theatrical repertoire is Luigi Pirandello's dramas and comedies by 18th-century Venetian Carlo Goldoni and 20th-century Neapolitan Eduardo de Filippo. Major foreign playwrights are also performed from time to time.

The best classic productions are staged at the **Teatro Argentina**, **Teatro Quirino**, **Teatro Valle**, **Teatro Eliseo** and **Teatro Piccolo Eliseo**. **Teatro Argentina** is state-owned and home of Rome's permanent theater company. Its sister theater, **Teatro India**, stages more innovative works. The **Quirino** and **Valle** host productions from other Italian cities. The latter shows both great Italian classics by famous companies and lesser-known modernist works. Plays at the **Quirino** often feature famous Italian actors. The **Eliseo** and **Piccolo Eliseo** are among the best private theaters.

Agatha Christie and Alfred Hitchcock are often on at the **Teatro Stabile del Giallo**, which runs crime and detective thrillers, while **Teatro Vittoria** goes in for Noël Coward or Neil Simon. At **Teatro Sistina** you can see musicals by visiting foreign companies and shows by popular Italian actors.

CONTEMPORARY THEATER

THE HOMES OF contemporary theater are the **Tordinona**, **Politecnico**, **Ateneo** (situated inside the university), plus a host of small theaters, ingeniously rigged up in cellars, garages, small apartments or tents.

The **Colosseo** hosts some alternative fringe-type productions (known here as *teatro off*), while the **Tordinona**, the **Politecnico** and the **Ateneo** tend to stage works by contemporary authors and occasional avant-garde productions. Some of them, like the **Teatro dei Cocci**, also put on drama school productions.

FOLK, CABARET AND PUPPET THEATER

ROMAN AND Neapolitan folk songs and cabaret can be enjoyed in one of Trastevere's lively tourist-trade restaurants like **Fantasie di Trastevere** or **Meo Patacca**.

Puppet theater is another Roman tradition. Shows take place early in the evening on weekends and sometimes during the week at **Teatro Verde**; **Teatro Mongiovino** and the **Puppet Theatre**, where recitals will be in English if there is enough demand. In summer, traveling Neapolitan and Sicilian marionette companies give special performances.

OPEN-AIR THEATER

THE OPEN-AIR summer theater season usually features Greek and Roman plays at **Ostia Antica** *(see pp270–71)*.

The **Anfiteatro Quercia del Tasso** in the Janiculum park takes its name from the oak tree under which 16th-century poet Tasso used to sit. Comedy shows are staged here in July and September, when the weather permits. In winter the company performs at the **Teatro Anfitrione.**

Nearby is a Neapolitan street puppet theater booth featuring *Pulcinella* (the Italian original of Punch). Shows are usually in the afternoons, with morning shows on Sundays.

DIRECTORY

MOVIES

Alcazar
Via Card. Merry del Val 14.
Map 7 C1.
06-588 0099.

Barberini
Piazza Barberini 52. **Map** 5 B3. 06-482 7707.

Cinema Roma
Piazza Sonnino 37. **Map** 7 C1. 06-581 2884.

Farnese
Piazza Campo de' Fiori 56.
Map 4 E5.
06-686 4395

Fiamma
Via Bissolati 47. **Map** 5 C2. 06-482 7100.

Nuovo Olimpia
Via in Lucina 16. **Map** 12 E1. 06-686 1068.

Quirinetta
Via M Minghetti 4.
Map 5 A3 & 12 E2.
06-679 0012.

Rivoli
Via Lombardia 23. **Map** 5 B2. 06-488 0883.

ART MOVIES

Azzurro Scipioni
Via degli Scipioni 82. **Map** 3 C2. 06-3973 7161.

Dei Piccoli
Viale della Pineta 15. **Map** 5 B1. 06-855 3485.

Filmstudio
Via degli Orti d'Alibert 1c.
Map 4 D4.
06-6819 2987.

Nuovo Sacher
Largo Ascianghi 1. **Map** 7 C2. 06-581 8116.

Palazzo delle Esposizioni
Via Nationale 194. **Map** 5 B4. 06-474 5903.
www.palaexpo.com

Tibur
Via degli Etruschi 36.
06-495 7762.

ENGLISH-LANGUAGE FILMS

Quirinetta
See left.

Pasquino
Piazza S. Egidio 10. **Map** 7 C1. 06-580 3622.

MAINSTREAM THEATER

Teatro Argentina
Largo Argentina 56.
Map 4 F4 & 12 D4.
06-6880 4601.
www.theatrodiroma.it

Teatro Eliseo
Via Nazionale 183.**Map** 5 B4. 06-488 2114.
www.theatroeliseo.it

Teatro India
Lungotevere dei Papareschi.
Map 7 C5.
06-553 0089

Teatro Piccolo Eliseo
Via Nazionale 183. **Map** 5 B4. 06-488 5095.

Teatro Quirino
Via delle Vergini 7.
Map 5 A4 & 12 F2.
06-679 4585.
www.theatroquirino.it

Teatro Sistina
Via Sistina 129. **Map** 5 B2. 06-420 0711.

Teatro Stabile del Giallo
Via Cassia 871.
06-3031 1335.

Teatro Valle
Via del Teatro Valle 21.
Map 4 F4 & 12 D3.
06-6880 3794.
www.theatrovalle.it

Teatro Vittoria
Piazza S. Maria Liberatrice 8.
Map 8 D3.
06-574 0170.

CONTEMPORARY THEATER

Teatro Anfitrione
Via di San Saba 24. **Map** 8 E3. 06-575 0827.

Teatro Ateneo
Viale delle Scienze 3.
Map 6 F3.
06-4991 4435.

Teatro Colosseo
Via Capo d'Africa 5A.
Map 9 A1.
06-700 4932.

Teatro dei Cocci
Via Galvani 69.
Map 8 D3.
06-578 3502.

Teatro Politecnico
Via Tiepolo 13A. **Map** 1 B3. 06-321 9891.

Teatro Tordinona
Via degli Acquasparta 16.
Map 4 E3 & 11 C2.
06-6880 5890.

FOLK, CABARET, PUPPET THEATER

Fantasie di Trastevere
Via di Santa Dorotea 6. **Map** 4 D5. 06-588 1671.

Meo Patacca
Piazza dei Mercanti 30. **Map** 8 D1. 06-581 6198.

Puppet Theatre
Piazza dei Satiri.
06-589 6201.

Teatro Mongiovino
Via Genocchi 15.
06-513 9405.

Teatro Verde
Circonvall. Gianicolense 10.
Map 7 B4.
06-588 2034.

OPEN-AIR THEATER

Anfiteatro Quercia del Tasso
Passeggiata del Gianicolo.
Map 3 C5.
06-575 0827.

Nightclubs

Tʜᴇ ᴄᴇɴᴛᴇʀ ᴏғ ʀᴏᴍᴀɴ ɴɪɢʜᴛ ʟɪғᴇ is no longer the Via Veneto area so effectively portrayed by Fellini in *La Dolce Vita*. The place still offers plenty of venues, but elsewhere more informal and more affordable clubs have emerged, with a more vibrant atmosphere appealing to a younger and more diverse crowd.

With the new clubs come new areas. Venues are always springing up in the historic center and Trastevere, while the once working-class districts of Testaccio and the Via Ostiense have also become new meccas for young Roman clubbers.

Wʜᴀᴛ's Oɴ

As ɪɴ ᴀɴy major city, Rome's nightlife is constantly changing. Roman club-goers are an extremely varied group and most clubs arrange different nights to appeal to different tastes – so it is essential to keep up-to-date on what's happening by checking listings magazines (*see p340*) that hit the newsstands every Thursday. Remember that most city clubs close from mid-June to mid-September, transferring to summer premises along the coast or to one of the open-air venues of the Roman Summer celebrations.

For a more direct source of information, head for the bars around the Via della Pace and Campo de' Fiori areas. At about 10.30pm the narrow streets and piazzas swarm with people and any interesting event will soon become common knowledge. *Buoni* (free or reduced price tickets) may be handed out.

Pʀᴀᴄᴛɪᴄᴀʟɪᴛɪᴇs

Pʀᴇғᴇʀʀᴇᴅ ᴄʟᴜʙʙɪɴɢ nights are Friday and Saturday, when the cars and scooters of revelers block the streets of the city center. Lines at the most popular places can be long at peak entrance time (around midnight) so get there an hour earlier.

Instead of an entrance fee, some clubs require a *tessera* (membership card) which you can buy on the spot. A ticket or *tessera* usually includes a free first drink, but your second could well be expensive – as much as €15.

In smarter places look is all important: for men a jacket and tie are a must and you might even need an invitation or a personal introduction. There is no problem getting into the more youth-oriented discos, with average dress codes ranging from smart casual to decidedly distressed. Beware: all-male groups are never welcome, and in some exclusive clubs neither are unaccompanied men.

Cʟᴜʙs ᴀɴᴅ Bᴀʀs

Aɴ ᴇʟᴇɢᴀɴᴛ ɴɪɢʜᴛ ᴏᴜᴛ could start in one of the American-style bars on the Via Veneto or in smaller *centro storico* bars like **Tartarughino** and **Giulio Passami l'Olio**. If you prefer something more bohemian, go straight to **La Vineria** in Campo de' Fiori or **Bar del Fico** and the **Antico Caffè della Pace**, both a short walk from Piazza Navona.

To brush shoulders with parliamentary under-secretaries and TV starlets, make for **Gilda**, a favorite with the Roman jet set and hangers-on, with its glitzy dancefloor and restaurant. The famous Sixties nightclub, **Jackie O**, has been revamped in lavish style, with a lush interior and an expensive eatery. In a similar vein is the nearby **Club 84** where booking is "strongly advised."

Alien is a safe option for commercial music among Roman twenty-somethings, though **Heaven** is slightly funkier with its marked preference for house. The more traditional disco is at its best at **Piper**, which changes look each season and organizes

imaginative floor shows and other happenings. **Blackout** is a huge disco south of S. Gionvanni, with a large dance area dedicated to rave. There are some disco pubs worth noting too, like city-center venue **Rock Castle**, or some of the smaller hangouts in Trastevere like **Main Frame**. More alternative, and a little farther out, is the **Circolo degli Artisti**, a social center with a large dance floor and frequent live concerts.

Undoubtedly, the coolest clubs for the young and trendy are dotted around Monte Testaccio and along the nearby Via Ostiense. These include **Bush**, a temple to tribal and hip-hop, the **Ex Bocciodromo** (former bowls club), the trend-setting **Mount Gay Club** and **Hangout**, which offers commercial hits and slick nostalgia. **Alpheus** has four separate dance floors with a different beat in each, while the ultra-hip **Goa** serves up everything from trip-hop to bhangra. In the same area, the **Ex-Magazzini** is worth going to if you enjoy indie and breakbeat. An unforget-table place to dance till you drop is **Radio Londra**, designed to look like a WW2 bunker, where dj-skills and free entrance attract huge crowds until the small hours. The Testaccio-Ostiense area offers something for most tastes, with a host of venues which open, have a moment of glory and then decline swiftly, awaiting rebirth.

Gᴀʏ

Tʜᴇʀᴇ ɪs ᴀ ɴᴜᴍʙᴇʀ of bars and clubs for gay men in Rome. Apart from the justly-famous **Alibi** disco, with its explosive mix of house and Seventies hits, there are also city-center bars like the legendary **Hangar** or newcomer **Side**, situated on what has been named Rome's Gay Street. Look out too for the various gay one-nighters, the best being Tuesday's **Gorgeous Goa** night or Friday's Mucca

Assassina (Killer Cow) event at the **Alpheus**, organized by the city's **Mario Mieli** center. This is one of the few mixed evenings in Rome, though younger lesbians may also enjoy Saturday evening's women-only bash at the **Jolie Coeur**. Pride week at the end of June / early July is a time when gay Romans hit the streets for seven days' partying.

JAZZ, SALSA AND AFRICAN SOUNDS

THERE ARE plenty of venues for jazz, from trad and swing to modern fusion (see p344). Many jazz and Latin American clubs combine live music with dancing – and eating and drinking. For South American style music,

Fonclea and **Ariba Ariba** (see p345) or **Alpheus** all pay homage to Latin American and world music, though **Caffè Latino** is probably the best place to visit on the weekend.

CLUBBING IN SUMMER

IN SUMMER when everything closes down in the city, head for the various open-air Roman summer events or don your designer casuals and get down to the nearby seaside resort of Fregene where many of the nightclubs transfer for the June-September period. Take your swimwear too, as much of the fun takes place in and around the pools. Beach venues include **Gilda on the Beach** (now with its

world music offspring Mary'y'Sol) and **Miraggio**, popular with the younger, weekend crowd. Most seaside clubs also have their own fish and seafood restaurants.

AFTER HOURS

MOST ROMAN clubs stay open until 2am or 3am. However, night-owls may find one or two dance havens that see in the dawn, especially during the beach-party season. Before heading off to bed, join other die-hard clubbers (and an exceptionally varied fauna) for a final drink at one of the city's 24-hour bars – or else make for one of the early-morning bakers and feast on sweet breakfast cornetti straight from the oven.

DIRECTORY

Alibi
Via di Monte Testaccio 44.
Map 8 D4.
06-574 3448.

Alien
Via Velletri 13. **Map** 6 D1.
06-841 2212.

Alpheus
Via del Commercio 36/8.
Map 8 D5.
06-574 7826.

Antico Caffè della Pace
Via della Pace 3–7.
Map 4 E4 & 11 C2.
06-686 1216.

Bar del Fico
Piazza del Fico 26/8.
Map 11 B2.
06-686 5205.

Blackout
Via Saturnia 18
Map 9 C3.
06-7049 6791.

Bush
Via Galvani 46.
Map 8 D4.
06-5728 8691.

Caffè Latino
Via di Monte Testaccio 96.
Map 8 D4.
06-5728 8556.

Circolo degli Artisti
Via Casilina Vecchia 42.
Map 10 F1.
06-7030 5684.

Circolo Mario Mieli di Cultura Omosessuale
Via Corinto 5 (off Via Ostiense south of Basilica San Paolo).
06-541 3985.

Club 84
Via Emilia 84. **Map** 5 B2.
06-482 7538.

Ex Bocciodromo
Via di Monte Testaccio 23.
Map 8 D4.
0339-764222.

Ex-Magazzini
Via dei Magazzini Generali 8 bis. **Map** 8 D5.
06-575 8040.

Gilda
Via Mario de' Fiori 97.
Map 5 A2 & 12 F1.
06-678 4838.

Giulio Passami l'Olio
Via di Monte Giordano 28.
Map 11 B2.
06-6880 3288.

Goa
Via Libetta 13 (to the south of Stazione Ostiense).
06-574 8277.

Hangar
Via in Selci 69.
Map 5 C5.
06-488 1397.

Hangout
Via Ostiense 131h (south of Mercati Generali).
06-578 3146.

Heaven
Viale di Porta Ardeatina 119.
Map 9 B5.
06-574 3772.

Jackie O
Via Boncompagni 11.
Map 5 B2.
06-4288 5457.

Jolie Coeur
Via Sirte 5 (north of the city centre).
06-8621 5827.

La Vineria
Campo de' Fiori 15.
Map 4 E4 & 11 C4.
06-6880 3268.

Main Frame
Via Fonte Dell' Olio 5.
Map 7 C1.
06-581 2798.

Mount Gay
Via Galvani 54.
Map 8 D4.
06-574 6013.

Piper
Via Tagliamento 9 (north of the city centre).
06-855 5398.

Radio Londra
Via di Monte Testaccio 67.
Map 8 D4.
06-575 0044.

Rock Castle Café
Via B Cenci 8.
Map 12 D5.
06-6880 7999.

Side
Via Verra 1.
Map 9 B1.
348 692 9472.

Tartarughino
Via della Scrofa 1.
Map 4 F3 & 12 D2.
06-686 4131.

Villaggio Globale
Ex-Mattatoio
Lungotevere Testaccio.
Map 8 D4.
06-5730 0329.

SUMMER CLUBS

Gilda on the Beach
Lungomare di Ponente 11.
Fregene
06-6656 0649.

Miraggio
Lungomare di Ponente 95.
06-6656 0369.

Sports

Do not be surprised if the peace of a Sunday afternoon in Rome is interrupted by people shouting and honking car horns. It simply means that one of the home soccer teams has won at the stadium, and the whole town will vibrate with the excitement.

Soccer is the national sport but other sports also manage to attract a large following. Roman sports fans are never at a loss for varied events and activities.

Times and venues for most spectator sports are listed in *Trovaroma* or *Roma c'è (see p340),* as well as the local sections of *La Gazzetta dello Sport* or *Corriere dello Sport.*

SOCCER

An Italian soccer match is an experience not to miss for the quality of the play and the fun atmosphere, though troublemakers are becoming more common.

Rome has two teams, Roma and Lazio, and they take turns playing at the **Stadio Olimpico** on Sunday afternoons at 3pm, in the Campionato Italiano (Italian championship league).

Seats can be scarce, so get tickets in advance from the stadium (€22 to €78). The cheapest tickets are in the Le Curve stand; middle-range and most expensive, are in Le Gardinate and La Tribuna, respectively.

On Wednesday evenings, there may be international competitions – the UEFA cup or the Coppa dei Campioni (European Championship Cup). In between these, teams battle it out for the national Coppa Italia.

TENNIS

A major event, the International Championships go on at **Foro Italico** for two weeks in May. The world's top tennis stars thrash it out on clay courts at 1 and 8:30pm from Tuesday to Friday, and at 1pm only on weekends. Buy tickets in advance either directly from the Foro Italico or from a ticket agency.

If you wish to play yourself, there are now over 350 tennis clubs in Rome. It is often essential to reserve at least a week in advance, and there is usually a moderate court fee.

Clubs where membership is not required are the **Tennis Lazio** and the **Circolo Tennis Stampa** in northern Rome and the **Oasi di Pace**, just off the Via Appia Antica. The big hotels offer tennis for a reasonable price. **St. Peter's Holiday Inn** requires a small annual membership fee on top of the court price, which includes the gym and the pool (in the summer).

HORSE RACING, TROTTING, AND LEISURE RIDING

Important races include the Derby in May and the Premio Roma in November. There are trotting races at the **Ippodromo di Tor di Valle** and flat races and steeple chases at the **Ippodromo delle Capannelle**.

The International Horse Show is held in May in Piazza di Siena, Villa Borghese *(see p258).* It is organized by the Federazione Italiana Sport Equestri (**FISE**) and is one of the most important social and sporting events in the calendar. The setting makes it a great attraction.

Through the FISE, it may be possible to find a riding club that will take you on a hack in the countryside around Rome, but most do not accept short-term members.

GOLF

Even the most elite golf clubs will accept a touring golfer with a home membership and handicap. Most clubs are closed on Mondays and on weekends, when they host competitions, and guests cannot play. Prices range from €21–€62.

Olgiata Golf Club is open to everybody from Tuesday to Sunday, though it is best to call first if you want to play at the weekend. **Country Club Castel Gandolfo** is the newest club, and **Circolo del Golf di Roma** the oldest and most prestigious. Within the city ring road is the course at the **Sheraton Golf Hotel** (closed Tuesday).

One of the many important competitions on the various golf courses around Rome is the Circolo Gold Roma Coppa d'Oro (Gold Cup) in April.

CAR AND MOTORCYCLE RACING

Formula 1 and Formula 3 races take place on Sundays at **Vallelunga**; be prepared for some expensive entrance fees. Frequently on Saturdays official trials are open to spectators, and on some nonracing Sundays Italy's car designers show new models.

RUGBY

Rugby has taken off recently, particularly since Italy joined the Six Nations tournament. This means that in winter (usually Jan–Feb) there are a couple of international matches in Rome. The home team is drawn against two other member "nations" each year: France, England, Scotland, Ireland or Wales.

ROWING

In mid-June, a British Oxbridge crew challenges the historic Aniene crew to a race taking place alternately on the Thames and the Tiber. The best place to view this from is between the Margherita and the Sant' Angelo bridges. The race usually starts at around 6pm. Another event is the battle between the Roma and Lazio crews, from Ponte Duca d'Aosta to Ponte Risorgimento, on the same variable date as the Roma-Lazio soccer Derby.

SWIMMING

SWIMMING POOLS are few and definitely not geared to the short-term visitor. You often have to pay an expensive membership plus a monthly fee. Most pools also require you to produce a medical certificate assuring your good health, and have lane-only swimming, so check to see if free swimming (*nuovo libero*) is possible. The state-owned pools can be slightly cheaper, but you still have to pay an initial membership fee.

The **Shangri-La Hotel** opens its pool to non-residents in the summer months, as does the **Hilton Hotel**, for a higher entrance fee. The best deal is on Sunday when the sports club and swimming pool **La Margherita** opens to non-members from 10am–1pm for a reasonable charge. **Piscina delle Rose** in EUR is an Olympic-sized pool (often deserted in the morning) open from June to September 9am to 5:30pm during the week, 9am to 7pm at weekends.

HEALTH CLUBS

JUST AS THE swimming pools, Roman health clubs usually require both a membership fee and monthly payments. For a short stay in Rome, it is much more sensible to try the facilities in your hotel, or, if you are willing to pay, head for one of the private clubs. Use of club facilities may be negotiable.

The **Roman Sports Center** welcomes day members for a reasonable price, and you can use the swimming pools, the gym and sauna. The facilities are open 9am–10pm. Be sure to wear Lycra because shorts made from other materials are not allowed.

JOGGING AND CYCLING

ROME'S PERFECT climate and stunning scenery attract thousands of well-dressed joggers and cyclists into the city's many parks. Early weekday mornings or at any time on a Sunday, you'll find the more popular locations

looking more like a high-speed fashion show than a track to work up a sweat. Each March, however, more serious runners take part in the Rome Marathon.

At **Villa Doria Pamphilj** (*see p267*), is an extensive park situated above the Janiculum, where you can choose among three tracks, plenty of open spaces and a network of paths. **Villa Borghese** (*see p258*) is another vast popular place with a running track.

Alternatively, jog under the acacia trees and palms at Villa Torlonia; on the spotlit track at Villa Glori; or combine sport with culture by running the **Via Appia Antica** (*see p265*) branching off into Parco Caffarella. Other favorite places are Viale delle Terme di Caracalla, Circo Massimo, Parco degli Aquedotti and Parco di Colle Oppio.

All of the above are also ideal for cyclists, and you can rent bikes from many places, including **Collalti**, **Via del Corso** and **I Bike Roma**.

DIRECTORY

SOCCER

Stadio Olimpico
Viale dei Gladiatori 2.
06-368 51.

TENNIS

Circolo Tennis Stampa
Piazza Mancini 19.
Map 1 A2.
06-323 2454.

Foro Italico
Viale dei Gladiatori 31.
06-321 9021.

Oasi di Pace
Via degli Eugenii 2.
06-718 4550.

St. Peter's Holiday Inn
Via Aurelia Antica 415.
06-663 1572.

Tennis Lazio
Lungotevere Flaminio 55.
Map 1 A3.
06-361 0349.

HORSE RACING AND RIDING

FISE
Viale Tiziano 74. **Map** 1 A1. 06-3685 8326
www.fise.it

Ippodromo delle Capannelle
Via Appia Nuova 1255.
06-71 67 71.

Ippodromo di Tor di Valle
Via del Mare km 9.
06-52 47 61.
www.ippocity.com

GOLF

Circolo del Golf di Roma
Via Appia Nuova 716a.
06-780 3407.

Country Club Castel Gandolfo
Via di Santo Spirito 13, Castelgandolfo.
06-931 2301.

Olgiata Golf Club
Largo dell'Olgiata 15.
06-3088 9141.

Sheraton Golf
Viale Parco de'Medici 165.
06-655 3477.

CAR RACING

Vallelunga
Autodromo di Roma,
Via Cassia km 345.
06-904 1027.

RUGBY

Federazione Italiana Rugby
Lungotevere Flaminio 80.
06-323 6059.
www.federugby.com

SWIMMING

ARCA Swimming Club
Via Monti Tiburtini 511.
06-451 0552.

Hilton Hotel
Via Cadlolo 101.
06-350 91.

Piscina delle Rose
Viale America 20.
06-5425 2185.

Shangri-La Hotel
Viale Algeria 141.
06-591 6441.

HEALTH CLUBS

Roman Sports Center
Viale del Galoppatoio 33.
Map 5 A1.
06-320 1667.

JOGGING AND CYCLING

Collalti
Via del Pellegrino 82.
Map 4 E4 & 11 B3.
06-6880 1084.

I Bike Roma
Via del Galoppatoio 33.
Map 5 A1.
06-322 5240.

Maratona di Roma
06-406 5064.
www.maratonadiroma.com

Via del Corso
Piazza S. Lorenzo in Lucina.
Map 4 F3 & 12 E1.

CHILDREN'S ROME

ITALIANS LOVE HAVING children around, and you can be sure yours will be made welcome wherever they go. But there are few special facilities for children, and the heat, crowds and lack of clean public bathrooms mean that Rome is not an ideal city for a vacation with those under seven. It does, however, have plenty to offer slightly older children, especially those who may have an inter-

Renaissance cherub from the Villa Farnesina

est in history or art. The temptation may be to wear yourself and your children out by packing too many sights into one day. Plan in advance and leave plenty of time to wander around the city, looking at the unusual fountains and monuments, watching knife grinders at work in the markets and spending hours agonizing over the choice of ice-cream flavors and special pizza toppings.

PRACTICAL ADVICE

IF YOU ARE bringing your children to Rome, try to come in early spring or late autumn, when the weather is good, but not too hot. Easter is best avoided, since the city is more crowded than usual, and you're constantly jostled on packed buses and streets. Where you stay is crucial. A hotel near the Villa Borghese park will give your children plenty of chance to relax and let off steam, though you may end up spending a lot of time and money to get to and from the town center. A hotel in the old center is ideal, so you can easily go back during the day for a rest and a clean bathroom.

Jogging in Villa Borghese

Since hygienic toilets and changing facilities are rare within the city, it is really not advisable to bring a baby to Rome unless you are visiting friends or family. As with many historic cities, Rome may not instantly appeal to all children, but there is plenty to inspire their imaginations. Use this book to make the buildings and history come alive. Children might also enjoy learning a few Italian words and phrases so they can order food and buy things by themselves.

If lingering over drinks on the café terraces is what you enjoy best, bring your offspring something to keep them busy once they have finished with their treat: crayons and paper, a computer game or a Walkman. Alternatively, most other adults are very tolerant of children running around and making a noise while they relax and, if yours are reasonably outgoing, they could join in with the local children playing ball games in early evenings on piazzas like Campo de' Fiori.

If you feel the need for a total break, most hotels will be able to provide a babysitter or help you to contact a qualified baby-sitting agency.

In the event of sickness or an accident, see pages 360–61 for information and a list of emergency numbers.

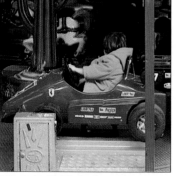

Fairground in the Villa Borghese park

GETTING AROUND

BUMPY COBBLES, narrow streets without sidewalks and overcrowded buses make pushing strollers around the city tiring work. However, mothers with young children are usually allowed ahead in lines and may be offered seats on buses. The Metro is often less crowded. Kids under 3 ft 3 in (1 m) tall travel free on public transportation.

Although the city is not good for cyclists, families with older children could rent bikes to ride along the Tiber on the cycle tracks to the north of the city or to take on a regional train into the country. The bikes, tandems and rickshaws for hire in Villa Borghese are good fun, and the bike rental hut in the Pincio gardens has free baby seats.

Anyone over the age of 14 can ride a scooter under 50 cc, although Rome is not the best place for novices (*see p378*).

A rental bike with free baby seat

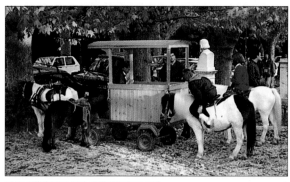

Pony-pulled trains in the Villa Borghese park

EATING OUT

CHILDREN ARE normally warmly welcomed in neighborhood pizzerias and trattorias, and highchairs are often available for toddlers and babies. If there is no highchair, you can expect the waiters to improvise for you with armloads of cushions or telephone directories. Most places are perfectly happy to serve half portions or to let children share meals.

In trattorias it can sometimes be difficult to be exactly sure what a certain dish contains (especially when there is no menu, and the dishes of the day are reeled off, usually at top speed, by the waiter), so picky eaters are likely to be happier in pizzerias *(see pp318–21)*. Here they can choose their own topping (remember that *prosciutto,* which is usually translated in menus as ham, is cured). The most entertaining pizzerias for kids are the old-fashioned ones where they can watch the chefs pound, stretch and flip the pizza dough. The best places get busy from around 8:30pm, so it is wise to go early to avoid having to get in line. If all else fails, there are many branches of McDonald's.

PICNICS

PICNICS IN THE parks are ideal, and shopping for the food is often half the fun. There is no problem finding small cartons of fruit juice and branded canned drinks, but these are expensive unless you go to a supermarket – the branch of Oviesse on Viale Trastevere is the most convenient. Water from the drinking fountains is potable, so it is worth carrying plastic cups around.

In addition to picnic food from bakeries and markets, there are lots of scrumptious takeout foods. Many of them are appealing but messy, so it is wise to bring paper napkins. Try deep-fried fruit and vegetables from Cose Fritte on Via di Ripetta and *supplì al telefono,* rice croquettes with a gooey string of mozzarella inside, from *pizza al taglio* or *pizza rustica* outlets. A *tramezzino* comes quite close to an American sandwich, but if your kids are miserable without peanut butter, you can find it (and other foreign foods) at Castroni on Via Cola di Rienzo.

Feeding pigeons on Piazza Navona

ICE CREAM

ROME, OF COURSE, is famous for ice cream; you and your children are likely to be tempted at every turn. Real ice-cream fans may even want to plan their day's sight-seeing around one of the best *gelaterie (see pp319–21)*. It is far cheaper to buy either a cone or tub of ice cream to eat in the street, but in some of the more traditional places it is worth paying to sit down. At Fassi, they have an old-fashioned ice cream-making machine on display, and at Giolitti, you can enjoy gargantuan sundaes in the elegant parlor *(see p109)*.

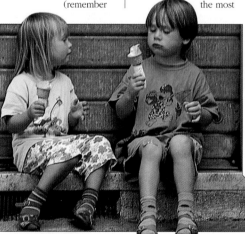

Investigating some of the hundreds of Italian ice-cream flavours

Sightseeing with Children

Entrance to the Villa Borghese Zoo

GENERAL TIPS

ROME DOES NOT have many museums with the sort of hands-on exhibits and activities that many other cities provide for children. However, Bernini's marble elephant *(see p108)* and the fat *facchino*, or porter *(p107)*, delight most children. The Capuchin cemetery at Santa Maria della Concezione *(p254)*, the catacombs *(pp264–6)* and the Mamertine Prison *(p91)* will grab more ghoulish imaginations, and children will enjoy putting their hands into the Bocca della Verità *(p202)*.

Look for details like the dirty toenails on figures in Caravaggio's paintings; the Etruscan votives, which were offered to the gods, at the Villa Giulia *(pp262–3)*; and the illusory collapsing ceiling in the Chiesa Nuova, as well as the fake dome of Sant' Ignazio di Loyola *(see p106)*.

Museums your children will enjoy include the Museo delle Arti e Tradizioni Popolari at EUR, with its antique toys and nativity scene *(p266)*, and the Museo delle Mura, which explores the length of the Aurelian Wall *(p196)*.

Among the churches, St. Peter's, where they can climb to the top of the dome *(see p230)*, and San Clemente, where they can descend to the underground mithreum *(see pp186–7)*, are most fun. At the Vatican children will like the statues and mosaics in the Animal Gallery and the Sistine Ceiling *(p246)*, especially when they find out that Michelangelo had to paint it hunched up on a scaffolding platform.

ANCIENT RUINS

THE ANCIENT RUINS best appreciated by children are the Colosseum *(see pp92–5)*, and Trajan's Markets *(see pp 88–9)*. You can still make out what both these buildings looked like from their remains. The scant ruins of the Forum and Palatine, on the other hand, may not appeal so strongly. Ostia Antica, where the remains include a theater, shop and 20-seater public toilet, is much more likely to interest them *(see pp270–71)*.

Mosaic from the Vatican

MOSAICS

THERE ARE SCORES of vivid, sometimes quirky, mosaics in buildings all over Rome. Many of these are particularly appealing to children. Details in the mosaics range from brilliantly colored flowers, leaves, animals and buildings (in the churches of San Clemente, Santa Prassede and Santa Maria in Trastevere, *see p186, p171 and pp212–13*) to the debris of a banquet (in the Vatican's Museo Gregorio Profano, *see pp234–5*).

Model trains in Villa Borghese

ENTERTAINMENT

ROME'S CULTURAL offerings for children are a bit sparse. To find out what's on, check the movie pages of the newspapers and the listings in *Trovaroma, Roma c'è, Wanted in Rome* and entertainment websites *(see p340)*. Most theaters and cinemas have reduced entry fees for children, but these are only useful if your children can speak Italian.

Language is not a barrier in cartoons and puppet shows. There are cartoons at Villa Borghese's Cinema dei Piccoli and traditional puppet shows every afternoon except Wednesday up on the Janiculum hill. Otherwise, try the cartoons on TV at your hotel!

Stall at the Christmas toy fair on Piazza Navona

Resting on the curb side

One of the most appealing times for children to be in Rome is over Christmas, when Piazza Navona hosts the Christmas toy fair, where stalls sell toys and sweets.

PARKS

VILLA BORGHESE *(see p258)* has rowboats to rent; pony-cart rides; bikes to rent; a mini-cinema; a small fun fair; and a zoo. Villa Celimontana *(see p193)* has bike trails, and open-air theater performances in the summer. The old-fashioned amusement park LUNEUR at EUR *(see p266)* can be fun. Also in EUR is the Piscina delle Rose, a swimming pool open in the summer *(see p351)*. The Bomarzo Monster Park, 60 miles (95 km) north of Rome, was built in the 16th century for a mad duke.

Children can clamber over its giant stone monsters.

TOYS

A VISIT TO a Roman toyshop can be a lot of fun. **Città del Sole** sells a range of delightful educational toys and games, while **Al Sogno** is a wonderland of stuffed animals.

Città del Sole
Via della Scrofa 65. **Map** 4 F3 & 12 D2.
📞 06-687 5404.

Al Sogno
Piazza Navona 53. **Map** 4 E4 & 11 C3.
📞 06-686 4198.

CHILDREN'S CLOTHES

Italians adore dressing their children up, and on Sunday afternoons in particular, you are likely to encounter young children dressed as if they had walked straight out of a costume drama: girls in frills and flounces and boys in velvet breeches or knee-length shorts.

Many shops sell beautifully handcrafted children's shoes and clothes – the downside is that they can often be expensive and impractical: dry-clean-only clothes are common, and shoes are not made for mud.

Lavori Artigianili Femminili sells handmade silk and wool clothes for children up to eight. **Baby House** offers *haute couture* for children, including clothes by top designers, and **Bennetton** sell smart casuals.

Baby House
Via Cola di Rienzo 117. **Map** 3 C2.
📞 06-321 4291.

Bennetton
Via Cesare Battista 129. **Map** 5 A4 & 12 F3. 📞 06-6992 4010.

Lavori Artigianali Femminili
Via Capo le Case 6. **Map** 5 A3 & 12 F1.
📞 06-679 2992.

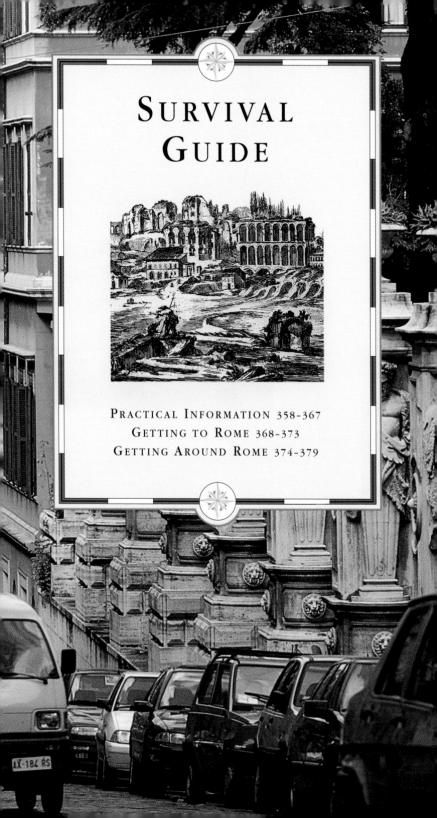

SURVIVAL
GUIDE

PRACTICAL INFORMATION

Romans often seem unconcerned by the priceless art treasures and ancient ruins which lie casually among the buildings and workings of their hectic 20th-century city. Visitors nearly always find these wonders very exciting, but it is not always easy to make the most of them. Relaxed local attitudes make for hundreds of variations in opening hours. Many places close for several hours over lunch and reopen in the late afternoon; some museums are open in the mornings only. Bank and shop hours can be just as difficult to pin down. On a more positive note, many of the main sights are within easy walking distance of one another. Start your day early and wear comfortable shoes for the Roman cobblestones. It can be a delightfully informal city to visit, but remember to observe dress rules to cover up in churches, since this is one area where the Italians are very strict.

MUSEUMS AND MONUMENTS

Many museums are now open all day, although most close on Mondays. If you are particularly keen to see a specific monument or museum, make sure it is open before you set out. Many museums don't allow visitors to enter in the last half an hour or so before they close.

L'Evento, **the guide to exhibitions**

There is usually an admission charge for museums and monuments, although some are free on Sundays. Many museums offer a reduced entrance fee for children under 18, students with the appropriate ID and senior citizens from the European Union. If you don't see any reductions advertised it is always worth asking. Entrance to all churches is free, and many contain works of art that are worthy of the world's greatest museums. Some of Rome's sights are accessible only on personal application or by written appointment. Examples include Nero's Aqueduct or the gardens at the Vatican.

The *Area by Area* section of this guide gives opening times for each sight and tells you whether there is an admission charge. The **APT** publishes a useful booklet called *L'Evento*, which gives details of current exhibitions at Rome's main museums and galleries.

Typical traffic congestion in Via delle Quattro Fontane

TOURIST INFORMATION

Pick up details of special tours here at the main tourist office (**APT**). APT will also help with accommodations *(see p289).* Information kiosks run by the Comune di Roma have English-speaking staff providing free maps, leaflets and advice. Or ring the **Rome City Council Tourist Information Call Center** for information in English. Besides the official tourist offices, good travel agents such as **CIT**, **Wagons Lits** or the **American Express** office can also be helpful to visitors. For information on Italian cities and areas outside Rome, contact **ENIT** (the National Tourist Board), who have offices in all the main cities.

A word of warning: prices and opening times can be closed for what seem to be unbelievably long periods of restoration (*chiuso per restauro*) or because of a strike (*sciopero*).

ENTE NAZIONALE ITALIANO PER IL TURISMO

ENIT logo

An electric minibus: useful for the historic center

ENTERTAINMENT INFORMATION

THE WEEKLY *Trovaroma*, in the Thursday edition of *La Repubblica*, and *Roma c'è*, published on Wednesdays, are the main guides to what's on. English listings are also in *Wanted in Rome*. Full entertainment information can be found on page 340.

Trovaroma

GUIDED TOURS

SEVERAL COMPANIES offer tours with English-speaking guides; these include **CIT**, **American Express**, **Green Line Tours**, **Carrani Tours**, **Rome Revealed Tours** and **Through Eternity Tours**. Full-day city tours including lunch cost around €75; half-day tours around €30. Alternatively the No. 110 ATAC bus passes many of the main sights on a 3-hour circuit. The journey costs around €8 and leaves from Termini every 30 minutes between 10am and 6pm. Tour guides can be hired at many of the major sights, such as the Roman Forum *(see pp78–87)*. Employ only the official guides and establish the fee in advance; they charge around €50 for a half-day tour.

ATAC, the Rome bus company

VISITING CHURCHES

MANY OF ITALY'S churches are very dark, but they usually have light meters to illuminate chapels and works of art. The meters are coin-operated. Recorded information in several languages is often available at coin-operated machines. Dress codes are firmly upheld in churches; St. Peter's *(see pp230–33)* is especially strict – you cannot wear shorts.

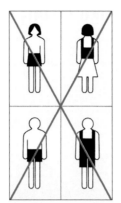
Unacceptable dress in church: both sexes should cover torsos and upper arms

ETIQUETTE

PEOPLE IN ROME are generally courteous and friendly to foreign visitors. Italians are delighted at any effort to speak their language, so it is worth learning a few phrases *(see p431)*. Italians tend to drink only with meals and are unlikely to be seen drunk – obvious drunkenness is frowned upon. Smoking is common in bars, restaurants and on streets, but banned on public transportation.

TIPPING

FOREIGNERS ARE expected to tip, although Italians themselves don't always do so. Leave a few coins in bars or cafés; in restaurants where service is not included, leave around 10 percent. Keep change handy for taxi drivers, sacristans, chambermaids, doormen and porters.

ROME FOR THE DISABLED

ROME is not particularly well organized to cater for the disabled. Look before crossing at traffic lights and pedestrian crossings – not all vehicles stop when you expect. The seriously disabled will need help getting around. Ramps, elevators and modified toilets exist in an increasing number of places, including Termini station and the Colosseum. It may be worth asking before entering restaurants, since some have wheelchair access to the dining area but not to the toilet. If you have no escort, consider a specially designed package tour, or contact an organization for disabled travelers before you set off. The Vatican Museums, Sistine Chapel and St. Peter's are all accessible by wheelchair. The Vatican Museums recently received an EU award for improving accessibility for the disabled and staff offer help if needed.

Public Toilets

PUBLIC TOILETS are few and far between. There are clean ones by the Colosseum (with facilities for the disabled), at St. Peter's and in the Rinascente store *(see p323)*. Most cafés let you use theirs if you ask. Take your own paper.

USEFUL ADDRESSES

American Express
Piazza di Spagna 38. **Map** 5 A2.
(06-676 41.

APT
Via Parigi. **Map** 5 C3.
Open 9am–7pm.
(06-4889 9253.

Carrani Tours
Via V. E. Orlando 95. **Map** 5 C3.
(06-488 0510.

CIT
Piazza della Repubblica 65.
Map 5 C3. (06-462 0311.
W www.citgroup.net

ENIT
Via Marghera 2. **Map** 6 E3.
(06-497 11.

Green Line Tours
Via Farini 5A. **Map** 6 D4.
(06-481 5764.

Rome City Council Tourist Information Call Center
(06-3600 4399.
W www.romaturismo.it

Rome Revealed Tours
(06-9016 0167.
W www.tiscali.it/romerevealed

Through Eternity Tours
Via Sinuessa 80. **Map** 9 C3.
(06-700 9336.
W www.througheternity.com

Personal Security and Health

O N THE WHOLE, Rome is a safe, unthreatening place for visitors, but petty street crime is a problem. Do not carry more money than you need for the day and leave other valuables or documents in a hotel safe. Cameras are less likely to be snatched if they are in a carrier bag rather than an obvious case. Take particular care in crowded places, such as stations, or on full buses, and steer clear of bands of innocent-looking children – they may be skillful professional pickpockets.

Pharmacy sign

ADVICE FOR VISITORS

T AKE OUT ADEQUATE property insurance before you travel (it is difficult to arrange once you are in Italy), and guard your belongings all the time once you are in Rome. Some hotels have personal safes in the bedrooms. You can program these with your own number. (Do not use your date of birth; it is on your passport and registration slip.) To be prepared for all eventualities, keep a separate photocopy of all your vital documents, such as your passport, to minimize the problem of replacing them, and take a spare photograph or two. Travelers' checks are the safest way to carry large amounts of cash. Keep the receipts separate from the checks for a refund in case you lose them.

Be wary of bag-snatchers on mopeds who operate on quiet streets. Carry your bag on the side away from the road or use a discreet money belt or a securely fastened,

Mounted police

long-strapped shoulder bag. Equipment like video cameras should be disguised. Pickpockets (sometimes children) adopt highly sophisticated distraction techniques with cards or newspapers while they deftly separate you from your possessions in seconds. Be especially cautious in market places or on public transportation. Bus route No. 64, between Termini station and the Vatican, is notorious for pickpockets.

Thefts from cars are common. Nothing portable like a jacket or bag should be left visible inside a car on Rome's streets, and do not carry luggage on a roof rack. The streets east and south of Termini station and around the Colosseum are well known for prostitution and drug-peddling and are unsavory at night.

Women traveling alone (or even in small groups) may need to take extra care. Italian society is male-dominated, and women who are out without male escorts attract more attention than they do in much of the rest of Europe and North America.

Beware of unauthorized minicab drivers, who are probably not insured and frequently overcharge. They operate in particular near the airport, waiting to profit from

Distinctive *carabinieri* motorcycle

***Carabiniere* – a member of the military police**

***Carabiniere* in traffic police uniform**

Municipal policeman directing traffic

new arrivals. Avoid unofficial vendors and tour guides; instead stick to the official tourist agencies (see p289 and pp358–9).

Police car

POLICE

THE VIGILI URBANI, or municipal police, wear blue uniforms in winter and white in summer and can most often be seen regulating traffic. The *carabinieri* are the military police, in red striped trousers. They deal with everything from fine-art thefts to speeding offenses. *La polizia* (state police) wear blue uniforms with white belts and berets. Any of these should be able to help you.

Green cross ambulance

Italian fire engine

MEDICAL MATTERS

NO INOCULATIONS are needed for Rome, but take mosquito repellent and sun screen in the summer. The Tiber is polluted, but the water from taps and street fountains is piped straight from the hills, and is fresh and palatable.

Non-EU visitors should take out insurance to cover everything, including emergencies. For insurance claims, make sure you keep all receipts for medical treatment and any medicines prescribed.

For urgent medical attention, contact the First Aid (Pronto Soccorso) department of a main hospital such as **Policlinico**

Carabinieri in dress uniform

Umberto I, Ospedale San Giacomo or Ospedale Fatebenefratelli or check the Yellow Pages (Pagine Gialle) for a doctor (medico) or dentist (dentista). For children, the Ospedale Pediatrico Bambino Gesù is renowned.

English speaking doctors can be found at the **Rome American Hospital** or by looking in the English Yellow Pages, available at some hotel receptions and international bookshops. Pharmacists post late-opening rosters on their doors (several stay open all night), and can usually supply the local equivalent of foreign medicines. The **Vatican Pharmacy** stocks some American and British pharmaceutical products.

Many of the words for minor complaints and remedies are similiar in Italian: for example *lassativo* (laxative) and *aspirina* (aspirin).

Ospedal Fatebenefratelli
Piazza Fatebenefratelli 2. **Map** 4 C4.
[06-683 7299.

Ospedal Pediatrico Bambino Gesù
Piazza S. Onofrio 4.
Map 3 C4.
[06-685 9235.

Ospedal San Giacomo
Via Canova 29. **Map** 4 F2.
[06-362 61.

Policlinico Umberto I
Viale del Policlinico 155. **Map** 6 F2.
[06-499 71.

Rome American Hospital
Via Emilio Longoni 69. **[** 06-225 51.

Vatican Pharmacy
Via di Porta Angelica.
Map 3 C2. **[** 06-686 4146.

LOST PROPERTY

FOR ITEMS LOST on a bus or Metro, contact the numbers below. Otherwise, ask at a police station. To make an insurance claim, report your loss to a police station and get a signed form. For lost passports, contact your embassy or consulate; for lost travellers' cheques, the issuing company's office (see p362).

Commissariato di Polizia

Lost Property on Buses
[06-581 6040. **Open** 8.30am–5.30pm Mon–Fri.

Lost Property on the Metro
Line A **[** 06-487 4308. **Open** 9am–noon Mon, Wed & Fri. Line B **[** 06-5753 2264. **Open** 7.30am–6.30pm Mon–Sat.

EMERGENCIES

Ambulance
[118 (free from any telephone).

Automobile Club d'Italia
[803116.

Fire
[115 (free from any telephone).

General SOS
[113 (free from any telephone).

Police
[112 (Carabinieri) (free from any telephone) or 06-4686 (Polizia).

Samaritans
[06-7045 4444.
Line open 1–10pm daily.

Traffic Police
[06-676 91.

Banking and Local Currency

MONEY SERVICES are not always fast in Rome. Transactions can involve considerable paperwork and a lot of waiting around. On the whole, bank exchange rates are more favorable than those in travel agents and hotels – the deal just takes longer to complete. Small change is indispensable, since coins are needed for telephones, tips and for illuminating works of art and chapels in churches *(see p359)*.

Eagle sculpture on the Ministry of Finance

CHANGING MONEY

IT IS BEST to have a few euros when you arrive, so you won't have to change money immediately. However, there are increasing numbers of convenient electronic exchange machines at arrival points. There are now several throughout the city too. Multilingual instructions are available. You simply feed in bills of a foreign currency, and should get some euros back. Exchange rates vary from place to place. The Banco di Santo Spirito office at Fiumicino airport offers reasonable rates.

For the best rates, change money at a bank (look for the sign *Cambio*). Hotels tend to give poor rates, even if they charge modest commissions. At the Vatican Museums *(see p235)*, you aren't charged any commission. The American Express office *(see p359)* offers good rates and is open on Saturday mornings. Cardholders may withdraw up to $1,000 (or £500) a week from the cash machine, but you have to pay a fee for this service and need to organize a PIN (personal identification number) linked to your account before you travel.

Automatic exchange machine

CREDIT CARDS

CREDIT CARDS, which used to be regarded with great suspicion in Italy, are now much more widely accepted in hotels, restaurants and shops. All major credit and charge cards (American Express, Access/MasterCard, Visa, Diners Card) are well known. Banks and cash dispensers are more likely to accept Visa cards for cash advances, but Access (MasterCard) is accepted by many retail outlets in Italy. Take both if you have them. Paying for anything in foreign currency will almost always be expensive.

Some restaurants and shops set a minimum expenditure level, below which they will not accept credit card payment. Check you have some cash just in case.

TRAVELERS' CHECKS

IF YOU OPT for travelers' checks, choose a well-known name such as Thomas Cook or American Express, or take those issued through a major bank. Most issuers charge 1 percent commission on travelers' checks. Get some small denominations, so you won't be left with huge amounts of euros at the end of your trip. But don't forget that the minimum commission charged for each transaction (and the amount of time involved) may make changing small amounts of money uneconomical.

Always record the travelers' check numbers and refund addresses separately from the checks themselves in case they are stolen. Some places will charge you for each check.

Check the exchange rates before you travel and decide whether euro, dollar or sterling checks are more appropriate.

OPENING HOURS

BANKS ARE USUALLY open 8:30am–1:20pm and 3–4:30pm Mon–Fri, but opening times vary and banks are closed for public holidays and at weekends.

Bureaux de Change have more generous opening times, similar to shop hours. The exchange offices at Termini station *(see p372)* are also open on Sundays.

USING BANKS

LINES IN BANKS can be long and the form-filling involved in changing money can take up a lot of valuable vacation time. You usually have to line up first at the *cambio*, then at the *cassa* to obtain your cash. Take some form of identification with you, such as a passport. Metal objects may set off emergency detectors as you enter.

Exchange office at one of the Italian national banks

One of the major Italian banks

The Bank of Rome, which has branches in other Italian cities

THE EURO

TWELVE COUNTRIES have replaced their traditional currencies, such as the Italian lire, with the euro. Austria, Belgium, Finland, France, Germany, Greece, Ireland, Italy, Luxembourg, Netherlands, Portugal and Spain chose to join the new currency; the UK, Denmark and Sweden stayed out, with an option to review their situation. The euro was intro-duced on January 1, 1999, but only for banking purposes. Bills and coins came into circulation on January 1, 2002. A transition period allowed both euros and local currencies to be used simultaneously, but all the old currencies were phased out by mid-2002. All euro bills and coins can be used anywhere inside the participating member states.

Bank Notes

Euro bank notes have seven denom-inations. The 5-euro bill (gray in color) is the smallest, followed by the 10-euro bill (pink), 20-euro bill (blue), 50-euro bill (orange), 100-euro bill (green), 200-euro bill (yellow) and 500-euro bill (purple). All bills show the stars of the European Union.

5 euros

10 euros

20 euros

50 euros

100 euros

200 euros

500 euros

2 euros   1 euro   50 cents   20 cents   10 cents

Coins

The euro has eight coin denominations: 1 euro and 2 euros; 50 cents, 20 cents, 10 cents, 5 cents, 2 cents and 1 cent. The 2- and 1-euro coins are both silver and gold in color. The 50-, 20- and 10-cent coins are gold. The 5-, 2- and 1-cent coins are bronze.

5 cents

2 cents

1 cent

Communications

IN RECENT YEARS the telephone system in Rome has undergone a number of major upheavals. Many phone numbers have been changed and a new generation of equipment has been installed alongside the old, which is in the process of being phased out. Since the deregulation of the system, Albacom and Infostrada phones compete with the national Telecom Italia service. It is important to note that any telephone number dialled in Italy – even a local number – needs to have the full relevant local code (including the zero) dialled in front of it.

Telephone company logo

CALL CHARGES

THE CHEAPEST times to phone within Italy are between 6:30pm and 8am Monday to Friday, after 1pm Saturday and all day Sunday. Check what time of day is best if you are making international calls: time variations throughout the world can make quite a difference.

As a general rule, it is considerably cheaper to dial direct for international calls rather than going through the operator or making collect or credit card calls.

Telephone calls from hotel rooms are usually very expensive and are sometimes marked up by as much as several hundred percent. Normally telephone calls cost more from Italy than they do from either the UK or the US.

TELEPHONE OFFICES

TELEPHONE OFFICES are run by Telecom Italia and private "call centers," and they offer a convenient way of making long-distance or private calls. There are several metered telephones, each in its own sound-proofed booth. An assistant will assign you a booth, and meter your call once you have been connected to the number you want. You do not need large amounts of change as you pay at the desk when you have finished. There is no extra charge for this service, but opening hours do not always coincide with Italy's cheapest-rate calling times. Those in Termini Station are an exception. The Telecom Italia office on the main concourse is open from 8am to 8pm daily and also offers fax and internet services while the Call Net office in the forum shopping complex below is open from 6am to midnight daily.

To send an international telegram, you can either go to a main post office or dial 186 and dictate it over the telephone.

USING PUBLIC TELEPHONES

IN THE WAKE OF the cell phone revolution, demand for public telephones has decreased considerably. However, there are still plenty of payphones around the city. New-style payphones are rounded, steel models, and from these you can dial long-distance and most inter-national calls direct. These phones only take telephone cards (ask for a *scheda* or *carta telefonica),* available in several denominations.

You may also see some orange payphones which take both cards and coins, but these are being phased out. If you do use one of these older payphones to make a long-distance direct-dial call, make sure you have plenty of change ready. If you do not put enough coins in to start with, the telephone retains your money and disconnects you.

USING A TELECOM ITALIA CARD TELEPHONE

1 Lift the receiver and wait for the dial tone.

2 Insert a phone card in the slot.

3 The display shows how much credit is left.

4 Dial the number and wait to be connected.

5 If you still have credit and want to make a second call, press the "follow-on call" button.

To use a card, break off the marked corner and insert, arrow first.

Telephone cards are available from shops, bars and tobacconists displaying the black-and-white T sign. Break off the marked corner, insert the card arrow first, and the value of the unexpired units will show on a display window. After your call, the card can be retrieved and reused until it expires.

For long-distance calls you can also go to a call center to find a metered phone *(telefono a scatti)*. Ask the attendant if you can phone and the call will be metered. You pay afterwards.

Public telephone sign

ELECTRONIC COMMUNICATIONS

For those wishing to send and check e-mails there are an increasing number of Internet cafés springing up

throughout Rome, where, for a generally modest fee, you can access your account or go online to search the Internet. These establishments offer a variety of refreshments ranging from alcohol and coffee to light snacks. Most are close to the center and therefore easily accessible to visitors.

Aexis
Via Marghera 11B. **Map** 6 E3.
06-6000 7425.

easyEverything
Piazza Barberini. **Map** 5 B3.
06-4290 3388. **Open** *24 hours.*

Internet Café
Via Cavour 213. **Map** 5 C4. 06-4782 3051. **Open** *9am–1am. daily*

The Netgate
Piazza Firenze 25. **Map** 12 D1.
06-689 3445.
Open *10.30am–9pm Mon–Sat.*
Forum Termini, Piazza Cinquecento.
Map 6 D3. 06-8740 6008.
Open *6am–11.30pm daily.*

Sending Letters

The Italian postal service is not especially efficient and it is said that letters traveled faster in the days of the old Roman Empire than they do today, in spite of modern technology. For postcards, the service is usually fine but it is particularly slow in August

Rome letters Other destinations

Vatican postage stamps

Post office sign

when it can take up to a month for a postcard to reach the UK. For important items, it is better to use the new "priority post" *(posta prioritaria)* with its own stamp which can be bought, like ordinary stamps *(francobolli)*, at tobacconists, as well as in post offices. For urgent items, use the post office's express or registered service.

Sub-post office hours are generally from around 8:30am until 2pm (8:30am–noon on

VATICAN MAIL
The Vatican postal service costs the same as the state post, but is faster. Buy cards and stamps at the post office near the Vatican Museums entrance, or in Piazza San Pietro. Letters bearing Vatican stamps can only be posted in blue Vatican post boxes.

Saturdays and the last day of the month), but main offices stay open until well into the evening for some services (such as registered mail). Italian mail boxes are red, though some, for foreign destinations (marked *estero*), are blue.

POSTE RESTANTE

Letters and parcels which are to be picked up at the post office are sent care of *(c/o)* Palazzo delle Poste, Roma, *Fermo Posta*. Print the surname clearly in block capitals and underline it to make sure the letters are filed correctly. To collect your post, you have to show your passport and pay a small charge. American Express *poste restante* is free to clients.

Postage stamps Airmail sticker

Additional Information

Fiumicino airport, point of arrival for most visitors to Rome

CUSTOMS AND IMMIGRATION

EUROPEAN UNION nationals and citizens of the US, Canada, Australia and New Zealand do not need visas for stays of up to 3 months. All visitors are required to present a full passport on entry and, officially, need to declare their presence to the Italian police within 8 days of arrival. If you are staying in a hotel or on a campsite, this will be done for you. Otherwise, contact the local **Questura** (police station).

Anyone wishing to stay for more than 3 months (8 days for citizens from countries other than those mentioned above) will have to work their way through complicated Italian bureaucracy to obtain a *permesso di soggiorno* (permit to stay). You can apply for a permit at any main police station, *Questura*. Depending on your motive for staying, you must apply for either a permit to work *(lavoro)* or a permit to study *(studio)*. Visitors should always check requirements before traveling.

Duty-free allowances are as follows. Residents of the EU can bring duty-free goods into Italy for their own use: 800 cigarettes, 200 cigars, 400 cigarillos, 1 kg of smoking tobacco, 10 liters of spirits, 90 liters of wine and 100 liters of beer. Limits for non-EU citizens are stricter: 400 cigarettes, 100 cigars, 200 cigarillos or 500 grams of tobacco, 1 liter of spirits or 2 liters of wine and 50 grams of perfume. To find out what you can take back from Italy to a non-EU country, contact that country's customs department. The refund system for Value Added Tax (IVA in Italy) for non-EU residents is very complex *(see p323)*.

Questura
[C] *06-46 86.*

Students on the steps of Santa Maria Maggiore

STUDENT INFORMATION

AN INTERNATIONAL Student Identity Card (ISIC) or a Youth International Educational Exchange Card (YIEE) are worth having for reductions on museum and other charges. Contact the **Centro Turistico Studentesco** for general student information. The **Associazione Italiana Alberghi per la Gioventù** (the Italian YHA) has four hostels in the city. **Wasteels** has information on rail discounts for students.

ISIC card

Associazione Italiana Alberghi per la Gioventù
Via Cavour 44. **Map** 3 D3.
[C] *06-487 1152.* [FAX] *06-488 0492.*
[W] www.hostels-aig.org

Centro Turistico Studentesco
Via Genova 16. **Map** 5 C3.
[C] *06-462 0431. Also branches at Termini station (06 4411 1519) and*

Corso Vittorio Emanuele 297
(06-6830 7883).

Wasteels
Termini station. **Map** 6 D3.
[C] *06-482 5537.*

CATHOLIC SERVICES

FOR MANY CATHOLICS, a visit to Rome means an audience with the pope. General audiences are usually held every Wednesday at 11am (10am in hot weather) in St. Peter's Square, the Audiences room, or at the summer residence at Castel Gandolfo. To attend an audience, apply by fax to the **Prefettura della Casa Pontificia** *(see p231)*. Rome travel agencies may be able to arrange an audience as part of a coach tour during your stay. There is no charge. Mass is held daily in the main churches of Rome (High Mass is on Sunday). Churches where confession is heard include St. Peter's *(see pp230–33)*, San Giovanni in Laterano *(pp182–3)*, San Paolo fuori le Mura *(p267)*, Santa Maria Maggiore *(pp172–3)*, the Gesù *(pp114–15)*, Santa Sabina *(p204)* and Sant'Ignazio *(p106)*. English-speaking Catholic churches include San Silvestro (Piazza San Silvestro) and San Tommaso di Canterbury (Via Monserrato 45).

Prefettura della Casa Pontificia
Città del Vaticano. **Map** 3 B3.
[C] [FAX] *06-6988 5863.*

Pope John Paul II during an audience in St Peter's Square

OTHER RELIGIOUS SERVICES

Anglican
All Saints, Via del Babuino 153.
Map 4 F2. **C** 06-3600 1881.

American Episcopal
St. Paul's, Via Napoli 58. **Map** 5 C3.
C 06-488 3339.

Jewish
Sinagoga, Lungotevere Cenci.
Map 4 F5 & 12 D5. **C** 06-684 00661.

Methodist
Via XX Settembre 123. **Map** 5 C3.
C 06-481 4811.

Mosque
Viale della Moschea 85 (Parioli district).
Map 2 F1. **C** 06-808 2167.

Presbyterian
St. Andrew's, Via XX Settembre 7.
Map 5 C3. **C** 06-482 7627.

The Mosque in Parioli

SIGHTSEEING PERMITS

To visit certain sights in Rome, you need to obtain a written permit and book your visit in advance, particularly for archaeological sites, which may sometimes be closed during excavations. Write to the address below, stating your name, the number of people in your party, the reason you wish to visit the sight (for example, study or tourism) and the days you are able to make the visit. Try to include a contact phone number in Rome. It is best to send the request by fax. Call a few days before to confirm your visit.

Ufficio Monumenti Antichi e Scavi
Via del Portico d'Ottavia 29. **Map** 4 F5
& 12 E5. **C** 06-6710 3819. **FAX** 06-689 2115. **W** www.romacultura.org

Newspapers available in Rome

NEWSPAPERS, TV, RADIO

Rome's main newspapers are *La Repubblica* and *Il Messaggero*. British and American newspapers are readily available, as are the *International Herald Tribune* and the *Guardian Europe*. The state TV channels are RAI Uno, Due and Tre, matched by four private channels. The advent of satellite and cable TV means there are European channels in many languages, plus sport and CNN news in English. The BBC World Service is broadcast on 648, 6195 and 12095MHz (shortwave) depending on the time of day. Vatican Radio on 93.3MHz and 105MHz (FM) broadcasts news in English.

EMBASSIES AND CONSULATES

If you lose your passport, or need other help, contact your national embassy or consulate as listed below.

Australia
Via Alessandria 215. **C** 06-85 27 21.
W www.australianembassy.it

Canada
Via Zara 30. **C** 06-44 59 81.
W www.canada.it

New Zealand
Via Zara 28. **C** 06-441 7171.
W www.nzembassy.com

United Kingdom
Via XX Settembre 80A. **Map** 6 D2.
C 06-420 001.
W www.ukinitalia.it

United States
Via Veneto 119A/121. **Map** 5 B2.
C 06-467 41. **W** www.usembassy.it

ROME TIME

Rome is one hour ahead of Greenwich Mean Time (GMT). Examples of the time difference with Rome for other major cities are as follows: New York: -6 hours; Dallas: -7 hours; Los Angeles: -9 hours; London: -1 hour; Perth: +7 hours; Sydney: +9 hours; Auckland: +11 hours; Tokyo: +8 hours. These figures can vary slightly for brief periods with local changes in summer. For all official purposes, the Italians use the 24-hour clock.

CONVERSION TABLE

Imperial to Metric
1 inch	= 2.54 centimeters
1 foot	= 30 centimeters
1 mile	= 1.6 kilometrer
1 ounce	= 28 grams
1 pound	= 454 grams
1 US pint	= 0.5 liters
1 US gallon	= 3.8 liters

Metric to Imperial
1 centimeter	= 0.4 inches
1 meter	= 3 feet 3 inches
1 kilometer	= 0.6 miles
1 gram	= 0.04 ounces
1 kilogram	= 2.2 pounds
1 liter	= 2 US pints

ELECTRICAL ADAPTORS

Electric current in Italy is 220V AC, with two- or three-pin round-pronged plugs. Adaptors can be bought in most countries. Most hotels of three or more stars have hair dryers and shaving points in all bedrooms.

Shaving point in hotel bedroom for 110V or 220V

Italian plugs often have two pins

GETTING TO ROME

M ANY NATIONAL AIRLINES, including Italy's Alitalia, fly direct to Rome from most European cities and several in North America and Australia. There are no direct flights from New Zealand, but passengers can catch connections from either Frankfurt or London. Rome's Fiumicino airport expanded considerably in the late 1990s to accommodate the growing number of visitors. Rome also has train and coach links with the rest of Europe. These take a lot longer than flights (about 24 hours from London, compared with about 3 hours by air), but tend to cost about the same, so are only really worthwhile if you want to travel overland. The trains are often crowded in summer.

Alitalia aircraft

Part of the new extension to Fiumicino airport

BY AIR

IF YOU'RE FLYING from the United States, **Delta**, **US Airways**, Continental and **Alitalia** operate regular direct scheduled flights to Rome, with services from Philadelphia and New York. Flying time is about 8½ hours. **Air Canada** and Alitalia fly from Toronto; **Qantas** from Melbourne and Sydney. The Italian state airline, Alitalia, also flies between Rome and San Francisco, Los Angeles, Boston, Chicago, Montreal, and Sydney, though most of these intercontinental flights involve changing at Milan. It may be considerably cheaper for intercontinental travellers to take a budget flight to London, Paris, Athens, Frankfurt or Amsterdam and continue the journey to Rome from there. **British Airways** and Alitalia operate direct scheduled flights from London Heathrow to Rome (Fiumicino), and you can also fly from Gatwick and Manchester. Among the airlines using Rome as an intercontinental transit point is Ethiopian Airlines: fares are cheaper, but flights are less frequent and are sometimes subject to long delays.

Alitalia flight tickets

Excursion fares generally offer the best value in scheduled flights, but you must purchase them well in advance. They are subject to penalty clauses if you cancel, so it is advisable to take out insurance as soon as you buy your ticket. If you are based in the UK, it is worth looking on the Internet. You can book low-cost tickets direct from companies such as the cheap flight options **Ryanair** and **Go**, to Ciampino from Stansted and Bristol). Those traveling with Go have the option of buying tickets for a chartered coach which

Check-in area at Fiumicino, Rome's main international airport

connects Ciampino Airport with the city center.

Regular charter flights for Rome's Ciampino airport run all year round. Most leave from Stansted, Gatwick and Luton, but there are a few flights from Manchester, Glasgow and Birmingham. Fares vary, peaking in summer, and in Holy Week for the Pope's Easter blessing. In Rome, the **American Express** travel office will also book flights.

Easy-to-follow signs at Ostiense

AIRLINE NUMBERS

Air Canada
06-659 1300.
www.aircanada.com

Alitalia
06-656 43 (information),
06-656 42 (international flights),
06-656 41 (domestic flights).
www.alitalia.com

American Express
06-676 41.

British Airways
199 712 266.
www.britishairways.com

Delta Air Lines
800 864 114.

Go
www.go-fly.com

Quantas
06-5248 2725.
www.quantas.com

Ryanair
www.ryanair.com

US Airlines
06-420 3261. www.usair.com

PACKAGE HOLIDAYS

Package holidays to Rome can be much better value than traveling independently. For European visitors there are weekend packages and two- or three-centre holidays; Rome is frequently packaged with Florence and Venice.

Those from further afield can visit the city during Europe-wide tours. Most package companies include transfers from the airport to your hotel.

FIUMICINO AIRPORT

Rome has two international airports. Leonardo da Vinci – often known as Fiumicino – handles most scheduled flights, and is about 30 km (18 miles) southwest of the city. The airport has recently expanded and now has three terminals. Terminal A for domestic flights, Terminal B for international flights within the European Community, and Terminal C for international flights.

From Fiumicino there are two types of train to Rome: one runs every 15–30 minutes (6:27am to 11:27pm) around Rome to Fara Sabina station, stopping at Trastevere, Ostiense, Tuscolana and Tiburtina but not at Termini. The other, "Leonardo Express", is faster and more expensive, running non-stop to Termini every half hour (7:37am to 10:37pm). If the ticket office (which also sells Metro tickets) is not open, tackle the automatic ticket machine. Remember to specify which train you want when buying your ticket.

Ostiense is linked with Piramide Metro (Line B) where you can catch an underground train to the city center from 5.30am until 11.30pm every day. It can be difficult to find a taxi at Ostiense after 9pm, but there is a bus (the No. 95) to Piazza Venezia.

In addition, car rental is available, from offices at the

Shuttle bus to car-hire lots at Fiumicino

The train linking Fiumicino airport to Stazione Termini

airport *(see p379)*. Efforts have been made at Fiumicino to improve both the airport and the surrounding area. These developments include the institution of a raised pedestrian walkway for traveling between car parks, the railway and various points within the airport, the expansion of Terminal A, and a four-star hotel located near to the terminals.

CIAMPINO AIRPORT

The other airport that services Rome is Ciampino, about 15 km (9 miles) south-east and used by the majority of charter flights. Major car hire firms have a rental office at the airport, though you may find it less harrowing to get into the city center from public transport or by taxi.

Although it is more difficult to travel to and from Ciampino via public transportation than Fiumicino, the swiftest way to get to the centre of Rome from Ciampino is by bus to Anagnina Metro station, then by underground train to Termini. If you take a taxi from the airport be careful to only use official cabs. In addition, make sure that the fare meter is switched on and showing only the mini-mum charge before you leave the airport.

Ciampino, a more basic airport used by most charter flights

Arriving in Rome

THIS MAP shows the main bus, rail and Metro links used by travelers arriving in Rome. The connections between Rome's two airports and the city center are shown, as well as links between Rome and the rest of Italy and the international rail routes from neighboring European countries. Travel information, including details of journey times and service frequency, is listed separately in each box.

FS *National connections*
*Links to Flaminio from **Viterbo** (2 hrs), **Bracciano** (90 mins).*

Flaminio

M *Line A, northbound*
Stops after Ottaviano, S. Pietro are: Cipro Musei Vaticani, Valle Aurelia, Baldo degli Ubaldi, Cornelia and Battistini (end station).

Lepanto

Piazza di Spagna

Spagna

Ottaviano S. Pietro

Barberini

FS *Coastal route from Northern Italy*
Links with Termini station.
***Marseille** (11 hrs), **Nice** (9 hrs), **Turin** (7 hrs 30 mins), **Genova** (6 hrs), **Pisa** (3 hrs 30 mins).*

Vatican

Piazza Navona

Piazza della Rotonda

San Pietro

Campo de' Fiori

Capitol

KEY

Janiculum

Largo Argentina

Forum

✈ Airport *see pp368–9*

Palatine

FS Railway *see pp372–3*

🚌 Coach & Bus Link *see p373*

Trastevere

M Metro *see pp376–7*

— Airport Link *see pp368–9*

— State Rail Link *see pp374–5*

— Metro Line A *see pp376–7*

— Metro Line B *see pp376–7*

Circo Massimo

•• Walkway

Aventine

— Tram 8

Piramide

✈ LEONARDO DA VINCI (FIUMICINO)
Direct train links to Ostiense, Tiburtina and Termini.
FS *Fiumicino–Fara Sabina (via Trastevere, Ostiense, Tiburtina) every 15–30 mins; **Fiumicino–Termini** every 30 mins.*

Trastevere

Ostiense

M *Line B, southbound*
Stops after Piramide are: Garbatella, Basilica San Paolo, Marconi, EUR Magliana, EUR Palasport, EUR Fermi and Laurentina (end station).

FS *International and Northern Italy*
Links with Termini. Trains arriving after midnight terminate at Tiburtina.
Paris (15 hrs), **Vienna** (14 hrs), **Geneva** (14 hrs), **Basle** (13 hrs), **Munich** (11 hrs), **Verona** (7 hrs), **Milan** (5 hrs), **Bologna** (3 hrs 30 mins), **Florence** (2 hrs).

Coach connections into Rome
International and national bus links at **Piazza dei Cinquecento** (in front of Termini). Buses for the Lazio region link at **Lepanto**, **Anagnina** or **EUR Fermi**.

Rome is well served by coaches

Piazza Bologna

M *Line B, northbound*
Stops after Tiburtina are: Monti Tiburtini, Pietralata, Santa Maria del Soccorso, Ponte Mammolo and Rebibbia (end station).

Policlinico

Via Veneto

Castro Pretorio

Tiburtina

Repubblica

Quirinal

Roma Termini

FS *Eastern Italy*
Links with Termini station.
Pescara (4 hrs),
L'Aquila (3 hrs 30 mins).

Cavour

Vittorio Emanuele

Esquiline

Colosseo

Manzoni

Lateran

FS *Southern Italy*
Links with Termini station.
Palermo (12 hrs), **Reggio Calabria** (9 hrs 30 mins), **Bari** (6 hrs 30 mins), **Naples** (2 hrs).

San Giovanni

Caracalla

Re di Roma

Tuscolana

Ponte Lungo

M *Line A, southbound*
Stops after Ponte Lungo are: Furio Camillo, Colli Albani, Arco di Travertino, Porta Furba, Numidio Quadrato, Lucio Sestio, Giulio Agricola, Subaugusta, Cinecittà and Anagnina (end station).

CIAMPINO
Bus link to Anagnina Metro station (on Line A).
COTRAL bus every hour to Anagnina Metro station (20 mins). Metro line A links with Termini station.

Termini Metro station

Reaching Rome by Train, Coach or Car

Aɴʏ ᴏᴠᴇʀʟᴀɴᴅ journey to Rome is fastest by train, though there are coach connections to most major European cities. Within Italy, journeys between large cities are usually also best done by train, but when traveling from towns which are not on the main Intercity rail routes, coaches can be quicker. For drivers, the Italian Automobile Club *(see p361)* provides free assistance and excellent maps to members of affiliated automobile clubs from all over the world.

The Eurostar – Italy's fastest train

The concourse at Stazione Termini

Sᴛᴀᴢɪᴏɴᴇ Tᴇʀᴍɪɴɪ

Sᴛᴀᴢɪᴏɴᴇ ᴛᴇʀᴍɪɴɪ, Rome's main train station, is also the hub of the urban transit system. Beneath it is the only interchange between the city's two Metro lines, and outside, on Piazza dei Cinquecento, is the central bus terminus. Though it is one of Rome's most stunning 20th-century buildings and has recently had a major facelift, it also has unsavory aspects, so don't linger longer than necessary.

FS logo

If you arrive late, aim to leave the neighborhood as swiftly as you can. There are usually taxis (go to the official line) even in the small hours, and many of the city's night buses start at Termini.

In summer the station gets very crowded, and you can expect long lines at ticket booths, bureaux de change and at both the transportation and tourist information offices. There is a left luggage office, a police station where you should report anything lost or stolen on a train or in the station, and a small Citalia office where you can exchange money as well as get travel information. There is an international telephone office *(see p364)*, a bookstore, a post office and tobacconists (where you can buy bus and Metro tickets). Other facilities at the station include a bar and restaurant on the mezzanine floor with more eateries and shops on the lower, Termini Forum level. The new Multi-Service gallery near platform 1 has desks for car-rental firms as well as reduced train fare companies. Note, however, that there are no waiting rooms.

Of Rome's other stations, four are most likely to be of

BINARIO 17
Platform sign

← uscita
Exit sign

interest to tourists. They are Ostiense and Trastevere, for trains to Fiumicino airport and Viterbo *(see p271)*; Tiburtina, for some of the late-night trains on the north-south line through Italy; and Roma Nord for trains to Prima Porta.

Tʀᴀᴠᴇʟɪɴɢ ʙʏ Tʀᴀɪɴ

Iᴛᴀʟɪᴀɴ ꜱᴛᴀᴛᴇ ʀᴀɪʟᴡᴀʏꜱ (Ferrovie dello Stato or FS) have several levels of service, from Locale trains which stop at every station, to the Eurostar, a super-fast and extremely luxurious train, which offers first- and second-class service. The Eurostar runs between Rome and Milan, Turin, Genoa, Bari, Naples and Venice. You have to reserve and you are charged hefty supplements for the privileges of speed, hostess service and free newspapers. You also pay a supplement on Intercity trains. These trains are for fast long-distance journeys and have both first- and second-class carriages. They run from Rome to Venice, Milan, Florence, Naples and other cities. You should book in high season

Termini, the heart of Italy's rail network and Rome's transport system

An international Eurocity train

and on weekends. Booking is obligatory on services which are marked in the timetable by a boxed R on a white background. Tickets for immediate travel can be bought at the station, but allow plenty of time to line up. To book a ticket in advance or make a seat reservation it is often far quicker to go to a travel agent displaying the FS symbol. From Rome you can also take international or Eurocity (EC) trains to destinations all over Europe.

Ferrovie dello Stato
☎ 848 888 088.
w www.fs-on-line.com

MACHINES FOR FS RAIL TICKETS

These machines are easy to use, and most have instructions on screen in a choice of six languages. They accept coins, notes and credit cards.

1 Select your destination.

2 The price is shown on the display.

3 Insert coins, notes, or a VISA, American Express or Diners Club card.

4 Take your ticket and change.

5 You must insert your ticket here to validate it for your journey.

COACH TRAVEL

Most regional and long-distance coaches are blue

LONG-DISTANCE coaches terminate at Tiburtina, which is the city's main coach station. Information and tickets for Eurolines coaches to European cities are available from **Lazzi Express**. The **Appian Line** offers regular services within Italy. Its itineraries include Florence, Naples, Capri, Sorrento and Pompei, and, in summer, Venice and Assisi. Local buses, serving villages and towns within the Lazio region, are run by **COTRAL**. All bus stations used by COTRAL are linked

to Metro stations. Tickets are bought on the spot and cannot be booked in advance. Some day trips from Rome by bus are described on pages 268–71.

Appian Line
Piazza dell Esquilino 6–7. **Map** 6 D4.
☎ 06-48 78 61.

Lazzi Express
Via Tagliamento 27.
☎ 06-884 08 40.

COTRAL
☎ 06-57531.

TRAVELING BY CAR

TO DRIVE YOUR OWN car in Italy you need an international Green Card (for insurance purposes) and the vehicle registration document. A translation of your driving licence, available at Italian tourist offices abroad, is also

Blue signs showing A roads and green signs showing motorways

useful. Wearing seatbelts is compulsory in Italy. You must also carry a warning triangle in case of breakdown. Main routes to Rome connect with the Grande Raccordo Anulare (GRA), Rome's ring-road.

Tolls are charged on all Italian highways. You can buy magnetic highway toll cards from motoring organizations before entering Italy.

Eurolines coach running between Rome and the rest of Europe

GETTING AROUND ROME

ROME'S CENTER is compact, and, although walking absolutely everywhere would be far too overly ambitious, it is a city in which you can spend much of your time on foot. Since the main streets in the center are usually clogged with traffic, driving and cycling are not recommended, but courageous motorcycle or scooter riders can have great

Crash helmets, compulsory on all motorcycles and scooters

fun buzzing around on a rented Vespa. Traveling by bus and tram can be very slow, so use overland public transportation only when you have a long way to go. The Metro, designed to connect the suburbs with the center, has no stops in the historic city center near the Pantheon or Piazza Navona, though it is the swiftest way of crossing the city.

WALKING

WANDERING through Rome's old center is one of the most enjoyable aspects of being in the city. You can take in the architectural details while absorbing the streetlife and stopping as you want at will, or peek into any church, shop or bar that catches your eye. You can easily see several of the main tourist sights in a few hours. The Colosseum, for example, is only about 1.5 miles (2.5 km) from the Spanish Steps. Your route could pass by the Forum, Piazza Venezia and several churches; other sights, such as the Trevi Fountain, the Galleria Doria Pamphilj and the Pantheon, are just a short detour away.

Explore the city area by area, using public transportation when distances are too far.

Although some parts of the historic center are closed to cars, this does not stop these streets being used by cyclists and scooter riders. There have been many plans to create more traffic-free zones, and even to ban anything on wheels from some parts of the city – but imposing such measures on a population as insubordinate as Rome's is not easily done.

If you find the summer heat hard to bear, remember that the narrow cobbled streets get little sunlight and remain relatively cool, while walking into an open piazza can be like stepping into a furnace.

During the height of summer, you'll have a more enjoyable time if you follow the example of the Italians. Walk slowly on the shady side of the street; have a long lunch followed by a siesta in the hottest part of the day. You can continue exploring in the late afternoon, when churches and shops reopen and the streets are at their liveliest. Wandering at night is worthwhile, for the streets are cool and many façades floodlit.

Directions for walkers

Pedestrian crossing: only slightly safer than the open road

CROSSING ROADS

FIRST IMPRESSIONS suggest there can be only two sorts of pedestrian in Rome: the quick and the dead. Even if you cross roads by sets of traffic lights and pedestrian crossings strictly in your favor, there is sure to be some van or Vespa hurtling toward you with apparently homicidal intent. Fortunately, Roman drivers have quick reactions. The pious would attribute this to the protection of Santa Francesca Romana (see p87), cynics to the fact that, according to Italian insurance law, drivers are responsible for any road accident. Whatever the inspiration, accidents are quite rare. The best tactic is to be as alert and confident

Avanti: go! Pedestrians have right of way

Alt: stop! Traffic has right of way

Pedestrian crossing   Watch out for children

as Romans. The roads are very busy. When crossing try to leave as large a gap as possible between yourself and oncoming traffic. Step purposefully into the road, facing approaching motorists with a determined glare. The trick now is to keep going steadily: do not hesitate or change your course and do not run. As long as a driver can see you, he or she should stop or at least swerve, albeit at the last moment.

Pedestrians and drivers must both take particular care at night, when the traffic lights are switched to a constantly flashing amber, turning the crossings into free-for-alls.

STREET SIGNS

THEORETICALLY, although it may not always seem to be the case, pedestrians have right of way at crossings when the green *avanti* sign is lit up. The red sign *alt* means you must wait. Underground crossings are indicated by a sign reading *sottopassaggio*.

It is easy to get lost in the maze of streets and piazzas that comprise the historic center. Until you know your way around, you can follow the yellow signs marking routes between the sights and piazzas of particular interest to tourists. Routes leading to general landmarks are indicated by signs on a brown or gray background.

No stopping

No parking

One-way street

No through road

DRIVING

DRIVING IN CENTRAL Rome can be an extremely intimidating experience for visitors. The flamboyant aggression of Italian drivers is notorious; pedestrians step out into the roads without warning; and the one-way system operating in much of the center makes retaining a sense of direction impossible. You'll also find motorists passing on the wrong side,

Directions to parking areas

while scooters and Vespas zoom among the lanes of traffic and go the wrong way down one-way streets. A rule to remember is to give way to the right. Unless you are accustomed to driving in Italian cities, leave your car at home – or, failing that, in a guarded parking area.

Car thefts are rife in Rome, so never leave anything of value in your car, even out of sight: areas such as Campo de' Fiori are patrolled by gangs watching for anyone leaving cameras, fur coats and other costly items in their trunks. You should also remove your car radio – you won't be the only person carrying one into a bar, restaurant or disco.

Take extra care driving at night. Not only do traffic lights switch to flashing amber, but many Italians are astonishingly cavalier about driving under the influence of alcohol or drugs.

PARKING

THE MOST convenient parking area is below the Villa Borghese. Much of the city center is reserved for residents with permits, but there are around 2,000 metered parking spaces (from 8am–8pm). If you do find a legal place to park, however, you may return and find that you have been hemmed in by double-parked cars. Locations of some of the most useful parking areas are on page 379.

GASOLINE

GAS IS VERY expensive. It can be bought from roadside pumps (many of which are self-service, operated by bills or credit cards) as well as from regular garages. Check whether your car uses lead-free gas (*benzina senza piombo* or *benzina verde*) or not. Late-night gas stations are listed on page 379.

The state petrol company logo

ILLEGAL PARKING

Rome's traffic police are vigilant. If you've parked illegally, your car may be clamped or (if it's causing an obstruction) towed away, so call 06-67 691 to check before reporting it stolen. No-parking zones should be clearly marked, but look carefully, in case the sign is hidden by a tree.

Signpost for a tow-away area (*zona rimozione*)

A tow truck at work

Traveling by Bus, Tram and Metro

ROME'S PUBLIC TRANSPORTATION system is comparatively cheap, comprehensive and as efficient as the busy streets allow. Priests, nuns, tourists, pilgrims, businessmen and pickpockets all pile aboard, transforming the buses and trams into mobile saunas during the summer. Short distances are better covered on foot, because heavy traffic often blocks the roads. Getting off at the right stop can be difficult, but other passengers will usually help if you ask for directions. Always keep a tight hold on your valuables.

Weekly travelcard

Monthly travelcard

BUSES AND TRAMS

ROME'S PUBLIC bus and tram company is called **ATAC** (Azienda Tramvie e Autobus del Comune di Roma). Scores of buses and several trams cover most parts of the city. They run from early morning until about midnight. There are also a few night buses.

Apart from a few electric minibuses (115, 116, 117, 119), no buses can run through the narrow streets of the historic center. But there are plenty of bus routes to take you within a short walk of the main sights (see map inside back cover).

Bus stops comprehensively list the details of routes taken by all the buses using that stop. Night buses are marked with a blue owl on the bus stop.

J LINES

THE J BUSES, managed by a private company, run on the main tourist routes with fewer and longer stops for getting on and off. Recognizable by their orange-and-blue livery, J buses have wheelchair access and air-conditioning. Single tickets last 75 minutes, but there are also 1-, 2- and 3-day tickets as well as weekly and monthly passes. Tickets may be bought on the buses.

Rome–Gubbio bus

Unfortunately, though, J-line bus stops are difficult to find, the routes are poorly publicized and the company's map is misleading. Ask a J-bus driver for information or call (toll-free) 800 07 62 87.

USING BUSES AND TRAMS

THE MAIN TERMINUS is on Piazza dei Cinquecento outside Termini station, but there are other major route hubs throughout the city, most usefully those at Piazza San Silvestro, Piazza Venezia and Piazza del Risorgimento. Information on public transport can be obtained from ATAC kiosks or the ATAC website (see below). Tickets can be purchased from automatic machines found at main bus stops as well as at Metro and train stations, newsstands and tobacconists.

Most day buses have only a driver; night buses usually also have a conductor who issues tickets. (You can't buy tickets on day buses.) In the day, if you have a normal ticket, you should board the bus at the back. There will be an orange machine there to time-stamp your ticket, or a yellow equivalent which automatically cancels the new electronic tickets. Timed tickets, *biglietto integrato a tempo* (BIT), can be used on all means of transport.

INFORMATION

ATAC
Piazza dei Cinquecento.
Map 6 D3. 📞 06-46 951.
W www.atac.roma.it
Open 7am–7pm daily.

Ticket for one day's unlimited travel

Ticket valid for 75 minutes

TICKETS

TICKETS FOR CITY buses, trams and Metros have to be bought before you travel and stamped in the appropriate machine as soon as you start your journey. You can buy tickets at bars, newsstands and tobacconists, as well as at Metro stations and bus termini. Look out for places displaying ATAC (bus), Metroferro (Metro and tram) and FS (train) stickers. There are also automatic ticket machines at main bus stops and train and Metro stations that take coins and bills and distribute change.

BIT tickets are valid for 75 minutes, during which time you can take one Metro ride and hop on and off as many buses and trams as you like. If you are going to make four or more journeys in one day, it is worth buying a *biglietto integrato giornaliero*

FERMATA

Bus stop listing details of routes served

One of Rome's red and grey ATAC buses

(BIG) ticket. These give you a day's travel on the buses, trams and the Metro. To travel farther afield in Lazio, consider buying a regional BIRG ticket. There are also available weekly tickets and monthly (calendar month) passes which are valid for the whole transport system, with discounts for students and people over 65. Fare-dodging is common, but incurs a hefty on-the-spot fine.

METROPOLITANA

Rome's underground system, the Metropolitana, has two lines (A and B) which cross the city in a rough X-shape, converging at Termini station (*see inside back cover and pp370–71*). Line A (red) leads from Battistini in the west to Anagnina in the

southeast of the city, from where buses go to Ciampino airport. Line B (blue) runs from Rebibbia in the northeast, down to EUR in the southwest, where buses leave for the coast. Stations are clearly marked by the Metro logo, a large white M on a red background.

The system was designed to ferry commuters in from the suburbs, so is not very useful within the center, but the Metro is a relatively speedy way of crossing the city. Among the most useful stations are Colosseo, Spagna, San Giovanni, Ottaviano S. Pietro and Piramide (for trains to Fiumicino). Both metro lines run from 5:30am until 11:30pm every day.

Metro logo

USEFUL BUS AND TRAM ROUTES

This map shows some of the buses that go through interesting parts of Rome with good views of major sights. The 40 Express and 64 are always full of tourists, since they go from Termini to St. Peter's (40) and Vatican (64). The other routes are likely to be less crowded. The 3 tram follows a long leisurely route around the southeast of the city, while bus 23 goes along the Tiber.

KEY

Ⓜ	Metro station
🔲 FS	Train station
▬	Tram route 8
▬	Tram route 3
▬	Bus route 23
▬	Bus route 62
▬	Bus routes 40 Express and 64
▬	Bus route 116
▬	Bus route 117

BIKE AND MOPED HIRE

Rome's narrow streets and heavy traffic, combined with the seven steep hills on which it was built, make it a challenging place for even the most serious of cyclists. However, there are a few areas, such as the Villa Borghese, the banks of the Tiber and some pockets in the historic center (around the Pantheon and Piazza Navona), where cycling can be a relaxing way to see the city. Make sure that you have a loud bell though – places that are good for cyclists tend to be popular with walkers and strollers too.

Mopeds *(motorini)* and scooters – like the classic

A Vespa scooter and helmet

Horse-drawn carriages outside the Pantheon

Piaggio Vespa, meaning "wasp" and named after the buzzing noise it makes – are good for getting through the traffic. You may want to stick to quiet streets to begin with, though.

Motorcyclists have to wear helmets by law, and they have finally started to do so.

You can hire helmets from most hire shops in Rome.

Bikes and mopeds can be hired from **Collalti**, **Roma Rent**, **Scoot-a-Long**, **Happy Rent** and **Scooters for Rent**. **Biciroma** rents from several spots around the city and a **telephone hire service** operates in the summer and autumn.

You may be asked to leave a credit card number or cash as a deposit when you pick up the bike.

HORSE-DRAWN CARRIAGES

These are not as popular in Rome as in Florence, but you can hire horse-drawn caleches *(carrozzelle)* for a gentle tour of the historic center. Carriages carry up to five people and can be hired from many points: Piazza di Spagna, the Colosseum, Trevi Fountain, St. Peter's, Via Veneto, Villa Borghese, Piazza Venezia and Piazza Navona. Trips last half an hour, an hour, half a day or a day. They tend to be expensive, but prices for longer rides are negotiable; establish the price before you set off and make sure you understand whether the rate is per person, or for the whole carriage.

TAXIS

Official taxis in Rome are yellow or white and must bear the "taxi" sign on the roof. Only use these taxis, not the ones offered by touts at stations and tourist spots; official taxi drivers do not tout for customers. Official taxis can be hailed either at specially marked stands or on the street (drivers are not meant to stop in the street but many of them do). You can nearly always find them at the main tourist sights, at airports and stations (including

TAXI

Taxi-stand signpost

Termini and Ostiense). Roman taxi drivers are not renowned for their friendliness and may even refuse to take you too far from the lucrative city center.

Taxis are not a particularly cheap way of getting about, so, unless you have heavy luggage or screaming toddlers, public transport is usually a better option. Taxi drivers always charge supplements for baggage, night journeys (10pm–7am), journeys on Sundays or public holidays, and fares to or from the airport. As with taxis elsewhere, the meter continues running while you

Taxis lining up at Fiumicino

are at a standstill, so traffic jams can become expensive. Drivers may also take suspiciously circuitous routes. While native Romans generally tip taxi drivers small amounts, visitors are expected to give 10 per cent of the fare. You can book in advance (but will incur a surcharge) from: **Pianeta Taxi 2000**, **Cooperativa Autoradiotaxi Romana 35–70** or **Società la Capitale Radio Taxi**. For a good value taxi service to and from the airports call **Airport Connection Services**.

Official taxi with Comune di Roma sign

CAR HIRE

IN ITALY car hire is expensive, and fuel is among the highest-priced in Europe. Major international companies, including **Avis**, **Europcar**, **Hertz** and **Italy By Car Thrifty** have rental offices at the airports, Termini station and within the city center. However, you may be able to get a better deal by booking a car before you arrive through a travel agent or tour operator. Local firms (such as **Maggiore**) are generally a lot cheaper, but check that breakdown service and collision damage waiver are included in the hire price.

Prospective renters should be aged 21 or over and have held a driving license for at least one year. Theoretically you should also hold an international license (available from your national automobile association) but most car rental firms do not insist on this. What they do insist on is a deposit. Usually your credit card number is sufficient.

If the expense does not discourage you, the aggressive style of driving might. Accident rates on Italian roads are very high, so make sure you are fully insured against all eventualities. It is also a good idea to join an internationally affiliated automobile association (such as the AA in Britain or the AAA in the US). If you are unfortunate enough to break down, it is best to phone the **ACI** (Italian Automobile Club) for assistance. Although they will tow any car without charging, only members of affiliated associations are entitled to free repairs.

Details of current road and traffic conditions (in Italian) are available from a special **Road Conditions** number. For more information about driving and parking, see page 375.

Car rental offices at Fiumicino airport

DIRECTORY

BIKE AND MOPED HIRE ADDRESSES

Biciroma
Piazza del Popolo.
Map 4 F1.
Also: Piazza di Spagna.
Map 5 A2.
Also: Il Pincio in Villa Borghese.
Map 4 F1.

Collalti
Via del Pellegrino 82.
Map 4 E4 & 11 C4.
📞 06-6880 1084 *(bikes)*.

Happy Rent
Via Farini 3.
Map 6 D4.
📞 06-481 8185 *(mopeds and scooters)*.

Scoot-a-Long
Via Cavour 302.
Map 5 B5.
📞 06-678 0206 *(mopeds and scooters)*.

Scooters for Rent
Via della Purificazione 84.
📞 06-488 5485 *(bikes and mopeds)*.

TAXI BOOKING NUMBERS

Airport Connection Services
📞 06-338 3221.

Cooperativa Autoradiotaxi Romana 35–70
📞 06-35 70.

Pianeta Taxi 2000
📞 06-881 77.

Società la Capitale Radio Taxi
📞 06-49 94.

CAR HIRE ADDRESSES

Avis
📞 06-41999 *(centralized booking number)*.
🖥 www.avis.com
Also: Ciampino airport.
📞 06-7934 0195.
Also: Fiumicino airport.
📞 06-6501 1531.
Also: Via Sardegna 38A.
Map 5 C1.
📞 06-4282 4728.

Europcar
📞 800 014410 *(centralized free booking number)*.
🖥 www.europcar.it

Also: Fiumincino airport
📞 06-6501 0879.
Also: Via Lombardia 7.
Map 5 B2.
📞 06-487 1274.

Hertz
Via Gregorio VII 207.
📞 06-3937 8808.
🖥 www.hertz.it
Also: Stazione Termini.
Map 6 D3.
📞 06-474 0389.
Also: Fiumicino airport.
📞 06-6501 1448.

Maggiore
Stazione Termini.
Map 6 D3.
📞 06-488 0049.
Also: Via Po 8A.
Map 5 C1.
📞 06-854 8698.
🖥 www.maggiore.it

Italy By Car Thrifty
Via Ludovisi 60.
Map 5 B2.
📞 06-482 0966.
🖥 www.italybycar.it
Also: Fiumicino airport.
📞 06-652 9134.
Also: Ciampino airport.
📞 06-7934 0137.

CAR BREAKDOWN SERVICES

ACI Breakdown
📞 803 116.

Autosoccorso CARA
Via Salk 80.
📞 06-332 0119
(24-hour rescue service).

Road Conditions
Via Magenta 5. **Map** 6 E3.
📞 166 664 477.

MAIN CAR PARKS

Acqua Acetosa station.
Map 2 E1.
Also: Lepanto Metro station. **Map** 4 D1.
Also: Villa Borghese.
Map 5 A1.
Also: EUR Palasport Metro station.

USEFUL 24-HOUR GAS STATIONS

Trastevere
Lungotevere Ripa.
Map 8 D1.

Portuense
Piazza della Radio.
Map 7 B5.

STREET FINDER

MAP REFERENCES given with sights, restaurants, hotels, shops and entertainment venues refer to the maps in this section (*see* How the Map References Work *opposite*). A complete index of the street names and places of interest marked on the maps follows on pages 382–91. The key map below shows the area of Rome covered by the *Street Finder*. This includes the sightseeing areas (which are color-coded) as well as the whole of central Rome with all the districts important for restaurants, hotels and entertainment venues. Because the historic centre is so packed with sights, there is a large-scale map of this area on pages 11 and 12.

0 kilometers   2

0 miles   1

How the Map References Work

The first figure tells you which Street Finder map to turn to.

Trevi Fountain ❼

Fontana di Trevi. **Map 5** A3 & 12 F2 🚌 52, 53, 61, 62, 63, 71, 80, 95, 115, 116, 119.

The letter and number are a grid reference. You will find the letters at the top and bottom of the map and the numbers at the sides.

The second reference refers to the large-scale maps of central Rome (11 & 12). It is read in exactly the same way as the first.

The map continues on map 8 of the Street Finder.

The key to the abbreviations used in the Street Finder is on page 382.

Key to Street Finder

- 🟧 Major sight
- 🟩 Places of interest
- 🟪 Train station
- Ⓜ Metro station
- 🚌 Bus terminus
- 🚊 Tram terminus
- 🅿 Main car parks
- ℹ Tourist information office
- ✚ Hospital with emergency unit
- 🚓 Police station
- ✝ Church
- ✡ Synagogue
- ⊠ Post office
- ═ Railroad line
- → One-way street
- ═ Steps
- ▬ City wall

Scale of Maps 1–10

| 0 meters | 250 |
| 0 yards | 250 |

1:13,000

Scale of Maps 11 & 12

| 0 meters | 150 |
| 0 yards | 150 |

1:8,000

Street Finder Index

KEY TO ABBREVIATIONS USED IN THE STREET FINDER

B.go	Borgo	**M.te**	Monte	**Reg.**	Regina
d.	di, del, dell',	**P.**	Piazza	**S.**	San, Sant', Santa
	dello, della, dei,	**P.etta**	Piazzetta	**S. M.**	Santa Maria
	delle, degli	**P.le**	Piazzale	**SS.**	Santi, Santissima
Gall.	Galleria	**Princ.**	Principe	**V.**	Via
L.go	Largo	**P.ta**	Porta	**Vic.**	Vicolo
Lungot.	Lungotevere	**P.te**	Ponte	**V.le**	Viale

General Index

Acknowledgments

MANAGING EDITOR Douglas Amrine,
MANAGING ART EDITOR Geoff Manders,
SENIOR EDITOR Georgina Matthews,
SERIES DESIGN CONSULTANT Peter Luff,
EDITORIAL DIRECTOR David Lamb,
ART DIRECTOR Anne-Marie Bulat.

DORLING KINDERSLEY would like to thank the
following people whose contributions and
assistance have made the preparation of this
book possible.

MAIN CONTRIBUTORS
Olivia Ercoli is an art historian and tour guide
who has lived all her life in Rome. Bilingual in
English and Italian, she lectures on art history
and writes on a range of subjects for English
and Italian publications.

Travel writer Ros Belford conceived the idea
of the Virago Woman's Guides, of which she
is now series editor, and wrote the *Virago
Woman's Guide to Rome*. She has traveled
widely in Europe and as well as writing guide
books contributes to a variety of publications,
including *The Guardian*.

Roberta Mitchell heads the editorial section of
the UN's Publishing Division in Rome, where
she has lived for many years. An experienced
writer and editor with extensive knowledge of
the city, she has contributed to a number of
guides to Rome, including the *American
Express Guide to Rome*.

CONTRIBUTORS
Sam Cole, Mary Jane Cryan Pancani, Daphne
Wilson Ercoli, Laura Ercoli, Lindsay Hunt,
Adrian James, Christopher McDowall,
Davina Palmer, Rodney Palmer, Debra Shipley.

DORLING KINDERSLEY wishes to thank the
following editors and researchers at Websters
International Publishers: Sandy Carr, Matthew
Barrell, Siobhan Bremner, Serena Cross,
Valeria Fabbri, Annie Galpin, Gemma
Hancock, Celia Woolfrey.

ADDITIONAL PHOTOGRAPHY
Max Alexander, Demetrio Carrasco, Andy
Crawford, Philip Enticknap, Steve Gorton,
John Heseltine, Neil Mersh, Poppy, David
Sutherland, Martin Woodward.

ADDITIONAL ILLUSTRATIONS
Anne Bowes, Robin Carter, Gillie Newman,
Chris D. Orr.

ADDITIONAL PICTURE RESEARCH
Sharon Buckley.

CARTOGRAPHY
Advanced Illustration (Cheshire), Contour
Publishing (Derby), Euromap Limited
(Berkshire). Street Finder maps: ERA Maptec
Ltd. (Dublin) adapted with permission from
original survey and mapping from
Shobunsha (Japan).

CARTOGRAPHIC RESEARCH
James Anderson, Donna Rispoli, Joan Russell.

RESEARCH ASSISTANCE
Janet Abbott, Flaminia Allvin, Fabrizio Ardito,
Licia Bronzin, Lupus Sabene.

DESIGN AND EDITORIAL ASSISTANCE
Hilary Bird, Lucinda Cooke, Vanessa Courtier,
Kristin Dolina-Adamczyk, Claire Edwards, Jon
Eldan, Simon Farbrother, Vanessa Hamilton,
Marcus Hardy, Sasha Heseltine, Sally Ann
Hibbard, Stephanie Jackson, Steve Knowlden,
Mary Lambert, Janette Leung, Jane Middleton,
Ian Midson, Fiona Morgan, Helen Partington,
Naomi Peck, Carolyn Pyrah, Salim Qurashi,
Sands Editorial, Jane Shaw, Clare Sullivan,
Rachel Symons, Andrew Szudek, Daphne
Trotter, Karen Villabona, Diana Vowles,
Lynda Warrington, Stewart J. Wild.

SPECIAL ASSISTANCE
Dottore Riccardo Baldini, Signor Mario di
Bartolomeo of the Soprintendenza dei Beni
Artistici e Storici di Roma, Belloni, Dorling
Kindersley picture department, Peter Douglas,
David Gleave MW, Debbie Harris, Emma
Hutton and Cooling Brown Partnership,
Dottoressa Todaro and Signora Camimiti at
the Ministero dell'Interno, Trestini.

PHOTOGRAPHY PERMISSIONS
DORLING KINDERSLEY would like to thank the
following for their kind permission to
photograph at their establishments:
Bathsheba Abse at the Keats-Shelley
Memorial House, Accademia dei Lincei,
Accanto, Aeroporti di Roma, Aldrovandi
Palace, Alpheus, Banco di Santo Spirito at
Palazzo del Monte di Pietà, Rory Bruck at
Babington's, Caffè Giolitti, Caffè Latino,
Comune di Roma (Ripartizione X), Comunità
Ebraica di Roma, Guido Cornini at
Monumenti Musei e Gallerie Ponteficie,
Direzione Sanitaria Ospedale di Santo Spirito,
Dottoressa Laura Falsini at the
Soprintendenza Archeologica di Etruria
Meridionale, Hotel Gregoriana, Hotel

Majestic, Hotel Regina Baglioni, Marco Marchetti at Ente EUR, Dottoressa Mercalli at the Museo Nazionale di Castel Sant'Angelo, Ministero dell'Interno, Plaza Minerva, Ristorante Alberto Ciarla, Ristorante Filetti di Baccalà, Ristorante Romolo, Signor Rulli and Signor Angeli at the Soprintendenza Archeologica di Roma, Soprintendenza Archeologica per il Lazio, Soprintendenza per i Beni Ambientali e Architettonici, Soprintendenza per i Beni Artistici e Storici di Roma, Daniela Tabo at the Musei Capitolini, Villa d'Este, Villa San Pio, Mrs. Marjorie Weeke at St. Peter's.

PICTURE CREDITS

t = top; tl = top left; tc = top center; tr = top right; cla = center left above; ca = center above; cra = center right above; cl = center left; c = center; cr = center right; clb = center left below; cb = center below; crb = center right below; bl = bottom left; b = bottom; bc = bottom center; br = bottom right.

Every effort has been made to trace the copyright holders and we apologize in advance for any unintentional omissions. We would be pleased to insert the appropriate acknowledgments in any subsequent edition of this publication.

Works of art have been reproduced with the permission of the following copyright holders: © DACS: Città con Cattedrale Gotica, 1925 by Paul Klee 241b.

The publishers are grateful to the following individuals, companies and picture libraries for permission to reproduce their photographs:

ACCADEMIA NAZIONALE DI SAN LUCA, Rome: 160b; AFE: 57b, 61cr; Sandro Battaglia 59c, 61clb, 61br, 324br; Louise Goldman 157t; G. La Malfa 251t; AEROPORTI DI ROMA: 368b; AGENZIA SINTESI: Fabio Fiorani 360br, 361t, 361b; Antonella di Girolamo 361c; Marco Marcotulli 360bc; R. Venturi 360bl; AGF FOTO: 38–39c; ALDROVANDI PALACE HOTEL: 291b; ALITALIA: 368t, 369cl; ALLSPORT: David Cannon 39br; ANCIENT ART AND ARCHITECTURE: 16bl, 20tl, 21tl, 25bc, 34crb, 35tc, 44cl; ARTOTHEK, Stadelsches Kunstinstitut Frankfurt, Goethe in the Roman Campagna by J.H.W. Tischbein 136t.

BIBLIOTECA REALE, Torino: 28–29c; BRIDGEMAN ART LIBRARY, LONDON/NEW YORK: 18br, 37tr; Agnew & Sons, London 51tr;

Antikenmuseum Staatliches Museum, Berlin 19bl; Biblioteca Publica Episcopal, Barcelona/Index 114bl; Bibliothèque de la Sorbonne 28c, British Museum, London 27ctr; Chateau de Versailles, France/Giraudon 33tr, 54cl; Christie's, London 40, 55tr, 68b, 95t; The Fine Art Society, London 151tr, 279tl; Galleria degli Uffizi, Florence 31bl; Greek Museum, University of Newcastle-upon-Tyne 16br; King Street Galleries, London 33br; Louvre, Paris/Lauros-Giraudon 56br; Louvre, Paris/Giraudon 26br; Roy Miles Gallery, 29 Bruton St, London 228t; Musée des Beaux-Arts, Nantes 53t; Museo e Gallerie Nazionali di Capodimonte, Naples, Detail from the predella of San Ludovico by Simone Martini 26tr; Musée Condé, Chantilly f.71v Très Riches Heures, 26tc; Museum of Fine Arts, Budapest 110bl; Museo Archeologico di Villa Giulia 48cl; Museo Poldi Pezzoli, Milan 54tr; Palazzo Doria Pamphilj, Rome 107b; Piacenza Town Hall, Italy/Index 27br; Private Collection 19br, 22bl, 24br, 27tr, 178b; Pushkin Museum, Moscow 111t; Sotheby's, London 18bl; Vatican Museums & Galleries 41ca, 237tr.

CAPITOLINE MUSEUM, Rome: 73cr; CEPHAS PICTURE LIBRARY: Mick Rock 306tr; VANESSA COURTIER: 355t.

IL DAGHERROTIPO: 118clb, 145cra, 322t, 323bl, 366br, 372cla, 377t; Stefano Chieppa 152cl, 378b; Museo di Roma/Giorgio Oddi 118b; Stefano Occhibelli 12c, 116; Giorgio Oddi 53cl; Paolo Priori 204tr; Giovanni Rinaldi 374t; CM DIXON: 17bl, 24c, 268b, 269t, 269b.

ECOLE NATIONALE SUPERIEURE DES BEAUX-ARTS: 21cr, 22–23, 248t, 284–285b; ENTE NAZIONALE ITALIANO PER IL TURISMO: 358cl, cr; ET ARCHIVE: 14, 17tr, 17clb, 18tr, 19tc, 23t, 27cl, 28tl, 31br, 32br, 37br, 48tl, 306tl; MARY EVANS PICTURE LIBRARY: 9, 18cl, 23cl, 24cl, 29br, 30cb, 30b, 31t, 34tl, 34cr, 34bl, 54tl, 56tl, 67bl, 74t, 81b, 91t, 92b, 94bl, 127c, 135t, 213b.

CORALDO FALSINI: 39tl, 340b, 341t, 341c; FERROVIE DELLO STATO: 373tr; WERNER FORMAN ARCHIVE: 17cr, 20bl, 22tl, 23cr, 23bl, 23br, 47tr, 155t, 163tr, 175c; FOLKLORE MUSEUM, Rome: 210br.

GARDEN PICTURE LIBRARY: Bob Challinor 172cb; GIRAUDON: 15b, 28br, 36br, 55tl; JACKIE GORDON: 364bl; RONALD GRANT: 52br, 340t.

SONIA HALLIDAY: 19c, 22br, 25cl; Laura Lushington 24bl; ROBERT HARDING PICTURE LIBRARY: 23cra, 32bl, 79cr, 177t, 268c, 353c,

Mario Carrieri 35tr; Caffè Greco, Rome by Ludwig Passini 309tr; John G. Ross 38tl, 59cl, 341b; Sheila Terry 39cl; G. White 59br; MICHAEL HOLFORD: 70b; HULTON DEUTSCH: 36tl, 38bc, 57cr, 63, 175b, 287c, 357c.
MAGNUM: Erich Lessing 15t, 17tl, 89br; MANSELL COLLECTION: 19tr, 25bl, 26bc, 31cl, 54bc, 55tc, 56cl, 57cl, 75cl, 75cr, 78tc, 93b, 112c, 122t, 125tr, 126tl, 132br, 133cr, 136bl, 139bl, 139br, 162tr, 172bl, 172 br, 183br, 192bl, 196bl, 210c, 220bl, 227cr, 229cr; Alinari 80br, 141bl, 174t, 254b; Anderson 78cr, 138bl, 163tl, 228b; MARKA: V. Arcomano 33cr; Roberto Benzi 325crb; Piranha 325cra; Lorenzo Sechi 224br; MORO ROMA: 36cl, 37cl, 38br, 39tr, 39bl.

NATIONAL PORTRAIT GALLERY, London: 55cr, 55b, 56tr, 57tr; GRAZIA NERI: Vision/Anna Caltabiano 358b; Vision/Giorgio Casulich 112br, 156br 325crc; Vision/Roberta Krasnig 124tr, 283t; © NIPPON TELEVISION NETWORK CORPORATION, Tokyo 1999: 244b and all pictures on 246–7.

LA REPUBBLICA TROVAROMA: 359tl; REX FEATURES: Steve Wood 39cr.

SCALA GROUP S.P.A.: 94t, 125tl, 278cl, Casa di Augusto 97t, Chiesa del Gesù 115t, Galleria Borghese 32cla, 260tr, Galleria Colonna 157b, Galleria Doria Pamphilj 46br, 105cr, Galleria Spada 46cl, Galleria degli Uffizi 16–17, 27bl, Museo d'Arte Orientale 174t, 174br, Musei Capitolini 47bl, Museo della Civiltà Romana 48tr, 48b, Museo delle Terme 21tr, Museo Napoleonico 49cr, Museo Nazionale, Napoli 21cl, Museo Nazionale, Ravenna 22cl, Museo del Risorgimento, Milano 36clb, 36–37c, Museo del Risorgimento, Roma 37tl, Museo di San Marco 54bl, Palazzo Barberini 253bl,

Palazzo Ducale 8, 19tr, Palazzo della Farnesina 220ct, Palazzo Madama 20cl, Palazzo Venezia 47cr, 66bl, San Carlo alle Quattro Fontane 33cl, Santa Cecilia in Trastevere 32tl, San Clemente 35bl, Santa Costanza 24–25c, Santa Maria Antiqua 24tl, Santa Maria dell'Anima 121t, Santa Maria Maggiore 43tr, Santa Maria del Popolo 139tr, 139c, Santa Prassede 26bl, 28bl, Santa Sabina 25tc, 29cl, Vatican Museums 19bc, 25t, 25cr, 25cra, 27cr, 29tl, 29cr, 30tl, 30ct, 31cr, 31bc, 32cr, 32clb, 41tr, 46tl, 48cr, 49bl, 224bl, 225cr, 235t, 238tl, 238br, 240t, 240b, 241t, 241c, 241b, 242tl, 242c, 242b, 243t, 243c, 243b, 245 (all 4), 246cl, 246cr, 246b, 247tl, 247c, 247cr, 247b.

TONY STONE IMAGES: Richard Passmore 1c; TOPHAM PICTURE SOURCE: 38cl.

ZEFA: 2, 230cl, 231br, 356–7, 358t, 372t; Eric Carle 58t; Kohlhas 231t.

JACKET: All special photography except: BRIDGEMAN ART LIBRARY, LONDON/NEW YORK: front cover cl; TONY STONE IMAGES: Richard Passmore spine c.

Thanks also to Dottoressa Giulia De Marchi of L'ACCADEMIA NAZIONALE DI SAN LUCA, Rome for 160b, Rettore Padre Libianchi of LA CHIESA DI SANT'IGNAZIO DI LOYOLA for 106t, ENTE NAZIONALE PER IL TURISMO, HASSLER HOTEL, Rome for 293tl, GRAND HOTEL, Rome for 293crb and to LA REPUBBLICA TROVAROMA.

All other images © Dorling Kindersley. For further information see: www.dkimages.com

Phrase Book

IN EMERGENCY

Help!	**Aiuto!**	*eye-yoo-toh*
Stop!	**Fermate!**	*fair-mah-teh*
Call a doctor	**Chiama un medico**	*kee-ah-mah oon meh-dee-koh*
Call an ambulance	**Chiama un' ambulanza**	*kee-ah-mah oon am-boo-lan-tsa*
Call the police	**Chiama la polizia**	*kee-ah-mah oon pol-ee-tsee-ah*
Call the fire department	**Chiama i pompieri**	*kee-ah-mah ee pom-pee-air-ee*
Where is the telephone?	**Dov'è il telefono?**	*dov-eh eel teh-leh-foh-noh?*
The nearest hospital?	**L'ospedale più vicino?**	*loss-peh-dah-leh pee-oovee-chee-noh?*

COMMUNICATION ESSENTIALS

Yes/No	**Si/No**	*see/noh*
Please	**Per favore**	*pair fah-vor-eh*
Thank you	**Grazie**	*grah-tsee-eh*
Excuse me	**Mi scusi**	*mee skoo-zee*
Hello	**Buon giorno**	*bwon jor-noh*
Good bye	**Arrivederci**	*ah-ree-veh-dair-chee*
Good evening	**Buona sera**	*bwon-ah sair-ah*
morning	**la mattina**	*lah mat-tee-nah*
afternoon	**il pomeriggio**	*eel poh-meh-ree-joh*
evening	**la sera**	*lah sair-ah*
yesterday	**ieri**	*ee-air-ee*
today	**oggi**	*oh-jee*
tomorrow	**domani**	*doh-mah-nee*
here	**qui**	*kwee*
there	**la**	*lah*
What?	**Che cosa?**	*keh-koh-sah?*
When?	**Quando?**	*kwan-doh?*
Why?	**Perchè?**	*pair-keh?*
Where?	**Dove?**	*doh-veh*

USEFUL PHRASES

How are you?	**Come sta?**	*koh-meh stah?*
Very well, thank you.	**Molto bene, grazie.**	*moll-toh beh-neh grah-tsee-eh*
Pleased to meet you.	**Piacere di conoscerla.**	*pee-ah-chair-eh dee coh-noh-shair-lah*
See you soon.	**A più tardi.**	*ah pee-oo tar-dee*
That's fine.	**Va bene.**	*va beh-neh*
Where is/are ...?	**Dov'è/Dove sono ...?**	*dov-eh/doveh soh-noh?*
How long does it take to get to ...?	**Quanto tempo ci vuole per andare a ...?**	*kwan-toh tem-poh chee voo-oh-leh pair an-dar-eh ah...?*
How do I get to ...?	**Come faccio per arrivare a ...?**	*koh-meh fah-choh pair arri-var-eh ah...?*
Do you speak English?	**Parla inglese?**	*par-lah een-gleh-zeh?*
I don't understand.	**Non capisco.**	*non ka-pee-skoh*
Could you speak more slowly, please?	**Può parlare più lentamente, per favore?**	*pwoh par-lah-reh pee-oolen-ta-men-teh pair fah-vor-eh*
I'm sorry.	**Mi dispiace.**	*mee dee-spee-ah-cheh*

USEFUL WORDS

big	**grande**	*gran-deh*
small	**piccolo**	*pee-koh-loh*
hot	**caldo**	*kal-doh*
cold	**freddo**	*fred-doh*
good	**buono**	*bwoh-noh*
bad	**cattivo**	*kat-tee-voh*
enough	**basta**	*bas-tah*
well	**bene**	*beh-neh*
open	**aperto**	*ah-pair-toh*
closed	**chiuso**	*kee-oo-zoh*
left	**a sinistra**	*ah see-nee-strah*
right	**a destra**	*ah dess-trah*
straight ahead	**sempre dritto**	*sem-preh dree-toh*
near	**vicino**	*vee-chee-noh*
far	**lontano**	*lon-tah-noh*
up	**su**	*soo*
down	**giù**	*joo*
early	**presto**	*press-toh*
late	**tardi**	*tar-dee*
entrance	**entrata**	*en-trah-tah*
exit	**uscita**	*oo-shee-ta*
toilet	**il gabinetto**	*eel gah-bee-net-toh*
free, unoccupied	**libero**	*lee-bair-oh*
free, no charge	**gratuito**	*grah-too-ee-toh*

MAKING A TELEPHONE CALL

I'd like to place a long-distance call.	**Vorrei fare una interurbana.**	*vor-ray far-eh oona in-tair-oor-bah-nah*
I'd like to make a collect call.	**Vorrei fare una telefonata a carico del destinatario.**	*vor-ray far-eh oona teh-leh-fon-ah-tah ah kar-ee-koh del desstee-nah-tar-ree-oh*
I'll try again later.	**Ritelefono più tardi.**	*ree-teh-leh-foh-noh pee-oo tar-dee*
Can I leave a message?	**Posso lasciare un messaggio?**	*poss-oh lash-ah-reh oon mess-sah-joh?*
Hold on	**Un attimo, per favore**	*oon ah-tee-moh, pair fah-vor-eh*
Could you speak up a little please?	**Può parlare più forte, per favore?**	*pwoh par-lah-reh pee-oo for-teh, pair fah-vor-eh?*
local call	**la telefonata locale**	*lah teh-leh-fon-ah-ta loh-kah-leh*

SHOPPING

How much does this cost?	**Quant'è?**	*kwan-teh*
I would like ...	**Vorrei ...**	*vor-ray*
Do you have ...?	**Avete ...?**	*ah-veh-teh.. ?*
I'm just looking.	**Sto soltanto guardando.**	*stoh sol-tan-toh gwar-dan-doh*
Do you take credit cards?	**Accettate carte di credito?**	*ah-chet-tah-teh kar-teh dee creb-dee-toh?*
What time do you open/close?	**A che ora apre/chiude?**	*ah keh or-ah ah-preh/kee-oo-deh?*
this one	**questo**	*kweh-stoh*
that one	**quello**	*kwell-oh*
expensive	**caro**	*kar-oh*
cheap	**a buon prezzo**	*ah bwon pret-soh*
size, clothes	**la taglia**	*lah tah-lee-ah*
size, shoes	**il numero**	*eel noo-mair-oh*
white	**bianco**	*bee-ang-koh*
black	**nero**	*neh-roh*
red	**rosso**	*ross-oh*
yellow	**giallo**	*jal-loh*
green	**verde**	*vair-deh*
blue	**blu**	*bloo*
brown	**marrone**	*mar-roh-neh*

TYPES OF SHOP

antiques dealer	**l'antiquario**	*lan-tee-kwah-ree-oh*
bakery	**la panetteria**	*lah pah-net-tair-ree-ah*
bank	**la banca**	*lah bang-kah*
bookshop	**la libreria**	*lah lee-breh-ree-ah*
butcher's	**la macelleria**	*lah mah-chell-eh-ree-ah*
cake shop	**la pasticceria**	*lah pas-tee-chair-ee-ah*
department store	**il grande magazzino**	*eel gran-deh mag-gad-zee-noh*
delicatessen	**la salumeria**	*lah sah-loo-meh-ree-ah*
drugstore	**la farmacia**	*lah far-mah-chee-ah*
fish seller	**la pescheria**	*lah pess-keh-ree-ah*
florist	**il fioraio**	*eel fee-or-eye-oh*
greengrocer	**il fruttivendolo**	*eel froo-tee-ven-doh-loh*
grocery	**alimentari**	*ah-lee-men-tah-ree*
hairdresser	**il parrucchiere**	*eel par-oo-kee-air-eh*
ice cream parlor	**la gelateria**	*lah jel-lah-tair-ree-ah*
market	**il mercato**	*eel mair-kah-toh*
newsstand	**l'edicola**	*leh-dee-koh-lah*
post office	**l'ufficio postale**	*loo-fee-choh pos-tah-leh*
shoe store	**il negozio di scarpe**	*eel neh-goh-tsioh dee skar-peh*
supermarket	**il supermercato**	*su-pair-mair-kah-toh*
tobacconist	**il tabaccaio**	*eel tab-bak-eye-oh*
travel agency	**l'agenzia di viaggi**	*lah-jen-tsee-ah dee vee-ad-jee*

SIGHTSEEING

art gallery	**la pinacoteca**	*lah peena-koh-teh-kah*
bus stop	**la fermata dell'autobus**	*lah fair-mah-tah dell ow-toh-booss*
church	**la chiesa**	*lah kee-eh-zah*
	la basilica	*lah bah-seel-i-kah*
garden	**il giardino**	*eel jar-dee-no*
library	**la biblioteca**	*lah beeb-lee-oh-teh-kah*
museum	**il museo**	*eel moo-zeb-oh*
railway station	**la stazione**	*lah stah-tsee-oh-neh*
tourist information	**l'ufficio turistico**	*loo-fee-choh too-ree-stee-koh*
closed for the public holiday	**chiuso per festa**	*kee-oo-zoh pair fess-tah*